ZOLTÁN

Books are to be returned on or before
the last date below.

**7 – DAY
LOAN**

LIBREX-

LIVERPOOL JOHN MOORES UNIVERSITY
Aldham Robarts L.R.C.
TEL. 0151 231 3701/3634

LIVERPOOL JMU LIBRARY

3 1111 01267 3727

The English, French and Hungarian language versions
of this book are published with identical page-setting.
The empty space at the bottom of certain pages is due to an attempt
to make each page correspond to the layout of the French and Hungarian text.

ZOLTÁN HORVÁTH

HANDBOOK
ON THE EUROPEAN UNION

Third edition in English,
translation of the seventh Hungarian edition.

Lap- és Könyvkiadó Kft.

© Zoltán Horváth

Hungarian text revised by:
Tamás Számadó

Translated by:
Péter Szűcs

English text revised by:
Ros and Tom Glaser

Manuscript completed on July 2007

Budapest, 2007
Published by HVG-ORAC Publishing House Ltd.
Responsible publisher: Éva Lipovecz, managing director

ISBN 978 963 258 000 5

All rights reserved.
No part of this publication may be reproduced or transmitted in any form or by any means, electronic, mechanical, photocopying, recording or by any information storage and retrieval system, without the prior written permission of the publisher.

Responsible editor: Ádám Frank
Typesetting and technical editing by: Zsolt Przymuszala
Proofreader: Katalin Szalóki
Printed in Hungary by Multiszolg Bt. – Vác

CONTENTS

PART II
THE POLICIES OF THE EUROPEAN UNION

ANNEX
REFORM TREATY BASED ON THE CONSTITUTIONAL TREATY
What changes will the Reform Treaty bring on its entry into force compared to the treaty framework currently in effect?

ABBREVIATIONS AND GLOSSARY OF TERMS

APPENDIX

INTRODUCTION

It gives me great pleasure to recommend this third English edition of the *Handbook on the European Union* by Zoltán Horváth. This clearly-structured, informative, technical and eminently readable work is one of the most popular titles on the EU in Hungary, and has become a key textbook at several universities and colleges. The Handbook has reached its seventh edition in Hungarian, and tens of thousands of copies have been published, helping civil servants, entrepreneurs and students to become acquainted with the European Union. Former editions were also translated into English, French and Slovak with – among others – the help of the European Commission, and proved to be an instant success in several EU Member States. This seventh edition, whose text was completed in July 2007, is being published simultaneously in Hungarian, English and French in an identical layout, which must be an unprecedented feat for a specialised volume on the EU.

This book owes much of its success to the fact that it evolves together with the European Union, keeping its readers abreast of the latest changes in Europe's architecture. One would be hard pressed to find many volumes that follow the EU's development so closely, with subsequent editions published so frequently. To illustrate how up-to-date it is, let it suffice to note that it analyses in detail the Reform Treaty, which is expected to enter into force in 2009.

The Handbook's enormous stock of knowledge is not only useful but essential for any present and future Union citizen seeking to make conscious decisions on EU-related matters. Economic and legal experts, civil servants and businessmen would be well advised to keep a copy of the Handbook within reach on their desk. It is also a useful volume for students as well as their teachers, whatever their field of specialisation, as European integration encompasses all areas of life. The Handbook should be particularly helpful for citizens of new and future EU Member States due to its special focus on enlargement, which includes analyses of the key elements required for successful accession and explains how to make the most of EU membership.

The European Union is often accused of being an opaque, bureaucratic organisation. I am convinced that those who want to learn more about the European Union (its functioning, institutional set-up, decision-making and legal systems), and discover why

European integration is so complicated and cumbersome, will find the answers to their questions in the pages of this Handbook. The book sets out to cover not only the legal and institutional architecture, but also to explore all policy areas, ranging from economic policy to environmental protection, from cultural affairs to justice and home affairs, from trade to foreign policy.

European integration is a long and laborious process, but – nevertheless – it is the best way to ensure the prosperity of Europe's peoples, as has been demonstrated by recent historic achievements, such as the introduction of the euro and the reunification of Europe through the accession of Central and Eastern European countries that were not long ago separated from the rest of the continent by the Iron Curtain. Throughout history, there have always been ups and downs and successes are inevitably followed by crises, such as the referenda rejecting the Constitutional Treaty a few years ago. However, it is my conviction that such decisions are usually due to misinformation or a lack of information. This Handbook contributes to a better understanding of European integration and provides its readers with comprehensive up-to-date information to enable them to make the best use of the opportunities that the EU has to offer. The success of a united Europe hinges on well-informed citizens. I wish all readers a successful future in the European Union.

Katalin Szili
Speaker of the Hungarian National Assembly

FOREWORD

Copies of the former editions of the *Handbook on the European Union* published in Hungarian, English, French and Slovak have made their way to the bookshelves of many readers wishing to know more about European integration. Much to my delight, it has proved to be useful for politicians, public officials, journalists, students and even the general public. The Handbook, promoted and disseminated by the Hungarian Parliament, the European Commission and the Hungarian Ministry of Foreign Affairs, has become a standard part of the curriculum in many universities and colleges, as well as the courses of the Hungarian Institute for Public Administration. The English and Slovak editions were published with the financial assistance of the European Commission while, for the first French edition, I am grateful for the support of the French Institute. It gives me great pleasure to see the new edition in English and French being published at the same time as the seventh Hungarian edition, all three with identical layouts.

This book aims to assist the work of practitioners dealing with the EU in their daily work, but hopefully it can also serve as a course book in its own right. I wanted to compile a book that could meet the expectations of all those interested in European integration from the legal, economic or political perspective. By attempting to incorporate all of these three aspects, I have aimed to provide a comprehensive view of the European Union, to help readers understand the motives of EU actions and decisions, the reasons behind the achievements and potential failures of integration, and the future direction of the EU.

During the writing of this book, I have been able to draw inspiration from my experience as a lecturer at universities, colleges and EU training courses for public officials, journalists, teachers, entrepreneurs and students, whose questions and feedback keeps me in touch with real needs, in particular in respect of those areas of European integration which are the most obscure to the average reader. That may be one of the reasons why the book has become such a popular reference book for people preparing for recruitment competitions (*concours*) of the EU institutions.

The *Handbook on the European Union* attempts to provide information which is essential for anybody looking to become an expert on European affairs. The Handbook focuses on the most topical and controversial issues, such as the consequences of the new Treaty framework expected to take effect in 2009, the key questions of implementing individual policies in the 2007–2013 budgetary period or future prospects for the enlargement process.

The *Handbook* devotes special attention to the provisions of the Reform Treaty, which is expected to enter into force in 2009. The Reform Treaty will replace the now defunct Constitutional Treaty, which was rejected by the Dutch and French electorate in referenda in 2005. This book attempts to provide a comprehensive analysis of the changes that the new Treaty will make to the provisions of the current Treaties and how they relate to those which were proposed in the Constitutional Treaty. As the Reform Treaty will probably only enter into force in 2009, its provisions are presented separately in the Annex. For ease of use, the Annex follows the same structure as the body of the book. This should enable readers to compare more easily the present situation in different policy areas with the provisions which will apply once the new Treaty enters into force, following its ratification by the Member States.

The Handbook is divided into two main parts. Part One provides a comprehensive introduction to the history and evolution of the European Union (with a separate section devoted to eastern enlargement) as well as the legal, institutional, decision-making and budgetary arrangements underpinning the EU's functioning. Part Two focuses on the general framework, objectives and functioning of Community policies in all three pillars of the Union. These two parts are followed by an Annex presenting the changes to be introduced by the Reform Treaty and a Glossary of Terms, containing brief definitions of over 300 key concepts, which will hopefully be a useful guide to EU terminology and may even serve as a stand-alone pocket reference book. In order to ensure that searching the Glossary is fast and user-friendly, terms that have an entry of their own are printed in italics in the text of the definitions. The book also contains four Appendices. Appendices I and II enumerate areas which require unanimity for decision-making according to the current Treaties, and which will continue to require unanimity on the entry into force of the Reform Treaty. Appendices III and IV provide a guide to the legislative procedures used in various areas of EU competence under the current Treaties and those which will apply on the entry into force of the Reform Treaty.

I am grateful to Péter Sárdi, the Head of the Office for Foreign Relations of the Hungarian Parliament, for his commitment to this English edition of the *Handbook*. I owe special thanks to Ros and Tom Glaser, whose immense help and devotion in proofreading the English edition was instrumental to the launch of this volume. Special acknowledgements go to the translator Péter Szűcs, for his meticulous work.

I genuinely hope that this book will prove to be useful in disseminating information about European integration and will thereby contribute to a better understanding of the opportunities that the European Union has to offer.

The author

PART I

THE DEVELOPMENT OF THE EUROPEAN UNION, ITS STRUCTURE AND FUNCTIONING

CHAPTER 1
HISTORY AND DEVELOPMENT OF EUROPEAN INTEGRATION

1.1. The issue of integration in Europe after the Second World War

Many are inclined to identify the concept of an integrated Europe with the present European integration – the European Union. However, the idea of united European states is rooted in common European thinking much earlier, and its emergence cannot be attributed exclusively to the political and economic conditions that prevailed in the period after World War II. Various idealistic concepts had been formulated before in the works of artists, philosophers and scientists, including Dante, Comenius, Erasmus of Rotterdam, or Immanuel Kant. As early as 1849, Victor Hugo used the term 'United States of Europe' to indicate a goal to be aimed at by each European country. Viewing industrialisation as it was gaining ground, Saint-Simon, on the other hand, also studied the economic and technical conditions of European integration, pointing out the need for establishing a comprehensive European organisation, a kind of European Parliament.

Then, in the first half of the 20th century, several plans were put forward to realise European unity in an institutionalised form. In this respect, special mention should be made of Richard Coudenhove Calergi, a citizen born in the Austro-Hungarian Monarchy, who published his book entitled 'Pan-Europa' in 1923. The book lists concrete proposals for uniting Europe. The 'Pan-European Movement', organised on the basis of his work in the 1920s, formulated a concept of economic integration as well.

Yet, a basis for actually creating an institutionalised Europe was provided through the lessons learned from the destruction caused by World War II. It was then that many realised that cooperation created on a loose intergovernmental basis, similar to that of the League of Nations which operated between the two world wars, could not provide a sufficient guarantee for peaceful coexistence and development of the states of Europe. The League of Nations failed to draw together European states either politically, economically, or culturally, and it even failed, as a result of its weakness as an institution for one thing, to prevent the most horrible war in the history of Europe from happening. This failure showed that member states do not look upon an organisation operating without supra-national control and based on loose intergovernmental relations as a guarantee of sustainable cooperation. Furthermore, it became evident that if a state finds that its national interests are better served if cooperation is called off and even if a war is launched, it may not hesitate to do so.

Also, the western part of the Europe that was divided after World War II, realised quite early that the old continent would be able to increase its largely diminished political and economic weight and influence in the nascent bipolar arrangement of the world only through integration. Regional economic cooperation appeared indispensable for the development of the countries of Europe with fragmented national markets, and also for regaining and strengthening the position occupied in the world economy. In addition, economic cooperation was necessary, in the face of the restructuring of the world economy and the competitive advantage of the United States (market scale, technological level, etc.), as well as for the sake of technological and structural modernisation.

Thus, following the devastation brought about by the World War, politicians in Western Europe started to discuss the feasibility, rather than the necessity, of integration. The main issue was whether a political, military, or economic orientation, or a combination thereof, was needed to preserve peace in Europe and enable the countries of Europe to recover; also, it had to be determined which countries would take part in the unfolding process of integration.

After 1945, the idea of unity became so popular that various movements aimed at European integration were formed one after the other in nearly every European country, except those controlled by the Soviet Union. The development of the idea of European unity is evidenced by the fact that parties belonging to differing political families started to set up their European organisations with the aim of creating a federalist Europe.

A feature shared by the various national and international movements was the intention to create a united Europe on the basis of a common system of institutions. These ideas centred around a federalism that included, directly or indirectly, the establishment of a European system of institutions on a supranational basis.

Most governments of the European countries, however, appeared reluctant to make a definitive step in this direction and took a standpoint that preferred looser cooperation primarily based on intergovernmental cooperation, in line with the tradition of policy making by nation-states. This was the approach taken in the setting up of the Council of Europe on 5 May 1949 by ten countries of Western Europe. The Council of Europe, however, did not represent a bloc aiming at integration in terms of competence, operation or activities; rather, it appeared to be a regional international organisation in its traditional sense.

The Council of Europe

The Council of Europe (CoE) was established by 10 countries of Western Europe (Belgium, Denmark, France, Ireland, Italy, Luxembourg, the Netherlands, Norway, Sweden and the United Kingdom) in London on 5 May 1949. Later on, practically all Western and Southern European countries with a democratic establishment joined the Council of Europe, and then, after the communist systems had collapsed, the countries of Central and Eastern Europe also joined the organisation, to be followed by Ukraine, Russia and other republics of the former Soviet Union. With further ex-Soviet and Yugoslav republics joining, the membership of the Council of Europe has grown to 47. Belarus is the only European country not admitted to the Council of Europe (while the Vatican has observer status).

The Council of Europe is a regional intergovernmental organisation with the following main aims: strengthening pluralist democracy, maintaining the rule of law, protecting human rights, promoting and developing European cultural identity, and seeking solutions to problems facing society. The activity of the Council of Europe is best characterised by the nearly 200 conventions elaborated by the Council, predominantly dealing with issues concerning human rights and various aspects of society and culture, including, for example, the European Convention on Human Rights ('Convention for the Protection of Human Rights and Fundamental Freedoms'), the European Social Charter, the Convention for the Protection of National Minorities, and the European Charter for Regional or Minority Languages, all of which have become part of national law following their ratification by the member states. The headquarters of the Council of Europe is in Strasbourg. Its main bodies include the Committee of Ministers, the Parliamentary Assembly, and the Secretariat headed by the Secretary General. An important role is fulfilled by the European Court of Human Rights – often referred to as the 'Strasbourg court' – established within the framework of the European Convention on Human Rights, which represents the highest judicial forum for the protection of human rights in Europe.

Of the Western European countries, it was the United Kingdom, with its colonial and commonwealth interests still playing an important role, that did not intend to join an organisation aimed at integration in which national sovereignty was restricted through the operation of supranational institutions. On the other hand, other countries – the Benelux states, for example – promoted the idea of the establishment of an organisation based on economic cooperation realising mutual interests. Belgium, the Netherlands, and Luxembourg had already decided to set up the Benelux Union in 1944, which was created in 1948. The cooperation between the Benelux states represented real integration, rather than a mere customs union.

By 1949, the problem of what to do with Germany – a question on the table since the end of World War II – had become crucial. The Americans considered the military strengthening of West Germany as an increasingly urgent task, while France and the other Western European allies were reluctant to support this measure for lack of appropriate safety guarantees. It was clear that resolving French-German relations was a critical issue for the future of Europe. Promoters of the idea of European unity were convinced that the resolution of the century-old German-French conflict was a precondition for creating a common Europe.

For the French, fear of a new German recovery raised the issue of how Germany and its strength could be controlled, since the alternative of taking punitive revenge had obviously failed after World War I. Promoters of a unified Europe saw a guarantee for building a peaceful and strong Europe through institutions with a supranational character that could embrace France and Germany alike.

Considerable impetus for the acceleration of Western European integration was stimulated by developments taking place in Central and Eastern Europe. Following World War II, the establishment of single-party states and communist regimes in countries occupied by the Soviet Union proceeded at a high speed. The countries of Central and Eastern Europe falling under Soviet orientation attempted to split away from the democratic orientation of Western European countries from a political and also economic perspective. Finally, the economic division of Europe was institutionalised through the Marshall Plan[1] of 1947. After the countries of Central and Eastern Europe under Soviet influence and the Soviet Union itself rejected the aid, the participating countries of Western, Northern and Southern Europe established, together with the United States, the OEEC (Organisation for European Economic Cooperation) in 1948. Its aim was to promote European trade, economic stability and development, and also to coordinate and distribute assistance received from America under the Marshall Plan. In 1961, the OEEC was redesigned considerably in terms of its objectives and operation: it converted from a European organisation of reconstruction into a cooperation organisation for the industrialised countries. Thus, the OECD (Organisation for Economic Cooperation and Development) was created.

The OECD

Twenty member states of the OEEC (Austria, Belgium, Canada, Denmark, the Federal Republic of Germany, France, Greece, Iceland, Ireland, Italy, Luxembourg, the Netherlands, Norway, Portugal, Spain, Sweden, Switzerland, Turkey, the United Kingdom, the United States), signed the founding Convention on the Organisation for Economic Cooperation and Development (OECD) in Paris on 14 December 1960, which then became effective on 30 September 1961. Japan joined the

---

[1] The Marshall Plan, named after Secretary of State of the United States of America George C. Marshall, was initially proposed as an American aid package offered by the USA to all European states for reconstruction after the war. However, the Marshall Aid was utilised only by countries of Western, Northern and Southern Europe, while countries of Central and Eastern Europe under Soviet influence rejected the plan on the instructions of the Soviet Union.

organisation in 1964, and so did Finland in 1969, Australia in 1971, New Zealand in 1973, Mexico in 1994, the Czech Republic in 1995, the Republic of Korea, Poland and Hungary in 1996, and Slovakia in 2000, increasing OECD membership to 30. The organisation, with its headquarters in Paris, unites countries with advanced market economies and provides member countries with an institutional framework for coordinating economic and social policy. Its main aim is to promote economic growth in member countries, maintain employment and financial stability at a high level, and contribute to the development of worldwide trade. The activity of the OECD is expressly targeted at the cooperation of the member states, rather than at a kind of integration. Cooperation between member states embraces a wide scope of economic and social life (social issues, employment, environmental protection, education, trade liberalisation, cooperation with developing countries, aid policy). Activities of the OECD are prepared and carried out in more than 200 specialised committees and working groups. The organisation frequently prepares studies and forecasts on the state of the world economy and the economic situation in individual regions and countries.

Although the OEEC (and later on, the OECD) could not be viewed as an organisation aimed at integration – similarly to the Council of Europe – its emergence signalled differing economic paths of progress taken by the western and the eastern sides of Europe due to political divisions. The political and economic detachment of Central and Eastern Europe and its binding to the Soviet Union was indicated by the formation in 1949 of an organisation that was guided by the Soviet Union and which represented a characteristic economic integration of the communist countries, i.e. the Council for Mutual Economic Assistance (COMECON). Nevertheless, the COMECON could not be considered as an example of *par excellence* integration either since its activity was primarily confined, at least in the early period, to barter agreements.

The sight of an Eastern Europe forming a political and also economic cluster had a fundamental influence on integration ambitions in Western Europe which, however, pursued a different course in terms of politics and economics. The setting up of NATO (North Atlantic Treaty Organisation) in 1949 represented political, military, and defence security against the Soviet threat. While the presence of the United States in NATO meant a guarantee for Western Europe in military terms, the area of economic thinking was more predominantly characterised by integration ambitions that could counter-balance the communist threat while at the same time make the western part of Europe independent of America.

NATO

The North Atlantic Treaty, the document that set up NATO, was signed in Washington on 4 April 1949 by 10 Western European countries (Belgium, Denmark, France, Iceland, Italy, Luxembourg, the Netherlands, Norway, Portugal, and the United Kingdom) and the United States and Canada. This intergovernmental political and military organisation was expanded by Greece and Turkey in 1952, the Federal Republic of Germany in 1955, Spain in 1982, and, a decade after the changes of the political system in Central and Eastern Europe, by the Czech Republic, Hungary and Poland in 1999. The first three ex-Soviet bloc countries were followed by Bulgaria, Estonia, Latvia, Lithuania, Romania, Slovakia and Slovenia in 2004; as a result, NATO now has 26 members. At the time of its establishment, the primary aim of NATO was to protect member states through political and military means against the military power of the Soviet Union. The reason for creating NATO, which became the most important military and political organisation of the western world during the decades of Cold War, appeared defunct after the collapse of the communist regimes in 1989–1990, and the disintegration in 1991 of the Soviet Union and the Warsaw Pact set up by it in 1955 as a military alliance. As a result, NATO has gone through a major transformation in the nineties. On the one hand, it has built partnerships with the countries of Central and Eastern Europe (CEECs) and former Soviet Republics (with Russia as a key partner), leading to NATO membership for CEECs. On the other hand, its strategy increasingly focuses on crisis management, peace-keeping, ensuring overall European security and combating terrorism and the proliferation of weapons of mass destruction. Notwithstanding the changes that have taken place in world politics, the basic mission of the organisation seated in Brussels continues to be related to the collective defence and security of its member states. France left the military structure of NATO in 1966 while Spain, which had not joined the military structure on its accession to NATO, became a member of the military structure in 1996.

1.2. Establishment of the European Coal and Steel Community

In the beginning, the movements cherishing the idea of creating a federal Europe on the basis of supranational institutions looked upon political integration as the right source of impetus for expanding the process of integration. Following the establishment of the symbolic Council of Europe, however, they began to review their standpoint. It appeared more and more appropriate to start building European integration from the direction of economic cooperation.

Relying on an approach to the integration process from the aspect of economic cooperation and with the intention of preventing the emergence of a renewed conflict between France and Germany and paving the way toward security guarantees for French-German cooperation, Robert Schuman, the then French Minister for Foreign Affairs, put forward a proposal on 9 May 1950 that was prepared together with Jean Monnet, head of the planning department of the French government. The proposal that became known as the Schuman Plan laid the foundation of European integration, the present European Union.

Dedicated to the idea of European unity and French-German reconciliation, Schuman and Monnet set the objective of creating a European federation along a French-German axis. They saw clearly that this objective could be reached only step-by-step. Therefore, in order to realise their programme, they selected as a basis for European integration an area of crucial importance for maintaining peace in Europe. Their concept relied on the assumption that central control over the coal and steel industries would make preparations for launching a war impossible. Thus, the Schuman Plan was targeted at creating a common market for German coal and French iron ore, which would offer a number of economic benefits in addition to providing security for maintaining peace. At the turn of the forties and fifties, considerable shortages were recorded in both coal and steel and thus the coordinated utilisation of the available stocks provided an economic justification for the integration of these areas.

France initiated the creation of an integration motivated by security policy considerations, but built on economic objectives. The Schuman Plan proposed that French-German coal and steel production be placed under a single high authority in the framework of a system that would be open to other countries as well. The French proposal was warmly received in the Federal Republic of Germany, led by Chancellor Konrad Adenauer. The British, however, were reluctant to go beyond the confines of traditional intergovernmental cooperation and rejected joining an organisation formed on a supranational basis. On the other hand, the Benelux states, which favoured integration, and Italy, which was trying to escape post-war isolation, signalled their intention of joining the organisation.

Finally, on 18 April 1951, Belgium, France, the Federal Republic of Germany, Italy, Luxembourg and the Netherlands (also known as 'the founding Six') signed the Treaty establishing the European Coal and Steel Community (ECSC) which entered into force on 25 July 1952.

In the course of elaborating the institutional system of the ECSC, a supranational, federal feature came to the fore. According to Monnet's concept, the organisation would be headed by a 'High Authority', consisting of independent officials as members, nominated by their respective governments but acting fully independently when making decisions on the basis of the interests of the community as a whole. Eventually, the High Authority was not established completely in accordance with the concept, since the Council was created from competent ministers of the Member States to counterbalance the supranational orientation. The Council of Ministers operated as an intergovernmental body supervising the activity of the High Authority and also fulfilling a legislative function. Pursuant to the. ECSC Treaty, the Assembly was established, which consisted of delegates from the Member State parliaments and which had a consultative function, as well as the Court of Justice of the ECSC that provided a forum for settling legal disputes. The first President of the High Authority was Jean Monnet.

1.3. From the failure of the European Defence Community to the Treaty of Rome

Impressed by the warm reception given to the ECSC, the promoters of federalism found that the time was also ripe for creating political integration in Europe. The European Defence Community (EDC), which was to be set up to form a common European defence force, again at the initiative of the French government, was intended to serve as the foundation stone. The idea was based on the Pléven Plan named after the French Prime Minister and announced in October 1950. Promoters of European unity, however, were disappointed that – in addition to the British with their traditional aloofness – France itself did not intend to give up its independence in this area, which it considered as having crucial relevance for retaining national sovereignty. Following several years of hesitation, the National Assembly of France refused to give its assent to the European Defence Community Treaty on 30 August 1954 – the treaty that had been proposed by the French and signed more than two years earlier by the Ministers for Foreign Affairs. Failure of the EDC brought with it a stoppage of the attempts aimed at establishing a European Political Community (EPC)[2], and it became apparent that the conditions for the political integration of Europe had not been created. Although six Member States of the ECSC and the United Kingdom created a defence organisation in 1954 to replace EDC, under the name Western European Union (WEU)[3], this was based on a much weaker foundation than the EDC, with no intention of setting up a common defence force, restricting its mission to adherence to the principle of collective defence.

Once the EDC failed, federalists had to resort again to the field of economics to promote the process of integration.

---

[2] During 1953 and 1954, both the ECSC Assembly and the Ministers for Foreign Affairs discussed the issue of establishing a European Political Community (EPC). Rejection of the EDC, however, also fixed the fate of the EPC.

[3] For details, see 23.2.

At the initiative of the Benelux states, Member States of the ECSC met on 1 and 2 June 1955 in Messina to discuss the issue of deepening and expanding economic integration, with institutional issues of possible cooperation in the area of atomic energy and a common market in general. The committee, headed by Paul-Henri Spaak[4] and set up after the Messina conference, prepared its report by April 1956 summarising a plan for realising a common market based on a customs union.

The Spaak Report proposed an institutionalised community structure for the would-be organisation of integration in which issues pertaining to general politics and the operation of the common market were to be handled separately. While the former would remain within the competence of the Member States, a body with authority and community responsibility would be set up with the function of ensuring the operation of the common market.

The Spaak Committee evaded reference to supranational status. As Spaak acknowledged later on, its aim was to create working institutions. The caution exercised by the Spaak Committee was not unfounded: the French had developed a more hostile attitude toward supranational institutions since the EDC failure, and even the Germans made critical remarks about the ECSC High Authority and referred to it as being "dirigiste" on several occasions.

The pragmatic approach of the Spaak Committee appeared successful in working out a concept that was acceptable to all the six ECSC Member States. Similarly to earlier occasions, the United Kingdom was requested to join in, but nevertheless, London rejected the offer once again and decided to set up EFTA instead.[5] Thus, the governments of Belgium, France, the Netherlands, Luxembourg, the Federal Republic of Germany, and Italy signed the treaties establishing the European Economic Community (EEC) and

---

[4] Paul-Henri Spaak, a Belgian politician, was one of the most dedicated representatives of European federalists. He was the first president of the OEEC, and went on to become the Chairman of the Parliamentary Assembly of the Council of Europe after its establishment; when he realised that the Council of Europe was unlikely to realise the process of European unity, he resigned. Later on, as the Foreign Minister of Belgium, he acquired considerable fame for his work in preparing the EEC and Euratom Treaties.

[5] Unlike the six ECSC Member States, the United Kingdom intended to take part in free trade cooperation only. As a consequence, the European Free Trade Association (EFTA) was established on a British initiative, which was basically comprised of Western European countries left out from the EEC. EFTA started off as a competitor of the EEC, but most of its founding Member States – including the UK – finally joined the EEC (or later on the EU), which offered closer cooperation and more profound integration. For details on EFTA and its members joining the European integration process, see 1.9.

the European Atomic Energy Community (Euratom) in Rome on 25 March 1957, known as the Treaties of Rome, which became effective on 1 January 1958.

The institutional model applied to the EEC and Euratom was that of the ECSC, with the difference being a shift in the scope of decision-making competence away from the Commission, that played the role of High Authority with respect to these treaties, to the Council as the body representing the governments. Thus, an intergovernmental model, rather than a supranational one, was established as a consequence of the general political climate after the failure of the EDC. The Commission became the main initiator of decisions, equipped with some decision-making authorisation but more restricted than that enjoyed by the High Authority of the ECSC. The Council of Ministers, on the other hand, being the main decision-making body, had more power than its ECSC counterpart. The Assembly was assigned a similar role to that in the ECSC, of consultation, authorisation and very limited supervisory competence. The Court of Justice received the task of interpreting and securing compliance with emerging Community law. These latter two institutions operated as common bodies of the ECSC, the EEC, and the Euratom, while the Commission (the High Authority of the ECSC) and the Council were separate institutions for each of the three organisations.

The Treaty of Rome that established the EEC, set the establishment of a common market as the overall aim of the Community; furthermore, it indicated as its task the "...harmonious and balanced development of economic activities... raising of the standard of living ... economic and social cohesion and solidarity among Member States ... through gradual convergence of economic policy" (Article 2 of the Treaty).
Meeting the overall aim was to be achieved by fulfilling the following main specific objectives (Article 3): the elimination of customs duties and quantitative restrictions, and of all other measures having equivalent effect; establishment of a customs union and adherence to a common commercial policy against countries outside the Community; free movement not only of goods and services, but also of labour and capital within the Community; a common policy in the areas of agriculture, transport, and competition; approximation of national laws.
The Treaty of Rome that established Euratom set as one of its aims the quick establishment and development of the atomic energy industry, identifying a number of tasks from common research to the effective utilisation of atomic energy and the provision of nuclear safety.

Forms of integration

Free trade area: *trade between countries within the area is liberalised (members abolish customs duties and quotas between each other) while each member country pursues its national trade policy with those outside the area.*

Customs union: *trade between countries within the area is liberalised (members abolish customs duties and quotas between each other); the movement of goods and services is unrestricted between the member countries, while a common customs tariff is imposed on those outside the area, and a common commercial policy is pursued.*

Common market: *more than a customs union in that (in addition to free movement of goods and services) the flow of production factors (capital and labour) is also liberalised, thereby creating the 'four fundamental freedoms' (the free movement of goods, services, capital and workers).*

Single (internal) market: *an advanced version of a common market where, in addition to the lifting of customs and quantity limitations, obstacles of a 'non-customs character' (of a non-commercial nature) – be they physical (border formalities, border controls), fiscal (budgetary or tax rules) or technical (resulting from the differences between the laws, standards or regulations of Member States) – which hinder the free movement of goods, services, capital, and workers are all eliminated.*

Economic union: *in addition to a common/single market, integration of economic policies is also realised, which means that national economic policies are coordinated, harmonised and, as the final aim, unified at the community level; an important element of economic union is the use of a single currency and the monetary union thereby established.*

Political union: *gradual transfer of governance and legislation to the community level; an important element of this process is the shaping of a common foreign policy and handling of home affairs and justice issues at the community level.*

1.4. The first fifteen years of the EEC

The first fifteen years following the enactment of the Treaty of Rome[6] and ending with the first oil crisis can be characterised by rapid internal integration. The removal of customs and quantitative restrictions between the Member States was completed by the middle of 1968, two years before the planned date in 1970, and common customs tariffs were also introduced. As the customs union which had been created and the common market which had been introduced both ensured the integration of industrial markets only, a

---

[6] Unless indicated specifically whether the EEC Treaty or the Euratom Treaty is involved, the term 'Treaty of Rome' used on its own, without specific reference to one or the other, will always mean, in line with the general usage applied in the literature, the Treaty establishing the EEC. This book adheres to the same principle. When reference is made to the Treaty of Euratom, this is specifically indicated.

decision was made in 1962 on working out a common agricultural policy that would lead to unification within the Community in terms of agricultural protectionism – a result of the specificity of the sector at hand.[7] The elaboration of a common agricultural policy had immense importance and served as an example that confirmed the ability of the Member States to carry out cooperation in areas where a considerable reallocation of revenues was involved – from one country to another.

In the period between 1958 and 1973, trade between the member countries grew dynamically as a result of trade liberalisation and customs union. While overall foreign trade produced an annual growth rate of 8 %, annual expansion of trade within the Community achieved a rate of 12 % and, as a result, trade inside the Community accounted for more than 50% of the overall trade of the Member States in 1973. The establishment of integration coincided with an economic boom. That period was characterised by fast technical development, radical modernisation of the structure of the economy, dynamic expansion of consumption, and an annual 5% rate of increase in GDP. Inspired by this success, the leaders of the European Community were elaborating plans for introducing monetary union as early as 1969 and 1970. However, the Werner Plan[8] that dealt with the details failed within a short time, due to the financial crisis of the early seventies and the oil crisis of the same period.

While it was easy to introduce the customs union, the free movement of capital and labour appeared hard to implement. Although the general conditions of free movement were liberalised, the pure form of a theoretical common market could not be achieved in practice. In addition, operation of the policies aimed at various specialised community areas (e.g. transport, social matters, etc.) was also in its infancy.

The main confirmation of the success of the EEC was provided through the re-evaluation of the British political attitude. Seeing the results of integration of the six Member States, the United Kingdom indicated its intention to join the Community in July 1961. The French President, General De Gaulle, who had been in office already for three years and viewed British entry as a threat related to increasing American influence, set a veto on the application, and he did the same in 1967 when the United Kingdom indicated its intention to join the Community once again.

The radical approach taken by President De Gaulle considerably affected not only the external relations of the Communities but also the internal functioning of integration.

---

[7] For details regarding the beginnings of a common agricultural policy, see 11.1–11.3.

[8] For details, see 8.1.

The General, who – contrary to previous French policy – proclaimed the idea of the 'Europe of Nations' and intended to steer the Communities towards purely intergovernmental cooperation, unleashed a serious crisis in 1965 when he boycotted participation in Community institutions for a half year period through his "empty chair" policy, because he did not agree with the proposals made for financing agricultural policy. This crisis could be resolved later on only by way of a solution that has become known as the 'Luxembourg compromise'. The compromise meant that, where a Member State declared that its fundamental national interest was at stake in a given situation, a solution could be accepted only if unanimous agreement was reached.[9] This provision, defended by De Gaulle as a security for the individual Member States, appeared to considerably hinder and slow down decision-making in the Community.

1.5. The Merger Treaty and its institutional impact

In the mid-sixties, the institutions of the three integration organisations were united. In pursuance of the Merger Treaty, adopted in 1965, the parallel institutions of the ECSC, the EEC and Euratom were merged by July 1967. In addition to the common Court of Justice and the Assembly (which was renamed as the European Parliament in 1962) of the three Communities, the Commission and the Council were reorganised to serve all three institutions. The High Authority of the ECSC was merged with the Commission. The name European Communities (EC) has been used since that time, although it has to be noted that the three Communities have preserved their independent international legal status and only their institutions became common institutions.

Further, it has to be noted that, since the Maastricht Treaty[10] of 1992, the acronym EC has been used to denote the EEC. The Maastricht Treaty renamed the European Economic Community (EEC) as the European Community (EC). Thus, the term EC refers to the former EEC and not the three Communities collectively. A further complication is that it is not always easy to distinguish between the notions 'Community' and 'Communities'. As a general rule, when Community is used in the singular form, it is mostly the context that reveals which of the three communities is being referred to. When no explicit reference is made, then the European (Economic) Community is meant; the ECSC and Euratom are usually referred to through specific reference.

In clarifying the scope of competence of the three Communities, it should be pointed out that the EEC (since Maastricht, the EC) operates as an organisation with general competence in issues related to the common market, as opposed to the ECSC and Euratom.

---

[9] On the Luxembourg compromise, see also 2.3.5.
[10] See 1.8.

While the latter two have clearly delineated scopes of activities and fields of application, the EEC Treaty must be applied, as a general rule, in areas not specifically regulated by the ECSC[11] and the Euratom Treaties.

1.6. The Six become Twelve –
Enlargements of the European Communities

In 1969, De Gaulle resigned, and thus the main obstacle to British entry was removed. In June 1970, accession negotiations were started with the United Kingdom, and also with Denmark, Ireland, and Norway. The negotiations were completed by January 1972, and, following a ratification procedure, Denmark, Ireland, and the United Kingdom became members of the European Communities on 1 January 1973. The Norwegian population, however, rejected accession in a referendum.

As a result of the enlargement, the importance of the European Communities in the world economy grew considerably – primarily owing to the British entry. This development could be observed through a change in American policy towards the Communities. While the United States had intensively supported the economic rebuilding and development of Europe before and, hence, the process of integration as well, the USA started to see the European Communities more and more like a competitor after the latter's enlargement in 1973. The Americans frowned at the European protectionist aspirations which presented themselves in a common trade policy, the trade relations established with socialist countries, and also the increased trade in Europe with the developing countries. It became apparent in the seventies that the competition between the three major actors in the world economy, i.e. the Triad consisting of the USA, Japan, and the European Communities, would play a dominant role.

Nevertheless, in spite of the growth in economic potential, the first years of the European Communities following enlargement to nine countries were not recorded as a period of success.
The world oil shock triggered by the Arab-Israeli War of 1973 – which was further

---

[11] Here it should be noted that the ECSC Treaty lapsed on 23 July 2002, as it was concluded for a period of fifty years only. As regards the other two treaties, there is no time limitation so they will not terminate. The expiry of the ECSC Treaty did not cause special problems because most of the ECSC provisions continue to remain effective within the EC due to the general validity of the EC Treaty. The financial consequences of the expiry of the ECSC Treaty are dealt with in a protocol annexed to the Treaty of Nice (see 1.11.).

aggravated by the earlier collapse of the Bretton Woods system[12] in 1971 (set up following World War II to ensure the stability of the international monetary system) – had a rather negative impact and hindered further integration considerably. As a result of the crisis and, basically, the increase in oil prices, together with the related growth in proportion of the oil in trade, trade within the Community was affected most. This is illustrated by the fact that the amount of internal trade in 1982 was somewhat below the level achieved in 1973. As a consequence of prolonged crises, the Member States often resorted to protectionist measures, which presented an obstacle to closer integration and the realisation of a fully-fledged common market.

British membership also made it difficult to proceed with integration, as the British government fought for a reduction in British contributions to the budget over a long period. Owing to increasing costs related to agricultural policy and also to the United Kingdom's position as an importer of agricultural products, the British were constant net budget contributors.[13]

On the other hand, mutual dependence within the Community increased even over this period. Relations between the Member States became more and more intensive in terms of micro- and macro-economics. A common commercial policy[14] had been fully implemented by the mid-seventies, which resulted in a more uniform economic and trade attitude amongst the Member States towards third countries. The major achievement of the period was the launching of the European Monetary System in 1979[15], which created financial stability within the Community and represented the first major step towards economic union. The establishment and successful operation of the European Monetary System indicated a higher level of inter-dependence than that in the late sixties and early seventies. Yet the period from 1973 to the end of the oil crisis (1982–1983) is better characterised by eurosclerosis than a deepening of integration.

From the institutional perspective, the key development of the seventies was that, from 1974 on, consultation between the Member States at the level of Heads of State or Government became a regular exercise. As top-level political leaders had to be involved in forging compromises between Member States in order to improve the efficiency of decision-making in Europe, the so-called European Council, namely the meeting of the Heads of State or Government, became the forum for taking the key decisions on

---

[12] For more, see 8.1.

[13] See also 7.3.1. and 7.3.3.

[14] For more details, see 9.2.

[15] For more details, see 8.2.

strategic issues, compromises and guidelines. The European Council was not created as a separate institution; the task of adopting legislative acts and specific decisions remained with the ministerial Council. Nonetheless, the role of the European Council as a top-level forum has become so decisive that, since it started, many consider the history of European integration as a series of European summit meetings.[16]

Then, in the eighties, the further development of integration received a new impetus from the enlargements of the European Communities. Greece – which had concluded an association agreement with the EEC back in 1962 – was allowed to join the European Communities in 1981, following a democratisation and modernisation period that started in 1974 when the military junta fell from power. A much longer period of transition was prescribed for Portugal and Spain after they had acquired freedom from military regimes. After many years of negotiations, the Iberian countries were able to become members in 1986. This southern enlargement brought with it new problems as a consequence of the accession of poorer states. The issue of economic and social cohesion within the Community appeared to have much larger importance than before and the activities and policies dealing with this issue increased in number.[17] The homogeneous organisation of the European Communities in terms of economy and geography turned into a heterogeneous integration block, comprising regions with varying potentials, and considerably enlarged from a geographical and political point of view.

1.7. Adoption of the Single European Act –
A single market coming true

Due to the oil crises and periods of recession, 'non-customs-related restrictions' multiplied within the Community in order to protect national markets. Not only did these restrictions make it impossible to realise a common market as set forth in the Treaty of Rome, they also represented a threat to the results already achieved. The elimination of these restrictions was a fundamental task for the creation of a pure internal, common market. During the lengthy period following the second oil crisis, it became increasingly apparent that the only recipe for boosting European competitiveness was deregulation. The elimination of various national-like administrative regulations would have been impossible if the system of unanimous voting had been maintained. Therefore, some restructuring of Community decision-making was called for, which, however, could be performed only by way of amending the Treaty of Rome. The requisite political conditions appeared to have been ripe because the coincidence of national and community interests made the Member

---

[16] For more on the European Council, its links with the Council of Ministers and how the two levels are interrelated, see 2.3.3.

[17] For details, see 7.3.1. and 13.1.

States inclined to sacrifice a part of their national sovereignty for the sake of escaping the crisis together and giving a new impetus to integration.

Making the markets more flexible and creating a real common market became an urgent issue for the European Communities of the middle eighties. For Western Europe, which had lagged behind the United States and Japan in technological and structural terms, the strengthening of market integration seemed indispensable. This necessity was recognised in 1985 by Jacques Delors, the newly appointed President of the European Commission, who understood and made the Member States accept that a prerequisite for development in the technology-intensive period of economic growth was a large and deregulated internal market. In 1985, the European Commission prepared a White Paper[18] under the guidance of Lord Cockfield – a member of the European Commission who was responsible for the internal market – which contained a plan for a single market, to be implemented by 1992. The White Paper was aimed at removing all restrictions hindering the establishment of a real common market (the so-called single or internal market), such as obstacles of a physical nature (border formalities and controls), financial (budgetary and taxation rules) or technical nature (differing Member State legislation, standards and other national – typically technical – regulations). With this in mind, the White Paper identified about 300 specific tasks which required legislation.

The realisation of these tasks required the consent of the Member States, which also involved disregarding unanimity and adopting majority decision-making, a necessary change for the accomplishment of such a large-scale legislative undertaking. This is why the political climate in the Member States in the mid-eighties was crucial, since the States were ready to further restrict their sovereignty for the sake of the legal rules that were to be created. That was how the Single European Act amending the Treaty of Rome came to be adopted. The Act was signed in Luxembourg on 18 February 1986 and entered into force on 1 January 1987. According to its provisions, a single market was to be created by 31 December 1992. In order to observe this deadline, intensive community legislation and legal harmonisation among the Member States became a characteristic feature in the following years. As a consequence of the single market programme, the amount of Community legislation increased immensely, which made subsequent accession to the integrated Community more difficult, too.

In fact, a single market programme meant harmonisation of Member State legislation on the basis of about 300 Community directives between 1987 and 1992. The purpose of this intensive legislative programme was to remove any barriers that still hindered the free movement of goods, services, capital, and labour, whether technical, physical, or

---

[18] In Community parlance, a White Paper means a plan containing a package of initiatives aimed at a major legislative action, which is issued by the Commission to be used as a proposal or plan prior to the accomplishment of strategic tasks.

financial. The programme of creating a single market thus included, among other things, the elimination of various protectionist national regulations and standards, the removal of obstacles to the movement of capital, the harmonisation of public procurement rules and the liberalisation of a range of service sectors.

The Single European Act did not only address the issue of deregulation that was necessary for the single market. It also brought with it substantial institutional changes through amending the Treaty of Rome in a number of respects, associated with the need for intensive legislative activity and other requirements that had emerged earlier. For example, the Single European Act extended the influence of the European Parliament (which had been elected directly since 1979)[19], widened the scope of competence of the Commission and made changes to the voting system of the Council, increasing the importance of qualified majority voting[20] that had had a minor role compared to unanimous decision-making.

1.8. From the Communities to a Union – The Maastricht Treaty

The intention to create a union of European nations had already been formulated in the Preamble to the Treaty of Rome. The transformation of the Communities into a union, however, was not politically feasible for decades. On the other hand, the political atmosphere of the eighties, that replaced the eurosclerosis of the seventies, promoted the deepening of integration – with the Single European Act as one of its indicators – and provided an appropriate background for the further development of European integration toward an economic and political union. Thus, it was already decided at the time of the adoption of the Single European Act, that the Member States should investigate the feasibility of a transition to an economic and political union in the framework of an Intergovernmental Conference (IGC)[21].

---

[19] For more details, see 2.4.1 and 4.1.1.3.

[20] See 2.3.5.

[21] An Intergovernmental Conference is a series of negotiations of representatives of the Member State governments that is convened when the Member States intend to amend the Founding Treaties, generally with the aim of deepening integration. As the outcome of an IGC is the transfer of certain Member State competencies within national sovereignty to the Community level, an important feature of IGCs is that they are not held within the Community institutional framework, but rather have the form of traditional diplomatic negotiations where each state is represented as a sovereign power. Therefore, decisions at IGCs can be made in total harmony, upon consensus only. The outcome of Conferences, i.e. the treaties thus prepared, must be confirmed (ratified) by each signatory state in accordance with its internal constitutional rules of ratification. An IGC was held prior to the adoption of the Single European Act and the elaboration of the treaties prepared later on (Maastricht, Amsterdam, and Nice). On the role of

It was fairly simple to identify the ways in which integration had to be deepened in order to establish the Union in terms of the economy. As regards political cooperation, however, arriving at a common standpoint appeared much more difficult.

In the area of the economy, for the achievement of a true common market, the next step in the integration process and the creation of an instrument for facing world economic competition, necessitated the introduction of a common currency[22], particularly because the establishment of a monetary union had been on the agenda since the late sixties. However, the early failure of the Werner Plan indicated that the necessary conditions were not within reach. By the early nineties, the successful operation of the European Monetary System, strengthening of inter-dependence and increasing economic integration provided a much more stable setting for the creation of a currency union.

Efforts aimed at establishing a political union took shape with much more difficulty. It was clear that if European integration was to gain the political weight commensurate with its economic power on the stage of world politics, a much more coordinated and uniform foreign policy would be needed to reduce the unsustainable situation of being 'an economic giant but a political dwarf'. It was also apparent that, in a globalising world, several phenomena posing a threat to internal security (illegal migration, terrorism) are linked to the permeability of borders and could be combated more successfully through joint action. That is why the inclusion of foreign policy and justice and home affairs in integration had been on the agenda for a long while. The turning point leading to such a decision was finally provided by the political changes in Central and Eastern Europe and, specifically, the issue of German reunification. The summit meeting of July 1990 decided on convening an Intergovernmental Conference for preparing a treaty on political union. Since a decision had been made earlier on the need for an IGC dealing with economic and monetary union, the summit held on 15 December 1990 could launch parallel IGCs dealing with economic and monetary union as well as political union, with the purpose of working out a treaty on a new European Union.

The Treaty establishing the European Union was signed in the Dutch city of Maastricht on 7 February 1992. The Maastricht Treaty – which made significant amendments to the original treaties – brought fundamental changes to the integration process.

IGCs, see also 5.2.1.

[22] A disadvantage of the EC (EU), usually mentioned in comparison with the United States or Japan, was the lower level of integration of its economy, which was largely attributed to the lack of a single currency.

To deepen economic integration, the Member States decided to join in an economic and monetary union (EMU) and introduce a single currency by not later than 1999. To promote closer political integration, they decided to create a common foreign and security policy, and common aims were identified in the area of home affairs and justice. EU citizenship was introduced[23] and, through a wider interpretation of free movement of labour – extension of the right to each citizen of the Union – the full freedom of people's movement was also decided on.[24]

The Maastricht Treaty introduced the name 'European Union' (EU). While this notion refers to deeper and more comprehensive cooperation compared to the earlier 'European Communities', it should be pointed out that the European Union did not replace the three communities established earlier. On the one hand, it did not terminate them and, on the other hand, the EU does not have an independent legal status, which has remained a privilege of the three Communities. Thus, the European Union is not a legal entity; rather it represents a political notion. European Union means all aspects of European integration in their entirety. Since Maastricht, European integration has been generally referred to through the notion of 'European Union'.

As regards the Communities, the Treaty of Maastricht changed the term 'European Economic Community' to 'European Community', thereby implying, on the one hand, a general scope of competence of this Community with respect to the common market, compared to the restricted competence of the other two Communities and, on the other hand, indicating that the Community is more than just a form of economic cooperation, especially since the Maastricht Treaty gave the Community competence in a number of non-economic policy areas (e.g. health, culture, education).

Despite the introduction of the name 'European Community'; the three Communities are jointly referred to as the 'European Communities'.

---

[23] Accordingly, everyone who is a citizen of a Member State is also a citizen of the Union. Union citizenship does not replace citizenship of a Member State; rather, it is complementary and grants extra rights. Union citizenship grants four specific rights: a citizen of the Union can 1. freely move, travel and stay in any country of the EU; 2. participate in municipal and European parliamentary elections in the Member State in which he resides, can take part as a candidate and can be elected; 3. request protection while in a country outside the Union from diplomatic bodies or consulates of any other EU Member State if his own country has no representation there; 4. submit petitions to the European Parliament and complaints to the European Ombudsman.

[24] Since Maastricht, the four core freedoms of the Union (the common or single market) have been the free movement of goods, services, capital, and also people. For more details, see 6.2.

Thanks to the Maastricht Treaty, a specific three-pillar structure was established.[25] The first pillar was determined as the three Communities that were already in operation, i.e. the European Communities[26], including the tasks related to the new aims of the economic and monetary union. As they did not want to establish very close Community-type cooperation in the areas aimed at creating a political Union, there was a need to create two new cooperation arrangements of a looser type, i.e. to set up two new pillars. The second and the third pillars were the new Common Foreign and Security Policy and Cooperation on Justice and Home Affairs organised on an intergovernmental basis, where competences of the Community institutions remained rather limited. The three pillars together constitute the European Union.[27]

At the time of preparing the Maastricht Treaty, more effective and democratic decision-making was also set out as a fundamental aim. For this reason – and as a continuation of the process begun by the Single European Act – the Treaty extended the scope of competence of the European Parliament considerably and widened the sphere of application of qualified majority voting in the Council, while restricting decisions requiring unanimity.

One of the purposes of the Maastricht Treaty was to finally settle disputes emerging in connection with coinciding scopes of Community and Member State competence. To this aim, the Treaty included the principle of subsidiarity in Community decision-making. According to this principle, an issue should be decided on at the Community level if the aim concerned cannot be realised at the national level and the measure proposed can probably be carried out with better success and efficiency at the Community level owing to its extent and effects.

1.9. The EU after Maastricht – Results following initial difficulties: a new enlargement and the introduction of the single currency

The Maastricht Treaty represented an enormous step toward closer integration. Yet the years following the signing of the document passed again in an atmosphere of eurosclerosis. After Maastricht, many thought that the leaders of the Union had gone too far, especially by setting monetary union and the single currency as an aim. This opinion manifested itself in the difficulties of ratifying the Treaty experienced in the Member States. For example, the Treaty was adopted by the referendum held in one of the key states of integration, France, by a mere 1% majority, while in Denmark it was rejected. Thus, to

---

[25] The text of the Treaty does not contain the word 'pillar'; this term became generally used and accepted later on.

[26] As the first pillar was in fact the earlier European Communities, the term Community (Communities) continued to be used after the establishment of the European Union as a reference to the first pillar of the EU.

[27] On the three pillars, see Chapter 3.

evade a crisis endangering the existence of the Union as such, the referendum had to be repeated in Denmark in 1993. The result was positive, although the Danes were given an 'opt-out', similarly to the British, who had presented the same request at the time of signing the Treaty[28]; this gave them an option to voluntarily withdraw from the monetary union. The Maastricht Treaty became effective on 1 November 1993 after the difficulties had been eliminated and the constitutional concerns in Germany had been dispelled.

The economic recession that took place in the early nineties did not appear favourable for integration either. It had a strong impact on the monetary system so that meeting the conditions for monetary union and introducing the single currency by the established date appeared rather difficult. The voices that criticised the idea of a monetary union as premature intensified and demanded its postponement.

In these hard times, however, more and more applicants knocked at the door of the Union. The establishment of the EU represented a bloc of close integration and staying away from it entailed the risk of lagging behind and possible isolation in a world undergoing intensive globalisation. Thus, it came as no surprise that four EFTA Member States, Austria, Finland, Norway, and Sweden, which had submitted their application before, became keen to join and were followed by the states of Central and Eastern Europe, that had rid themselves of the communist regime and signed association agreements with the EU.[29] In the first half of the nineties, however, the option of joining the EU was only realistic for the EFTA Member States.

EFTA

In the fifties, the British who traditionally favoured free trade, intended to establish a free trade association embracing all of Western Europe. However, it became clear

---

[28] The 'opt-out' clause allows the United Kingdom and Denmark to decide individually on joining the monetary union, which means giving up their national currencies and introducing the single currency. The other Member States are not granted this option; joining the monetary union for them is in essence mandatory, provided that they fulfil the required criteria. Opt-out-like solutions were also applied to issues other than the single currency. The Danes were granted similar rights in relation to other aspects of the Maastricht Treaty (in justice and home affairs).

[29] Officially, the association agreements are concluded with the EC and not the EU, as international treaties can only be concluded by the Community due to the fact that the Union does not have a legal personality. The countries of Central and Eastern Europe and the eastern enlargement of the EU are discussed in detail in 1.13.

with the establishment of the EEC that 'the Six' had a different idea about European integration. Thus, the British had to realise their plan without the six states, so they set out to establish the European Free Trade Association (EFTA). The agreement on establishing EFTA was signed by the founding members Austria, Denmark, Norway, Portugal, Sweden, Switzerland and the United Kingdom on 4 January 1960. Later, Iceland, Finland, and Liechtenstein joined the Association. However, some member countries left the organisation and decided to join the European Communities (or, later on, the European Union). First, the British themselves, having reviewed their integration policy, entered the EC together with the Danes in 1973, and so did Portugal in 1986, followed by Austria, Finland and Sweden in 1995. Thus, EFTA was reduced to an organisation of minor importance, since it now has only four small, geographically distant member states (Iceland, Liechtenstein, Norway, and Switzerland).

Free trade in industrial products between the European Communities and EFTA had already been implemented in 1977, and relations remained at this level for more than a decade. But because the Community had decided on creating a single internal market, negotiations were started on how the EFTA countries, with a similar level of development in terms of market economy, could be included and a yet wider single European market established. Finally, the European Communities and six EFTA Member States decided to create a large European economic area through extending the single market to EFTA and started negotiations in June 1990. As a result, the twelve European Community member countries and the six EFTA members (Austria, Finland, Iceland, Norway, Switzerland, Sweden) signed the Treaty on the establishment of the European Economic Area (EEA) on 2 May 1992, which became effective on 1 January 1994, with the participation of 17 states only, since a referendum in Switzerland had rejected entry into the EEA. Later on, the number of EEA members rose to 18 when Liechtenstein joined this economic association in May 1995. The importance of the EEA is related to the fact that the EFTA states concerned took over approximately 80% of the rules regulating the single market so as to provide for the internal market conditions required for the common economic area; practically all legal provisions except those pertaining to agriculture and fishery were adopted by the EFTA states. Another important feature of participation in the EEA is that non-EU EEA members are consulted in the course of the elaboration of new Community legislation falling within its sphere of competence (that is, the single market).

As a result of establishing the EEA, an economic block with a population of more than 370 million people was created. Its importance, however, declined within a short time because Austria, Finland, Norway and Sweden started accession negotiations with the EU in 1993 and managed to conclude them in 1994, with 1 January 1995 being the date set for actual accession. In the end, however, only Austria, Finland, and Sweden joined the European Union because the citizens of Norway rejected accession for a second time, as it had in 1972. Thus, the number of European Union Member States grew to 15 on 1 January 1995.[30] Of course, the three new ex-EFTA member countries continued to be members of the EEA, representing this time, however, the EU. On the other hand, the importance of the EEA as an institution diminished to a minimum as it meant barely more than the EU itself, since the EEA embraces, in addition to the EU Member States, just one small state (Norway) and two mini states (Iceland and Liechtenstein) with less than 5 million inhabitants in total.

The economy and the weight in the world economy of the EU increased further through the enlargement in 1995 and the establishment of the European Economic Area. This increase was necessary for the organisation which experienced some economic and political crises after Maastricht. Pursuant to the Maastricht Treaty, the Union (which was to face another enlargement wave after the applications had been received from countries of Central and Eastern Europe) had to accomplish, before the turn of the millennium, its perhaps most important undertaking – the introduction of the single currency. The political problems undermining the Maastricht optimism around 1992–1993, followed by an economic recession lasting well into the mid-nineties, together with rising unemployment and increasing budgetary difficulties, had made the introduction of the single currency hard to achieve. However, the stringent measures taken in 1996–1997 on economic policy and the return of prosperity appeared to make the launch of the single currency viable by 1998. Hence, the common European currency, named the 'euro', could be launched as planned, on 1 January 1999, with 11 of the 15 Member States participating. On 1 January 2001, Greece joined as the 12th state. Thus, only Denmark, the United Kingdom, and Sweden stayed out of the largest EU advance for many years. The culmination of the introduction of the single currency was reached on 1 January 2002, when euro banknotes and coins were introduced in cash transactions. As a result, not just a single currency but also European integration became a tangible reality for many citizens of the Union. On 1 March 2002, after a two month period of parallel use, old national currencies were withdrawn in the 12 Member States concerned, called 'countries of the eurozone', and the euro became the sole legal tender. It is no exaggeration to state that the introduction of the single currency marked the beginning of a new era for the European Union and opened new horizons for European integration, undoubtedly offering new opportunities both economically and in the area of political union.[31]

---

[30] It should be noted that a sort of enlargement had also taken place before the EFTA countries joined the Union; the former Eastern Germany, the GDR (German Democratic Republic) was integrated with the EU in 1990 when Germany was re-united.

[31] For details concerning the circumstances of the introduction of the single currency, see Chapter 8.6.

1.10. Maastricht continued: the Amsterdam Treaty

Since the Member States were unsure about the consequences of the implementation of the Treaty's provisions at the time of the signature of the Maastricht Treaty, and could not foresee how the system that was new in several respects would function, they provided in one of the articles of the Maastricht Treaty (Article N.) that another Intergovernmental Conference should be convened in 1996 to review and possibly amend the Treaty. Launching the IGC in the mid-nineties became justified for an increasing number of reasons.

Many thought, after Maastricht, that the organisation that had developed from the Communities into a Union, and which had obtained in Maastricht several new rights and tasks as a result of deepening integration, was not functioning satisfactorily in a number of respects. They called attention to the fact that more and more areas and related decisions were transferred to the Community level, whereas the functioning of the Community institutions was inappropriate in terms of both democratic control and efficiency. In addition, decision-making that was still significantly based on unanimity between the Member States became rather difficult in the fifteen-member Union. For the Union that was facing further enlargement, with the countries of Central and Eastern Europe, the restructuring of an institutional system originally designed to accommodate only six Member States was becoming an increasingly urgent task.

The Intergovernmental Conference which opened in Turin in March 1996 was meant to assist in a comprehensive reform of the operation of the Union as a kind of supplement to, or revision of, the Maastricht Treaty. However, the large number of current problems considerably expanded and prolonged the programme of the conference. The negotiations could only be ended nearly one and a half years later, in June 1997, when a new Treaty amending the treaties on which the EU is based was prepared in Amsterdam. The Amsterdam Treaty was signed on 2 October 1997 and entered into force following the required ratification by the Member States on 1 May 1999.

According to general opinion, the importance of the Amsterdam Treaty failed to meet expectations, because no agreement was reached on issues that appeared necessary for the further enlargement of the EU and for making the institutional system more efficient. The crucial issues requiring the most difficult compromises were postponed and the hardest decisions to be made by the Union were actually put off. Amsterdam was supposed to definitively resolve three institutional issues with regard to EU enlargement: extension of Council decisions requiring qualified majority voting (reducing the application of unanimity-based decision-making to a minimum); re-weighting of votes in the Council;

determination of the composition and size of the Commission. These three issues left open in Amsterdam were named Amsterdam leftovers.[32] Despite the failure in the area of institutional restructuring, the Amsterdam Treaty brought some progress. Positive – albeit not revolutionary – changes were made in the area of Common Foreign and Security Policy[33], and – perhaps the largest achievement – considerable progress was made in intensifying cooperation on justice and home affairs (primarily through the integration of the areas of external and internal border controls, immigration, asylum and judicial cooperation on civil matters into the first pillar).[34] A further achievement of the Amsterdam Treaty involved raising the issue of employment policy to Community level – an issue that was especially interesting for Member State citizens because of the increase in unemployment that had taken place in the previous couple of years. Pursuant to the Treaty, and as a supplement to the harmonisation of economic policies, the Member States were required to coordinate the orientation and purposes of their respective national employment policies along guidelines adopted mutually each year.[35]

The Amsterdam Treaty managed to produce results in making the decision-making mechanism more democratic and efficient. First of all, the significant widening of the decision-making competence of the European Parliament, the simplification of the co-decision procedure and the significant extension of its application were considerable innovations[36]. Also, the Treaty expanded the range of issues requiring a qualified majority vote, albeit to an extent much smaller than expected. A main aim of the Amsterdam Treaty was to improve decision-making by making it more transparent and citizen-friendly. Mention should be made in this respect of the declaration on opening up access to Union-related information and documents, making this a basic right, and on making the Treaties establishing the European Union and the Communities more transparent[37].

In spite of the major innovations and progress made by the Amsterdam Treaty, it left the impression of a semi-finished Treaty, as it failed to solve some of the most important problems that the Union was to face and it also failed to provide the expected results on issues that were considered by many as a precondition for eastward enlargement. This entailed

---

[32] The 'Amsterdam leftovers' were finally settled by the Treaty of Nice that envisaged this task as its main aim.

[33] For details, see 23.3.

[34] For more details, see 24.3.

[35] For details, see Chapter 14.

[36] A more thorough presentation is given in Chapter 4.1.1.3. and 4.1.2.4.

[37] This involved re-structuring and re-numbering the titles and articles of the Treaties for the sake of transparency; thus the articles of the Treaties have been effective since the Amsterdam Treaty with the new numbering, which this book also uses (the numbering used earlier is only indicated when relevant).

Table 1.1. Development of European integration from customs union
to political union

Integration level	Legal base	Objective	Implementation
Customs union	Treaty of Rome (signature: 25. 03. 1957 entry into force: 01. 01. 1958)	Customs union: until 1970	1968
Common market	Treaty of Rome (signature: 25. 03. 1957 entry into force: 01. 01. 1958)	Common market: no specific final deadline	Ongoing implementation
Single market	Single European Act (signature: 18. 02. 1986 entry into force: 01. 01. 1987)	Single market: Single Market Programme by 01. 01. 1993	01. 01. 1993 (implementation of specific programme) Ongoing implementation
Economic and monetary union	Treaty of Maastricht (signature: 07. 02. 1992 entry into force: 01. 11. 1993)	Monetary union: by 01. 01. 1999, the latest Economic union: no specific final deadline	⇒ 1999.01.01. ⇒ Ongoing implementation
	Treaty of Amsterdam (signature: 02. 10. 1997 entry into force: 01. 05. 1999)	Coordination of employment policy: no specific final deadline	⇒ Ongoing implementation
Political union	Treaty of Maastricht (signature: 07. 02. 1992 entry into force: 01. 11. 1993)	– EU citizenship – Common Foreign and Security Policy – cooperation in justice and home affairs	⇒ 01. 11. 1993 ⇒ Ongoing implementation ⇒ Ongoing implementation
	Treaty of Amsterdam (signature: 02. 10. 1997 entry into force: 01. 05. 1999)	– Strengthening of foreign and security policy – Communitarisation of most of justice and home affairs within 5 years	⇒ Ongoing implementation ⇒ 01. 05. 2004

statement by several Member States and the European Parliament itself according to which a new round of enlargement would be supported only when all problems left over had been settled. Thus, less than a month after the Amsterdam Treaty entered into force, the Member States decided at the Cologne Summit held on 3 and 4 June 1999 to convene another Intergovernmental Conference in the first half of 2000 that would close by the end of 2000; it was intended that this would allow for the decisions necessary for institutional reforms and for the amendment of the EC Treaty and the EU Treaty.

1.11. The precondition for enlargement: the Treaty of Nice

Although several Member States considered that the institutional failure of the Amsterdam Treaty did not enable the institutional and decision-making system of the Union to accept more Member States, the unanimous opinion of the Member States was that this did not affect the commencement and continuation of accession negotiations with candidate countries.

The institutional reform of the EU before enlargement was necessary because more countries had applied for membership than at any time before. By the middle of the nineties, a total of 13 countries had indicated their intention to join the EU: Bulgaria, Cyprus, the Czech Republic, Estonia, Hungary, Latvia, Lithuania, Malta[38], Poland, Romania, Slovakia, Slovenia, and Turkey. The Community institutional system, originally designed for 6 Member States, was already operating with some difficulty with the 15 Member States. Although the system might have been able to manage with some new members, it would probably fail if the number of member countries nearly doubled. That was why the EU decided in Cologne, in the summer of 1999, to complete the reforms left over from Amsterdam before commencing with eastern enlargement. On the other hand, the Member States fully agreed that accession negotiations could be conducted even though the reforms would need to be completed before the first new member was admitted.

In line with the above, the EU decided at its Luxembourg Summit held in December 1997 to launch its largest ever enlargement process, which officially commenced on 30 March 1998 at the ceremonial meeting of the Ministers for Foreign Affairs. One day later, in pursuance of the Luxembourg decision of the EU, accession negotiations were opened with the most advanced group of candidate countries, including five Central and Eastern European countries (the Czech Republic, Estonia, Hungary, Poland, and Slovenia), plus Cyprus. At the same time, the EU started to maintain closer ties with the other candidate countries (and in fact began preparatory work aimed at opening negotiations with them).

---

[38] Although Malta suspended its accession application in 1996, it re-applied for membership in 1998.

The EU had to specify a financial framework for funding the enlargement process and accepting new Member States. Since all of the candidate countries in Central and Eastern Europe lagged far behind the average level of development of the EU, it was apparent that their entry would require a considerable EU budget increase and/or re-structuring of the most expensive policies of the EU. The EU had to settle this problem prior to accession. The Heads of State or Government of the Member States made an effort at their Berlin Summit on 25 March 1999 to handle this issue within the framework of the Agenda 2000 programme, representing a budget and reform package. Agenda 2000 determined the EU's financial perspectives (budgetary framework) for the 2000–2006 period, in which provisions were made, from the year 2002, in the form of a budgetary item with concrete figures, to allow for the possible admission of new Member States.[39]

An important point in the process of enlargement was the Helsinki Summit held in December 1999, when the EU decided to commence negotiations with six other candidate countries and offered candidate country status to Turkey. Thus, in addition to the six countries that had been carrying out negotiations for nearly two years, another six countries (Bulgaria, Latvia, Lithuania, Romania, Slovakia, and Malta) began accession negotiations with the European Union on 15 February 2000. It was also decided in Helsinki that the EU would start another Intergovernmental Conference in February 2000 to discuss the reforms left over from Amsterdam, according to the schedule specified in Cologne; this IGC would finish by the end of 2000. The Treaty to be worked out would specify the required institutional reforms and enable the Union to admit new Member States. The Member States also committed themselves in Helsinki to concluding the ratification process of the new Treaty by not later than the end of 2002, to prepare the European Union for enlargement from 1 January 2003. This was the decision by which the Member States specified, for the first time, an earliest date for eastern enlargement. Nevertheless, due to the road map adopted at the Nice Summit in December 2000, it became gradually clear that a more realistic date of accession would be 2004 in the case of the best-prepared candidates.

The Intergovernmental Conference launched on 14 February 2000 pursuant to the Helsinki decisions mostly concentrated on the institutional issues left over by the Amsterdam Treaty[40] and ended with the Nice Summit of 7–10 December 2000 after 10 months of intensive negotiations. The new treaty amending the Founding Treaties

---

[39] For details on Agenda 2000, see 7.3.4., 11.5., and 13.3.

[40] Amsterdam leftovers: increasing the scope of decisions to be made in Council by qualified majority voting, re-weighting of Council votes, determination of the composition and the size of the Commission.

of the EU, i.e. the Treaty of Nice, was born, which was directly aimed at reforming the institutional system and the process of decision-making. The Treaty of Nice formulated at the summit of December 2000 was finally signed on 26 February 2001, and entered into force on 1 February 2003 following a long ratification process, which was particularly problematical in Ireland.[41]

Although the Treaty of Nice can be viewed as a continuation of the process of deeper integration aimed at by the Single European Act, the Maastricht Treaty, and the Amsterdam Treaty, it did not focus on including more fields in the integration process and transferring new areas of competence to the EU level – as did the treaties concluded earlier – rather, it aimed at speeding up decision-making in connection with decisions concerning existing scopes of competence and at facilitating agreement among Member States, so as to enable the EU to operate efficiently after the large-scale increase in its members. Thus, the Treaty of Nice carried on the process that began with the Single European Act and was aimed at further extending the role of qualified majority voting in EU decision-making against unanimity-based decisions and at modifying Member State participation in decision-making so that population weights would be better reflected in the decision-making bodies of the EU. The Treaty extended decisions made through qualified majority voting to a number of areas, thereby restricting the option to set a Member State veto, and further increased the influence of the European Parliament in passing decisions (though to a lesser extent compared to the Single European Act, Maastricht, or Amsterdam). As regards Community institutions, the Treaty of Nice specified the weights to be assigned to each country in the new 27-member Union (comprising the then 15 Member States and the 12 candidate countries still engaged in negotiations). Furthermore, with a view to the growing number of Member States, the Treaty facilitated the use of enhanced cooperation[42], making it possible for countries intending to proceed with integration at a faster rate to deepen their integration in certain areas, even if some other Member States decided not to. With these provisions, the Treaty of Nice made significant steps toward preserving the efficiency of an enlarged EU, although it has to be noted that the Treaty fell behind expectations

---

[41] The referendum on the Treaty of Nice held in Ireland on 7 June 2001 produced a record-low turnout (34.79%) and a negative outcome, with 53.87% of the voters rejecting the Treaty, partly due to the strong NO-campaigners who misinterpreted the Treaty. In order to avoid a potential crisis, which could have even delayed enlargement, the Irish government decided to put the Treaty of Nice to the popular vote a second time. The second plebiscite held on 19 October 2002 mobilised 48.9% of the electorate, 62.89% of whom cast their ballot in favour of the Treaty.

[42] For details, see 4.1.1.2.

in several respects compared to federalist aspirations. Major criticism was directed at the insufficient expansion of the scope of qualified majority decision-making and of the competence of the European Parliament (unanimity-based decisions were retained in a relatively large number of cases[43]), and the preservation (and even further complication) of a decision-making system that still lacked transparency for the average citizen. Yet the undoubted importance of the Treaty of Nice was that its entry into force opened the way to the historical eastward enlargement, which foreshadowed a new dimension to the European Union.

Nonetheless, Nice did not solve several problems related to efficiency, transparency and democratic operation, which could only be eliminated within the framework of a more comprehensive reform. With a view to this, the Member States decided in a Declaration annexed to the Treaty of Nice, to convene another Intergovernmental Conference in 2004 where a longer term, more profound institutional restructuring of the Union would have to be discussed – with the inclusion of the new members and candidate countries which would have signed their accession treaties by then.

Two major factors played a crucial role in the issue of the Nice Declaration, annexed to the Treaty of Nice. On the one hand, an opinion – albeit then only a minority opinion – had already been on the agenda of the EU prior to the IGC of 2000, to the effect that the EU should not exclusively address enlargement-related institutional issues but should also adopt global reforms to fundamentally restructure the institutions. On the other hand, the modest results attained by the Treaty of Nice made it clear that the time was ripe for the EU Member States to consider more thoroughly the issue of the orientation of integration, namely the way they wanted the future Europe to look. The need for further reforms received impetus from the fact that the bargaining-style politics typical of IGCs failed in Nice and from the growing feeling that closed IGCs were unsuitable for making major reforms and that a complementary working method was required. Thus, the Member States, in issuing the Nice Declaration, made a decision not simply on which issues should be dealt with during the next institutional reform (a more precise separation of competences of the

---

[43] Although decision-making by unanimity had already been used much less frequently than qualified majority voting before Nice, the main problem was related to the quality, rather than the quantity, of those decisions. Several issues crucial for the deepening of integration still required the full consent of the Member States even after Nice (see Appendix I), and that might hinder flexible progress and further deepening of the EU.

EU and the Member States, reflecting the principle of subsidiarity; determination of the status of the Union's Charter of Fundamental Rights[44]; simplification of the Treaties; role of the national parliaments in the European architecture) but also on providing a new, more transparent and democratic framework than before, that would be necessary for outlining and proposing the reforms.

1.12. The European Union at the beginning of the 21st century: the parallel processes of deepening and widening

1.12.1. Enlargement

The Nice Summit of December 2000 marked a turning point in enlargement of the European Union from two aspects. The summit gave birth to the Treaty of Nice, considered a prerequisite for enlargement, and it also saw the adoption of an enlargement strategy, containing a detailed roadmap. On this basis, the Heads of State or Government expressed their hope that they could conclude accession negotiations with the most advanced candidate countries before the end of 2002, and that the citizens of these countries could already take part in the next elections to the European Parliament in June 2004, implying that eastern enlargement would begin by that date. The Nice roadmap was confirmed at the Laeken Summit in December 2001, where ten candidate countries that had a good chance of early entry were named (Cyprus, the Czech Republic, Estonia, Hungary, Latvia, Lithuania, Malta, Poland, Slovakia and Slovenia). Due to the accelerated pace of accession negotiations in 2001 and

---

[44] The Cologne European Council of 3–4 June 1999 took the view that the fundamental rights applicable at Union level should be consolidated in a single document. As a result, the Charter of Fundamental Rights of the EU was adopted at the Nice European Council in December 2000 and was proclaimed subsequently by the Community institutions. However, the Charter – which is more than a symbolic text, as it also defines social rights – could not become legally binding due to the disagreement between the Member States; decisions concerning the Charter's legal status and its place in Community law were postponed. This was because some countries, such as the UK and certain Scandinavian countries, feared that if the charter became legally binding, it would create new legal obligations that would undermine their national sovereignty. Hence, even though most of the Member States would have liked to see a legally binding Charter, it remained a political declaration. Nevertheless, it became clear that, at this level of European integration, the fundamental rights of European citizens had to be laid down at the level of the Union. (For more on the Charter of Fundamental Rights, see 5.5. and Annex, Point 5.5.)

2002, the negotiations were concluded with these 10 countries at the Copenhagen Summit on 13 December 2002, and the date for their accession was set for 1 May 2004. The Accession Treaty were finally signed in Athens on 16 April 2003 and followed by the necessary ratification procedures in all the 25 countries involved (the 15 Member States and the 10 acceding countries). As part of this process, all the candidate countries except Cyprus[45] held a referendum on accession. After the successful referenda and the conclusion of parliamentary ratification procedures, the historic eastern enlargement of the European Union actually took place on 1 May 2004 with the accession of Cyprus, the Czech Republic, Estonia, Hungary, Latvia, Lithuania, Malta, Poland, Slovakia and Slovenia. Many referred to this enlargement as the reunification of Europe, which brought an end to the post-World War II division of Europe. The Iron Curtain had finally fallen for good, and a new phase of European development began with the main objective of managing the impact of enlargement and pressing ahead with deepening, that is completing the economic union and political union and reconciling the goals of further enlargement and deepening.

Following closely in the footsteps of the 2004 enlargement, the four-year negotiations with Bulgaria and Romania were concluded at the summit of 16–17 December 2004. With the accession of these two countries on 1 January 2007, the EU now has 27 Member States (four and a half times the original six), uniting almost half a billion citizens.

The accession of Bulgaria and Romania marked the end of the enlargement process that began in the early nineties, although the Union will probably continue to expand to the south-east. The December 2004 European Council decided that negotiations should be commenced with Croatia in March 2005 and with Turkey in October 2005. Accession talks began with both countries on 3 October 2005, when Croatia's cooperation with the International Criminal Tribunal for the former Yugoslavia (ICTY) – which deals with war crimes committed in the former Yugoslavia – was finally deemed satisfactory, which was a precondition for starting such negotiations. Croatia could realise its membership aspirations in the near future, while the accession of Turkey will probably be a more lengthy

---

[45] A referendum was held in Cyprus in April 2004 on the unification of the southern Greek-populated and the northern Turkish-populated parts of the island; the proposed unification was based on a UN proposal. The Greek Cypriots rejected unification since they found the UN plan unacceptable. As a result, on 1 May 2004, only the internationally recognised southern part of the island populated by Greek Cypriots acceded to the European Union.

process: the EU has proclaimed that it cannot happen before 2015.[46] It should be noted that some Member States (such as Austria and France) have expressed serious reservations in relation to Turkey's accession, which could influence the whole process of negotiations, already burdened with a number of difficulties. Due to Turkey's refusal to recognise Cyprus and open its ports to vessels flying the Cypriot flag, in December 2006 the EU decided not to open the eight negotiating chapters linked to the customs union until Turkey changed its position.

The possibility of a future continuation of the enlargement process was demonstrated by the Thessaloniki Summit of June 2003, where the EU offered the prospect of membership to the countries of the Western Balkans (Albania, Bosnia-Herzegovina, Croatia, Macedonia and the then State Union of Serbia-Montenegro which has since split up); this did not constitute a specific promise of accession but indicated the EU's commitment to this region. As a result, Macedonia followed in the footsteps of Croatia and submitted its application for membership in March 2004. The EU officially recognised Macedonia as a candidate country in December 2005, but has not yet adopted an official position concerning the opening of accession talks. Other countries of the Western Balkans are considered potential candidates for membership.[47]

As far as the continuation of enlargement is concerned, it should be emphasised that several Member States along with the European Parliament link any future enlargement beyond the current 27 inextricably with putting the EU on a new Treaty basis – a process which began well before 2004 but which will be completed in 2009 at the earliest.

1.12.2. The comprehensive reform of the Founding Treaties – From the Constitutional Treaty to the Reform Treaty

Already at the time of the adoption of the Treaty of Nice – considered a precondition to enlargement to Central and Eastern Europe – the EU recognised that the institutional framework modified in Nice would not guarantee the efficient functioning of the institutions in a Union of 25–27, and would not necessarily enable the Union to fulfil its ambitions for

---

[46] At the summit of December 2004, the Heads of State or Government stated that negotiations with candidate countries whose accession had considerable budgetary impacts could only be concluded after the financial perspectives for the period from 2014 are finalized. Consequently, Turkey – due to its size and its peculiar problems – obviously cannot become a member before that date.

[47] A comprehensive overview of eastern enlargement is given in 1.13. For details on the continuation of enlargement (Croatia, Turkey and the Western Balkans), see 1.13.8. For more on relations with the Western Balkans, see 9.4.2.1.

deepening and widening. This recognition provoked the Nice Declaration, annexed to the Treaty of Nice, in which the Member States decided to convene another Intergovernmental Conference in 2004 to discuss the comprehensive long-term institutional reforms, with the active participation of countries that had become members by then or had signed treaties of accession. To prepare the sweeping reforms, the Member States also decided in Nice that, for the first time in EU history, institutional changes should be shaped in the framework of a wide public debate, although its conclusion and final decision-making phase would again be an IGC.

The most important decisions concerning the content and organisation relating to the preparation of the IGC of 2004 were made at the Laeken Summit held on 14–15 December 2001. Before Laeken, three issues had to be tackled: whether a limitation should be imposed on the topics to be discussed at the IGC; what organisational form should be selected to prepare the Conference, so that transparency and democracy would be ensured; how candidate countries (i.e. future Member States) should be involved in the organisational framework, given that a majority of them would in all probability have the right of approval with respect to the results of the Conference.

Finally, the Heads of State or Government of the EU adopted a Declaration at the Laeken Summit concerning the future of the Union. The Laeken Declaration emphasised that the Union needed to make progress in three areas if it was to play a role in the world commensurate with its economic weight. These three areas were: making Europe more democratic, strengthening Europe's global participation and taking steps to better meet the needs of citizens. On the basis of these objectives, the Declaration identified the areas – representing a reconsideration of the four issues formulated in Nice – that should be addressed during the reform and on which the Union would be expected to produce results. These included: more appropriate definition and division of competencies within the Union; simplification of the instruments of the Union; increased transparency, democracy, and efficiency; and a constitution for the citizens of Europe.

A decision was also made in Laeken on the organisational framework in which these issues should be addressed and the Intergovernmental Conference of 2004 prepared. In order to provide for a more open, transparent, and democratic organisational framework, the Heads of State or Government of the Member States decided to set up a broad body called a Convention[48], whose work would be assisted not only by representatives of the national governments but also by representatives of national parliaments, as well as

---

[48] Its full name was: the Convention on the Future of Europe

representatives of the institutions of the Union.[49] It was evident that such an organisation could operate and work out proposals for the Intergovernmental Conference which would be convened at the end of the process for passing a final decision, and that this structure would give it more legitimacy. Based on these assumptions, the Laeken Declaration formulated a detailed decision concerning the tasks pertaining to setting up the Convention. Pursuant to the Laeken decisions, the Convention that was established on 28 February 2002 consisted of a Chairman (Valéry Giscard d'Estaing) and two Vice-Chairmen (Giuliano Amato and Jean-Luc Dehaene), and also one representative of the government of each of the 15 Member States, two representatives from each national parliament of the Member States, 16 Members of the European Parliament, and two delegates from the European Commission. An historic decision was made on the inclusion of the candidate countries in the debate on the Convention and the future of the EU. Accordingly, the candidate countries (all 13; the 12 engaged in accession talks and Turkey) were fully included in the work of the Convention, represented, similarly to the Member States, by one representative of each government and two representatives of each national parliament. The number of Convention members including candidate country representatives totalled 105.[50] The Convention had to report to the European Council and submit proposals to the Intergovernmental Conference.

When the Convention began its work, it was unclear what form its proposals to the IGC would take. As work progressed, the expectation became increasingly manifest that this broad-based body (comprising representatives of the key European and national institutions) should elaborate proposals in as specific a manner as possible. Finally, the Convention itself decided to prepare the draft of a new Treaty for the European Union to replace the system of treaties in force. To indicate the advanced level of integration and the closeness of relations between Member States, the draft Treaty was named the Constitutional Treaty, officially the *Treaty establishing a Constitution for Europe*. The name was supposed to reflect the balance between the fact that it was an international treaty

---

[49] The Charter of Fundamental Rights was already prepared in the framework of a similar 'Convention' and the positive experience served as a basis for the decision on establishing a similar body as the most suitable forum for work and debate concerning the preparation for the next Intergovernmental Conference.

[50] Except for the Chairman and the two vice-chairmen, all members had a substitute, who could also take part in the work of the Convention; thus, in practical terms, the Convention had 207 members.

(and not a constitution) and that, by emphasising its constitutional nature, politically speaking it symbolised the closeness of European unity.[51]

At the end of a period of almost 18 months, the Convention completed its work on 10 July 2003 by adopting the draft Constitutional Treaty, which it forwarded to the European Council to be used for opening the Intergovernmental Conference.

As a result of enlargement, the IGC debating the draft Constitutional Treaty put forward by the Convention began with the participation of 25 countries[52] on 4 October 2003, ahead of the Nice schedule. The IGC set itself the objective of adopting a new treaty framework to guarantee that the EU could function smoothly with 25, 27 or possibly even more Member States and at the same time make the Union's institutions and decision-making simpler, more democratic and more transparent for citizens.

The overhaul of the Union's functioning, legal and institutional set-up in the Convention was deeper and more thorough than any previous attempts. The result was the draft Constitutional Treaty. A number of Member States – particularly the most fervent advocates of deepening, namely the founding states – would have liked the IGC to endorse the Convention's proposal, maybe with some minor changes, and adopt it at the 2003 December summit, but due to disagreements on some issues, in particular the weighting

---

[51] The name 'Constitutional Treaty' is the result of a compromise between the more federalist supporters, suggesting the name 'European Constitution', and the less federalist-minded, who had difficulties with the word 'constitution" (the United Kingdom, for example, has no written national Constitution as such) and wanted to stick with the simple term 'Treaty'. The formulation 'Treaty establishing a Constitution for Europe' – or 'Constitutional Treaty' in short – emerged as a compromise. Although, in a legal sense, it was a traditional international treaty, politically its objectives went beyond traditional international treaties, and some of its provisions were of a constitutional nature.

[52] The 15 Member States and the 10 countries that joined on 1 May 2004 took part in the IGC on an equal footing from its beginning. It was already decided in the Nice Declaration that candidate countries could take part in the work of the IGC following the signing of their accession treaties (for the ten countries this happened on 16 April 2003), but their precise status remained unspecified. The 15 Member States granted equal rights to those 10 acceding countries as it was obvious that they would also have to sign the Constitutional Treaty, which would only enter into force after their accession. The then candidate countries (Bulgaria, Romania and Turkey) could also participate in the IGC as observers, having the right to take the floor but not to vote.

of votes, this was not possible. The negotiations continued into 2004 and, after over eight months of talks the IGC was finally concluded and the text of the Constitutional Treaty was adopted at the Brussels Summit on 17–18 June 2004. The IGC introduced about 80 significant changes[53] to the Convention's draft, while leaving its structure virtually intact. As a tribute to the Treaty of Rome of 1957, the 25 Member States signed the new Treaty on 29 October 2004 in Rome. The aim was to complete its ratification by 1 November 2006. The rather lengthy ratification process was warranted by the fact that ten Member States[54] indicated that they would hold a referendum, making it difficult to predict when the Constitutional Treaty would enter into force.

The Constitutional Treaty, born of a desire to improve the functioning of the European Union by simplification and to guarantee more transparency and efficiency, attempted to consolidate the existing treaties (the Treaty on the European Union and the Treaty establishing the European Community) into a single text, which had a clearer structure and was written in a simple, legible style.

The Constitutional Treaty sought to merge the three pillars, create a single legal framework and give the European Union legal personality. In order to compile all fundamental freedoms recognised in the Union into this key legal document, the Charter of Fundamental Rights – adopted in Nice but not yet a binding document – was incorporated into the Treaty as a separate part.

By providing a detailed list of the Union's competences, the Constitutional Treaty clearly specified the areas where the Union would have competence, the scope of its competences, where it could take decisions, and where it could act. By doing so, the Treaty also met the demand expressed by some Member States before the IGC to specify areas of exclusive national competence. It must be noted that the Constitutional Treaty did not set out to extend the scope of the EU's competence significantly. It rather tried to clarify the status quo and deepen integration, not by adding new areas but by making existing ones more transparent and effective. The Constitutional Treaty stated specifically the primacy of

---

[53] Many linguistic and editing changes were also made, but these did not concern the substance of the provisions of the Treaty.

[54] The Czech Republic, Denmark, France, Ireland, Luxembourg, the Netherlands, Poland, Portugal, Spain and the United Kingdom.

Union law over national law. The Constitutional Treaty also officially recognised the Union's symbols already used in everyday practice: the flag, the anthem and the motto.[55] Through the Constitutional Treaty, the Member States attempted to simplify decision-making by considerably reducing the number of types of decision-making procedures and forms of legal acts (using simpler terms, such as law and framework law), while clarifying the role that each EU institution should play in the process of decision-making and implementation. Possibly the most important provision of the Constitutional Treaty concerned the significant reduction in the number of areas where unanimity was required for decisions (in order to curb the right of national veto) and the redesigned system of weighted votes (the introduction of double majority voting, requiring the support of at least 55% of the Member States representing no less than 65% of the Union's population), which aimed at making decision-making simpler and quicker.

Key institutional changes included the extension of the European Parliament's powers and the introduction of two new posts: the permanent President of the European Council and the Union Minister for Foreign Affairs. The purpose of the latter – along with some other provisions – was to make the European Union's external action more effective and coherent, and to enable the Union to speak with a single voice on the stage of world politics. To ensure efficiency, the Constitutional Treaty also foresaw a cut-back in the number of Commissioners from 2014, when Member States were to designate their Commissioners according to a system of rotation.

Overall, although it may not have brought about revolutionary changes in the Union's daily life, the Constitutional Treaty – if successfully ratified – would have certainly provided a solid foundation on which to build a stronger and more modern Europe capable of meeting the new political, economic and social challenges posed by the 21st century and enlargement. Although the Constitutional Treaty was criticised, both by fervent federalist advocates of deeper integration (although not as heavily as the Treaty of Nice had been) and by sceptics wary of closer integration and further deepening, it was in fact a synthesis of Member-State views and the result of over two years of negotiations by and between the 25 Member

---

[55] The Union's flag is twelve golden stars (pointing upwards) in a circle on a blue background; its anthem is the prelude to 'The Ode to Joy', the 4th movement of Ludwig van Beethoven's 9th symphony; its motto is 'United in diversity'.

States in the Convention and the IGC. The European Union could certainly have had a more ideal Treaty, but this is how far the political reality of 2004 allowed them to go. All in all, the Constitutional Treaty, effectively a series of compromises, was a realistic response to the institutional and operational challenges the Union was facing at the time.

The ratification of the Constitutional Treaty began after it had been signed in late 2004: Lithuania and Hungary ratified it by a parliamentary decision. In the first half of 2005, Slovenia, Italy, Greece, Slovakia, Austria Germany and Latvia followed, also ratifying by parliamentary decision. The first referendum on the Constitutional Treaty was held in Spain on 20 February 2005, in which 76% of the citizens who turned out at the polls cast their vote in favour of ratifying the Treaty. The second referendum was held in France on 29 May 2005, which brought a high turnout (70%) and a decisive 'no' (54.8%). Three days later, on 1 June, it was the Dutch electorate's turn; out of the 63% who voted, 61.7% decided to say 'no' to the Constitutional Treaty. These two rejections put almost insurmountable obstacles in the way of the ratification of the Constitutional Treaty; legally speaking, it could only enter into force if and when all the 25 signatory states had ratified it.

After the two unsuccessful referenda, the Union had the following options: to press on with the ratification process; to abort the ratification process; to renegotiate the Constitutional Treaty; or to apply only certain provisions of the Constitutional Treaty, which would not require an amendment of the Treaties, within the Nice framework. These were the options and their implications that the Heads of State or Government had to choose from at their summit meeting in Brussels on 16–17 June 2005.

By aborting the ratification process, they would have killed off the Constitutional Treaty. Within the limits of the Nice framework, only a fraction of the Constitutional Treaty's provisions could have been applied. Renegotiating the Constitutional Treaty would have been unlikely to result in a better text (considering that the original text was the result of almost three years of hard talks and a balanced compromise of national positions). As the rejection of the Constitutional Treaty by French and Dutch voters was more due to dissatisfaction with domestic political leaders and with the EU in general than with the Constitutional Treaty as such, the Member States decided to extend the target deadline for concluding the ratification process to mid-2007 and to introduce a 'a period of reflection'; this gave Europe some time to think and Member States a chance to provide more information to their citizens about the Constitutional Treaty and its content, and explain why Europe needed such a new Treaty, if it wanted to become more efficient, more democratic, and more transparent. The main reason behind the negative outcome of the French and Dutch referenda was the electorate's dissatisfaction with the work of the domestic political elite, poor economic prospects, increasing unemployment, social insecurity and the problems of immigration, but – to some extent – disillusionment with the Union also played an important role. Some of Europe's citizens felt that the EU had been unable to find the right answers to the social and economic challenges that affected them most directly; instead, it had been too preoccupied with enlargement. Paradoxically, the French and Dutch publics let their anger out on the very document that could have enabled the Union to make decisions quicker and respond to economic, social and political challenges more flexibly. These two referenda clearly indicated that the European Union should devote more attention to the day-to-day problems of Europe's economies and societies[56], and come up with concrete steps for solving these problems. In that context, the Union and its Member States had a lot of explaining to do: what the Union had done for its citizens, how they benefited from EU membership in their daily lives, how the Constitutional Treaty would create the legal framework for more efficient functioning, and why it was not the task of such a Treaty to provide specific answers to daily economic and social problems.

The French and Dutch 'no' undoubtedly shook the European Union and its vision of the future, raised uncertainty about the prospects of further integration and left the EU's reputation in tatters, both internally and externally.

The period of reflection gave the remaining Member States the opportunity to ratify the Constitutional Treaty, but only Luxembourg (in a referendum), Belgium, Cyprus, Estonia, Finland and Malta (all five through their national parliaments) decided to do so. With Bulgaria and Romania added, the ranks of countries that had ratified the Treaty swelled to 18. In the wake of the two unsuccessful referenda, seven Member States (the Czech Republic, Denmark, Ireland, Poland, Portugal, Sweden and the United Kingdom) decided to suspend their national ratification processes.

As it became increasingly obvious that neither France nor the Netherlands would want to put the Constitutional Treaty to the popular vote again, while the countries with ratifications

---

[56] Problems caused by globalisation, e.g. *delocalisation* (companies relocating production to countries offering cheaper labour), problems such as the sustainability of high social expenditure (compared to cheap labour costs in other regions), together with concerns over Europe's ageing population and immigration (which seems necessary economically but causes social tensions).

pending would not make any move until France and the Netherlands budged, the period of reflection could only lead to one conclusion: the EU had to abandon the original text and go back and amend the Treaty, but it was unclear what changes would make the text palatable for the electorate.

The period of reflection could not be concluded without a change in the French and Dutch domestic political landscapes, which came with the Dutch national elections in November 2006 and the French presidential and parliamentary elections in April-June 2007. By this time, however, it was apparent that France and the Netherlands were not the only two countries forming the bottleneck: Polish and Czech political leaders became increasingly critical of certain provisions of the Constitutional Treaty.[57] Less openly, the United Kingdom was also trying to use the situation to remove from the new text those provisions it had only agreed to in 2004 to avoid deadlock over the Treaty reforms. As the sticking points were slowly but surely identified, the task of forging a compromise fell upon Germany, which assumed the Council Presidency in the first half of 2007. Germany had the unenviable job of reconciling the position of the few Member States mentioned that wished to amend the text with the position of the majority, who preferred maintaining the provisions of the Constitutional Treaty as much as possible.

From its first day in office, the German Presidency demonstrated impressive commitment to finding the common denominator between the two groups of Member States and reaching an agreement on the future of the new Treaty before the end of the semester. This determination was reflected in the Berlin Declaration signed on 25 March 2007 on the 50th anniversary of the Treaty of Rome. The Declaration, which was signed by only the Presidents of the three major political institutions but was agreed by the Member States themselves, enumerated the achievements of European integration and the shared values of Europe, outlined the challenges facing the Union and emphasised the common aim of placing the European Union on a renewed common basis before the European Parliament elections in 2009, although without specific reference to the Constitutional Treaty. The Berlin Declaration had three implications for treaty reforms: i) the Member States were ready to do all that was necessary to resolve the impasse by adopting a new Treaty; ii) they were prepared to ratify that Treaty by 2009; and iii) the new Treaty would not have to be "constitutional".

---

[57] Poland was especially outspoken in its criticism of a key (according to many, the most important) achievement of the Constitutional Treaty: double majority voting. Poland would be the biggest loser of the new system of voting, since its strong (and currently rather preferential) voting position would be considerably weakened.

The decision on the new Treaty had to be taken at the summit of 21–22 June 2007, wrapping up the German Presidency. The agreement reached by the Heads of State or Government mirrored the conclusions of the two-year period of reflection since the two failed referenda. The Member States decided to discard the adjective 'constitutional' (both as a name and as a goal) and place the Union on a new basis by means of a Reform Treaty amending the current Treaty on European Union and the Treaty establishing the European Community. Contrary to the Constitutional Treaty, the new Reform Treaty will not replace the EU and EC Treaties, only amend them (as the Treaties of Amsterdam and Nice did). It will, however, rename the EC Treaty as the 'Treaty on the Functioning of the European Union', thereby conferring legal personality on the EU and abolishing the three pillars. These changes reflect the Reform Treaty's aspiration to incorporate the provisions of the Constitutional Treaty into the current treaty structure instead of fundamentally changing them. With this solution, the Member States have scrapped the Constitutional Treaty, both as a concept and as a name, but have managed to save most of its elements through the Reform Treaty.

At the summit meeting of 21–22 June 2007, the Member States agreed on a mandate for a new Intergovernmental Conference convened for 23 July 2007 to finalise the Reform Treaty before the end of the year, giving enough time for the Member States to ratify it and allowing the new Treaty to enter into force in time for the next elections to the European Parliament in June 2009. As the Reform Treaty amends rather than replaces the existing Treaties – as the Constitutional Treaty would have done – most Member States will not have to put it to a referendum, which should simplify its ratification considerably. That is one of the reasons why the name 'Constitution' was scrapped: the symbolic C-word made many citizens feel that the Union's competences were becoming excessive to the detriment of the individual countries (when in fact the Constitutional Treaty hardly extended EU competences, but mainly just clarified them).

On the whole, the Reform Treaty is practically a dressed-down version of the Constitutional Treaty. Nonetheless, due to the reservations concerning the provisions of the Constitutional Treaty, which were expressed by some Member States during the period of reflection, it was decided at the 2007 June summit that an IGC should be convened to draft the new Treaty, omitting certain provisions of the Constitutional Treaty. Most of these changes mean a step backwards.

Contrary to the Constitutional Treaty, the Reform Treaty does not state explicitly the supremacy of Community law; that will only be stated in the declaration to be adopted by the IGC. The Reform Treaty does not include references to the Union's symbols – the flag, the anthem and the motto – either. Another provision of the Constitutional Treaty not taken up by the Reform Treaty is the introduction of the names European law and framework law, which would have replaced the current terms of regulations and directives. The Reform Treaty does not incorporate the Charter of Fundamental Rights into the Treaties, but it does include a reference to the rights enshrined in the Charter. In practice, this means that the Charter will become legally binding upon the Reform Treaty's entry into force, although it will only be applicable in UK courts with strong restrictions. The Union Minister for Foreign Affairs proposed by the Constitutional Treaty will be replaced by the name 'High Representative of the Union for Foreign Affairs and Security Policy', even though the person's competences remain pretty much the same. Just as in the case of the Constitutional Treaty, the hottest potato at the 2007 June summit was the new system of qualified majority voting. Poland tried until the last minute to sabotage the introduction of the system of so-called double majority voting. According to the final compromise, double majority voting will only be used from 1 November 2014 (and not from 2009 as originally proposed), with an extra safeguard clause allowing Member States to request the application of the current qualified majority voting system for individual decisions until 31 March 2017.

Apart from all the watering down, the Reform Treaty is an improvement on the Constitutional Treaty in two aspects. Firstly, reflecting the greater emphasis on an integrated climate change and energy policy, the Treaty will make specific reference to solidarity among the Member States on energy issues and on combating climate change. Secondly, the role of national parliaments is strengthened in comparison to the Constitutional Treaty in an effort to ensure greater democratic control.[58]

All in all, with their decisions at the summit of 21–22 June 2007, the Member States reconfirmed their conviction that an enlarged Union facing increasing global competition must rest on a treaty basis better suited to the present challenges. With the entry into force of the Reform Treaty, the Union will be able to continue deepening and widening, integration will regain its momentum and the institutions their tarnished

---

[58] The provisions of the Reform Treaty replacing the Constitutional Treaty and the changes it will bring compared to the current Treaty framework are discussed in detail in the Annex.

reputation. Even though the Reform Treaty discards some of the ambitious aims of the Constitutional Treaty, it takes up most of its progressive provisions. Once in force, the Reform Treaty will enable the EU to turn the page, close the chapter of 'amending treaties' – going on for two decades now – and move away from institutional, legal and decision-making issues. What the European Union needs to focus on now is finding the answers to the burning economic and social questions that affect its citizens' daily lives, reinforcing the single market and pressing on with building an economic and political union.

1.12.3. Building an economic and political Union

In addition to preparing and implementing the eastern enlargement and elaborating institutional reforms leading to a new Treaty framework, the evolution of the EU in the early 21st century has been first and foremost characterised by efforts aimed primarily at building an economic and political union. Without these efforts, the enlarged Union and its Member States would be unable to maintain or strengthen their political and economic competitiveness in the world. At the beginning of the 21st century, as the European Union is accomplishing its biggest ever enlargement while facing its most critical ever political, economic and social challenges due to globalisation, harmonising the objectives of deepening and widening is more important than ever before. The 50 years of European integration, however, prove that the process of deepening and widening can reinforce each other.

1.12.3.1. Strengthening economic integration: the role of the Lisbon strategy in improving the Union's competitiveness

As regards economic integration, the greatest achievement of the European Union at the turn of the millennium was undoubtedly the historic introduction of the single currency. Following the enlargement of 2004, the introduction of the euro in the new Member States and in the 'older' members that decided to stay out of the eurozone became an important task. Slovenia was the first of the new Member States to meet the preconditions, changing over from the tollar to the euro on 1 January 2007. Slovenia will be joined in the eurozone by Cyprus and Malta on 1 January 2008, as the 14th and 15th members of the eurozone. Based on their national convergence programmes the other Member States that acceded to the EU in 2004 and 2007 are expected to join the eurozone between 2009 and 2013.[59]

---

[59] For more on the enlargement of the eurozone, see 8.6.3. and 8.7.

On the whole, improving the competitiveness of the Member States, enhancing European citizens' prosperity, managing globalisation-related challenges, and further shaping the economic union have also remained fundamental tasks and priorities of the EU since the introduction of the euro. To accomplish all of the above tasks, the Member States launched a new strategy at the Lisbon Summit held on 23–24 March 2000, aimed at a more specific harmonisation of Member States' economic policies, thereby complementing the provisions set out in Maastricht in connection with the economic union and the coordination of employment policy as decided in Amsterdam. The concept announced as the 'Lisbon strategy' is aimed at strengthening employment, economic reforms and social cohesion, parallel with building a knowledge-based society. The essence of this complex strategy is that the EU should face major economic and social challenges (such as unemployment and an ageing population) through the use of the key elements of a modern economy (including, for example, the Internet, e-commerce, biotechnology, and telecommunications). The central objective of the strategy announced in March 2000 is to make the EU the most competitive and dynamic, knowledge-based economy in the world by 2010, one that is capable of maintaining sustainable development while creating more and better jobs through greater social cohesion. To accomplish this, the Member States will harmonise and coordinate their economic policies more closely than before and identify specific mutual objectives along common guidelines and tied to specific deadlines.[60]

According to the Lisbon Summit, this decade-long strategy is reviewed and supplemented by the Heads of State or Government of the Member States at their now regular spring summit, which is dedicated completely to economic and social issues. The first such summit meeting of the European Council was held in Stockholm on 23–24 March 2001, where

---

[60] Within the framework of the Lisbon strategy, it was decided that the 61% employment rate of 2000 should be raised to 70% by 2010; the proportion of young people aged 18–24 and not enrolled in higher education should be reduced by half, each school should be connected to the Internet by 2001 and each teacher should be trained to use the Internet by 2002; a financial services single market should be established by 2005; the liberalisation of gas, electricity, mail services should be accelerated, etc. Another basic element of the strategy is that the annual rate of economic growth in the Union should be kept above 3%.

a number of Lisbon objectives were further specified and updated, and new guidelines were set.[61] The Barcelona Summit held on 15–16 March 2002[62], and the Brussels Summits of 20–21 March 2003[63] and 25–26 March 2004[64] also contributed to the realisation of the Lisbon strategy through a number of concrete decisions.

Halfway through the decade, the Member States recognised that the strategy was not being implemented at the necessary speed and that the competitiveness of Europe vis-à-vis the US was not improving – in fact the gap was widening; achieving the desired aim of making the EU the world's most competitive region appeared increasingly unlikely. The underlying reason was that the tasks outlined in the Lisbon strategy mostly fell outside the Community's scope of competence, remaining under national authority. In most of these areas, the so-called *open method of coordination* was applied, when common goals are set which the Member States tried to attain, the aim being to find and spread best practice.

In order to identify the difficulties and determine the tasks for the second half of the decade, the summit of 22–23 March 2005 carried out a *mid-term review* of the Lisbon process. As it became apparent that the strategy could only be successful if the Member States showed more commitment towards implementing the strategy, the mid-term review focused on

---

[61] In Stockholm, decisions were made, for example, on establishing integrated securities markets by 2003, and increasing the employment rate to 67% by 2005 (to 57% in the case of women and above 50% for the population aged 55 to 64).

[62] The Barcelona Summit set one of the key Lisbon objectives that by 2010 the EU should spend 3% of its GDP on research and development, one third coming from public funds and two thirds borne by the private sector. The other outstanding achievement of the Barcelona Summit was the liberalisation of the gas and electricity sectors, according to which non-household users would be able to choose their gas and electricity suppliers freely by 2004, and household users from 2007.

[63] The spring summit of 2003 focused on increasing employment and social cohesion, strengthening innovation and enterprises, reinforcing the internal market and developing environmental and employment objectives to promote growth.

[64] The 2004 spring summit set four priorities in order to enhance European competitiveness: completing the internal market, better regulation, higher rates of R&D and effective institutional arrangements.

national action.[65] As the key change, it was recognised that the ambitious objective of making the EU the most competitive economy in the world by 2010 was not achievable; thus this objective was no longer mentioned in specific terms. The renewed strategy focused on creating the conditions for economic growth in Europe while boosting competitiveness. Accordingly, the original aims were redirected at growth and employment. The strategy placed at its heart the aspiration that the EU and its Member States should contribute to growth and employment (that is job creation) to a greater extent and in more practical terms. In order to promote the implementation of the objectives on the ground and the monitoring thereof, the new approach is based on three-year cycles, the first one beginning in 2005 with a review in 2008. The Commission's *strategic report* provides a starting-point for the cycle. The relevant Council bodies examine the report, and then the Heads of State or Government (the European Council) elaborate political guidelines for the economic, social and environmental parts of the report. Based on the European Council's conclusions, the Council adopts *integrated guidelines* consisting of two parts: *broad economic policy guidelines* (BEPGs) and *employment policy guidelines*. On the basis of the integrated guidelines, the Member States within their own competence draft their *national reform programmes* according to their individual needs and circumstances. The Member States conduct consultations on these programmes with the stakeholders and, to intensify internal coordination, they appoint a national coordinator for the Lisbon strategy. Similarly, the Commission draws up a *Community Lisbon programme* covering all activities that should be implemented at Community level to promote growth and employment. In addition, the Commission prepares an annual report assessing the implementation of the strategy's three dimensions. On the basis of the Commission's assessment, at each spring summit meeting, the Heads of State or Government review the progress made and decide if the integrated guidelines need to be adjusted. At the end of each three-year cycle, the integrated guidelines are revised, taking into account the experiences of the national reform programmes and of the Community Lisbon programme. The integrated guidelines for the first three years were adopted at the summit meeting of 16–17 June 2005. The package, which contains 24 specific guidelines, focuses on coordinating the objectives and activities of micro- and macroeconomic policies and employment policies.

---

[65] At the request of the EU Heads of State or Government, prior to the mid-term review, an expert group headed by former Dutch Prime Minister Wim Kok prepared a report on the results of the strategy. The *Kok Report* expressed disappointment at the achievements of the strategy, mainly due to the lack of political commitment. The report stressed the need to maintain the three pillars (economic, social and environmental) of the Lisbon strategy, but also to devote more attention to faster economic growth and higher employment, which contribute to social cohesion and environmentally sustainable development.

The first review of the updated Lisbon strategy based on the objectives of growth and employment was carried out by the 23–24 March 2006 European Council, which set specific targets and tasks in the areas of investing in knowledge and innovation, employing young people, and dismantling the obstacles hampering the development of SMEs. The European Council of 8–9 March 2007 put the emphasis on strengthening the internal market, better regulation (improving lawmaking) and sustainable development (a renewed energy policy). The March 2007 summit concluded that the renewed Lisbon programme had yielded the first results: growth was up (with an average of 2.7% forecast for 2007), employment figures showed a rebound (from below 64% to 66% predicted for 2007/2008). The Council conclusions also referred to the promising start in implementing the national reform programmes.

The Gothenburg Summit of 15–16 June 2001 was an important milestone in the harmonisation of economic policies: complementing the Lisbon strategy, the Member States agreed that the EU should have a sustainable development strategy and that the individual countries should elaborate national strategies aimed at the same objective. Sustainable development, in essence, means an integrated approach to economic growth, social progress and the environment in the EU's future strategy. With the three-pronged strategy of sustainable development, the Gothenburg Summit added a new, environmental dimension to the socio-economic initiatives of Lisbon. The two strategies must be coordinated and implemented hand in hand. The sustainable development strategy is renewed every five years. The first review of the strategy carried out by the June 2006 summit recognised the need for a gradual change in the current, unsustainable consumption habits and production practices and the need to integrate that attitude horizontally in every policy. The strategy identified seven priority areas where joined-up EU action based on common objectives was needed and should be incorporated into individual policies. These priority areas for action are: climate change and green energy, sustainable transport, sustainable consumption and production, public health threats, better management of natural resources, social exclusion and demographic and immigration-related challenges, combating global poverty.

One of the key issues linked to the Lisbon strategy is the completion of the internal market. In relation to competitiveness, two areas merit mention: the programme of better regulation and the further liberalisation of the services market.

Better regulation has been on the Union's agenda since the turn of the millennium, and is receiving more and more attention. The programme of better regulation aims to simplify and improve the regulatory environment both at the national and Community level. Complicated, often overlapping legislative acts are replaced by simple, transparent ones, which reduce the administrative burden, create a citizen- and business-friendly legal environment, and thereby yield significant savings. The Commission estimates that reducing the administrative burden of national and EU legislation by 25% would eventually lead to a saving equivalent to 1.5% of the GDP. Consequently, at its meeting on 8–9 March 2007, the European Council decided that the administrative burden of EU legislation should be cut by 25% by the year 2012 and that the Member States should set similarly ambitious targets by 2008.[66]

The area of services has been at the forefront of internal market activities in recent years. Despite the freedom to provide services, Member States have been protecting their national markets heavily against 'intruders', removing several sectors from the scope of EU competition rules. Services account for close to 70% of the Union's GDP, and therefore it is of paramount importance to ensure that internal market rules are applied to enable the EU to realise its competitive potential. In that context, the gas and electricity markets became fully liberalised in mid-2007, and international roaming charges for mobile telephony were considerably reduced. Liberalisation is underway in the railway sector and postal services are expected to become fully liberalised in 2011–2012. The Services Directive adopted in late 2006 is a major step forward and will bring considerable improvements by making it easier to provide services across national borders. The Directive, which Member States are required to transpose into domestic law before December 2009, stipulates that a Member State where a service is provided cannot discriminate against service providers established in another Member State.[67]

The need to renew European energy policy, which is closely linked with both the Lisbon strategy and sustainable development, has become a pressing task because of increasingly evident climate change and the security of energy supply, which is a growing headache due to the EU's increasing import dependence and the uncertain political climate in supplier countries. Therefore the European Council meeting on 8–9 March 2007 marked a new turn in energy policy. Realising the interrelation between climate change and energy policy, the Heads of State or Government launched an integrated climate change and

---

[66] For more on better regulation, see 15.3.
[67] For more details see also 6.3.3.

energy policy, setting ambitious goals: limiting the global average temperature increase to not more than 2°C above pre-industrial levels, and to achieve this aim, to slash the EU's greenhouse gas emissions by 20% in 2020, partly by raising the share of renewable energy sources to 20% by 2020. This environmentally conscious policy may mean higher costs and a competitive disadvantage for the Union at first, but can be turned into a competitive advantage in the long run. However, as climate change can only be tackled globally, the EU has been engaged proactively in trying to convince other leading economic powers to make similar pledges.[68]

1.12.3.2. Strengthening internal and external security

The other element constituting the deepening of the EU, complementing the element of economic integration, is closer political integration. The two priority issues on the way to a political union are: increasingly closer cooperation in justice and home affairs and the creation of a more uniform foreign policy.

In making cooperation on justice and home affairs closer, the central element of the integration process is the objective of creating an *area of freedom, security, and justice* that was announced by the Amsterdam Treaty. In accordance with the Amsterdam Treaty, the EU takes more and more justice and home affairs issues within Community competence (external and internal border controls, asylum policy, immigration policy and judicial cooperation in civil matters) and adopts relevant Community legislation in these areas. As a part of this process, not only has it introduced a common visa policy but internal border checks of persons between the 15 old Member States were abolished years ago – except for the two islands of the United Kingdom and Ireland. Border control has been transferred to the external borders of the EU and has to be performed according to common rules. The ten Member States that acceded to the EU in 2004 are expected to join the so-called Schengen area on 1 January 2008, while Bulgaria and Romania can become part of the Schengen zone a few years later.[69]
The increasing importance of justice and home affairs is indicated by the fact that the EU held a special summit dedicated to this issue in Tampere on 15–16 October 1999, where a multi-annual package of justice and home affairs measures, the so-called *Tampere programme,* was adopted. As a follow-up, at the summit of 4–5 November 2004, another multi-annual package, the *Hague programme*, was adopted, its key element being the

---

[68] For more on the integrated climate change and energy policy, see 16.3. and 18.2.5.
[69] For more details see 24.2. and 24.3.2.

fight against terrorism. Following the terrorist attacks against the United States on 11 September 2001, the fight against terrorism became one of the main priorities in the European Union as well, which has yielded a number of results: police and judicial cooperation between the Member States has become closer than ever before; as a logical follow-up to the establishment of *Europol* (the agency responsible for exchange of information between member-state police forces) in 1999, *Eurojust* was set up to promote the exchange of information between prosecuting and investigating authorities; the European Police Chiefs' Task Force was called into existence; intensive links were built between intelligence services, judicial authorities and police forces; the European arrest warrant and extradition convention were elaborated; and combating money laundering for the purpose of financing terrorism was placed on new foundations. Apart from the fight against organised crime and terrorism, immigration is the area attracting the most attention in justice and home affairs. The EU is intensifying cooperation on immigration in an effort to combat illegal immigration and to better control legal immigration necessary for demographic and labour shortage reasons.

Overall, on the basis of the legislative work aimed at creating an area of freedom, security and justice, one can safely say that justice and home affairs have been at the forefront of European integration in recent years. This is the area where the *acquis communautaire* has progressed in giant strides, and if the pillar structure is abolished when the Reform Treaty enters into force, this momentum is likely to continue in the years to come.[70]

Within the process of deepening the EU, the strengthening of foreign and security policy received a new impetus after the Cologne Summit of June 1999. The Member States began to forge an independent EU defence policy, with the main aim of building up and reinforcing its crisis management military capacity, to ensure that European countries can solve regional crises on their own, unlike in the past when they needed NATO (i.e. the US) to do so. The main element of the *European Security and Defence Policy (ESDP)* adopted by the Helsinki Summit of December 1999 and thereby formed was the establishment of a rapid reaction force of 50–60,000 troops, which became a reality by 2003 thanks to Member State pledges. Following the Helsinki Summit and in relation to ESDP tasks, the institutional framework of the EU's Common Foreign and Security Policy underwent an overhaul

---

[70]   For more on the Tampere and Hague programmes and developments in the field of justice and home affairs, see 24.4. and 24.6.

in 2000, which was also confirmed by the Treaty of Nice. The operational deployment of the crisis management force could only begin in parallel with the conclusion of a political agreement with NATO (and the US) in December 2002, stipulating that the EU would only conduct crisis management operations if NATO (or more exactly the US) does not wish to act in a given case and that, during its operations, the EU can use NATO resources and thus does not have to establish unnecessary parallel capacities. The first EU-led military and police crisis management operations took place from 2003 in Macedonia, Bosnia-Herzegovina and Congo. The first really large-scale EU military peacekeeping operation was launched under the name *Althea* in December 2004, with the deployment of 7,000 troops on the ground in Bosnia-Herzegovina.

Unfortunately, the recent division among Member States on the issue of the Iraq war cast a shadow over efforts aimed at developing a truly common foreign policy. Following the US decision in early 2003 to go ahead with the war on Iraq, several Member States and candidate countries fully supported US action, while others (such as France and Germany) were opposed to military action in Iraq. This inability to agree on a common EU position was an acutely clear indication of just how far the EU still is from being able to speak with one voice on world issues of gravity. The tensions resulting from this clash of opinions on Iraq seemed to have slackened by the turn of 2003 and 2004, as was demonstrated by the European Security Strategy adopted in December 2003, the decision in May 2004 to set up rapid deployment combat units (thirteen units of 1,500 troops), and the increasing number of EU military and civilian crisis management missions in various parts of the world. Due to these developments – and especially with the eventual entry into force of the Reform Treaty – there is renewed hope that, by reinforcing its crisis management capacity and defence cooperation, the EU could increase its weight in world politics and narrow the gap between its economic potential and its political and military might.[71]

---

[71] For more on the creation of a European security and defence policy and the evolution of the Common Foreign and Security Policy, see 23.6. and 23.7.

1.13. The history and process of eastward enlargement

1.13.1. The institutionalisation of relations with Central and Eastern European Countries

Following the creation of the European Economic Community, its relations with Central and Eastern European countries (CEECs), which had been forced to join the Soviet bloc, were characterised by political antagonism and minimal economic relations. Foreign trade relations of CEECs were determined by their membership in the COMECON, which had a rather confrontational position towards the Community. Mutual non-recognition and political conditions governed by ideological differences hampered closer economic and trade cooperation. The Common Commercial Policy only allowed EEC Member States to conclude single trade agreements while, for political reasons, the COMECON refused any agreement with the Community as an organisation, and insisted on entering into agreements with individual Member States. Without an EEC-COMECON trade agreement, the Community put COMECON countries in the least favourable category of so-called state-trading countries. It is a curious fact that this label was kept for Hungary, a COMECON member that signed up to the GATT in 1973. As a result, it could not benefit from the preferential treatment that was theoretically applicable to all GATT members; the Community often applied discriminatory protective measures even vis-à-vis Hungary. Trade relations between the EC and CEECs even lacked the most-favoured-nation clause.

Following decades of political opposition and icy economic relations, the collapse of Communist regimes in Europe and the end of the bi-polar world order was a great success for the western world, and for the Community. Despite being freed from state party rule and Soviet oppression, CEECs posed an enormous political, security and economic challenge for European integration. Both the newly independent Central and Eastern European states and Western European countries felt that new democracies might become rather unstable on their own, both economically and politically. The previous 40 years of European integration had demonstrated that the key to the future, security and prosperity of Europe was unity. Thus, it was evident to both sides that countries formerly united in opposed military, political and economic blocs should establish closer relations.

Naturally, the needs and expectations concerning the depth and intensity of cooperation were very different in the west and the east.

The EEC was quick to initiate talks on improving relations with Hungary and Poland, the first two countries to cut themselves off from the Soviet regime. Of course, the first steps were aimed at restoring and developing trade. These aspirations were embodied in the trade agreement between the Community and Hungary signed on 26 September 1988, in which the Member States agreed to remove former discriminatory trade measures vis-à-vis Hungary. At the Paris G7 summit on 14 July 1989, the world's seven greatest economic powers decided to provide economic assistance to the two leading reform countries (Hungary and Poland) and to channel this through the EEC's PHARE programme[72], an initiative later accepted by all the OECD countries; the European Commission was put in charge of coordinating and managing the programme. In addition to funding, PHARE also included trade policy measures, which granted the countries involved the benefit of GSP (General System of Preferences) status.[73] Parallel to political changes, PHARE was extended to other Central and Eastern European countries, and it became the European Communities' (later the EU's) assistance programme in the CEECs.

At the turn of 1989 and 1990, events started to speed up. After Poland and Hungary, other countries in the region, one after the other, also witnessed democratic changes, and expressed their wish to reinforce relations with the Community; in some cases, even the idea of membership was raised.

Recognising that it was facing a new situation, the Community was quick to respond. In April 1990, the Dublin European Council, in addition to endorsing German reunification, proposed that associated status[74] should be offered to those Central and Eastern European countries which were most advanced in the reform process: namely the Czech and Slovak Republic, Hungary and Poland, and also Romania and Bulgaria, and this time even Yugoslavia was mentioned.

---

[72] PHARE is an acronym of 'Poland and Hungary Assistance for the Reconstruction of the Economy'. The acronym is also supposed to evoke the association with the Greek word for 'lighthouse', which indicates the role of the programme.

[73] For details on the GSP (generalised system of preferences) and other preferential instruments of the common trade policy, see Chapter 9.

[74] See also 9.4.2.1.

Finally, negotiations on association with the Czech and Slovak Republic, Poland and Hungary began in December 1990 and lasted about a year. The Association Agreements and the so-called Interim Agreements with these three countries were signed on 16 December 1991; the latter enabled the Association Agreements' trade provisions to become applicable immediately (or to be more exact on 1 March 1992). This solution was necessary because, according to the EC Treaty, Member State parliaments had to ratify Association Agreements, which usually takes a long time.

Following the long process of ratification, the Agreements with Hungary and Poland entered into force on 1 February 1994, while the Agreements with the Czech Republic and Slovakia (by then two separate states, whose agreements had to be renegotiated due to their separation), as well as Romania and Bulgaria, took effect on 1 February 1995. Later, the Community[75] concluded similar Association Agreements with the three Baltic states of Estonia, Latvia and Lithuania and with Slovenia[76], which increased the number of Central and Eastern European associated countries to ten. These Association Agreements, which – apart from differences due to national peculiarities – were very similar in content, were collectively called the 'Europe Agreements'. This collective name indicated their historic significance and distinguished them from other association agreements, which aim at reinforcing trade relations but do not include provisions on political cooperation and approximation of legislation.

Europe Agreements mainly dealt with the four fundamental freedoms, which were the original objectives of European integration. While they contained few specific provisions relating to capital, labour and services, they went quite far in the area of the free movement of goods (except for agricultural produce). Consequently, it is not surprising that trade provisions made up the bulk of the Agreements and set the ultimate aim of full free trade in industrial products (which – for example – in Hungary's case was achieved by 31 December 2000). The EU agreed to dismantle obstacles to trade (customs duties and quotas) asymmetrically, which meant that the EU removed these obstacles by the mid-nineties, while CEECs only had to do so at a slower pace. (for example, in Hungary's case, the deadline for the EC to dismantle trade barriers was 31 December 1995, except

---

[75] Despite the existence of the EU, using the term *Community* is justified because the Association Agreements are concluded by the European Community (not the European Union). External treaties and agreements can only be concluded by the Community(ies), since the Union does not have legal personality in international law.

[76] Association Agreements with the Baltic States were signed in June 1995 and entered into force in February 1998. In the case of Slovenia, the Agreement was signed in June 1996 and entered into force in February 1999.

for textiles, where the deadline was 31 December 1997.) For agricultural produce, the achievements were more modest. The parties only agreed to provide mutual preferences and the option of free trade was not even suggested. The EU with its rather protectionist Common Agricultural Policy (CAP)[77] did not want – and under the CAP rules was not able – to open its agricultural markets to a greater extent to CEECs.

The Europe Agreements also clarified a number of other trade-related questions. They contained provisions on competition, rules of origin, and the approximation of customs legislation.

The various safeguard clauses, however, enabled the parties to restrict trade and derogate from the Agreements' provisions by reintroducing customs duties for a limited period in justified cases, for instance for emerging industries, crisis-struck sectors and anti-dumping measures.

It must be noted that, although the EU became the number one trading partner of CEECs[78], which was primarily attributable to the Association Agreements, initially the Member States realised a larger trade surplus because the economic transition in ex-Communist States drastically reduced the volume of exportable products. Despite the asymmetric dismantling, EU Member States, which had a competitive advantage in industrial products, could carve out a larger share of markets in associated countries than the other way around. The trade balance of CEECs turned negative in comparison to the former surplus. This was due to the delays in market liberalisation in the agricultural sector, which made it impossible to compensate for the increasing imports of industrial products by boosting agricultural exports. On the other hand, it is true that in a number of CEECs, following the change of regime, agricultural subsidies fell to a fraction of the EU average, which prevented these countries from realising their competitive advantage in agri-food products. Indeed, the growth of Community exports of agricultural produce exceeded the rate of increase in agri-exports of CEECs to the EU. Nonetheless, on the whole, Europe Agreements undeniably contributed to the dynamic integration of CEECs into the economy, trade and market of Western Europe. In the late nineties, trade trends shifted in favour of associated countries, a few of whom managed to build up a trade surplus with the EU.

---

[77] For details, see Chapter 11.

[78] By the second half of the nineties, associated CEECs conducted over 60% of their trade with EU Member States.

Table 1.2. Trade between associated CEECs and the EU in 1994 and 1998

	Exports to the EU (million ECU)		Imports from the EU (million ECU)		Trade balance with the EU (million ECU)		Trade with EU in % of all trade	
	1994	1998	1994	1998	1994	1998	1994	1998
Bulgaria	1 195	1 922	1 157	2 003	38	−81	34.1	47.3
Czech Republic	5 804	14 807	6 593	16 255	−789	−1 448	43.8	63.2
Estonia	210	1 594	335	2 566	−125	−972	36.2	58.1
Hungary	4 588	14 959	5 542	14 698	−954	261	47.7	68.3
Latvia	232	916	261	1 572	−29	−656	26.3	55.8
Lithuania	438	1 258	520	2 439	−82	−1 181	26.0	43.6
Poland	9 087	17 198	10 426	27 660	−1 339	−10 462	59.8	66.8
Romania	2 492	4 776	2 731	6 093	−239	−1 317	46.9	60.5
Slovakia	1 598	5 336	1 456	5 842	142	−506	27.3	52.7
Slovenia	3 398	5 287	3 506	6 259	−108	−972	58.1	67.6

Source: Eurostat

In addition to trade provisions, in the Europe Agreements, the associated countries undertook to align their legislation with Community norms in certain areas. The obligation for the approximation of legislation was a forward-pointing element of the Association Agreements in terms of alignment with the single market and eventual membership.

Compared to other types of association agreements, the Europe Agreements carried a unique element: the intention of tightening political cooperation. These Agreements opened up major opportunities for cooperation for the associated countries: building extensive and institutionalised intergovernmental relations, participating in Community programmes, or joining joint foreign policy actions or positions.

Although the Agreements included no specific financial provisions, they referred to previously created financial instruments such as PHARE.

For every associated CEEC country, the Europe Agreements created an institutional framework corresponding to Community institutional levels to run the association relationship.

Association Councils, consisting of members of the EU Council, Commission and members of the government of the relevant associated country, became the main decision-making bodies of association agreements. It is important to underline that individual Europe Agreements could also be amended or improved by the decision of the Association Councils, as happened in several cases.

The Association Committees, which consisted of senior officials of the governments of individual associated countries, the EU Council and the Commission, became the main bodies for preparing decisions related to the Association Agreements.

The task of Joint Parliamentary Committees, which consisted of members of the European Parliament and of the Parliaments of individual associated countries, was to monitor and control the association process.

Altogether, Europe Agreements created a new form of association status, which can be considered an innovation among Association Agreements. Europe Agreements had several elements that were not included in the previous Agreements that had created association status. Key elements were the creation and conducting of political dialogue, the inclusion of obligations for the approximation of legislation and the 'evolution clause'[79], which gave the Association Council the power to further develop the Agreement.

Thus, Europe Agreements brought a number of significant results for CEECs but failed to live up to expectations in one respect. CEECs would have liked the EU to make promises concerning subsequent full membership in the Agreements – just as it had in the sixties in Mediterranean association agreements – but the EU was unwilling to assume any such specific obligations. All that associated countries could achieve was to indicate in the preambles of the Europe Agreements that their aim was full membership, which the Community merely acknowledged.

1.13.2. The conditions of accession for Central and Eastern European countries

The provisions of the Treaty of Rome allowed any European state to apply for membership. The Amsterdam Treaty added the criterion that a candidate country has to be a functioning

---

[79] It is important to note that the evolution clause did not mean that Europe Agreements were evolutionary, i.e. that they were directly aimed at membership. The evolution clause only gave the Association Council (the associated parties) the opportunity of further developing association.

democracy that respects human rights and the rule of law, which most CEECs fulfilled easily in the early nineties. Nevertheless, accession for CEECs was not yet within reach because, in reality, applicant countries had to meet a much more complex set of economic, institutional, legal and other criteria, which were not laid down in the Treaty, but had a more decisive role in a political sense. That is why it became necessary for the EU to define these criteria clearly, which it finally did at the Copenhagen Summit in June 1993, when Member States essentially approved the possibility of eastern enlargement.

At the time of the conclusion of the Europe Agreements, the Member States lacked the political will for the integration of CEECs into the EU; thus they tried to avoid linking Association Agreements to promises of future membership. The shift in the official position of Member States came about one year after the signing of the Europe Agreements – though before their entry into force – when the Copenhagen European Council confirmed the legitimacy of Central and Eastern European applications for membership and also defined the criteria which applicants would have to meet before they could join the Community. These criteria, which have come to be known as 'the Copenhagen criteria', concern:

– the stability of institutions guaranteeing democracy, the rule of law, human rights and respect for and protection of minorities (political criteria);
– the existence of a functioning market economy as well as the capacity to cope with competitive pressures and market forces within the European Union (economic criteria);
– the ability to take on the obligations of membership (i.e. the adoption and enforcement of the *acquis communautaire*)[80] including adherence to the aims of political, economic and monetary union (legal and institutional criteria).

Member States at the Copenhagen Summit also added the conditions of the EU's capacity to take in new members and the need to preserve the level and intensity of integration. With this, the EU indicated to applicants that its internal processes and problems of restructuring were inseparable from enlargement and that widening could only happen parallel to deepening. This led later and indirectly to the Treaty of Nice and the Constitutional Treaty.

---

[80] For details, see 5.2.4.

The Copenhagen criteria can be considered a political declaration, whose significance lies in the fact that it was the first time in its history that the European Union defined the conditions that applicant countries had to meet before accession. With the Copenhagen criteria, the EU redefined the conditions for joining the European integration process, because the Treaty of Rome only said that any European state could become a member of the Community. In the light of the evolution of integration, it is not surprising that, as a result of increasingly closer cooperation in the areas of the economy and approximation of legislation, the criteria of having a functioning and competitive economy and the ability to take on board the *acquis* were added. Only these criteria together can guarantee that the achievements of the Union are preserved.

The procedure of accession of new Member States to the EU

The procedure of accession is more elaborately regulated in the Treaties than membership criteria. According to the provisions on the procedure of accession, contained in Article 49 of the Treaty on European Union, applications for membership should be addressed to the Council. The Council then requests the Commission to prepare a report, a so-called 'Opinion' (also known by its French name 'avis') on the applicant country's readiness for joining the EU.[81] On the basis of the Commission's report – which is not binding[82] – the Council decides by unanimity whether to accept or reject the application for membership. If the Council's decision is positive, the EU begins accession negotiations with the candidate country. Officially, the accession negotiations are conducted on a bilateral basis between the governments of the Member States and the candidate country in the framework of an Intergovernmental Conference, but their length and content is not regulated. The Presidency of the Council makes proposals concerning the agenda and timetable, which the Council adopts after consulting the candidate country. Following the conclusion of the negotiations, immediately before the signing of the Treaty of Accession and after the political agreement between the governments of the Member States and the candidate country, the European Parliament in the framework of the assent procedure[83], acting with an absolute majority (more than 50% of all MEPs), endorses or rejects the candidate country's accession before the Treaty of Accession is signed. The Parliament may not make proposals; it can only say yes or no to admission.

---

[81] In its opinion, the Commission assesses not only the applicant country's preparedness for accession, but also the impact of its prospective membership on the functioning of the Union.

[82] For example, in the case of Greece, the Member States decided to start accession negotiations despite the Commission's negative opinion.

[83] See 4.1.2.3.

If the Parliament has given its assent, the Member States and the candidate country sign the Treaty of Accession, which then has to be ratified by all the contracting states in accordance with their respective constitutional requirements. This is usually done by the national parliaments. Usually, accession is confirmed by a referendum in the candidate country. Theoretically this is not compulsory, but since most of the time accession entails a constitutional amendment, accession is usually put to a referendum. Political leaders of new Member States also tend to insist on a referendum because it gives an unquestionable legitimacy to this major step, which fundamentally concerns national sovereignty.

1.13.3. From the Copenhagen criteria to accession negotiations

Following the declaration of membership criteria in Copenhagen, it was suggested that the EU should elaborate a strategy to help CEECs meet the criteria and thus facilitate their accession. The Essen European Council in December 1994 embarked upon a so-called 'pre-accession strategy' to prepare the associated countries for membership and accelerate the integration process. The Essen Summit confirmed the EU's commitment to closer cooperation with associated countries in a number of areas (such as infrastructure development, trans-European networks, transport, telecommunications, research, environment, education and culture). To be able to fulfil the tasks, the Member States and CEECs created a structured institutional dialogue, which provided a framework for meetings of Heads of State or Government (once or twice a year), of foreign affairs, justice and home affairs ministers (twice a year) and of other ministers (usually once a year).

In December 1994 in Essen, the Member States decided to issue a White Paper, which served as a guideline for associated countries in their preparation for the single market. The Commission drafted the White Paper in the first half of 1995, which was then adopted by the Cannes European Council in June 1995. This White Paper, which recommended about 1,100 measures containing mainly legislative tasks, could be considered a comprehensive programme package facilitating preparations for the internal market and defining priorities for the harmonisation of legislation, with the primary aim of orientating the legislative work of applicant countries.

In Cannes, the Heads of State or Government also asserted that, six months after the conclusion of the 1996 IGC, accession negotiations should begin with Cyprus and Malta, which had applied for membership in 1990. Central and Eastern Europe was not mentioned; this was partly justified by the fact that the two Mediterranean countries had applied for membership earlier, and the Commission had already expressed a positive opinion about Cyprus and Malta, proposing the commencement of negotiations.

Table 1.3. The dates of signature and entry into force of the 13 Association Agreements and of the submission of the applications for membership

	Signing of the Association Agreement	Entry into force of the Association Agreement	Submission of application for membership
Bulgaria	March 1993	February 1995	December 1995
Czech Republic	October 1993	February 1995	January 1996
Estonia	June 1995	February 1998	November 1995
Hungary	December 1991	February 1994	April 1994
Latvia	June 1995	February 1998	October 1995
Lithuania	June 1995	February 1998	December 1995
Poland	December 1991	February 1994	April 1994
Romania	February 1993	February 1995	June 1995
Slovakia	October 1993	February 1995	June 1995
Slovenia	June 1996	February 1999	June 1996
Cyprus	December 1972	June 1973	July 1990
Malta	December 1970	April 1971	July 1990
Turkey	September 1963	December 1964	April 1987

Source: European Commission

At the Madrid Summit in December 1995, Member-State Heads of State or Government called upon the Commission to prepare country opinions for all Central and Eastern European applicant countries, and submit them to the Council immediately following the conclusion of the Intergovernmental Conference. The European Council also instructed the Commission to prepare a report on the impact of enlargement on EU policies, particularly structural and agricultural policies, and the financing of the common budget.

The Madrid European Council pledged that it would adopt a decision on the launching of accession negotiations in the light of the Commission's reports and opinions as soon as possible after the completion of the IGC. The Heads of State or Government also expressed their hope that this would coincide with the beginning of negotiations with Cyprus and Malta.

The IGC was finally concluded at the Amsterdam Summit of 16–17 June 1997, where Member States adopted the draft Amsterdam Treaty. The Treaty fell short of expectations: failing to achieve its main objective, it only brought modest results in the key area of institutional reforms indispensable for going ahead with enlargement. Thus it was clear that another IGC and another treaty would be necessary prior to enlargement. (This is how the Treaty of Nice, remedying the 'Amsterdam leftovers' came to be adopted in December 2000.) Nevertheless, the Amsterdam Treaty secured one major achievement for enlargement: it closed the IGC. According to the Madrid Conclusions, this was a precondition for starting accession negotiations with Cyprus (the only certain candidate with the withdrawal of Malta[84]) and CEECs deemed fit by the European Council based on the Commission's proposal. Following Amsterdam, the applicants (the ten CEECs, Cyprus and Turkey, which had submitted its application back in 1987) were primarily interested in which countries could begin negotiations six months after the end of the IGC.

The only legal condition for commencing negotiations with a prospective candidate country is the Commission's Opinion, in the light of which the Council (not necessarily following the Commission's recommendation) decides on launching negotiations. In December 1995, the Madrid European Council instructed the Commission to prepare its Opinions on the candidate countries following the IGC and a report on the potential impact of enlargement on Community policies and their financing.

Acting upon the Council's request, on 16 July 1997, the Commission issued Agenda 2000, a document containing the EU's draft strategy for the first years of the new millennium – including the reform of Community policies and the Community budget, and aligning them to the consequences of enlargement – with the Commission's Opinions on the ten CEECs annexed.

---

[84] When the Labour Party took power in 1996, Malta suspended its application for membership, and thus was not considered a candidate country in 1997. When the Nationalist Party returned to government in autumn 1998, it revised this decision, and resubmitted its application for membership.

Agenda 2000 was the first major paper to take account of the prospect of an EU enlarged to the east. The main significance of Agenda 2000 – which bears the subtitle 'For a stronger and wider Europe' – was that the Commission dealt with the EU's internal reforms, future strategy and enlargement in a single document. The programme outlined in Agenda 2000 proposed a strategy for reform in the subsequent years (in the 2000–2006 period) and laid down a framework for enlargement. It even specified the financial conditions for the accession of new Member States, to the extent that the Commission's financial perspectives for the 2000–2006 period included a separate budget line for expenses related to new Member States. The 'stronger' and 'wider' Union, i.e. deepening and widening, appeared as common and inseparable objectives in the Commission's communication. Agenda 2000 also pointed out the feasibility of eastward enlargement while preserving common and Community policies. Moreover, it attributed an overall positive impact to enlargement from the entire EU's perspective.[85]

In Agenda 2000, the Commission not only put forward a concrete concept for an enlargement strategy, but in the annexed Opinions – prepared on the basis of a comprehensive and objective evaluation[86] of the extent to which the ten applicant countries met the Copenhagen criteria – the Commission recommended that accession negotiations start with Cyprus and five Central and Eastern European countries: the Czech Republic, Estonia, Hungary, Poland and Slovenia (known as the 'Luxembourg group' or the '5+1'). The Commission did not find the other candidates adequately prepared for starting negotiations, due to their inability to meet the Copenhagen criteria to a satisfactory extent (in the case of Slovakia for political reasons and, in the case of Latvia, Lithuania, Bulgaria and Romania, for economic reasons). Turkey, which was first assessed by the Commission in a country report in 1989, was still not accepted as a candidate country. The Commission's opinion highlighted that the persistent violation of civil and human rights, the excessive influence of the army on political life, sustained macroeconomic instability and the lack of modernisation in certain sectors (e.g. agriculture) were all reasons for to which Turkey could not be considered as an eligible candidate in 1997.

---

[85] For the budgetary provisions of Agenda 2000, see Chapter 7.3.4. For the decisions of Agenda 2000 on the CAP, see Chapter 11.5. For the decisions of Agenda 2000 on structural and cohesion funds, see Chapter 13.3.

[86] The Opinions on applicant countries were largely prepared on the basis of the thousands of pages of documentation that associated countries submitted in response to the 150-page questionnaire the Commission sent them in 1996. The aim of the Commission's questionnaire was to take stock of the progress made by applicant countries in adopting and implementing the *acquis*. The Commission primarily wanted to see to what extent candidate countries met the Copenhagen criteria.

Following the publication of Agenda 2000 and the 'Country Opinions', attention focused on the Council and Member States again. The Commission, as the institution responsible for preparing but not making decisions, only made a proposal for the framework of enlargement and submitted its assessment of candidate countries, but the decision – as ever – was in the hands of the Member States. The Member States had to decide with which countries to begin negotiations six months after the end of the IGC. The conclusion of the IGC was interpreted flexibly: the point of reference was the signing of the Amsterdam Treaty, i.e. 2 October 1997.

The Commission's opinions and proposals stirred heated debate in certain Member States as well as in applicant countries not proposed for accession. The key question was which countries the EU should begin negotiations with. Should it follow the differentiated approach proposed by the Commission (negotiating with 5+1 countries: the Czech Republic, Estonia, Hungary, Poland, Slovenia + Cyprus) or adopt the 'regatta principle'[87] advocated by the European Parliament and a few Member States (Greece, Denmark and Sweden) and launch negotiations with all 12 candidates, except Turkey.

Although most Member States were in favour of the differentiated approach, due to the insistence of a few Member States, the decisions of the Luxembourg European Council in December 1997 were difficult to predict. The left-outs argued that the differentiation could further increase the gap between candidates, and could have negative consequences both politically and economically. Some even talked about a re-division of Europe. The Commission and leading candidates emphasised that negotiations with 11 countries at the same time could not work efficiently and that the EU (EC) had never negotiated with more than 4 countries at a time. They also pointed out that it would be unjust for more advanced countries to adapt to the pace of slower ones, let alone have to wait for those lagging behind.

The Member States had to make the final decision concerning the Commission's proposals at the Luxembourg Summit held on 12–13 December 1997. The European Council meeting in Luxembourg turned out to be an historic milestone for eastward enlargement, as the Heads of State or Government committed themselves to enlarging the EU to the east. The Luxembourg Summit put an end to the uncertainty that had surrounded enlargement in

---

[87] The regatta principle means that all candidates begin accession negotiations at the same time, and individual countries cross the finishing line when they have met the accession criteria. According to advocates of this principle, differentiation among candidate countries should only be based on their performance at the negotiating table.

the CEECs since the early nineties. According to the Luxembourg Conclusions, it became possible to launch the enlargement process at the beginning of 1998 and thus put an end to the artificial division of Europe once and for all.

The significance of the Luxembourg decisions was that Member States managed to find a compromise, by endorsing a form of enlargement that allowed for the commencement of negotiations with the best-prepared candidates (the 5+1 countries proposed by the Commission), which was also acceptable both to countries left out of the 'Luxembourg group' and to those in favour of the regatta solution. The essence of the Luxembourg formula was that the enlargement process would involve all candidates, but negotiations would only begin with the most prepared countries. The Council's decision stipulated that enlargement was a comprehensive process involving all candidate countries except Turkey, which would be conducted in phases based on the individual performance of applicants.

Accordingly, the solemn meeting of the Ministers of Foreign Affairs of the 15 Member States, the 10 CEECs and Cyprus on 30 March 1998 marked the official start of the enlargement process. The accession negotiations with the 5+1 countries began one day later on 31 March, observing the six-month period from the signing of the Amsterdam Treaty. This differentiation between the candidates did not mean a sharp and final dividing line between the two groups of countries. According to the Luxembourg formula, accession would depend solely on the preparedness of the individual country; the process would be open and inclusive, with an opportunity for any country to catch up with others that began negotiations earlier. This was guaranteed by the annual assessment of the progress made by individual countries towards accession in the form of the comprehensive Regular Reports prepared by the Commission. An important element of the process was that the status of countries left out of the first round did not remain unchanged, and the EU reinforced ties with them. For these countries, the Luxembourg decisions talked about an acceleration in preparing negotiations, which meant an analytical review of the *acquis communautaire*, though not as detailed as the negotiations themselves.

The eastern enlargement was really decided upon in Luxembourg, not only because negotiations were launched with certain CEECs, but also because a new institutional framework was set up, which made it clear that the ultimate objective for all candidate countries was full membership.

Within the framework of a so-called accession strategy, the Luxembourg European Council placed relations between the EU and candidate countries on a new basis. The declared aim of the accession strategy was to help all applicants become fully-fledged members of the EU after they had taken on board as much of the *acquis communautaire* as possible. This was facilitated by the so-called Accession Partnerships, proposed by the Commission in Agenda 2000. Accession Partnerships, which were drawn up for each candidate country, irrespective of whether or not they had begun negotiations, provided an assessment of the priority areas in which the country needed to make progress in order to prepare for accession. Each country's Accession Partnership was complemented by its own National Programme for the Adoption of the *Acquis* (NPAA), which set out the timetable for adopting the *acquis* and putting it into practice. The implementation of the Accession Partnerships and the NPAAs, which were adopted following consultations between the two sides, was monitored by the association institutions created on the basis of the Europe Agreements. A key element of Accession Partnerships was the technical assistance and financial aid provided by the EU. Financial support was provided primarily through the pre-accession funds.

The European Council in Luxembourg also decided to considerably increase allocations for the pre-accession funds in the new budgetary period starting in 2000. The exact extent of this increase was only decided when the 2000–2006 financial perspectives together with Agenda 2000 were adopted. The new system of pre-accession funds was laid down at the Berlin Summit in March 1999. The Berlin European Council also finalised the formula put forward by the Commission in the 1997 draft of Agenda 2000. In addition to the reinforcement of PHARE, this proposal also called for the establishment of new pre-accession funds, similar to the Structural and Cohesion Funds, to help CEECs in their preparations for membership. The Berlin European Council decided to finance candidate countries in the seven-year budgetary period with an annual sum of EUR 3.12 billion from three separate funds[88]. The remodelled PHARE programme provided EUR 1.56 billion in aid per year, which financed the following two main priorities: 1) institution building in public administration and the judicial system (30%); 2) adopting and implementing the *acquis communautaire* (70%).[89] In addition to PHARE, two new pre-accession funds were set up in 2000:

---

[88] In practice, until 1999, financial assistance provided by the EU to Central and Eastern Europe meant the PHARE programme, with an annual budget of EUR 1.3 billion in 1999.

[89] According to its new orientation introduced in 1998, PHARE funds could only be used for strictly accession-related and legal approximation-related measures.

SAPARD[90], which financed agricultural restructuring with an annual amount of EUR 520 million; and ISPA[91], which could be considered as a forerunner of the Cohesion Fund and provided EUR 1.04 billion for infrastructure development.[92]

In addition to setting up pre-accession funds, the other key decision of Agenda 2000 concerning enlargement was that, from 2002 on, a separate budgetary heading with a fixed amount was set aside for the future Member States. Even though the sums involved were relatively minor in the context of the whole EU budget, it was a manifestation of the EU's willingness to welcome new Member States from 2002. It was also declared that the funds in this budgetary heading could only be used for financing costs related to new Member States, and could not be reallocated to other areas.

The enlargement process set out in Luxembourg (and financially reinforced by Agenda 2000) was built on close and continuous cooperation between the EU and candidate countries, in which all parties had defined tasks, candidate countries (approximation of legislation, institution building, economic preparation) as well as Member States (providing technical and financial assistance to applicants, reforming the EU, implementing the necessary internal reforms in time). The process hinged on dialogue and individual preparation. However, the specific conditions of accession for individual countries were decided at various stages of the accession negotiations, which were part and parcel of the enlargement process, but did not immediately commence with all candidates involved in enlargement.

1.13.4. Accession negotiations – An outline

Accession negotiations are typically divided into two parts: an initial analytical examination of Community legislation and the negotiations proper.

---

[90] Special Accession Programme for Agriculture and Rural Development
[91] Instrument for Structural Policies for Pre-Accession
[92] The EU adopted the Regulations on the establishment of the two new Funds in the summer of 1999, so the preparation of projects to be implemented with ISPA and SAPARD funding began in 1999. In the case of ISPA, this ensured smooth absorption in the initial phase. On the other hand, in the case of SAPARD, the complicated system of national administration required by the EU slowed down the launching of the programme (to various extents in different candidate countries), delaying its start until 2001–2002.

The initial phase of the process begins with the 'screening of the *acquis*'[93], during which the negotiating parties go through EU legislation divided into chapters. For the countries that became Member States in 2004 and 2007, there were 31 chapters to negotiate; for Turkey and Croatia, negotiations began in 2005 with 35 chapters to go through.

The screening of each chapter comprises two phases. First, the European Union presents the *acquis* to negotiating countries. Then the EU representatives sit down separately with candidate countries, which outline how fast they would be able to transpose the legislation in question. Those parts of the *acquis* which candidate countries pledge to adopt by the time of accession – provided the undertaking is plausible and acceptable for the EU – are theoretically taken off the table. Those parts for which either of the parties have remarks or requests for transitional exemptions, are placed on the negotiating table during the substantive phase, which constitutes the second part of the process.

For the substantive negotiations of a chapter, which can begin when its screening has been completed, both the candidate country and the EU elaborate a so-called *position paper*, which serves as a starting point. First, the candidate country submits its position paper to the EU, which then elaborates its position paper in response. The EU's position papers are drafted by the Commission and adopted by the consensus of the Member States.

Similarly to the screening exercise, the negotiations proceed on a chapter-by-chapter basis, but, contrary to the process of screening, a chapter is closed only when there are no unresolved questions left on either side. However, chapters are only provisionally closed and can be reopened at the request of the parties, the principle being that "nothing is agreed until everything is agreed". Consequently, the final closure of chapters occurs when the Treaty of Accession is signed. If there are questions on which the two sides cannot come to an agreement and the positions do not converge, the chapter is put aside.

---

[93] The expression 'screening of the *acquis*' is a unique mixture of Community jargon and 'Brussels-speak' (from the French word 'acquis' and the English term screening). For more details on the *acquis communautaire*, see 5.2.4.

When all chapters have been visited, the chapters that have been put aside are revisited and outstanding questions are negotiated in a single package. This is usually the longest and most unpredictable phase of the negotiations, where everything depends on the willingness of the two sides to find a compromise.

It is expedient to separate the screening phase from the substantive negotiations, since the screening is managed by the Commission's Negotiating Working Group acting at the request of the Council; thus, in practice it takes place between the candidate countries' governments and the Commission. The negotiations proper, on the other hand, are conducted by the government of the candidate country and the governments of all the Member States within the framework of an Intergovernmental Conference, which means that one country is negotiating with all the Member States. While screening can be considered as an introductory stage, the outcome of the negotiations is clearly decided at the IGC. This is where Member States decide in which areas a candidate can be granted transitional exemptions from the application of the *acquis*, what technical modifications to Community legislation are needed (e.g. changes in the area of the EU, or the incorporation of trademarks registered in the future Member State), what payments the future Member State will have to make to the common budget, how much Community funding it will be eligible for, and how it can take part in the work of the EU's institutions (e.g. the number of representatives or the weighting of the votes).

Concerning exemptions, it must be noted that these are of a strictly transitional nature, and are only granted in cases when they do not limit the functioning of the single market excessively or for long periods. Before starting accession negotiations with the countries of Central and Eastern Europe, the EU made it clear that it would not agree to any opt-outs or perpetual exemptions.

It should be pointed out that transitional periods can be requested by both sides; the EU or a Member State can also request and be granted temporary exemptions. In this case, during a transitional period, certain rights (such as eligibility for budgetary funds, or free movement of persons) are not granted to a new Member State. On the other hand, when a transitional period is requested by a candidate country, it usually means a temporary exemption from meeting certain obligations of membership (such as enforcing environmental or veterinary standards, or applying fiscal rules).

1.13.5. The accession negotiations of eastern enlargement

Following the official opening of negotiations with the 6 Luxembourg-group countries on 31 March 1998, the EU immediately started screening the *acquis*, which was concluded by July 1999.[94] The first round of substantive negotiations was held on 10 November 1998 and dealt with the seven chapters screened first. Accession talks continued gradually, though not too dynamically, with usually one or two negotiating rounds every six months, leading to the closure of three to six chapters during a Presidency.

Two years after enlargement was officially launched at the Luxembourg European Council, the Helsinki Summit of 10–11 December 1999 brought further important decisions concerning the enlargement process. Looking at the first 18 months of negotiations with the first six applicants, an increasing number of Member States were of the opinion that negotiations should begin with the remaining candidate countries as well. Despite the clear differences in progress made by some of these countries, the majority of Member States supported the idea of launching negotiations with the five CEECs left out in Luxembourg and with Malta, which re-submitted its application in 1998. Although there were a number of reservations concerning the preparedness of Bulgaria and Romania, on the basis of the recommendations of the European Commission's Regular Reports published in autumn 1999, the Member States decided in Helsinki to start negotiations with all the remaining six applicants in early 2000. The Helsinki European Council pointed out that the commencement of negotiations with all candidate countries put an end to their division into two groups. Underlining the role of judging candidates on their own merits, the Member States emphasised that the principle of differentiation in practice meant the possibility of differentiation within the 'Luxembourg group', and therefore the possibility for countries in the 'Helsinki group' to catch up those candidates who began negotiations earlier.

The Helsinki European Council also took major decisions concerning Turkey, officially acknowledging its candidate status, but not mentioning the launching of negotiations. Nonetheless, the EU pledged to prepare an Accession Partnership for Turkey and to assess it similarly to other candidate countries. The European Council also called upon Turkey to meet the accession criteria, particularly concerning respect for human rights. Overall, the Helsinki Conclusions on Turkey could be considered as a political gesture, which theoretically opened the way for the accession of a predominantly Muslim and partly Asian country to the EU, but gave no indication of the timeframe.

---

[94] Of course, this did not mark the end of the screening exercise; subsequently adopted Community legislation (the so-called 'pipeline *acquis*') had to be reviewed during the negotiations.

In relation to the implementation of institutional reforms necessary for enlargement, the Helsinki European Council took an important decision on the possible date of enlargement. The Member States asserted that the European Union had to complete institutional reforms before the end of 2002 at the latest and be ready to take in new members by 1 January 2003. This meant in practice that the EU considered 1 January 2003 as the first possible date for enlargement.[95] However, the EU only expressed the possibility of the first entries in 2003 and did not make any commitments for 2003. The Union also confirmed that, from that date, the preparedness of individual candidate countries would be the only factor which would determine the precise date of accession.

Following the Helsinki conclusions, the EU officially opened negotiations with Bulgaria, Latvia, Lithuania, Malta, Romania and Slovakia on 15 February 2000. The fact that the *acquis* screening had already taken place enabled these six countries to start negotiating with great momentum, making quick progress in the early stages. Due to this dynamic start and the loss of momentum of negotiations with the Luxembourg six, Malta, Slovakia and Latvia had almost caught up with the Luxembourg group by the end of the year. In the EU, the year 2000 was clearly all about the IGC preparing the Treaty of Nice on the institutional reforms considered essential for enlargement. In this political situation, accession negotiations with the Luxembourg group were somewhat pushed into the background, breaking their momentum. In the second half of 2000, after almost two years of talks, the negotiations were still far from entering the intensive stage, when problematical questions are on the table and the parties try to forge a compromise. The chapters forming the hard core of the negotiating package were not put on the table; only those chapters were provisionally closed which involved no difficult issues, where neither Member States nor candidate countries had made requests for transitional periods. This made it very difficult to predict when the negotiations could be concluded. The dynamism of negotiations was further hindered by the fact that – even though the Luxembourg six had submitted their position papers on all chapters before the end of 1999 – the Member States were either unable to come to an agreement on their common position or had not even started consultations on certain difficult chapters, such as agriculture.

---

[95] 2002, the earliest possible date of accession indicated by the enlargement heading of Agenda 2000, was thereby taken off the agenda once and for all.

The time of the conclusion of negotiations became questionable, as the EU had no common concept on the timetable for accessions.[96] The failure of the EU to come up with a specific scenario for itself and the candidates on how enlargement should take place did not help the situation. Thus, during the course of 2000, political discourse focused most frequently on two extreme alternatives. According to the first scenario, the first round of enlargement, which should take place as soon as possible, would only include a handful of leading candidate countries, which would then be followed by other waves of enlargement, as and when candidates could fully meet the Copenhagen criteria. The second scenario, which seemed to enjoy increasing support in summer 2000, outlined a so-called 'Big Bang' enlargement, including as many countries as possible (up to ten applicants, except Bulgaria and Romania). This could give enlargement an historic significance, but could also mean that applicant countries would have to wait for the slowest one to catch up.

This situation created growing uncertainty among leading candidates, and raised doubts as to whether the EU would really apply the principle of differentiation in the enlargement process. Candidate countries thus repeatedly asked the EU to set a precise timetable for their accession, particularly for the conclusion of negotiations. In the middle of 2000, the EU seemed rather reluctant to do so, which intensified scepticism over enlargement both in Central and Eastern Europe and within the Union. Realising the long-term danger of such a situation, the Member States finally began to accept that, in addition to institutional reforms, the Nice European Council of December 2000 should also deliver some concrete encouragement to candidate countries, preferably by means of some kind of schedule.

The primary significance of the Nice European Council held from 7 to 10 December 2000 was that, by adopting the Treaty of Nice, it concluded the institutional reforms and opened the way for enlargement. This was a clear indication to the candidate countries, but Member States went further and tried to specifically outline the future of the enlargement process. In Nice, the EU's Heads of State or Government expressed their support for a concrete negotiating timetable, which confirmed that it should be possible to conclude negotiations with the most advanced candidate countries in 2002, provided that they had demonstrated their ability to assume the obligations of membership. The Member States decided that accession negotiations should progress as far as possible during the course of 2001, leaving

---

[96] The commencement of negotiations with some less developed members (i.e. Bulgaria and Romania) of the Helsinki group had a certain effect on leading candidates, who felt a danger that simultaneous negotiations with 12 countries might absorb all of the EU's capacities, with the result that the EU might opt for the more convenient method of adjusting the pace of talks to the slower countries. On the other hand, the fact that countries lagging years behind the leading candidates in terms of preparedness were only one or two years behind in the negotiations created some political uncertainty.

only the most outstanding substantial issues in the negotiations, particularly those with the greatest budgetary implications and the institutional chapter, to be addressed in 2002. In cases where a chapter could not be provisionally closed, but the number of remaining problems was very limited, the Commission proposed to modify the approach and instead of leaving such a chapter on the negotiating table, to 'set aside' the chapter with a specific written annotation that it would be revisited later at the appropriate moment. This approach ensured that a few unresolved problems would not delay negotiations of other chapters and facilitated agreement on the final package. The so-called 'road map' proposed by the Commission and adopted by the European Council in Nice set out a priority schedule for the negotiations in the subsequent 18 months, listing the chapters that should be provisionally closed in each of the three semesters, to enable the parties to agree on a package deal of outstanding issues in late 2002.

The Nice European Council Conclusions stated that the EU should be in a position to welcome new members from the end of 2002. In Nice, the Heads of State or Government also expressed their hope that citizens of candidate countries would be able to participate in the next European Parliament elections in June 2004. This was a forward-pointing element in the time-frame for enlargement, turning around the atmosphere of enlargement from the scepticism of 2000.

The positive impact of the decisions taken in Nice already made itself felt in the negotiations early in 2001. The first half of 2001 brought a breakthrough, when the first difficult chapters (environment, free movement of capital, free movement of persons) were provisionally closed with a few candidate countries, and the EU granted the first transitional measures with a significant scope or duration (for environment and the free movement of capital). The Gothenburg European Council of 15–16 June 2001 confirmed and specified the Nice timeframe by setting the express objective of concluding negotiations with the best prepared applicants by the end of 2002, in order that they could take part in the elections to the European Parliament in 2004 as full members.

While the first six months of 2001 only brought a real breakthrough in the negotiations with a few countries of the Luxembourg group[97], the second half of the year yielded major results for both the Helsinki and the Luxembourg groups[98], which practically eliminated differences between the two groups with the exception of Bulgaria and Romania in terms

---

[97] In these six months, Cyprus and Hungary made particularly good progress (Hungary closing 8 chapters in the first half of the year).

[98] Latvia, Lithuania, Slovenia, Slovakia and the Czech Republic made outstanding headway by closing 5 to 7 chapters in 6 months.

of the number of chapters closed. It became clear that ten countries (Cyprus, the Czech Republic, Estonia, Latvia, Lithuania, Hungary, Malta, Poland, Slovakia and Slovenia) might be able to conclude negotiations within the foreseeable future, possibly all at the same time, while Bulgaria and Romania had no chance of doing so.[99]

On this basis, assessing the progress made at the negotiating table, the Laeken European Council of 14–15 December 2001 could conclude that, during the course of 2001, the Nice roadmap had been observed. The Heads of State or Government welcomed the significant progress made and the fact that earlier delays had been partly compensated. Confirming the Nice and Gothenburg conclusions, at the Laeken Summit, the Member States committed themselves to completing negotiations before the end of 2002 with countries that were ready, and which could thus participate in the EP elections in 2004. The Laeken Summit was of significance because – for the first time in the enlargement process – the EU named the potential first-round countries. It was officially pronounced that, if the pace of negotiations was maintained and if candidate countries continued with their internal reforms, then Cyprus, the Czech Republic, Estonia, Latvia, Lithuania, Hungary, Malta, Poland, Slovakia, and Slovenia would be able to keep to the Nice roadmap and might be in a position to conclude negotiations before the end of 2002. However, in Laeken, the Member States also wanted to demonstrate that they had not forgotten about Romania and Bulgaria either, by acknowledging their efforts and encouraging them to make further progress. For these two applicants, the Laeken Summit expressed the objective of opening all negotiating chapters by the end of 2002 and mentioned the possibility of preparing a roadmap similar to the one adopted in Nice.

Altogether, the Laeken European Council supported the Big Bang concept of enlargement, as negotiations in the first six months of 2002 confirmed. Having closed most of the chapters related to the adoption of the *acquis*, for 2002 the ten candidate countries indicated in Laeken only had the budgetary chapters (agricultural, regional policy, budget) and the institutional issues to discuss, which nevertheless formed the most difficult hard core of the package. In this phase, it was highly unlikely that different candidate countries would close these chapters at very different times. Since the EU handled budgetary issues in a single package, it submitted its offer to all ten countries at the same time.

---

[99] By the end of 2001, the 10 countries had provisionally closed 20–26 chapters (Slovenia leading the way with 26, with Poland and Malta bringing up the rear with 20 each). Bulgaria and Romania had managed to close 14 and 9 chapters, respectively.

The main question left for 2002 was not so much which countries would join in the first wave, but rather whether Member States and candidate countries would be able to agree on the financial conditions of enlargement, and whether this enlargement, involving the greatest number of new Member States in the history of the European Union, would really take place in 2004.

The concept of a Big Bang enlargement and the Nice roadmap were confirmed by the Seville European Council of 21–22 June 2002, where a decision was made that, on the basis of the Commission's proposals, the Brussels Summit to be held in October 2002 would determine the list of countries with which the EU could conclude the negotiations at the Copenhagen European Council in December 2002. The European Council meeting in Brussels on 24–25 October 2002 – as had been expected – named all ten candidates already singled out in Laeken. At the Brussels Summit, the Member States also managed to adopt a common position on budgetary questions – the thorniest of issues for the conclusion of negotiations. This agreement was made possible by a Franco-German deal on the future financing of the EU's most costly policy: the Common Agricultural Policy.[100] In Brussels, the Member States decided that the Common Agricultural Policy would only be extended to the new Member States gradually: direct payments to farmers in new Member States would start at 25% of the Community level and would increase to 100% over a period of 9 years, while in the financial perspectives for the period 2007–2013, Community spending on agriculture could not grow by more than 1% annually. Concerning structural and cohesion policy, Member States decided that, for the interim period of 2004–2006, preceding the next budgetary period, new Member States would benefit from proportionately lower funding than eligible regions in old Member States.[101]

In line with the conclusions of the Brussels Summit, the Copenhagen European Council of 12–13 December 2002 had to make the final decisions concerning negotiating chapters with financial implications and bring the negotiations to a successful conclusion. By slightly improving the budgetary terms of its offer, the EU managed to forge a compromise, and the final package of the accession negotiations was agreed upon with the 10 countries on 13 December 2002. The process, which had begun at the Copenhagen Summit in June 1993 with the elaboration of the accession criteria, ended in Copenhagen nine and a half years later with the decision that Cyprus, the Czech Republic, Estonia, Hungary,

---

[100] For details, see 11.6.
[101] For more on the budgetary periods 2000–2006 and 2007–2013, see 7.3.4. and 7.3.5.

Latvia, Lithuania, Malta, Poland, Slovakia and Slovenia – provided that their Accession Treaty was ratified – would become fully-fledged members of the European Union on 1 May 2004. It was also decided at the Copenhagen Summit that these ten countries could take part in the work of the next Intergovernmental Conference on an equal footing, and that the new Treaty (which was to become the Constitutional Treaty) would only be signed following enlargement, to demonstrate that this would be a Treaty of all 25 Member States.

The Heads of State or Government emphasised in Copenhagen that the results of the negotiations provided a sound basis for the integration of the 10 new Member States and ensured the efficient operation of the enlarged Union, and noted that the final package included all the transitional measures necessary for the acceding countries to meet their obligations of membership.

Accession negotiations were concluded one by one with each of the 10 countries, according to their needs, interests and level of preparedness. Nonetheless, since the ten countries – with the exception of Cyprus and Malta – were very similar both in terms of their situation and preparation, the final packages agreed upon in their respective accession negotiations were also rather similar. The two key issues of accession negotiations – the budgetary sums involved and transitional measures – were also similar for all candidate countries. This enables a general summary to be made of the financial projections for all ten countries.

The enlargement financial package that the 15 Member States and the 10 candidate countries agreed to in Copenhagen specified budgetary obligations and rights, i.e. how much each country had to contribute to and could receive from the EU budget until 2006, the end of the financial period laid down in Agenda 2000. Only in the area of agriculture (or more precisely, of direct payments) did they adopt decisions reaching beyond the current financial perspective, setting the terms of eligibility for Community budgetary funding for the next period from 2007 to 2013. With the exception of this one policy area, the Copenhagen financial deal only applied for the years until 2006, which meant that the new Member States participated in the talks on the financial perspectives for the period 2007–2013 with a right of veto.[102] According to the Copenhagen financial package, the ceiling for enlargement-related financial commitments in 2004–2006 was EUR 40.85 billion, out of which 14.5 billion was covered by contributions from new members. This meant that in practice, in the first two and a half years, enlargement cost the 15 old Member States

---

[102] Substantive talks on the financial perspectives for 2007–2013 began in the second half of 2004, when the new Member States had equal rights. (For more, see 7.3.5.)

EUR 26 billion. It is interesting to note that the sum of 40.85 billion is 1.5 billion below the 42.59-billion ceiling fixed in Berlin in 1999 for the last 3 years of the 2000–2006 budget, even though in Berlin the accession of only 6 countries was foreseen. Despite all the efforts by the candidates, the Member States – resorting to the use of the argument of the unfavourable economic situation (slow growth, high unemployment and particularly budgetary deficits, the latter important for eurozone membership)[103] – were unwilling to exploit the Berlin ceiling to the full.

Table 1.4. The Copenhagen financial package for enlargement
The Union's enlargement-related financial commitments in 2004–2006 vis-à-vis the ten Member States that joined in 2004 (at 1999 prices, in million euros)*

	2004	2005	2006	Total
Agriculture	1897	3748	4147	9792
from which:				
– Common Agricultural Policy (CAP)	327	2032	2322	4682
– Rural development	1570	1715	1825	5110
Structural operations	6069	6907	8770	21746
from which:				
– Structural Funds	3453	4755	5948	14156
– Cohesion Fund	2617	2152	2822	7590
Internal policies and supplementary interim expenditure	1457	1428	1371	4255
from which:				
– Current policies	846	881	916	2642
– Nuclear safety measures	125	125	125	375
– Institution building expenditure	200	120	60	380
– Schengen measures	286	302	271	858
Administrative expenditure	503	558	612	1673
Budgetary compensation	1273	1173	939	3385
Total financial commitment	11199	13813	15840	40851

* 'Total' figures may differ from the sums of individual chapters due to rounding-up.

Source: European Commission

---

[103] At the Copenhagen Summit, the net contributors and particularly Germany, the main financing state of the Community budget, dug in their heels, which made it practically impossible to further increase enlargement spending. Germany and the other net contributors argued that increasing contributions would put too much pressure on their national budgets and could jeopardise their commitment to meeting their eurozone obligations to keep their budget deficits below 3% of GDP. These Member States also emphasised that the economic situation and growth prospects had weakened since 1999.

Concerning the two key areas of agriculture and structural and cohesion funding, the agreement reached in Copenhagen maintained the EU proposal on direct payments adopted in Brussels. According to this formula, in 2004, farmers of 'new' Member States received only 25% of direct payments that 'old' member-state farmers were entitled to, which increased to 30% in 2005, 35% in 2006 and 40% in 2007; from 2007, the amount will grow by 10% annually, reaching 100% in 2013. The original formula was improved somewhat by the possibility of 'topping-up', which allows the new Member States to top up direct payments from the national budget by 30%, meaning that ultimately, in 2004, 2005 and 2006, farmers received 55, 60 and 65% respectively, which can reach the full 100% of direct payment funding by 2010 – of course only if their governments so decide.[104] Structural and cohesion funding to new Member States from 2004 to 2006 was set at below EUR 22 billion, hardly in the same order of magnitude as sums available to eligible regions of old Member States. However, according to the agreement, from 2007 no distinction is made between 'new' and 'old' Member States in structural and cohesion operations. In the new financial period, the ten new Member States must be treated equally[105], except in the area of agriculture, where they will only receive equal treatment from 2013.

On the whole, the Copenhagen financial package enabled the EU to proceed with enlargement, and met the candidates' goal that their budgetary position should improve upon accession. However, the extent of this improvement was far from what these countries had hoped for at the beginning of their accession process or even from what they had anticipated at the time of the adoption of Agenda 2000. Copenhagen did, however, pave the way for, and necessitate significant positive changes in the financial position of new Member States from 2007 on. Once the transitional period ended for structural and cohesion policy, considerable Community funding opened up for them, making most of these countries major net recipients for a long time.[106]

---

[104] See also 11.6.
[105] See also 13.3.
[106] See Table 13.7.

Apart from the financial deals, other important elements of the accession negotiations (except for national peculiarities) demonstrated several similarities, with the same areas usually posing the sticking points. Questions such as the free movement of persons and capital, the environment, competition and justice and home affairs were the subject of heated debate in all the candidate countries.

When it came to the free movement of persons, several Member States – mostly those neighbouring one or more candidate countries – expressed concerns that removing restrictions on the free movement of labour would lead to a wave of workers arriving from the new Member States, which could disturb the domestic labour market, push up unemployment and thus create significant social tensions, thereby turning public opinion against enlargement and the new Member States. The solution the negotiators came up with was to grant old Member States a transitional period of 2+3+2 years. This formula allowed Member States not to open their labour markets fully in the first two years after enlargement, and then they could choose to extend this transitional period by another three years. After five years, however, they could only maintain such restrictions if they could prove that the influx of workers from new Member States really distorted the domestic labour market.

In the chapter on free movement of capital, it was the new Member States who requested transitional exemptions, primarily for property and land ownership. This was in response to a popular fear that opening these segments of their capital markets to richer Member States would induce extensive speculative buying of cheap land and real estate, which would in turn drive up prices, making it less affordable for local citizens to purchase property and thus causing major tensions. Different acceding countries found different solutions to this problem, generally placing bans or restrictions of some sort on citizens of other Member States on acquiring property in the first few years of EU membership.

Important requests for transitional exemptions were put forward by acceding countries in the area of environment, where the magnitude of investment required made compliance with the rules upon accession practically impossible. One example was municipal sewage, where a number of countries were granted transitional periods of sometimes around ten years to build sewage systems in towns lacking these. An equally difficult problem was the modernisation of certain power plants, where significant transitional concessions were granted (both under the energy and the environment chapters).

In the chapter on competition, the major clash between the two negotiating sides was usually over state aids. Several candidate countries had introduced incentives aimed at attracting foreign investors and boosting local enterprise development, which included forms of state aid (such as tax breaks) not allowed under Community rules. Following long and tough negotiations, compromises emerged, allowing these countries to maintain such forms of state aid, normally for periods of between one to two years and in some cases between five to seven years.

The main issue in the chapter on justice and home affairs related to border controls and accession to the Schengen area.[107] According to Community law, the new Member States had to join the Schengen area, dismantle internal border checks and establish common border controls. But since this would involve major institution-building tasks for the authorities, primarily in staffing and technology, the decision was taken that new Member States would only become full members of the Schengen area a few years following their accession, some time around 2007. The precise date was finalised in December 2006: provided that they meet the relevant criteria, the Member States that acceded to the EU in 2004 can join the Schengen area on 31 December 2007, which in practical terms means that internal land border controls will be abolished on 1 January 2008.[108]

A special demand put forward by the EU side during negotiations concerned the possibility of monitoring and introducing sanctions against new Member States if they failed to meet the obligations laid down in the Accession Treaty. The solution came in the form of so-called *safeguard clauses*, which enable the Council acting on the Commission's proposal to impose transitional restrictions on the rights of a Member State in the areas of the economy (including agriculture), the internal market, as well as justice and home affairs. The Commission could have activated these safeguard clauses if serious and persistent problems had arisen in the specified areas.

Negotiations with Bulgaria and Romania were concluded two years later with a similar result as for the ten countries of the previous round of enlargement. The formulae for financial questions (for agriculture and structural operations) and legislative issues (the free movement of capital and persons) as well as safeguard clauses that had been applied to the ten countries were used for Bulgaria and Romania too. A major difference between the two rounds of enlargement was that Bulgaria and Romania were granted

---

[107] For details, see 24.2. and 24.3.2.

[108] For airports, the date was adjusted to the first day of the new timetables: 29 March 2008.

longer transitional periods in some areas (such as the environment) and that a super-safeguard clause was enacted, which would have enabled the EU to delay the two countries' accession by one year, had they been judged to be ill-prepared for membership. For more on the accession of Bulgaria and Romania, see 1.13.7.

1.13.6. The enlargement of 1 May 2004

The conclusion of accession negotiations put the enlargement process in a clear, well-defined timeframe. The key date was that of actual accession: 1 May 2004. This date was in line with the European Union's commitments made in Nice, reinforced in Gothenburg, Laeken and Seville, to enable the citizens of the new Member States to take part in the elections to the European Parliament in June 2004. This date also gave enough time for ratification in all 25 states following the Copenhagen Summit. (A date as late as possible was also desirable due to the limited funds available for enlargement.) In practice, 1 May 2004 was set as the latest possible date for accessions in the Nice roadmap. Previous accessions had always been set for the first day of the calendar year[109], making eastern enlargement special for yet another reason. Of course, what really made this round of enlargement unprecedented in the history of European integration was its sheer size (ten new countries, a two-thirds increase in the number of Member States) and the fact that it finally reunified a Europe divided by the Iron Curtain for four decades.

The most important date between the conclusion of negotiations and accession was 16 April 2003, when leaders of the 25 old and acceding Member States gathered in Athens for the signing of the Treaty of Accession. The signing ceremony, held in Stoa of Attalos, the ancient Agora of Athens, at the foot of the Acropolis, marked the beginning of a new phase for the ten candidate countries; they were now acceding states with observer status in the Community decision making institutions: the Council and Parliament. From that day, the Interim Agreement annexed to the Treaty of Accession gave their government or parliamentary representatives the right to express their views during decision-making, though not yet the right to vote.

---

[109] The only exception was the "special accession" of the German Democratic Republic, which became part of the Federal Republic of Germany and the EU (or, more precisely, of the EC) on 3 October 1990, upon German reunification.

The signing of the Accession Treaty also marked the beginning of the ratification process, when the 25 signatory states had to ratify the Treaty they signed in Athens according to their own constitutional rules. The national parliaments of the 15 old Member States gave their seal of approval to eastern enlargement without any difficulties, usually with a decisive majority. In nine of the ten acceding countries, the Treaty of Accession was not only ratified by Parliament but also approved by the electorate in a referendum. In most cases, the result of the referendum showed clear popular support for membership; only in Malta did the 'no' camp manage to convince enough voters to make the result a relatively close one.[110]

The only country not to hold a referendum on accession was Cyprus. The primary reason was that, as a divided country with control over only the southern part of the island, the Treaty of Accession was signed by the Greek Cypriot government recognised by the international community. Negotiations between the northern Turkish and southern Greek Cypriots were going on in parallel about reunification, and the two sides – in the hope of success – were looking to hold a referendum on reunification instead. Confirming the EU's previous position, the Copenhagen Summit emphasised that the southern part of the island would accede to the EU on 1 May 2004, irrespective of the outcome or approval of the reunification talks. The final results of the negotiations – conducted under the aegis of the UN according to the so-called Annan Plan – was not acceptable to the Greek Cypriot leaders; thus the reunification plan was rejected by the Greek Cypriot side in the referendum by a wide margin.[111] Despite the broad support of the Turkish Cypriots, it was only the Greek Cypriot half of the island that acceded to the European Union on 1 May.[112] The European Union, however, decided that, in the hope of future reunification, it would foster closer ties with the northern Turkish Cypriot community and help them align to the single market. To that end, the EU decided to adopt legislation on the free movement of goods and persons between Northern Cyprus and the Union, as well as to earmark funds (EUR 259 million) for boosting economic recovery in the under-developed northern part of the island.

---

[110] Turnout / the percentage of 'yes' votes: the Czech Republic – 55.2% / 77.3%; Estonia – 64% / 66.9%; Hungary – 45.6% / 83.8%; Latvia – 72.5% / 67.7%; Lithuania – 63.3%,/ 91%; Malta – 91% / 53.7%; Poland – 58.9% / 77.5%; Slovakia – 52.5% / 92.5%; Slovenia – 60.3% / 89.6%.

[111] Greek Cypriot leaders in fact indicated their support for reunification and talks thereon, but not under the terms of the Annan plan.

[112] In the referendum held on 24 April 2004, the reunification plan proposed by UN Secretary General Kofi Annan was approved by 64.9% of Turkish Cypriots and rejected by 75.8% of Greek Cypriots. (Turnout was 88% and 87%, respectively.)

Overall, the ratification of the Treaty of Accession went without major hitches in all 25 Member States. Consequently, the first eastern enlargement of the EU took place on 1 May 2004, completing the fall of the Iron Curtain. The ten new Member States became fully-fledged members; their delegates began to take part in the work of the Community institutions. Just over a month after enlargement, the elections to the European Parliament were held between 10 and 13 June, with citizens electing MEPs from all 25 Member States.

The accession of ten new Member States on 1 May 2004 was by no means the end of a process; it was just the end of a beginning: the beginning of eastward enlargement, which was followed by a second wave of enlargement in 2007 and which is expected to continue in coming years with more enlargement rounds.

1.13.7. The enlargement of 1 January 2007

At the Copenhagen Summit of December 2002, specific decisions were taken concerning Bulgaria and Romania, engaged in accession negotiations since 2000. In Copenhagen, the Member States adopted a roadmap for these two countries (similar to the one adopted in Nice for the Ten), setting clear objectives and pronouncing that – provided that the membership criteria were fulfilled – the EU wished to welcome the two countries as members in 2007. The Copenhagen Council also decided that supplementary resources be made available within the pre-accession funds for these two candidates in the run-up to their accession. (Available funding increased by 20, 30 and 40% in 2004, 2005 and 2006 respectively, compared to the 2001–2003 average.)

The Thessaloniki Summit of June 2003 amended the roadmap by setting a target date for the conclusion of negotiations the following year. Building on these developments, negotiations with Bulgaria and Romania progressed smoothly and swiftly during the course of 2003 and 2004, enabling Bulgaria to close the last chapter in June 2004 and Romania to do the same in December. Thus the Heads of State or Government, at their summit meeting of 16–17 December 2004, could decide on the official closure of negotiations and set 1 January 2007 as a target date for accession. Compared to the accession of the ten new Member States, the Treaty of Accession of Bulgaria and Romania included a new kind of *'super safeguard clause'* (postponement clause), which left open the option of postponing accession by one year should the two countries fail to fulfil the membership criteria on time. This special, unprecedented safeguard clause was necessary because the Commission's assessment indicated that Bulgaria's and Romania's levels of preparedness (in fulfilling the commitments they made at the negotiating table) were behind schedule compared to the situation of the ten Member States that joined in 2004 before their accession.

The accession negotiations with Bulgaria and Romania concluded – as outlined in 1.13.5. – with similar results as for the ten Member States that joined in 2004. The only major difference was the super safeguard clause and the longer transitional exemptions for certain chapters of the *acquis*. The financial agreement, however, closely followed the format used for the Ten in 2004. Direct payments to Bulgarian and Romanian farmers are phased in gradually: they start at a level of 25% in 2007, increasing by 5% annually to reach 40% in 2010; from that point, they go up by 10% each year and reach the full 100% in 2016. Both countries have the possibility to top up direct payments from their national budgets by a maximum of 30%; thus their farmers could be receiving the full amount as soon as 2013.[113] Structural and cohesion funding is also to be introduced gradually: in the first three years of their membership, Bulgaria and Romania are entitled to a reduced amount. From 2010, however, they will enjoy full eligibility, which will mean major funding opportunities for the two countries and their regions.[114]

The financial package agreed upon during the accession negotiations included the following sums earmarked for Bulgaria and Romania for the years 2007–2009 (calculated at 2004 prices): EUR 8.274 billion for structural and cohesion funding, EUR 3.041 billion for rural development, EUR 1.12 billion for agricultural market measures, EUR 1.312 billion for direct payments to farmers, EUR 210 million for nuclear safety and EUR 82 million for institution building. On top of these sums, another EUR 799.3 million has been pledged in the form of budgetary compensation over the three years to ensure that the net balance of the two countries contributions to and receipts from the EU budget remains positive from year one.

The Treaty of Accession with Bulgaria and Romania was signed on 25 April 2005 in Luxembourg. The European Council of 16–17 June 2005 also decided that these two countries could participate in the work of the decision-making bodies (the European Council, the Council of Ministers and the European Parliament).

Once the Treaty of Accession was signed and sealed, its ratification could begin in the 25 Member States and the two acceding countries. Unlike the ten Member States that joined in 2004 before them, Bulgaria and Romania decided not to hold a referendum on accession, and instead left it to their national parliaments to rubberstamp the Treaty, which they did by a large majority. Ratification by the Member States took longer than

---

[113] See 11.6.
[114] See 13.4.

in the case of the previous round of enlargement, not because there were now 25 of them, but because due to the slower pace of Bulgaria's and Romania's preparations, the Commission waited for the 11th hour to commit itself and say whether it considered the two countries fit for membership. In the absence of such a positive Commission assessment, some Member States decided to postpone ratification. The European Commission finally published its last monitoring report on Bulgaria and Romania on 26 September 2006, which gave a favourable assessment and proposed the date of 1 January 2007 for accession. As Bulgaria and Romania could breathe a sigh of relief with the sword of Damocles in the form of a super safeguard clause no longer hanging over their heads, the Commission stressed that both countries had to make further efforts to fully meet their pledged commitments. In order to minimise the risks associated with the remaining phase of preparation, the Commission introduced a number of post-accession flanking measures. It established a control mechanism with special benchmarks, whereby the two countries have to report twice a year on the progress towards achieving these benchmark goals. If unsatisfied with that progress, the Commission may initiate the application of the safeguard clauses as stipulated by the Treaty of Accession.

Following the publication of the Commission's positive monitoring report, the remaining four Member States (Belgium, Denmark, France and Germany) completed the ratification procedures and Bulgaria and Romania became members of the European Union on 1 January 2007. With nearly 30 million new citizens and two new Member States, the EU now unites more than 490 million people and 27 countries.

Nonetheless, the accession of Bulgaria and Romania further increased the disparities within the Union. While the average per capita GDP of the ten countries of the 2004 enlargement wave exceeded half of the EU average at the time of their accession, in the case of Bulgaria and Romania this figure was just above one third of the EU average.

1.13.8. Continuing eastward enlargement

The accession of Bulgaria and Romania marked the end of an historic phase, the enlargement process that began in the early nineties with the conclusion of the Europe Agreements had reached its end. Nonetheless, enlarging the Union to the east and southeast remains a top priority on the Union's agenda, due to former commitments towards Turkey and countries of the Western Balkans.

The accession of Turkey is of paramount importance for enlargement. The Helsinki Council of December 1999 recognised Turkey as a candidate country, but the start of negotiations remained out of the question at the time. The Turkish side had hoped that the time would come at the Copenhagen Summit of December 2002 for the EU to make up its mind on commencing membership talks with Ankara, but finally the Member States decided it was too early to adopt a common position on the issue. The main criticism against Turkey was that it did not even meet the political criteria of membership in relation to the development of properly functioning democratic institutions and ensuring respect for human rights. According to the EU's principles declared earlier, meeting the Copenhagen political criteria is a precondition for starting negotiations on the economic and legal terms of accession. With a view to the low level of preparedness demonstrated by Turkey, the decision was deferred by two years. According to the Copenhagen conclusions, the European Union – on the basis of a report by and the recommendations of the European Commission – had until December 2004 to decide, though it was added that if Turkey fulfilled the Copenhagen political criteria, the Union would launch negotiations without delay.

In its much-awaited report, which was finally published on 6 October 2004, the Commission – based on its assessment of political criteria – recommended that negotiations be opened with Turkey, with the proviso that it fulfilled certain tasks immediately. Once Turkey undertook to fulfil the tasks set by the Commission by the December 2004 summit, following a lengthy debate, the Member States decided to commence negotiations with Turkey on 3 October 2005. Some Member States and political groups in the European Parliament suggested that negotiations should not begin with the declared aim of membership, instead it should be decided in the light of the progress made by Turkey whether the aim was membership or some other special status.[115] This proposal was finally disregarded, but it was added that the negotiation process was open-ended with no guarantees concerning its outcome: taking into consideration all of the Copenhagen criteria, if the candidate country cannot fully assume the obligations of membership, it must be ensured that it is linked to European structures as closely as possible.

In view of Turkey's special situation, and following the recommendations of the Commission's October 2004 report, a new negotiating approach was adopted, including

---

[115] This would have been unacceptable for Turkey anyway. The Turkish government declared early on that its aim was full membership, and it would only be willing to negotiate full membership.

several novel elements. The Council sets the basic conditions for the preliminary closure of each individual chapter, and may also require Turkey to make certain legal commitments prior to the opening of a chapter. The Commission had also pointed out that long transitional periods would probably be needed and that in some areas – such as structural and cohesion policy as well as agricultural policy, which have the greatest financial implications – special arrangements might be desirable (because extending these Community policies to Turkey in their present form seemed unfeasible with the available funding).[116] In the case of the free movement of workers, the EU may consider the application of a permanent safeguard clause. Since the accession of Turkey will have a significant impact on the Union, from both the institutional and the financial aspect, the key figures of the financial perspectives for the period following 2014 should be set before the conclusion of accession negotiations (implying that the earliest date for Turkey's accession would be 2015–2016). In the course of the negotiations, the Commission not only monitors the preparations by Turkey for membership, but also assesses the EU's readiness to welcome new members.[117] In response to concerns that Turkey might violate the political criteria (particularly respect for human rights), a special arrangement has been added, allowing for the suspension of negotiations – initiated by the Commission or one third of the Member States and decided by a qualified majority vote in Council – in the event of a serious and sustained violation of freedom, democracy, the rule of law, human rights and fundamental liberties.

A precondition set by the EU for kicking off accession talks was that Turkey should officially recognise the extension of the 1963 customs union under the Ankara Agreement to the countries that became Member States on 1 May 2004. The customs union between the EU and Turkey has been operating since 1 January 1996, and was to be extended to all the ten new Member States upon their accession. However, there was a sensitive political dimension to the issue: Turkey refused to recognise Cyprus (since its division in 1974), which the EU tried to achieve indirectly. Finally, on 1 August 2005, Turkey signed the Protocol to the Ankara Agreement extending the customs union to the new Member States, but with a diplomatic sleight of hand it issued on the same day a unilateral declaration stating that

---

[116] Turkey's membership would turn the present structural and cohesion policy upside down. The accession of Turkey would increase the EU's area by 18.3% and its population by 14.7%, while reducing GDP per person by 10.5%. As a result, several countries and regions currently receiving support from the Funds would suddenly find themselves above the threshold and lose their eligibility to structural and cohesion funding.

[117] Along with its report, the Commission also published an impact assessment, assessing the timespan and impact of Turkey's accession. In this assessment, the Commission noted that membership poses a major challenge both for Turkey and the Union, and confirmed its previous opinion that preparations for Turkey's accession are likely to last a decade.

the extension of the customs union does not mean the recognition of Cyprus. With that trick, it managed to fulfil the EU's wishes without changing its policy on Cyprus. The EU kept its word and opened accession negotiations with Turkey on 3 October 2005.

As usual, negotiations began with screening the *acquis communautaire*. Accession talks with Turkey and Croatia, which began on the same day, are conducted on the basis of 35 chapters. The screening phase was completed by the end of October 2006, and substantive negotiations could commence. In 2006, only one chapter (science and research) was opened, which the parties closed the same year. Towards the end of 2006, EU-Turkey relations became troubled anew: contrary to the spirit of the Ankara Agreement, now extended to the new Member States, and despite repeated requests from the EU, Turkey refused to allow ships flying Cypriot flags to enter Turkish ports. As a consequence, the Council of the EU – following the Commission's proposal – decided on 11 December 2006 to suspend eight chapters related to the customs union[118] and not to re-open them until Turkey fully implemented the Ankara Agreement. Apart from the eight suspended chapters, accession talks can continue if the usual conditions are met (in the first half of 2007, three chapters were opened).

These developments are a good indication of how Turkey's accession is riddled with several political problems, making a swift conclusion of the process highly unlikely. Since accession talks began, the Commission has criticised Turkey repeatedly for practices running counter to the Copenhagen political criteria (in areas such as freedom of speech, religious freedom, women's rights, minority rights, trade union rights, civilian control of the military or judicial practice). Recently, there has been a rise in several Member States of the sentiment that Turkey should be offered some kind of special status instead of membership proper. Austria, for example, insisted until the last moment before accession talks began that the outcome of the negotiations could a privileged partnership rather than membership. In the end, Austria only accepted a milder formula ("an open-ended process, the outcome of which cannot be guaranteed") in return for the launching of negotiations with Croatia at the same time. The French position is particularly ambivalent towards

---

[118] These eight chapters are the following: free movement of goods, right of establishment and the freedom to provide services, financial services, agriculture and rural development, fisheries, transport, customs union and external relations.

Turkey; the French Constitution, amended in February 2005, calls for a referendum on all accessions in the future. The only countries to which this provision does not apply are Bulgaria and Romania (which have already joined) and Croatia.[119] With these strings attached, the constitutional amendment is clearly tailored to the case of Turkey, whose potential membership enjoys very little public support in France. To add insult to injury, the new French President Nicolas Sarkozy has repeatedly expressed strong views on Turkey, advocating the prospect of special status over full membership and seeking a Union-wide debate on the issue.

It is safe to conclude that Turkey will not become a member of the EU in the next few years, but the exact timeframe of its accession process is rather difficult to predict. Nevertheless, the decision to open talks with Turkey was a milestone in the history of European integration, and the decision itself was much more important than the actual date of Turkey's eventual accession. By this decision, the European Union committed itself to the accession of a country only partly European in geographical terms and with a different religious culture. The unconcealed aim of this commitment was to demonstrate to the world that western-type democracy and the European economic model can work successfully in a Muslim country too. Consequently, the EU reconfirmed the key motive and objective of European integration: guaranteeing peace, security and stability in Europe and the world, and thereby extending prosperity.

Similar motives led the Member States at the Thessaloniki Summit of June 2003 to offer the prospect of EU membership to the countries of the Western Balkans. The so-called Thessaloniki Agenda states that the future of these then five countries (Albania, Bosnia-Herzegovina, Croatia, Macedonia and Serbia-Montenegro, including Kosovo)[120] is in the European Union. The Thessaloniki Agenda does not mean candidate status (only potential candidacy), and does not give any specific dates, but does stipulate that the EU's aim is to take these countries on board and continue eastern enlargement, extending the area of

---

[119] These three countries were removed from the scope of this constitutional provision on the grounds that the EU had decided to launch negotiations with them before 1 July 2004.

[120] Montenegro has since become independent, following the referendum of 21 May 2006, in which 55.5% of Montenegrins expressed their desire to break off from Serbia. Montenegro proclaimed its independence on 3 June 2006. According to the current state of play in the negotiations in the UN, there is a serious chance that Kosovo, which is still under UN administration, could become an independent state as well.

political stability and economic prosperity further south-east. However, the EU – pointing out the differences in development between the countries of the Western Balkans – emphatically stressed that the accession of each individual country would be conditional on the fulfilment of the Copenhagen criteria and based on individual merits.

The EU's commitment to the Western Balkans was demonstrated by the decision of the Brussels Council meeting of June 2004 to grant candidate status to the region's most advanced country, Croatia (which submitted its application for membership in February 2003). Six months later, at the summit of December 2004, the Member States decided to begin negotiations with Croatia on 17 March 2005. Finally, the EU decided not to open negotiations after all, because some Member States felt that Croatia failed to cooperate fully with the International Criminal Tribunal for the former Yugoslavia in the Hague. The negotiations were finally opened with Croatia on the same day as Turkey (3 October 2005), when Croatia's cooperation with the ICTY was deemed satisfactory. Another important factor was Austria's insistence that accession talks with Turkey should only begin if they were also opened with Croatia. It became clear early on that the two sets of negotiations would be very different and Croatia would be able to proceed much more quickly; therefore the two accession processes are not linked in any way. By mid-2007, Croatia had opened 12 of the 35 chapters, while Turkey had only opened four, and the Commission's annual reports have consistently emphasised Croatia's steady progress. Nevertheless, Croatia will only be able to close the negotiations and accede to the EU once the ratification of the Reform Treaty amending the Founding Treaties is successfully concluded and is certain to enter into force, since several Member States and the European Parliament consider the entry into force of the new Treaty an essential precondition for any further enlargement.

The 35 chapters of the accession negotiations with Croatia and Turkey*

Free movement of goods
Free movement of persons
Freedom of establishment and
    freedom to provide services
Free movement of capital
Public procurement
Company law
Intellectual property rights

Social policy and employment
Enterprise and industrial policy
Trans-European networks
Regional policy, structural instruments
Justice and fundamental rights
Freedom, security and justice
Science and research
Education and culture

Competition policy
Financial services
Information society and media
Agriculture and rural development
Food safety, plant and
  animal health
Fisheries
Transport
Energy
Taxation
Economic and monetary union

Environment
Consumer and health protection
Customs union
External relations
Foreign and security policy
Financial control
Financial and budgetary provisions
Statistics
Institutional issues
Miscellaneous

*The 33 chapters of the acquis plus 'Institutional issues' and 'Miscellaneous' (the latter two were not part of the screening process).

The second country from the region of the Western Balkans to submit its formal application for membership was Macedonia, in March 2004. The European Commission published an Opinion on Macedonia on 9 November 2005, on the basis of which the European Council meeting of 15–16 December 2005 decided to grant Macedonia candidate status. This gave Macedonia's accession prospects a whole new dimension: the EU officially declared that it counts Macedonia as a future Member State, although no specific date has been given for the opening of accession talks. The Commission report of November 2006 emphasised that Macedonia's recognition as a candidate for EU membership was a form of encouragement, especially with a view to the peaceful cohabitation of the Macedonian and Albanian populations. The European Council of December 2006 stressed that candidate status was an acknowledgement of the reforms Macedonia had carried out, but that further major progress was required for the accession process to move on.

As far as the other countries of the Western Balkans are concerned, membership is clearly a very distant prospect; the primary goal is to implement the stabilisation and association agreements (SAAs)[121] they have been offered. Still, the EU considers all of these countries (Albania, Bosnia-Herzegovina, Montenegro and Serbia, including Kosovo, under interim UN administration) as potential candidates for EU membership. In the stabilisation and association process, Albania has made the greatest leap forward by signing the SAA in June 2006. Negotiations on the SAA began with Serbia – then still Serbia and Montenegro – in October 2005,

---

[121] The EU has offered SAAs (which are similar to the Europe Agreements once offered to Central and Eastern European countries) to all countries of the Western Balkans. For mor,e see 9.4.2.1.

but were suspended in May 2006, because the EU deemed the country's cooperation with the International Criminal Tribunal for the former Yugoslavia (ICTY) in the Hague as insufficient. Negotiations re-commenced in June 2007, but they will only be concluded and the SAA will only be signed if Serbia fully cooperates with the ICTY. Negotiations on the SAA with Montenegro commenced following its independence in June 2006 and were completed before the end of that year; the Agreement could be signed sometime during 2007. The EU opened SAA talks with Bosnia-Herzegovina in January 2006 and formally concluded them by the end of 2006, but the Agreement itself will only be submitted for signature after Bosnia-Herzegovina has fulfilled the reform criteria set by the Union.

The EU's commitment towards candidate and potential candidate countries is demonstrated by the significant funding earmarked for the 2007–2013 period in the form of accession and pre-accession support. From 1 January 2007, all existing pre-accession-type funds (PHARE, ISPA, SAPARD, Turkey's pre-accession support and CARDS for the Western Balkans) were merged into a single Instrument for Pre-accession Assistance (IPA), which covers candidate countries (Croatia, Macedonia and Turkey) as well as potential candidates (Albania, Bosnia-Herzegovina, Montenegro and Serbia, including Kosovo). The IPA has five constituent strands, each supporting one priority area: transition assistance and institution building, regional development, cross-border cooperation, human resources development and rural development. The latter three are only available to candidate countries and are aimed at preparing them for the management of Structural Funds. IPA will provide a total amount of EUR 11.47 billion over the 2007–2013 period. The breakdown of the total envelope is decided annually on the basis of a three-year indicative financial framework. In the first three years from 2007 to 2009, IPA will have at its disposal EUR 4 billion, divided between Turkey and the Western Balkans in a ratio of 40% to 60%.

Table 1.5. IPA funding by country from 2007 to 2009
(EUR million)

	2007	2008	2009	Total
Albania	61.0	70.7	81.2	212.9
Bosnia - Herzegovina	62.1	74.8	89.1	226.0
Croatia	138.5	146.0	151.2	435.7
Kosovo	63.3	64.7	66.1	194.1
Macedonia	58.5	70.2	81.8	210.5
Montenegro	31.4	32.6	33.3	97.3
Serbia	186.7	190.9	194.8	572.4
Turkey	497.2	538.7	566.4	1 602.3
Regional and horizontal programmes	100.7	140.7	160.0	401.4
Administrative expenditure	55.8	54.0	56.5	166.3
Total	1 255.2	1 383.3	1 480.4	4 118.9

Source: European Commission

The case of Turkey and the Western Balkans shows that there is a lot to do still in the enlargement process, which will undoubtedly remain high on the agenda in the coming one to two decades. At the same time, it is increasingly likely that a debate will have to be held on – and an answer will have to be given to – the question of how far European integration can go, how far the Union can enlarge and where the geographical boundaries of the united Europe end.[122]

In that context, the issue of absorption capacity (sometimes also referred to as integration capacity) has received increasing attention. Absorption signifies the Union's capacity to welcome new members. At their summit meeting on 14–15 December 2006, the Heads of State or Government devoted special attention to the question of absorption capacity, after a number of Member States had expressed their opinion that there is a limit to how

---

[122] The rejection of the Constitutional Treaty in the French and Dutch referenda may have been partly attributable to the public mistrust towards enlargement with certain candidate countries.

many countries the EU can integrate. The European Council of December 2006 concluded that there was a need to adapt the approach to enlargement: namely, to apply accession criteria more rigorously, focus more on the fulfilment of certain basic requirements from the beginning of negotiations, and take into consideration the Union's ability to welcome new countries. Nonetheless, the Heads of State or Government did not set new conditions for countries already on the road to accession, did not change or amend the Copenhagen criteria[123] and did not even debate where the boundaries of Europe lie. Thereby they left the door of the Union open to not only countries with a clear prospect of membership, but also to countries that have expressed an interest in accession but that the EU has not made any commitments to yet.[124]

The gates of the Union remain open to all countries interested in membership. The real question is to what extent will domestic political rows of the present Member States put the issue of enlargement at the heart of national political debate. France's decision to amend its Constitution and introduce the requirement of holding referenda on future accessions shows what can be expected in the future. If the new membership of new entrants requires successful referenda, and if public opinion remains as it is now, it is highly questionable whether the Union will be 'enlargeable'. To encourage a swing in the public mood, the EU will first have to deliver tangible results on economic and social issues affecting its citizens and thereby convince them of the importance of enlargement. The European public needs to understand that enlargement is the best means to further peace, security, stability and prosperity.

---

[123] The recent change of attitude in the Union is indicated by the decision of the European Council of 21–22 June 2007 to add a new provision in the Reform Treaty to the loosely worded Treaty Article on accession criteria (TEU Article 49). The new wording stipulates that beside the criteria defined in the Treaty additional conditions set by the European Council must be taken into consideration as well. In practical terms, this means that the European Council can set extra criteria for acceding countries.

[124] Let it suffice to mention the examples of Moldova and Ukraine, who have repeatedly expressed their aspirations for integration and accession, but who are part of the EU's neighbourhood policy only (see 9.4.2.3.) and are not even considered as potential candidates for membership.

CHAPTER 2
THE INSTITUTIONAL STRUCTURE OF THE EUROPEAN UNION

2.1. The character of the institutional structure

The European Union is a unique construct in international law. It is unlike any traditional international organisation or state. Intergovernmental and supranational[1] characteristics exist side by side in the operation of the European Union and form a distinctive blend. On the one hand, the EU cannot be seen as a simple intergovernmental organisation since it has its own competences, its own legal entity through the Communities and endorses legal acts set by the Community institutions. On the other hand, it is not a supranational federation in which national governments and parliaments are subordinated to central federal institutions.

The decision-making and operating mechanisms of the EU are essentially guaranteed by four main institutions. The system based on the cooperation of the Council, the Commission, the Parliament and the Court of Justice creates the characteristic institutional structure in which intergovernmental and supranational features inter-weave in a unique way. While the Council is an intergovernmental organisation, in the other three institutions supranational elements prevail. The Commission's scope of duties involves the recommendation, preparation, formulation and, to a lesser degree, implementation of decisions. The main decision-making and legislative institution is the Council, while the Parliament functions partly as a co-decision maker and co-legislator and partly as a consultative and monitoring body along with the Council. In practical terms, these three institutions represent three different interests that need to be taken into account in Community decisions: national interests expressed by the member-state governments in the Council, citizens' (political) interests represented by the political parties in Parliament, and the Community's interests guarded by the Commission's supra-national administration. The work of these three

---

[1] The concept of supranationality generally means that the participating states do not have full control over the development and decisions of the organisation, i.e. that in certain cases, they may be compelled to adopt decisions (taken by the majority of the states or by a common institution) with which they disagree or may even have to act contrary to their position. Supranationality is more than the traditional cooperation between states since it entails the partial pooling and limitation of national sovereignty.

institutions is complemented by the Court, which ensures that Community law is upheld and uniformly implemented.[2]

The Maastricht Treaty also granted the Court of Auditors, whose task is to check the accounts of the EU, the same institutional status as the Council, the Commission, the Parliament and the Court of Justice.

In addition to the main institutions, the other bodies of the Union also have important responsibilities. These bodies, established by the Treaties, are: the two Advisory Committees, namely the Committee of the Regions and the Economic and Social Committee; the financial institutions, namely the European Investment Bank and the European Central Bank (which manages the single currency of the monetary union and the European System of Central Banks); and the European Ombudsman.

In this Chapter, we introduce the Community institutions[3] as they function now according to the Treaty of Nice, which entered into force on 1 February 2003, and the Accession Treaties of the ten Member States that acceded to the Union on 1 May 2004, as well as the two that followed on 1 January 2007.

It must be pointed out that the Constitutional Treaty signed on 29 October 2004 would have introduced significant changes in the composition and functioning of certain Community institutions. Following the failure of the ratification of the Constitutional Treaty, the Heads of State or Government decided at their summit of 21–22 June 2007 to abandon the constitutional approach and put the EU on new foundations by the means of a Reform Treaty amending the current EU Treaty and EC Treaty. The Reform Treaty is largely based on the Constitutional Treaty and takes on board most of its provisions on Community institutions. These provisions are presented separately from the current framework in Point 2 of the Annex for the practical reason that they will probably only come into effect in 2009.

---

[2] The method described herein is characteristic of the first pillar of the European Union, the European Communities. Within the framework of the second and third pillars, the functions of the institutions are partly different. On these differences, see also 3.2., 23.4. and 24.3.3.

[3] Community institutions are EU bodies whose establishment and operation are stipulated by the EC Treaty. However, it must be mentioned that, in certain cases, specific duties (usually of a technical nature) are assigned to other, less significant EU organisations whose establishment is not stipulated by the Treaty but by a legal norm set by the Union (by the Council, or by Council and Parliament). These are the so-called Agencies, which perform specific professional (technical, scientific) duties or function as managing authorities. Such Agencies include, for instance, the European Training Foundation, the European Environmental Agency, the European Monitoring Centre for Drugs and Drug Addiction, etc. The EU Agencies are not discussed in this Chapter but some of them are mentioned in the Chapters on individual policies.

2.2. The Commission

The European Commission (in short, the Commission) is the body responsible for the EU's daily work, including preparing decisions, making proposals and taking initiatives, as well as performing monitoring, representative and, in certain cases, decision-making and executive duties.

The term 'Commission' may either denote the institution's leading political body (the so-called College of Commissioners with 27 Members called Commissioners, which functions similarly to national governments) or the institution as a whole (the Commissioners and the nearly 30,000 officials under their control).

The Commission is generally seen as a supranational body since it does not serve the Member States directly but rather the Union as a whole; as a guardian of Community interests, in the course of fulfilling its responsibilities, it serves and represents the interests of the Union and not the individual Member States.

The Commission is an institution that functions similarly to national governments, as it is headed by a political body whose members divide the tasks of the individual areas of policy amongst themselves and who manage the administrative machinery, which is arranged according to areas of competence. Nevertheless, the Commission does not govern the European Union, as its decision-making and executive powers are limited. Within the EU, the major decisions are taken by the Council and the Parliament, while the executive power is mainly exercised by the Member States.

The Commission's seat is in Brussels, where the majority of staff is also located, although a considerable number of officials work in Luxembourg and at several other locations inside or outside the Union.

2.2.1. The members of the Commission

As stipulated by the Treaty of Nice and the amending Accession Treaty of the ten countries joined on 1 May 2004, from 1 November 2004 each Member State nominates one Commissioner. Accordingly, the Commission began its term of office with 25 members in November 2004, who were then joined by a Bulgarian and a Romanian Commissioner on 1 January 2007.[4]

---

[4] For a transitional period between 1 May 2004 and 22 November 2004, there were 30 Commissioners in office: the 20 from before enlargement and one from each new Member State. The first Commission to follow the 'one country – one Commissioner' principle took office on 22 November 2004.

Prior to enlargement in the EU-15 the practice was that, each of the five 'big' Member States (France, Germany, Italy, Spain and the United Kingdom) nominated two Commissioners while the other Member States nominated one each, adding up to a Commission of 20. Due to the big increase in the number of Member States, the old system was no longer sustainable; thus the Treaty of Nice had to rearrange the system to suit post-enlargement conditions.

By maintaining the '2 per big country, 1 per small country' formula in a Union of 27 the Commission could have grown to a college of 34–35, much more than the number of portfolios available. It was clear that the big Member States would have to give up one of their Commissioners[5] but, with 27 Member States, even that arrangement would mean 27 Commissioners; thus it was uncertain whether the 'one Member State – one Commissioner' solution was acceptable in the long run.[6] There were two alternatives to choose from in Nice: applying the principle of 'one Member State – one Commissioner' or limiting the maximum number of Commissioners (e.g. at 20) and introducing a system of rotation.

Finally, the Treaty of Nice opted for the 'one Member State – one Commissioner' principle for a transitional period, with the proviso that the conditions for converting to a rotational system would have to be elaborated in the future. The Protocol on enlargement annexed to the Treaty of Nice set out a two-phase approach. When the next Commission took office, there would be one Commissioner from each Member State. When the number of Member States reached 27, the Council – acting by unanimity – would have to set the number of Commissioners in a way that there would be fewer Commissioners than Member States. The Council would also have to take a unanimous decision on the arrangements for a fair system of rotation, bearing in mind that all Member States would be treated on an equal footing and that each Commission would have to satisfactorily reflect the different demographic and geographic characteristics of the Member States. Until the number of Member States reached 27, each new Member State would nominate one Commissioner. With the number of Member States reaching 27 on 1 January 2007, the next Commission would have to be formed (probably in autumn 2009) according to the new rules.

---

[5] The big Member States were compensated by increased weighting of their vote in Council. See 2.3.5.

[6] The 'one Member State – one Commissioner' principle is generally rejected by committed federalists who point out that Commissioners are required to act independently of their Member States, in the interests of the Community. With one member for each Member State, the representation of national governments creeps back into the Commission, strengthening the EU's intergovernmental nature rather than the Community model.

It must be noted that, compared to the Treaty of Nice, the Constitutional Treaty would have introduced the system of rotation one term later, from 2014, with two thirds of the Member States nominating Commissioners at a time. This provision was incorporated into the Reform Treaty, which means that if the new Treaty is ratified the principle of one Commissioner per Member State will remain unchanged for one more term until 2014.[7]

The Commission is headed by a President, who provides political and strategic leadership. The President sets the main guidelines of the Commission's work, shapes its working style and its relations with the other institutions. The Treaty of Nice strengthened the role of the Commission President, due to the increased number of Commissioners. It is up to the President to decide on the internal organisation of the Commission. The President allocates portfolios to individual members, and may reshuffle the allocation of those responsibilities during the Commission's term of office. The President may also request the resignation of members of the Commission.

Presidents of the European Commission

January 1958 – July 1967	*Walter Halstein* (Germany)
July 1967 – July 1970	*Jean Rey* (Belgium)
July 1970 – March 1972	*Franco Maria Malfatti* (Italy)
March 1972 – January 1973	*Sicco Mansholt* (Netherlands) (interim)
January 1973 – January 1977	*François-Xavier Ortoli* (France)
January 1977 – January 1981	*Roy Jenkins* (United Kingdom)
January 1981 – January 1985	*Gaston Thorn* (Luxemburg)
January 1985 – January 1995	*Jacques Delors* (France)
January 1995 – July 1999	*Jacques Santer* (Luxembourg)
July 1999 – September 1999	*Manuel Marin* (Spain) (interim)
September 1999 – November 2004	*Romano Prodi* (Italy)
November 2004 –	*José Manuel Durão Barroso* (Portugal)

The members of the Commission (the Commissioners) have portfolios, similarly to the Ministers of national governments. The portfolios vary in their significance and political weight, which is often a source of conflict between the Member States (and their nominees) when appointing a new Commission. Hence, the allocation of the portfolios is always

---

[7] For more details see 2.1.2.

preceded by a lengthy political reconciliation procedure. The competences assigned to the individual portfolios undergo constant modifications and are re-defined whenever a new Commission is appointed, in the light of political and national interests and preferences and the changes in the Members of the Commission. Although the Commissioners are by no means the subordinates or representatives of the Member States, the national governments always set into motion significant forces to win the particular portfolio for their Commissioner which they see as crucial to influence the Commission's work in the most effective manner. To counterbalance this trend, the Treaty of Nice introduced a new system whereby it is the President who decides on the allocation of tasks and responsibilities among the Commissioners. Thus the President of the Commission who took office in November 2004 was free to decide how to allocate portfolios among the members of his Commission.

The Commission also has a varying number of Vice-Presidents. The number of Vice-Presidents to be appointed used to be decided by the Member States, but the Treaty of Nice gave this power to the President. The Prodi Commission of 1999–2004 had two Vice-Presidents, while the Barroso Commission now has five.

The Commissioners are appointed for a renewable period of five years by the common accord of the governments of the Member States, and with the assent of the European Parliament according to the method instituted by the Treaty of Maastricht, which was later amended and reinforced by the Treaty of Amsterdam.[8] The Treaty of Nice enacted further changes to the procedure of appointment of the Commission, not affecting Parliament's role, but replacing unanimity in nominating members with qualified majority voting, to take account of the increased number of Member States.

Under the Treaty of Nice, the Council (in this case meeting at the level of Heads of State or Government) nominates the President of the Commission by a qualified majority vote.[9] This choice has to be approved by the European Parliament. Afterwards, the Commissioners

---

[8] The Commission is appointed for the same term as the European Parliament; however, the Commission's term starts and ends a few months later (previously in January of the given year, but from 2004 in November). The Parliament always holds its constitutive meeting in July after the elections that take place in June every five years. For a few months, the EP works together with the outgoing Commission, devoting most of its time to the nomination, hearing and appointment of the new College of Commissioners.

[9] It has to be noted that the Member States try to nominate the President by consensus, as the personality of the President can have great influence on the work of the whole Commission. The office of the Commission President is a particularly significant position, and therefore finding the right person for the job has always been a lengthy process of consultation, which remains largely unchanged by the introduction of nomination by qualified majority.

are nominated by the Council (in accordance with the proposals of each Member States and in agreement with the President-designate) by qualified majority voting. The entire Commission is then subject to the vote of approval of the Parliament. The European Parliament may not disapprove of individual candidates, only the entire Commission[10]; if it grants approval, the Council appoint the new Commission by a qualified majority.

As far as the track record of Commission members is concerned, in recent years the appointed Commissioners have generally been politicians who have held high office in their home countries. Previously, in the larger Member States, who had the right to nominate two Commissioners each, the government and the opposition usually shared the two seats, while in the smaller Member States, the nominee generally belonged to the leading party of the government in office. Now, with the Nice system of 'one Member State – one Commissioner', the members of the Commission are in practice nominated from the ranks of leading politicians of government parties.

Upon their appointment, members of the Commission pledge to perform their duties independently of their national governments and the Council and to abide by the interests of the Community. Therefore, once appointed, Commissioners can no longer be considered as representatives of their respective governments.

The Commission is appointed for a period of five years, but its mandate can expire in the event of resignation. Apart from such a scenario, the Commission can only be required to resign if the European Parliament passes a motion of censure. The Council has no right to dismiss the Commission; only the European Parliament can do so, with a majority

---

[10] The European Parliament can indeed exert considerable influence on the choice of individual Commissioners, as it can bring the appointment procedure to a halt, even if it dislikes only one or two of the Commissioners-designate, and thereby informally force the Commission President and Member-State governments to put forward new nominées. This was demonstrated by the events of Autumn 2004 when various political groups in the European Parliament objected to some nominees (particularly to the Italian candidate, Rocco Buttiglione), thus Commission President José Manuel Durão Barroso – wary of the consequences of a rejection by the EP – decided not to put the College to the vote. Instead, with the assent of the Member States he reshuffled his Commission, replacing Rocco Buttiglione of Italy with Franco Frattini and Ingrida Udre of Latvia with Andris Piebalgs and assigning László Kovács of Hungary to another portfolio. With these changes, the EP was willing to compromise, hence the Commission obtained the majority required for the EP's assent but only on 18 November 2004. As a result, the new Commissioners officially took office only on 22 November instead of 1 November as foreseen in the Treaty of Accession, with their mandate ending on 31 October 2009.

of two thirds of its members present.[11] Although the Parliament has never dissolved the Commission, there have been a number of precedents for votes of no confidence.[12]

Members of the European Commission (November 2004 –) and their portfolios

José Manuel Durão Barroso (Portugal)	President
Margot Wallström (Sweden)	Vice-President, institutional relations and communication strategy
Günter Verheugen (Germany)	Vice-President, enterprise and industry
Jacques Barrot (France)	Vice-President, transport
Siim Kallas (Estonia)	Vice-President, administrative affairs, audit and anti-fraud
Franco Frattini (Italy)	Vice-President, freedom, security and justice
Joaquín Almunia (Spain)	economic and monetary affairs
Joe Borg (Malta)	fisheries and maritime affairs
Stavros Dimas (Greece)	environment
Benita Ferrero-Waldner (Austria)	external relations and European neighbourhood policy
Ján Figel (Slovakia)	education, training, culture
Mariann Fischer Boel (Denmark)	agriculture and rural development
Dalia Grybauskaite (Lithuania)	financial programming and budget
Danuta Hübner (Poland)	regional policy
László Kovács (Hungary)	taxation and customs union
Neelie Kroes (Netherlands)	competition
Markos Kyprianou (Cyprus)	health
Peter Mandelson (United Kingdom)	trade
Charlie McCreevy (Ireland)	internal market and services
Louis Michel (Belgium)	development and humanitarian aid

---

[11] Even the EP cannot dismiss individual members, only the whole of the Commission with a motion of censure. However, both of the last two Presidents, Prodi and Barroso pledged upon their appointment that if the EP loses confidence in one of their Commissioners, they would seriously consider requesting the resignation of the member in question. Apart from the President, the European Court of Justice can also dismiss members of the Commission if they no longer meet the conditions required for the position or have committed a serious breach of duty.

[12] See 2.4.1.

Andris Piebalgs (Latvia)	energy
Janez Potocnik (Slovenia)	science and research
Viviane Reding (Luxembourg)	information society and media
Olli Rehn (Finland)	enlargement
Vladimir Spidla (Czech Republic)	employment, social affairs and equal opportunities
Meglena Kuneva (Bulgaria)	consumer protection
Leonard Orban (Romania)	multilingualism

2.2.2. The administrative structure of the Commission

The administrative structure of the Commission is composed of the Directorates-General (DGs), Services and Offices, both with responsibilities similar to those of Directorates-General. All of them operate under the respective Commissioner's supervision. DGs used to be designated by numbers. The Commission appointed in September 1999 and headed by Romano Prodi modified the former structure of the institution; the number of administrative units was somewhat decreased, and the DGs' traditional identification with numbers was brought to an end. The Commission's organigram currently includes 40 administrative units.

The administrative units report to the Commissioners, some of whom are responsible for one DG or Service, some for several. The allocation of the Directorates-General and Services to the Commissioners takes place in the framework of the division of the portfolios. The DGs and Services are further divided into Directorates, which in turn are divided into Units.[13]

The Commission has a staff of about 30,000 people.[14] Because of this number, the Commission is often seen as an over-sized bureaucratic system. However, it is worth noting that the individual administrations of many European cities often employ more staff. Considering the 450-million strong population of the Union, this staff level is relatively small, bearing in mind the extensive responsibilities of the Commission.

---

[13] The Directorates-General are often compared to government ministries. Although this comparison may facilitate the understanding of the division of the Commission, it is misleading in several respects. The DGs, as well as the entire Commission, are primarily responsible for preparing decisions and presenting proposals and only to a limited extent for implementing legislation (which is an extremely important task of national line ministries).

[14] According to the Staff Regulations that entered into force on 1 May 2004, permanent officials working at EU institutions are divided into two categories: administrators (AD) and assistants (AST). AD officials perform independent, policy-making and executive tasks while AST officials play a role as support staff with secretarial and other duties. Within the categories, grades run from AD5 to AD16 (the latter indicating Director General level), and from AST1 to AST11.

The Commission's Directorates-General and Services

Secretariat General
Legal Service
Communication DG
Publications Office
Statistical Office (Eurostat)
Interpretation DG
Translation DG
European Anti-Fraud Office
Personnel and Administration DG
Energy and Transport DG
Research DG
Joint Research Centre
Information Society and Media DG
Fisheries and Maritime Affairs DG
Agriculture and Rural Development DG
Regional Policy DG
Employment, Social Affairs
    and Equal Opportunities DG,
Taxation and Customs Union DG
Enterprise and Industry DG
Data Protection Officer
Education and Culture DG

Heath and Consumer Protection DG
Justice Freedom and Security DG
External Relations DG
Trade DG
Development DG
Enlargement DG
Bureau of European Policy Advisers
Internal Market and Services DG
Economic and Financial Affairs DG
Environment DG
Competition DG
Budget DG
Internal Audit Service
Office for Infrastructures and
    Logistics – Brussels
Office for Infrastructures and
    Logistics – Luxembourg
Informatics DG
EuropeAid – Cooperation Office
Humanitarian Aid Office (ECHO)
Office for Administration and Payment
    of Individual Entitlements

The Cabinets of Commissioners, consisting of staff working directly to support their respective Commissioner's work, play a key role in linking the Commissioners and the Commission services. Cabinet members are closely linked to the person in office, as they are appointed by the Commissioners themselves.[15] Some of the cabinet members come from the same country as the Commissioner, often former colleagues, but nowadays they are mostly Commission officials. The Head of Cabinet is in most cases of the same

---

[15] The number of staff working in a cabinet varies between 18 and 20. About 6 to 9 of them are administrators (AD officials), the others are assistants and secretaries (AST).

nationality as the Commissioner, but then the Deputy must come from another country.[16] The task of a cabinet is to liaise with Commission services, prepare decisions, ensure coordination among Commissioners (which is mainly done in the framework of weekly meetings of heads of cabinet, where the next meeting of the College of Commissioners is prepared), support and organise public appearances by the relevant Commissioner, as well as maintain links with the Commissioner's home country. Overall, cabinets have considerable informal influence on the activities of Commissioners.

2.2.3. The competence of the Commission

The founding Treaties of the Communities entrust the Commission with a wide range of responsibilities that involve making proposals (preparing decisions and initiating legislation), as well as executive, decision-making, control and representative functions.

The Commission plays a key role in the decision-making process within the EU, as it initiates legislation in the areas falling within the Community's competence. Because of its right of initiative and presentation of legislative proposals, it has the exclusive right to submit legislative proposals to the decision-making and legislative institutions, namely the Council and the Parliament. In its proposals and initiatives, the Commission aims at aligning the provisions of Community legislation with the Treaties.

In certain areas, the Commission also has limited secondary decision-making and legislative powers. In the areas (e.g. competition, agriculture, trade) assigned to it by the Treaties[17] or by the decisions of the legislators (the Council or the Council and the Parliament), it has the right to set certain legal norms.

---

[16] Commissioners used to pick and choose compatriots for almost all positions in their cabinets, but according to the 1999 reform of the then Commission President Romano Prodi, cabinets must be multinational, while heads of cabinets and their deputies must be of different nationalities. This reform was necessary because cabinets often worked as an extended arm of the national administration, which ran in the face of the requirement that the Commission should act in the defence of Community interests.

[17] The term 'the Treaties' always refers to the Founding Treaties in force at the time. Since the original Founding Treaties have been amended and overwritten on several occasions (for example by the Maastricht Treaty, the Amsterdam Treaty and the Nice Treaty), the term 'Treaty' in the singular always implies the document in force applying to the Community in question (EC or Euratom) or to the Union at a given time. See also 5.2.1.1.

In specific cases, the Commission is also responsible for implementing the decisions and legislation adopted by the EU's legislative bodies. It must be stressed, however, that implementation is first and foremost the responsibility of the Member States. Nevertheless, the Commission, as the institution responsible for the implementation of Community objectives, also has certain executive duties and, consequently, a monitoring function in several areas (e.g. competition).

With regard to the Community budget, the Commission has the right of initiative, as it is responsible for the preparation of the draft budget and for its presentation to the Council and to the Parliament. As the executive body of the Union, it manages the adopted budget, for example running and monitoring Community programmes and Community funds.

As the guardian of the Treaties, it ensures that the provisions of the Treaties and acts adopted by the Community institutions are applied properly, both in the public and private spheres. It may institute legal proceedings against those Member States and enterprises that fail to comply with the Treaties or with their obligations under Community legislation. First, it calls upon the State or company in question to redress the situation and, as a last resort, brings them before the European Court of Justice.

The Commission's scope of duties involves filing regular reports on the economic, social and legal situation of the Union as well as submitting annual reports on its own activities.

The Commission represents the Union on the international stage and negotiates international, mainly trade agreements falling within the Community's competence (e.g. association or cooperation agreements). It also represents the European Communities at the meetings of certain international economic organisations, such as the OECD and the WTO. The Commission negotiates on the Union's behalf in the multilateral trade rounds with the WTO (the former GATT).

The Commission is accountable to the Parliament, which may even dissolve the college of Commissioners with a two-thirds majority vote. The Commission is obliged to explain and justify its actions to the Parliament and, when requested, must provide written or oral answers to questions by the MEPs.

2.3. The Council

2.3.1. The Council of the European Union

The Council of the European Union (in short, the Council) is the Union's principal, but not exclusive, intergovernmental decision-making and legislative body. The Council functions as the institution representing the interests of the Member States, where they can put forward their points of view. The Council's decisions are adopted as the common result of the Member States' national interests.

The Council is composed of one representative at ministerial level from each Member State, usually the Minister responsible for the relevant subject; but it is for the Member States to decide who to delegate to the Council meetings. Accordingly, the Council meets in the configuration of the agenda and the policy area under discussion at a given meeting. The Council is often referred to as the Council of Ministers.

The name of the Council of Ministers varies, depending on which ministers are to meet. The bodies of the competent ministers are the so-called sectoral Councils. For example, Financial Ministers (responsible for economic and financial affairs) meet as the Economic and Financial Affairs Council (ECOFIN), while the Ministers of Agriculture meet as the Agriculture Council. The General Affairs and External Relations Council (originally known as the General Affairs Council and frequently referred to as the Council of Foreign Ministers) falls into a separate category: it deals with politically more significant, general, horizontal or sensitive issues and often also functions as an appeal forum for the sectoral Councils.

The last modification to the structure of the Council of Ministers was introduced by the Seville European Council[18] of 21–22 June 2002, which changed the name of the General Affairs Council to General Affairs and External Relations Council and merged various configurations to reduce the number of sectoral Councils to nine.

In order to best organise proceedings of the General Affairs and External Relations Council with regard to the two main areas of activity covered by this configuration, it has to hold separate meetings dealing respectively with:

a) preparation for and follow-up to the European Council, institutional and administrative questions and horizontal dossiers which affect several of the Union's policies;

b) the whole of the Union's external actions, namely Common Foreign and Security Policy (CFSP), European Security and Defence Policy (ESDP), foreign trade, development cooperation and humanitarian aid.

The Council configurations were reduced by the Seville decisions to the following 9:

- General Affairs and External Relations;
- Economic and Financial Affairs (including the budget);
- Justice and Home Affairs;

---

[18] See 2.3.3.

- Employment, Social Policy, Health and Consumer Affairs;
- Competitiveness (internal market, industry and research, including tourism);
- Transport, Telecommunications and Energy;
- Agriculture and Fisheries;
- Environment;
- Education, Youth and Culture (including audiovisual affairs).

It was agreed in Seville that several ministers would be able to participate as full members of the same Council configuration, with the agenda and the organisation of proceedings being adjusted accordingly. In the case of the General Affairs and External Relations Council, each government would be represented at the different meetings by the Minister or State Secretary of his choice. The significance of this is that certain Member States delegate their Minister (or State Secretary) for European affairs to replace or accompany their Ministers for Foreign Affairs at meetings of general affairs, while external relations meetings fall exclusively within the competence of the Ministers for Foreign Affairs.

The General Affairs and External Relations Council, Agriculture and Fisheries Council, the Economic and Monetary Affairs Council usually meet once a month, the Justice and Home Affairs Council almost on a monthly basis, while the other Councils meet less frequently, around two to six times a year.

The Council is based in Brussels, but meets at fixed intervals (in April, June and October) in Luxembourg. In addition, so-called informal meetings are held in the country that holds the office of the Presidency[19].

The smooth running of the Council and the Presidency is assisted by the General Secretariat with approximately 3,500 officials, whose principal responsibility is to prepare the meetings of the Council and the related bodies. It is headed by the Secretary General, an independent official mainly responsible for foreign and security policy affairs who acts as the High Representative for CFSP (Common Foreign and Security Policy).[20] The Deputy Secretary General manages the General Secretariat's day-to-day work, i.e. the preparation of Council meetings.

2.3.2. COREPER and the Council's working groups

Although the Ministers meet more and more frequently, their meetings cannot ensure continuity. The 1–2 day long meetings of the sectoral Councils usually scheduled every 1 to 3 months cannot possibly ensure the adequate preparation and comprehensive

---

[19] See 2.3.4.
[20] For more on the role of the Secretary General, see 23.3. and 23.4.

discussion of the decisions taken. The time available is only enough to deal with the issues concerned at a political level. Community decision-making, which in essence involves legislation, the elaboration and the adoption of Community laws in different areas, calls for much more frequent discussions and – in view of the complexity of issues discussed – for more in-depth preparation. This is why, early on, a body was established to assist and prepare the work of the Council, the so-called COREPER[21]. This is the Committee of Permanent Representatives, which consists of the ambassadors, i.e. the heads of the permanent representations of the Member States in Brussels, or their deputies. COREPER's principal responsibility is to try to reconcile and harmonise the positions of the Member States on the questions discussed at this expert, diplomatic level and to prepare the specific recommendations to be discussed by the Ministers at political level. Furthermore, COREPER is responsible for maintaining communication between the governments of the Member States and the institutions of the Union (principally the European Commission) and for mediation and coordination between Community and national administrations. The Committee meets once a week at two separate levels. COREPER II is the forum of the Permanent Representatives, while COREPER I consists of their Deputies. COREPER II deals with issues of a political nature, while COREPER I is responsible for issues of a more technical nature, although it should be noted that, at this level, every issue has political dimensions. In practice, it is the permanent representatives who decide which issues they deal with and which ones they leave to their deputies. However, the general practice is that COREPER II is in charge of preparing the General Affairs and External Relations Councils, Economic and Monetary Affairs Councils, as well as Justice and Home Affairs Councils, while COREPER I is given responsibility for all other Council bodies.

It may be interesting to point out that, owing to its special character, the Council of Agricultural Ministers is assisted by the so-called Special Committee on Agriculture. The Article 133 Committee, the special committee which prepares trade policy decisions, established by Article 133 of the EC Treaty, plays an equally special role. In the framework of the second pillar, it is the Political and Security Committee, while, in the third pillar, it is the Coordinating Committee (generally known as the Article 36 Committee after the related article of the EU Treaty, which used to be referred to as the K4 Committee), which execute preparatory, coordinating duties similarly to COREPER. It is worth pointing out that, even though these bodies often do the work of COREPER, the final word before

---

[21] The acronym comes from the French abbreviation of the Committee of Permanent Representatives (COmité des REprésentants PERmanents).

Council meetings always belongs to COREPER, where the draft agenda and proposals for decisions for the ministers are formally adopted (mostly without reopening the debate on issues already dealt with in the Political and Security Committee, for example).[22]

Due to the increased workload and frequency of meetings of COREPER, there was a need to establish bodies preparing the work of COREPER. The so-called *Antici Group* (named after its first chairman and set up in the seventies) prepares Coreper II proceedings and also conducts important preparatory work for European Council meetings. The so-called *Mertens Group* (also named after its first chairman and set up in the nineties) fulfils the same role but for COREPER I. Both groups are made up of diplomats working at the Permanent Representations.[23]

The work carried out by COREPER and related bodies has become so extensive and technical that the Member States' Permanent Representations in Brussels have had to be significantly enlarged. Generally, in addition to the senior diplomats, experts of the competent Ministries of the Member States are also delegated to the Permanent Representations in Brussels. In this way, each significant Community area has its own expert who maintains non-stop relations with both the national administrative bodies and the Community institutions, first and foremost with the Commission.[24]

Since certain impasses are extremely difficult to overcome, the work of the Council and COREPER is assisted by another 250 permanent and *ad hoc* Council working groups, arranged according to specific subjects. The number and duties of these working groups frequently vary, depending on the topical issues on the agenda. The members of these working groups are officials from the Member States' government offices (mostly Ministries) responsible for a particular issue, but the meetings are usually also attended by competent officials of the Permanent Representations. In the course of constant conciliation and occasional meetings, members of working groups prepare the decision plans at a technical level to be discussed later by the Council and COREPER. Hence, the

---

[22] Occasionally there may be rivalry between these bodies (particularly between the PSC and COREPER II), but the primacy of COREPER over the other – relatively recently created – bodies remains undoubted.

[23] Antici and Mertens posts are prestigious and highly regarded in national diplomatic services, and thus usually awarded to diplomatic high flyers. Being responsible for preparing European Council meetings, at EU summits members of the Antici group are located in a room adjacent to the meeting room of the Heads of State or Government. 'Anticis', who are orally briefed by Council officials about the proceedings, keep other members of their national delegation informed of how the discussions are progressing.

[24] A medium-sized Permanent Representation employs about 100 staff, about half of whom enjoy diplomatic status.

corresponding officials of the Ministries of the Member States remain in non-stop contact with each other. The working groups are extremely active. This is shown by the total of some 2,500 working group meetings held every year.

The recommendations discussed in the working groups are first forwarded to COREPER and then to the Council. If agreement is reached on an issue at a lower level, the Council of Ministers generally makes its decision without further deliberation. The work of COREPER and the working groups of the Council permits the Council of Ministers to deal with the purely political aspects of the issues discussed. Technical discussions and coordination are mostly settled at the lower levels. This division of labour guarantees the smooth decision-making of the Council.

2.3.3. The European Council

Due to the peculiarities of the EU's decision-making and institutional setup, the European Council – the body composed of the Heads of State or Government of the Member States and the President of the European Commission – must be discussed together with the Council. Although not part of the Council from an institutional point of view, it is an integral element of the structure of the Council, since it is the forum of the Heads of State or Government of the Member States. The European Council functions as the top organisation of the Union.

The European Council did not feature in the Community's first Treaties. It evolved from the practice of organising meetings of the Heads of State or Government of the Member States, which became regular occurrences following the Paris Summit of December 1974. This arrangement of the European Council was formalised by the Maastricht Treaty, which stipulated that it should meet at least twice a year, but did not define it as an institution in its own right.

Apart from the Heads of State or Government, the European Council's meetings are also attended by the President of the Commission. The Member States' Ministers of Foreign Affairs and a Member of the Commission assist the European Council's work. Whether it is the Head of State or Government that represents a Member State depends on the constitutional system of the particular country.[25]

The European Council settles vital, strategic issues and defines the general political guidelines for the development of the EU. However, it does not enact any laws (apart from defining the principles, general guidelines and common strategies in the field of the common foreign and security policy)[26]; this is the exclusive responsibility of the Council

---

[25] Generally, the meetings are attended by the Prime Ministers of the Member States, but e.g. France due to its presidential system is represented officially by the President of the Republic, who is accompanied by the Prime Minister.

[26] See 5.2.2.2.

(or the common task of the Council and Parliament). Accordingly, opinions vary as to whether the European Council is part of the Council's hierarchy, whether it represents a separate, higher level or is entirely independent of the Council. The latter argument is supported by the fact that the meetings of the European Council are not conducted according to the Council's decision-making, procedural order, but items on the agenda of the European Council are prepared in Council. The question is further complicated by the provision of the Maastricht Treaty, which stipulates that when making certain decisions, the Council shall be convened at the level of Heads of State or Government[27]; nevertheless, in such instances, the Heads of State or Government officially meet not as the European Council but as the Council.[28]

During the past decades, the significance and the role of the European Council have gradually increased as it became the primary scene for the Member States to forge political compromises.[29] Often, the disputes between the Member States can only be arbitrated by the Heads of State or Government, who enjoy the necessary political overview and authority. Grasping the complexity of issues, they have the ability to arrive at compromises through so-called *package deals*.[30] The ensuing decisions are then adopted as legal acts by the sectoral Councils, observing the European Council's guidelines, with or without preparation by the European Commission (depending on whether the Council requests this). Hence the task of final shaping does not lie with the European Council.

The European Council holds four regular meetings every year (usually in March, June, October or November and December) but – if necessary – more extraordinary, or so-called informal meetings are held. Previously, European Council meetings used to be held in the

---

[27] Such a provision is included in Article 112 of the EC Treaty on the economic and monetary union or Article 7 of the EU Treaty (introduced by the Treaty of Amsterdam) on the violation of fundamental rights stated and sanctioned by the Member States.

[28] The status of the European Council was supposed to be clarified by the Constitutional Treaty by making it a full-blown institution, an objective taken on by the Reform Treaty as well. (See Annex, Point 2.2.)

[29] This is essentially the reason why this formerly non-existent forum of the Heads of State or Government was established in the first place: to achieve compromises in situations of major importance, where agreement is often very difficult.

[30] Although these deals are literally called 'package deals', they could just as easily be termed 'package diplomacy', as they refer to compromises reached after inter-linking several unrelated issues and are often the lowest common denominator of the Member States. This, in practical terms, means that a Member State relinquishes its position on a certain question in order to win it in another dispute. This can only be conducted at the level of the Heads of State or Government.

country holding the Presidency, but according to the Declaration annexed to the Treaty of Nice from 2002 on, each Presidency had to hold at least one European Council meeting in Brussels and, once the number of Member States reached 18, all European Council meetings were to be held in Brussels. With the accession of 10 new Member States in May 2004, bringing the number of Member States well above 18, the official site of European Council meetings is now Brussels, but this rule does not apply to informal (unofficial) summit meetings, which the Presidency-in-office can still hold in its home state.

Since it is more often than not the meetings of the European Council (the summits) where the decisions vital to the future of the EU are adopted, it is no coincidence that these meetings attract the attention of the media and the public.

2.3.4. The Presidency of the Council

The Presidency of the Council plays a vital part in the organisation of the work of the institution. It rotates between the Member States every six months. The presiding Member State convenes the Council, presides not only over the Council of Ministers but also over other bodies related to the Council (European Council, COREPER, working groups), oversees the voting and signs the adopted acts. Since the State holding the Presidency plays a decisive role in the arrangement of the agenda and in the preparation of voting, it has significant influence over the issues discussed. The State holding the Presidency of the Council also plays a key role in the international representation of the Union as well as in presenting the Union's position in the field of foreign policy. The Presidency is a highly prestigious office for the Member States; therefore, the national governments make major preparations and serious efforts to fulfil their presidential duties successfully. The presidential periods are synchronised with the regular 'end-of-Presidency' meetings of the European Council (June and December), which are held in the final month of the six-month Presidency, in effect wrapping up the Presidency and its work.

When drafting the Constitutional Treaty, the Member States introduced changes to the system of the rotating Presidency. Some of these changes were linked to the ratification of the Constitutional Treaty and thus remain ineffective[31], but others – such as the order in which the Member States would hold the Presidency – remain valid anyway.

---

[31] The Constitutional Treaty would have given the European Council a permanent president and would have created a separate Foreign Affairs Council. The majority of the relevant provisions in the Constitutional Treaty are adopted in the Reform Treaty. For more, see Annex, Point 2.3.2.

According to the decision taken in December 2004, from 2007 onwards, the Member States assume the responsibilities of the Presidency in groups of three for periods of 18 months. Within every such group of three, each Member States still holds the Presidency for six months according to a system of rotation. The point of having 18-month cycles is to enable the countries to coordinate their programmes, which ensures predictability and continuity. During the six months all duties related to the Presidency are carried out by the one Member State holding the Presidency-in-office, while the other two members in the group help the country in question run the Presidency according to the common programme. The order adopted for the period from 2007 to 2020 is the following:

2007/I.	Germany	2007/II.	Portugal	2008/I.	Slovenia
2008/II.	France	2009/I.	Czech Republic	2009/II.	Sweden
2010/I.	Spain	2010/II.	Belgium	2011/I.	Hungary
2011/II.	Poland	2012/I.	Denmark	2012/II.	Cyprus
2013/I.	Ireland	2013/II.	Lithuania	2014/I.	Greece
2014/II.	Italy	2015/I.	Latvia	2015/II.	Luxembourg
2016/I.	Netherlands	2016/II.	Slovakia	2017/I.	Malta
2017/II.	United Kingdom	2018/I.	Estonia	2018/II.	Bulgaria
2019/I.	Austria	2019/II.	Romania	2020/I.	Finland

2.3.5. Voting system in the Council

The Council may adopt its decisions by three different types of voting: by a *simple majority*, by a *qualified majority* or *unanimously* (consensus). The Treaties in effect identify which voting system is to be applied in each case. The Member States may vote by a simple majority in the Council only in relation to procedural issues or when no other system is stipulated by the Treaties. For substantive matters, such as legislative acts, a qualified majority or unanimity is required. In the past, the Council decided almost exclusively on a unanimous basis (consensus); however, as a result of the amendments of the Treaties, in the vast majority of the cases, the Member States now decide by a qualified majority vote (QMV). However, even today, many of the most significant or sensitive decisions[32] must be adopted unanimously. In practice nevertheless, the voting procedure often does not take place, as the President in office generally aims at reaching a consensus during the course of the meetings (even when the issue discussed could be carried by a qualified majority

---

[32] These sensitive decisions usually concern areas linked to national sovereignty (for exampe foreign and security policy, fiscal harmonisation, culture), in which the Member States have been reluctant to relinquish their right of veto.

vote). If a consensus is reached, the President asserts the lack of objections and the issue is considered decided.[33]

In the case of qualified majority voting, the votes of the Member States carry different weight according to their population. The weighting of the votes however is not in direct proportion to the population – the actual weightings are the result of political deals. The current system clearly favours Member States with a smaller population, but does not take into account economic, political or territorial differences at all.

By introducing the qualified majority system, the founding Member States of the Communities wanted to emphasise the supranational character of the Council. This concept, however, was damaged right at the start when De Gaulle in 1966 pushed through the so-called 'Luxembourg compromise'. Issues involving a 'vital national interest' of a Member State henceforth required unanimous decisions.[34] The adoption of the Luxembourg compromise emphasised the intergovernmental character of the Council. However, from the second half of the 1980s, following the adoption of the Single European Act, the compromise was suspended, as the Act stated explicitly when decisions could be adopted by a qualified majority and when they required unanimity.

The application of qualified majority voting was hampered again by the so-called 'Ioannina compromise', which was introduced under British pressure during the 1995 enlargement round. At the time, the Member States shared a total of 87 votes. When a Commission proposal was involved, a qualified majority was obtained when at least 62 votes supported the decision. In other cases, these 62 votes

---

[33] It should be pointed out that, due to enlargements, this compromise-seeking practice is increasingly difficult to maintain. The exact number of votes cast has to be counted more and more frequently, with regular 'test votes' at lower levels of Council as well. It is not without precedent for a working group chair to ask the national delegates how their minister would vote on a particular issue, thereby testing the possibility of reaching decisions on the matter. If the indicated voting preferences yield an obvious qualified majority, the chair does not aim to reach a consensus at all costs, as that would be extremely difficult with 27 Member States.

[34] It must be noted, however, that the Luxembourg compromise has not institutionalised any kind of national right of veto, since the compromise itself is merely a remark in the Protocols of the Council meeting of 18 January 1966, which says that the Member States undertake to continue negotiations until reaching a consensus when a vital national interest is involved. The application of the compromise is not included in any legal norm, the Treaty or any other source of Community law.

had to be cast by at least 10 Member States. While 26 votes were required to oppose the adoption of a decision, the casting of between 23 and 25 votes against a decision necessitated further negotiations (a 'blocking minority'). This meant that, although the qualified majority theoretically required 62 votes, a proposal could only be adopted by a qualified majority with 65 votes. The 23 votes of the blocking minority reflected the situation before the 1995 enlargement round. This was precisely the British intention, namely that, even with the accession of the 3 new Member States, the same number of countries would be needed to block a decision. The decision could not be adopted until the Council managed to find a solution that could be agreed to with 65 votes. With the new weightings of the votes introduced by the Treaty of Nice prior to the enlargement of May 2004, the Ioannina compromise became pointless.

The Treaty of Nice brought changes in qualified majority voting as, by the end of the 90s, it had become clear that a large-scale enlargement would be impractical if the old weighting of the votes were maintained and applied to the future Member States.
The Treaty of Nice, which was signed on 26 February 2001 and entered into force on 1 February 2003, set the institutional framework of a Union of 27 and defined a new voting system.
One of the principal aims of the Treaty of Nice was to make the operation of the Council more effective, by extending qualified majority voting to new areas, thus narrowing the range of issues settled by unanimity, and by adjusting the number of votes required for a qualified majority to the needs of an enlarged Union.
The restriction of unanimous voting in the enlarged Union became necessary because, even with 15 Member States, it was difficult to reach full consensus, while with 27 Member States it promised to be even more problematic. Therefore, the Treaty of Nice, similarly to the previous ones, extended qualified majority voting to about 30 further areas. Nonetheless, several key issues of integration (e.g. taxation, important fields of social policy, and the bulk of justice and home affairs) continued to require unanimity.[35]

---

[35] For a detailed list of areas under unanimity following the Treaty of Nice, see Appendix I.

[36] This ratio would have been reached if, for example, the most populous Member State, Germany, voted against a decision together with another big country, for example, France, and the largest of the middle-sized States, the Netherlands (the total population of these three States represented about 42% of the entire population of the Union).

The modification of the weighting of qualified majority votes was essential, as sustaining the former system after enlargement could have resulted in certain imbalances. The former weighting of votes strongly favoured Member States with smaller populations. As a result, it could well happen that a qualified majority of 71.26% of the votes (62/87) in effect only represented a mere 58% of the population of the Member States.[36] With the successive accession of countries with small populations (and the majority of applicant countries fell into this category), that system could have led to a decision adopted by a qualified majority but representing less than half of the Union's population – quite a controversial situation in a democracy. Therefore, in the interest of Member States with larger populations, the weighting of votes had to be modified prior to the accession of the applicant countries; and the Treaty of Nice accomplished just that.[37]

An interesting feature of the Treaty of Nice was that the new system of qualified majority voting was not going to be introduced upon the Treaty's entry into force on 1 February 2003, but only on 1 January 2005. Therefore, it had to be stipulated in the Accession Treaty of the ten acceding countries what the allocation of votes would be between 1 May 2004 and 1 January 2005. In the end, it was decided that the new members would get the same number of votes as old members with a similar population, which increased the total number of votes from 87 to 124, and the qualified majority from 62 to 88. The Treaty of Accession finally stipulated that the Nice system of voting would be introduced on 1 November 2004, together with the new Nice rules on the Commission.[38] The transitional period, therefore, only lasted six moths from May to November.

The new system of qualified majority voting introduced by the Treaty of Nice established a kind of triple majority based on the following:

a) The central element of the new system was the re-weighting of votes. In order to underline the differences in the size of population of the Member States, the former weights between 2 and 10 are extended into a wider band between 3 and 29, but maintaining the favoured position of smaller countries. Accordingly, the former system – in which out of the total of 87 votes, 62 were required for the adoption of a decision – was also modified. In the Union of 27 Member States, out of the total of 345 votes,

---

[37] The bigger Member States strongly supported this solution in order to be compensated for the introduction of the 'one Member State – one Commissioner' system, which meant giving up one of their two Commissioners. See also 2.2.1.

[38] The changes affecting the Commission were only put into effect on 22 November. (See 2.2.1.)

255 are required for a qualified majority, thus the threshold of a blocking minority is set at 91 votes. (During a transitional period from 1 May 2004 until the accession of Bulgaria and Romania on 1 January 2007, the number of votes required for a qualified majority in the Union of 25 was set at 232 out of the total of 321.)

b) When an issue concerns Commission proposals or initiatives, the qualified majority must also represent over half of the Member States. (When the voting does not relate to a Commission initiative, two thirds of the Member States must support the decision to be adopted.) In other words, the adoption of a decision proposed by the Commission in the present Union of 27 requires that at least 14 countries vote in favour.

c) The Treaty of Nice also introduced a sort of 'population filter', which functions as a security monitoring mechanism – a blocking option. This entails the possibility for a Member of the Council to request verification that the qualified majority (i.e. the countries in favour of the decision) represents at least 62% of the total population of the Union. If this condition is not met, the decision will be considered as not adopted.[39]

2.4. The European Parliament

The European Parliament (EP) is a representative body elected directly by the citizens of the Union. Its essential function is to express the will of the Union's citizens in the Community decision-making process hand-in-hand with the Council, representing the interests of the Member States, and the Commission, ensuring Community interests. The Members of the European Parliament (MEPs), working in European political groups, perform their duties on behalf of the Union's citizens and try to represent their interests. Over the years, the Member States have gradually extended the powers of the Parliament, which was originally a consultative body. Today, in respect of the majority of the Community's legislative process, the Parliament shares with the Council the power to take decisions and to adopt European legislation and therefore acts increasingly as the co-decision-making, co-legislative body, alongside the Council. It also shares budgetary authority with the Council. Furthermore, the European Parliament approves the composition of the European Commission and exercises supervision over its activities.

---

[39] This population threshold was introduced on the insistence of Germany, which had the same number of votes as France, the UK and Italy, even though its population exceeded that of the other three by about 20 million. However, due to this third population condition, Germany may be able to use its relative advantage in population to block certain decisions.

Table 2.1. The allocation of votes among Member States
in qualified majority voting in a Union of 15, 25 and 27

Member State	Population (1,000)	Votes in a Union of 15 until 1 May 2004	Votes in a Union of 25 from 1 May to 1 November 2004	Votes in a Union of 25 from 1 November 2004 to 1 January 2007	Votes in a Union of 27 from 1 January 2007
Germany	82 438	10	10	29	29
France	62 999	10	10	29	29
United Kingdom	60 393	10	10	29	29
Italy	58 752	10	10	29	29
Spain	43 758	8	8	27	27
Poland	38 157	–	8	27	27
Romania	21 610	–	–	–	14
Netherlands	16 334	5	5	13	13
Greece	11 125	5	5	12	12
Portugal	10 570	5	5	12	12
Belgium	10 511	5	5	12	12
Czech Republic	10 251	–	5	12	12
Hungary	10 077	–	5	12	12
Sweden	9 047	4	4	10	10
Austria	8 265	4	4	10	10
Bulgaria	7 718	–	–	–	10
Denmark	5 427	3	3	7	7
Slovakia	5 389	–	3	7	7
Finland	5 255	3	3	7	7
Ireland	4 209	3	3	7	7
Lithuania	3 403	–	3	7	7
Latvia	2 295	–	3	4	4
Slovenia	2 003	–	3	4	4
Estonia	1 345	–	3	4	4
Cyprus	766	–	2	4	4
Luxembourg	459	2	2	4	4
Malta	404	–	2	3	3
Total	492 965	87	124	321	345
Qualified majority		62	88	232	255
Blocking minority		26	37	90	91

Source: Eurostat – population data on 1 January 2006

2.4.1. The development of the European Parliament's institutional role

The Assembly of the ECSC, whose Members were delegated from amongst the members of the Member States' national parliaments, was established immediately after the Treaty on the European Coal and Steel Community came into effect in 1952. After the Treaty of Rome was signed in 1957, the Assembly also became the parliamentary institution of the European Economic Community and the Euratom. Initially, the Assembly – which in 1962 came to be known as the European Parliament[40] – functioned as a mere debating forum of the Communities. Although the Treaty of Rome assigned advisory and monitoring rights to the Parliament, it did not invest it with legislative powers. Under the Treaty, the Council was obliged to consult the Parliament in certain cases; however, it was under no obligation to follow the advice given. The Parliament was first granted considerable powers in 1970 and in 1975 with the two Budgetary Treaties, when it came to share budgetary authority with the Council. Since then, the Parliament's budgetary powers have been reinforced and the budget may not be implemented without the approval of the Parliament.[41]

The Parliament started gaining true momentum when the first direct elections were held in 1979. The European Parliament became the first international parliamentary assembly in the world to be elected by direct universal suffrage. The primary significance of the direct elections was that, once they were introduced, the Parliament could be considered as the body guaranteeing democratic legitimacy for the Community and, as such, it gained the right to demand – on the basis of its mandate from the citizens – a wider range of competences in Community legislation and decision-making.

Even after 1979, the Parliament only enjoyed consultation and limited monitoring functions and its transformation into a true legislative body did not begin until the Single European Act came into effect in 1987. It was at this moment that the Parliament took the course which was later reinforced by the Treaty of Maastricht in 1992, the Treaty of Amsterdam in 1997 and pursued by the Treaty of Nice (and is also one of the key ambitions of the Reform Treaty), namely that of expanding its role as the co-legislative and co-decision-making institution of the Union, alongside the Council. Although even today, the European

---

[40] The German and Dutch language versions of the original Treaty already used the name *European Parliament*, thus in 1962 the Parliament decided to adopt the same name in Italian and French as well. The change in name was officially recognised at Treaty level in 1986 by the Single European Act.

[41] The two treaties amending the budgetary procedure and adopted in 1970 and 1975 are called the 'Budgetary Treaties'.

Parliament is not a decision-making institution equal in rank to the Council, it must be emphasised that, since the Single European Act came into force, the number of areas where no decision may be adopted without the approval of the Parliament has been constantly growing. Even where the Treaty does not require Parliament's opinion to be taken into account, the Parliament's power to influence the decision-making process and its presence is progressively more pervasive and effective. Nevertheless, the Parliament has no legislative power of its own (and this will remain unchanged even when the Reform Treaty enters into force): it assumes the role of the co-legislator of the Council (i.e. of the Member States). In many cases however (as regards the majority of decisions now), this role is a key one.

Besides the boost in its legislative powers and the gaining of the right of final say on the adoption of the Community budget, the Parliament also acquired significant authority over the nomination and monitoring of the Commission under the Treaty of Maastricht and the Treaty of Amsterdam. The Treaty of Amsterdam made the nomination of the Commission's President, and subsequently of the entire body, subject to Parliament's approval. The Parliament also exercises supervision over the greater part of the Commission's activities. It even has the right to censure the Commission with a two-thirds majority of the votes cast (with the majority of MEPs present), which in practice means that the Commission must resign.[42] The Commission is also obliged to report on its activities to the Parliament.

International agreements concluded between the Communities and other countries are also subject to the Parliament's assent. Thus, the various trade agreements and the accession treaties concerning enlargements of the Union must be approved by the Parliament.

---

[42] In fact, Parliament has never dissolved a Commission, but there have been twelve motions of censure. On two occasions, the motions were withdrawn, while in the remaining cases, the vote of no confidence went in favour of the Commission. The closest Parliament ever came to dissolving a Commission was in January 1999, when almost half of the MEPs supported the motion calling for the resignation of the Jacques Santer Commission (552 of the 626 voted, 232 votes were cast in favour and 293 against, with 27 abstentions). The motion of censure failed, but the close result of the vote indicated a loss of confidence, which eventually led to the resignation of the Commission a few weeks later, after the Commission failed to fully clear itself of allegations of irregularities. By bringing down the Santer Commission, the European Parliament strengthened its weight and its power of scrutiny.

One of the important tasks of the Parliament is to take political initiatives demanding the expansion and modification of existing Community programmes and the launch of new ones. Parliament may also request the Commission to submit legislative and decision-making proposals.[43]

Considering all aspects of the development of the Parliament as an EU institution, it can be stated that, as a result of the introduction of the direct elections and the extension of its powers initiated by the Single European Act, the EP is becoming more and more akin to a 'true' national parliament. When established, the European Parliament did not truly possess any of the fundamental parliamentary powers, such as the right of legislation, nomination, control and adoption of the budget. It has now managed to acquire all these powers, even if it can only exercise them together with the Council.

2.4.2. The election and political composition of the European Parliament

Today, the Members of the European Parliament (MEPs) – just as their colleagues sitting in national parliaments – represent the citizens of the Union directly. Another trait that the MEPs share with national assemblies is that they also form political groups; they perform their duties according to the stance taken by their relevant affiliation. The European Parliament however was not always structured in this manner. The present configuration of the institution was established in 1976, when the Heads of State or Government of the European Communities – finally complying with the Parliament's request of 15 years – gave their assent for the EP to be elected directly by the Union's citizens. In this manner, they also approved the European Parliament's ambition of becoming a true parliamentary body ensuring the democratic legitimacy of European integration. The first historic European elections were held between 7 and 10 June 1979. Since then, the Members of the European Parliament have been elected directly by the citizens of the Member States for a period of five years.

The European elections are similar to the elections of national parliaments, in that it is usual for the same political forces to be pitted against each other. The main difference, however, manifests itself in the way in which, in the European Parliament, the elected members of the national parties group into multinational political groups according to their

---

[43] The right of submitting the actual text of a legislative proposal rests exclusively with the Commission.

political affiliations. These European parties, similarly to the parties represented in national parliaments, perform their work on the strength of their common concerted interests. Today, it is characteristically much more the political affiliation of the MEPs than their nationality that shapes their opinion regarding the issues discussed and determines which way they vote. At the same time, the importance of nationality is under-pinned by the MEPs' right to deliver their speeches in any of the EU's 23 official languages.[44]

Despite the transnational nature of the political groups, the conditions under which the European elections are held in the various Member States still differ in many ways. Although there have been attempts to form a unified European electoral system, only common principles have been adopted that provide a framework for European elections. On the basis of these principles, it is up to the Member States to determine which system they draw on to elect their European representatives. The main common principle is that each State has to adhere to the principle of proportional representation when electing its Members to the European Parliament, applying either the party list system or the single transferable vote.

In 20 of the Member States (Austria, Bulgaria, Cyprus, the Czech Republic, Denmark, Estonia, Finland, Greece, Hungary, Latvia, Lithuania, Luxembourg, Malta, the Netherlands, Portugal, Romania, Slovakia, Slovenia, Spain and Sweden), the whole country forms a single constituency, and citizens vote for a national list. In 6 Member States (Belgium, France, Ireland, Italy, Poland and the United Kingdom), territorial constituencies are used and the people vote for regional lists (except for Ireland, which uses the single transferable vote[45]). Germany is a unique case, because its election system allows political parties to set up lists at the national or at the Länder level, but the seats are allocated nationally.

At the European elections, any Union citizen of voting age may elect a representative and be elected one in the country of his residence.

The number of mandates allocated to each Member State depends on the number of inhabitants, yet the system favours the smaller Member States (although to a lesser degree than the system applied in the Council) who, in relation to the size of their population, have more seats than the more populous Member States. The number of seats in the European Parliament is determined by Article 189 of the EC Treaty, which was last amended by

---

[44] The EU has 23 official languages, these being Bulgarian, Czech, Danish, Dutch, English, Estonian, Finnish, French, German, Greek, Hungarian, Irish, Italian, Latvian, Lithuanian, Maltese, Polish, Portuguese, Romanian, Slovak, Slovene, Spanish, and Swedish.

[45] Within the United Kingdom, Northern Ireland is somewhat special as instead of the regional lists it also uses the system of single transferable votes, like in Ireland.

the Treaty of Accession of Bulgaria and Romania on 1 January 2007. From that day until the end of the 2004–2009 parliamentary term, the EP has 785 members; from 2009, candidates in the elections to the European Parliament will contest 736 seats.

The Treaty of Nice, which paved the way for eastern enlargement, placed a cap of 732 on the number of seats in the European Parliament of a Union of 27. However, under the Treaty of Nice the allocation of mandates among the 27 Member States could only become effective following the accession of all 12 then-candidate countries. Thus, the Treaty of Nice stipulated that, if the number of seats in the EP remained below 732 due to fewer than 12 acceding to the Union, a proportional correction mechanism would be applied, increasing the number of MEPs from each Member States so as to make the total as close to 732 as possible. On this basis in 2004 the Accession Treaty distributed the EP seats among 25 Member States, sharing out the 17 and 33 seats of Bulgaria and Romania. This arrangement, however, meant that upon the accession of Bulgaria and Romania, on 1 January 2007, the number of EP Members temporarily exceeded the ceiling. For this temporary period, the proportionality principle entitled both countries to an increased number of seats (18 for Bulgaria and 35 for Romania); thus, until the next elections, the total number of MEPs stands at 785.

The European Parliament should return to 732 seats in 2009, but since the Treaty of Accession of 2004 acknowledged and corrected the error made in the Treaty of Nice (which gave the Czech Republic and Hungary 2 seats fewer than the 22 of Belgium, Greece and Portugal despite their comparable population), there should be 736 seats available in the 2009 EP. Nevertheless, according to plans, by 2009, the Reform Treaty will have entered into force and on that basis the European Council could set a different number of seats upon the proposal of the European Parliament.[46]

In the European Parliament, the Members do not sit in national delegations but according to their political affiliations in factions of European political parties – in so-called political groups. The political groups play a key role in the work of the Parliament; they determine the composition of the institution's bodies, nominate the President and Vice-presidents of the

---

[46] See Annex, Point 2.5.2.

Table 2.2. The national composition of the European Parliament
in the EU of 25 and 27

Member States	Number of seats – EU 25	Number of seats – EU 27 January 2007 – June 2009	Number of seats – EU 27 From June 2009 – (according to the EC Treaty in effect)
Germany	99	99	99
France	78	78	72
United Kingdom	78	78	72
Italy	78	78	72
Spain	54	54	50
Poland	54	54	50
Romania	–	35	33
Netherlands	27	27	25
Greece	24	24	22
Portugal	24	24	22
Belgium	24	24	22
Czech Republic	24	24	22
Hungary	24	24	22
Sweden	19	19	18
Austria	18	18	17
Bulgaria	–	18	17
Denmark	14	14	13
Slovakia	14	14	13
Finland	14	14	13
Ireland	13	13	12
Lithuania	13	13	12
Latvia	9	9	8
Slovenia	7	7	7
Estonia	6	6	6
Cyprus	6	6	6
Luxembourg	6	6	6
Malta	5	5	5
Total	732	785	736

Parliament and assign the chairmen and Members of the Committees. It is the political groups' responsibility to draw up the agenda, to appoint the rapporteurs responsible for reports by the Committees and to decide the allocation of speaking time in the plenary session.

The European political groups are generally formed by MEPs with similar political values. As the political groups must reflect their trans-national character, a minimum number of

20 members from at least one fifth of the Member States (6 Member States in the Union of 27) can form a political group.

After the elections, the existing political groups are reformed and new ones are created. There are traditional groups (that have been operational for decades) and groups that are formed for only one parliamentary term, since their member organisations, i.e. national parties form *ad hoc* leagues. The traditionally large political groupings have founded political parties that are European both in their name and financing; the two largest ones – the European People's Party, drawing together the majority of Christian Democrats and Conservatives, and the Party of European Socialists, assembling the Socialist and Social Democratic Parties – determine the course of activities taken by the European Parliament.

The dominant role of the two largest political groups is reflected by the fact that, usually, each occupies about one fourth or one third of all the seats, while together they often hold over 60% of the mandates. The large groups have Members from all or almost all Member States. Because of their size, they do not only have a significant influence on the decision-making process but, not surprisingly, they nominate the leaders of the Parliament.

In addition to the two main groupings, the Liberals – who used to be the third large group in the 50s and 60s – have had the biggest impact on the work of the Parliament. Their significance has dwindled in the last three to four decades, but have remained a steady third behind the big guns. Outside the three traditional political families, some other stable political forces have also been factors to reckon with in the Parliament: the communist-oriented United Left, the Greens, and the group of more eurosceptic right-wing parties (the Union for a Europe of Nations). In the last two legislatures Members opposed to the current form of the EU or European integration in general were able to set up quite a group under the name Independence/Democracy, but remain unable to influence decisions in the European Parliament. The accession of Bulgaria and Romania enabled parties with extreme right wing views to clear the threshold needed for a parliamentary group, and with the help of some MEPs from these two newcomer countries they set up the political group Identity, Tradition, Sovereignty.

2.4.3. The office-holders and bodies of the European Parliament

The structure of the European Parliament is similar to that of national assemblies, although its organisation of labour is somewhat different, owing to its international character. At the same time, the division of labour and the responsibilities of the top officers are essentially identical with the arrangements of national parliaments. In other words, the bulk of the

Table 2.3. The political composition of the European Parliament in June 2007

EPP-ED Group of the European People's Party and European Democrats	278
PES Socialist Group in the European Parliament	217
ALDE Group of the Alliance of Liberals and Democrats for Europe	103
UEN Union for Europe of the Nations Group	44
Greens/EFA Group of the Greens/European Free Alliance	42
GUE/NGL Confederal Group of the European United Left – Nordic Green Left	41
IND/DEM Independence/Democracy Group	24
ITS Identity, Tradition, Sovereignty	23
NI Non-attached Members	13
Total	785

work, namely the technical debates, takes place in the standing Committees of experts while the plenary session, responsible for the political debates, examines only the issues prepared in advance by the Committees. The European Parliament is also headed by a President, who is assisted by the Vice-presidents.

Every two and a half years, that is, at the start and in the middle of each parliamentary term, the MEPs elect the President of the Parliament by secret ballot by a majority of the Members voting. The President manages the European Parliament, chairs, opens and closes the parliamentary sessions, acts as chair at the sessions of the management bodies – the Conference of Presidents and the Bureau – and represents the European Parliament at meetings with other EU institutions and non-member states. Furthermore, the President signs the budget of the European Union and those Community acts in which the Parliament acts as co-legislator with the Council.

Table 2.4. The national composition of political groups in the European Parliament as of June 2007

	EPP-ED	PES	ALDE	Greens/EFA	EUL/NGL	IND/DEM	UEN	ITS	Non-	Total
Austria	6	7	1		2		1	1		18
Belgium	6	7	6		2			3		24
Bulgaria	5	5	5					3		18
Cyprus	3		1		2					6
Czech Republic	14	2				6	1		1	24
Denmark	1	5	4	1	1	1	1			14
Estonia	1	3	2							6
Finland	4	3	5		1	1				14
France	17	31	11		6	3	3	7		78
Germany	49	23	7		13	7				99
Greece	11	8				4	1			24
Hungary	13	9	2							24
Ireland	5	1	1	4		1	1			13
Italy	24	15	12	13	2	7		2	3	78
Latvia	3		1	4	1					9
Lithuania	2	2	7	2						13
Luxembourg	3	1	1		1					6
Malta	2	3								5
Netherlands	7	7	5		4	2	2			27
Poland	15	9	5	20				3	2	54
Portugal	9	12				3				24
Romania	9	12	8					6		35
Slovakia	8	3							3	14
Slovenia	4	1	2							7
Spain	24	24	2		3	1				54
Sweden	6	5	3		1	2	2			19
United Kingdom	27	19	12		5	1	10	1	3	78
Total	278	217	103	44	42	41	24	23	13	785

Source: European Parliament

Concurrently with the President of the Parliament, the MEPs also elect 14 Vice-presidents from among themselves for the term of two and a half years. The Vice-presidents are elected by secret ballot, not according to their nationality but as nominated by the political groups.

European Parliament Presidents

1952–54	*Paul-Henri Spaak* (Belgium, Socialist Group)
1954–54	*Alcide De Gasperi* (Italy, Christian Democrat Group)
1954–56	*Giuseppe Pella* (Italy, Christian Democrat Group)
1956–58	*Hans Furler* (Germany, Christian Democrat Group)
1958–60	*Robert Schuman* (France, Christian Democrat Group)
1960–62	*Hans Furler* (Germany, Christian Democrat Group)
1962–64	*Gaetano Martino* (Italy, Liberal Group)
1964–65	*Jean Duvieusart* (Belgium, Christian Democrat Group)
1965–66	*Victor Leemans* (Belgium, Christian Democrat Group)
1966–69	*Alain Poher* (France, Christian Democrat Group)
1969–71	*Mario Scelba* (Italy, Christian Democrat Group)
1971–73	*Walter Behrendt* (Germany, Socialist Group)
1973–75	*Cornelis Berkhouwer* (Netherlands, Liberal Group)
1975–77	*Georges Spenale* (France, Socialist Group)
1977–79	*Emilio Colombo* (Italy, Christian Democrat Group)
1979–82	*Simone Veil* (France, Liberals and Democrats Group)
1982–84	*Pieter Dankert* (Netherlands, Socialist Group)
1984–87	*Pierre Pfimlin* (France, European People's Party Group)
1987–89	*Lord Plumb* (UK, European Democrats Group)
1989–92	*Enrique Barón* (Spain, Socialist Group)
1992–94	*Egon Klepsch* (Germany, European People's Party Group)
1994–97	*Klaus Hänsch* (Germany, Party of European Socialists Group)
1997–99	*José Maria Gil-Robles* (Spain, European People's Party Group)
1999–02	*Nicole Fontaine* (France, European People's Party and European Democrats Group)
2002–04	*Pat Cox* (Ireland, European Liberal Democrat and Reform Party Group)
2004–07	*Josep Borrell* (Spain [Catalan], Party of European Socialists Group)
2007–	*Hans-Gert Pöttering* (Germany, European People's Party and European Democrats Group)

The day-to-day work of the European Parliament is managed by two central bodies: the Conference of Presidents and the Bureau, which take decisions on matters relating to legislative planning and organise the Parliament's work. The President of the Parliament and the leaders of the political groups comprise the Conference of Presidents, which is responsible for taking political decisions concerning the Parliament's work. Its scope of duties involves the drawing up of the agendas of the sessions, the decision on the composition of the Committees, the reconciliation of any conflict arising between the Committees regarding their competences and the supervision of the Parliament's relations with the other EU institutions, the national parliaments and the Member States. The Bureau's members are the President of the Parliament and the 14 Vice-presidents. The Bureau manages the sessions and administers the organisational, financial and administrative matters of the Parliament and matters relating to the institution's operation. Meetings of the Bureau are attended by the five non-voting Quaestors, who are responsible for financial and administrative issues relating to Members' work. Quaestors are elected for a term of two and a half years.

In the European Parliament, as by and large in any parliament, the standing Committees are in charge of the in-depth discussion and detailed preparation of topics. It is the Committees that prepare the issues for political debate at the plenary session. During the 2004–2009 term, the European Parliament has 20 Committees, which deal with the areas that fall within the competence of the European Union.

Committees of the European Parliament in the 2004–2009 term

Committee on Foreign Affairs[47]
Committee on Development
Committee on International Trade
Committee on Budgets
Committee on Budgetary Control
Committee on Economic and Monetary Affairs
Committee on Employment and Social Affairs
Committee on the Environment, Public Health and Food Safety
Committee on Industry, Research and Energy
Committee on Internal Market and Consumer Protection
Committee on Transport and Tourism
Committee on Regional Development
Committee on Agriculture
Committee on Fisheries
Committee on Culture and Education
Committee on Legal Affairs

---

[47] From July 2004, the Foreign Affairs Committee has two sub-committees as well: Subcommittee on Human Rights and Subcommittee on Security and Defence.

Committee on Civil Liberties, Justice and Home Affairs
Committee on Constitutional Affairs
Committee on Women's Rights and Gender Equality
Committee on Petitions

Each Committee is headed by a Chairman and three or four Vice-Chairmen, who are elected on the basis of agreements between the political groups at the Committees' constituent meetings, so that the number of chair and vice-chair positions allocated to each political group should reflect its size. The political groups are also responsible for assigning the Members of the Committees, bearing in mind that the composition of each Committee should mirror the structure of mandates in the Parliament. The Committees vary in size from 28 to 86. The decision on the size, members and heads of the Committees is taken at the beginning of the new parliamentary term. Two and a half years thereafter, in the middle of the term, the positions are re-allocated and a new Chairman and Vice-Chairmen are elected (Vice-Chairmen and Committee Chairmen are often re-elected). As a rule, each MEP is a Member with full rights in at least one Committee and acts as a substitute in at least one other Committee. The substitutes are entitled to speak at Committee meetings and, if any of their respective political groups' full members is absent, to take part in the vote.

Committee work is usually organised by reports on various issues (legislative proposals, other parliamentary resolutions). The MEP responsible for drafting a particular report and thus preparing Parliament's resolutions is called the *rapporteur*. The rapporteurs are appointed by the committee on the basis of deals between the political groups. The number of rapporteurships is generally proportionate to the weight of a political group in a Committee as they are allocated on the basis of a quota system. Committee work largely focuses on debating draft reports, which take their final shape after amendments thereto have been debated and voted upon. Once a draft report is adopted in Committee, it is submitted to the plenary session for final adoption. Amendments may still be submitted in plenary, which MEPs vote on before voting on and adopting the final text of the report.

Besides the standing Committees, the Parliament has the right to set up sub-committees, temporary committees and temporary committees of inquiry. The Parliament also maintains close contacts with parliamentary bodies of third countries and groups of countries that are either connected to the EU by association or cooperation and partnership agreements or are key economic-political partners. The structured dialogue with these parliamentary assemblies is conducted through Interparliamentary Delegations, of which there are 34 at present. In the case of associated countries these Delegations are called Joint Parliamentary Committees.

2.4.4. The working order of the European Parliament

The European Parliament's official seat is in Strasbourg, but Brussels and Luxembourg also play an important role in the work of the institution. For that reason, the Parliament may be called a body with three seats, which conducts its work in three venues alternately. The Parliament normally meets in plenary session in Strasbourg, while the Committees meet in Brussels and the 5,000-strong administrative staff, the General Secretariat, is located in Luxembourg.

A Protocol attached to the Treaty establishing the European Community specifies that the Parliament should have its official seat in Strasbourg, where the 12 monthly part-sessions, which are normally one-week long (from Monday to Thursday), should be held. However, as the Parliament generally holds over 12 plenary sessions a year, the extraordinary sessions – which are generally no longer than 1 or 2 days and therefore are known as mini-sessions – are held in Brussels. Mini-sessions are held 6 to 7 times a year. There are exceptions also to the venue of Committee meetings. Since the Committees do not always manage to conclude their discussions in Brussels prior to the plenary meetings, they may hold brief sittings in Strasbourg during plenary weeks.

The European Parliament works in 4-week periods. Besides the plenary week and the two weeks for the Committees, the political groups also have one week when they have the opportunity to outline their strategies and reconcile their internal differences. Although the political groups hold their meetings in Brussels, they frequently convene in the Member States or in Strasbourg during the plenary week prior to voting-sessions.

The General Secretariat, which functions as the EP's administrative staff and has responsibility for the background work, is officially located in Luxembourg. However, as an increasing part of the parliamentary work is conducted in Brussels – despite the official seat being in Strasbourg – that part of the Secretariat supporting Parliament's legislative work has also relocated to Brussels, accompanying the MEPs to Strasbourg during plenary sessions, of course. In reality about half of the General Secretariat is posted in Luxembourg.

Since every MEP has the fundamental right to address a meeting in his mother tongue, the working languages of the European Parliament are all the official languages of the European Union.

2.5. The Court of Justice

2.5.1. The tasks of the Court of Justice

The European Court of Justice (ECJ) (officially the Court of Justice of the European Communities) has its seat in Luxembourg. Its establishment is related to the creation of Community law. With the establishment of the Communities, the concept of Community law was created, which has become an integral part of the legal systems of the Member States but has remained independent of national jurisdictions.[48] Community law, like any other legal system, needed effective judicial protection to ensure its implementation and observation. This protection is primarily guaranteed by the European Court of Justice, as the judiciary of the Communities.

The Court of Justice ensures that Community law is uniformly interpreted and implemented in each Member State, supervises the observance of Community law and monitors and ensures that the Community institutions act in line with their competences as stipulated by the Treaties. Another task of the Court is to give its opinion on the compatibility with Community law of any international agreement to be concluded by the EU or the Member States.

The Court of Justice has played a fundamental role in the development of European integration by executing its duties pursuant to the Treaties, that is, by interpreting Community law (clarifying the role of Community law and the European institutions and the relationship between Community law and national law). Having delivered several historic judgements, the Court of Justice has provided an impetus for the development of closer European integration. The Treaties founding the Communities, for example, do not spell out explicitly the supremacy of Community law over national law. This deficiency was remedied by the Court of Justice in its case law.[49] As a result of the Court's interpretation of Community law, the so-called principle of direct effect, which permits natural and legal persons to invoke Community law before their national courts, has also become general.[50]

---

[48] On the characteristics of Community law in detail, see 5.3.

[49] In 1977, in the so-called Simmenthal case, the European Court of Justice stated (see European Court of Justice case No. 106/77) that 'Every national court shall... ignore any element of national law that may be at variance with Community law...'.

[50] On the supremacy of Community law, the principle of direct effect and the interpreting activities of the ECJ in detail, see 5.3.2.

The institutional significance of the ECJ is that it is the only forum that has jurisdiction to interpret Community law and to verify the legality of acts adopted by the EU institutions.

2.5.2. The composition of the Court of Justice

The ECJ comprises one judge from each Member State, nominated by national governments and appointed by the common accord of the governments of the Member States. The judges hold office for a renewable term of six years. Every three years, half the judges are replaced or re-appointed, which ensures continuity of jurisdiction. The judges perform their duties independently of the Member States or any institution and cannot be dismissed before the end of their mandate. The judges select one member to be President for three years.

The Court of Justice may sit in plenary session (which happens quite rarely) or in chambers of three or five judges. It sits as a full court when a Member State or a Community institution that is a party to the proceedings so requests, or in particularly important and complex cases. Other cases are heard by a chamber. The Treaty of Nice established a Grand Chamber comprised of 13 judges (the President of the Court, the Presidents of the Chambers of 5 judges and other judges by rotation), which essentially took over cases to be heard in full court, although the possibility of sitting as a full Court remains open for particularly important cases.

Eight Advocates General assist the Court in its task, whose appointment and status are similar to those of the judges. The Council can increase the number of advocates general upon the Court's request and acting by unanimity. They also hold office for six years. The Member States select 4 advocates general every three years. The duties of the advocates general are to give a summary of a particular case and submit an opinion in writing to the Court. This written opinion must include the list of acts that the Advocate General responsible considers to be applicable in the given case. The advocates general must also submit specific recommendations for the Court's decision, which are not binding on the Court.

As the European Court of Justice became increasingly overloaded with cases, the Court of First Instance was established in 1989 to reinforce the judicial protection of Community law, facilitate faster and more effective jurisdiction and relieve the Court by assuming some of its tasks so that it could concentrate on its primary duty, namely the uniform interpretation of Community law.

The Court of First Instance is composed of at least one judge from each Member State, with the exact number of judges defined in the Statute of the Court. This arrangement leaves the door open for increasing the number of judges at the Court of First Instance to a number exceeding that of the Member States. (The Statute of the Court can be amended by the Council by a unanimous decision.) Such an increase could be necessitated by the growth in the number of cases, in particular pursuant to enlargement. The aim of this provision introduced by the Treaty of Nice was to provide for a mechanism of reducing the case overload of the Court or of the Court of First Instance, if necessary.

Members of the Court of First Instance are appointed by the common accord of the governments of the Member States for a renewable term of six years. Every three years, half the judges are replaced or re-appointed. The judges of the Court of First Instance also select one of their number to be President. The Court of First Instance sits in chambers of three or five but it may also sit as a full Court in particularly important cases.

In order to reduce the case overload of the Court of Justice and the Court of First Instance, the Treaty of Nice introduced the possibility of setting up judicial panels with special competences, to act as specialised courts and deliver rulings in the first instance. Such judicial panels can be set up by the Council acting unanimously on a proposal by the Commission or a request by the Court of Justice after consulting the Parliament. At the end of the IGC preceding the Treaty of Nice, the Member States requested the Court of Justice and the Commission to initiate the setting up of a judicial panel to hear disputes between the Community and its civil servants, in view of the growing number of such cases. As a result, the Civil Service Tribunal was established.[51]

2.5.3. The procedures of the Court of Justice

A procedure by the European Court of Justice can be initiated for a variety of reasons. The various forms of procedure currently employed by the Court are the following:

a) *Proceedings for failure to fulfil an obligation* (vis-à-vis the Member States): one of the most important proceedings is when an action is brought by the Commission to the Court of Justice to determine whether a Member State has fulfilled its obligations under the Treaties. It must be mentioned that the Commission does not automatically bring an action against a Member State that fails to fulfil its obligations under the Treaties. As a first step, it serves a reasoned opinion on the particular Member State. Should the Member State fail to comply with the opinion within the deadline specified therein, the Commission initiates legal proceedings before the Court of Justice. In such cases, the Commission acts as the plaintiff. The Treaties also permit the Member States to initiate such proceedings against each other, although such disputes are generally settled in the

---

[51] See Decision 2004/752/EC, Euratom.

Council or the Commission. If, at the end of a proceeding, the Court finds that the Member State concerned failed to fulfil its obligation, the Member State must comply with the Court's ruling. Should it fail to comply, the Commission may initiate further proceedings and the Court may impose a fixed or periodic penalty on the Member State.

b) *Proceedings for annulment:* the Court of Justice also reviews the legality of the acts of the Community institutions. If it finds a misuse of competence or power, an absence of competence, a violation of a substantial procedural requirement, or a breach of the Treaties or of any act of Community legislation, the Court may annul the ensuing legal measure. Such annulment of a Community act may be initiated by a Member State, the Council, the Commission or the Parliament. Natural and legal persons may seek the annulment of a legal measure that is of direct and individual concern to them.

c) *Proceedings for failure to act* (vis-à-vis the Community institutions): the Court of Justice may also review the legality of a failure to act by a Community institution. In such cases, for example the failure to legislate, it is a Member State, the Community institutions, or natural and legal persons who are directly and individually concerned, who may initiate the legal proceedings.

d) *Actions for damages:* the Court of Justice may rule on the liability of the EU institutions or servants in the performance of their duties in actions for damages, based on non-contractual liability.

e) *Request for an opinion:* the Council, the Commission, a Member State or the Parliament may seek the opinion of the Court of Justice to determine the compatibility of an envisaged international agreement with the provisions of the EC Treaty. If the Court decides that there is an incompatibility, the agreement may not be put into force.

f) *Preliminary rulings:* one of the key responsibilities of the Court of Justice is to cooperate with the national courts in order to facilitate the uniform interpretation and application of Community law. The courts of each Member State cooperate with the European Court of Justice inasmuch as, when in doubt as to the interpretation or validity of a Community rule in a case involving Community law, they seek a preliminary ruling from the Court on the relevant questions. The national court to which the ruling is addressed must apply the interpretation of the Court. Subsequently, the preliminary ruling on interpretation by the Court of Justice also serves as a guide for other national courts. Several important principles of Community law (such as the principle of primacy or direct effect) have been laid down in preliminary rulings by the Court of Justice.[52]

---

[52] For more on the case law of the ECJ and its key preliminary rulings, see 5.3.2.

Appeals can be considered a special type of proceeding. The Court of Justice may hear appeals against the judgements given by the Court of First Instance, in effect acting as a court of appeal on such occasions.

Generally, a distinction is drawn between requests for preliminary rulings and the other procedures, since the former are 'indirect actions', where the case before the Court of Justice is based on what happened before national courts, while the latter are 'direct actions', where those concerned resort directly to the Court of Justice.

The procedure before the Court of Justice always has a written stage and almost always an oral stage. The written stage is generally more significant.
With direct actions, as soon as the written application is sent to the Court, the judges appoint an advocate general and a judge-rapporteur from their members who are responsible for the given case. The application is also sent to the defendant, who has one month to lodge a defence. The applicant then submits a reply and the defendant a rejoinder (the time allowed being one month in each case). After hearing the judge-rapporteur's report and the advocate general's opinion, it is decided whether the case should be dealt with by a Chamber or by the full Court and the date is set for the public hearing. In a report for the hearing, the judge-rapporteur summarises the facts and the arguments of the parties. At the public hearing, the judges may put questions to the parties. Some weeks later, again in open court, the advocate general delivers his opinion to the Court, in which he proposes his solution to the problem. The oral procedure then ends. The judges deliberate alone, the judge-rapporteur presents his draft judgment; the draft is modified on the basis of changes proposed by the other judges and is then adopted by a majority vote; no dissenting opinions are attached to the final judgment, which is given in open court.
During the procedure of preliminary rulings, after the national court submits its questions to the ECJ, the ECJ has the request translated into all the official languages of the EU – since an interpretative ruling may be of interest to all Member States – and then serves it on the Member States, as well as the Commission and the Council. The parties, the Member States and the Community institutions have two months within which to submit their written observations and opinions to the Court. From this point on, the procedure is basically the same as that for direct actions. All those who submitted written observations may present their arguments orally at the hearing.

The Treaty of Nice – in order to improve the efficient operation of the Court necessitated by enlargement – brought major changes in the division of labour between the Court of Justice and the Court of First Instance. The primary goal of these changes was to extend the jurisdiction of the Court of First Instance to as many procedures as possible, thereby allowing the Court of Justice itself to focus on its principal task of providing a uniform interpretation and enforcement of Community law. As a result of the Treaty of Nice, the Court of First Instance became the general judicial body in almost all direct actions, such as actions for annulment, for failure to act and for damages. The Court of Justice retains responsibility for actions for failure to fulfil obligations and questions referred for a preliminary ruling, but the Statute (with the unanimous decision of the Council) can entrust certain proceedings even in these matters to the Court of First Instance. The idea behind the distribution of responsibilities under the Treaty of Nice is to maintain disputes concerning essential Community issues within the Court of Justice, as the jurisdictional supreme body of the European Union, while relegating other cases to lower level judicial bodies. Appeals against the rulings of the Court of First Instance under its jurisdiction may be submitted to the Court of Justice in cases defined in its Statute. In contrast, no appeal can be made against the judgements of the Court of Justice.

2.6. The Court of Auditors

2.6.1. The composition of the Court of Auditors

The European Court of Auditors was established as the independent body entrusted with the supervision of Community finances in 1977. The Court of Auditors sits in Luxembourg.
The Court of Auditors consists of one member from each Member State. The members of the Court of Auditors are appointed for a renewable period of six years by a qualified majority of the Council, after consulting the European Parliament. The Court's members elect their President for a renewable term of three years.

2.6.2. The work of the Court of Auditors

The European Court of Auditors was set up to represent the interests of Community tax payers. Its task is to examine whether the European Union manages its finances in accordance with the budgetary rules and the set objectives. The Court of Auditors is often referred to as the 'financial conscience of the Union', since this institution guarantees that the Community's expenditure is incurred in compliance with proper accounting, administrative and moral constraints. At the same time, the Court of Auditors examines not only expenditure but also whether EU budgetary revenue has been received and the financial management has been sound. The institution also checks whether management objectives have been met and at what cost.

The Court of Auditors may audit any institution or organisation receiving Community funds. In addition to the Community institutions, national, regional and local bodies, independent organisations receiving Community funds and even third countries (e.g. candidate states) in receipt of Community aid are also obliged to supply data regarding the utilisation and management of the Community resources allocated to them.

The Court of Auditors publishes an annual report on its work and the results produced, which is deliberated on by the Parliament and debated by both the Council and the Parliament. Acting on its own initiative or in response to requests by another Community institution, the Court of Auditors may also decide to compile special reports on any subject related to the implementation of the Community budget.

The Court of Auditors also has an advisory function, since the Community institutions may ask the Court for an opinion on the management of Community finances or on legislation relating to financial matters or the budget. The Court must be also consulted on budgetary regulations, as well as on measures aimed at preventing and combating fraud.

2.7. The Economic and Social Committee

2.7.1. The composition of the Economic and Social Committee

The Economic and Social Committee (ESC) is one of the Union's two advisory bodies, the other being the Committee of the Regions. The ESC was set up by the 1957 Treaty of Rome in order to involve the various economic and social interest groups in Community matters and in the preparation of Community decisions. The body comprises the representatives of economic and social interest groups, who are divided into three different groups: Employers' Group, Workers' Group and Various Interests' Group. The third group represents a wide range of interest groups from environmentalists, consumer protection activists, self-employed people and scientists to farmers, teachers and cooperative members, in practice from numerous areas falling outside the first two groups.

According to the Treaty of Nice, the number of members of the Economic and Social Committee may not exceed 350. Currently, in a Union of 27 the ESC has 344 members, who are nominated by the Member States and appointed by the Council, acting by a qualified majority, for a renewable term of four years. (The division of members by nationality is shown in Table 2.5. together with the Committee of the Regions.) The members of the ESC are appointed on an individual basis; the appointed members perform their duties independently of any external institution and may not take instructions from any organisation. Nevertheless, during their term of office, the members are free to engage in any other occupation.

The ESC elects its President, two Vice-presidents and a Bureau from its members every two years. The Bureau is made up of 24 members, 8 from each interest group; its task is to coordinate the work of the Committee. The President and the two Vice-presidents are chosen from each of the three groups in rotation. The President is responsible for the orderly conduct of the Committee's business and represents the ESC in relations with outside bodies.
The seat of the ESC is in Brussels.

2.7.2. The activities of the Economic and Social Committee

The role of the Economic and Social Committee is to forward the opinions of the various economic and social interest groups of the Union to the Community's decision-making bodies so that they can be taken into account in the decision-making process. The ESC's task is to advise the European Commission and the Council on economic, social and employment policy issues. Consultation of the ESC by the Commission or the Council is mandatory in certain (mainly economic and social) matters stipulated by the Treaty but the institutions are by no means obliged to follow the opinion of the Committee. The powers of the ESC are limited, which is shown by the fact that the Committee must comply with a set deadline when issuing its opinion. Consequently, it cannot delay and thereby exert influence on the Community decision-making process (unlike the Parliament) by holding back its opinion. The ESC may also adopt opinions on its own initiative on any issue concerning Community legislation.
The scope of action and opportunity of the ESC as a consultative body to influence Community decisions is relatively limited. This is also demonstrated by the fact that the most significant interest groups have built direct lobby channels to the Commission, the Parliament and the Member States (for example by opening offices in Brussels), to keep abreast of the decisions and the latest acts in the initial preparatory phase and to attempt to influence them.

The full Committee meets in plenary session ten times a year and in so-called section sessions in between. At the plenary sessions, the opinions of the Committee are adopted on the basis of section opinions. Presently, the ESC has six sections:
 – Agriculture, Rural Development and the Environment
 – Economic and Monetary Union and Economic and Social Cohesion

- Employment, Social Affairs and Citizenship
- External Relations
- The Single Market, Production and Consumption
- Transport, Energy, Infrastructure and the Information Society

The ESC also has the right to set up temporary sub-committees for specific issues. These sub-committees operate on the same lines as the sections.

2.8. The Committee of the Regions

2.8.1. The composition of the Committee of the Regions

The Committee of the Regions has a relatively brief history as a Community institution compared to the other advisory body, the Economic and Social Committee. It was set up by the Maastricht Treaty to provide a forum for local and regional authorities to express their points of view on Community decision-making.

According to the Treaty of Nice, the number of members of the Committee of the Regions may not exceed 350. At present, in the Union of 27, the Committee has 344 members (and the same number of substitute members), who represent local and regional authorities. They are mostly mayors or leaders of local governments or provinces appointed by direct democratic elections, or persons who are politically accountable to a local or regional elected body of representatives and who do not hold office as a result of delegation. The members are nominated by the Member States and appointed by the Council by a qualified majority for a renewable term of four years. The division of members by Member State is the same as in the Economic and Social Committee (see Table 2.5.).

The members of the Committee perform their duties independently of any external institution and may not take instructions from any organisation. Nevertheless, during their term of office, the members are free to remain in their positions in their respective local or regional bodies.

The members of the Committee elect their President, a Vice-president from each Member State and a Bureau from their members every two years. The Bureau's task is to coordinate the work of the Committee. The 58 members of the Bureau comprise the President, the Vice-presidents, a further 27 members and the leaders of the political groups. In practical terms, seats on the Bureau are allocated in the following way: three delegates from each big Member State of the Union, 2 delegates from medium-sized countries and 1 from each of the smaller ones.

The seat of the Committee of the Regions is in Brussels.

Table 2.5. The number of seats in the Economic and Social Committee and the Committee of the Regions allocated to the Member States in the Union of 27

Germany	24	Austria	12
France	24	Bulgaria	12
United Kingdom	24	Slovakia	9
Italy	24	Denmark	9
Spain	21	Finland	9
Poland	21	Ireland	9
Romania	15	Lithuania	9
Netherlands	12	Latvia	7
Greece	12	Slovenia	7
Czech Republic	12	Estonia	6
Belgium	12	Cyprus	6
Hungary	12	Luxembourg	6
Portugal	12	Malta	5
Sweden	12	Total	344

2.8.2. The activities of the Committee of the Regions

The Maastricht Treaty states that the Committee of the Regions must be consulted as a matter of course prior to the adoption of decisions which will have repercussions at regional level. Pursuant to the Maastricht Treaty, the Committee must be consulted on the areas of education, culture, health, trans-European networks and economic and social cohesion. The Treaty of Amsterdam gave the Committee another five areas of compulsory consultation: employment policy, social policy, the environment, vocational training and transport. The Committee also has the right to issue own-initiative opinions on matters having an impact at local or regional level.

The opinion of the Committee of the Regions is similar to the ESC's opinion, that is, it must be issued in compliance with a set deadline. The Council and the European Commission however are by no means obliged to follow the opinion of the Committee. Consequently, similarly to the ESC, the power of the Committee to influence Community decisions is relatively limited. Therefore, it is by no means an accident that the majority of the Union's regions have set up offices in Brussels, which engage in direct lobbying of the Community institutions.

The Committee meets in plenary session five times a year. The bulk of the work is done in the internal commissions, which are appointed every four years and whose task is to draft

the opinions to be adopted at the plenary session. At present, there are 6 commissions:
- Commission for Territorial Cohesion
- Commission for Economic and Social Policy
- Commission for Sustainable Development
- Commission for Culture and Education
- Commission for Constitutional Affairs and European Governance
- Commission for External Relations

2.9. The European Investment Bank

The European Investment Bank (EIB) was created under the 1957 Treaty of Rome. The Luxembourg-based EIB's objective is to contribute to the balanced economic development of the Communities through financing capital investments.

Since the Member States subscribe jointly to the EIB's capital (their respective contributions reflecting their economic weight in the Union), they are the shareholders of the Bank. The subscribed capital of the EIB has been raised on several occasions, the last time to EUR 165 billion. The Bank may have a maximum of loans outstanding equivalent to 250% of its capital.

The EIB grants loans mainly by borrowing on the international capital markets, usually through issuing bonds. With its AAA rating on the capital markets, it can raise credit on the best terms and, consequently, it can grant loans under highly favourable conditions. Since the EIB secures the majority of its resources from the international financial markets, it can finance significant investments without debiting the Member States or the Community budget.

2.9.1. The organisational structure of the European Investment Bank

The supreme body of the EIB is the Board of Governors, which consists of Ministers nominated by each Member State, usually Ministers of Finance. The Board of Governors lays down the general guidelines on credit policy, approves the balance sheet and the annual report, decides on capital increases and appoints the leading officers of the EIB.

The Board of Governors appoints the Board of Directors based on the nominations of the Member States and of the European Commission for a term of 5 years. The Board of Directors consists of 28 Directors and 18 Alternates.[53] Its task is to adopt decisions concerning borrowings, granting of loans and guarantees.

---

[53] The 27 Member States and the European Commission nominate one Director each, while Alternates are nominated either by a country or a group of countries.

The Board of Governors also appoints the Management Committee, which comprises the President and eight Vice-presidents, for a renewable term of six years. Under the supervision of the Board of Directors, the Management Committee oversees day-to-day business at the EIB, prepares borrowing and lending decisions and ensures that the decisions of the Board of Directors are implemented.

The three members of the Audit Committee appointed by the Board of Governors monitor the Bank's operations and book-keeping. Meetings of the Audit Committee are also attended by three observers.

2.9.2. The tasks of the European Investment Bank

The EIB's task is to grant loans to finance projects that are in accordance with the economic aims of the Community. The Bank's most important missions are: to help the development of economically weaker regions; to support the improvement of the international competitiveness of the EU's industry, in particular by means of support for small- and medium-sized companies; to grant loans for projects guaranteeing the Community's energy supply, the protection of the environment and the quality of life. Recently, at the initiative of the Council, the EIB has played a decisive role in the development of the transport and communications infrastructures of the Union. In 1997, to fight the alarming unemployment rates in the 1990s, the Council set a new guideline for the EIB, namely to support job-creating investments, requesting the Bank to mobilise its reserves to this end.

Every year, the EIB grants new loans amounting to EUR 30–40 billion. Roughly 90% of the Bank's loans are granted for the Member States of the Union. At the same time, in its activities outside the Community, the EIB makes a considerable contribution to development policy in accordance with the economic aims of the Community. Outside the Union, the EIB grants loans to candidate countries, some 80 African, Caribbean and Pacific countries enjoying EU preferential treatment, the Mediterranean countries (which have concluded financial protocols with the Bank), the fast-developing Asian and Latin American countries and neighbouring countries to its East.

The EIB's activities are complemented by the related European Investment Fund (EIF)[54], established in 1994. The EIF's task is to finance the establishment, growth and

---

[54] The EIF's majority shareholder is the EIB. Other shareholders include the European Commission and several European banks and financial institutions.

development of small- and medium-sized enterprises. The registered capital of the EIF is around EUR 2 billion. The EIF does not grant direct loans to SMEs but to the intermediary institutions and venture funds financing them. The EIF operates in the Member States and in candidate countries as well.

2.10. The European System of Central Banks and the European Central Bank

The Maastricht Treaty established the programme of the economic and monetary union (EMU)[55], involving the establishment of the single European currency in the third phase of the programme and, at the latest, by 1999. In order to establish the required institutional structure to manage the European currency and the monetary union, the Treaty of Maastricht also provided for the establishment of the European System of Central Banks (ESCB) and the European Central Bank (ECB). However, the precise date of their launch was not specified in the Maastricht Treaty; the Member States were to decide later depending on the rate of progress. On 1 January 1994, the European Monetary Institute (EMI) was established for the lifetime of the transitional period. As the forerunner of the European Central Bank, the EMI was given the task of carrying out preparatory work on the future monetary union, executing transitional duties.

At the Madrid Summit in December 1995, the Member States agreed to launch the third stage of the EMU on 1 January 1999. Consequently, the ESCB and the ECB had to be set up by that time. On 2 May 1998, the Council of the European Union confirmed the date and decided which Member States would adopt the single currency, the euro, in the final and third stage of EMU. On 25 May 1998, the Member States, having consulted the European Parliament, appointed the Executive Board of the ECB. The appointment took effect from 1 June 1998 and marked the establishment of the ECB and the ESCB. The EMI went into liquidation and merged with the European Central Bank, which, similarly to the EMI, has its headquarters in Frankfurt. This institutional framework opened the way for the introduction of the single currency on 1 January 1999. Euro coins and banknotes were put into circulation on 1 January 2002.

---

[55] On the economic and monetary union in detail, see Chapter 8.

2.10.1. The European System of Central Banks

With the adoption of the single currency, the European System of Central Banks became the leading institution of the Union's financial policy. The ESCB is composed of the European Central Bank and the national central banks (NCBs) of the Member States. In accordance with the Treaty, the primary objective of the ESCB is to maintain price stability. The basic tasks carried out by the ESCB are:

– to define and implement the monetary policy of the Community;
– to conduct foreign exchange operations;
– to hold and manage the official foreign reserves of the Member States;
– to promote the smooth operation of payment systems.

The operation of the ESCB was prepared by the transitional European Monetary Institute, which went into liquidation on the establishment of the European Central Bank.

The European Monetary Institute

In accordance with the timetable of the Monetary Union established by the Maastricht Treaty, the EMI commenced operations at the start of the second stage of the EMU, on 1 January 1994. The EMI's main tasks were to prepare the third stage of the EMU, by strengthening monetary policy, coordination and cooperation between the Member States, and to carry out the preparations required for the establishment of the European System of Central Banks and the European Central Bank. The competences of the EMI were however much more limited than those of its successor, since its sole task was coordination; it had no responsibility for the conduct of monetary policy in the EU and no competence regarding foreign exchange operations.

The decision-making process of the ESCB is centralised through the European Central Bank. The ECB is a completely independent institution; it may not seek or take instructions from the governments of the Member States, from the Community institutions or any other external body. The ECB, assisted by the NCBs, guarantees that the duties assigned to the ESCB are carried out. Although the national central banks of the single currency zone (the eurozone) cannot be seen as mere subordinates of the ECB, they perform their duties in compliance with the ECB's guidelines and instructions; for example, they are authorised to issue banknotes exclusively with the ECB's consent.

To guarantee the coordinated and effective operation of the ESCB prior to its establishment, the Member States had to synchronise the statutes of their national central banks and institute the model of the independence of the central banks from their governments, similarly to the operating principle of the ECB.

The NCBs are the sole subscribers to the capital of the ECB. The subscription of capital is based on the EU Member States' respective shares in the GDP and population of the Community, each with a weighting of 50%.

It is important to mention that the NCBs of the Member States, which do not participate in the eurozone, are members of the ESCB but with a special status; they do not take part in decision-making with regard to the single currency or the implementation of such decisions.

The European System of Central Banks has no separate decision-making bodies and, therefore, the decision-making is centralised through the decision-making bodies of the European Central Bank.

2.10.2. The institutions of the European Central Bank

The main decision-making body of the ECB is the Governing Council, which comprises all the members of the Executive Board and the presidents of the NCBs of the Member States that have joined the currency union (the 'eurozone'). The President of the Council and one member of the Commission may attend the Governing Council's meetings without the right to vote. The Governing Council adopts the guidelines and takes the most important decisions for the performance of the ESCB. It formulates the monetary policy of the Community, including decisions relating to monetary objectives of the ESCB, like key interest rates and the supply of reserves. The members of the Governing Council generally adopt decisions by a simple majority; however, on some issues, mainly relating to the ECB's capital, they vote on the basis of the subscribed capital. In such cases, the vote is carried when the decision is supported by two thirds of the subscribed capital and half of the shareholders.

The Executive Board comprises the President, the Vice-president and four other members, chosen on the basis of their recognised financial expertise. They are appointed by the common accord of the governments of the Member States at the level of the Heads of State or Government (after consultation with the European Parliament and the Governing Council of the ECB) for a non-renewable period of up to eight years. The members of the Executive Board perform their duties independently of governments and the other Community institutions and may not engage in any other professional activity during their terms of office. The President and the Vice-president of the Executive Board are also the President and Vice-president of the European Central Bank. The President of the Executive Board chairs the sessions of the bodies of the ECB and, in the case of a tied vote, his vote is decisive. However, when the members of the Governing Council vote on the basis of the subscribed capital, the votes of the members of the Executive Board do not carry any weight.
The Executive Board's responsibility is to implement monetary policy in accordance with the guidelines laid down by the Governing Council and, in doing so, to give the necessary instructions to the NCBs. Furthermore, the Governing Council may occasionally delegate further powers to the Executive Board. The Executive Board prepares the meetings of the Governing Council.

The General Council comprises the President, the Vice-president of the Executive Board and the presidents of the NCBs of all the Member States, irrespective of whether they fully participate in the monetary union, namely whether or not they have joined the eurozone. The primary responsibility of the General Council is to settle issues involving Member States not participating in the eurozone, such as the relationship and dealings of these countries with the single currency. Nevertheless, it also deals with other matters pertaining to each Member State, for instance it performs advisory functions and collects statistical data.

2.11. The European Ombudsman

The Maastricht Treaty vested the European Parliament with responsibility for appointing the Ombudsman of the European Union. The first European Ombudsman was appointed in 1995. The Ombudsman holds his office for a renewable period of five years with an official seat in Strasbourg, just like the European Parliament.

The Ombudsman is empowered to receive complaints from any citizen of the Union or any social organisation or undertaking with headquarters registered in any of the Member States who have suffered maltreatment or have a grievance involving an institution of the Union. Examples of such cases are where a Community institution or body has failed to act when it is obliged to, has acted in a manner which infringes Community law or has failed to administer its tasks correctly (instances may include administrative errors, inequitable actions, discrimination, misuse of power, failure to provide information or unwarranted delay in acting).

The Ombudsman's responsibility is to conduct an investigation regarding the complaints. A complaint may only be filed with the Ombudsman if the complainant has already voiced his concern to the institution involved.
The Ombudsman may not intervene on behalf of national, local and regional governments and does not deal with pending cases or cases already settled with a final judgement.

When receiving a complaint, the Ombudsman first decides if he has authority in the given matter. If so, he launches an investigation, which is as a rule a public investigation but which can also be confidential, if requested by the complainant. If the Ombudsman substantiates the complaint, he seeks a solution to redress the problem and, if necessary, submits draft recommendations to the institution concerned. If the institution concerned fails to act upon the recommendation, the Ombudsman reports the case to the European Parliament.

CHAPTER 3
THE UNION'S COMPETENCES –
THE UNION BASED ON THREE PILLARS

3.1. The development of the three pillars

The objective of creating a union of European peoples was enshrined in the preamble of the Treaty of Rome. Transforming the Communities into a union was not a political reality for many decades. The idea of closer European integration became stronger in the '80s, and the creation of a European Union was increasingly on the agenda. The so-called 'Solemn Declaration'[1], published by the Heads of State or Government in Stuttgart on 19 June 1983, was the first time the Member States specifically mentioned transforming the Communities into a European Union. This Solemn Declaration, together with the European Parliament's Spinelli Draft Treaty on the European Union[2], served as a basis for the Single European Act (SEA), which entered into force on 1 January 1987. The SEA, however, did not bring about the institutional reforms that would have justified renaming the Communities a Union. For many, the Union also meant a higher form of political integration, which was missing from the SEA.

The problem with the Union always lay in the fact that the concept of the Union was not completely clear; it meant different things for different Member States, politicians and schools of thought. Thus, there was no universally accepted method of how to change over to the Union. While in the area of the economy, it was clear that, after the single market, the next phase of integration would be an economic union, meaning the harmonisation and coordination of economic policies and the introduction of a single currency, the concept of a political union was more elusive. It is not surprising that it was much more difficult for the Member States to come to a common position on political integration when substantive negotiations about the creation of a European Union began at the turn of the '80s and '90s.

---

[1] The Stuttgart Solemn Declaration called for institutional reforms to prepare for the creation of a Union, and also included the objective of an economic and monetary union.

[2] The Italian politician, Altiero Spinelli, one of the most committed advocates of a federal Europe, was a Commissioner in the '70s and later an MEP. Acting on Spinelli's initiative, the first directly elected European Parliament adopted a so-called Draft Treaty on the European Union, which proposed the foundation of the European Union. This was, however, premature at the time (March 1984) given the position and will of the Member States.

Moreover, the Member States seemed to be less committed to closer political integration than to forging ahead with economic integration. So, while the idea of giving up their own national currencies and relative independence in shaping their economic policies was acceptable to the majority of Member States, they were more reluctant to limit their political independence, which many considered more important for national sovereignty, especially in the area of foreign and defence policy. This atmosphere determined the shaping of the Treaty on the European Union and created the peculiar structure of the three pillars.

When creating the European Union, the Member States had two objectives in mind. On the one hand, they were willing to deepen economic integration within the familiar framework of the European Communities. On the other hand, although they agreed on the need for, and even set themselves as a goal, the creation of some kind of political union, they did not wish to grant Community institutions any competence in the area of political integration, which they wanted established on a purely intergovernmental basis. This led to the birth of the three pillars.[3]

The complicated three-pillar architecture was the result of political evolution. In the first four decades of European integration, the emphasis was on the economic areas, where Member States were willing to forge close integration and pool some of their sovereignty. This led to the emergence of the so-called *Community method*, which comprises several supranational elements and self-imposed restrictions on the sovereignty of the Member States, involving either delegating competences to the Community level or sharing competences with other Member States.[4]

At the turn of the eighties and nineties, when Member States recognised that integration should be extended to political areas (foreign and security policy and justice and home affairs) as well[5], they were reluctant to apply the closer Community method to these areas.

---

[3] The Treaty itself does not use the term 'pillar' (thus it is not a legal concept), this descriptive term only came into use later following a Dutch proposal.

[4] This means that a Member State has to accept and implement a decision even if it disagrees with that.

[5] By the second half of the '80s, it was apparent that, if European integration was to gain the political weight commensurate with its economic power on the stage of world politics, a much more coordinated and uniform foreign policy would be needed to reduce the unsustainable situation of being 'an economic giant but political dwarf'. It was also apparent that, in a globalising world, several phenomena posing a threat to internal security (illegal migration, terrorism) are linked to the permeability of borders and could be combated more successfully through joint action. That is why bringing foreign policy and justice and home affairs into the sphere of European integration had been on the agenda for a long while.

The Treaty of Maastricht – which was signed on 7 February 1992 and entered into force on 1 November 1993 – created the European Union, while preserving the former European Communities (which form the first pillar). Common Foreign and Security Policy (the second pillar) and cooperation on justice and home affairs (the third pillar) were, however, left to the looser framework and different operating mechanisms of intergovernmental cooperation. The Treaty of Amsterdam, which entered into force on 1 May 1999, reduced the scope of the third pillar to police and judicial cooperation on criminal matters, elevating other areas of justice and home affairs (namely, external and internal border control, asylum, immigration policy and judicial cooperation on civil matters) to the Community level by placing them in the first pillar.

All areas that formerly fell within the competence of the three Communities (European Coal and Steel Community – ECSC, European Economic Community – EEC or EC, European Atomic Energy Community – Euratom), tasks relating to closer economic integration – primarily the introduction of the economic and monetary union[6] – and a few other new Community policies where the Communities had no competence before, formed the first pillar of the European Union created by the Treaty of Maastricht. In short, the first pillar was defined as the extended European Communities.

An important decision on matters of principle introduced by the Treaty of Maastricht was that the European Economic Community was renamed the European Community, indicating that it was more general in nature and not just economic. The institutional, decision-making and legislative systems of the three European Communities were integrated into the European Union, preserving the unique supranational character of the Communities. In the field of political integration, the Member States did not want to maintain the structure of the Communities. This is how the second pillar, the Common Foreign and Security Policy (CFSP), and the third pillar, cooperation on justice and home affairs (which the Treaty of Amsterdam limited to police and judicial cooperation in criminal matters), were born. These two pillars were created on a purely intergovernmental basis, independent of – or, more precisely, parallel to – Community cooperation.

The European Union created in Maastricht is the sum of the three forms of cooperation, namely the three pillars. However, it must also be pointed out that the European Union did not receive a legal personality of its own; that was reserved for the three Communities of the first pillar. Thus, the concept of the European Union is not a strictly legal category, although

---

[6] For details, see Chapter 8.

this somewhat contradicts the fact that the Treaty on the European Union defined the ncept of Union citizenship and related rights.[7] The European Union is more of a political concept, implying the full cooperation of its Member States and embodying all elements of European integration. According to the architecture created by the Treaty of Maastricht, the Union is based on three elements: the European Communities, the Common Foreign and Security Policy and cooperation in the area of justice and home affairs (now police and judicial cooperation in criminal matters). Precisely because of its comprehensive nature, since Maastricht, the concept of the European Union has become a synonym for European integration, irrespective of which pillar we are referring to.

The structure of the three pillars

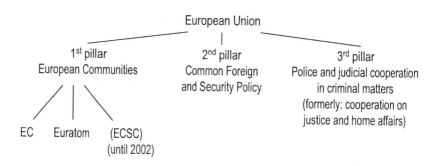

3.2. The division of the three pillars

The legal bases for the operation of the three pillars are laid down by the European Union's Founding Treaties, the so-called 'Treaties', which consist of four separate treaties: the Founding Treaties of the three Communities (ECSC, EC, Euratom – the Treaty establishing the European Coal and Steel Community lost its effect on 23 July 2002, as it was only concluded for 50 years, leaving only two Community Treaties in force)[8], and the Treaty on

---

[7] See 6.2.2.

[8] Its expiry did not cause any problems, however, because the EC Treaty has a general effect in relation to the operation of the internal market, and so the provisions of the ECSC remain valid. The financial implications of the expiry of the ECSC Treaty are governed by the relevant Protocol of the Treaty of Nice, which ensures integration into the EC.

the European Union, signed in Maastricht. Although the three Community treaties appear in the Treaty on the European Union as Titles II, III and IV amending these treaties, from the legal point of view they are considered as separate treaties.

The Community Treaties apply to the European Communities, that is the EU's first pillar, while the Treaty on the European Union is divided among the three pillars. Titles II-IV of the EU Treaty refer to and provide a link between the three Communities, while the provisions of Title V and VI form the legal bases for the second and third pillars, respectively. The remaining Titles I, VII and VIII of the EU Treaty essentially apply to all three pillars.[9]

The first pillar, the European Communities, and the other two, the Common Foreign and Security Policy and police and judicial cooperation in criminal matters (formerly justice and home affairs cooperation), are all based on an independent set of rules. Nonetheless, the institutional system is hard to split up according to pillars; Article 3 of the EU Treaty stipulates that the Union shall have a single institutional framework, which in practice means that the EU, which has no legal personality, can use the institutions of the Communities. However, only the Council and the European Council can be considered as bodies that have comprehensive competence in respect of all three pillars. The other Community institutions are only 'borrowed' by the second and third pillars, which work on an intergovernmental basis.

While supranational institutions (the Commission, Parliament and Court of Justice) have a central role in the first pillar, they have a limited say in the intergovernmental second and third pillars. Cooperation between the Member States is the basis for the functioning of the second and third pillars. Under the first pillar, the Commission has the exclusive right of initiative, preparing decisions but also exercising certain executive, decision-making, supervisory and representative powers; the Parliament is a co-decision-maker and co-legislator, but is also partly a consultative and supervisory body; the Court of Justice interprets the *acquis communautaire* and ensures its enforcement and uniform implementation. Under the second and third pillars, however, these three institutions have limited competence: the Commission has the right of proposal, but not an exclusive right as Member States can also put forward proposals and take initiatives; the Parliament is either consulted or usually just informed about the decisions taken; the Court of Justice only has jurisdiction if the Member States request its ruling but, under the third pillar, it has the relatively important power of delivering preliminary rulings on interpretation.

---

[9] For details of the Treaties, see 5.2.1.1.

Even the Council's internal division of labour varies from one pillar to the other. The substantive work of the Council of Ministers is primarily assisted not by COREPER, which is nonetheless responsible for preparing meetings in respect of all three pillars, but by the Political and Security Committee in relation to the second pillar, and by the Coordination Committee (formerly called the K4 Committee, now called Article 36 Committee) in relation to the third pillar.

A major difference is that, in the case of the intergovernmental pillars, decisions are predominantly taken unanimously (except as regards procedural issues), while in the case of the first pillar, qualified majority voting is more typical.

Another indication of the differences between the three pillars is that legislation created by the Community institutions (so-called secondary legislation[10]) takes different forms according to which pillar is being used; the sources of law differ from one pillar to another. The three-pillar structure is further complicated by the fact that the three pillars as such, (i.e. the European Union itself,) have no legal personality; only the Communities of the first pillar do.[11]

The three pillars differ not only in terms of the nature of integration and the role of the institutions, but also in terms of the intensity of integration and the dimension of the areas involved. While the second and third pillars essentially cover well-defined areas, the scope of the first pillar extends not only to practically the whole economy, but to several other important areas of life as well (e.g. education, healthcare). In the last 50 years, within the first pillar, the Community has created close and comprehensive integration, which has a fundamental impact on the operation of the economy and citizens' daily lives. Thus, while the functional and institutional structure of the two intergovernmental pillars is relatively simple, the first pillar has a rather complex institutional, legal and economic system. The first (Community) pillar includes measures regulating the key objectives of European integration, the single market, the four fundamental freedoms (the free movement of goods, services, persons and capital), and the duties arising from the creation and operation of the economic and monetary union. In order to ensure the single market and the economic and monetary union, a comprehensive and continuously expanding legal system was created within the first pillar, complemented by the joint action of the Member States through common policies and Community activities. A carefully regulated system of Community decision-making forms the framework for approving Community legislation and creating common policies and Community activities.

---

[10] For more on secondary legislation, see 5.2.2.

[11] Both the European Community and the European Atomic Energy Community have a legal personality of their own, thus they – unlike the Union itself – have the capacity to conclude international treaties.

3.3. The three pillars and the problem of defining the Union's scope of competence

The competences of the European Union are defined by the Founding Treaties of the Union and of the Communities. All of the Founding Treaties currently in force (the Treaty on the European Union, the Treaty establishing the European Community and the Treaty establishing the European Atomic Energy Community) are so-called *framework treaties*.[12] Their characteristic feature is that they do not usually stipulate specific measures, but rather set tasks and objectives, whose implementation through concrete measures is left to Community institutions. The Treaties regulate lawmaking by Community institutions and the implementation of various policies in detail.

However, the Treaties do not always include unambiguous provisions as to the division of competences between the Community and Member States in the case of individual policy areas, which sometimes leads to serious political and legitimacy problems. Often it is still unclear to the citizens which decisions are taken at the EU level, what achievements are attributable to Europe, and what each institution does. As a consequence, the EU/ EC over-regulates some areas while – in the absence of an appropriate legal base – it has no competence to act in others, where citizens expect action. There are areas where the Treaties define competences exhaustively, but there are also several fields where the division is not clear-cut, which may give rise to disputes between the Union and the Member States. This is also problematic because, at the current level of integration, further deepening is only conceivable and feasible if the Member States can clearly see what tasks will remain within national competence in the future, i.e. what are the areas where integration poses no 'danger' to national sovereignty. At the time of the adoption of the Nice Treaty in 2001, when the Member States decided to place the European Union on new foundations, this problem highlighted the necessity of finding a clearer definition and division of competences during the preparation and elaboration of the new Treaty framework and, also, of abolishing the complicated three-pillar structure. The issue of competences, therefore, became a key element of the Constitutional Treaty. Following the failure of the ratification of the Constitutional Treaty, its successor, the Reform Treaty pursues this key aspiration.

Redefining competences became particularly necessary due to the difficulties created by the three-pillar structure. Despite efforts to sharply divide the three pillars, they do sometimes

---

[12] For details on the features of framework treaties, see Chapter 5.2.1.2.

overlap, creating complications in defining competences and responsibilities. A classic example of overlapping pillars is foreign and security policy (second pillar) and foreign trade (first pillar), where the line between the scope of competence of Council and Commission is sometimes unclear. Currently, on certain occasions, it is debated whether the Commissioner for external relations or the Council's Secretary General, wearing his hat of High Representative for the Common Foreign and Security Policy, should act.

Defining competences is equally difficult in the first pillar, because competences differ in scope and type from one policy area to the other. Competences are not catalogued or clearly divided. The terminology currently in use is also ambiguous: the EC Treaty talks about common policies, Community actions and measures, but fails to set up concrete categories. The term 'common policy' usually, though not always, refers to areas where the Community has exclusive decision-making competence (e.g. trade policy), while 'Community action' and 'measure' imply that the Community and Member States have shared competence to take decisions (e.g. on the environment).

Monitoring how the principles of subsidiarity and proportionality – fundamental to decision-making in the Union and to its functioning – are put into practice is another unsolved issue.
According to the principle of *subsidiarity*, action should be taken as close to the grass roots as possible; the Community/Union should only act if there is added value in Community action, that is if the Member States cannot achieve the desired results in a satisfactory manner, and thus the planned action, due to its scope or impact, can be better implemented at Community level. The principle of *proportionality* stipulates that Union/Community actions should only extend as far as they achieve the objectives set in the Treaty.
Although the European Commission can only initiate the adoption of a piece of legislation if it has examined whether it does not violate these principles, the control mechanisms are not in place or not appropriately enforced. Thus, during the drafting of the Constitutional Treaty, the Member States insisted on laying down new rules to ensure that the principles of subsidiarity and proportionality should be respected, particularly because shared competence has become general in most areas, and this trend is likely to continue. The Reform Treaty replacing the Constitutional Treaty will seek to make further progress in this area.

Another issue related to the principles of subsidiarity and proportionality was the strengthening of the role of national parliaments. Ultimately, the competences of the EU originate from the Member States, indirectly from the national parliaments, who usually ratify treaties which enhance integration in the name of the Member States, thereby yielding some of their sovereign decision-making power to the EU. Consequently, at the Community level, if the principles of subsidiarity and proportionality are violated, it generally affects the decision-making sovereignty of national parliaments; thus these parliaments have the most legitimate claim to assume responsibility for the monitoring of the application of these principles.

Given these difficulties, it was suggested that it might be useful to have a catalogue of competences or some other, more flexible method of resolving the problem of the division of competences. With a view to these questions, in the Constitutional Treaty, the Member States sought to settle the issue of abolishing the three pillars, by bestowing legal personality on the Union, clarifying competences and ensuring more effective monitoring of the principles of subsidiarity and proportionality through closer involvement of the national parliaments, while maintaining the instruments that ensured the flexibility needed to attain the objectives of the Union.[13] Following the failure of the ratification of the Constitutional Treaty, the new Reform Treaty will take on board the relevant provisions. With the entry into force of the Reform Treaty, anticipated for 2009, these provisions will bring about fundamental changes to the Union's legal architecture.[14]

---

[13] A key instrument in resolving the conflicting competences and in ensuring that the Union has the ability to act is Article 308 of the EC Treaty, which allows the Community to take appropriate measures even when the Treaty does not provide the necessary powers, if action by the Community should prove necessary to attain, in the course of the operation of the common market, one of the objectives of the Community. In such cases, the Council adopts measures acting unanimously, on a proposal from the Commission and after consulting the European Parliament.

[14] For more on the Reform Treaty and the Constitutional Treaty, see Annex, Point 3.

CHAPTER 4
DECISION-MAKING AND LEGISLATION IN THE EUROPEAN UNION

The unique institutional structure of the European Union has led to the development of a singular decision-making mechanism. However, while the Community's institutional structure has proved to be relatively permanent, the decision-making mechanism has been modified by the amended Treaties four times[1] in the past two decades for several reasons. On the one hand, the institutional development of the various organs of the Community and especially the demand for the European Parliament's greater involvement in decision-making, have had a significant impact on the development of the decision-making mechanism. On the other hand, the increased powers of the Communities and the increased number of areas covered by integration necessitated the intensification of legislation – which in turn also stimulated the modification of the decision-making mechanism, with the aim of making it more dynamic. Finally, as a result of the repeated enlargements of the EU and the significantly higher number of Member States, the decision-making system designed for six Member States became cumbersome and failed to function smoothly.

Despite the succession of changes, decision-making has never been radically simplified, although there has been a marked reduction in the length of time taken to reach decisions. The Community decision-making mechanism – modified several times as a result of the hard-won compromises reached by the Member States – still functions as a rather complex system, which outsiders find difficult to understand. Consequently, the Union decision-making mechanism is still often criticised by both the federalist proponents of integration and by those opposed to integration. However, it should be pointed out that, in the face of constant expansion and various other external and internal challenges, the decision-making mechanism of the European Union has invariably managed to maintain its functioning and to ensure a clearly continuous – albeit not very rapid – progress of integration. The complexities of the decision-making mechanism may also be attributed to those 'fundamentals' of the European Union which imply that more is required than simply reconciling the national interests of the 27 Member States, since decisions have to mirror the Community's interests (as represented by the Commission) and the interests of the citizens (as represented by the Parliament), which also have to be taken into account in the decision-making process. Furthermore, there are numerous other Community bodies (especially the Committee of the Regions and the Economic and Social Committee) as well as thousands of economic, social and cultural lobby organizations and interest groups that try to influence decision-making to suit their interests.

---

[1] These treaties are the Single European Act (date of entry into force: 1 January 1987); the Treaty of Maastricht (date of entry into force: 1 November 1993); the Treaty of Amsterdam (date of entry into force: 1 May 1999), and the Treaty of Nice (date of entry into force: 1 February 2003).

This Chapter will provide an overview of decision-making in the European Union in its present state, as last modified by the Treaty of Nice. Firstly, the operation of the first pillar – a key slice of Union decision-making – will be discussed, dealing in detail with the adoption of legislative acts, i.e. the legislative process. Then a summary of decision-making in the somewhat narrower scope of the second and third pillars follows, identifying differences with the first pillar. A detailed description of the operation of policies in these two pillars is provided in Chapters 23 and 24.

It should be stressed that the Constitutional Treaty signed on 29 October 2004 would have brought major changes in the decision-making system; the key motivation behind the Constitutional Treaty was the need to make the Union's decision-making simpler, more efficient and transparent. However the ratification of the Constitutional Treaty was not successful in all Member States, which prevented its entry into force. Following the failure of the ratification of the Constitutional Treaty, the Heads of State or Government decided at their summit of 21–22 June 2007 to abandon the constitutional approach and put the EU on new foundations by means of a Reform Treaty amending the current EU Treaty and EC Treaty. The Reform Treaty is largely based on the Constitutional Treaty and takes on board most of its provisions on Community decision-making. These provisions are presented separately from the current framework in Point 4 of the Annex, for the practical reason that they will probably only come into effect in 2009 (while probably the most important new rule on qualified majority voting will only come into effect in 2014).

4.1. Community decision-making

4.1.1. The role of the Commission–Council–Parliament Triangle in Community decision-making

Decision-making in the European Union was initially restricted to cooperation between the Commission, which drafted proposals, and the decision-making Council. However, the Parliament – through decades of hard effort – managed to attain more and more rights in the area of direct participation in decision-making and in influencing decision-making. This led to significant changes in the original line-up, although the Council retained its role as the principal decision-making organ. Simply put, in accordance with the first-pillar decision-making structure of the European Union, the right of initiative at present falls within the competence of the Commission, and the Council – in conjunction with the Parliament, or by itself – decides on the Commission's proposal after hearing the Parliament's opinion and having included it in the decision-making process. In certain cases, the Council may also request the opinion of the Economic and Social Committee or the Committee of the Regions; however, this opinion has no binding force.

Within the framework of this system, developed over the decades, joint decisions are made and Community legislation is realised through cooperation between the three most significant Community institutions: the Commission, safeguarding Community interests; the Council, representing the Member States, and; the Parliament, representing the citizens through political parties. It must be noted that, although the European Council does not take part in the legislative process as such, by adopting strategic guidelines and making decisions that set the framework for legislative issues, it sets the course of and determines the progress of the legislative process.

4.1.1.1. The development and significance of the Commission's role in preparing decisions

The federalist founding fathers, including Schuman and Monnet, conceived of the High Authority of the ECSC, and later the EEC Commission, as the beginning of a European government – an organisation run by officials who believed in Europe and who could not be influenced by the Member States, and who would thus be able to enforce Community interests in the most efficient way possible. This model – based on the dominant role of the High Authority (continuously being delegated powers from the Member States), and later that of the Commission – was already 'diluted' in its form when it was established by the ECSC Treaty. In the years following the introduction of the model, its limitations became increasingly evident, so much so that Monnet (the first President of the High Authority of the ECSC) stepped down in 1954, having recognised with disappointment that his original concept could not be realised because of the opposition of Member States to the delegation of their powers.

In the Treaty of Rome, which established the European Economic Community, the principal decision-making powers were unequivocally conferred upon the Council, i.e. an organisation that brought together the respective governments of the Member States. As the 'Guardian of the Treaty', the primary role of the Commission was to exercise its right of initiative and, to a lesser degree, its rights of implementation and control. At the same time, the founding fathers provided leeway for the subsequent expansion of the Commission's powers, as Article 155 of the Treaty (currently Article 211) foreshadowed the time when the Commission would be gradually delegated powers from the Member States, provided that it had authorisation from the Council. Thus, for instance, in the early years of the Communities, the Council invested the Commission with autonomous decision-making powers in the area of competition policy. Subsequently, the Commission was delegated significant powers in realising and implementing the common agricultural policy. However, this trend was discontinued, as the Member States backed down. After the 1966 Luxembourg compromise[2] – which in practice meant a victory for consensus (unanimity) based decision-making in the Council, and also put an end to the expansion

---

[2] See Chapter 2.3.5.

of the Commission's decision-making powers – the Commission eventually assumed a prominent role in proposing, initiating and preparing measures. The 'Council-based model' was born. In contrast to the concept of having an active Commission and a passive Council, this model is based on the reduced role of the Commission in decision-making as well as on discussion of proposals in Council – up to the very last minute.

Thus, in accordance with the Treaty of Rome, the Commission became an organ that essentially dealt with preparing decisions and submitting proposals, and subsequent Treaties amending the Treaty of Rome have not resulted in changes with respect to the role of the Commission. At the same time, this role should not be undervalued, as the Commission has 'exclusive' rights in this area – at least with regard to the first pillar.[3] This does not mean that the Council, the European Council or the Parliament cannot initiate legislation; on the contrary, they often exercise their rights to this end.[4] However, the actual wording and submission of the proposal is the exclusive task of the Commission and thus the other institutions have to call upon the Commission to carry out its duties. This exclusive right of wording and proposal means that, in accordance with the rules and regulations, a Commission proposal can only be amended by the Council, acting by a unanimous decision. In addition, before a Community act is adopted by the Council, the Commission may withdraw its proposal at any time, should it consider the amendments proposed with respect to that proposal to be unacceptable.[5]

Because representatives of the Commission are present at all levels of negotiations in the Council (and in the Parliament), the Commission is able to constantly follow any attempts by the Member States to amend the original proposal. Should the Commission fail to agree to the proposed amendments, it has the right to withdraw its proposal. However, if this happens, no act will be adopted on the given matter and, naturally, this is not in the interests of the Commission either. It is common practice in the case of a withdrawn proposal for the Commission to revise and then resubmit its proposal.

The significance of the Commission is enhanced by the fact that, through its duties laid down in the Treaty, it may initiate Community legislation by itself. Thus, the Commission plays a defining role in deciding what issues are to appear on the Community decision-making agenda. Naturally, proposals that do not have the support of the Member States

---

[3] In the second and third pillars, the Commission shares the right of proposal with the Member States, which means that both the Member States and the Commission may submit proposals. However, in the second and third pillars, the role of the Commission is diminished by the fact that the Council is not obliged to discuss the Commission's proposals.

[4] This is particularly characteristic of the European Council, as the body which defines strategic guidelines for the Union. It is general practice in the case of strategic decisions and programmes for the European Council to identify a list of specific areas (sometimes with deadlines) where it expects the Commission to initiate legislation.

[5] Proposals that reach the conciliation phase during the co-decision procedure (see 4.1.2.4.) are an exception to this rule.

(and/or the European Parliament) do not go very far and, in this respect, the Commission's options are rather limited. At the same time, however, it depends on the Commission what direction a particular draft decision or draft act takes, what its defining provisions are and what these focus on; this gives it considerable influence. This is especially so in the light of the continuously growing number of Member States: the more players there are, the more important this agenda-setting competence is.

With so many Member States, the Commission – whose proposals can only be amended by unanimity and who can withdraw a proposal if it finds the amendments to it unacceptable – has a quasi right of assent in Community legislation. This power must not be overrated, though; it must be considered in the light of the fact that the Commission needs to win the support of the Member States (or at least a qualified majority thereof) and often also that of Parliament (or at least the majority thereof). The Commission can only ensure such support if it shows enough flexibility in amending and revising its proposals. The Commission's quasi right of assent is in practice accompanied by a high degree of flexibility (often amounting to a complete revision of the text or re-evaluation of its position), without which decision-making would be impossible in the Council or Parliament.

In describing the significance of the Commission, it also has to be emphasised that, besides its exclusive policy-proposing role in Community matters, the Commission also carries out tasks related to implementation and normative decision-making with regard to issues concerning certain policies (e.g. agriculture, commerce, competition) and, in doing so, it significantly influences these areas, assuming a critical role. This 'derived' implementing and decision-making role of the Commission is discussed in 4.1.3.

4.1.1.2. The Council as the principal decision-making organ – decision-making in the Council

The system of Council-based decision-making has created conciliation mechanisms between the Member States, which are so intricate that they are very difficult for the outsider to understand. In this system, consensus can only be reached within the framework of an extremely laborious and long-winded process. This means that certain bodies – functioning at various levels, and connected with the Council of Ministers – have acquired an increasingly significant role in the system. Although final decisions are made at the ministerial level, lower level forums play an important role in preparing and reaching consensus, while in matters of great importance, it is the direction given by Heads of State or Government that is important.

Within the Council, the COREPER (the Committee of Permanent Representatives) plays a significant role in coordination. In addition, the formulation of a common position is a task carried out by numerous working groups.

The COREPER is the primary link between the Commission and the Member States. In every case, the Commission first forwards its proposal for a decision or legislation on a given matter to the Permanent Representations of the Member States in Brussels, who forward the proposal to the competent national government offices. Once the national positions on these matters are formulated, the proposal is first discussed by working groups composed of various officials from the Member States, then by the COREPER itself. The ministers deal with the matter only in the final phase, when an agreement is near. If there is full consensus on a matter discussed in the COREPER, then the ministers often adopt the proposal without discussing the matter. Community jargon refers to these as 'A' matters. Thus, within this system, the COREPER is charged with a rather comprehensive task. The scope of activities carried out by the COREPER and the Representations include the maintenance of contacts between national governments and Community institutions, involvement in coordinating the work of national governments, coordination between the Commission and the Council and, finally, the preparation of decisions within various working groups.

About 250 working groups[6] assist continuously and carry out the preparations for the work of the Council and the COREPER. The Council working groups are usually composed of one or two ministerial experts from the Member States[7] (who are usually accompanied by the competent official working at the country's Permanent Representation)[8] and the competent representatives of the Commission. The scope and intensity of their work is aptly illustrated by the fact that, on typical weekdays, more than 3,000 national officials from the Member States participate in various meetings in the Council building in Brussels. The role of the working groups is to prepare the Commission's proposal in a professional manner in anticipation of the political debates that take place in the COREPER. The working groups strive for consensus and, if they reach consensus, a decision in principle on a particular matter is often already developed at this stage. Having discussed the decision in the COREPER, the Council often adopts the proposal without further deliberations (as A points). For about 85% of the items on the Council's agenda, agreement is reached at a

---

[6] This number constantly changes, depending on how many matters there are on the agenda.

[7] Usually senior officials of line ministries.

[8] It can sometimes happen – indeed it happens quite often with smaller Member States – that national ministries do not send officials to working group meetings and the Member State is only represented by an official of the Permanent Representation responsible for the given area. There are working groups where attendance by Permanent Representation officials only is common practice.

lower level (70–75% in working groups, 10–15% in COREPER). At the same time however, a large proportion of cases do not get past the working groups. Thus the groups act as a kind of filter, which facilitates the work of the Council. The significance of the working groups lies in the fact that the Member States' officials and experts, who deal with the same issues and are in charge of the same areas, get to know each other, and the so-called 'engrenage' develops between them; this popular term from the literature on integration refers to the 'inter-twining' of national administrations.

The above shows that, throughout the decades, the complexity of matters has called for the increased and more intense involvement of national administrations in the Community decision-making process. This has also meant that officials, working at the same level, have also become acquainted which, in turn, has often facilitated the resolution of matters in dispute.

Through the participation of national administrations, this system seemingly enhanced the dominance of intergovernmental cooperation. At the same time, it is worth noting that, within the framework of this system, the Council itself became supranational, as national administrations and officials came to be inter-linked at various levels. This in turn led to the establishment of stable and inter-twined relations between the governments and officials of the Member States.

In the model based on the Council's dominant role in decision-making, the country that had the Presidency assumed a predominant role in the process of conciliation between the Member States and in making compromises. The role of the Presidency, originally established with the sole purpose of presiding over Council meetings, assumed increasing prominence from the mid-sixties, with the development of the Communities. The Presidents-in-office gained increasing influence over decisions reached during the term of their Presidency and their active role and capacity for initiation came to be a determining factor in terms of the legislative programme of the six-month period. In respect of the closure and outcome of complicated issues, it can be decisive whether the government of the country holding the Presidency is properly prepared and capable of forging a compromise. It has become the key role of the Presidency at every level of the Council, including in the European Council, to act as an intermediary between national delegations with opposing positions and to elaborate alternative solutions. The Presidency carries out its activities in close cooperation with the Commission.

As a result of the increasingly complicated process of making compromises, Heads of State or Government gradually came to be involved in decision-making, while the role of the President also gained in significance. In a situation where matters were often inter-twined and where sectoral Councils often had conflicts of interest, the top political leadership was required to make the most essential compromises and to lay down the rules of cooperation, acting as a body administering justice and having appellate jurisdiction. As a result, the European Council, i.e. the "Council" of Heads of State or Government, was consolidated in 1974, and European summits became a standard practice. The significance of the European Council's establishment was so great that, in the opinion of some, the post-1975 history of the EC is the history of summits. As exaggerated as this conclusion may be, the fact remains that, today, every strategic decision in connection with matters of any political significance is a decision reached at the meetings of Heads of State or Government. In consequence, summits were organised more and more often, and their agenda also expanded.

In order to understand the logic behind the decision-making process, it has to be emphasised that in every single body related to the Council (from working groups to the European Council itself), this process is dominated by a constant effort to make compromises. It is a characteristic feature of the debating culture that, in reaching a final decision, the Member States generally try to avoid open confrontation. Even though this culture encourages the Member States to be more inclined to implement decisions, it is also increasingly becoming an obstacle to decision-making, as the number of Member States continues to rise.

As the Council is the primary decision-making organ of the European Union, one of the most serious problems facing the institutional structure of the Union lies with the fact that, even after repeated amendments to the Treaty, the requirement to have unanimous decision-making still applies to a number of matters that are relevant to the advancement of integration. Although the Single European Act, the Treaty of Maastricht, the Treaty of Amsterdam and – as one of its primary objectives – the Treaty of Nice all increased the number of areas that fall under the scope of the qualified majority procedure, there remain matters of great importance which, even after the entry into force of the Treaty of Nice, require unanimous support to be resolved. These areas include taxation, most social policy matters, certain issues related to commercial policy and certain justice and home affairs issues. For an exhaustive list of areas requiring unanimity, see Appendix I.

Although most decisions are taken in areas that fall under the scope of qualified majority voting, abolishing the requirement of unanimity in certain areas – particularly due to enlargement from 15 to 27 (the number of Member States almost doubled in a few years) – is essential if the EU is to continue to evolve and be able to meet external and internal challenges. That is exactly why extending qualified majority voting was set as a key objective of the Constitutional Treaty, and although in the end it did not enter into force, the Reform Treaty it is replaced by maintains this same objective.[9]

---

[9] See Annex, Point 4.1.

As the demand for unanimity is still present in numerous key matters before the Council, the application of the concept of 'enhanced cooperation' may become more common within the decision-making process of the EU in the future.

Enhanced Cooperation

The application of the mechanism of 'enhanced cooperation' may be applied if certain Member States wish to establish closer integration in a given area and accelerate progress, while others are not inclined or not able to do so. Enhanced cooperation essentially means that certain Member States strengthen their integration, while others may choose not to enter into cooperation. Those who shun cooperation can still fall into line with the 'forerunners' later on, if they wish to do so. The possibility of entering into enhanced cooperation must always be open to every single Member State. However, within the framework of enhanced cooperation, only those Member States that are already involved in the cooperation have the right to vote.

The option of choosing enhanced cooperation was introduced by the Treaty of Amsterdam but, as the implementation of enhanced cooperation was conditioned by rather strict requirements, it has not been applied so far.[10] In accordance with the Treaty of Amsterdam, the implementation of enhanced cooperation required the participation of more than half of the Member States and the unanimous permission of all Member States. In such conditions, the realisation of enhanced cooperation would have been increasingly impossible, following the enlargement of the EU. However, with the expanding EU becoming increasingly heterogeneous, the 'instrument' of enhanced cooperation may become essential. Consequently, the Member States made the task of facilitating and simplifying enhanced cooperation one of the primary objectives of the Treaty of Nice. In accordance with the Treaty of Nice, 8 Member States may initiate enhanced cooperation, irrespective of the total number of Member States, and a qualified majority is enough to establish the cooperation. However, in areas that fall under the scope of the co-decision procedure[11], the consent of the European Parliament is also a prerequisite to the initiation of enhanced cooperation.

---

[10] Yet there are certain areas where processes similar to enhanced cooperation were developed earlier. For instance, participation in the introduction of the single currency is regarded as a similar kind of cooperation, as here, too, there are Member States that choose to stay out but still have the option of joining the single currency later. Nevertheless, the conditions for the introduction of the single currency are dealt with separately in the Treaty, thus this process cannot be regarded as a classic example of enhanced cooperation. Despite this, the monetary union does play a role in the establishment of the institution of enhanced cooperation, in that it is very likely that countries within the monetary union will endeavour to strengthen their integration in other areas as well. Consequently, it will be these countries that will be able to initiate the introduction of enhanced cooperation in other areas.

[11] See subchapter 4.1.2.4.

In the interest of maintaining unity within the European Union, it is further stipulated in the Treaty that enhanced cooperation cannot be launched if that cooperation would undermine the functioning of the single market and weaken economic and social cohesion. The former prohibition is based on the fact that the essence and core of the EU's functioning lies with the single market. Closer cooperation that affects the single market would not serve to deepen unity within the single Europe; on the contrary, it would create a kind of 'à la carte' Europe. The latter prohibition is there to ensure that wealthier nations do not initiate any kind of cooperation that would exclude states just because they are less developed. The option of choosing enhanced cooperation should be available to every Member State, and the Commission must encourage Member States to enter into enhanced cooperation if they have not done so already. Since the entry into force of the Treaty of Nice, enhanced cooperation (excluding cooperation in the area of defence policy or military matters) is also possible in the second pillar of the EU – an option that the Treaty of Amsterdam had not allowed for. However, unanimity between the Member States is still a prerequisite in this respect. Nevertheless, after Nice, enhanced cooperation in the third pillar, as in the first, can be launched by a qualified majority.

The rules on how enhanced cooperation can be initiated and operated was to be amended by the Constitutional Treaty, and these provisions are largely taken on board by the Reform Treaty.[12]

The European Parliament has been assigned increasingly important co-legislative tasks recently, as shown in the following point of this chapter. Yet, on the whole, the Council (i.e. the respective governments of the Member States) remains the principal decision-maker in matters of the greatest significance, including those that affect the future development of the EU.

In a system based on the primacy of the Council, the way in which institutional 'cards' are dealt has significant implications (not only for the various bodies of the Union, but also within the Member States), since an essential feature of this system is that various organs (e.g. national parliaments) of the Member States can only take part in the Community decision-making process via their respective governments. This requires the Member States to adjust their internal legislative systems in accordance with the above, in a way that: on the one hand, allows for the democratic formulation of a national position prior to a Community decision being made (which means that national parliaments and national interest groups are allowed to become involved), and; on the other hand, provides a solution for the national implementation of Community decisions. However, there is no general Community rule determining how Member States should deal with these tasks. Member States usually develop their national coordination schemes in EU-related matters in accordance with their own constitutional systems and in keeping with their political traditions, and the level of involvement of various national organs other than the government varies from State to State.

---

[12] See Annex, Point 4.3.

The involvement of national parliaments also varies from State to State, but the various approaches can be grouped into three categories. In some Member States, the government's activities in Council are closely scrutinised by parliament and in practical terms the government needs a negotiating mandate from parliament every time it enters into substabtive talks in Council. In most Member States, the government has a full reporting obligation to parliament concerning negotiations in Council and tries to elaborate its negotiating position based on parliament's proposals but can deviate in justified cases. In the least restrictive, third model, there is constant consultation between government and parliament, but in practice the government has a free rein during negotiations in Council. As a result of efforts to reduce the democratic deficit of the Union (see more details about this in the next point), increased involvement of national parliaments has become an important objective.[13]

4.1.1.3. The expansion of the Parliament's powers – assuming the role of co-legislator

It took decades for the Parliament to gain ground in the system dominated by the Council and the Commission. The European Parliament had no real legislative powers like national parliaments, except for the budgetary powers it was granted in 1970 and 1975. The system of direct elections introduced in 1979 was the first major step on the way to becoming a 'real' parliament. This system endowed the organisation with strong legitimacy because, starting from that date, the EP – as an organ assuring the democratic legitimacy of the European Communities – could act on behalf of the European citizens and, as a result, it could argue more efficiently for the expansion of its own powers.

---

[13] A Protocol attached to the Treaty of Amsterdam includes provisions on the involvement of national parliaments in Community decision-making. As a key rule, governments must be given enough time before negotiations in Council to consult the national parliament about their negotiating position. According to the Protocol, at least six weeks must elapse after a Commission legislative proposal is made before it can be placed on the Council's agenda for adoption. During this period, the national parliaments have time to deliberate and consult the government on the negotiating position. The Constitutional Treaty sought to extend the provisions of this Protocol and introduce new safeguards for the involvement of national parliaments. These provisions are taken on board by the Reform Treaty as well. (See Annex, Point 3.1.)

However, the increase in the significance of the European Parliament after 1979 had no effect on the organisation's legislative and controlling role, which remained insignificant. A change was brought about by the Single European Act, which resulted in the European Parliament's considerable institutional advancement. In accordance with the Act, the so-called cooperation procedure was introduced in ten community areas. Consequently, in certain matters, the Parliament received significantly greater powers than it had had within the framework of the earlier consultative mechanism. However, the Parliament still had no genuine decision-making rights. The other great innovation of the Single European Act was the introduction of the so-called 'assent powers', which granted substantially higher institutional significance and real decision-making powers to the Parliament. However, these powers were restricted to a few specific areas. In essence, the notion of assent powers meant that the Council could decide on a specific matter only after having secured the prior assent of the Parliament.

The Treaty of Maastricht carried the process initiated by the Single European Act even further, and expanded the decision-making and legislative powers of the Parliament in order to strengthen the democratic legitimacy of the European Union, and to decrease the much talked about 'democratic deficit'.[14] The Maastricht Treaty expanded the assent powers of the Parliament to cover a small number of new areas and, as the most significant improvement, also introduced the so-called co-decision procedure, which, in certain areas, made the Parliament a decision-maker equal in rank to the Council. The significance of this new form of decision-making, in comparison with the cooperation procedure, is that the Parliament may now act as a decision-maker, and no decision can be made without its agreement. With the co-decision procedure, in effect, Parliament was, in practical terms, granted the co-legislative function that it had been seeking for decades. At the same time, the significance of this improvement was very much diminished by the fact that, in accordance with the Treaty of Maastricht, the Parliament could only exercise its rights in 15 areas (accounting for about a quarter of all legislative work). A major breakthrough in this respect was brought about

---

[14] A major reason for the expansion of the Parliament's powers (and also an argument that is often used by the Parliament with a view to expanding its own powers) is related to the issue of the so-called *democratic deficit*, which has become increasingly talked about since the eighties. The term 'democratic deficit' is meant to draw attention to the fact that the representation of citizens in EU institutions (especially in the Council and in the Commission) is indirect in more than one respect, while at the same time, too much power is concentrated in the hands of civil servants who are nominated and not elected. Many see the expansion of the European Parliament's decision-making powers and its greater involvement in the decision-making process as a means of reducing the democratic deficit. This might be one of the reasons why the EP has been able to gain increasingly significant powers during the past few years. Another key question in relation to increasing the role of elected bodies and reducing the democratic deficit, which has been on the agenda to a varying extent in various Member States, is strengthening the role of national parliaments in integration. It must be noted, though, that the democratic deficit is not only related to the role of parliaments, but implies more generally that citizens have become distanced from the decisions.

by the Treaty of Amsterdam, which expanded the scope of the co-decision procedure to cover 23 other areas, thereby making the co-decision procedure a key decision-making mechanism. The Treaty of Nice took this process one step further, by extending Parliament's co-decision power to five new areas and allowing for the possibility of extending co-decision to certain social policy and first pillar JHA issues by a unanimous decision of the Council. As a result, co-decision has evolved into the most commonly used decision-making procedure. The European Parliament has become a true co-legislator on an equal footing with regard to approximately half of the Community acts adopted by the Council.

Since 1987, the institutional status of the Parliament has undergone significant changes. While, in the mid-eighties, the European Parliament was hardly anything more than a consultative body, by the end of the nineties it had challenged the decision-making and legislative primacy of the Council and, in certain areas, had attained equal footing with the Council, as a co-decision-maker. Although the Parliament still does not have significant powers in several matters that are critical to the functioning of the European Union (such as the common agricultural policy, or cooperation in justice and home affairs), defining it as a co-decision-making institution is now much more justified than referring to it as a consultative organ of the Council. The Member States intend to reinforce this institutional set-up based on Parliament's role as a co-decision-maker. Therefore in the Constitutional Treaty they wished to introduce co-decision as the general rule. The Reform Treaty – which replaces the Constitutional Treaty – has taken up this aspiration, and when it enters into force (probably in 2009) it will bring institutional changes consolidating the European Parliament that can only be compared in magnitude to those introduced by the Maastricht Treaty: extending co-decision to almost 80% of legislative areas.[15]

With the increase in the significance of the European Parliament, many are already comparing EU decision-making to a kind of bicameral parliamentary system (characteristic of federal states), in which the European Parliament, i.e. the organ directly elected by and representing the citizens, is the Lower House, while the Council, which brings together the governments and representatives of the respective Member States, acts as an Upper House. Doubtless, this simile aptly illustrates the features of decision-making but this comparison may be inappropriate in the sense that – in deviating from the traditions of double-chamber parliaments characteristic of certain civil democracies – in the EU context, the powers of the 'quasi-lower-house' (the Parliament) are much more limited

---

[15] See Annex, Point 4.1.

The European Union's decision-making mechanism

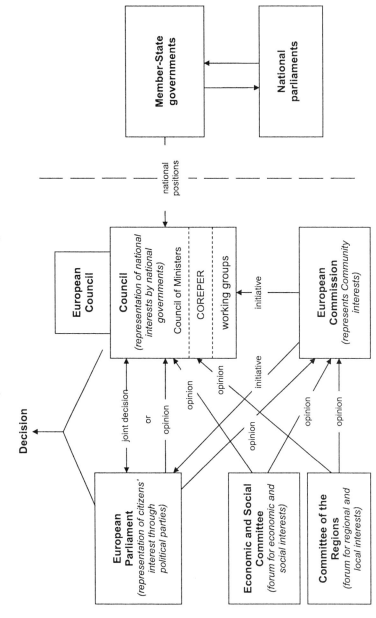

than those of the 'quasi-upper-house' (the Council), which clearly has a defining role. Consequently, the significance of this simile lies in the fact that it delineates the policy that has characterised the EU's decision-making and institutional system in recent years. However, with respect to the consolidation of the Parliament, the fact remains that, to date, the Parliament still has no independent decision-making and legislative powers, and it practices joint decision-making with the Council, while the Council continues to make numerous decisions independently, without the Parliament.

4.1.2. Decision-making procedures according to Parliament's participation

Due to the fact that the participation of the Parliament in the decision-making process has not been uniform, the past fifty years of European integration have seen the development of an exceedingly intricate decision-making mechanism. The Treaty contains separate provisions for every single matter as to the conditions of Parliament's participation in decision-making. In the case of certain matters, it is sufficient to inform the Parliament, while in others, the Parliament acts as a legislator, cooperating with the Council on an equal footing. On the whole, depending on the extent of Parliament's participation, theoretically there are seven separate procedures through which decisions can be made. Yet the situation is somewhat simpler now, as Community legislation is realised through four procedures (that of consultation, cooperation, assent and co-decision). Besides these legislative procedures, there are other additional procedures (information, budgetary and those created by Inter-Institutional Agreements) that are applied in well-circumscribed cases. The picture is further simplified by the fact that as regards legislative procedures, the application of the cooperation procedure is limited to a few areas related to the economic and monetary union (where practically there are no longer legislative acts), while the assent procedure is also applied quite rarely, and only in the case of matters of great significance. As a result, Community legislation today is essentially characterised by the application of the consultation and co-decision procedures. The text of the Treaty clearly establishes what decision-making procedures are to be applied in what matters, and it also defines whether a Council voting procedure should be based on a qualified majority vote or on a unanimous vote.

4.1.2.1. The consultation procedure

Prior to the introduction of the Single European Act, the consultation procedure was essentially the only legislative procedure. Even though its scope came to be somewhat limited (as the assent, cooperation and co-decision procedures gained ground), the consultation procedure is still regarded as the primary legislative procedure along with the co-decision procedure. The significance of the consultation procedure lies with the fact that, due to this, practically every single legislative initiative passes through the Parliament, which serves as proof of the increasing importance of the European Parliament.

The Treaty does not require the participation of the Parliament in every case. However, as early as the sixties, the Council already took upon itself to consult with the Parliament, and from the mid-seventies onwards it has consulted with the Parliament on practically every legislative matter, except in the case of technical and interim proposals.[16]

The Parliament's power to enforce its interests is at its most restricted during consultation; nevertheless, its capacity cannot be regarded as negligible, as the whole point of the procedure is that the Council may only decide on a matter after it has obtained the Parliament's opinion. Although the Council is not obliged to take the Parliament's opinion into account, it cannot make a decision in the absence of such an opinion. Taking advantage of this situation, the Parliament may stall decision-making for a while by dragging out the process of delivering its opinion, in cases where it does not agree with a certain proposal or the details of that proposal. The Parliament cannot postpone indefinitely the delivery of its opinion, it must cooperate with the Council in good faith.[17]

By delaying its position, Parliament may be able to have its proposals for amendment taken into consideration, especially in matters that require a swift decision, and the Commission may have to revise the original proposal. The Parliament may make its opinion available to the Council only after the preparation of a version that it finds acceptable is complete. Technically, this can be done as follows: the Parliament first votes on its amendments, which it then submits to the Commission. The Parliament only adopts a position with regard to the complete legislative initiative if the Commission has incorporated the Parliament's proposed amendments. Only after having received the Parliament's position can the Council make a decision. This is important, because if the Commission adopts the amendments requested by the Parliament, those amendments also become Commission proposals, which the Council can only reject with a unanimous vote.

In practice, the Commission is generally inclined to incorporate amendments by the Parliament (in three out of four cases). The Council is much less inclined to adopt amendments and usually gives its support to roughly half of the Parliament's motions. This is due to the fact that the Council's debate commences prior to the Parliament's position being heard (almost concurrently with the Parliamentary debate) and, if the Member States

---

[16] In 1960, the Council first agreed to consult the Parliament voluntarily on legislative issues 'of importance'. In 1964 the 'important' condition was removed, hence the Council consults the European Parliament in practice on all legislative issues, even the ones not placed under the consultation procedure by the Treaty.

[17] In former times, the Council did not always wait for Parliament's opinion in all cases, and sometimes went ahead and took a decision without it. In the Isoglucose case of 1980, the Parliament requested the European Court of Justice to annul a Regulation that the Council had adopted without waiting for Parliament's position. The Court of Justice ruled that Council had to obtain Parliament's opinion before adopting a legal act, which changed the practical application of the consultation procedure.

reach an agreement, they are usually not too keen on reopening the discussions that have been closed simply to accommodate a motion by Parliament, as the compromises they make are often reached after very tough bargaining.[18] The fact that the consultation procedure is often coupled with unanimous decision-making in the Council impedes the incorporation of the Parliament's opinion into the hard-won agreements concluded between the Member States.[19] Nevertheless, the Parliament's bargaining position in consultation

The consultation procedure

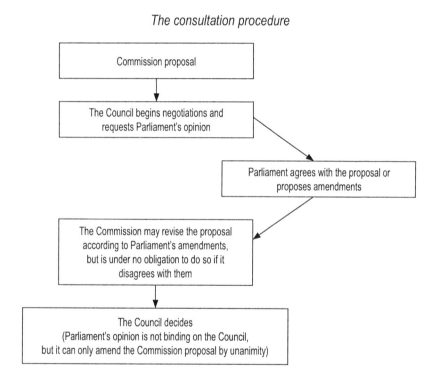

---

[18] However, should the content of the legislative initiative significantly change as a result of the Council debate, following the delivery of the Parliament's opinion, the Parliament must be consulted again.

[19] In the past, consultation was generally coupled with Council decisions based on unanimity and, despite the fact that the Treaty of Nice extended qualified majority voting over approximately 30 areas (the majority of which fall within the scope of the consultation procedure), a large proportion of consultation cases is still coupled with unanimous decision-making by the Council.

procedures has improved concurrently with the intensification of the Parliament's role as a co-decision-maker in other procedures. This is because the Member States are making an effort to consider more thoroughly the Parliament's position in order to facilitate easier agreement in areas falling under co-decision or assent, where Parliament's agreement is required.

For a complete list of areas under the consultation procedure, see Appendix III.

4.1.2.2. The cooperation procedure

It was the Single European Act that introduced the cooperation procedure, which allowed the Parliament a greater say in Community matters. Even though this was a marked improvement over having a mere consultative role, the Parliament did not become a legislative organ in the strictest sense of the word.

The 1987 introduction of the cooperation procedure was considered as a major step for the Parliament. Within the framework of cooperation, Parliament had the new right – compared with the consultation procedure – of receiving the legislative proposal for a second reading, this time with the Council's proposed version, also known as a *common position*.

During the second reading, Parliament has three options:

1. It can accept the Council's common position, in which case the Council only has to confirm its decision.
2. It can reject the common position by an absolute majority (with more than half of all its members voting in favour), in which case the Council can only adopt it by unanimity.
3. It can propose amendments, in which case the same procedure is followed as in consultation, i.e. if the Commission supports the amendments, they can only be rejected by the Council by a unanimous vote.

It is the possibility inherent in option 2 that really strengthens Parliament's role in the cooperation procedure compared to consultation: when elaborating its position, the Council has to take into account the fact that, if it fails to take on board enough of Parliament's amendments proposed in the first reading, it runs the risk of its position being rejected by Parliament. In such a case, the Council can then only adopt the common position – that is the new legislative act – with a unanimous decision.

Thus, although the Parliament is not yet an equal partner with the Council in this procedure, its power is demonstrated by the fact that if – following its rejection of the common position – it wins the support of a single Member State, its proposals will either be adopted or the entire act will have to be withdrawn. If Parliament proposes amendments again in the second reading, in effect it falls back upon the same competences as it has in the consultation procedure. The most noteworthy significance of the cooperation procedure is that it allows Parliament to set the agenda (since its proposed amendments are placed on the agenda), even though it has no decision-making power or the right of veto.

However, the importance of the cooperation procedure was reduced to a minimum owing to the Treaty of Amsterdam as, in accordance with the provisions of the Treaty, many of the areas that had previously fallen within the scope of this procedure were placed within the scope of the co-decision procedure. Since the entry into force of the Treaty of Amsterdam, the cooperation procedure – regarded as a milestone at the time of the Single European Act – has been applied only in four areas related to the economic and monetary union (EMU). When drawing up the Treaty of Nice, the possibility of abolishing the procedure was even discussed but, as certain Member States were reluctant to have the co-decision procedure introduced in the area of the EMU while others did not wish to return to consultation, the cooperation procedure was retained. In practical terms, however, this procedure is no longer used, as there have been no legislative acts in the area of the economic and monetary union since the introduction of the euro.

For a complete list of areas under the cooperation procedure, see Appendix III.

4.1.2.3. The assent procedure

The assent procedure, introduced by the Single European Act, essentially means that the Parliament has the right of veto in areas placed within the scope of this procedure by the Treaties. These are usually high priority areas in terms of the EU's development. Within this decision-making procedure, obtaining the Parliament's assent prior to the decision by the Council is a necessary condition for adopting a proposal on a specific matter. However, the Parliament is not allowed to submit any amendments during the procedure. Should the Parliament reject a proposal, the Council will not be allowed to vote on the proposal.

The assent procedure is not a standard legislative procedure. It is only applied in the case of some important decisions. For a complete list of areas under the assent procedure, see Appendix III.

There are two forms of the assent procedure. The 'yes' vote of the majority of the MEPs present (i.e. a simple majority) is generally sufficient for adoption. However, there are cases when adoption requires an absolute majority, which means that the support of more than half of all the MEPs is needed. An absolute majority is required in the case of accession treaties[20], decisions on situations where there is a risk that fundamental rights may be seriously breached, decisions on the existence of such a breach, and in connection with decisions concerning the establishment of a common European electoral system.

Assent provides the Parliament with quite significant decision-making powers as, without the Parliament, no decisions can be made in areas falling within the scope of this procedure under the Treaties. At the same time, however, these powers also have a rather negative effect, since the Parliament is not allowed to propose amendments to submitted proposals – it may only adopt or reject proposals. The option of choosing between 'yes' or 'no' is equivalent to the right of veto, and it is also a serious hindrance for the Parliament in view of the fact that Parliament's assent is imperative while, in the case of dismissal, Parliament must assume sole political responsibility for its decision. Consequently, the European Parliament, in the absence of any power to propose amendments, and because it does not want to be seen as adopting a negative attitude, endeavours to assert its position (in the form of preliminary decisions, statements or informal means, such as letters by its President or during discussions) by drawing the attention of the Member States and the Commission to those aspects that it deems important with respect to its assent. Thus, the Commission or the Member States have a chance to incorporate Parliament's key demands into the text they then submit to Parliament. In the case of certain international agreements (Association Agreements), this method was successfully applied by the Parliament to have its human rights related demands with regard to the partner country in question taken into account in the conclusion of an agreement, by simply setting these demands as a condition for its assent.

---

[20] With regard to enlargement, it is very important that the Parliament's assent is required for the Accession Treaties. The Parliament may assume its powers to this end in the first phase of the accession process, following negotiations, and after the full text of an Accession Treaty has been drawn up. The Parliament can then – prior to the final signature by the Council – adopt or reject the Treaty. If the Parliament rejects the Treaty, the document will not be submitted to the Council for signature. Should this be the case, the Treaty has to be re-negotiated, or to be more precise, the conditions laid down by the Parliament have to be met, in order for the Treaty to be adopted. Once this has taken place, the Treaty can be submitted again to the Parliament. Consequently, the European Parliament has quite significant powers with regard to the expansion of the European Union. At the same time, however, this role of the Parliament assumes significance only when the Accession Treaty is finalised, and it only concerns the adoption of the Treaty. The Parliament cannot intervene in the accession process and, until the stage of the final text of the Treaty its only option is to formulate a position. However, neither the Council nor the Commission are obliged to take into account the Parliament's opinion. Nevertheless, during negotiations, both the Commission and the Council have an obligation to provide information to the Parliament. The Parliament may request information on the course and status of the negotiations and the Council and the Commission must provide such information to the competent parliamentary special committees. This facilitates the Parliament's assent later on.

4.1.2.4. The co-decision procedure

The Treaty of Maastricht introduced the co-decision procedure in 15 Community areas. The procedure's significance was greatly enhanced later by the Treaty of Amsterdam, which placed 23 additional areas[21] under its scope. This in turn not only invested the procedure with a defining role but also consolidated the Parliament's status as a co-legislator. The Treaty of Nice carried this process even further, although not at the same pace as its predecessors. Even so, the new Treaty expanded the Parliament's co-decision powers to five additional areas and, in the case of certain social policy issues and first pillar justice and home affairs, also allowed for the prospective expansion of the scope of the co-decision procedure to additional areas, in accordance with the unanimous decision of the Council. In that spirit, the Council brought another five areas of justice and home affairs under the scope of the co-decision procedure with effect from 1 January 2005. For a complete list of areas under the co-decision procedure, see Appendix III.

The introduction and broader application of the co-decision procedure is of remarkable significance in the context of the institutional development of the European Union, because it was the co-decision procedure which made the Parliament a co-legislator of the Council. The scope of the co-decision procedure has steadily expanded, and correspondingly, the Parliament's role as a decision-maker has become increasingly strong. The significance of co-decision lies in the fact that it amalgamates the powers enjoyed by the Parliament in the assent, cooperation and consultation procedures. Parliament's role in the assent procedure is essential (it has a right of veto) but it may not introduce its own amendments, while in the case of cooperation and consultation, the Parliament may make amendments but it cannot act as a decision-maker. Within the framework of the co-decision procedure, the Parliament may make amendments, and its consent is also a prerequisite to making a final decision. Consequently, in the co-decision procedure, the Parliament acts as a co-decision-maker with a rank equal to that of the Council.

The Treaties (of Maastricht, Amsterdam and Nice) introduced the co-decision procedure in areas that directly concern the interests of citizens (e.g. free movement of workers, employment, social policy, public health, and consumer protection). Consequently, the participation of the European Parliament, and the strengthening of the democratic legitimacy of the European Union, which is realised through Parliament's participation, is particularly justified. The Treaty of Amsterdam made the co-decision procedure somewhat simpler; following the Treaty of Maastricht, the procedure was often criticised for being complicated. The simplified formula was conducive to the further consolidation of the Parliament's role, and it also made the procedure shorter, which in turn made co-decision by the Council and the Parliament more rapid.

---

[21] Out of these, 8 are areas introduced by the Treaty of Amsterdam (i.e. new areas that were placed under the competence of the Community) while the other 15 are areas that used to fall within the scope of the cooperation or consultation procedures.

Co-decision is a procedure potentially involving three readings, which can end after the first or second reading if there is agreement between the Council and Parliament.

In co-decision, as a first step of the procedure, the Commission forwards its proposal to the Council and Parliament. Simultaneous submission to both institutions is an important feature of co-decision, because the Commission must treat the two institutions equally in this procedure.
The debate on the proposal also begins in parallel in the two institutions but, officially, Parliament has the right to go first and decide whether it supports the Commission proposal as it stands, with amendments or not at all. The Council can start debating the proposal at the same time as Parliament, but can only make its decision once it has learned Parliament's opinion. The Council and the Commission have to inform Parliament or its competent committee regularly about the state of play of the negotiations (especially in the Council working groups). For the Commission, this obligation stems from the right of Commission officials to attend Council meetings.
The Parliament thus is the first one to deliver its opinion on the Commission proposal, which may also comprise proposals for amendments. Should the Council agree with the proposal from the Parliament, it may also adopt the act, which brings the procedure to a close. However, if the Parliament does not have the Council's agreement on every aspect of the matter (which often tends to be the case), the Council submits its own proposal, the so-called common position, to the Parliament. The Parliament considers the common position in a so-called second reading.

From the second reading – or more precisely: once the Council has adopted its common position – strict deadlines are defined for the procedure.[22] The Parliament must then choose from one of the following four options within a period of three months (extendable by one month):
1. not to deliver an opinion;
2. adopt the Council's position;
3. reject the Council's position, acting by an absolute majority;
4. propose amendments to the Council's position.[23]
In the first two cases, the legislative act is deemed adopted according to the text of the Council common position, and the procedure is completed.

---

[22] Since there are no binding deadlines in the first reading, occasionally it can last as long as a year or even years. However, once the Council has adopted its common position, the procedure must follow a strict timetable.

[23] For an amendment to be acceptable, it has to: be in line with Parliament's first-reading opinion (i.e. partly or fully restore EP proposals against Council's common position); be a compromise amendment agreed upon by the Council and Parliament; or be aimed at amending those parts of the Council's common position that concern issues not featuring in the original Commission proposal.

In the third case, the proposal is regarded as being rejected, the procedure is terminated without a result and the proposed act does not enter into force.

In the fourth case, after the Commission has considered the proposal, the Parliament sends it back to the Council, in effect for a second reading, which the Council has to produce within a period of three months (extendable by one month). Should the Council adopt every proposed amendment coming from the Parliament during this period, the act is final (according to the text of Parliament's opinion in the second reading) and the procedure is completed. If, however, the Council fails to agree with the Parliament on every aspect of the matter, then the special third reading begins.

In the third reading, a so-called Conciliation Committee is convened within a period of six weeks (which may be extended by two weeks). The Conciliation Committee is composed of the members of the Council (one from each Member State, generally deputy permanent representatives[24]) and an equal number of representatives of the European Parliament[25] from each Member State (currently 27). Representatives of the Commission also take part in the proceedings of the Committee.

The task of the Conciliation Committee is to establish a compromise between the two institutions within a period of six weeks (extendable by two weeks) and to adopt a compromise text, with the support of the qualified majority of Council representatives and the majority of MEPs.

The 6+2 week deadline for the Committee's work starts with the Committee's first meeting, but preparatory work begins earlier. The 6+2 week timeframe before the deadline for convening the Committee is already used for approximating the positions in the framework of informal so-called *trialogue* meetings between Council, Parliament and Commission. These trialogue meetings held before the first meeting of the Conciliation Committee often allow for a successful conclusion of the conciliation procedure during the first Committee meeting.

There are three possible outcomes of the conciliation procedure:

1. An agreement is reached, and the Conciliation Committee prepares a joint text, which is approved by the Parliament acting by a simple majority of the votes cast in plenary session, and by the Council acting by a pre-defined voting procedure (generally, by a qualified majority of the votes cast) within a period of six weeks (extendable by two weeks), after which the act shall be deemed to have been adopted, and the procedure is completed;

---

[24] Except in the case of the state holding the Presidency, since it is often the President of the Council, i.e. the competent minister of the state holding the Presidency, who participates in the meeting.

[25] The delegation of the European Parliament is set up in proportion to the number of seats held by each political group in the Parliament. In each case, the delegates are nominated prior to the particular conciliation process. However, three Vice-Presidents of the Parliament are permanent members of the delegation, appointed for this task upon being elected, and the Chairman of the competent parliamentary committee and the rapporteur on the subject matter are also members of the delegation. In practice, this means that decisions have to be made only with respect to the remaining positions (but in a way that, in the allocation of positions, the permanent members are also considered as representatives of the political groups).

2. An agreement is reached, but one of the two institutions fails to approve the joint text, thus the proposed act is deemed not to have been adopted, and the procedure is terminated without having reached a result;

3. Members of the Conciliation Committee fail to come to an agreement, the proposed act is not adopted, and the procedure is terminated without having reached a result.

Concerning the Conciliation Committee's work, it should be noted that the Commission's role in this stage of the procedure is more limited than in other procedures. The Commission may repeal the draft act at any point before the Conciliation Committee is convened if it cannot agree with the way in which it was amended (furthermore, the Commission's opinion delivered after the second reading can only be amended by a unanimous Council decision). However, once the Conciliation Committee is convened, the Commission's powers of influence are essentially exhausted. From thereafter, everything depends on whether the Council and the Parliament can come to an agreement, and neither of them is required to take into account the Commission's position when making a decision, relegating the Commission to the role of a mediator.

Initially, the co-decision procedure received a lot of criticism as, due to the lengthy conciliation process, decision-making became slower, while legislation was also delayed. In the beginning, the passage of an act took an average of approximately two years within the framework of the co-decision procedure (and, in some cases, legislation was even protracted for 3–4 years).[26] However, it must be noted that, in most cases, it was the adoption of the Council's position (i.e. reaching an agreement between the Member States) that took the longest time – and, generally, not because of the Parliament's involvement. But as the co-decision process was gradually 'eased', the length of the procedure was markedly reduced. In the case of legislative proposals published in 1997, the average time for adopting a proposal dropped to 344 days. This more expeditious decision-making process was consolidated by the Treaty of Amsterdam, which attached specific deadlines to each step of the procedure, thereby guaranteeing that matters already in progress would not be dragged out for years. The improved efficiency of the co-decision procedure is also corroborated by the fact that an increasing number of cases come to a close prior to the stage of conciliation, and there are also fewer cases that demand the convening of the Conciliation Committee.

During the roughly five-and-a-half-year period between the entry into force of the Treaty of Maastricht and the Treaty of Amsterdam (between 1 November 1993 and 1 May 1999), the Conciliation Committee had to be convened in about 40% of the cases[27], or on a total of 66 occasions. In addition, there were only three cases where the conciliation procedure was

---

[26] Even so, co-decision procedures proved to be substantially shorter than cooperation procedures; nor were they significantly longer than consultation procedures.

[27] A total of 165 co-decision procedures were completed within this period.

terminated without having achieved a result. The bargaining clout of the Parliament in the conciliation process is demonstrated by the fact that, in the 66 cases mentioned, out of the Parliament's 913 proposals for amendment, 711 (74% of the proposals) were incorporated into the acts during conciliation, and in a way acceptable to the Parliament.

Following the entry into force of the Treaty of Amsterdam, the efficiency of the co-decision procedure was further improved. In the 1999–2004 parliamentary term, the Conciliation Committee had to be convened in only 22% of the cases, while 28% of the cases were closed already in the first reading, which serves as proof of the fact that the average length of the procedure had been reduced even further. This was made possible by a significant increase in the scope of the procedure. Prior to the entry into force of the Treaty of Amsterdam, an average of 30 co-decision procedures had been completed annually, whereas in the first year following the Treaty of Amsterdam, this figure increased by 100%, to 65 completed cases. This proves that co-decision has become a routine procedure.

The efficiency of co-decision improved further in the years that followed. In the first half of the 2004–2009 parliamentary term, out of the 169 co-decision procedures concluded by 31 December 2006, 63% ended in the first reading and only in 6.5% of the cases did a Conciliation Committee have to be convened. This huge improvement was mainly due to intense use of informal trialogues in the first reading.

An important condition for the success of the co-decision procedure is that, in addition to conciliation with the Parliament, Member States should be able to reach an agreement on the act to be adopted. During the co-decision procedure, the position of the Parliament is presented alongside the respective positions of the Member States and it would be rather difficult to arrive at an agreement with the Parliament, if full consensus between the Member States were required; as a result, in accordance with the provisions of the Treaty, in the co-decision procedure, the Council generally acts by a qualified majority. There are only three cases where unanimity is required by the Council in the context of the co-decision procedure.[28]

---

[28] The exceptions are the following: Culture: incentive measures (EC Treaty Article 151(5)); Social policy: social security for migrant workers (EC Treaty Article 42) and the taking up and pursuit of activities of self-employed persons, training and access to work (EC Treaty Article 47).

The co-decision procedure

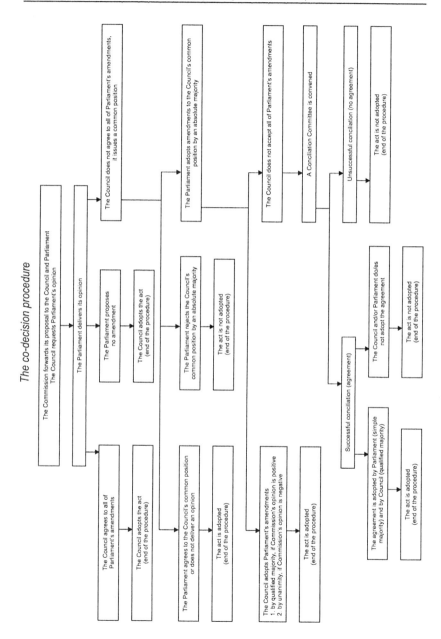

The Commission forwards its proposal to the Council and Parliament
The Council requests Parliament's opinion

The Parliament delivers its opinion

The Council agrees to all of Parliament's amendments

The Council adopts the act (end of the procedure)

The Parliament agrees to the Council's common position or does not deliver an opinion

The act is adopted (end of the procedure)

The Council adopts Parliament's amendments
1. by qualified majority, if Commission's opinion is positive
2. by unanimity, if Commission's opinion is negative

The act is adopted (end of the procedure)

The Parliament proposes no amendment

The Council adopts the act (end of the procedure)

The Parliament rejects the Council's common position by an absolute majority

The act is not adopted (end of the procedure)

Successful conciliation (agreement)

The agreement is adopted by Parliament (simple majority) and by Council (qualified majority)

The act is adopted (end of the procedure)

The Council and/or Parliament do/es not adopt the agreement

The act is not adopted (end of the procedure)

The Council does not agree to all of Parliament's amendments, it issues a common position

The Parliament adopts amendments to the Council's common position by an absolute majority

The Council does not accept all of Parliament's amendments

A Conciliation Committee is convened

Unsuccessful conciliation (no agreement)

The act is not adopted (end of the procedure)

4.1.2.5. Other decision-making procedures

In addition to the four legislative procedures, other decision-making procedures are also applied in certain matters.

In accordance with the Treaty, the European Parliament must be informed – within the framework of the so-called information procedure – about certain monetary and economic measures[29] taken by the Council (or the Commission). For instance, in accordance with Article 99(2) of the EC Treaty, the Council must inform the Parliament of the broad guidelines of the economic policies adopted by the Council acting on a recommendation of the Commission. One type of information procedure is carried out in accordance with Article 133 of the EC Treaty, concerning the Common Commercial Policy. Within the framework of this procedure, the Council must inform the Parliament of trade agreements concluded in accordance with Article 133; however, as the Council informs the Parliament only after the adoption of the agreement, the Parliament in practice has no influence in the matter.
Overall, the Parliament has practically no competence to stand up for its interests in the information procedure. In essence, this procedure guarantees that, in areas where Parliament is not involved in decision-making but which are closely related to other areas where it has significant influence, Parliament is kept informed of new developments. This is important for ensuring the transparency of Community decision-making.

The budgetary procedure, introduced by the 1970 and 1975 Budgetary Treaties, is also a quite unique decision-making procedure, which specifically deals with the Community budget adoption process, marking out in detail the tasks of the three institutions (the Commission, the Council and the Parliament). The preparation of the budget falls within the competence of the Commission. The adoption of the budget falls within the competence of the Council and the Parliament. In this procedure, as in the case of co-decision, the Parliament has both a right of veto and a right of amendment, which means that the Community budget can only be adopted with its agreement. In some areas, the Parliament's amendment capacity and options for modification are more limited, while in others they are greater, when compared to the Council. The course and features of the budgetary procedure are described in detail in 7.4.

---

[29] See EC Treaty Article 60(2) (measures against the movement of capital), Article 99(2) (guidelines on economic policies), Article 99(4) (the results of multilateral surveillance), Article 100(2) (grant of Community financial assistance to a Member State), Article 104(11) (Community measures in case of excessive governmental deficit in Member States), Article 111(1) (adjustment of the central rates of the ECU), Article 114(3) (setting up of the Economic and Monetary Committee).

The European Parliament may also participate in decision-making if the Treaty contains no separate provisions for this but the other institutions (i.e. the Council and the Commission) are willing to assume certain obligations. So-called Inter-institutional Agreements (IIAs) can be concluded by the common accord of the institutions. Within the framework of these agreements, the Council, the Parliament and the Commission undertake to engage themselves to facilitate certain relations and connections that exist between them. For instance, relations between the Parliament and the Commission (information flow, maintaining contacts between Commissioners and Parliamentary committees, comparison of the legislative programme, etc.) are also regulated by such Inter-institutional Agreements, which refine relations between the two institutions. But practical questions of the co-decision procedure not defined in the EC Treaty (such as coordinating the work programme of Council and Parliament and ensuring a smooth flow of information between the two institutions) are also regulated by IIAs.

Within the framework of Inter-institutional Agreements, they may even set up decision-making procedures. Thus, for instance, in 1975 the three institutions agreed on the possible applications of the so-called *conciliation procedure*[30], which is carried out between the Council and the Parliament, with the active participation of the Commission. The aim of the conciliation procedure is to have official positions reconciled with respect to those generally applied Community acts which have significant financial implications and whose adoption is not regulated by separate norms. The procedure was essentially introduced because the Parliament was invested with its budgetary powers around that time and a forum of conciliation was needed to avoid cases where the Parliament would have to reject the entire budget, due to the fact that, in the case of certain budget-related acts (where it only has rights of consultation), its opinion is not taken into account. Thus, the conciliation procedure essentially functioned as a kind of complement to the consultation and budgetary procedures. Within the framework of the procedure, conciliation was carried out in a Conciliation Committee, which was similar to the one involved in the co-decision procedure. However, that is where the similarity between the two procedures ends. Since the introduction of the now prevalent, more recent decision-making procedures (especially co-decision), the conciliation procedure, introduced in 1975 and successfully applied in cases in the seventies and eighties, is no longer used. The Inter-institutional Agreement concluded on 6 May 1999, which made inter-institutional consultation on the budget a general rule, can be considered as a kind of successor to the 1975 conciliation procedure. In essence, the 1999 IIA stipulates that, each year, the three institutions conduct consultation complementary and prior to the budgetary procedure. This is done in the form of *trialogue* meetings, where representatives of the three institutions set priority figures for the annual budget before the Commission adopts

---

[30] The final phase of the co-decision procedure is also called *conciliation*, which may create some confusion, thus it must be pointed out that the two are separate and unrelated 'conciliations'.

the first draft. During the course of the budgetary procedure, another three trialogue meetings follow, where the institutions are represented by the President of the Budget Council (ECOFIN), the Chairman of the EP's Committee on Budgets and the Commissioner responsible for Budgetary Affairs. On the whole, this type of consultation cannot be regarded as a separate decision-making procedure in its own right, as it merely complements the budgetary procedure.

4.1.3. The Commission as a delegated decision-maker – How comitology works

Within the framework of the legislative work of the Council, or of both the Council and the Parliament, it would be impossible to make the necessary decisions on every matter in every area. There are specific areas (e.g. measures concerning the adjustment of agricultural prices, setting rebates on exported agricultural products, licensing food additives, etc.) where smooth operation requires a decision-making process more continuous than that offered by the Council and the Parliament (or their meeting and operational mechanisms). Thus, such decisions and acts are adopted by the Commission, based on a broader skeleton act adopted by the Council or by both the Council and the Parliament. In such cases, the Commission essentially makes 'implementing' decisions in cases delegated to it by the Council or by the Council and the Parliament. The significance of these decisions is represented by the fact that there have been years when the number of norms (implementing measures) issued according to this method exceeded 4,000 (although this number has substantially decreased following the implementation of the Single Market Programme, currently totalling around 1,500 annually), while the number of acts adopted by the Council, or by the Council and the Parliament, approximately amounts to 'a mere' 3–500, annually.

However, the Council in many cases does not completely relinquish these normative decision-making tasks to the Commission, and it continuously controls or, in some cases, even vetoes such activities of the Commission. The Council performs these activities by means of various committees composed of the representatives of the Member States. In Community jargon, this procedure is referred to as comitology[31].

The establishment of such control committees, composed of civil servants from the Member States and chaired by Commission officials, had already started in the sixties in the area of agriculture and, later, it became common in the case of other policies as well. Eventually, in 1987, a Council Decision categorised the committees into the following three types: Advisory Committee (Type I), Management Committee (Type II), and Regulatory

---

[31] The term 'comitology' was coined from the word 'committee' and refers to the practice of using committees in the Council.

Committee (Type III), which offer three different levels of member-state control from weak to strong. With a June 1999 Decision, the Council simplified the system of committees even further: while earlier there had been two sub-types in the case of both the management and the regulatory committees (IIa, IIb and IIIa, IIIb), these were merged into one. In July 2006, a Council Decision amended the 1999 Decision and introduced a new type of comitology procedure, complementing the other three in the case of acts adopted through co-decision. The Regulatory Procedure with Scrutiny Committee is supposed to guarantee that not only the Council but also the co-legislator Parliament can control the implementation of legal acts adopted by co-decision and block the Commission's implementing decisions under certain conditions.

The European Parliament and Comitology

In terms of democratic supervision over the EU's operation, the participation of the Parliament in comitology is an interesting issue. Earlier, the Parliament was in essence totally excluded from the task of supervising implementing measures. Even though the Parliament had issued several warnings to the Council that the principle of democratic legitimacy was being violated in comitology (as the decisions made by the Commission's officialdom were subject to surveillance only by national officials) and that theoretically the Commission has a reporting obligation towards the Parliament (Parliament controls the Commission), the Council failed to involve the Parliament in the supervision of the implementing measures adopted by the Commission. As a result, the Parliament contested before the European Court of Justice how comitology functioned but the Court did not uphold the arguments of the Parliament.

After the introduction of the co-decision procedure, the Parliament was able to bring forth new arguments for seeking to become involved in the surveillance of implementing measures adopted by the Commission, claiming that the Community acts adopted during the co-decision procedure were not only acts of the Council, but also joint acts of the Council and the Parliament; therefore, the Parliament should also be entitled to carry out the surveillance of the tasks delegated to the Commission, which would also provide democratic legitimacy for the measures taken by the Commission. Although this argument was not clearly accepted by the Council or the Court, the Council eventually partly granted the Parliament's request, for the very reason that some acts could not be adopted within the framework of the co-decision procedure because the Parliament did not give its assent to the common procedure for the introduction of comitology. Parliament was particularly reluctant to give its assent especially to the setting up of Type IIIb Regulatory Committees, which restricted the Commission's role the most. The Parliament was not going to just sit back and watch the Commission having its hands tied by the increasing influence of the Member States.

On the one hand, to a certain extent it acted as an ally of the Commission, but on the other hand it did so in an attempt to increase its supervisory role over the Commission, using the principle of the Commission's reporting obligation to Parliament.

Finally, the disagreement between the Council and Parliament was partially alleviated by the December 1994 agreement between the Parliament and the Council, also called the 'Modus Vivendi'. While this agreement expanded the rights of the Parliament, it still did not make it an equal partner with the Council in comitology. In accordance with the agreement, the Parliament (or in practice, its competent parliamentary committee) must receive from the Commission the draft of every generally applicable implementing measure, and also the deadline for its adoption. Furthermore, the Commission must "take the utmost account of the opinion" of the Parliament, and also inform the Parliament of this. On the other hand, the Council may adopt a measure only after having informed the Parliament (namely its competent committee) and having laid down an acceptable period of time for the Parliament to formulate its position. Should the Parliament deliver a negative opinion, the Council undertakes to "make an attempt at" finding a solution. However, the Council was not legally bound to come to an agreement with the Parliament and MEPs could not attend Comitology meetings and thus control the Commission in parallel with the Council.

The December 1994 'Modus Vivendi' was eventually amended by the June 1999 Council Decision. This provided additional rights for the Parliament, especially with respect to acts adopted by co-decision. Firstly, the Decision abolished the Type IIIb Regulatory Committee that Parliament had protested against as unacceptable, as well as leaving only one type of Management Committee. Secondly, the Decision provided that the Parliament must receive the draft of all implementing measures to be taken within the framework of the act adopted by co-decision; furthermore, it must be informed of the agenda of committee meetings, and receive the minutes of the meetings.

The 2006 Council Decision further extended Parliament's competences. During the implementation of acts adopted by co-decision, the Parliament may carry out a Regulatory Procedure with Scrutiny Committee and veto the Commission's implementing decisions, but only if it believes that the proposed measures go beyond the implementing powers provided for by the act, are incompatible with its aims or violate the principles of subsidiarity or proportionality.

Despite these significant changes, the Decision did not entitle Parliament to direct participation in committee meetings and in the work of committees set up by the Council, which meant that Comitology committees remained bodies of the Council and Commission.

In accordance with the June 1999 Council Decision (1999/468/EC), the three types of Council Committees function as follows:

a) The Commission enjoys the largest degree of autonomy when the Council sets up an *Advisory Committee* (Type I). In this case, the Commission submits to the Advisory Committee a draft of the measure to be taken. The Committee delivers its opinion on the draft (it may also adopt the opinion acting by simple majority). However, this opinion is not binding on the Commission, which only has to take "the utmost account" of the opinion delivered by the Advisory Committee, and inform the Committee of this.

b) When the Council sets up a *Management Committee* (Type II), the Commission submits to the Management Committee a draft of the measure to be taken. The Committee delivers its opinion on the draft, acting by qualified majority. The Commission then adopts the implementing measure. However, if certain elements of the measure are not in accordance with the opinion of the Management Committee, they must be communicated by the Commission to the Committee. In addition, the Commission may defer application of the measure for a determined period (but not exceeding three months). The Council, acting by qualified majority, may of its own accord modify the Commission's measure within the given period of time. However, should it fail to come to an agreement with the Commission by the expiry of that period, the Commission's decision will take effect.

c) The Commission enjoys the smallest degree of autonomy in decision-making when the Council sets up a *Regulatory Committee* (Type III). Again, the Commission submits to the Committee a draft of the measure to be taken. If the Regulatory Committee supports the draft, acting by qualified majority, the Commission adopts the measure. However, if there is no qualified majority support in the Regulatory Committee, or if an opposing opinion is delivered, the Commission turns to the Council. The Council then adopts the proposal, acting by qualified majority, within the period of time laid down in the measure (which must not exceed three months), or it adopts a different unanimous decision. If, within that period, the Council indicates by qualified majority that it opposes the proposal, the Commission re-examines it, and re-submits it to the Council. However if, on the expiry of that period, the Council has neither adopted the proposal, acting by qualified majority, nor indicated its opposition to the proposal, the proposed measure can be adopted by the Commission and take effect. (In the case of Type IIIb the Council used to be able to block Commission decisions with a simple majority even if it could not agree on an alternative solution.)

Council Decision of July 2006 (EC/512/2006) added a fourth procedure complementing the other three in the case of acts adopted through co-decision: the Regulatory Procedure with Scrutiny Committee:

d) In the case of the Regulatory Procedure with Scrutiny Committee, the Commission submits to the Committee a draft of the measures to be taken. If the measures are in accordance with the opinion of the qualified majority of the Comitology Committee, the Commission submits the draft measures for scrutiny to the European Parliament and the Council. The European Parliament, acting by a majority of its component members, or the Council, acting by a qualified majority, may oppose the adoption of the draft by the Commission, justifying their opposition by indicating that the draft measures proposed by the Commission exceed the implementing powers provided for in the basic legal act, or that the draft is not compatible with the aim or the content of the basic legal act or does not respect the principles of subsidiarity or proportionality. If, within three months from the date of referral to them, the European Parliament or the Council opposes the draft measures, they cannot be adopted by the Commission. In that event, the Commission may submit to the Committee an amended draft of the measures or present a new proposal. If, on expiry of the three-month period, neither the European Parliament nor the Council has opposed the draft measures, they are adopted by the Commission.

Things get more complicated if the measures proposed by the Commission are not in accordance with the opinion of the Comitology Committee. In this case, the Commission submits without delay a proposal relating to the measures to be taken to the Council and forwards it to the European Parliament at the same time. The Council acts on the proposal by a qualified majority within two months from the date of referral. If, within that period, the Council opposes the proposed measures by a qualified majority, the measures are not adopted. In that event, the Commission may submit to the Council an amended proposal or present a new proposal. If the Council envisages adopting the proposed measures, it submits them without delay to the European Parliament. The European Parliament, acting within four months by a majority of its component members may oppose the adoption of the measures in question, justifying their opposition with the reasons already mentioned above. In this case, the measures are not adopted and the Commission may submit to the Committee an amended draft of the measures or present a new proposal. If, on expiry of the four-month period, the European Parliament has not opposed the proposed measures, they are adopted by the Council or by the Commission, as the case may be.

4.2. Decision-making in the second pillar

The operation and decision-making of the second pillar is described in detail in Chapter 23. This point outlines briefly the ways in which it differs from the decision-making of the first and third pillars.

Decision-making in the second pillar (common foreign and security policy), as regulated by the EU Treaty, differs from the first pillar; it uses the Union's institutional system but functions in the framework of intergovernmental cooperation. Thus, the main responsibility for operation and decision-making in the second pillar lies fundamentally with the Council and the European Council.

The European Council plays a lead role at the strategic level of the common foreign and security policy, defining principles and general guidelines for the CFSP (including issues with a defence implication) and formulating common strategies to be implemented by the Union.
The Council ensures unity, coherence and effectiveness of Union action; it adopts decisions required for operating the common foreign and security policy: joint actions, common positions and other decisions necessary for their implementation.[32]
The common foreign and security policy falls within the scope of competence of the General Affairs and External Relations Council. Its work is assisted by COREPER II and by committees set up specifically for the second pillar. The most important job of daily consultation is the task of the Political and Security Committee, assisted on defence and military issues by the European Union Military Committee and the European Union Military Staff.[33]

Commission and Parliament involvement is much more limited than in the first pillar. The Commission's right of initiative is not exclusive but is shared with the Member States. Every Member State or the Commission can put forward proposals to the Council concerning issues relating to the common foreign and security policy.

The Council Presidency consults the European Parliament on the key aspects of the common foreign and security policy and also ensures that Parliament's views are appropriately taken into consideration. This obligation to consult Parliament is much looser than in the first pillar or even the third pillar; it is a general obligation without any specific reference to individual decisions or deadlines. However, the Presidency and the Commission have to inform the Parliament regularly about developments in the Union's common foreign and security policy. Parliament can pose questions and make recommendations to the Council.
Decisions pertaining to the second pillar are taken by the Council acting in unanimity. The abstention of members present or represented by other members does not pose an obstacle to adopting a decision (this is known as *constructive abstention*). The abstaining Member State is under no obligation to apply the decision, but accepts the fact that the Union is bound by its decision. To a limited extent, qualified majority voting is also used

---

[32] For legal acts in the second pillar (general guidelines, common strategies, joint actions and common positions and decisions for the purpose of implementing the aforementioned), see 5.2.2.2.

[33] For more on the operation of these committees, see 23.6.

in the second pillar for implementing-type decisions of less importance.[34] Nonetheless, in such cases, any member of the Council can block a decision by objecting to the adoption of a decision by qualified majority on the grounds of an important, specified national interest. The qualified majority of the Council can then request that the issue be put to a unanimous decision by the European Council.

4.3. Decision-making in the third pillar

The operation and decision-making of the third pillar is described in detail in Chapter 24. Mention should be made here of the ways in which it differs from the first and second pillars.

The third pillar is regulated by the EU Treaty and covers police and judicial cooperation in criminal matters. According to the general rule, in this pillar any Member State and the Commission can initiate legislative acts. Thus – just like in the second pillar – the Commission's right of initiative is not exclusive, but is shared with the Member States.

Similarly to the second pillar, decisions are made in the Council, with a less determinant role assigned to the European Council, essentially confined to strategic guidelines.
In the third pillar, the Council can adopt common positions, framework decisions, decisions and conventions,[35] acting unanimously in all cases. The Council can only use qualified majority voting for adopting measures necessary for implementing decisions.
Police and judicial cooperation in criminal matters falls within the scope of competence of the Justice and Home Affairs Council. Its work is assisted by COREPER II and by the Coordination Committee (also known as the Article 36 Committee) set up specifically for the third pillar, whose work is supplemented by several other Council Working Groups.

In the third pillar, the European Parliament has a consultative role when the Council is adopting framework decisions, decisions or conventions. However, this right to be consulted is more limited than in the first pillar, because Parliament has to express its opinion on third-pillar issues by a deadline set by the Council, which may not be less than three months.

---

[34] For more on the use of qualified majority voting, see 23.4.

[35] On legal acts of the third pillar (common positions, framework decisions, decisions and conventions), see 5.2.2.3.

CHAPTER 5
EUROPEAN UNION LAW

5.1. The creation of a Union legal order

A binding legal system ultimately enforceable by public law enforcement authorities is the basis of the operation of every state. Even though the European Union is by no means a state, and has no public powers similar to those of states, the tasks it has been entrusted with are quite similar to tasks that are normally the responsibility of states. A legal system was necessary if the EU was to perform these tasks. The EU is not an international organisation in the traditional sense of the term, where states cooperate for common benefits; the EU is much more than that: it is a Community whose Member States have pooled some of their rights – with the tasks that go with them (such as policy-making and implementation), which are exercised jointly or by a Community institution.

The aims underpinning the creation of European integration, the European Community – which can be considered the core of today's European Union – are laid down in Article 2 of the EC Treaty. According to this Article, the Community shall have as its task to promote throughout the Community:
– a harmonious, balanced and sustainable development of economic activities;
– a high level of employment and of social protection;
– equality of men and women;
– sustainable (and non-inflationary) growth;
– a high degree of competitiveness and convergence of economic performance;
– the protection and improvement of the quality of the environment;
– the raising of the standard of living and quality of life;
– economic and social cohesion and solidarity among Member States.

In order to achieve these objectives, the signatories of the EC Treaty defined three tasks of outstanding importance for the Community: the establishment of a common market; the creation of an economic and monetary union; and the implementation of common policies and Community activities. A common market entails the free movement of goods, services, workers (and later, legal and physical persons) and capital; economic and monetary union means the harmonisation of economic policies and the introduction of a single currency, while the implementation of common policies and Community activities implies tasks such as the setting up of common external tariffs, agricultural prices and subsidies, establishing common environmental and consumer protection rules, or the common planning and financing of infrastructure developments.

As can be seen from the complexity of objectives set for and tasks (traditionally under state responsibility) transferred to the Community, these cannot be achieved and performed without an enforceable (binding) body of law. From the creation of the Community, there emerged – by definition – a need for a legal system to define the tasks and competence of both Community institutions and Member States, regulate the decision-making process and set up an independent judicial body to oversee the uniform interpretation and application of law. These were the reasons for the creation of Community law.

Community law, however, is simply one element, although a key one, of a working Community, which lays the foundations for the special character that sets the Union apart from other international organisations. In addition to Community law, common policies and Community activities are additional means for meeting the EU's objectives. Community law can be regarded as the basis of a functioning Community, while common policies and Community activities are more like a set of tools used to achieve Community goals.[1]

Community law and Community-level policies are, however, inseparable. It is difficult to see how these policies could be made to work in the absence of a body of legal instruments interpreted in a uniform way. A common commercial policy would be unworkable without uniform customs tariff rules, just as the common competition policy would be meaningless without a uniform regulation of state subsidies.

The creation of the European Union in Maastricht added to the complexity of the European legal order; second and third-pillar legislation together with Community law now form European Union law.

The goals of the Treaty on the European Union are, however, very similar to the objectives of the EC Treaty. In Article 2 of the EU Treaty, the Union sets itself the following objectives:

– to promote economic and social progress which is balanced and sustainable, in particular through the creation of an area without internal frontiers, through the strengthening of economic and social cohesion and through the establishment of economic and monetary union, ultimately including a single currency in accordance with the provisions of this Treaty;

– to assert its identity on the international scene, in particular through the implementation of a common foreign and security policy including the eventual framing of a common defence policy, which might in time lead to a common defence force;

– to introduce a citizenship of the Union;

– to create an area of freedom, security and justice, in which the free movement of persons is assured in conjunction with appropriate measures with respect to external border controls, asylum, immigration and the prevention and combating of crime;

– to maintain in full the '*acquis communautaire*' and build on it.

---

[1] Part II of this book covers common policies and Community activities.

Concerning the operation of European Union law, currently organised into three pillars, it must be noted that the legal order changes from one pillar to the other, with significant differences between the Community first pillar and the intergovernmental second and third pillars. Having regard to the fact that in practice the pillars often overlap, this chapter will deal with Community law and European Union jointly. Nevertheless, since the bulk of European integration happens within the first pillar, making Community law the most extensive body of legislation, and since it is mostly within the first pillar that the Court of Justice has jurisdiction, Community law is the most exciting part of the EU's legal system. That is why this chapter will mainly focus on Community law, providing a comprehensive overview thereof in 5.3. It is important to stress the difference between the concepts of Community law and European Union law; the two terms are not interchangeable and should never be confused. In this book, Community law only refers to the first pillar of the EU, i.e. the European Communities.

This chapter presents European Union law as things stand now. It should be stressed that the Constitutional Treaty signed on 29 October 2004 would have brought major changes in the Union's legal order. The ratification of the Constitutional Treaty was not successful in all Member States, which prevented its entry into force. Following the failure of the ratification of the Constitutional Treaty, the Heads of State or Government decided at their summit of 21–22 June 2007 to abandon the constitutional approach and put the EU on new foundations by the means of a Reform Treaty amending the current EU Treaty and EC Treaty. The Reform Treaty scraps many of the Constitutional Treaty's provisions, but takes on board a number of its provisions on the Union's legal order, which will bring significant changes in the Community legal framework upon the Treaty's entry into force. These provisions are presented separately from the current framework in Point 5 of the Annex for the practical reason that they will probably only come into effect in 2009.

5.2. Sources of European Union law

European Union law is based on various sources. The Founding Treaties of the European Union (the 'Treaties'), legal acts adopted by Community institutions, judgements and interpretative rulings of the European Court of Justice, international treaties concluded by the Communities and the Member States and general principles of law are all sources of European Union and Community law.

5.2.1. Primary legal sources: the Treaties

Among the legal sources, the Treaty on European Union and the three Treaties establishing the Communities, as well as subsequent amendments, occupy a central role. Collectively known as the 'Treaties', they established the institutions of European integration and provided a basis for the operation of the EU.

Treaties are always the products of so-called Intergovernmental Conferences (IGCs) among the governments of the Member States. An IGC can be considered as a series of traditional, diplomatic negotiations, where all the Member States are present as sovereign powers. As a result, all decisions must be reached with the agreement of all parties (consensus). Any treaty emerging as a result of an IGC must always be ratified by all signatories, in accordance with their own internal constitutional requirements. A treaty will not enter into force until ratified by all parties. Any amendment of the Treaties must also be agreed to at an IGC and ratified by Member States. Treaties are amended for two reasons: either when the content of the treaty is amended (extension of competence, the definition of new tasks or actions or the modification of existing ones); or when a new Member State is admitted (the most important changes affect the territorial scope of the Founding Treaties and the composition of Community institutions). Both types of amendment are prepared within the framework of Intergovernmental Conferences. In the first case, the IGC is attended by the Member States; in the second case it is attended by the Member States and the applicant country(-ies). IGCs producing amendments are conducted – in a legal sense – outside the framework of the EU, as, on the one hand, they are about how sovereign states should transfer part of their sovereignty to the EU, while, on the other hand, the Member States, in their capacity as subjects of international law, negotiate how the Union – in which they pool part of their sovereignty – should work in the future.

5.2.1.1. The concept of the 'Treaty' and 'the Treaties'

The European Union was founded on four treaties: the three Community Treaties, establishing the European Community (EC) (formerly known as the European Economic Community), the European Coal and Steel Community (ECSC) and the European Atomic Energy Community (Euratom), as well as the Treaty on European Union. It should be noted that the ECSC Treaty expired on 23 July 2002, having only been concluded for 50 years. Therefore, only three treaties remain in force, but they were all concluded for an indeterminate period. Despite the expiry of the ECSC Treaty, its provisions 'live on' within the EC due to the general common market effect of the EC Treaty. The financial implications of the expiry of the ECSC Treaty were dealt with in a Protocol annexed to the Treaty of Nice.

The previously four, now three treaties, are collectively known as the 'Treaties' in EU-jargon. 'Treaty' always refers to one of the three Treaties. In other words, if we use the term 'Treaty', it can refer to the EU Treaty, the EC Treaty or the Euratom Treaty, depending on the context in which the term is used. Without a clear reference, the term 'Treaty' refers to the EC Treaty in the literature on European integration. There is always an unambiguous reference if the author means the EU or the Euratom Treaty.

A clear definition of the 'Founding Treaties of the Union' is made even more difficult by the numerous amendments made to the four Treaties. The Treaty establishing the ECSC was signed originally as the Treaty of Paris on 18 April 1951; the Treaty establishing the EEC (later renamed EC) was first known as one of the two Treaties of Rome, the other being the Treaty establishing the Euratom, both signed on 25 March 1957. The Treaty on European Union was signed at Maastricht on 7 February 1992. These Founding Treaties were amended by various other treaties (e.g. the Single European Act or the Treaty of Amsterdam). Thus these subsequent treaties are not independent instruments; they are only treated as such because of the need to have all Member States sign up.[2] The new treaties are merely instruments amending or modifying the first three Treaties (the Treaty of Paris and the two Treaties of Rome) or the more recent fourth Treaty (the Treaty on European Union signed in Maastricht) and are not parallel effective instruments. New treaties always overwrite old ones. In other words, the Treaty of Nice is not a treaty in its own right, but an instrument containing amendments to the EC, the Euratom and the EU Treaties. The provisions of the Treaty of Nice are consolidated into these Treaties; the Treaty that has legal force is not the Treaty of Nice but the EC, the Euratom and the EU Treaties, as amended by the Treaty of Nice. In that sense, the terms 'Treaty' and 'Treaties' always refer to the amended versions of the old treaties, namely the provisions that are in force

---

[2] The Maastricht Treaty is unique among the Treaties due to its dual nature: it is a founding treaty (creating the Treaty on European Union) as well as an amending treaty (amending Community Treaties, for example renaming the European Economic Community as the European Community).

LIVERPOOL JOHN MOORES UNIVERSITY
LEARNING & INFORMATION SERVICES

at that time. These treaties are published in a consolidated form (Consolidated Treaties), and references are also made to the consolidated text. The Treaty on European Union provides some kind of framework for the relationship between the Treaties. The Treaty on European Union contains provisions concerning the EU as a whole (i.e. all pillars) as well as the second and third pillars. The Treaties establishing the three Communities, together with the amendments, are defined as three separate Titles within the EU Treaty. However, legally speaking, the Treaties of the Communities continue to function as separate, independent treaties.

The Constitutional Treaty, signed on 29 October 2004, would have put the treaty structure on a new footing upon its entry into force. One of the paramount aims of the drafting of a Constitutional Treaty was to simplify the Treaties both in terms of their structure and their wording. The Constitutional Treaty would have consolidated the EC Treaty and the EU Treaty into a single legal document, while bestowing legal personality on the European Union, abolishing the three pillar division, and thereby placing the EU in a single institutional and legal framework. Following the failure of the ratification of the Constitutional Treaty, the Heads of State or Government decided at their summit of 21–22 June 2007 to abandon the constitutional approach and put the EU on new foundations by the means of a Reform Treaty amending the current EU Treaty and EC Treaty. The Reform Treaty (similarly to the Treaty of Amsterdam and the Treaty of Nice) will not replace the current EU and EC Treaties, only amend them. The amending Treaty will also rename the EC Treaty the *Treaty on the Functioning of the European Union.*[3] The Reform Treaty will bring about some fundamental changes: it bestows legal personality on the Union and abolish the three-pillar division. These provisions are presented separately from the current framework in Points 3 and 5 of the Annex for the practical reason that they will probably only come into effect in 2009.

5.2.1.2. The nature of the Treaties: the framework treaty structure

Even to this day, the Treaties reflect the system laid down in the Treaty of Paris and the two Treaties of Rome. The aim of the most important of these three treaties, the Treaty of Rome establishing the EEC, was to ensure the free movement of goods, services, labour and

---

[3] It must be noted that the Constitutional Treaty would not have integrated the Euratom Treaty, which will remain an independent treaty in its own right even with the Reform Treaty.

capital and to establish a common market, which basically involved the extension of the sectoral integration brought about by the ECSC Treaty to the whole of the economy. The primary objective of the EEC Treaty was to establish a common market, but not all of its provisions were about the common market. The Treaty of Rome provided for the setting up of common policies and Community activities and defined economic and social objectives; conspicuously, it did not lay down specific measures but defined tasks and objectives, entrusting the Community institutions and the Member States with their implementation. The Treaty of Rome and its various amendments are like a programme, containing no detailed obligations, but instead offering an opportunity for the elaboration of various policies and the deepening of cooperation and of harmonisation. The policy content of the programme is rather varied: some objectives are fully worked out, together with deadlines, while others are surprisingly general. For this reason, it is not unfair to consider the Treaty of Rome and its amended versions as a framework treaty, in which the contracting parties – the Member States – entrust the institutions of the Community with drawing up the legislation necessary for implementing these principles. The Treaties thus provide a legal point of reference for future Community instruments that are adopted to achieve the objectives.

The Treaties, which are binding for all Member States after ratification, are referred to as primary legislation. Legislative powers conferred on Community institutions under the Treaties, in order to achieve the objectives, perform the tasks and carry out the programmes and policies laid down in the said Treaties, are defined as secondary legislation, which yield secondary legal acts. Secondary legislation is always based on the Treaties (or, more precisely, on the legal bases indicated therein); its purpose is to implement the provisions of the Treaties within the legal framework created by the Treaties. Community decision-making is effectively synonymous with secondary legislation. The decision-making mechanisms and the procedures were dealt with in Chapter 4.

5.2.1.3. The primary sources of law

The Founding Treaties, their amendments and other supplementary treaties based thereon are also known as primary legislation under the framework treaty structure. Secondary legislation consists of legal instruments based on primary legislation and produced by Community institutions (see 5.2.2.).

Primary sources of law, in other words the Founding Treaties and subsequent amendments, include (the first date in brackets is the date the treaty was signed, the second date is when it came into effect):

- The *Treaty of Paris* establishing the European Coal and Steel Community (ECSC) (18 April 1951; 25 July 1952)
- The *Treaty of Rome* establishing the European Economic Community (EEC) (25 March 1957; 1 January 1958)
- The *Treaty of Rome* establishing the European Atomic Energy Community (Euratom) (25 March 1957; 1 January 1958)
- The Treaty establishing a Single Council and a Single Commission of the European Communities – *Merger Treaty* (8 April 1965; 1 July 1967)
- The *Single European Act* (18 February 1986; 1 January 1987)
- The Treaty on European Union – *Treaty of Maastricht*[4] (7 February 1992; 1 November 1993)
- The *Treaty of Amsterdam* (2 October 1997; 1 May 1999)
- The *Treaty of Nice* (26 February 2001; 1 February 2003)
- The so-called *Budgetary Treaties* of 1970 and 1975, regulating the budget of the EU and amending the Founding Treaties, also belong to the category of primary legislation,
- as do the *Treaties of Accession* signed whenever a new Member State is admitted (Denmark, the United Kingdom, Ireland – 1972, Greece – 1979, Portugal, Spain – 1985, Austria, Finland, Sweden – 1994, Cyprus, the Czech Republic, Estonia, Hungary, Latvia, Lithuania, Malta, Poland, Slovakia, Slovenia – 2003, Bulgaria, Romania – 2005).

5.2.2. Secondary legal sources: Community legislation

Legal instruments implementing the principles, objectives and tasks laid down in the Treaties are referred to as secondary legislation. They are the products of the legislative work of Community institutions, as discussed in Chapter 4. The legislative work of Community institutions is regulated in the Treaties. The Treaties serve not only as points of reference, by defining what aspects should be taken into account when the Community draws up a new piece of legislation to achieve a Treaty objective in a certain field, but also establish the legislative procedure in all areas and define the role and tasks of the institutions, including which legislative procedure to follow (consultation, co-decision, etc.), or what type of vote the Council must take (unanimous or qualified majority).

---

[4] In addition to establishing the European Union, the Treaty of Maastricht also amended the Community Treaties. (One of its key amending provisions was renaming the European Economic Community the European Community.)

The significance of the EU's secondary legislation is highlighted by the fact that the Council on its own, or in conjunction with Parliament (in the co-decision procedure) adopts between 300 and 500 legal acts each year, in addition to the around 1,500 executive-type legal norms issued by the Commission in the framework of the implementing measures delegated to it (an annual figure of 4–5,000 was not unusual in earlier days).[5]

Due to the differences in nature and operation of the three pillars, the sources of law differ in each of the three pillars as laid down in Article 249 of the EC Treaty[6] for the first pillar, in Article 12 of the EU Treaty for the second and Article 34 of the EU Treaty for the third.

5.2.2.1. Legal acts in the first pillar

Article 249 of the EC Treaty differentiates between binding and non-binding legal acts. There are three types of binding legal acts: regulation, directive and decision. There are two types of non-binding legal acts: recommendation and opinion.[7]

A *regulation* is a legal act that has general application, is binding and directly applicable in all Member States; in other words, Member States are not required to issue a separate legal act, since the regulation becomes applicable in its entirety (with the same text) in the legal systems of all Member States when it takes effect. Regulations are adopted to lay down precise and detailed rules for a policy area. Regulations can be adopted by the Council, jointly by the Council and Parliament, the Commission and the European Central Bank.

A *directive* is a Community legal act that requires each Member State to which it is addressed to achieve certain aims but leaves to the national authorities the choice of form, procedure and instrument of implementation, in other words the way in which they wish to fit it into their legal system. Unlike in the case of a regulation, Member States are under a

---

[5] The number of legal instruments issued by the Commission fell due to the successful implementation of the Single Market Programme. The historic high point of 4–5,000 was typical at the turn of the eighties and nineties.

[6] Identical with Article 161 of the Euratom Treaty.

[7] The sources of law described in this chapter apply to the EC (formerly the EEC) and Euratom; the sources of law under the ECSC Treaty, which have lapsed, were somewhat different (see Art. 14 of the ECSC Treaty). As far as the ECSC is concerned: a 'general decision' was a near-equivalent of a 'regulation'; a 'recommendation' was similar to a 'directive' (in other words, they were legally binding); the counterpart of 'decision' was something called an 'individual decision'; non-binding legal instruments (soft law) under the ECSC were called 'opinions'.

legal obligation to adopt national legislation that conforms to the directive by a specified deadline (known as a *'transposition'* deadline). Member States are free to chose their method, it being up to them whether they wish to adopt a new legal act or amend an existing one, and to decide what kind of legal instrument they wish to adopt (law, decree etc.). What is important is that they achieve in their national legal order the aim laid down in the directive by the specified deadline. Directives are generally less detailed than regulations; their aim is to define general principles for the regulation of a certain policy area. Directives can be adopted by the Council, jointly by the Council and Parliament, and the Commission.

A *decision* is a legal act addressed to a specified entity concerning a specific issue. The addressee can be a state (often all Member States), a legal entity or an individual. Decisions can be issued by the Council, jointly by the Council and Parliament, the Commission and the European Central Bank. Decisions are usually administrative in nature, can pertain to specific issues (establishing a financial fund, granting permission for disbursement of subsidies from a Community fund, imposing fines and anti-dumping measures, etc.) or can be used in conjunction with the implementation of other Community legal instruments (in this case they usually contain normative rules).

In Community decision-making, it is possible to issue non-binding legal acts such as *recommendations* and *opinions*. A recommendation usually states what kind of action or approach is expected from the addressee, whereas an opinion usually sets out the position taken by the issuer, often at the request of a third party. Though neither of these instruments is legally binding, when deciding cases under Community law, national courts must take both recommendations and opinions into account, though not as legal norms; this is especially true if the recommendation was issued to help the interpretation of Community law. The European Court of Justice also takes them into account before delivering a ruling.

In addition to the legal instruments defined in the Treaty, mention must be made of *sui generis decisions*, which are usually without a specific addressee. These sui generis decisions evolved because Article 249 of the EC Treaty understandably gave a narrow scope of definition for legal acts, including decisions, without providing for separate legal acts for decisions of a certain type (for example, procedural or staff-related). Union institutions adopt their internal rules of procedure with the help of such sui generis decisions, and the President of the European Parliament also uses this type of legal instrument to promulgate the annual budget.

5.2.2.2. Legal acts in the second pillar

According to the provisions of Article 12 of the EU Treaty, in pursuing its objectives in the area of common foreign and security policy the Union has the following means at its disposal: to define the principles of and general guidelines for the common foreign and security policy, decide on common strategies, adopt joint actions, and adopt common positions.

The *principles* of and *general guidelines* for the common foreign and security policy, including matters with defence implications, are defined by the European Council.

The European Council also decides on *common strategies* to be implemented by the Union in areas where the Member States have important interests in common. Common strategies define the political guidelines to be pursued in relation to either a country, a region, or an international political problem. Common strategies set out their objectives, duration and the means to be made available by the Union and the Member States.

Joint actions are adopted by the Council. Joint actions address specific situations where operational action by the Union is deemed to be required. They lay down their objectives, scope, the means to be made available to the Union, if necessary their duration, and the conditions for their implementation. Joint actions commit the Member States in the positions they adopt and in the conduct of their activity.

Common positions are also adopted by the Council. Common positions define the approach of the Union to a particular matter of a geographical or thematic nature. Member States ensure that their national policies conform to the common positions.

As well as these four instruments, Articles 13 and 14 of the EU Treaty also refer to *decisions*, which are different from decisions in the first pillar, but which are available for implementation purposes. Article 13 (3) stipulates that "The Council shall take the decisions necessary for defining and implementing the common foreign and security policy on the basis of the general guidelines defined by the European Council", while Article 14 (2) reads "If there is a change in circumstances having a substantial effect on a question subject to joint action, the Council shall review the principles and objectives of that action and take the necessary decisions".

5.2.2.3. Legal acts in the third pillar

Under Article 34 of the EU Treaty, in the third pillar there are four types of legal acts available to the Council, which has exclusive competence for adopting legal acts in this area. These four types of legal acts are: common position, framework decision, decision and convention.

Common positions are adopted by the Council acting unanimously. The aim of common positions is to define the approach of the Union to a particular matter.

Framework decisions are adopted by the Council by unanimity for the purpose of approximating the laws and regulations of the Member States. Framework decisions – similarly to first-pillar directives – are binding upon the Member States as to the result to be achieved but leave to the national authorities the choice of form and methods. Framework decisions – unlike directives and the principles related thereto laid down by the Court of Justice – entail no direct effect.

Decisions are adopted by Council in unanimity, for any other purpose consistent with the objectives of the third pillar, excluding any approximation of the laws and regulations of the Member States. These decisions are binding but have no direct effect. The Council can adopt the measures necessary to implement these decisions acting by a qualified majority.

Conventions are adopted by the Member States in accordance with their respective constitutional requirements, which always makes the process a lengthy one. Since the Amsterdam Treaty, the Council has to set a time limit for Member States for ratification procedures. Conventions enter into force once adopted by at least half of the Member States. Conventions are adopted by unanimity, but implementing measures are adopted within the Council by a majority of two thirds.

5.2.3. Other legal sources

International treaties that the Community is part of (e.g. WTO Agreements, Association Agreements, the Lomé Convention) can also be considered as sources of Community law.
Other sources of Community law include agreements between Member States (but not international agreements between a Member State on its own and a third country).

Since the Communities have international legal personality, in a sense the general rules of international law (e.g. those applying to the conclusion of international agreements or immunity arrangements) can also be considered as sources of Community law.

The sources of Community law also include the unwritten rules of law, the so-called general principles, as the Treaties authorise the European Court of Justice to ensure that, in the course of the interpretation and implementation of the Treaties, the general principles of law are observed. Thus, in its jurisprudence and interpretations, the European Court of Justice takes into consideration general principles of law such as proportionality, the prohibition of discrimination or the presumption of good faith (bona fides).

Over the decades, the case law of the European Court of Justice has grown to play an increasingly important role as a source of Community law. Although case law is traditionally not considered a prominent source of national law in the Member States (with the exception of common-law countries), the practice of the European Court of Justice in its rulings is of outstanding importance. Due to the sometimes ambiguous wording of the Treaties, a number of principles of Community law (such as its primacy and direct effect) have been established by the judgements and interpretations of the Court of Justice. Thus, the judicial practice of the European Court of Justice, consisting of its judgements and interpretative rulings, can undoubtedly be considered a source of Community law.

5.2.4. The notion of the acquis communautaire

The entire body of Community law and elements derived from it are collectively called the *acquis communautaire*[8] or, in short, the *acquis*.

The *acquis communautaire* consists of norms and legal practice, including primary and secondary legislation, as well as all other legal acts, principles, agreements, declarations, resolutions, opinions, objectives and practices (including the practice or case law of the European Court of Justice) applying to the Communities, whether legally binding or not. The fact that the *acquis communautaire* includes both binding and non-binding norms is recognition of the fact that, in the evolution of law, certain legal acts first appear as non-binding declarations or recommendations, and only become legally binding later on.

It must be noted that the term '*acquis*' (without the adjective communautaire) is increasingly used to refer to the Union as such ('Union achievements').

---

[8] The term comes from French and literally translates to 'community patrimony/heritage'.

The notion of the *acquis communautaire* primarily appears in relation to EU-membership, since it encompasses the set of rights and obligations that Member States have to accept and apply. Consequently, the *acquis communautaire* is of key importance to countries aspiring to become members of the European Union, as a fundamental condition of accession to the EU is the recognition, acceptance, adoption and application of the *acquis*. Thus, the accession negotiations are always conducted on the basis of the *acquis*, and the entire accession process is mainly about the transposition of the *acquis* into the national law of the state seeking membership.

5.3. The features of the Community legal system

5.3.1. The relationship between Community law and international law

The law of the European Communities has created a new legal order different from both international law and the internal legal order of the Member States.
Even though, originally, Community legislation was created according to the standards of international law through treaties between states, it differs from international law in a number of ways. Unlike international law, which primarily regulates inter-state relations, with the states being the legal subjects, Community law comprises a full set of rights and obligations applying to the Member States, and private and legal persons within those States. Community law is binding on both the Member States and its citizens.
Another difference between Community and international law is that, while the latter is usually based on international treaties/agreements, the sources of Community law include the Treaties but also the Communities' own legal acts – secondary legal acts created by the Community institutions. Community law is a unique legal order that has its own institutions, legislative procedures and legal acts.
An unusual feature in international law lies in the fact that Community law has become an integral part of the legal order of the Member States, which the national courts are bound to apply.

5.3.2. The relationship between Community law and the national legal order of the Member States: the notions of primacy, pre-emption, direct applicability, direct and indirect effect

Community law has primacy (supremacy) over the national legislation of the Member States. Although this is not explicitly stipulated in the Founding Treaties, in its interpretative rulings, the European Court of Justice has clarified the relationship between Community law and national law, defining the primacy of the former. The primacy of Community law means that, in the case of a conflict between Community and national law, the former takes precedence.

The primacy of Community law was first established by the European Court of Justice in 1964 in *Costa v. ENEL*[9], when it made the important observation that, by creating a Community with its own institutions, legal personality and competences, the Member States have transferred sovereign rights to the Community (limiting their own sovereignty in certain areas) and have thereby created a legal order binding on the Member States themselves as well as on their legal subjects. In 1971, in *Commission v. France*[10], the Court of Justice pointed out that the competences conferred upon the Community cannot be reversed by means of subsequent unilateral measures. In 1978, in *Simmenthal II (Amministrazione delle Finanze v. Simmenthal)*[11], the ECJ confirmed the supremacy of Community law even more clearly by stating that Member State courts shall interpret national legislation in the light of the provisions of the *acquis*, safeguard the rights established therein and disregard provisions of national legislation which are inconsistent with Community law.

Community law enjoys primacy not only over earlier national law, it also has a limiting effect on laws adopted subsequently; thus, the Member States cannot amend or overwrite Community law by subsequent national legislative acts. National legislators cannot unilaterally amend or annul Community law.

Community law has priority over national law, irrespective of the level of the piece of national legislation in the country's legal order. The European Court of Justice has consistently upheld this finding and has, in fact, also confirmed the principle of primacy with regard to the relationship between Community law and national constitutions.

The principle of *pre-emption* is closely linked to the supremacy of Community law; the principle means that, in certain areas where Community legislation is exhaustive or in which the Communities have exclusive powers, no national legislation shall be adopted. There are pieces of Community legislation that specifically stipulate that, in the given area, Community law is exhaustive, but there are cases when the exhaustive nature of Community law is established by the European Court of Justice.

---

[9] ECJ 6/64.

[10] ECJ 7/71.

[11] ECJ 106/77.

Certain pieces of Community legislation are directly applicable in the Member States, i.e. no further national legislative action for transposition is required. Among secondary legal acts, the Treaty provides for the *direct applic*ability of regulations.

A significant part of Community law has *direct effect* in the Member States, which means that natural and legal persons can refer to Community law in national courts and request the court to base its decision on Community law. Similarly to the principle of primacy, the notion of direct effect was developed by the interpretative rulings of the ECJ.

The principle of direct effect was first identified in 1963, in the *Van Gend & Loos* case[12]. The action prompting this case was brought by the Dutch transport company Van Gend & Loos against the Dutch fiscal authorities for having imposed a customs duty on imports from Germany. This practice infringed the principle of the free movement of goods, or more precisely Article 12 of the EEC Treaty (currently Article 25 of the EC Treaty). Uncertain as to whether a legal person could refer to an Article of the Treaty, the Dutch court referred the case to the ECJ for a preliminary ruling. The Court of Justice ruled that Community law can have direct effect and that Article 12 is one of the provisions that has direct effect in the Member States.

Treaty provisions usually have direct effect, regulations practically always, while directives and decisions often have direct effect. However, direct effect is not automatic; it depends on the content (unambiguous and unconditional wording), nature and structure of the relevant provision of Community law. Pieces of Community law can have direct effect in two ways: 1) a natural or legal person can rely on Community law before a national court against the state ('vertical direct effect'); 2) in cases between natural or legal persons, the parties may request the national court to base its ruling on Community law ('horizontal direct effect'). A provision having vertical direct effect may or may not have horizontal direct effect, depending on its content.

The uniform application of Community law was aided by the ECJ's ruling in the *Marleasing* case[13] of 1990, which established the principle of *indirect effect*. The issue of indirect effect emerged in relation to the failure to implement a directive. The case was brought against the Spanish company, La Comercial Internacional de Alimentacion SA, by one of

---

[12] ECJ 26/62.
[13] ECJ 106/89.

its creditors (Marleasing SA), who alleged that the company in question was null and void. The main argument was that the memorandum and articles of association on the basis of which the company had been formed were not valid. This argument was justified according to Spanish civil law; however, Company Law Directive 68/151/EEC did not mention this ground as a reason for annulling a company. At the time when the main action was brought, Spain had not as yet implemented the directive. The European Court of Justice – introducing the principle of indirect effect – ruled that national courts had an obligation to interpret national legislation in the light of directives, which had primacy over conflicting national law, regardless of whether the national transposing legislation has been adopted or not. The Court of Justice based this obligation on the duty imposed by the EC Treaty on member-state courts to take all appropriate measures to ensure the achievement of the result envisaged by the directive (in practice irrespective of whether the directive in question has been transposed into national law appropriately or not).

The 1991 ECJ ruling in the *Francovich* case[14] can also be considered a milestone in the relationship between Community and national law. Andrea Francovich and his fellow plaintiffs brought proceedings against the Italian state for its failure to transpose into national legislation Directive 80/987/EEC, which stipulates the obligation to set up a guarantee fund to provide compensation to employees following the insolvency of their employer. In the absence of such a guarantee fund, the applicants could not obtain compensation following the bankruptcy of their employer. The ECJ ruled that Member States were liable for damage caused by their failure to implement Community law (by not transposing a directive). The Court of Justice held that, if natural or legal persons had no justified claim for compensation in such cases, the full effectiveness of Community law would be impaired. The significance of the Francovich case is that natural or legal persons may refer to Community law even when it has no direct effect.

5.4. Approximation of legislation in the EU

The need to align the legal systems of the Member States emerged as early as the foundation of the Community itself. The Treaty of Rome institutionalised the approximation of legislation as the main form of legal alignment of the Member States' laws and, under the

---

[14] ECJ 6/90, 9/90.

EC Treaty, the Member States have focused on the harmonisation of their national laws by removing major inconsistencies, rather than on creating a completely uniform legal system.

The EU requires the alignment of national legislation to the extent necessary for the proper functioning of the common (now single) market. Thus, the need for the approximation of legislation stems from the single market embodied by the four freedoms; the underlying objective of the approximation of legislation is to ensure equal competition and the unobstructed functioning of the single market by guaranteeing the same market conditions for the free movement of goods, services, capital and persons (prior to the Maastricht Treaty, 'persons' only extended to workers and legal entities).

The main instrument of legal harmonisation is secondary legislation, particularly directives, which can reconcile without major conflicts the dual objectives both of securing the necessary uniformity of Community law and of respecting national traditions and structures. A directive is binding on the Member States as regards the objective and deadline by which it has to be achieved, but leaves it to the national authorities to decide on how the agreed Community objective is to be incorporated into their domestic legal systems. It is the task of the European Commission and ultimately of the European Court of Justice to monitor the harmonisation of legislation, determining whether the form and methods used to transpose Community obligations into domestic law are adequate.
The Treaty of Rome did not stipulate the form of legal act that the Member States should adopt in transposing a Directive. Nevertheless, the Court of Justice has defined a set of criteria which such transposing legal sources must meet. They have to be general, binding and effective. Recently the approximation of legislation has been mostly done through Acts.

In the last four decades, there have been two generations of directives. In the early years, directives included rather precisely worded rules aimed at total harmonisation. However, the adoption of such directives was a lengthy and cumbersome procedure, and was sometimes even impossible, due to the clash of national interests. From the eighties, a new generation of more optional directives became prevalent. These ‚softer' directives gave the Member States more room to manoeuvre, making their adoption much simpler. The second-generation directives proved to be particularly productive and efficient in the accelerated legislative process following the adoption of the Single European Act. Even though they do not result in the unification of legislation, the significance of softer directives lies in the fact that they have enabled the Community to approximate the different national legislations in areas where harmonisation had been inconceivable before.

By amending the Treaty of Rome, the Single European Act introduced new rules that intensified the process of harmonisation of legislation. According to certain interpretations, the Single European Act added recommendations to directives as a means of legal alignment. It has to be acknowledged that, although recommendations have no binding effect and thus cannot be fully considered part of Community law, they do play a role in the harmonisation of legislation in areas where the use of binding pieces of Community legislation would be too premature.

Although not considered as legal harmonisation in the true sense, the Community legislative process achieved through regulations should also be mentioned, as it creates a closer link between the national legal orders of the Member States than legal harmonisation. The significance of regulations is that, instead of trying to align the national laws of the Member States, they create directly applicable and directly effective uniform Community law.

Although the approximation of legislation of the Member States is one of the EU's main instruments, harmonisation has certain limits, also acknowledged by the EC Treaty. Since national legislation may be stricter or regulate a given area better than Community law, in certain cases (particularly in areas of a non-economic nature), there may be a need to safeguard the integrity of domestic law *vis-à-vis* the *acquis*. Article 95 of the EC Treaty stipulates that, if harmonisation measures contradict higher-level legislation of a Member State, in certain cases the Member State may impose restrictions on the transposition of the Community act in question, with the approval of the European Commission. The areas covered relate to: public morality, public policy or public security; the protection of health and life of humans, animals or plants; the protection of national treasures possessing artistic, historic or archaeological value; or the protection of industrial and commercial property or environmental protection. The Commission investigates whether the national provisions are a means of arbitrary discrimination or a disguised restriction on trade between Member States. If this is not the case, the Commission approves the Member State's request for maintaining its higher level protective national provisions and proposes new Community measures to adapt to this higher-level legislation at Community level.

5.5. The Charter of Fundamental Rights

Parallel with deepening economic integration, intensifying single market law-making and creating the economic and monetary union, there had been growing criticism of the Union for adopting a mass of Community legislation affecting the daily lives of European citizens (from plastic softeners in children's toys to audiovisual broadcasting), while failing to produce any protection for the basic rights of citizens. The fundamental rights of Union citizens had never been summarized, even though respect for human rights and civil liberties had always been a cornerstone of the Union's construction.

The Cologne European Council of 3–4 June 1999 took the view that at the stage of its development, the European Union could greatly benefit from a Charter of Fundamental Rights setting out the basic rights that European citizens have in a clear format. The extraordinary EU summit on justice and home affairs, held in Tampere on 15–16 October 1999, acted by giving responsibility to a body for drawing up the draft Charter, which later on took the name of 'Convention'. The Convention[15] (composed of members of the national parliaments of the then 15 Member States, members of the European Parliament, representatives of the Heads of State or Government of Member States and the responsible European Commissioner) drafted the EU Charter of Fundamental Rights by the end of 2000; the Charter was proclaimed at the Nice European Council on 7–10 December 2000 by a Joint Declaration of the Member States, the Parliament and the Commission. However, the text was not incorporated into the Treaties at the time; decisions concerning the Charter's legal status and its place in Community law were postponed. Consequently, the Charter remained a non-binding text, a mere political declaration.

The key significance of the Charter of Fundamental Rights, which was proclaimed in Nice, is that it consolidates the various principles present in national and international law – hitherto fragmented – into a single document. Its novelty lies in the fact that it includes all personal rights. The Charter, contrary to the previous practice of many similar European and international documents, does not separate civil and political rights from economic and social rights. Instead, it organises various rights around fundamental principles.

The Charter includes 54 Articles, most of which are a collection of rights borrowed from various sources. The 1950 European Convention on Human Rights ('Convention for the Protection of Human Rights and Fundamental Freedoms') of the Council of Europe forms

---

[15] Due to its success, it served as a model for the Convention on the future of Europe, which drafted the Constitutional Treaty.

the backbone of the document, but the Charter is more comprehensive than the Convention, since it draws on other sources too (the constitutional traditions and international obligations of the Member States, the EU Treaty, the EC Treaty, the Social Charters of the Council of Europe and the European Union, and the jurisprudence of international courts and tribunals) and it deals with not only classic human rights but also certain economic and social rights (the latter provoking opposition in Nice to the adoption of the Charter as a legally binding document).

The Charter consists of a Preamble and seven Chapters. The Preamble sets out the values and principles on which the Charter is based, as well as the objectives it seeks to achieve. It professes that a peaceful future of the Union should be built on the common universal values of human dignity, freedom, equality and solidarity. It is through respect for these values that one of the Union's long term aims can be achieved and an area of freedom, security and justice can be created. While these are common values, the cultural diversity of the Union must be preserved. The seven chapters that follow the Preamble cover the following areas: *dignity, freedoms, equality, solidarity, citizens' rights, justice, general provisions.*

The Charter organises fundamental rights into a hierarchy. Firstly, it states that human dignity is inviolable and that everyone has the right to life. These absolute rights are followed by freedoms offering the individual protection against groups and third persons. Some of the traditional political rights and civil liberties can be limited under certain conditions (e.g. the freedom of assembly and association or the freedom of expression may be restricted for the sake of public security, public morals or public health). Economic and social rights come next, which presuppose active action by the state, such as the provision of a high level of social protection. The Charter also lays down rights that had never been recognised and guaranteed as fundamental rights before, such as the right to good administration, the right to the protection of personal data and rights related to bio-ethics.

When it was proclaimed in Nice in 2000, not only was the Charter not incorporated into the EU Treaty or the EC Treaty, and thus did not become legally binding, but neither was any reference to it included in the Treaties, contrary to what the Parliament, the Commission and several Member States would have liked. Some countries, such as the United Kingdom, feared that if the charter became legally binding, it would create new legal obligations that would undermine their national sovereignty. The British anxiety was that the incorporation of the Charter into the Treaties would reinforce the role of the Union vis-à-vis the Member States in the area of civil liberties and social policy. Thus, following its proclamation in Nice, the Charter can really be considered no more than a political declaration, which means that it may be taken into account by the European Court of Justice, but is not legally binding.

However, the Convention and the subsequent IGC incorporated the Charter of Fundamental Rights into the Constitutional Treaty as Part II. Therefore, if the Constitutional Treaty had entered into force, the fundamental rights of the citizens of the Union would have been defined in the principal legal act of the Union for the first time in the history of European integration. The Reform Treaty amending the current EU and EC Treaties and replacing the Constitutional Treaty – as one of the key elements of the compromise between the Member States – will not integrate the Charter into the Treaties formally. In a cross-reference, however, it will acknowledge the rights enshrined in the Charter, and thus the Charter will probably become legally binding with the Reform Treaty's entry into force – foreseen for 2009. This also means that the respect and promotion of those rights and freedoms will have to be guaranteed during the Union legislative process and interpreted by Member-State courts and the Court of Justice, albeit with some limitations. Therefore it must be noted that the Charter still does not create a legal basis for the adoption of Union legal acts, and does not create new competences or tasks either. As far as the United Kingdom is concerned, the Charter can only take effect with strict limitations as – in practice – it cannot be directly enforced in British courts.[16]

---

[16] For the relevant provisions of the Constitutional Treaty and of the Reform Treaty, see Annex, Point 5.5.

CHAPTER 6
THE SINGLE MARKET AND THE FOUR FREEDOMS

The fundamental aim of establishing the European Economic Community was to create a common market of its Member States. The common market – replaced by the concept and objective of a single market or internal market after the Single European Act – is, and has always been, the fundamental motivation for European integration, taking primacy over all other ends.

The common market is an area where *goods, services, capital* and *workers* move freely without any restrictions. Following the Treaty of Maastricht, the principle of free movement was extended from workers to persons in general.
Although the Community was supposed to complete the building of a common market in the '70s, that aim was only partially accomplished. Therefore the programme of the single market outlined in the Single European Act (SEA), signed on 18 February 1986, was aimed at achieving the four fundamental freedoms through the dismantling of various obstacles which still remained: physical (frontier formalities and border controls), financial (budgetary and tax rules) and technical (differences in Member-State legislation, standards and other rules). The creation of the single market necessitated the application of many deregulatory measures by the Member States as well as the adoption of about 300 pieces of Community legislation by 1 January 1993, the deadline set by the SEA for the completion of the internal market. However, the legislative process related to the single market continues even today.

To guarantee the 'four fundamental freedoms' (the free movement of goods, services, persons and capital), a comprehensive legal framework was needed between the Member States, which originally had different regulatory systems and traditions. As guaranteeing the single market and the four freedoms was the pivotal aim of European integration, it is not surprising that Community legislation related to these areas provides the backbone of the *acquis communautaire*. Both the EC Treaty and secondary legal acts focus primarily on ensuring the efficient functioning of the single market. The four fundamental freedoms are guaranteed on the one hand by negative integration, that is, through the dismantling of factors that hinder free movement, and on the other hand by positive integration, that is through the adoption of common rules, common policies and Community actions. It needs to be added that the building of the single market is a process that is still continuing, and it will probably take a long time until it is completed. Although the *acquis communautaire* now extends to a wide range of areas, ensuring a single or harmonised legal framework, there are still a number of major obstacles to the full implementation of the single market. There are several financial, technical, legal or administrative regulations rooted in the differences in taxation systems, standards, state or national traditions that prevent the European Community from fully realising the dream of the single market.

This chapter provides an overview of the instruments that ensure the four fundamental freedoms in practice, of the functioning of the single market and of the achievements of the last 50 years of integration.

6.1. The free movement of goods

The essence of the concept of a single market is that the EU is a single economic area, functioning similarly to a national market. Thus the free movement of goods is possibly the most fundamental element of not only the single market, but also the Community as such. The free movement of goods (which is about free trade within the EU), is guaranteed by the creation of a customs union and the abolition of quantitative restrictions between Member States.

6.1.1. Establishing the customs union

The customs union means the elimination of customs duties and charges having equivalent effect to customs duties within the Community, as well as the pursuance of a common commercial (or trade) policy[1] based on common customs tariffs applied vis-à-vis third countries.

6.1.1.1. The abolition of customs duties and charges having equivalent effect

In order to achieve the aim of a customs union, as enshrined in the Treaty of Rome, the Member States abolished existing (and refrained from introducing new) customs duties and charges having equivalent effect levied on trade between each other. The Council Decision of 26 July 1966[2] set the deadline of 1 July 1968 for achieving that aim and this date was observed.

Discriminatory taxation is also prohibited in the EU, which means that a Member State cannot directly or indirectly levy higher taxes on products coming from another Member State.

---

[1] For more on the Common Commercial Policy, see Chapter 9.2.

[2] Decision 66/532/EEC

There are, however, three exceptions when charges having equivalent effect may be levied. In certain exceptional cases (with strictly defined conditions), Member States may levy charges on importers or exporters if the authorities provide essential services of a general interest to them (e.g. phytosanitary tests). A similar case is when a Community system (e.g. the common agricultural policy) necessitates the levying of such charges on exporters or importers. The third (strictly defined) exception concerns levies on foreign products that have no domestic competition or no similar domestic substitutes, and thus the aim of the levy is clearly not to protect domestic producers or limit competition.

6.1.1.2. The system of Common Customs Tariff

In addition to the abolition of customs duties and charges having equivalent effect, the setting up of a Common Customs Tariff (or Common External Tariff) forms another important element of the customs union. The Common Customs Tariff is the main instrument for regulating trade with third countries. The Common Customs Tariff means that the customs duty levied on a product from a third country is the same, irrespective of which Member State imports the product, and that once the customs duty has been levied in one Member State, the product can be freely transported to any other Member State. Collected customs duties are paid into the Community budget, and not into the budget of the collecting country. However, Member States can keep part of the collected customs duties for administrative costs. (This ratio used to be 10%, but was changed to 25% from 2001.) Common customs tariffs are thus a precondition for guaranteeing the free movement of goods within Member States. The Common Customs Tariff was originally set in a Council Regulation in 1968, which, of course, has been subsequently amended and updated several times.[3] This Council Regulation is put into effect by the Commission in the form of implementing regulations, which for example set the exact rate of tariffs. In addition to setting common tariffs, the Member States have also harmonised their customs regulations and procedures, simplified border control formalities and developed forms of cooperation in the field of customs.

---

[3] The original Regulation 950/68/EEC was replaced in 1987 by Regulation 2658/87/EEC, which is also regularly updated.

6.1.2. Abolition of quantitative restrictions and removal of measures with equivalent effect

In order to guarantee the free movement of goods, in addition to the removal of customs duties, quantitative restrictions (trade and customs quotas) and measures with equivalent effect also had to be prohibited. Thus the Treaty of Rome provided for their elimination. While the removal of quantitative restrictions, just as in the case of customs duties, was relatively easy (quotas were removed by 31 December 1961), the elimination of measures with equivalent effect to quantitative restrictions posed serious difficulties and continues to do so even today, because such measures appear in diverse forms in individual Member States and have proved to be one of the most effective instruments of restricting trade.

For a long time, even attempting to define measures with equivalent effect was problematic. Originally, the Commission derived the ban on such measures from a 1970 Directive[4]. This Directive prohibited all national measures that did not create an equal framework for imported and domestic products or that made imports from other Member States more costly or difficult. Finally, in its ruling in the *Dassonville case*[5] of 1974, the European Court of Justice gave a uniform definition of the concept of measures with equivalent effect to quantitative restrictions, which was wider than the scope of the Directive.[6] In this particular case, the Belgian Public Prosecutor had brought criminal proceedings against a French trader called Dassonville, who had imported a consignment of Scotch whisky from France to Belgium without having a valid certificate of origin issued by the British customs authorities, as was required by Belgian law. The Court discovered that it was very difficult for someone importing whisky from a country other than the United Kingdom to obtain such a certificate, and therefore this requirement impeded trade, and was thus considered a measure with equivalent effect to a quantitative restriction. The ECJ took advantage of this opportunity to set down a general formula defining the scope of the concept of measures with equivalent effect to quantitative restrictions: "All trading rules enacted by Member States which are capable of hindering, directly or indirectly, actually or potentially, intra-Community trade are to be considered as measures having an effect equivalent to quantitative restrictions." This has become known as the *'Dassonville formula'*.

---

[4] Directive 70/50/EEC.

[5] European Court of Justice, Case 8/74.

[6] The definition of the Court of Justice prohibited not only differences in conditions for domestic and imported products, but also any differentiation between importers.

However, there is an exception to the ban on imposing restrictions on trade. Article 30 (ex Article 36) of the EC Treaty stipulates that the prohibition of quantitative restrictions and measures with equivalent effect shall not preclude restrictions on grounds of: public morality, public policy or public security; the protection of health and life of humans, animals or plants; the protection of national treasures possessing artistic, historic or archaeological value; or the protection of industrial and commercial property. Article 30 also stipulates that such measures shall not constitute a means of arbitrary discrimination or a disguised restriction on trade between Member States. Following the rulings of the European Court of Justice, restrictions within these categories may only be applied if they are proportionate to the objective to be achieved, namely that the objective could not be achieved by less restrictive means.

Another landmark ruling of the ECJ was in the so-called *Cassis de Dijon*[7] case of 1979, which – together with the *Dassonville formula* – was a milestone not only in the removal of trade barriers, but also in the entire process of the approximation of legislation. It arose when a German firm was refused permission to import a consignment of French *Cassis de Dijon* liqueur because of its inadequate alcoholic strength (15–20%). This rendered it incompatible with German legislation, which fixed a minimum alcohol percentage of 25% for fruit-based liqueurs. The case was brought before the ECJ, where the German authority argued in its defence that if it gave up its stricter regulations, it would have to align itself with the lowest common standards in the Community. Another argument raised by the defence and refuted by the Court was that there was an issue of public policy to consider, in that fixing a minimum alcohol content for liqueurs discouraged the proliferation of alcoholism among young people. The Court did not accept these arguments[8], and gave a ruling that was to have a profound impact on the *acquis communautaire*: the Court ruled that a product which has been lawfully produced and marketed in one Member State should be able to circulate lawfully throughout the entire Community. (This is known as the *principle of equivalence*). The *Cassis de Dijon* judgment pioneered the concept of *mutual recognition*, which means that obstacles to movement within the Community resulting from disparities between national laws must be accepted only insofar as those provisions are recognised by the ECJ as being necessary in order to satisfy mandatory requirements relating in particular to the effectiveness of fiscal supervision, the protection of public health, the fairness of commercial transactions and the protection of the consumer.

---

[7] European Court of Justice, Case 120/78.
[8] The Court of Justice pointed out that the indication of a product's origin and alcohol content on its packaging and labelling sufficiently informs the consumers, and thus it meets the condition of protecting public interest, consequently the placing on the market of a product cannot be restricted on those grounds.

The possible restrictions listed in the *Cassis de Dijon* judgment are generally referred to as *mandatory requirements*, which should be strictly distinguished from the general and permanent exemptions from the prohibition of measures having equivalent effect to quantitative restrictions, listed in Article 30 (ex Article 36) of the Treaty. Mandatory requirements set by the Court are not valid forever but only until Community legislation covers the relevant field (thus different protective measures by Member States are only acceptable until then). A Member State can refer to mandatory requirements in cases when national measures apply without distinction to imported and domestically produced goods alike. The Member State also has to be able to demonstrate that it restricts trade because the protection offered by the legislation in the country of origin of the product in question is in some way inferior to the level of protection that its own laws provide for consumers. (Germany failed to prove this in the *Cassis de Dijon* case.) The temporary nature of mandatory requirements is indicated by the Court's subsequent decisions, which extended their scope.[9]

The *Cassis de Dijon* ruling put an end to the Member States' practice of protecting their national products with various rules and standards. The principle of mutual recognition mounted an attack against protectionist national trade regulations and can be considered a turning point in establishing the truly unrestricted and free movement of goods. Mutual recognition effectively became a new harmonisation mechanism in Community law.
Mutual recognition however does not mean that Member States have to adjust to the lowest national standards and requirements. The aim of the continuous exercise of extensive and thorough approximation of standards and technical specifications is to provide a solution to this problem. The Community is particularly active in laying down common framework rules for safety requirements[10]. The enforcement of these rules is monitored by the Commission. This ensures confidence in the quality, reliability and effectiveness of quality control conducted by other Member States, which forms the basis for the practical implementation of mutual recognition. Member States must always inform the Commission in advance if they wish to introduce new standards or regulations.

---

[9] Based on the case law of the European Court of Justice, such areas include environmental protection (Case 302/86 Commission v. Denmark), support for the protection of culture (Cases 60, 61/84 Cinéthèque) and the protection of the freedom of press (Case 368/95 Familiapress v. Bauer Verlag).

[10] For instance, food safety and chemical safety are particularly important areas for Community-level regulations.

6.2. The free movement of persons

The universal right of free movement was not enshrined in the Treaty of Rome. In line with the main underlying objective of ensuring the proper functioning of the single market, the original Treaty only provided for the free movement of economically active persons (employees, self-employed people and service providers) and their families. This changed gradually over the years and, finally, the Treaty of Maastricht introduced the freedom of movement as a fundamental right that all EU citizens have, irrespective of whether they have an economic activity. There are still different rules for various groups, depending on the economic nature of their activities, if any.

6.2.1. The free movement of economically active, wage-earning persons

Three different freedoms apply to people taking up residence in another Member State for the purposes of work: the free movement of workers for employees, the freedom of establishment for self-employed people and the freedom to provide services for service providers. Nonetheless, the free movement of these three groups is based on the same underlying principle: *non-discrimination*. This means, for instance, that workers or self-employed entrepreneurs from other Member States have the same rights as those of the host state. It should be added, however, that the three freedoms – the free movement of workers, the freedom of establishment and the freedom to provide services – are not unlimited rights. They only mean that natural or legal persons of all Member States are entitled to equal treatment irrespective of their nationality or country of origin. The following two points outline the principles and rules that apply to workers and self-employed people. For more on the freedom to provide services, see 6.3.

6.2.1.1. The free movement of workers

The freedom of movement for workers is a fundamental pillar of European integration. Extending the conditions of labour mobility, on the one hand, expands employment opportunities and, on the other hand, makes it easier for employers to find people with the right qualifications and experience; this ultimately improves the employment situation and the efficiency of the economy in the Union as a whole. That is why the mobility of workers has been a key issue from the very beginning of the Communities. Nonetheless, the creation of specific conditions and the dismantling of various barriers in the Member States was a long and slow process. Even today, a mere 2% of the EU's active population works in another Member State.

The free movement of workers can be hampered by three conditions: 1) discrimination between workers based on nationality; 2) legislation or administrative action that sets different conditions for workers from different Member States; 3) the lack of coordination between social security systems. Thus, both the EC Treaty and subsequent Community legislation have been aimed at the abolition of such barriers. In addition to the prohibition of discrimination, in order to ensure the free movement of workers, Article 39 expressly stipulates the key rights of workers of the Member States, which are:
 – to accept actual offers of employment;
 – to move freely within the territory of Member States for the purpose of (seeking) employment;[11]
 – to stay in a Member State for the purpose of employment in accordance with the same provisions laid down by law, regulation or administrative action as those governing the employment of nationals of that State;
 – to remain in the territory of a Member State after having been employed in that State, subject to conditions embodied in relevant Community regulations.
The anti-discriminatory provisions of Article 39 also prohibit discrimination between workers from different Member States in terms of remuneration (including social and tax benefits), or any other conditions of work and employment.
Under the secondary legislation of the Union, workers are entitled to bring with them their spouses and dependants (or children under the age of 21), even if they are not nationals of any Member State.

However, the principle of the free movement of workers would not be very useful if workers lost their rights to social security benefits when moving from one Member State to another. For this reason, Article 42 of the EC Treaty stipulates that migrant workers can "carry over" the rights acquired (and the amounts accumulated, which are added to their entitlements in other Member States). This means that pensions are calculated aggregately on the basis

---

[11] According to the position of the European Court of Justice, EU citizens may stay within another Member State for a period of six months for the purpose of seeking employment.

of all entitlements in various Member States. Taking up employment in another Member State is also facilitated by the fact that workers can avoid not only double taxation, but also having to pay social security contributions in more than one Member State.

The aim of the Treaty is clearly not to harmonise the social security systems of the Member States (they remain completely under national competence), but to create the necessary coordination between – and interoperability of – those systems. The Treaty made this a task for Community legislation, on the basis of which the Council has adopted several regulations.[12] Council regulations are aimed at regulating the following areas: sickness pay, maternity allowance, family benefit, unemployment benefit, invalidity benefit, old-age pension, surviving spouse's pension, benefits payable for industrial accidents or occupational illnesses and death grants. Workers (in an employed or self-employed capacity) as well as their family members are entitled to social security benefits.

However, there are exemptions from the free movement of workers, whereby the Treaty allows for certain restrictions against foreign workers (from another Member State).[13] According to Article 39 of the EC Treaty, such restrictions must be justified on grounds of public policy, public security or public health. Article 39 also allows for limitations to be applied in relation to a state's public service. However, this does not mean that citizens of other Member States cannot be employed in the public service or that the employment of foreign citizens can be prohibited in every case. On the contrary, such limitations can only be an exception to the rule and have to be properly justified, as the rulings of the ECJ demonstrate. For example, in the public service – according to the interpretation of the Court – such a prohibition can only be applied to employees with truly public service duties.

---

[12] Regulation 1408/71/EEC is the key legal act laying down these rules, but there are several other regulations covering specific details.

[13] It should be noted here that, in addition to the above exceptions, the Treaty of Accession of 2003 allows the 15 'old' Member States to apply restrictive measures against workers from 8 of the 10 'new' Member States that acceded to the EU on 1 May 2004. These restrictions can be applied for a transitional period of 2+3+2 years (adding up to a total of 7 years). In the first two years after enlargement, the old Member States could freely decide not to open their labour market to workers from the new Member States and to apply national arrangements for a transitional period of two years. After the first two years, they could decide to continue with their national transitional arrangements for a further three years (most of them did not). At the end of this three-year period on 1 May 2009, they can only prolong these restrictions for another two years, if they can demonstrate that workers from the Member States that joined in 2004 pose a real threat of serious disturbance in the domestic labour market. The 25 Member States can apply the same 2+3+2 formula vis-à-vis the two newest Member States – Bulgaria and Romania.

6.2.1.2. The freedom of establishment

Self-employed persons form a separate category based on Community law. This category includes those working in the so-called liberal professions (e.g. physicians, lawyers and architects) as well as different activities (e.g. retailers, wholesalers, craftsmen, agents and transport operators), many of whom provide services[14]. These people are entitled to freedom of establishment, which means that they have the right to pursue their professional activities in any of the Member States, and to set up and run a firm or company according to the same rules that apply to the nationals of the host State.

The main barrier to the freedom of establishment, which concerns both the freedom to provide services and, to some extent, the free movement of workers, stems from the problem that professional qualifications are often needed for the pursuit of certain professional activities. However, qualifications may vary greatly from one Member State to another in terms of their content and length, which makes it more difficult for citizens of other Member States to obtain a licence for the pursuit of professional activities. At first, this problem seemed to pose a huge challenge for the approximation of legislation in the Community. In the beginning, Member States tried to harmonise certain professions, which they succeeded in doing in some cases – often only after decades of negotiations – for example as regards physicians, architects, chemists, etc., but eventually it became clear that extending this process to all professions was impossible. Thus, Member States extended the principle of mutual recognition, already introduced for the free movement of goods, to this area, with the adoption of two Directives[15]: the first relating to higher-education diplomas and the second to other professional education and training.

The mutual recognition of diplomas, degrees and certificates thus became a fundamental principle (both for people in a self-employed or employed capacity). In the case of the majority of professions, Member States mutually recognise diplomas issued by the others. Nonetheless, in certain professional fields (for example, law), the recognition of a person's qualifications has to be requested from the local authorities. If the authorities establish a major disparity between qualifications in terms of the length or content of education, they may require proof of professional experience, an adaptation period of no more than three years or an aptitude test.

---

[14] That is why the closely related concepts of the freedom to provide services and the right of establishment cannot be separated precisely.

[15] The first Council Directive 89/48/EEC covers the recognition of higher-education diplomas awarded on the completion of professional education and training of at least three years' duration, while Directive 92/51/EEC covers the recognition of diplomas awarded on the completion of professional education and vocational training.

The significance of the freedom of establishment is that it covers both natural persons and legal entities. For the latter, it means the right of so-called 'secondary establishment' in another Member State, meaning the right to set up a branch or a subsidiary of an existing firm or company in another State. The specific conditions covering the establishment of legal persons are regulated by Council directives adopted on the basis of the Treaty. These directives are collectively referred to as Company Law Directives.

It took the Member States 30 years of negotiations before they finally came to an agreement on the European Company Statute[16] at the Nice Summit in December 2000.[17] The European Company Statute is a legal instrument that gives companies the option of forming a European Company – known formally by its Latin name of 'Societas Europeae' (SE) – in one of four ways: by the merger of two or more existing public limited companies from at least two different Member States; by the formation of a holding company by public or private limited companies from at least two different Member States; by the formation of a subsidiary of companies from at least two different Member States; or by the transformation of a public limited company which has, for at least two years, had a subsidiary in another Member State. In practice, this means that European Companies are able to operate throughout the EU on the basis of a single set of rules and a unified management and reporting system.

There are exemptions from the freedom of establishment principle. Member States may impose certain restrictions on the grounds of public policy, public security or public health, as long as they are justified and proportionate to the objectives they are supposed to serve. According to Article 45 of the Treaty, such exemptions may be applied to activities that are connected, even occasionally, with the exercise of official authority. Similarly to restrictions on the free movement of workers, exemptions may only be applied in duly justified cases, appropriately supported by the strict interpretation practice of the European Court of Justice. The Council may, acting by a qualified majority on a proposal from the Commission, extend the scope of exemption to certain new activities.

6.2.2. The free movement of non-economically active persons

With the Treaty of Maastricht, the freedom of movement became a fundamental right of every citizen of every Member State of the European Union. This is due to the fact that the Maastricht Treaty created the institution of Union citizenship and made the right to

---

[16] Agreement was delayed because Member States found it difficult to come to a consensus on the form of worker participation (in certain Member States, employees have to be involved in company management decisions, while this is not characteristic of other states). Finally, an agreement was reached on involving employees through negotiations.

[17] This agreement finally took shape in Regulation 2157/2001/EC on the European Company Statute.

free movement a fundamental element of such citizenship. According to the Treaty, every citizen of any Member State is also a citizen of the Union. The latter does not replace nationality, but complements it by providing additional rights. Citizenship of the Union means four specific rights. A citizen of the European Union has the right:
- to move, travel and stay freely in all Member States of the EU;
- to vote and to stand as a candidate in municipal elections and elections to the European Parliament in the Member State of his residence;
- to receive the protection of the consular and diplomatic authorities of any Member State when in the territory of a non-Member State, if the citizen's own country has no such authority there;
- to petition the European Parliament or address a plea to the European Ombudsman for legal redress.

According to the principle of the free movement of persons, it is a fundamental right of all Union citizens to be able to freely cross borders between Member States without any restrictions.

There are no restrictions whatsoever on EU citizens on short-term visits (travelling). All citizens of the Union are free to travel to and stay in another Member State for a period of three months. All limitations on goods purchased by travellers were also removed under the principle of the free movement of goods and persons. Today, anybody can freely take any product purchased in another Member State for personal consumption back to his home country.[18] Taxes on these products (VAT, excise duties) have to be paid at the point of purchase.[19] As the EU is a single market, European citizens can no longer take advantage of 'tax-free' or 'duty-free' shopping at airports or ports; inside the Union, tax- or duty-free goods are only available for third-country citizens.

Free movement involves not only the right to travel freely, but also the right to stay in any Member State for a sustained period, which includes the freedom to work, study, reside and stay in all Member States. This also means that citizens of the EU are free to choose their domicile in the area of the Union. However, if they intend to stay in a Member State for a period longer than three months, they need a residence permit. These permits are automatically issued if certain conditions – which depend on the purpose of

---

[18] For certain products (alcohol, cigarettes) the extent of personal consumption is limited, but is set in a way that easily covers the needs of an average person. For instance, the limits for quantities than can be taken from one Member State to another are 90 litres of wine, 110 litres of beer, 20 litres of fortified wines and 10 litres of spirits.
[19] New cars are an exception to this rule. For new cars, the VAT must be paid in the country where they are first registered.

residence – are fulfilled. While for wage-earners, the conditions of free movement were already guaranteed by the Treaty of Rome and subsequent secondary legislation[20], for residence for other purposes the Council adopted three Directives on 28 June 1990, which regulate the general framework rules on the right of residence for non-economically active persons[21], the conditions governing the right of residence of people who have ceased their occupational activity (pensioners)[22] and the conditions applicable to persons staying in another Member State for educational purposes (students)[23].

The main aim of the Directives is to regulate the conditions upon which citizens of another Member State may be entitled to a residence permit. According to the provisions of the first Directive, nationals of Member States have the right of residence in other Member States, provided that they can demonstrate that they have sufficient resources to avoid becoming a burden on the social assistance system of the host Member State. The second Directive grants the right of residence to retired people, if they are recipients of a pension or an amount sufficient to avoid becoming a burden on the social security system of the host Member State. According to the provisions of the third Directive, students have the freedom to choose to attend an educational institution in any Member State, but have to obtain a residence permit for the duration of their studies. The permit is issued automatically, provided that the student is enrolled in a recognised educational establishment, is covered by sickness insurance and has sufficient resources to avoid becoming a burden on the social security system of the host Member State during his or her period of residence.

Free movement and travel to other Member States is facilitated by the fact that there are practically no border controls inside the EU. By integrating the Schengen Agreement[24] and subsequent Schengen legislation (the so-called Schengen *acquis*) into the European Union and the *acquis communautaire*, the Amsterdam Treaty largely removed controls on passenger traffic on borders within the Union, except for the United Kingdom and Ireland.[25]

---

[20] People who take up employment or run a business in another Member State, together with their families, are automatically entitled to a residence permit.

[21] Directive 90/364/EEC on the right of residence.

[22] Council Directive 90/365/EEC on the right of residence for employees and self-employed persons who have ceased their occupational activity.

[23] Council Directive 90/366/EEC on the right of residence for students, which was later replaced by Directive 93/96/EC. The Directive applies to students who reside in another Member State specifically for educational purposes, and who are not studying as family members of migrant workers or of self-employed persons. The latter enjoy the same rights as students who are nationals of the host Member State (e.g. they are entitled to social benefits to which foreigners are not generally entitled).

[24] For more on the Schengen Agreement, see 24.2. and 24.3.2.

[25] Border controls were not abolished either for the ten Member States that joined on 1 May 2004. Based on the accession negotiations an agreement was reached in December 2006, according to which new Member States that can fully apply the Schengen *acquis* will become part of the Schengen area on 31 December 2007 (in practical terms from 1 January 2008). Bulgaria and Romania, who acceded to the Union on 1 January 2007, will also have to wait a few years before becoming part of the Schengen area.

Border controls are now only carried out at the Union's external borders. Persons crossing from one Member State to another can do so freely, while those who have entered from a third country can move on freely without any controls to other Member States. Moreover, citizens of the Union can cross the border with their identity cards (rather than passports). In relation to the dismantling of internal border controls and the free movement of persons, in order to ensure their national security, Member States have adopted common regulations in the area of visa policy, asylum policy, external border controls and judicial cooperation in civil affairs; these issues fall within the field of cooperation in justice and home affairs, which are dealt with in detail in Chapter 24.

6.3. The freedom to provide services

6.3.1. The definition of services in Community law

The *acquis* (Article 50 of the EC Treaty) defines services as activities provided for remuneration, insofar as they are not governed by the provisions relating to the freedom of movement of goods, capital and persons. This definition was necessary because services are often difficult to distinguish from other activities and thus from the other fundamental freedoms. The majority of self-employed persons are engaged in providing services, while the distribution of goods is also closely linked to related services (e.g. transport) and the free movement of capital can also involve services (see financial services). That is why Community law had to provide a clear and detailed definition of what fell within the scope of the freedom to provide services.

For the sake of clarity, the freedom to provide services applies to those services which have a cross-border element, i.e. when the provider and the recipient of the service reside in different Member States. This does not mean that the service provider cannot temporarily pursue his activity in the state where the service is provided, and in fact he may even open a permanent representation there[26], but his activity must be fundamentally related to another Member State. If he were to permanently relocate his activities into the state where the services are provided, he would fall within the scope of the freedom of establishment.

---

[26] Travel agencies, for example, can have a local representation or local guide in another Member State.

For the freedom to provide services the emphasis falls on the temporary (non-permanent) and cross-border nature of such activities.[27]

It is also important to note that the service is provided for remuneration, since – to a certain extent – the essence of the freedom to provide services is to embrace all those activities which are exercised for remuneration but which do not fall within the scope of the other freedoms. The *acquis* stipulates that the remuneration must come from a private source, thus educational services paid by the state do not fall within the scope of the free movement of services.

In order to clarify the nature of services, Article 50 of the EC Treaty lists activities that – upon the fulfilment of the above conditions – are typically considered as services: activities of an industrial nature, activities of a commercial character, the activities of craftsmen and the activities of the professions.

To ensure a harmonised liberalisation of services, Article 51 of the Treaty stipulates that the freedom to provide services in the field of transport shall be governed by the provisions of the Title relating to transport (EC Treaty Title V) and that the liberalisation of banking and insurance services connected with capital movements shall be carried out in step with the liberalisation of capital movements (EC Treaty Title III Chapter 4).[28]

6.3.2. The prohibition of discrimination, the question of educational qualifications and the exceptions to the freedom to provide services

The prohibition on discrimination also applies to the free movement of services. This means that Member States may not impose different conditions on service providers who exercise their activities from another Member State or on recipients of services in another Member State. It is important to note here that recipients of services cannot be restricted or discriminated against, which means that they have the right to travel to another Member State to buy services. This is standard practice for a number of services. The most general case is that of tourists or persons travelling for business purposes, but there are also people who travel to another country to receive medical treatment. The Council Directive on the abolition of restrictions on movement and residence with regard to establishment

---

[27] A mason, who lives in a border region and occasionally crosses to another Member State to help build a few houses for a certain amount of remuneration, falls within the scope of the freedom to provide services. However, if he relocates his business to another Member State, he falls within the scope of the freedom of establishment.

[28] For more on the common transport policy and the free movement of capital, see Chapter 12 and 6.4.

and the provision of services[29] grants the right of residence for persons providing and receiving services for the period during which the services are provided.

In its judgements, the European Court of Justice has pointed out that not only is direct and indirect discrimination prohibited, but also restrictions that apply to both domestic and foreign providers (or recipients) of services where these in fact make it more difficult for foreign providers (or recipients) to pursue (receive) such activities or services. With its rulings, the Court has also extended the *Dassonville* formula, first applied to goods only, to services as well.

Similarly to the freedom of establishment, requirements pertaining to qualifications are a key issue. The application of different rules on qualifications to service providers by Member States would be an obstacle to the freedom to provide services. Therefore, the Directives on the mutual recognition of qualifications and the harmonisation of educational and training conditions also apply to the freedom to provide services.

Certain activities are exempt from the provisions on the freedom to provide services, as in the case of the freedom of establishment and the free movement of goods. These exceptions include activities which are connected with the exercise of official authority, and, as in the case of the other freedoms, restrictions on grounds of public policy, public security or public health, as long as they are justified and proportionate to the ends they are supposed to serve. This condition is very strictly interpreted by the Court of Justice, just as in the case of the free movement of persons and goods.

6.3.3. The liberalisation of the free movement of services in practice

Community law guarantees the freedom to provide services and the abolition of provisions restricting the movement of various services through means of directives. According to Article 52 of the Treaty, the Council shall, on a proposal from the Commission and after consulting the Economic and Social Committee and the European Parliament, issue directives acting by a qualified majority in order to achieve the liberalisation of a specific service.

---

[29] Directive 73/148/EEC on the abolition of restrictions on movement and residence within the Community for nationals of Member States with regard to establishment and the provision of services.

Compared to the free movement of goods, the realisation of the freedom to provide services progressed rather slowly and the adoption of certain directives failed. Finally, parallel to the programme of the single market, the liberalisation of intra-Community services gained new momentum in the late '80s and early '90s. Consequently, most services (e.g. banking, financial, air transport and telecommunications services) had been liberalised by the turn of the millennium. In recent years, there has been increased focus on the few remaining areas where the active ownership and regulatory role of the state has prevented liberalisation. Liberalisation in the energy sector is at a relatively advanced stage (the electricity and gas sectors were opened up fully to free competition from 1 July 2007)[30], while liberalisation of the railway sector is in the pipeline and liberalisation of postal services is high on the agenda.

The enforcement of the freedom to provide services has increasing significance for the functioning of the single market and the success and competitiveness of the European Union. The reason is that, in the world economy and in the EU alike, services play an increasingly dominant role, both in terms of the number of people employed and GDP produced. A large part of the Union's active population works in the service sector, with commercial services and public services combined accounting for 70% of GDP (50% and 20%, respectively). Due to their significance, services feature more and more noticeably in the EU's economic policy and legislation. In the light of these developments, the Lisbon Summit in March 2000 placed the so-called Internal Market Strategy for Services at the centre of the Community's new long-term economic policy. This new approach was needed because the traditional method of harmonisation and liberalisation, aimed at individual sectors, was no longer sufficiently effective. A new approach in the field of services was necessary for three reasons. Firstly, the traditional sectoral approach involved cumbersome legal harmonisation; moreover it led to overlapping and often contradictory legislation in various sectors. Secondly, in today's economy, even manufacturers provide comprehensive services, the complexity of which

---

[30] According to the decision on the liberalisation of the gas and electricity sectors taken at the Barcelona Summit on 15–16 March 2002, non-household consumers became free to choose their gas and electricity service providers from 1 July 2004, with household consumers followed from 1 July 2007. The electricity and gas sectors are regulated by Directive 2003/54/EC and Directive 2003/55/EC, respectively. See also 16.2.

makes it impossible to have a clear overview using the sectoral approach.[31] Thirdly, modern technology necessitates new directions in the liberalisation of services. The new Internal Market Strategy for Services thus strives to create a comprehensive horizontal regulatory framework applicable in all sectors and flexible enough to ensure that services based on new technologies can develop for the benefit of the single market. The new strategy hinges on three elements: 1) identifying (listing) obstacles to the implementation of Community legislation in Member States and subsequently removing them (if necessary by bringing Member States before the European Court of Justice); 2) introducing non-legislative measures (e.g. developing Codes of Conduct, launching information campaigns); 3) developing harmonisation provisions based on a horizontal approach, i.e. adopting new pieces of Community legislation. With the latter, the strategy aims at establishing horizontal rules covering services in all sectors, focusing particularly on the following six areas: removing all obstacles to the establishment of service companies and promoting cross-border services and purchases, distribution activities, promotional activities, sales activities (e.g. contracting and pricing rules) and after-sales activities.

The Directive on Services in the internal market (in short, the *Services Directive*)[32] adopted in December 2006, is a major step forward towards the completion of the single market. The Directive, presented by the Commission in the framework of the Lisbon strategy in January 2004, is aimed at establishing a truly single internal market in services by dismantling any remaining unjustified and discriminatory administrative obstacles to cross-border service provision. The unnecessarily complicated and costly administrative burdens still deter many companies (mainly SMEs) from providing services in other Member States. The Commission wished to introduce the principle of 'country of origin' to cross-border services, according to which service providers would be subject only to the law of their country of establishment rather than that of their country of operation, and the Member State where the service was provided could only impose additional requirements in justified cases. The application of this principle would also make the country of origin responsible for controlling the service provider and his services, even when provided in another Member State (also known as the principle of 'country of origin control'). The draft Services Directive became the centre of attention of stakeholders from the very beginning, provoking great controversy, primarily due to the country of origin principle,

---

[31] One of the best examples of this are car manufacturers, who, in addition to production, also provide banking, lending, insurance, marketing, advertising, after-sales servicing and other services, which are often sold in a package along with the product.

[32] Directive 2006/123/EC of the European Parliament and of the Council of 12 December 2006 on Services in the Internal Market.

which – due to pressure from some old Member States – was finally dropped and replaced by the principle of the freedom to provide services.[33] The Directive is based on the principle of non-discrimination, according to which Member States must respect service providers' rights to provide a service in a Member State other than that in which they are established. They must receive free access to and enjoy free exercise of a service activity in any territory. However, Member States can introduce requirements that are necessary to protect public policy, public security, public health and the protection of the environment, as long as they are strictly proportionate to the desired objectives. If a Member State authority requests service providers to present certificates or documents proving compliance with a requirement, it must accept equivalent certificates issued in another Member State.

By easing the administrative burden, the Directive could bring significant benefits and new market opportunities to small- and medium-sized enterprises, particularly in sectors such as tourism, the construction industry, household services, advertising or retailing. The Member States have until the end of December 2009 to transpose the Directive into their national legal orders.

6.4. The free movement of capital

6.4.1. The realisation of the free movement of capital

Article 56 of the EC Treaty prohibits all restrictions on the movement of capital, both between Member States and between Member States and third countries. This general prohibition was not characteristic of the *acquis* in the beginning. The Treaty of Rome originally only dealt with the movement of capital and payments as a supplementary freedom linked to the free movement of goods, services and workers.

---

[33] The draft Directive was primarily criticised by Member States with higher labour costs in the services sector, who were afraid of job losses caused by competition from (mainly Central and Eastern European) Member States with cheaper labour. The other common fear was that the draft Directive could jeopardise the quality of services, by giving Member States with the lowest regulatory standards a competitive advantage.

The EC Treaty includes provisions not only on the free movement of capital, but on the free movement of payments as well, but this distinction between capital and payments no longer made sense following the general liberalisation necessitated by the economic and monetary union; thus, nowadays, we only talk about the free movement of capital. It should also be noted that the category of capital includes not only traditional elements of the capital market, such as money, securities, etc., but also real estate, land and capital assets.

According to ex Article 67 of the Treaty of Rome, the free movement of capital and payments only had to be guaranteed to the extent required by the "proper functioning of the common market". The free movement of goods, services and workers would not have made much sense without, for example, allowing companies/people to take their profits/earnings back to their home state; accordingly, for a long time, the *acquis* mainly dealt with the free movement of capital connected with such cross-border activities. The wish to create a single market and, later, an economic and monetary union brought major changes in this field, and legislation hampering capital movements was quickly removed. The decisive moment came with the adoption of a Directive[34] in 1988, which liberalised capital transfers by abolishing all restrictions on movements of capital. This Directive entered into force on 1 July 1990, except for Greece, Ireland, Portugal and Spain, where the full application of the Directive was postponed for a few years. The realisation of the unrestricted, free movement of all elements of capital was reinforced by the Maastricht Treaty, which set the free movement of capital as a precondition for joining the economic and monetary union. Thus, by the beginning of the second phase of the EMU on 1 January 1994, all payments and capital movements had been fully liberalised.[35]

---

[34] Directive 88/361/EEC.
[35] For more on the economic and monetary union, see Chapter 8.

6.4.2. Exceptions to the free movement of capital

There are general exceptions to the free movement of capital.[36] The free movement of capital cannot encroach upon a Member State's right to prevent the infringement of national legislation on taxation or to ensure the supervision of financial institutions and, in relation to reporting obligations, the collection of information serving administrative and statistical purposes. In addition, just as in the case of the free movement of goods, persons and services, the free movement of capital may be restricted on grounds of public policy or public security.[37] The principle of a restriction being in proportion to the objective to be achieved applies here as well, which means that such restrictions are not permissible if the objective could be achieved by less restrictive means. This principle is strictly enforced by the European Court of Justice.

Exceptionally, and strictly vis-à-vis third countries, the free movement of capital can be limited for a maximum period of six months if capital movements to or from a third country risk posing serious difficulties to the functioning of the economic and monetary union. Such restrictions may also be imposed against third countries as an element of measures taken and instruments used within the framework of the common foreign and security policy (for example in the form of economic sanctions).

6.5. The single market and taxation

In order to ensure the four fundamental freedoms, certain rules on taxation are necessary, pursuant to Articles 90 to 93 of the EC Treaty. It must, however, be made clear that the aim is not to harmonise all taxes or create a single system of taxation; these do not even appear as objectives for the distant future. It should also be emphasised that the Treaty makes a clear distinction between rules on indirect and direct taxation. While significant progress has been made in harmonising indirect taxes[38], little has been achieved

---

[36] It must be noted that in addition to the above exceptions, according to the Treaties of Accession several of the ten Member States that acceded to the Union in 2004 and the two new Member States that joined in 2007 can apply transitional measures – with differing conditions and duration – for natural and legal persons of the 15 old Member States in relation to the acquisition of real estate and land, thereby putting transitional restrictions on the free movement of capital.

[37] The free movement of capital can be limited in the public interest if such restrictions are designed to combat money laundering or tax evasion.

[38] Indirect taxes are taxes levied on production and consumption and not directly on the taxable person or income. Indirect taxes include value-added tax, excise duties, and other turnover taxes.

in relation to direct taxes[39] as the Member States remain reluctant to give up their national sovereignty and share competences with the Union in this area.

Since indirect taxes are closely related to the free movement of goods and the freedom to provide services, a certain degree of tax harmonisation is necessary in these fields. To that end, Article 93 of the EC Treaty empowers the Council to adopt provisions for the harmonisation of legislation concerning turnover taxes, excise duties and other forms of indirect taxation, to the extent necessary to ensure the establishment and the functioning of the internal market. The Council adopts such harmonising measures acting unanimously on a proposal from the Commission and after consulting the European Parliament and the Economic and Social Committee. Article 93 has helped to create very detailed common rules on value-added tax and excise duties.

Value-added tax (VAT) was first introduced in the Community in 1970 with the aim of replacing the various different forms of consumption and turnover tax in the Member States. The creation of the single market in 1992 brought about the elimination of 'tax borders', which necessitated even closer harmonisation of VAT rates. The significant differences in VAT rates hindered the free movement of goods and services. According to a Directive adopted in 1992[40] on harmonising tax rates, the Member States have to apply a standard rate of VAT of a minimum 15%, with one or two reduced rates of no less than 5% applied for certain goods and services, serving primarily cultural and social purposes. Lower rates (e.g. 0%) of value-added tax may only be applied in cases specified in the Directive.

In order to guarantee the free movement of goods and services, in addition to harmonising certain tax rates, the place where tax liability arises (the issue of where taxes are payable) also has to be defined. The EU's long-term objective is to establish an origin-based Community VAT system. Nevertheless, it will probably take a few more years before that goal is realised, and until then the destination-based transitional system remains in place. For private individuals, the rule applies that VAT is payable at the place of consumption or purchase.[41]

---

[39] Direct taxes are taxes levied directly on taxable persons. Direct taxes include income taxes, corporate taxes and property/asset taxes.

[40] Council Directive 92/77/EEC supplementing the common system of value added tax and amending Directive 77/388/EEC (approximation of VAT rates).

[41] The purchase of a new motor vehicle is the only exception to that rule. If one buys a new car, the VAT must be paid in the country of destination, i.e. the country where the car is to be registered.

Since the introduction of the single market on 1 January 1993, excise duties have been payable at the place of consumption. Excise duties on alcoholic beverages, tobacco products and mineral oils are payable in the Member State of final consumption. Minimum rates of excise duty are also set at Community level.

Unlike for indirect taxes, the EC Treaty includes no specific provisions for direct taxes, which – following from the principle of subsidiarity – have traditionally fallen under national competence. The only condition concerning direct taxes is that national tax systems must respect the four fundamental freedoms. As a practical consequence, Community legislation adopted in this area is aimed at avoiding double taxation and facilitating cross-border business activities.

The only area of direct taxation where there has been a substantial will for harmonisation is company (or corporate) tax. The European Commission has proposed the harmonisation of the tax base (and not the actual tax rate), as it could put an end to the current practice of tax evasion through internal accounting mechanisms by companies with subsidiaries in several Member States. This proposal however does not enjoy the unanimous support of all Member States, which only goes to show how anxious the Member States are to hold on to their national independence in this field, where they demonstrate the least willingness to give up national competences.

Tax harmonisation is clearly one of the most sensitive issues of closer integration. Several Member States are understandably reluctant to pool their national sovereignty, as tax policy is the key fiscal instrument and a major component of each government's political programme. As a result, approval in the Council by unanimity has been maintained in the area of tax harmonisation. Replacing unanimity is so unrealistic that even the Constitutional Treaty (and the Reform Treaty it is to be replaced by) did not attempt to extend qualified majority voting to taxation.

Concerning taxation, it is worth mentioning several proposals designed to introduce some kind of Community tax, which would reduce the dependence of the Community budget's sources of income (so-called own resources)[42] on national budgets. These proposals have never been backed up by a majority of the Member States, and thus have always been put off the agenda.

---

[42] For more on 'own resources', see 7.2.1.

6.6. Decision-making related to the single market

Harmonising measures for the single market and decisions related to the free movement of workers and their right of establishment and the free movement of Union citizens and their right of residence, are adopted jointly by the Council and Parliament in the co-decision procedure. An exception to that rule is legislation on the social security of migrant workers, where – instead of the general rule of qualified majority voting applied for co-decision – the Council acts in unanimity.

Harmonising measures that do not have the internal market as their object but which affect the functioning thereof, are adopted by the Council acting in unanimity and through the consultation procedure.

For the liberalisation of a specific service, the consultation procedure is applied as well, but the Council acts by a qualified majority.

The free movement of capital is affected by the provision that, in special circumstances when capital movements to or from third countries pose a threat of causing a serious disturbance to the functioning of the EMU, the Council, acting on the Commission's proposal and after consulting the European Central Bank, may adopt protective measures with a qualified majority vote.

The consultation procedure and unanimity also apply in relation to taxation.

Upon its entry into force (foreseen for 2009), the Reform Treaty will bring about some minor modifications to single market legislation. These modifications – borrowed from the Constitutional Treaty and of a technical nature – are outlined in Point 6 of the Annex.

CHAPTER 7
THE BUDGET OF THE EUROPEAN UNION

7.1. Features of the EU budget

The budget of the European Union is unique, different both from that of international organisations and nation states. On the one hand, it is more extensive than the budgets of traditional international organisations, which usually only cover their own operations and administration. On the other hand, it is confined to fewer areas than a national budget: while Member State budgets have 30 to 50% of GDP at their disposal, the EU redistributes a little more than 1% of its total GDP. Another difference is that the Community budget finances public goods or services to an insignificant degree.

Unlike in the case of international organisations, the EU's budget has important regulatory and resource-redistribution functions; of course the EU's budgetary competences are more limited than those of Member States but its redistributional role is exceptional, especially because it redistributes between Member States, or to be more precise, between their producers and consumers.

Unlike with other international organisations, the EU's common budget is not only used for financing its own administration; in fact, administrative costs amount only to about 5% of all expenditure. The main aim of the Community budget is to finance and support common and Community policies, actions and objectives, such as measures aimed at strengthening economic and social cohesion between Member States, or providing financial aid to third countries.

The common budget is calculated in Euro (formerly in ECU), and it totals about EUR 120–130 billion annually. The budgetary year (called 'financial year' in the Treaty) coincides with the calendar year, starting on 1 January and ending on 31 December.

The draft budget is prepared by the Commission, and is approved by the Council and the Parliament.[1]

Unlike national budgets, the Community budget can have no deficit; revenue and expenditure must always be in balance.

---

[1] See budgetary procedure (7.4).

The European Commission's so-called MacDougall Report of 1977, which reinforced the regulatory, stabilising and redistributional functions of the common budget, laid down its fundamental principles:

– According to the principle of *externality*, the costs and incomes of certain activities may occur simultaneously in different Member States, which may entail the need for compensation.

– According to the principle of *indivisibility*, due to reasons of economy of scale, the financing of certain activities may not be divided among Member States, but must be implemented at Community level.

– According to the principle of *cohesion*, citizens of all Member States must be guaranteed a minimum standard of services, prosperity and development, which necessitates the transfer of resources from more prosperous countries to poorer ones. This means the implementation of the objective of economic and social cohesion, as laid down in the Treaty.

– According to the principle of *subsidiarity*, a given issue (expenditure item) should be solved (financed) as closely as possible to the citizens, unless there is an advantage in action at higher level.

7.2. Structure of the European Union's budget

7.2.1. The revenue of the common budget

While between 1958 and 1970, the common budget was financed from Member State contributions, in 1970, so-called 'own resources' were introduced to finance the common budget. The significance of these own resources was that the revenue of the common budget was made independent from the contributions of the Member States, which enabled the automatic (normative) financing of the common budget. This meant that the common budget was less dependent on the willingness of Member States to make contributions. Due to the insufficient level of own resources, the so-called 'fourth resource' (the GNP-based contribution of Member States) was introduced in 1980, supplementing the other three sources of financing. Since 1988, the former own resources cover a gradually decreasing part of the budget, which increases the importance of the fourth source of revenue. This means that the proportion of automatic financing has fallen, while direct contributions by Member States have grown to represent a higher percentage of revenue, which has put budgetary debates on a different level (see 7.3.1.).

The revenues of the common budget are the following:

a.) Traditional own resources (customs duties, agricultural duties, sugar levies):
All customs duties levied (according to common customs tariffs) on imports from third countries are paid into the common budget.[2] The collection of customs duties is the responsibility of the Member State through which the import is made, and it can only reserve for itself a fixed percentage (currently 25%) of the duties collected to cover its administrative expenditure.

Agricultural duties, which are now also considered part of customs duties, used to be called *agricultural levies*. Agricultural levies were continuously changing duties payable upon importation, which served to compensate for the difference between lower prices on the world market and the higher Community prices[3]. Agricultural levies imposed on imported produce under the Common Agricultural Policy were paid into the common budget by the importer. Agricultural levies, as a drastic instrument restricting trade, were in essence abolished from 1995 when, according to the decisions taken at the Uruguay Round of GATT (now WTO), they had to be converted into customs duties.[4] Thus, the difference is, in practical terms, that agricultural duties are often adjusted, so-called variable duties, while industrial duties are stable (and usually very low). The regime applicable to sugar is slightly different from other agricultural produce, with levies instead of duties.

Traditional own resources account for about 15% of the revenues of the 2007 budget.

b.) VAT-based resource:
Revenue from value-added tax (VAT) cannot really be considered a Community tax, because the rate at which it is collected is a pre-set rate of the VAT tax base (1% in earlier years, 0.75% from 2002, 0.5% from 2004 and 0.3% in the 2007–2013 period[5]) which is not added onto the national VAT rates. Member States transfer their payments on a monthly basis according to the annual budgetary perspectives and not according to actual economic figures.

VAT-based contributions make up 15% of the revenues of the 2007 budget.

---

[2] When establishing a customs union, the Member States abolished customs duties between them, and introduced common customs tariffs on imports from third countries. For more details, see 6.1.1.2. and 9.2.

[3] See also 11.2. on the Common Agricultural Policy.

[4] Except for the sugar sector, where duties of the same nature as agricultural levies continue to be imposed on sugar and other isoglucose products.

[5] For Member States that are the biggest net contributors to the EU budget, the VAT collection rate is even lower: 0.225% for Austria, 0.15% for Germany and 0.1% for the Netherlands and Sweden.

c.) GNI-based resource (formerly GNP resource):
This source of income was introduced by the 1998 budgetary reform[6] in order to supplement own resources. This became necessary during the EC's financing crisis in the mid-eighties, when the ratio of customs duties and agricultural levies in the revenue fell from 50% in 1980 to 34% in 1987 and VAT-based contributions rose to 66%. This significantly distorted the Member States' financial burden compared to their national product, which was rather unfavourable for some poorer Member States, and the financing of Community expenditure was no longer guaranteed. That is why the new resource was introduced, which is set on the basis of Member States' GNP (gross national product), and is aimed at counterbalancing the former own resources in a way that Member State contributions amount to a predetermined rate of the GNP (e.g. set at a maximum 1.27% of the EU's GNP for the 2000–2006 budgetary period). The EU decided to switch to GNI-based statistics in 2002. Due to the differences between the GNP- and GNI-based calculations, the new ceiling for the 2000–2006 budgetary planning period was set at 1.24% of GNI. This ceiling was maintained for the 2007–2013 financial perspective as well. However, the budget is usually well below that ceiling – the 2007 budget amounts to 1.08% of GNI based upon commitments and 0.99% based upon payments.
69% of the revenues of the 2007 EU budget come from the GNI-based resource.

d.) Other revenues:
This heading covers all other revenues of the Community budget and includes mostly unspent budget items from the previous year, as well as tax contributions by Community officials and bank interest.
Other revenues make up 1% of the revenues of the 2007 budget.

7.2.2. Expenditure of the common budget

Until 2006, Community expenditure was divided into six major headings[7], which were the following:
1) Common Agricultural Policy (CAP)
2) Structural operations

---

[6] See 7.3.3. on the Delors I package.
[7] Headings are also called categories of expenditure.

3) Internal policies
4) External actions
5) Administrative expenditure
6) Reserves
In addition, in the 2000–2006 financial planning period the budget included two additional enlargement-related items:
7) Pre-accession funds
8) Expenditure earmarked for new Member States

In the 2007–2013 Financial Perspective, the headings used in previous budgets were revised by the Member States with a view to a Union of 27 members. They chose a structure that was better suited to spelling out the European Union's key objectives and political priorities. As a result, from 2007 the budgetary framework contains 5 headings for expenditure.

Heading 1 – *Sustainable growth*
This heading is divided into two separate subheadings: Competitiveness (1a) and Cohesion (1b).
1a. Competitiveness for growth and employment, encompassing expenditure on research and technological development, education and training, the security and environmental sustainability of EU energy and transport networks, the internal market and accompanying policies, as well as employment and social policy (which used to feature among internal policies). Spending on research and technological development gives by far the biggest share of this subheading.
1b. Cohesion for growth and employment, covering economic and social cohesion policy, in practical terms the expenditure of Structural and Cohesion Funds. This subheading is designed to enhance convergence by the least developed Member States and regions, to complement the EU strategy for sustainable development outside the less prosperous regions through competitiveness and employment programmes, and to support European inter-regional cooperation through cross-border and trans-national programmes.
The Heading of Sustainable Growth accounts for 43.4% of the 2007 budget, 7.4% going to the Competitiveness Subheading (1a) and 36% to the Cohesion Subheading (1b). This also means that more than one third of the Community budget is spent on structural and cohesion policy (a small increase compared to earlier years, largely due to the accession of relatively less prosperous countries).[8]

---

[8] For more on the reform of Structural and Cohesion Funds, see 13.4.

Heading 2 – *Natural resources*
Heading 2 is aimed at the preservation and sustainable management of natural resources and includes the common agricultural and fisheries policies, rural development and certain environmental measures. Roughly 80% of expenditure under this heading goes to agricultural market measures, while most of the remaining 20% finances rural development.

It must be noted that the Common Agricultural Policy – the only Community policy exclusively financed from Community sources – was traditionally the single biggest item in the budget: it accounted for as much as two thirds in the eighties and only fell to 50% in the nineties because the total budget grew and not because agricultural spending was curbed. Considering that from 2007, expenditure on rural development falls into a separate subheading and shows a growing trend vis-à-vis traditional agricultural measures (such as market support and direct payments, effectively frozen by a 2002 European Council decision), traditional farm policy spending now makes up no more than one third of the Community budget.[9]

The Heading of Natural Resources accounts for 44.5% of the 2007 budget, 33.8% going to agricultural market support and direct payments and 9.8% to rural development.

Heading 3 – *Union citizenship, area of freedom, security and justice*
Heading 3 reflects the growing importance attached to these fields[10], and hence placed in a separate heading, which includes expenditure related to border management, asylum policy, institution building, access to public goods, food safety, public health, consumer protection, culture, audiovisual policy, youth, information and dialogue with the citizens. This heading accounts for 1% of the 2007 budget, evenly divided between Union citizenship and the area of freedom, security and justice.

---

[9] For changes in the Common Agricultural Policy see 11.4. – 11.8.
[10] Since the Treaty of Amsterdam, the term 'area of freedom, security and justice' reflects the policies under justice and home affairs cooperation. (TEU Title VI and TEC Part III Title IV.) See Chapter 24.

Heading 4 – *The European Union as a global partner*
Heading 4 covers all costs of external action of the Union, whether political or economic, including pre-accession instruments for candidate countries, neighbourhood policy, civilian crisis prevention and management, development policy aid for poverty reduction in developing countries, and humanitarian aid. This heading also includes the current reserves for emergency aid and loan guarantees.
This heading accounts for 5.4% of the 2007 budget.

Heading 5 – *Administration*
This heading covers operational expenditure for Community institutions (costs of buildings, officials' remuneration, translation and interpreting costs, etc.), including officials' pensions and the European Schools.
The administrative costs accounts for 5.5% of the 2007 budget.

As a result of the last round of enlargement on 1 January 2007, for a transitional period between 2007 and 2009, on top of the 5 headings above, the annual budgets include an extra heading: Compensation to new Member States. This heading is aimed at helping Bulgaria and Romania in the first three years of their membership when they are likely to face difficulties in absorbing EU funds. This compensation ensures that the two countries become net beneficiaries from year one and do not find themselves in a situation where they contribute more to the EU budget than they absorb. A similar heading existed from 2004 to 2006 for the ten Member States that acceded to the Union on 1 May 2004.
The Compensation Heading accounts for 0.3% of the 2007 budget.

Concerning budget headings, it should be noted that the Union budget is calculated in two ways, according to two appropriations. Each year there is an annual budget based on commitments and another one based on payments, with two different total sums. Commitment appropriations include sums committed in a given fiscal year, even though some of these sums are only spent in the following years. Payment appropriations take stock of items to be spent in a given year, on the basis of the commitments of the given year and of the commitments carried over from previous years.

Table 7.1. The 2007 budget of the EU

Commitment appropriations	Sums (in EUR billion)
1. Sustainable growth	54.9
1a Competitiveness	*9.4*
1b Cohesion	*45.5*
2. Natural resources	56.3
of which agriculture (market support and direct payments)	*42.7*
3. Citizenship - freedom, security, justice	1.2
Area of freedom, security and justice	*0.6*
Union citizenship	*0.6*
4. The EU as a global partner	6.8
5. Administration	6.9
6. Compensation to new MSs	0.4
Commitment appropriations – total	126.5
Commitment appropriations – % of GNI	1.08 %
Payment appropriations – total	115.5
Payment appropriations – % of GNI	0.99 %

Source: European Commission

7.3. Budgetary debates and multi-annual financial perspectives

7.3.1. The key issues of budgetary debates in the eighties and nineties

Since the mid-eighties, the debate on the common budget between the Member States has focused on three important and recurring issues.

The Common Agricultural Policy (CAP), its exorbitant costs and the outdated and sometimes unfair structure of its financing have been the subject of heated debate for quite a while. The debate is fundamentally between the main beneficiaries of the Community's agricultural policy (states such as France, which have a large agricultural sector producing mainly temperate products), the net contributors (states with relatively small agricultural potential, e.g. the United Kingdom), and the countries producing less-subsidised products (e.g. Portugal). Although the ratio of CAP expenditure within the common budget was reduced during the nineties, it was done by drastically increasing the budget as a whole and not by cutting subsidies in real terms. Strong Member-State agricultural lobby groups have always managed to prevent comprehensive reforms to the financing of agriculture, although external factors (such as WTO obligations and the need for maintaining competitiveness on the world market) have made these increasingly pressing.

The extent of structural and cohesion expenditure has been another key point in the budgetary debate. There has been a gap between less prosperous Member States, also known as cohesion countries (in the eighties and nineties Greece, Ireland[11], Portugal and Spain), and others. After they joined the EU, these four countries maintained the argument that, due to their lower level of development, the single market and economic and monetary union posed more difficulties for them than for more developed Member States; thus, they argued that – according to the principle of economic and social cohesion – the more prosperous Member States should compensate for the costs of continuous alignment through the common budget's redistributional (i.e. structural) measures. The amount of – and not the need for – these financial transfers was what poorer and richer Member States always debated.

A persistent problem was created by certain constantly apparent, often seemingly unjustified, differences between the contributor/beneficiary status of Member States. EU members benefit from agricultural and structural policies, the two biggest expenditure headings in the common budget, to various extents, according to the redistributional logic of these policies. These differences in the balance of payments into and transfers from the common budget, the so-called difference in net contributions, are a major source of tension, but the main reason for disagreement is that, contrary to proclaimed objectives, these balances often do not reflect the level of income and development of the different Member States. For example, over several years, Denmark, one of the most prosperous Member States, was a net beneficiary of the EU budget. In some years, in per capita terms, Denmark benefited more from the EU budget than Spain, which was one of the least developed member countries. Significant differences could also arise between countries of the same weight and at the same level of development. A good example of this is Germany and France: despite the fact that, in terms of per capita GDP, the two countries are almost identical, the net costs of

---

[11] Ireland no longer belongs to this group; its swift growth – facilitated by structural and cohesion funding – has increased per capita GDP well above the EU average, elevating Ireland to the level of the most prosperous Member States.

the EU – for example – in 1995 were five times higher for German taxpayers than for their French counterparts. The main – but not exclusive – explanation for these surprising disparities were the differences in size (France) and structure and efficiency (Denmark) of the agricultural sectors, which result in different levels of agricultural support.

In terms of net contributions, the United Kingdom was the most controversial Member State. Since the agricultural sector is relatively insignificant compared to the size of the country, and since the UK is at the European average in terms of development, the British are not entitled to much agricultural, structural and cohesion funding. Compared to other Member States, the UK only receives a small percentage of its contributions from the Community budget. To compensate for that 'loss', the system of 'rebate' was introduced in the seventies on an *ad hoc* basis subject to annual voting. Primarily due to the considerable pressure from Prime Minister Margaret Thatcher, the 'correction mechanism' was institutionalised by the decision of the Fontainebleau European Council in 1984. Essentially, the rebate is a fixed sum of annual compensation paid to the UK by the other Member States, effectively on a bilateral basis.

It should also be noted that sharing net contributions fairly seems to be practically impossible even today, since financial support to poorer Member States does not necessarily stay inside the beneficiary country. How much of such Community support actually ends up in donor states is difficult to calculate. Companies from more developed Member States are involved as contractors in many of the investments financed from the common budget and, therefore, part of Community funding to less prosperous countries is indirectly transferred back to the budget of the donor states (for example in the form of taxes). This puts the debate on net contributions in a completely different light.

7.3.2. The system of multi-annual financial perspectives

In order to solve the above controversy, to make the common budget more efficient and fair, four large reform packages have been adopted since the late '80s. Sharing the common objective of ensuring the stable operation and financing of EU policies for longer, thus assisting better planning, these packages set longer-term (5 to 7-year) budgetary planning periods. This was at first a major novelty, but it soon became standard practice to adopt comprehensive financial perspectives (the last three times for a 7-year period) on the basis of estimated own resources. These financial perspectives include ceilings for the overall budget and its key headings, which then serve as a framework for the annual budgets of subsequent years.

These multi-annual budgetary packages, so-called *financial perspectives* or *multi-annual financial frameworks*, are adopted at summit level meetings of Heads of State or Government. The peculiarity of multi-annual financial perspectives, which are not institutionalised in the Treaties and thus have no primary legal base[12], is that they are always adopted by a unanimous vote because, on issues of such great significance, Member States respect each other's interests as much as possible. Thus, the adoption of financial perspectives for a given budgetary planning period is preceded by heated debates lasting one to two years, which can usually only be resolved by complicated packages of compromises. However, the resulting financial perspectives guarantee stable and transparent financing for many years ahead. Another advantage is that the predetermined financial framework makes it easier for the Council and Parliament to agree on the annual budget and reduces the chances of conflicts between the institutions in establishing the budget.

Before the introduction of budgetary packages, in the eighties, the Council and Parliament regularly failed to come to an agreement on the annual budget in time, by the beginning of the financial year. Since multi-annual financial perspectives have been used, the annual budget has always been adopted on time. This is partly facilitated by the inter-institutional agreement between the Council and the Parliament, acknowledging and confirming the financial perspectives adopted by the Member States, in which Parliament in practice gives its consent to the perspectives, therefore it is expedient to consult Parliament during their preparation.

These longer budgetary planning periods also give ample time before the beginning of a period to review expenditure and revenue, to make the necessary changes, to solve problematic issues and to introduce reforms (e.g. in respect of own resources or the aim and functioning of various policies).

---

[12] The Constitutional Treaty would have institutionalised the system of multi-annual financial perspectives in the form of a multi-annual financial framework. This element is taken on board by the Reform Treaty (see Annex, Point 7.1.).

7.3.3. The Delors I and Delors II packages

During the Presidency of Jacques Delors, the European Commission put forward two major packages of reform proposals. These proposals, which are also known as the Delors I and Delors II packages, formed the basis for the decisions taken by Member States for the financial perspectives of subsequent years. The Delors I and II packages overhauled the common budget, with a view to solving the problems already outlined, and made the use of multi-annual financial perspectives standard practice.

The first longer-term budgetary framework was adopted by the Brussels European Council in February 1988, to boost revenue and rein in spending on agriculture. This Delors I package for the budgetary period 1988–1992, increased revenue by introducing the GNP-based resource (currently the GNI resource), and allocated the extra funds primarily for structural policy. In order to limit agricultural spending, it was decided that CAP expenditure should not grow by more than 74% of the Community's GNP growth. The Delors I package also introduced an overall ceiling for the Community's overall expenditure, set at 1.2% of the total annual GNP of the Member States.

The introduction of the GNP-based resource was a key step: it solved the acute problems of financing and ensured the stability of the common budget. At the same time, it also reduced the Community feature of the budget by accentuating Member State contributions. The reduced role of former own resources and the increased ratio of Member State contributions later sharpened the debate and conflict between the Member States.

The Delors II package, for the period 1993–1999, was adopted by the Edinburgh European Council in December 1992, allowing – in response to the demands of cohesion countries – an increase in the EU's overall expenditure from 1.2% to 1.27% of GNP by 1999, a gradual increase in the resources of the Structural Funds from ECU 19.7 billion in 1993 to 27.4 billion in 1999 (at 1992 prices), and the creation of a Cohesion Fund of ECU 15.1 billion for the period 1993–1999, to provide financial help for projects in the fields of environment and transport infrastructure in the four least developed Member States (Greece, Ireland, Portugal and Spain).

Another change introduced by the Delors II package was aimed at easing the VAT contribution burden of the less prosperous Member States. The role of this source of income, which had put a greater burden on countries with a higher rate of consumption, was modified, reducing VAT-based contributions for countries with GNP per capita below 90% of the Community average, and increasing VAT contributions for the other Member States. As a general rule, it was also decided that the maximum share of Member States' VAT revenue called in by the Community should be gradually reduced from 1.4% (1994) to 1% (1999).

The Delors II package was an important step for ensuring that the financial burden would be shared more evenly between Member States according to their economic strength, even if this was done by reducing the ratio of former own resources again. The new VAT–based resource system meant unfavourable changes for Denmark, for example. The United Kingdom continued to pay an unfairly large sum into the Community budget and so was permitted to keep its entitlement to a rebate of about 2/3 of its net contributions (i.e. negative net balance), which was institutionalised in 1984.

Overall, the Delors packages favoured the poorer Member States, which was only possible because of the willingness of more prosperous countries – especially Germany[13] – to finance the closer integration of backward regions in the single market and economic and monetary union, and thus create a more united and stronger European Union in the common interest of all Member States. The success of this policy was demonstrated by the gradual catching-up of less developed countries and their integration into the economic and monetary union.

This generous approach was possible in a favourable economic environment, but the recession of the '90s, increasing unemployment and budgetary difficulties, exacerbated by the austerity and restrictive measures necessitated by the preparations for monetary union, changed that optimistic climate. At the same time, finding a solution to the applications for membership submitted by CEECs also became an increasingly urgent task as the need for eastward enlargement began to be generally accepted. Enlarging the Union by a dozen or so poor countries with large agricultural sectors highlighted the prospect of drastic increases in Community spending, especially in agricultural and structural expenditure, and it was obvious that somebody would have to foot the bill. The biggest net contributors argued that their contributions were already unjustifiably high and raised the need to reduce their burdens, which, of course, triggered a negative

---

[13] Although Germany was not the most prosperous European country in terms of per capita GDP, during these years, its per capita net contribution was usually much higher than that of any other Member State.

Table 7.2. Changes in contributions to the EU budget due to the two Delors packages
(Net contributions to the EU budget in 1986 and 1995)

| Country | 1986 Net contribution | | | 1995 Net contribution | | | Per capita GDP in % of the EU average* |
	Total million ECU	Per capita ECU	rank	Total million ECU	Per capita ECU	rank	
Germany	3742	61.3	(2)	13431	164.6	(1)	106,7
United Kingdom	1438	25.3	(4)	4720	80.7	(6)	98.2
Netherlands	-217	-14.9	(8)	2005	129.7	(2)	100.4
France	561	10.1	(5)	1727	29.6	(9)	107.2
Sweden	–	–	–	937	105.5	(5)	95.3
Austria	–	–	–	905	112.9	(3)	109.3
Italy	195	3.4	(6)	614	10.7	(10)	101.7
Belgium	284	28.7	(3)	311	30.6	(8)	110.4
Finland	–	–		165	32.3	(7)	92.5
Luxemburg	59	160.3	(1)	45	110.6	(4)	128.2
Denmark	-421	-82.2	(10)	-306	-58.6	(11)	112.0
Ireland	-1230	-374.4	(12)	-1887	-526.8	(15)	85.3
Portugal	-219	-22.1	(9)	-2381	-241.8	(13)	67.9
Greece	-1273	-127.8	(11)	-3489	-333.0	(14)	60.0
Spain	-95	-2.5	(7)	-7218	-184.0	(12)	76.1

Source: European Court of Auditors

* Expressed in terms of PPS (purchasing power standard)

reaction from the biggest net beneficiaries. In addition to enlargement and the demand for a revision of net contributions, the need for the financial reform of the most expensive policies also became evident as a result of other internal and external factors necessitating restructuring, such as the obligations agreed to at the Uruguay Round of GATT (now the WTO). In the mid-nineties, it became clear that the comprehensive reform of the common budget and its main items – agricultural and structural policy – was inevitable, and that the issue would have to be solved before the next budgetary planning period starting in 2000. This resulted in a programme package published by the European Commission on 16 July 1997, which became known as Agenda 2000. This document was supposed to provide a solution to both traditional budgetary problems (agricultural policy financing, support for disadvantaged regions, and the issue of net contributions) and the new problems arising from enlargement, which only complicated things further.

7.3.4. The financial provisions of Agenda 2000

The Delors II package had set the expenditure of the EU budget until 1999, thus Member States had to adopt new financial perspectives for the years after 2000. The Madrid European Council (December 1995) requested the Commission to carry out an in-depth analysis of the impact of the EU's forthcoming eastern enlargement on its policies and, on that basis, propose a financing system for the next financial perspective. The Commission launched Agenda 2000 on 16 July 1997 with a view to assessing the financial implications of enlargement and the pressing need to reform the Common Agricultural Policy as well as structural and cohesion policy.[14] This action programme included the Commission's proposals for budgetary perspectives for the period 2000–2006, which included the implications of enlargement.[15]

The European Commission's proposed action programme soon became a rather controversial document, as it included several proposals on the rate of Member State contributions. Since Agenda 2000 was a complex financial package for a 7-year period, the Member States tried to defend their own interests until the last moment. Against such

---

[14] This comprehensive package outlined the key challenges the EU had to face in the years following 2000, as well as proposals for tasks, measures, reforms and a financial framework for facing those challenges.

[15] For more on Agenda 2000 and eastward enlargement, see 1.13.3.

a backdrop, it was not surprising that the adoption of Agenda 2000 took more than 18 months of negotiations but, finally, at the Berlin European Council of 24–25 March 1999, the Heads of State or Government finally adopted the financial perspective for the period 2000 to 2006.

The final text of Agenda 2000, as adopted by the European Council, differed from the original version on a number of points. Some of the Commission's reform proposals (particularly in the area of Common Agricultural Policy) were toned down, while in other areas (such as spending ceilings) Member States' demands were more rigorous than the Commission's proposals. Although the final document that was actually adopted can be criticised for leaving out or delaying some of the necessary reforms of the CAP, it has to be acknowledged that it undoubtedly created a budgetary framework that opened the way to enlargement while securing a sound financial basis for key policies. Member States decided to achieve this through covering the costs of enlargement primarily from the surplus revenue yielded by economic growth and only to a smaller extent from the reform of the budget and internal policies. This meant maintaining – or freezing – expenditure at 1999 levels in real terms and allocating surplus revenue generated by economic growth to the financing of the enlargement process. In the Berlin package, Member States intended to ensure that in the 2000–2006 period, Community funding to old Member States would not fall (although it should not increase either), while new Member States should also receive aid, although not what they would have been entitled to under the rules given their lower level of development. With this arrangement, Member States managed to solve the greatest contradiction: new Member States would enjoy the benefits of economic and social cohesion (i.e. Structural and Cohesion Funds), while the revenue of the poorer old Member States from the Community budget would not be immediately or radically cut down either. Despite all of these achievements, the failure to carry out a comprehensive structural and financial reform of the other key area, the Common Agricultural Policy, and the low level of agricultural support foreseen for new Member States made the sustainability of the financial framework uncertain. This foreshadowed the need for further reforms before the end of the financial perspective, and exacerbated the difficulties in the accession negotiations the parties were to encounter when it came to the chapter on agriculture.[16]

Another major factor of uncertainty was that, at the time of the elaboration of Agenda 2000, it was impossible to foresee the total number of countries that would become Member States between 2000 and 2006, in which year they would join and exactly how many countries each wave of enlargement would include. Agenda 2000 was thus originally

---

[16] The provisions of Agenda 2000 on agricultural policy and structural and cohesion policy are dealt with in detail in Subchapters 11.5. and 13.3.

based on the hypothesis of enlargement with 6 new Member States (i.e. a Union of 21 Member States) by 2006. This was due to the fact that, when Agenda 2000 was adopted in March 1999, the EU was negotiating with only six candidate countries. However, the Helsinki Summit of December 1999 decided to open negotiations with another six applicants. Moreover, the Member States declared that second-wave countries in the so-called 'Helsinki group' could catch up with applicants in the 'Luxembourg group', which four of them did.

Agenda 2000 introduced a number of changes concerning the structure of the budget. On the revenue side, the former own resources were maintained, but the rate of contributions was adjusted. The most important new measure was that the maximum call-in rate for the VAT-based resource would be gradually reduced from 1.0% to 0.75% in 2002 and 0.50% in 2004, which would be compensated for by increasing the GNP-based resource (from 2002, GNI resource). It was also agreed that the percentage of traditional own resources (customs duties and agricultural duties) retained by the Member States by way of collection (administrative) costs would be increased from 10% to 25% in 2001. While further reducing the role of real own resources to the detriment of the GNI resource, the Berlin European Council requested the Commission to undertake by 2006 an in-depth analysis of the possibilities of improving the system of own resources, including the introduction of new sources of revenue for the next financial perspectives from 2007.[17]

These changes on the revenue side favoured poorer countries with a higher rate of consumption, but moved in the direction of a more equitable sharing of the financial burden by Member States (e.g. by increasing the contributions of Denmark or Belgium). The interests and needs of net contributors (primarily Germany), who emphasised the excessive rate of contributions and asked for a reduction in their payments to the common budget, also had to be taken into consideration. This was mainly done by reining in spending on agricultural policy and structural measures. Despite the foreseeable high costs of enlargement, the financial framework laid down by Agenda 2000 kept the overall ceiling on expenditure at 1.27% of GNP (or 1.24% of GNI) for the entire period 2000–2006. This 1.27% ceiling included the possibility of a larger total budget, as the maximum budget had never been exhausted in previous years. The ceiling on expenditure set by the Delors II package for 1999 was 1.27% of GNP, but actual spending amounted to only

---

[17] During the negotiations on the 2007–2013 Financial Perspective, the issue of reforming the system of own resources was finally postponed until 2008–2009.

1.15%. During the 1993–1999 period, Community expenditure peaked in 1996 and 1997, when the EU budget redistributed 1.17% of Community GNP. This meant that about 0.1% of GNP remained unspent in previous years, which gave the EU some room for increasing spending. Agenda 2000 took account of these available resources as the other main source of financing enlargement along with surplus revenues generated by economic growth. When adopting Agenda 2000, the Member States emphasised that the budgetary balance guaranteed by the 1.27% ceiling indicated the Community's commitment to the

Table 7.3. The financial perspectives of Agenda 2000
(for the EU-21* for the period between 2000–2006, at 1999 prices, in million euros)

	2000	2001	2002	2003	2004	2005	2006
1. Agriculture	**40920**	**42800**	**43900**	**43770**	**42760**	**41930**	**41660**
Agricultural expenditure	*36620*	*38480*	*39750*	*39430*	*38410*	*37570*	*37290*
Rural development	*4300*	*4320*	*4330*	*4340*	*4350*	*4360*	*4370*
2. Structural operations	**32045**	**31455**	**30865**	**30285**	**29595**	**29595**	**29170**
Structural Funds	*29430*	*28840*	*28250*	*27670*	*27080*	*27080*	*26660*
Cohesion Fund	*2615*	*2615*	*2615*	*2615*	*2515*	*2515*	*2510*
3. Internal policies	**5900**	**5950**	**6000**	**6050**	**6100**	**6150**	**6200**
4. External action	**4550**	**4560**	**4570**	**4580**	**4590**	**4600**	**4610**
5. Administration	**4560**	**4600**	**4700**	**4800**	**4900**	**5000**	**5100**
6. Reserves	**900**	**900**	**650**	**400**	**400**	**400**	**400**
7. Pre-accession aid	**3120**	**3120**	**3120**	**3120**	**3120**	**3120**	**3120**
SAPARD	*520*	*520*	*520*	*520*	*520*	*520*	*520*
ISPA	*1040*	*1040*	*1040*	*1040*	*1040*	*1040*	*1040*
PHARE	*1560*	*1560*	*1560*	*1560*	*1560*	*1560*	*1560*
8. Enlargement			**6450**	**9030**	**11610**	**14200**	**16780**
Agriculture			*1600*	*2030*	*2450*	*2930*	*3400*
Structural operations			*3750*	*5830*	*7920*	*10000*	*12080*
Internal policies			*730*	*760*	*790*	*820*	*850*
Administrative expenditure			*370*	*410*	*450*	*450*	*450*
Total expenditure	**91995**	**93385**	**100255**	**102035**	**103075**	**104995**	**107040**

Source: European Council – Berlin conclusions (26 March 1999)

* The 15 old Member States and 6 new Member States (as foreseen by the state of play of accession negotiations in 1999) which Agenda 2000 did not name.

implementation of budgetary discipline[18] in connection with monetary union. It was also an instrument for the net contributor States that wanted to restrain any excessive spending that they would have to finance.

In order to establish a clear distinction between different types of expenditure, the cost of enlargement was included in the 2000–2006 financial perspectives in two separate new headings: 1) pre-accession aid to candidate countries; 2) spending reserved for possible new Member States. The Council decided to disallow any reallocation of resources between the budget lines for old Member States, candidate countries and new Member States.

Although preceded by long and tense negotiations, Agenda 2000, just like previous budgetary package deals, was based on comprehensive compromises between Member States. This is not surprising if we consider that, although the financial interests of Member States differ greatly, the adoption of a long-term financial perspective requires consensus among the parties. Despite the 18 months of heated debates on issues like reducing the financial burden of Germany (and, to some extent, the Netherlands, Austria and Sweden) or adjusting support for cohesion states (Spain, Portugal, Greece and Ireland), the gap between the position and demands of the Member States was so wide that no radical changes were possible in these areas. This was the situation reflected in the final version of Agenda 2000, which only made the most necessary changes and in practice upheld the status quo: Germany was unable to achieve a significant reduction in the level of its contributions, the special rebate paid to the United Kingdom was maintained (although the portion paid by Germany, the Netherlands, Austria and Sweden was reduced by one quarter of their normal share), support to cohesion states was not reduced although a ceiling was introduced, while France's strict opposition towards agricultural reform was reflected.

Concerning the implementation of the 2000–2006 financial perspective, it must be noted that the enlargement-related budget lines of Agenda 2000 had to be modified in line with developments during the enlargement process. By 2002, it had become clear that neither the hypothetical date of the first accessions (2002) nor the number of new members (6)

---

[18] See also 8.5. – 8.7.

would be the same as had been assumed originally. The Nice European Council in December 2000 made it clear that the earliest possible date of new accessions would be 2004, while the conclusions of the Laeken Summit in December 2001 (which talked about ten countries) made it very likely that the number of new Member States would exceed six. This meant that the budget lines of Agenda 2000 affecting the new Member States had to be finalised during the negotiations with the candidate countries, with the Berlin financial perspectives as a basis. The final deal reached in the accession negotiations (concluded on 13 December 2002 with 10 countries) concerning the 2004–2006 period (see Table 1.4.) was about 1.5 billion euros below the figure foreseen for the new Member States for that period in the Berlin financial perspectives, even though the original calculations were for 6 and not 10 new countries. This also resulted in the new Member States being entitled to significantly less Community funding in agricultural subsidies and structural measures than old Member States. According to the agreement reached at the negotiating table in Copenhagen, this differentiation was phased out in structural policy in 2007 and will be phased out in agriculture by 2013.[19]

The cuts in funding to new Member States were primarily due to worsening economic conditions. Agenda 2000 calculated with an outlook of 2.5% economic growth and hoped to finance enlargement from the surplus generated by that growth. As the actual figures were well below forecasts, net contributors demanded cuts in the annual budgets, which in turn led to lower spending on enlargement.

The economic slowdown, which hit the biggest net contributors, especially Germany, had an impact not only on the 2004–2006 finances, but on the perspectives from 2007 too. Net contributors increasingly pushed for the freezing of their contributions to the EU budget. In December 2003, six net contributors (Austria, France, Germany, the Netherlands, Sweden and the United Kingdom), in a letter to the European Commission (which was to become known as 'the letter of the Six'), called for the capping of the bloc's future budget, saying the expenditure side of the budget should not exceed 1% of the EU's gross national income. It was against this backdrop that the Member States had to begin talks in 2004 about the next financial perspective for the period 2007 to 2013.

---

[19] For more on the outcome of accession negotiations and the Copenhagen financial package adopted upon their closure, see 1.13.5.

Table 7.4. The budgetary contributions and receipts of Member States in 2005

Member State	National contribution without traditional own resources (EUR million)	Total contribution (all resources) (EUR million)	Total contribution (% of total EU revenue)	Total uptake from EU expenditure (EUR million)	Total uptake from EU expenditure (% of total EU expenditure)
Austria	1 955.5	2 144.0	2.13 %	1 785.8	1.86 %
Belgium	2 650.6	4 023.8	3.99 %	5 450.8	5.68 %
Cyprus	114.8	150.0	0.15 %	215.2	0.22 %
Czech Republic	844.1	990.2	0.98 %	1 074.8	1.12 %
Denmark	1 690.8	1 989.0	1.97 %	1 551.5	1.62 %
Estonia	83.7	99.7	0.10 %	248.7	0.26 %
Finland	1 352.2	1 464.9	1.45 %	1 349.7	0.63 %
France	15 516.8	16 854.1	16.72 %	13 617.1	14.18 %
Germany	17 411.9	20 136.3	19.97 %	12 282.7	12.79 %
Greece	1 601.9	1 801.6	1.79 %	5 596.0	5.83 %
Hungary	719.9	833.2	0.83 %	1 356.9	1.41 %
Ireland	1 260.2	1 442.5	1.43 %	2 492.9	2.60 %
Italy	12 204.8	13 546.7	13.44 %	10 693.9	11.14 %
Latvia	109.4	129.8	0.13 %	385.0	0.40 %
Lithuania	172.9	207.0	0.21 %	665.6	0.69 %
Luxemburg	211.2	227.0	0.23 %	1 100.4	1.15 %
Malta	38.2	50.1	0.05 %	134.6	0.14 %
Netherlands	4 462.7	5 947.1	5.90 %	2 092.7	2.18 %
Poland	2 055.2	2 327.2	2.31 %	4 029.0	4.20 %
Portugal	1 419.0	1 527.0	1.51 %	3 880.4	4.04 %
Slovakia	314.9	359.0	0.31 %	609.4	0.63 %
Slovenia	246.6	274.7	0.20 %	366.0	0.38 %
Spain	8 377.1	9 474.9	9.40 %	14 822.3	15.43 %
Sweden	2 303.2	2 654.3	2.63 %	1 561.8	1.63 %
United Kingdom	9 630.2	12 157.1	12.06 %	8 667.0	9.03 %
Total (EU)	86 748.0	100 811.1	100.00 %	96 030.6	100.00 %

Source: European Commission

Table 7.5. The net budgetary position of Member States (as a % of GNI) between 1993 and 2005

Country	1993	1995	1997	1999	2001	2003	2005
Austria	–	-0.44 %	-0.44 %	-0.32 %	-0.26 %	-0.15 %	-0.11 %
Belgium	0.12 %	0.21 %	-0.19 %	-0.14 %	-0.24 %	-0.28 %	-0.20 %
Cyprus	–	–	–	–	–	–	0.69 %
Czech Republic	–	–	–	–	–	–	0.19 %
Denmark	0.40 %	0.36 %	0.08 %	0.07 %	-0.13 %	-0.12 %	-0.13 %
Estonia	–	–	–	–	–	–	1.54 %
Finland	-0.06 %	-0.07 %	0.03 %	-0.17 %	-0.12 %	-0.02 %	-0.05 %
France	–	-0.08 %	-0.11 %	0.00 %	-0.14 %	-0.12 %	-0.17 %
Germany	-0.53 %	-0.58 %	-0.56 %	-0.43 %	-0.34 %	-0.35 %	-0.27 %
Greece	5.07 %	3.87 %	3.95 %	3.19 %	3.41 %	2.18 %	2.19 %
Hungary	–	–	–	–	–	–	0.72 %
Ireland	6.42 %	4.51 %	4.39 %	2.53 %	1.21 %	1.32 %	0.83 %
Italy	-0.14 %	-0.01 %	-0.03 %	-0.07 %	-0.16 %	-0.06 %	-0.16 %
Latvia	–	–	–	–	–	–	2.09 %
Lithuania	–	–	–	–	–	–	2.35 %
Luxembourg	-0.76 %	-0.38 %	-0.35 %	-0.48 %	-0.72 %	-0.27 %	-0.36 %
Malta	–	–	–	–	–	–	2.07 %
Netherlands	-0.05 %	-0.16 %	-0.31 %	-0.47 %	-0.51 %	-0.41 %	-0.52 %
Poland	–	–	–	–	–	–	0.80 %
Portugal	3.29 %	2.96 %	2.78 %	2.54 %	1.42 %	2.56 %	1.64 %
Slovakia	–	–	–	–	–	–	0.73 %
Slovenia	–	–	–	–	–	–	0.37 %
Spain	0.72 %	1.72 %	1.17 %	1.32 %	1.15 %	1.13 %	0.68 %
Sweden	–	-0.36 %	-0.52 %	-0.38 %	-0.40 %	-0.35 %	-0.30 %
United Kingdom	-0.14 %	-0.31 %	0.01 %	-0.20 %	0.06 %	-0.14 %	-0.08 %

Source: European Commission

7.3.5. The European Union's financial perspective for the period 2007–2013

7.3.5.1. The Commission's proposal

The Commission presented its proposal for the 2007–2013 financial perspective for an EU of 27 members on 10 February 2004, in the form of a Commission Communication entitled 'Building our Common Future: Policy Challenges and Budgetary Means for an Enlarged EU, 2007–2013'. Unlike the case of previous financial perspectives, the Commission chose a structure that was better suited to spelling out the European Union's key objectives and political priorities. The framework proposed by the Commission contained 5 headings, as presented in 7.2.2. above.

In its proposal, the Commission pointed out that expenditure for the period 2007–2013 was partly decided: in October 2002, agreement was reached among Member States on market and direct payments within the CAP until 2013[20]; due to the lower per capita GDP levels of the ten Member States that joined the EU in 2004, expenditure on cohesion policy would keep growing; the decision was made to grant membership on 1 January 2007 to another two less prosperous countries with big agricultural sectors (Bulgaria and Romania); several policy areas (such as internal market, transport, justice and home affairs) would require more and more funding due to the Treaties and certain secondary legal acts. The European Commission expressed its view that the level of financing proposed by the six net contributors (1% of GNI) would make it impossible for the Union to meet the commitment for farm spending, would undermine the gradual introduction of cohesion policy in the new Member States and could jeopardise the fulfilment of the new political priorities, including future enlargements ("we cannot build more Europe with less money".) In a 1% scenario, the EU would also be forced to curb its external aid programmes, cut rural development spending, backtrack on some of its international commitments and drastically reduce cohesion funding to 'old' Member States. Therefore the Commission's proposal represented 1.14% of EU GNI on average for the whole period 2007–2013 for covering the common expenditure of a Union of 27 members. In addition to retaining the principle of budgetary discipline, the Commission proposal would have also capped own resources at 1.24% of GNI, i.e. the ceiling applied from 2000 to 2006. The Commission stressed that due to the average drop of 0.1% in spending, this would still allow for a necessary degree of flexibility for unanticipated contingencies.

---

[20] For more details on this agreement see 11.6.

According to the Commission's proposal, commitment appropriations in 2007 should have totalled EUR 133.6 billion (at 2004 prices), which would grow to 158.5 billion by 2013. For the seven years of 2007–2013, the Commission would have liked to ensure EUR 1,025 billion for the Union.

The changes proposed by the Commission in the allocations to budgetary headings reflected the changing political priorities of the Union.
The most significant change in the Commission proposal is in Subheading 1a 'Competitiveness for growth and employment': an almost threefold increase from EUR 8.791 billion in 2006 to EUR 25.825 billion in 2013. With this increase, the Commission wished to put more emphasis on the economic policy objective enshrined in the Lisbon strategy: strengthening competitiveness, and so promoting sustainable growth and improving employment. As competitiveness fundamentally hinges on the performance, attitude and policies of the Member States, the Commission wanted to make available sufficient resources at EU level for reinforcing, complementing and supporting such national action.
The proposal called for a major leap in Subheading 1b 'Cohesion' from 2006 to 2007 when equal treatment of old Member States and those that joined in 2004 would have had to be applied and funding to new ones would have had to jump sharply. Overall, cohesion spending was to grow by about 25% from EUR 38.791 billion to 47.57 billion in just one year (2006 to 2007), but then not change significantly, edging up only to 50.96 billion by 2013. The Commission proposed maintaining the proportion of cohesion spending within the overall EU budget, but extending Structural and Cohesion Funds to the new Member States on equal terms. As a result, although in 2006 the 10 new Member States received only 22.5% of these Funds, for the 12 new Member States the Commission proposed 44.7% in 2007 and 53.3% in 2013.
As a key feature of Heading 2 'Preservation and sustainable management of natural resources', the Commission proposed the ceiling of market support and direct payments to farmers agreed by the Heads of State or Government in October 2002. With spending capped at a nominal maximum of 1%, CAP expenditure would not increase in the new financial period, while rural development would become more important (27% of the total expenditure in this heading, with market support and direct payments accounting for 70%,

Table 7.6. The European Commission's proposal for the financial framework 2007–2013
(in EUR million at 2004 prices)

Commitment appropriations	2006	2007	2008	2009	2010	2011	2012	2013	Total 2007–2013
1. Sustainable growth	47 582	59 675	62 795	65 800	68 235	70 660	73 715	76 785	**477 665**
1a. Competitiveness	*8 791*	*12 105*	*14 390*	*16 680*	*18 965*	*21 250*	*23 540*	*25 825*	*132 755*
1b. Cohesion	*3 8791*	*47 570*	*48 405*	*49 120*	*49 270*	*49 410*	*50 175*	*50 960*	*344 910*
2. Natural resources	56 015	57 180	57 900	58 115	57 980	57 850	57 825	57 805	**404 655**
of which agriculture (market support and direct payments)	*43 735*	*43 500*	*43 673*	*43 354*	*43 034*	*42 714*	*42 506*	*42 293*	*301 074*
3. Citizenship, freedom, security and justice	1 381	1 630	2 015	2 330	2 645	2 970	3 295	3 620	**18 505**
4. The EU as a global partner	11 232	11 400	12 175	12 945	13 720	14 495	15 115	15 740	**95 590**
5. Administration	3 436	3 675	3 815	3 950	4 090	4 225	4 365	4 500	**28 620**
Total appropriations for commitments	119 646	133 560	138 700	143 140	146 670	150 200	154 315	158 450	**1 025 035**
Total appropriations for payments	114 740	124 600	136 500	127 700	126 000	132 400	138 400	143 100	**928 700**
Payments as % of GNI	1.09%	1.15%	1.23%	1.13%	1.09%	1.12%	1.14%	1.15%	1.14%
Margin available	0.15%	0.09%	0.01%	0.11%	0.15%	0.12%	0.10%	0.09%	0.10%
Own resources ceiling as % of GNI	1.24%	1.24%	1.24%	1.24%	1.24%	1.24%	1.24%	1.24%	1.24%

Source: European Commission [COM(2004) 101 final (10 February 2004)]

fisheries 2% and environmental spending 1%). The weight of this heading would dwindle from 46.4% in 2006 to 36.5% in 2013.

The Commission proposed significant increases in Heading 3 'Citizenship, freedom, security and justice' (from EUR 1.381 billion in 2006 to 3.62 billion in 2013).

The Commission also proposed a relatively considerable increase in Heading 4 related to external actions (40% over six years) and Heading 5 related to administrative expenditures (30%).

On the whole, the Commission draft aimed to reduce the proportion of farm spending considerably, while putting much more emphasis on the new political priorities of competitiveness, Union citizenship, freedom, security and justice. The Commission proposal in practice would have left the rate of cohesion expenditure unchanged, but would have allocated a growing share of these funds to Member States that joined in 2004 and 2007.

7.3.5.2. The agreed Financial Perspective

Since it was published in February 2004, the Commission's proposal has created major divisions among the Member States. The six net contributors (Austria, France, Germany, the Netherlands, Sweden and the UK) took a firm stance, attacked the proposal and put their foot down, refusing to accept spending set at above 1% of GNI. At the same time, southern Member States rejected the 1% idea in no uncertain terms.

At the beginning of the debate, the net contributors mainly attempted to cut back cohesion spending in the old Member States (regions in the south of Europe) and reallocate those savings to the new Member States, but since this solution was the most unfavourable for the current main beneficiary countries, the southern Member States, they fought hard against the suggested 1% ceiling. However, the real sticking point preventing agreement among the Member States was not the 1% ceiling, but rather the issue of the British rebate and the financing of agricultural policy. Most Member States called for the abolition of the rebate, while the United Kingdom stuck to its guns, insistent on holding on to its rebate and right to special treatment[21] and only willing to accept cuts to the rebate in return for drastic reforms to the Common Agricultural Policy.

---

[21] In recent years, the UK has been reimbursed EUR 4 to 5 billion of its annual net contribution through the rebate mechanism.

The Member States were supposed to reach agreement on the financial perspectives for 2007–2013 before the end of the Luxembourg Presidency in June 2005. In an attempt to seal an agreement, the Luxembourg Presidency submitted a number of compromise packages during its six-month stint at the helm. The last compromise package was tabled prior to the closing summit of 16–17 June 2005, in which it proposed considerable cuts in the Commission's original proposal, capping commitment appropriations at only 1.06% of GNI.

The biggest cuts in the Presidency package would have slashed Subheading 1a (competitiveness) from the EUR 132 billion proposed by the Commission to just 72 billion over the seven-year period. In Subheading 1b (cohesion) the Presidency proposed to reduce the original Commission proposal from EUR 344 billion to 306 billion. The Presidency, with a view to the October 2002 agreement on agricultural spending, suggested only minor cuts (from 301 billion to 295 billion) in Heading 2 (agricultural market support and direct payments to farmers), but would have reduced both Headings 3 and 4 significantly (from 20 to 11 billion, and from 96 to 44 billion, respectively).

Interestingly, despite these major cuts, the new Member States were willing to accept the Presidency's package just to see a deal reached, and the southern countries – with the exception of Spain – were not hostile to it either. However at that point, the debate focused not so much on cohesion funding or key budget grand totals, but much more on the position of net payers and the extent to which they should contribute to the Community budget. Finally, the United Kingdom refused to accept any reduction or freezing of its rebate (which was a part of the Luxembourg Presidency package) until spending on the Common Agricultural Policy was reduced, the CAP reformed and the Community budget overhauled.[22] Securing agreement was all the more difficult because the Netherlands, the biggest net contributor in per capita terms, wished to improve its position by EUR 1.5 billion, and also because Sweden joined the UK in demanding CAP reforms and budget restructuring. But since France, along with some other Member States, was adamant about not linking farm policy reforms and the issue of the UK rebate (arguing that, in October 2002, the Member States took a unanimous decision about the financing of

---

[22] The UK was granted its rebate in the first place because of the way the Common Agricultural Policy was financed (in compensation for very low CAP funding). That is why they linked its reduction, freezing or abolition to CAP reform.

agricultural policy until 2013, which also served as the basis for the 2003 CAP reforms[23]), no agreement on the 2007–2013 financial perspectives was possible at the June 2005 summit and the negotiations had to continue. In July 2005, it was the UK's turn to take over the rotating Presidency, which added a special flavour to the budget talks.

During the British Presidency, it became clear that it was impossible to reach a political agreement on a comprehensive reform of the CAP before the 2007–2013 period as the UK would have liked. This meant that the British rebate would also remain largely unchanged. At the same time, the Member States were under increasing pressure to compromise as 2007 was approaching. For the new system to become operational from 1 January 2007, the Inter-Institutional Agreement with Parliament had to be signed in the first half of 2006, leaving enough time to adopt the implementing rules (particularly for the Structural and Cohesion Funds) in the second half of 2006. This implied that the Member States had to conclude the negotiations by the end of 2005.

In early December 2005, the British Presidency put forward a new proposal with further cuts to the Luxembourg package, with commitment appropriations at only 1.03% of GNI. Both the new Member States and Southern cohesion countries, as well as several net contributors, were critical of this proposal. Finally, at the European Council meeting of 15–16 December 2005, the Heads of State or Government agreed on a compromise halfway between the Luxembourg and the British proposals, capping commitment appropriations at 1.045% of GNI. According to the agreement at the 2005 December summit, the CAP financial package adopted in 2002 would remain in effect until 2013, and so would the British rebate (although not in its original form), but the EU would start discussing the reform of both the revenue and expenditure sides of the budget, especially the financing of the CAP, the system of own resources and the UK rebate. This deal forged by and between the net contributors was acceptable to net beneficiaries too. The compromise package was made more digestible for the new Member States: there was no further reduction in cohesion spending and the absorption rules of Structural and Cohesion Funds were relaxed. For the cohesion countries of the South, the phasing-out periods for regions suddenly finding themselves above the eligibility ceiling were long enough to sugar-coat the compromise package.

---

[23] See 11.6–11.7.

The final compromise had to be agreed by the European Parliament in the form of an Inter-Institutional Agreement. Negotiations between the Council and Parliament were never going to be easy; the Parliament supported the Commission's proposal and constantly criticised the Member States for the cuts they proposed. Similarly to the Commission, the Parliament stressed that "we cannot build more Europe with less money". However, the Parliament was ready to compromise in order to kick off the 2007–2013 financial perspective on 1 January 2007. In the end, the European Parliament managed to wring an EUR 4 billion increase spread over 7 years on top of the package agreed by the 2005 December European Council.[24] This meant that the Inter-Institutional Agreement finally signed by Council, Commission and Parliament on 17 May 2006 set commitment appropriations for the period 2007–2013 at 1.048% of Community GNI (84% of the figure originally proposed by the Commission).

The largest cuts to the Commission proposal were in Subheading 1a 'Competitiveness' although this still represented a yearly 7.5% increase on 2006. By 2013, spending under Subheading 1a will have gone up by 69%; research and technological development – which accounts for the largest chunk of this Subheading – by 75%.

For Subheading 1b 'Cohesion' the final agreement included a sum 10% below what was proposed by the Commission: EUR 308 billion (0.37% of GNI) for seven years. By 2013, structural and cohesion expenditure will have been augmented by 20% compared to 2006, with major shifts in favour of the Member States that joined in 2004 and 2007. The most favourable element of the financial perspective was the lowered minimum level of national co-financing and the introduction of new eligible fields of action.[25]

Expenditure under Heading 2 'Preservation and sustainable management of natural resources' was also curbed by roughly 10% compared to what the Commission proposed. The point of departure was the 2002 agreement on CAP financing, but with the

---

[24] The European Parliament primarily wanted to reintroduce sums in the original Commission proposal that the Member States had most reduced (Headings 1a, 3 and 4). Out of the 4 billion, the EP squeezed out of the Member States, 2 billion was incorporated into the expenditure ceiling, the rest appeared as reserve.

[25] For details, see 13.4.

incorporation of Bulgaria and Romania into the framework devised for 25 countries, which meant a proportional reduction in payments to individual Member States. Rural development funding enjoyed a major boost; over the seven-year period, it will amount to 24% of CAP market support measures and direct payments.

Final figures under Heading 3 'Citizenship and the area of freedom, security and justice' are hardly more than half of what the Commission proposed, but the EU will still spend 78% more in this area than it did in 2006.

Although Heading 4 'the Union as a global partner' was also cut to 50% of the Commission proposal, there will still be a small 8% hike from 2006 to 2013.

Another novelty of the 2007–2013 Financial Perspective is the decision of the Member States (approved by the Inter-Institutional Agreement) to set up a European Globalisation Adjustment Fund, with a view to providing complementary assistance for the restructuring efforts aimed at counterbalancing the negative impacts of globalisation and of world trade flows endangering European jobs. The annual budget of the Fund is EUR 500 million, financed mainly from unused expenditure of the previous budgetary year. The Financial Perspective also created a European Union Solidarity Fund with an annual budget of EUR 1 billion, which provides financial assistance to Member States and candidate countries in the event of natural disasters or terrorist attacks. The Emergency Aid Reserve, also a novel feature of the 2007–2013 Financial Perspective, enables the Union to respond rapidly to crisis situations in third countries and provide assistance for humanitarian aid, crisis management and civil protection, up to a maximum of EUR 221 million a year. In addition, a so-called Flexibility Instrument with an annual budgetary ceiling of EUR 200 million can supplement depleted headings of expenditure without a need for transfers.

One of the cornerstones of the agreement on the 2007–2013 Financial Perspective was the review clause, which served as a compromise solution to the most controversial budgetary issues (UK rebate, CAP reform) postponed to a later date. The review clause stipulates that both the revenue and expenditure side of the budget has to be reviewed. The Commission is instructed to carry out this comprehensive budgetary review during the course of 2008 and 2009, paying special attention to the British rebate and the Common Agricultural Policy. Based on the Commission's report, the European Council may then take decisions on areas covered by the review, the results of which will be taken into consideration when preparing the next Financial Perspective. Theoretically, such changes could be introduced before the end of the current financial period but, in practical terms, fundamental changes are likely only from 2014, provided that there is sufficient political will among Member States.

The Financial Perspective includes some key auxiliary rules for improving the budgetary position of net contributors. The VAT collection rate was capped at 0.3% (which meant a reduction), with special provisions for the four largest net contributors. For the years between 2007 and 2013, the maximum VAT collection rate for Austria is 0.225%, for Germany 0.15%, and for Sweden and the Netherlands 0.1%. On top of that, in these 7 years, the Netherlands and Sweden can withhold EUR 605 million and 150 million (respectively) of their GNI-based contributions.

The UK rebate was maintained in the form agreed by the 1999 Berlin European Council, except for the Member States that joined in 2004 and 2007, which can reduce their financial obligations vis-à-vis the United Kingdom (except for CAP direct payments) by 0% in 2007–08, by 20% in 2009, by 70% in 2010 and by 100% in 2011–13. The correction of the UK rebate over the seven-year period cannot exceed EUR 10.5 billion, roughly 20% of the total rebate; that is how much the UK was ready to sacrifice.

The biggest single structural change in the 2007–2013 Financial Perspective is the increased proportion of non-agricultural and non-cohesion internal policies (Headings 1a and 3). This is an important development even if the sums remain well below those proposed by the Commission. Another important structural change is the increase in rural development spending and the falling ratio of agricultural market support and direct payments within the budget. It may seem controversial that structural and cohesion expenditure has not gone up too radically, even though enlargement brought many new eligible regions. The question arises: how can a smaller budget (in terms of GNI proportion) finance a larger (wider and deeper) Europe? However, it would be

Table 7.7. The Financial Perspective adopted for 2007–2013
(in EUR million at 2004 prices)

Commitment appropriations	2007	2008	2009	2010	2011	2012	2013	Total 2007–2013
1. Sustainable growth	51 267	52 415	53 616	54 294	55 368	56 876	58 303	382 139
1a. Competitiveness	8 404	9 097	9 754	10 434	11 295	12 153	12 961	74 098
1b. Cohesion	42 863	43 318	43 862	43 860	44 073	44 723	45 342	308 041
2. Natural resources	54 985	54 322	53 666	53 035	52 400	51 775	51 161	371 344
of which agriculture (market support and direct payments)	43 120	42 687	42 279	41 864	41 453	41 047	40 645	293 105
3. Citizenship, freedom, security and justice	1 199	1 258	1 380	1 503	1 645	1 797	1 988	10 770
4. The EU as a global partner	6 199	6 469	6 739	7 009	7 339	7 679	8 029	49 463
5. Administration	6 633	6 818	6 973	7 111	7 255	7 400	7 610	49 800
6. Compensation to new Member States	419	191	190	–	–	–	–	800
Total appropriations for commitments	120 702	121 473	122 564	122 952	124 007	125 527	127 091	864 316
Commitments as % of GNI	1.10 %	1.08 %	1.07 %	1.04 %	1.03 %	1.02 %	1.01 %	1.048 %
Total appropriations for payments	116 650	119 620	111 990	118 280	115 860	119 410	118 970	820 780
Payments as % of GNI	1.06 %	1.06 %	0.97 %	1.00 %	0.96 %	0.97 %	0.94%	1.00 %
Margin available	0.18 %	0.18 %	0.27 %	0.24 %	0.28 %	0.27 %	0.30 %	0.24 %
Own resources ceiling as % of GNI	1.24 %	1.24 %	1.24 %	1.24 %	1.24 %	1.24 %	1.24 %	1.24 %

Source: Interinstitutional Agreement of the European Parliament, Council and Commission (OJ 2006/C 139/01)

a mistake to paint too tragic a picture; the 2007–2013 Financial Perspective was a logical consequence of how the EU currently operates. As long as decisions on financial planning and budgetary spending require a consensus of the Member States, no radical changes disadvantageous to some countries can be expected. It does not mean that the Member States will refuse all reforms, but they will take a firm stand on those that are not vital. If change entails major sacrifices by any Member State, agreement is only reached at the last moment, when change cannot be postponed any longer. This can be seen as a negative approach, but also as an expression of solidarity among Member States. And the Community budget is based on solidarity and the harmonisation of interests. As a direct consequence, the seven-year Financial Perspective and the annual budgets therein cannot have major losers or winners: in the European Union, compromises are forged along the lines of the lowest common denominator.

7.4. The budgetary procedure

The European Union's annual budget is adopted through the budgetary procedure, which is different from the other decision-making procedures discussed in Subchapter 4.1.2. The budgetary procedure is a unique decision-making process, which involves the Council, the Commission and the Parliament. The Commission prepares the Community budget, while the actual decision on its adoption is taken by the Council and the Parliament. That is why in this context 'eurospeak' refers to the Council and Parliament as the budgetary authority.

The budgetary procedure is conducted according to a strict timetable and conditions laid down in Article 272 of the EC Treaty. Every year, the Commission prepares a preliminary draft budget (PDB) according to the multi-annual financial perspectives set by the Council; the draft is sent to the Council by no later than 1 September. In practice, however, a 'pragmatic' timetable is applied by the three institutions, and the Commission adopts the preliminary draft budget in late April and tries to have as many rounds as possible of informal consultations ('trialogue meetings') with the Council and the Parliament. Having received the preliminary draft budget, both the Council and the Parliament start to elaborate their own positions on the draft.[26] The Council conducts its first reading of the

---

[26] The budgetary procedure has several levels within the Council. The draft is first discussed in a Council Working Group (Budgetary Committee), then by COREPER, and finally in the Council of Ministers (in its ECOFIN composition). The debate on the budget in the European Parliament is held in the Budget Committee, but the vote on Parliament's final position is – of course – taken in plenary session.

preliminary draft and establishes its version of the draft budget before 5 October, which it then sends to the Parliament. Both modifications to and adoption of the Commission's proposals require a Council decision by qualified majority voting.[27] Parliament conducts its first reading in a plenary session held within 45 days of the receipt of the Council's draft.[28] Parliament can either adopt the budget in its first reading (which is usually not the case), propose modifications to compulsory expenditure (obligations arising from the Treaties or from commitments under international agreements[29]) acting by an absolute majority of the votes cast, or make amendments to non-compulsory expenditure with an absolute majority of its members. These proposals and amendments are sent back to the Council, where a final decision is taken on compulsory expenditure by qualified majority voting (which cannot be rejected by Parliament separately, only if it rejects the budget as a whole). The Council adopts its own amended version on non-compulsory expenditure, also with qualified majority voting (this is the Council's second reading).

The draft budget, as amended, is returned to Parliament, which devotes most of its December part-session to reviewing non-compulsory expenditure, on which it can accept or refuse the Council's proposals. If the Council does not support Parliament's amendments for non-compulsory expenditure, Parliament has the power to overrule the Council's decision within a period of 15 days and, acting by a majority of its members and three fifths of the votes cast, can amend the amounts adopted by the Council. If Parliament is not satisfied with the final solution (especially with the Council's position on compulsory expenditure), it can reject the entire budget at its last plenary session in December by a two thirds majority, with more than half of the members present. This has happened on two occasions, in 1979 and in 1984; once (in 1982) the Parliament rejected an amending budget, and in the years between 1985 and 1988, the institutions failed to adopt the common budget by the beginning of the financial year. In such cases, until an agreement is reached and the new annual budget is adopted, the provisional twelfths laid down in Article 204 come into play, using the previous year's budget as a reference. In 1985 and 1988, the Council and Parliament reached an agreement on the budget only

---

[27] This is a peculiar feature of the budgetary procedure. Normally in the legislative process, the Council can only amend Commission proposals by a unanimous decision. (See 4.2.)

[28] If the Parliament fails to take a substantive decision within 45 days, the budget is considered adopted on the basis of the Council's first reading.

[29] These are budgetary items the payment of which are guaranteed by Community law, and are thus considered compulsory Treaty expenditure (currently accounting for 40% of the budget). The most important such items are agricultural price support and direct income. Similarly, external commitments such as trade preferences and aid granted to third countries, are also part of compulsory expenditure.

about half way through the fiscal year. However, since the introduction of the multi-annual budgetary packages (the financial perspectives), the adoption of the budget has been smoother; since 1988, the Council and Parliament have always managed to agree on the budget in time.

At the end of the budgetary procedure, the Parliament's President declares the budget adopted. The budget is then implemented by the Commission. The Court of Auditors has responsibility for controlling budget implementation and monitoring financial management. The European Parliament, though, has ultimate competence to decide whether discharge may be granted to the Commission in respect of budgetary management for the financial year in question.[30]

It should be noted that the Constitutional Treaty signed on 29 October 2004 would have introduced significant changes in the budgetary procedure. However, in response to the failure of the ratification of the Constitutional Treaty, the Heads of State or Government at their summit of 21–22 June 2007 decided to place the EU on new foundations by means of a Reform Treaty amending the current EU and EC Treaties. The Reform Treaty relies heavily on the Constitutional Treaty, adopting most of its provisions on the budget. The entry into force of the Reform Treaty will introduce two key changes: institutionalising the practice of multi-annual financial planning so far lacking a legal base in the Treaties and modifying the budgetary procedure. Since these provisions will probably only become effective in 2009, they are discussed in detail separately in Point 7 of the Annex 7.

---

[30] Although the Treaties stipulate no sanctions in the event of Parliament refusing to grant discharge to the Commission, such a decision has large political weight, comparable to that of a vote of no confidence. At the end of 1998, the Parliament delayed granting discharge because of the financial irregularities uncovered within the Commission. This led to a motion of censure against the Commission, which was not adopted by the EP, but which ultimately forced the entire Jacques Santer Commission to step down in the spring of 1999.

PART II

THE POLICIES OF THE EUROPEAN UNION

CHAPTER 8
THE ECONOMIC AND MONETARY UNION

8.1. The evolution of monetary integration

The Treaty of Rome establishing the European Economic Community did not include provisions on the monetary integration of the Community, let alone on genuine monetary union. At the time it seemed unnecessary since, at the turn of the fifties and sixties, the international monetary system, the Bretton Woods system – which was adopted after the Second World War and based on the supremacy of the dollar as a key currency and its convertibility into gold – guaranteed monetary stability for the international economy.

Nonetheless, the expansion of the common market soon raised the question whether the four fundamental freedoms could truly be achieved if the Member States pursued their own separate monetary policies. Since financial transactions between countries require currency exchange, the instability of the exchange rates and the unpredictability of fluctuations make the movement of goods, services, capital and labour risky from a business standpoint. Profit is more difficult to forecast and, as a result, the operation of a common market may become severely hampered. When the Member States outline their own monetary policies, exchange rates fluctuate corresponding to their internal economic and monetary processes. In the worst case, fluctuations may even generate a permanently unstable situation, which can undermine most advantages resulting from the customs union and common market.

This realisation, the necessity of eliminating exchange fluctuations, motivated the Member States to take the first steps towards establishing monetary integration and, ultimately, monetary union. For many, the objective of monetary union was a logical move, in view of the fact that integration theories envisaged economic union as the next step after establishing the common/single market and one of the most important elements of economic union is integrated monetary policy, and within it the single currency.

The serious need to converge the monetary policies of the Member States first emerged at the end of the 1960s, when the Bretton Woods system started to show the first signs of weakness. At the summit in The Hague in 1969, the creation of an economic and monetary union emerged as an official goal of European integration. A special committee was set up to draw up a report on how this goal might be achieved. The so-called Werner group submitted its report in 1970. It envisaged the achievement of economic and monetary union in several subsequent stages between 1971 and 1980.

As a first stage, it foresaw the reduction of the fluctuation margins between the currencies of the Member States to +/- 1% and, by gradually narrowing the band, its ultimate goal was the irrevocable fixing of exchange rates between the currencies. The collapse of the Bretton Woods system between 1971 and 1973 and the oil crisis of 1973 with its economic and political consequences, however, brought the realisation of the Werner Plan in its initial stage to an abrupt halt.[1]

After the collapse of the Werner Plan, the Member States attempted to fix the parities of the Community's currencies once again, but the British pound would not participate in this mechanism, while the weaker French franc and Italian lira could not. Finally, the plan was reduced to a zone of monetary stability comprising the permanently stable German mark and the currencies of some smaller States. Nonetheless, this cooperation could by no means guarantee the smooth operation of the Communities and the common market.

Due to the pervasive problems of the floating exchange rate system of the 1970s, the Member States renewed their efforts to establish a common monetary system. On a Franco-German initiative (the so-called Giscard-Schmidt proposal), the European Monetary System (EMS) was set up in 1979 without the participation of the United Kingdom. During the following two decades, the EMS guaranteed the sustainable monetary cooperation of the Member States.

8.2. The European Monetary System

The main objective of the European Monetary System (EMS) was to create exchange rate stability within the Community. The EMS was based on three elements: the Exchange Rate Mechanism (ERM), the European Currency Unit (ECU) and the European Monetary Cooperation Fund (EMCF).

The Exchange Rate Mechanism is based on the central parity-grid established by the national central banks for the participating currencies. A grid of bilateral rates was calculated for all the currencies. In 1979, the currency fluctuations had to be contained within a margin of +/-2.25%[2], which meant that the maximum fluctuation between any two

---

[1] Nonetheless, the objectives set in the Werner Plan continued to remain a matter of common political knowledge. The main aspects of the Werner Plan (the irrevocable fixing of exchange rates, complete convertibility, etc.) even served as the basis for the 1989 Delors Plan, outlining the concept of economic and monetary union (see 8.3. and 8.5.).

[2] With the exception of the Italian lira, which was allowed a margin of +/-6%. Later, when joining the system, the British pound was also allowed the same broader margin.

currencies was +/-4.5%; if the currency rates were not contained in the grid, the national central banks were obliged to intervene.

An important element of the EMS was the ECU, paving the road to the single currency. The ECU functioned as a basket of the currencies of all the Member States, and not only of those participating in the EMS, created by weighting the economic strength of the Member States. The exchange rate mechanism was also based on the ECU. The currencies of the Member States could fluctuate against the daily exchange rate of the ECU within a margin of +/- 2.25 %, otherwise the central banks had to intervene.

For their interventions, the central banks could draw on the short-term ECU credit facilities of the European Monetary Cooperation Fund, accumulated from the reserves of the Member States.

The launch of the European Monetary System coincided with the second oil crisis and, therefore, the initial stage was characterised by instability. The second stage of the EMS, which led to the stabilisation of the currency system, started in 1983. From September 1987, with the adoption of the Basel-Nyborg Agreement, a new era of the EMS set in. Under the Agreement, the central banks of the Member States intervened before their currencies reached the limits of the fluctuation margins. The new EMS brought about currency stability, first and foremost the stability of the franc-mark parity. The success of the European Monetary System is shown by the fact that the United Kingdom joined the mechanism (although with a 6% fluctuation margin) in 1990. Even Spain and Portugal, which entered the European Communities after the EMS had been created, joined the system in 1989 and 1992 respectively. Greece, which was struggling with an unremittingly high inflation level, was the only one of the then 12 Member States that did not participate in the EMS.

At the same time, the enduring recession at the beginning of the 1990s severely hampered the EMS. As a result of the 1992 monetary crisis, the British pound and the Italian lira exited from the mechanism and several currencies had to be devalued. Finally, in August 1993, the Member States were forced to raise the fluctuation margins from +/- 2.25% to +/-15%. This move was seen by many as the demise of the system, since with a 30% wide fluctuation band, one could hardly talk about an exchange rate mechanism. The end, however, did not come since, at the beginning of 1994, when the monetary crisis was over, the currency rates once again stabilised around the original narrow +/-2.25% margin.

Apart from the 1992–1993 monetary crisis, generally speaking, politicians and economists alike saw the European Monetary System as a positive development, whose advantages went way beyond its disadvantages. From 1979, the fluctuations between the currency rates of the Member States decreased significantly, while inflation rates converged considerably and stabilised at a low level. The EMS assisted the governments' anti-inflation policies and established the foundations for the coordination of the economic policies of the Member States, which was accepted as the basis for economic and monetary union.

The slowdown in economic growth, the increase in unemployment and the deterioration of the foreign trade balance are generally considered as the negative effects of the EMS, even though their relationship has never been substantiated.

The key importance of the EMS is that, by creating the ECU currency basket, it paved the road for the single currency. The ECU, which initially had been used solely for transactions between the central banks and for credit facilities, gradually started to fulfil a more diverse function. Although it always remained an accounting currency – it never existed as legal tender – it was introduced in the accounts stated between financial institutions and even in trading transactions. It had a key role in the bond market and came into general use as the base currency of credit cards; it also gained considerable popularity as a reserve currency since, being a currency basket, it retained an exceptionally stable value.

8.3. The Delors Plan

Following the collapse of the Werner Plan, the concept of monetary union was struck off the EC's agenda for a long time. However, the results of the EMS, the adoption of the Single European Act and the ensuing liberalisation of the capital market, placed it back on the agenda after 1987. This era is hallmarked by the name of the Frenchman Jacques Delors, who became the President of the European Commission in 1985.

Inspired by the success of the Single European Act, a committee chaired by Jacques Delors and mandated to define the objectives of monetary union, submitted its report in 1989. The Delors Report outlined the programme for establishing the economic and monetary union (EMU).

To this end, the Delors Report, similarly to the Werner Plan, proposed the complete liberalisation of capital movements, the complete and irrevocable convertibility of the national currencies, the elimination of fluctuation bands and the irrevocable fixing of the currency parities. As the key element of the system, it recommended the introduction of a single currency.

8.4. The advantages of the single currency

The idea of a single currency had been on the Community's agenda for quite a while even before the Delors Plan, yet the necessary conditions for its implementation had been missing. Ultimately, it was the programme of the common market that created the necessary foundation for introducing the single currency. The single currency itself is a key element for creating a truly free single market, as it eliminates the impediments deriving from exchange rate differences. At the turn of the 1980s-90s, however, it was assessed in a much wider dimension; besides guaranteeing the smooth operation of the single market, it was also expected to entail wide-ranging economic and political rewards.

During the era of the European Monetary System, severe exchange rate fluctuations led to the instability of economic processes. Hence, at the turn of the 1980s-90s, one of the most significant benefits of the single currency was expected to be the complete elimination of exchange rate fluctuations and risks. It was considered that this, in turn, would make the dealings and economic processes between the Member States more predictable and calculable, boosting cross-boundary transactions and stimulating economic growth and employment. Besides triggering economic prosperity as a result of exchange rate stability, a whole range of further benefits was associated with the introduction of the single currency.

In the monetary union, the elimination of uncertainties linked to exchange rate fluctuations was expected to bring about price stability, low inflation rates and falling interest rates. Consequently, the financing of national debts would become easier and the number of investments would grow, which would ultimately result in the acceleration of economic growth.

One of the gravest dangers threatening the stability of exchange rates is market speculation. It may have an especially devastating effect on smaller national economies, since there could be foreign exchange speculations on a greater scale (sales or purchase). The introduction of the single currency, on the other hand, creates an economy/currency zone on a scale that can only be compared to the American economy and the dollar and is far less likely to be jeopardised by any monetary speculation.

The introduction of the single currency also eliminates the transaction costs incurred by currency exchanges between the Member States. Furthermore, the prices in the Member States become easily comparable and the market opportunities discernible, which could give momentum to the dynamics of the single market, encourage competition and enhance economic growth and employment.

With the establishment of a common central bank, significant reserves are released, since national central banks without an independent monetary policy need smaller reserves. The released common reserves may be utilised to meet various economic policy objectives.

It is of key importance for the future of the European Union and its role in the world economy and international politics that the common European currency is on an equal footing with the American dollar and the Japanese yen. This further strengthens the Union's monetary sovereignty, independence and stability and increases its weight and influence in the political arena. The ensuing monetary autonomy and stability create a sound economic environment, which also gives momentum to economic growth and creates new jobs.

Monetary union also facilitates political union, since for countries sharing the same currency it makes sense to – for example – pursue coordinated foreign policies. The spill-over process – which means that monetary union intensifies the integration process and establishes closer links between the Member States in other areas – is seen by many, especially the federalists, as one of the supreme benefits of the single currency.

8.5. The Treaty of Maastricht and the EMU

The Treaty of Maastricht, signed on 7 February 1992, institutionalised the Delors Plan in a slightly modified form and established it as the official programme of the Union. Under the Maastricht Treaty, the Member States are legally bound to comply with the programme, with the exception of the United Kingdom and Denmark, who have obtained an opt-out[3] and may freely decide whether to join the single currency or not.

As the final objective of the economic and monetary union, the Maastricht Treaty stipulated that the single currency had to become the official currency by 1 January 1999. The Treaty also outlined the institutional framework of the monetary union and called for the future establishment of the European Central Bank (ECB) and the European System of Central Banks (ESCB).[4]

The Treaty provides for economic and monetary union to be introduced in three successive stages.

---

[3]   See also 1.9.
[4]   On the European Central Bank and the European System of Central Banks in detail, see 2.10.

The first stage was completed on 1 January 1994. Its main objectives were the liberalisation of capital movements, the establishment of the independence of central banks and the coordination of the economic policies of the Member States.

After the successful completion of the first stage, the founding of the European Monetary Institute (EMI), the precursor to the European Central Bank, on 1 January 1994, marked the start of the second stage. The task of the EMI was to make preparations for the conduct of the single monetary policy, to strengthen central bank cooperation, to monitor the European Monetary System and public finances and to extend the scope of application of the ECU.

Pursuant to the Maastricht Treaty, the second stage had to be completed by 1 January 1999. The transition to the third stage was subject to the achievement of certain criteria by the Member States and to the adoption of certain decisions of a technical and practical nature regarding the introduction of the single currency. The Treaty stipulated that the third and final stage of the EMU had to start on 1 January 1999 with the introduction of the single currency. The Treaty allowed for no loophole to the commencement of the third stage, that is, to the introduction of the single currency. It stipulated that, if no decision was adopted regarding the date of commencement of the third stage by the end of 1997, it would commence automatically as of 1 January 1999.

Under the Treaty of Maastricht, in order to join the single currency, the economies of the Member States must fulfil certain conditions vital to the monetary union, those being the stability of their economy, the existence of appropriate conditions for currency union and excellent monetary results. These requirements were set up because the Member States wanted to adopt a stable, inflation-free single currency, which would guarantee the predictability of the economy and which would be able to preserve price stability in the long run. The criteria were designed to ensure that these objectives were met. The relatively strict standards to be met by the Member States for the adoption of the single currency, the so-called Maastricht convergence criteria, are as follows:

- *Price stability:* the annual consumer price level (inflation) may not exceed the average rates of inflation of the three Member States with the lowest inflation rate by more than 1.5%.
- *The convergence of interest rates:* the annual long-term interest rates may not exceed by more than 2% the average interest rates of the three Member Sates with the lowest inflation rates.
- *Exchange rate stability:* a national currency may not be devalued during the two previous years within the exchange rate mechanism (ERM) of the European Monetary System.

- *The sustainability of the government financial position:* the annual budget deficit must remain below 3% of GDP and gross government debt must not exceed 60% of GDP (theoretically the public debt of a State may exceed 60% of GDP if it shows a falling trend).

It must be mentioned that, under the Maastricht Treaty, the Member States – with the exception of the United Kingdom and Denmark – are obliged to strive to meet the convergence criteria. Nonetheless, Member States that fail to comply with these conditions before their entry into the third stage of the EMU do not face sanctions.[5]

The importance of the convergence criteria lies in the fact that it is these provisions that the Heads of State or Government observe when deciding which Member States may enter the third stage of the monetary union.

8.6. The EMU after Maastricht – the introduction of the euro

8.6.1. Difficulties after the Treaty of Maastricht

During the years following the adoption of the Treaty of Maastricht, the introduction of the single currency seemed to be doomed to failure. In 1993 and 1994, a recession set in and the economic indicators which had to be taken into account for the transition to the third stage of the monetary union deteriorated significantly in almost all the Member States of the Union. The magnitude of the recession is shown by the fact that, while at the time of the adoption of the EMU, most Member States stood a good chance of meeting the convergence criteria, by 1994, Luxemburg remained the only Member State that managed to fulfil all the conditions. The recession led to the swelling of the national budget deficits, which was generally understood as the most important criterion. Germany, despite its renowned economic austerity, was no exception, since the reunification of the country placed an enormous burden on its national budget. Unemployment rose to an exceptionally high level; it ran as high as 10% throughout the EU. Many saw the rise in unemployment as a backlash of strict monetary policy and the European Monetary System's preoccupation with price stability. The conviction was growing, and not only in the circles of radical political forces, that the introduction of the single currency and the third stage should be postponed.

---

[5] Pursuant to the Stability and Growth Pact adopted in June 1997, the Member States that have entered the third stage of the EMU (i.e. who have met the criteria) could face sanctions for non-compliance. On the Pact, see 8.7. It must be noted that, in the case of countries eligible for the Cohesion Fund (for more details see Chapter 13), i.e. with per capita GNP below 90% of the EU average, repeated violation of the budget deficit ceiling could – as a last resort sanction – lead to a suspension of financing for cohesion projects. Although the Regulation on the Cohesion Fund includes this option, it has never been activated.

In the period 1994–1995, a general political debate raged in the EU about a potential rescheduling and its consequences.

Theoretically, however, it was impossible to reschedule the introduction of the single currency, as it would have required the amendment of the text of the Treaty establishing the European Community as adopted in Maastricht. Furthermore, the rescheduling entailed the potential threat that, once again, the monetary union might be brought to an abrupt halt as had happened after the demise of the Werner Plan, which would have hindered the possibility of introducing the single currency in the near future. This would have held up the entire integration process, which the leaders of the Member States wanted to avoid at any cost. Ultimately, the governments of the Member States decided to adopt rigorous budgetary measures to attempt to meet the most challenging convergence criterion on the budget deficit. In 1995, the Member States started competing against each other in bringing down their national budget deficits.

8.6.2. Decision about the euro and the timetable of its introduction

The determination of the political leaders of the Member States is shown by the fact that, notwithstanding the difficulties, in December 1995, at the Madrid Summit, they adopted a scenario for the unresolved questions of the third stage. The European Council in Madrid set 1 January 1999, the latest date specified by the Treaty, as the date for the start of the third stage, and agreed that the participating countries would be chosen at the beginning of 1998. The Heads of State or Government christened the European currency unit to be introduced as the 'euro'[6]. A chronological sequence of events was also announced for the changeover to the euro: the three-year transitional period would start on 1 January 1999 and culminate in the introduction of the euro as a legal tender.

---

[6] The Member States opted for the name *euro* because it can be easily understood in any of the 11 official languages of the Union at that time and it is spelled the same way (although pronunciations vary) in all the languages, except for Greek. The official Hungarian spelling according to the Hungarian Academy of Sciences is *euró*, which led to debates when the Constitutional Treaty was being translated into Hungarian. The Council insisted that the spelling *euro* be used in the Treaty and, in the end, this spelling became official in the translation. Hungary and Latvia declared in a Declaration on the spelling of the single currency to be annexed to the Constitutional Treaty that "without prejudice to the unified spelling of the name of the single currency of the European Union referred to in the Treaty as displayed on the banknotes and on the coins (…) the spelling of the name of the single currency, including its derivatives as applied throughout the Latvian and Hungarian texts of the Treaty, has no effect on the existing rules of the Latvian and the Hungarian languages". (In practical terms, this implies that spelling will not change on euro notes and coins once these countries introduce the single currency.)

According to the euro timetable adopted in Madrid, the exchange rates of the currencies of the Member States participating in the eurozone had to be irrevocably fixed against each other and the ECU with effect from 1 January 1999. The exchange rate of the ECU to the euro was set at 1:1. Initially, during a transitional period of three years, the euro would exist only as an accounting unit and not in "tangible" form. During the interim period, the national currencies would remain in circulation and function as denominational currencies of the euro (with their exchange rate irrevocably fixed against the euro). On 1 January 2002, the euro banknotes and coins would be put into circulation. Under the Madrid timetable, the national currencies were to be used as legal currencies parallel with the euro for a maximum period of six months. The dual circulation was to be applied up to 1 July 2002, when the national currencies would have to be withdrawn from circulation. In September 1999, however, ECOFIN, the Council of Economic and Finance Ministers of the EU, adopted a decision concerning the exact length of the dual circulation period and decided that the maximum duration should not exceed two to three months. Finally, the Member States agreed that the replacement of currencies and the withdrawal of national currencies from circulation would have to be completed by 28 February 2002 in the participating Member States and that the euro should become the sole legal tender as of 1 March 2002.

At the Madrid Summit, the Heads of State or Government also reached an understanding that, after specifying which Member States could participate in the third stage, the European Central Bank would be established and the members of its Executive Board appointed at the earliest possible time. The operational framework of the ECB and the ESCB would need to be put in place by 1 January 1999.

8.6.3. The third stage and the introduction of the single currency

In the period 1996–1997, the Member States were committed to introducing austere budgetary restrictions to repress inflation rates and to reduce public debt, in order to overcome their economic and financial difficulties. Despite their efforts, at the end of 1996, some Member States were still experiencing difficulties in meeting the budget deficit criterion, amongst them France and Germany, whose participation had a strategic importance for the introduction of the single currency.

By 1997, the criteria had to be met at any cost, as the following year the Member States had to adopt the final decision concerning the third stage to be commenced in 1999, which meant that they had to decide on the basis of the economic indicators of 1997.[7]

---

[7] With the exception of the exchange rate stability criterion, as the Treaty stipulated that the indicators of the previous two years, or rather whether a national currency had to be devalued during the two previous years within the ERM, must be taken into account.

By 1997, essentially all the Member States, except for Greece, managed to meet the convergence criteria (even though Sweden and the United Kingdom stayed out of the European Exchange Rate Mechanism). This achievement was partly due to the increase in economic growth, partly to restrictive economic policies and partly to certain accounting tricks[8].

In accordance with the decisions of the Madrid Summit, at the beginning of 1998 the Heads of State or Government of the Member States were to decide, on the basis of the Commission's recommendation, which Member States would enter the eurozone in 1999. The Commission submitted its report on 25 March 1998.

The Commission – whose report did not include Denmark and the United Kingdom, which had opted out of the eurozone[9] – decided that 11 of the 13 Member States were eligible to participate in the third stage. Greece did not fulfil any of the criteria[10]. The Commission reprimanded Sweden for not participating in the ERM. Sweden, however, did not intend to enter the eurozone in 1999, for reasons not unlike those of Denmark and the United Kingdom, and this was essentially one of the factors why it did not participate in the ERM. It must be mentioned that Sweden is an exceptional case as regards the Member States' entry into the third stage. Pursuant to the Treaty, any Member State that met the convergence criteria (with the exception of the two Member States which had opted out) was in theory required to introduce the single currency. Nevertheless, Sweden also made sure it stayed out by non-fulfilment of the criteria.

---

[8] In France, for example, the amount of 37.4 billion francs paid by France Télécom to be privatised to cover its future pension contributions was accounted as budgetary revenue. This amount decreased the deficit of the budget by 0.5 %, thus lowering it to the 3.0% ceiling. Other Member States also needed to resort to similar accounting tricks ("creative accounting") to meet the deficit criterion.

[9] Under the Treaty of Maastricht, Denmark and the United Kingdom had the right to opt out of the third stage. Both of these Member States met the convergence criteria effortlessly, even though the United Kingdom did not participate in the ERM. The United Kingdom and Denmark traditionally believe in a slower pace of integration. Generally, they are seen as the Member States that are most reluctant to give up their national sovereignty. As the public and the majority of politicians in both countries saw the national currency as an important symbol of national sovereignty, it came as no surprise that they got an opt-out in the Treaty of Maastricht. It must be mentioned, however, that neither country rejects the idea of the single currency per se. Their opt-out is most probably temporary and they would be ready to join the eurozone if the euro proves successful in the long run. In Denmark, a referendum was held on 28 September 2000 on the adoption of the euro, where the majority of the votes, 53.9%, were cast against the single European currency.

[10] Greece was, however, fully committed to the objectives of the EMU and ultimately managed to enter the third stage of the EMU and the eurozone on 1 January 2001, as a result of the country's steadfast economic policy and improving macro-economic indicators. However, later it turned out that the Greek government had reported false budget deficit figures and in 1999 (the year on the basis of which Greece was allowed to join the eurozone) it did exceed the 3% ceiling by a few decimal points.

Table 8.1. The fulfilment of the convergence criteria by the Member States in 1993, 1995 and 1997

Member States	Inflation rates			Long-term interest rates			Budget deficit (% of GDP)			Public debt (% of GDP)			Participation in the ERM in 1997
	1993	1995	1997	1993	1995	1997	1993	1995	1997	1993	1995	1997	
Austria	–	2.0	1.1	–	7.1	5.6	–	–6.2	–2.5	0	69.2	66.1	yes
Belgium	2.8	1.4	1.4	7.2	7.5	5.7	–6.6	–4.5	–2.1	136.9	131.2	122.2	yes
Denmark	1.3	2.3	1.9	7.3	8.3	6.2	–4.4	–1.4	0.7	79.5	73.3	65.1	yes
Finland	–	1.0	1.3	–	8.8	5.9	–	–5.6	–0.9	–	58.0	55.8	yes
France	2.1	1.7	1.2	6.8	7.5	5.5	–5.8	–5.0	–3.0	45.8	52.7	58.0	yes
Germany	4.1	1.6	1.4	6.5	6.8	5.6	–3.3	–3.5	–2.7	48.1	58.1	61.3	yes
Greece	14.5	9.0	5.2	23.4	17.3	9.8	–13.3	–9.2	–4.0	115.2	110.1	108.7	no
Ireland	1.5	2.4	1.2	7.7	8.3	6.2	–2.5	–2.4	0.9	96.1	82.3	66.3	yes
Italy	4.3	5.4	1.8	11.3	12.2	6.7	–9.5	–7.1	–2.7	118.6	124.2	121.6	yes
Luxemburg	3.6	1.9	1.4	6.9	7.6	5.6	1.1	0.3	1.7	7.8	5.9	6.7	yes
Netherlands	2.6	1.1	1.8	6.4	6.9	5.5	–3.3	–3.4	–1.4	81.4	79.0	72.1	yes
Portugal	6.5	3.8	1.8	10.0	11.5	6.2	–7.2	–5.4	–2.5	66.9	65.9	62.0	yes
Spain	4.6	4.7	1.8	10.2	11.3	6.3	–7.5	–5.8	–2.6	59.8	65.5	68.8	yes
Sweden	–	2.9	1.9	–	10.2	6.5	–	–8.1	–0.8	–	77.6	76.6	no
United Kingdom	1.6	3.0	1.8	7.5	8.3	7.0	–7.8	–6.0	–1.9	48.3	53.9	53.4	no
The Maastricht criteria	3.0	2.7	2.7	9.5	9.7	7.8	–3.0	–3.0	–3.0	60.0	60.0	60.0	yes

Source: European Commission

The Heads of State or Government decided in Brussels on 2 May 1998, following the recommendation of the Commission, that 11 countries – Austria, Belgium, Finland, France, Germany, Ireland, Italy, Luxemburg, the Netherlands, Portugal and Spain – would take part in the third stage of EMU commencing on 1 January 1999. They also decided on the irrevocable fixing of the exchange rates of the national currencies of the 11 Member States joining the eurozone and the necessary conversion rates. The Heads of State or Government in Brussels nominated the members of the Executive Board of the European Central Bank and, in May, they were appointed by the Council after consulting the European Parliament. Their appointment marked the establishment of the ECB and the ESCB on 1 June 1998. All the institutions necessary for the conducting of a single monetary policy were in place. On 1 January 1999, at midnight, what is perhaps the most tangible result of European integration, the single currency, in the form of the euro, set out on its historic journey with due solemnity.

The number of participating Member States increased to 12 on 1 January 2001, when Greece, having met the convergence criteria, finally entered the third stage. Thus the euro banknotes and coins were finally put into circulation in 12 Member States on 1 January 2002. As planned, the national currencies were withdrawn from circulation by 28 February 2002 and, as of 1 March 2002, the euro became the only legal tender in all 12 participating countries.[11] Thus, possibly the greatest venture of European integration was accomplished successfully and smoothly.

Since the introduction of the euro on 1 January 1999, the commencement of the single monetary policy and the readjustment of the payment system have proved to be successful. The integration of the European capital markets has made considerable progress and the euro has gained a position similar to that of the dollar in international bond issues. The main objective of price stability has been attained. The ECB has met its official objective established in its monetary policy strategy issued on 13 October 1998, under which, in the eurozone, the annual growth rate of the Harmonised Index of Consumer Prices (HICP)[12] must not exceed 2 per cent in the medium term. Although inflation rose to 2.4 per cent in the summer of 2000, this was mainly attributable to a sudden rise in energy prices; core inflation (the price index excluding energy and food) did not surpass 2 per cent.

Nonetheless, the exchange rate of the euro did more poorly than expected. In the two years following its introduction, it remained continuously low, triggering press headlines such as "euro goes into full nose-dive mode". The euro fell from the initial rate of 1.17 to 0.85 against the dollar by September 2000, and failed to bounce back to above

---

[11] The national banks, however, continued to exchange the former national currencies for a considerable time (in some countries for an indefinite period of time).

[12] The HICP counter-balances the differences in consumer baskets of the Member States.

USD 0.90 for quite a while.[13] It must be mentioned, however, that the European Central Bank did not intend to intervene in the euro-dollar exchange rate, since it attempted to focus on, and by and large was successful in, fulfilling its primary objective – the maintenance of price stability and internal balance. From a certain point of view – which however should not be over-estimated – the devaluation of the euro was even seen as beneficial to the European economy, since it facilitated export growth. In the autumn of 2002, the euro bounced back to parity with the dollar, and then continued to rise. Riding the 'weak dollar' wave in spring 2003, the euro catapulted to a high of USD 1.25, and a year later to USD 1.35, and has steadily held its position since in the 1.25–1.35 band.

The monetary strategy of the new Member States was proof of the stabilisation of the euro and the successful operation of the eurozone. The Member States that acceded to the EU on 1 May 2004 and on 1 January 2007 generally decided on a swift adoption of the single currency and tailored their economic policies accordingly. The target dates the new Member States have set themselves for eurozone membership vary from 2007 to 2013. The biggest challenge they face in meeting the convergence criteria is usually the stability of government finances, and mainly keeping the budget deficit below the 3% limit. Once the new Member States manage to push down budget deficits to the required level, they will probably face no major difficulties in meeting the other criteria (on inflation, interest rates and participation in ERM II[14]). Among the new Member States, Estonia, Lithuania and Slovenia were the first to join the ERM II (the euro 'waiting room') in June 2004, Cyprus, Latvia and Malta followed in May 2005 and Slovakia in November 2005. Bulgaria, a member since 1 January 2007, is planning ERM II membership for 2007.

---

[13] As a result of the monetary crises in the emerging markets and their increasing spread, investors tended to pull out of unsafe markets and invest mainly in American government securities, which contributed to this situation.

[14] With the introduction of the euro, the Exchange Rate Mechanism (ERM) of the European Monetary System was replaced by ERM II, which ensures the link between the eurozone members and those Member States that stayed out of the eurozone but wish to participate in the exchange rate mechanism. Participation in ERM II is a precondition for eurozone membership. Of the three old Member States that opted out of the eurozone, only Denmark and the Danish krone participated in ERM II. The British pound was also part of ERM II between 1990 and 1992 but had to leave during the 1992 financial crisis and has stayed out since. Sweden remains out of ERM II in order to not meet the Maastricht criteria and thereby avoids having to join the eurozone.

Table 8.2. Convergence indicators for government financial position
in the Member States (2003–2006)

Member States	Budget deficit (-) / surplus (+) (as a % of GDP)				Public debt (as a % of GDP)			
	2003	2004	2005	2006	2003	2004	2005	2006
Austria	–1.6	–1.2	–1.6	–1.1	64.6	63.9	63.5	62.2
Belgium	+0.1	0.0	–2.3	+0.2	98.6	94.3	93.2	89.1
Finland	+2.5	+2.3	+2.7	+3.9	44.3	44.1	41.4	39.1
France	–4.1	–3.6	–3.0	–2.5	62.4	64.3	66.2	63.9
Germany	–4.0	–3.7	–3.2	–1.7	63.9	65.7	67.9	67.9
Greece	–6.2	–7.9	–5.5	–2.6	107.8	108.5	107.5	104.6
Ireland	+0.4	+1.4	+1.0	+2.9	31.2	29.7	27.4	24.9
Italy	–3.5	–3.5	–4.2	–4.4	104.3	103.8	106.2	106.8
Luxembourg	+0.4	–1.2	–0.3	+0.1	6.3	6.6	6.1	6.8
Netherlands	–3.1	–1.8	–0.3	+0.6	52.0	52.6	52.7	48.7
Portugal	–2.9	–3.3	–6.1	–3.9	56.8	58.2	63.6	64.7
Slovenia	–2.8	–2.3	–1.5	–1.4	28.6	28.9	28.4	27.8
Spain	0.0	–0.2	+1.1	+1.8	48.8	46.2	43.2	39.9
Total – Eurozone	**–3.0**	**–2.8**	**–2.5**	**–1.6**	**69.2**	**69.7**	**70.5**	**69.0**
Bulgaria	–0.9	+2.2	+1.9	+3.3	45.9	37.9	29.2	22.8
Cyprus	–6.3	–4.1	–2.3	–1.5	69.1	70.3	69.2	65.3
Czech Republic	–6.6	–2.9	–3.5	–2.9	30.1	30.7	30.4	30.4
Denmark	0.0	+2.0	+4.7	+4.2	45.8	44.0	36.3	30.2
Estonia	+2.0	+2.3	+2.3	+3.8	5.7	5.2	4.4	4.1
Hungary	–7.2	–6.5	–7.8	–9.2	58.0	59.4	61.7	66.0
Latvia	–1.6	–1.0	–0.2	+0.4	14.4	14.5	12.0	10.0
Lithuania	–1.3	–1.5	–0.5	–0.3	21.2	19.4	18.6	18.2
Malta	–10.0	–5.0	–3.1	–2.6	70.4	73.9	72.4	66.5
Poland	–6.3	–5.7	–4.3	–3.9	47.1	45.7	47.1	47.8
Romania	–1.5	–1.5	–1.4	–1.9	21.5	18.8	15.8	12.4
Slovakia	–2.7	–2.4	–2.8	–3.4	42.4	41.5	34.5	30.7
Sweden	–0.9	+0.8	+2.1	+2.2	53.5	52.4	52.2	46.9
United Kingdom	–3.2	–3.1	–3.1	–2.8	38.8	40.3	42.2	43.5
Total – EU Member States	**–3.1**	**–2.7**	**–2.4**	**–1.7**	**61.8**	**63.2**	**62.9**	**61.7**

Source: Eurostat

Slovenia was the first of the ERM II countries to meet the Maastricht convergence criteria: on 1 January 2007, it became the first Central or Eastern European country to adopt the single currency and the 13th member of the eurozone. Eurozone membership will increase to 15 in 2008: according to the decision of the Heads of State or Government taken at their meeting on 21–22 June 2007, Cyprus and Malta will join the eurozone on 1 January 2008.

The accession of the new Member States to the eurozone will undoubtedly have an impact on the strategy of the old Member States who opted out of the single currency because, once all new Member States have adopted the euro, the euro will be used in most of the area of the Union. It should, however, be noted that although only 13 of the 27 Member States are part of the eurozone in 2007, these countries generate almost three quarters of the Union's economic output (GDP).

8.7. The economic and political dimensions of the EMU

Many tend to forget that EMU is both an economic and monetary union, and not just a monetary union. In addition to introducing the single currency, the programme of the EMU also aims at laying the foundations for economic union. Economic union, which entails as a first step the coordination of economic policies, followed by their harmonisation and finally their transfer into Community competence (unification), is in any case closely inter-twined with the concept of monetary union and one can hardly be achieved without the other.

The two most important instruments of any state's economic policy are monetary policy and fiscal policy, which are closely inter-related. Once monetary policy is relegated from the national to Community level, fiscal policy remains the main controlling instrument of the state. The autonomous implementation of fiscal policy, however, becomes an impossibility at this stage, since the common monetary policy means that the action of one Member State will affect the other members of the Community and *vice versa*.[15] Consequently, monetary union inherently entails the convergence of the economic policies of the Member States. Therefore, the Member States have adopted several measures that facilitate the coordination of their economic policies and thereby endorse the stability of the eurozone.

---

[15] This explains why it was the budget deficit criterion of the convergence criteria that the Member States focused on most and why essentially it became the decisive factor for the commencement of the third stage. Maintaining the stability and convergence of fiscal policies is crucial to monetary union.

Within the framework of establishing an economic union, and according to Articles 98 and 99 of the EC Treaty, the Member States conduct their economic policies with a view to contributing to the achievement of the objectives of the Community, particularly those of a harmonious, balanced and sustainable development of economic activity, a high degree of competitiveness, a high level of employment and social protection, sustainable and non-inflationary growth respecting the environment, and a high degree of competitiveness and convergence of economic performance. Within the framework of the coordination of economic policies, the Council formulates so-called *broad economic policy guidelines* (BEPGs) for the Member States, which used to be adopted annually but, since 2003, are adopted by the Council for three-year periods. Following the Treaty of Amsterdam, the Council also adopts *employment policy guidelines.*[16]

Economic policy coordination and BEPGs have been dominated by objectives serving the implementation of the Lisbon strategy[17], adopted in March 2000 as the Union's strategic economic objectives for the first decade of the new millennium. Since the publication of the Lisbon strategy, the Heads of State or Government have dedicated their annual spring summits exclusively to economic and social issues, reviewing and updating the strategy, and adopting Conclusions that then serve as a basis for the Council for formulating the BEPGs. The Brussels European Council of 20–21 March 2003 decided on a much closer integration of the economic and employment policy guidelines, formulating them together for the same three-year periods. At the mid-term review of the Lisbon strategy, at the summit of 22–23 March 2005, this method was confirmed and the formal decision was taken that the Council should adopt three-year *integrated policy guidelines*, consisting of broad economic policy guidelines and employment policy guidelines. On the basis of the integrated guidelines, the Member States would elaborate *national reform programmes* and the Commission would draw up a *Community Lisbon programme* covering all Community-level activities boosting growth and employment. At their annual spring summit, the Heads of State or Government would take stock of the progress made and decide on the modification of the integrated guidelines if necessary. At the end of each three-year programme, the integrated guidelines would be renewed, along with the national reform programmes and the Community Lisbon programme.

---

[16] For more on economic policy guidelines, see Chapter 14.2. and 14.3.
[17] For more on the Lisbon strategy, see also Chapter 1.12.3.1.

LIVERPOOL JOHN MOORES UNIVERSITY
LEARNING & INFORMATION SERVICES

The implementation of the broad economic policy guidelines falls completely within national competence, but the Council – within the framework of the so-called multilateral surveillance procedure – monitors the activities of Member States both within and outside the eurozone, with a view to closer coordination and alignment of their economic policies, and draws up a comprehensive assessment thereof on a regular basis. Where it is established that the economic policies of a Member State are not consistent with the broad guidelines, or that they risk jeopardising the proper functioning of economic and monetary union, the EC Treaty allows the Council, acting by a qualified majority on a recommendation from the Commission, to make the necessary recommendations to the Member State concerned and to make these recommendations public.

To guarantee the smooth operation of the single currency, the Member States must pursue an economic policy that does not jeopardise the stability of the monetary union and hence the economic stability of the other Member States. When framing their economic policies – and as its key element, their budgets – the Member States must act responsibly, taking into consideration the interests of other Member States. No Member State may be permitted to endanger the other Member States, the monetary union and monetary stability by engaging in a potentially irresponsible fiscal policy. Therefore, the Member States participating in the eurozone must continue to fulfil the convergence criteria once they have entered the third stage of the EMU. The most important convergence criterion is the avoidance of running an excessive budget deficit. Article 104 of the EC Treaty calls on the Member States to avoid excessive government deficits, and defines the procedure to be followed if a Member State fails to meet that criterion. The Commission monitors the development of the budgetary situation and of the stock of government debt in the Member States. If the Commission considers that an excessive deficit in a Member State exists or may occur, the Commission prepares an opinion to the Council. The Council, acting by a qualified majority on a recommendation from the Commission, and having considered any observations which the Member State concerned may wish to make, decides after an overall assessment whether an excessive deficit exists. Where the existence of an excessive deficit is decided, the Council makes recommendations to the Member State concerned with a view to bringing that situation to an end within a given period. If a Member State persists in failing to put into practice the recommendations of the Council, the Council may decide to give notice to the Member State to take, within a specified time limit, deficit reduction measures which are judged necessary by the Council in order to remedy the situation. If the Member State concerned fails to reduce its deficit, the Council may impose a fine as a sanction.

The so-called excessive deficit procedure (EDP), however, differentiates between Member States within and outside the eurozone. The financial sanctions cannot be applied to Member States with a derogation, which are not part of the eurozone.

To guarantee budgetary discipline in the long run, the Member States – mainly under pressure from Germany – adopted the Stability and Growth Pact at the Amsterdam European Council in June 1997. The Stability and Growth Pact complements the relevant EC Treaty provisions and clarifies the procedure applicable to Member States for non-compliance. Pursuant to the Pact, sanctions may be imposed on any Member State participating in the third stage that breaches the reference value of the deficit; the State in breach is obliged to pay up to 0.5% of its GDP as a fine.[18] The Stability and Growth Pact is a fundamental pillar to the monetary stability of the eurozone. Germany insisted on the adoption of the Pact before giving up the Deutschmark and changing over to the euro. The role of the Pact is to guarantee the preservation of the close convergence of the Member States, which was established in 1997–98.

In the first years of the third stage there were no major problems with the application of the Stability and Growth Pact. Paradoxically, the status of the Pact was weakened when its initiator – Germany – and the second biggest eurozone member – France – both exceeded the deficit reference value. With their political clout, France and Germany could ensure that, despite the Commission's proposal, there were not enough votes in the Council to reach a qualified majority to impose sanctions against the Franco-German duo, although other countries (Ireland and Portugal) had been sanctioned for smaller breaches. This move undermined confidence in the Pact and its credibility, prompting the Commission and a group of Member States to turn to the Court of Justice which, in its ruling, took the side of the European Commission. In an attempt to resolve this embarrassing situation, and under pressure from France and Germany, which both urged for the Pact to be more flexible and take difficult economic conditions into consideration, the Member States finally agreed that the Pact should be interpreted in a more flexible manner. The European Council of 22–23 March 2005 reached a political agreement on reforming the Stability and Growth Pact. According to the European Council Conclusions, the reformed Pact would take into consideration the specific economic conditions of individual countries, developments and trends in the economy, and the economic and financial processes behind the deficit, and the Pact would adopt a more flexible approach regarding the role of periods of recession

---

[18] The Member State first has to pay a non-interest bearing deposit of a maximum of 0.5% of GDP, which only becomes a fine if the Member State fails to adjust its deficit within two years. The financial sanction is not applicable to Member States outside the eurozone but there is also a sanction in their case: disbursement of Cohesion Fund payments may be suspended if they exceed – for a prolonged time – the deficit ceiling set in their own convergence programmes. It should be pointed out that so far such sanctions have not been imposed in either of the two cases.

in the evolution of budget deficits by focusing on the sustainability of public finances.[19] The 3% and 60% reference values remain unchanged.

After the euro became the official currency unit, ECOFIN, the Council of Economic and Finance Ministers of the Community Member States, remained the main forum of economic policy coordination. In accordance with Article 99 of the EC Treaty, ECOFIN outlines annually the broad economic policy guidelines to be followed by the Member States of the EU. The implementation of these guidelines is the responsibility of the Member States. To provide an informal forum for the reconciliation of their economic policies, the Member States participating in the eurozone established a down-sized ECOFIN, the so-called EuroGroup, which is the unofficial forum of the Finance Ministers of the Member States of the single currency area. The EuroGroup's primary objective is to provide an exclusive forum for the participating Member States to coordinate their economic and monetary strategies. It is convened prior to ECOFIN-sessions; however, its meetings are strictly informal, in that any official decision may only be adopted by the ECOFIN comprising the 27 Member States of the Union. Nonetheless, the President or a Member of the EuroGroup may attend certain international negotiations, such as the financial meetings of the G7 and the IMF, where the eurozone would otherwise not be represented (i.e. when the Presidency of the ECOFIN is held by a State which is not participating in the third stage). In that context, in September 2004, the Member States of the eurozone decided – although without a Treaty legal base – to appoint Jean-Claude Juncker, the Prime Minister and Finance Minister of Luxembourg as the first standing EuroGroup president for the period 2005–2007.

In certain cases, the Treaty itself makes a distinction between eurozone countries and Member States with derogation that have stayed out, where the latter have no right to vote. These cases are the following: the adoption of those parts of the broad economic policy guidelines which concern the eurozone generally; coercive means of remedying excessive deficits; objectives and tasks of the European System of Central Banks; issuance of euro

---

[19] Another element of the political agreement pointing towards flexibility stipulates that respecting budgetary goals cannot hinder structural reforms aimed at improving the long-term sustainability of public finances. Considering the demographic reality of Europe (its ageing population), and acknowledging the necessity and budgetary implications of reforms of the social security systems, special attention should be devoted to the introduction of a multi-pillar pension system. In the case of Member States implementing such reforms, they may slightly exceed the reference value on a temporary basis.

notes and coins; legal acts of the European Central Bank; measures governing the use of the euro; monetary agreements and other exchange-rate policy measures; appointment of members to the Executive Board of the European Central Bank; decisions establishing common positions on matters of particular interest for economic and monetary union within the competent international financial institutions and conferences; and measures to ensure unified representation within the international financial institutions and conferences.

It must be underlined that the introduction of the single currency – as forecast by the establishment of the EuroGroup – has resulted in closer than ever cooperation between the participating Member States in every area of the economy and politics. The single currency was partly put on the agenda of the European Union to give a new and more powerful momentum to closer integration and the programme of a unified Europe. It is evident that, today, when financial actions affect every aspect of life, the Member States operating with the single currency will unavoidably come closer and will be increasingly dependent on each other. Moreover, putting the euro into circulation made the reality of European integration, i.e. the European Union itself, tangible for all citizens. This helps to further strengthen the sense of inter-dependence and, in the long run, may encourage stronger public support for reinforcing the integration process. Therefore, monetary union is the key to strengthening European integration and particularly political union, since it would be inexpedient for Member States with a single currency and a common Central Bank to pursue radically different policies in areas such as foreign policy. Thus, the introduction of the single currency may trigger impulses carrying over to other areas of integration – mainly the second and third pillars – that may lead to the enhancement of cooperation. Further prospects are opened up by the institution of enhanced cooperation commenced by the Treaty of Amsterdam and facilitated by the Treaty of Nice, which in all likelihood will be further simplified with the entry into force of the Reform Treaty.[20] It is the Member States participating in the monetary union that are most likely to resort to enhanced cooperation, which guarantees closer integration in a given area between certain Member States if other Member States, which are committed to slower progress, do not wish to establish closer links in further areas of policy; this will be particularly so if those other Member States are those which also voluntarily refrained from introducing the single currency.
In this context, the process of deepening induced by the monetary union raises the question whether it is viable for certain Member States of the European Union to opt out of the eurozone in the long run. The answer is that this is unlikely. Presumably, the United

---

[20] On enhanced cooperation, see also 4.1.1.2. and Annex, Point 4.3.

Kingdom, Denmark and Sweden have adopted a wait-and-see attitude towards the single currency. If the euro and the eurozone are successful in the long run, these three non-participating countries are unlikely to stay outside the EMU for long, since this move may put them in an unfavourable situation on the single market, which constitutes the essence of European integration. Ultimately, they would fall out of the main current of the Union and might easily drift to the sidelines in relation to other important decisions too, since the opportunities to voice their opinion on certain decisive matters would diminish dramatically. This could reconfirm the validity of the principal characteristic of British policy, that it is better to be a reluctant insider and be able to actively shape things, than to opt out and try to adapt thinking passively from the outside. This has also been a key source of motivation for the ten Member States that acceded to the Union in 2004 as well as the two new Member States that joined in 2007, who all wish to join the eurozone as soon as possible; once they do so, it will become all the more difficult for the 'opt-out' states to stay outside the 'euro club' in the long run.

CHAPTER 9
COMMON TRADE POLICY AND
THE EU'S EXTERNAL RELATIONS

This chapter provides an overview of the EU's external relations, which fall within the first pillar (the competence of the European Communities), and in particular covers the common commercial policy. This chapter also deals with trade-related relations, which have evolved during the European integration process to extend beyond strictly foreign trade aspects. Along with economic relations, European integration has led to the establishment of a comprehensive system of external relations, which – through its complex web of agreements – encompasses nearly all regions of the world and almost all areas of life.

In must be noted that foreign trade relations and foreign policy are almost always two inter-twining and inseparable areas. The EU's common trade policy and development policy towards developing countries have always been interlinked with its Common Foreign and Security Policy as well.

Nonetheless, the Common Foreign and Security Policy is dealt with separately in Chapter 23, because trade policy and CFSP depend on different legal bases. The Common Foreign and Security Policy belongs to the second – intergovernmental – pillar, with its own peculiar decision-making rules, institutional set-up and legal acts. Other external relations, particularly trade policy are, on the other hand, one of the most 'Communitarised' policy fields falling under the first pillar.

The separation of these two areas is somewhat complicated by the fact that these two pillars are often linked and taken together in a coordinated manner. Foreign policy action often relies heavily on foreign trade instruments (such as politically-motivated economic sanctions). It should also be pointed out that the difference in legal base and the separation of competences has frequently given rise to debate. The Commission has limited powers in the second pillar, while playing a leading role in foreign trade. This has repeatedly led to an overlapping of competences between the Commissioner for External Relations and the Council's High Representative for CFSP. The link between these two areas is ensured by the European Council, and the relevant Council body, the General Affairs and External Relations Council. These two bodies are responsible for coordinating the Common Foreign and Security Policy and other, first-pillar external relations.

It must be noted that the Reform Treaty – which is expected to enter into force in 2009 – will make great strides towards putting an end to this separation of external relations and the foreign and security policy. The distinction in decision-making procedures will continue (trade policy will remain a Community competence, with foreign and security policy an intergovernmental one). However, the Reform Treaty will abolish the pillar structure, giving the Union legal personality, and will merge the positions of the external relations Commissioner and the Council CFSP High Representative (in the position 'High Representative of the Union for Foreign Affairs and Security Policy'), while creating a separate Foreign Affairs Council chaired by the High Representative, thereby bringing about fundamental changes in the way foreign affairs are dealt with in the Union. Since these changes will only come into effect with the entry into force of the Reform Teaty, they are dealt with in detail in Point 9 and 23 of the Annex.

This chapter first gives an overview of the Common Commercial Policy, then looks at how the Community can conclude international agreements, and analyses external relations in the first pillar (EC competence). Although the actual agreements to be introduced here are concluded within the framework of the first pillar, there are often strong underlying CFSP motivations in them, which shows why it is so difficult to draw a clear distinction between first- and second-pillar external actions. Finally, the chapter will present the EU's development policy for assisting developing countries.

9.1. The weight of the European Union in the world economy

The European Union is the main player on the world economy in several respects. Although GDP per capita is higher in both the USA and Japan, its key rivals, the EU has the biggest total GDP and is the most significant trading power. The main trading partners of the EU are the USA, China, Japan, recently industrialised Far-Eastern states, Switzerland, Norway, Russia, and the countries of the Mediterranean, but all the significant economic regions of the world trade with the EU as well.[1] Recently, the most dynamic development in EU trade relations has been with the countries of Central and Eastern Europe (with the volume of trade growing threefold or fourfold), but following their accession to the Union on 1 May 2004 and 1 January 2007, this trade is now conducted within the internal market.

---

[1] See table 9.2. for details of the share of the EU's trading partners in EU foreign trade.

Table 9.1. Some important indicators for the EU, the USA, Japan and China

	EU-25	USA	Japan	China
Population (million in 2005)	461	298	128	1 316
Percentage of world population (in 2005)	7.1	4.6	2.0	20.4
GDP (EUR billion in 2005)	10 817	10 037	3 672	1 796
Percentage of world GDP (in 2005)	30.1	28.0	10.2	5.0
GDP/capita (in 2005, EUR/capita)	23 400	35 000	25 500	1 420
Share of world trade in goods (in 2004, %)	18.1	16.7	7.0	7.9
Share of world export of goods (in 2004, %)	19.2	14.4	9.0	9.4
Share of world import of goods (in 2004, %)	16.0	19.1	5.7	7.1
Share of world trade in services (in 2004, %)	26.4	18.9	7.5	4.4
Share of global foreign direct investment outflow (2002–2004, %)	32	38	7	5
Share of global foreign direct investment inflow (2002–2004, %)	27	17	2	17
Official aid provided (in 2006, USD billion)*	58.9*	22.7	11.6	n.a.

* EU 15
Sources: Eurostat, OECD, UNCTAD, World Bank

The European Union also plays a leading role in making and attracting foreign direct investment. Almost one third of foreign investment in the world originates from the EU, and it is usually the number one destination of FDI.

The role and influence of the EU on the world economy is further strengthened by the fact that the European Union is the largest provider of aid in the world, way beyond its competitors, the USA and Japan. Through its development policy, which supports countries with developing and emerging economies, the EU and its Member States provide nearly half of officially registered aid, exceeding the USA and Japan together. Development policy is important both in terms of the budget (representing on average 5% of the expenses in the last decade) and in terms of the institutions[2].

The significance and weight of the EU in the global economy is evidenced by the fact that the majority of developing and emerging countries have signed trade agreements with the EU, which also cover trade preferences and financial subsidies.

The Member States of the EU apply a Common Commercial Policy when carrying out trade with foreign partners.

9.2. The functioning of the Common Commercial Policy of the European Union

The need to introduce a common commercial (or trade) policy stems from one of the main objectives of the formation of the Communities, the customs union. With customs union, the Member States delegated the regulation of trade with third countries to the Community level. The essence of a customs union is that customs duties should be abolished in respect of trade between Member States, and a common, uniform system of tariffs should be applied for countries outside the Community.

Title IX of Part III of the EC Treaty speaks of a Common Commercial Policy. Within this Title, on the basis of Article 133 (formerly Article 113), the following activities are normally understood to fall within the common trade policy:

- changes in tariff rates;
- the conclusion of tariff and trade agreements;
- the achievement of uniformity in measures of liberalisation;
- export policy;
- measures to protect trade, such as those to be taken in the event of dumping or unfair subsidies.

It is important to underline that the Common Commercial Policy relates to trade carried out with countries outside the EU and that, for trade within the EU, the rules for the single market apply.[3] Trade in agricultural products does not come under the Common Commercial Policy, but is governed by the provisions of the Common Agricultural Policy[4].

---

[2] A separate Directorate-General at the Commission and a standing committee in the Parliament deal with development aid provided abroad and with policies related to cooperation.

[3] See Chapter 6.

[4] See Chapter 11.

The Common Commercial Policy entered into force in 1970 after the permanent removal of customs duties between Member States, but certain of its elements only came into operation from 1975, due to the bilateral trade agreements in force for some Member States (e.g. agreements with the then socialist countries). From 1970, however, the Member States could no longer make bilateral trade agreements with countries outside the Community. With the introduction of the Common Commercial Policy, the individual Member States could no longer make decisions on questions of foreign trade, and trade policy became an exclusive Community competence. Specifying common customs tariffs and carrying out trade negotiations and measures for trade protection (e.g. anti-dumping) are matters which are dealt with at Community level. The main guarantee for the implementation and success of the trade policy is the common system of instruments (e.g. Common Customs Tariff, dumping procedures, etc.).

Since the customs union was established, the Member States have applied a Common Customs Tariff for goods coming into the EU[5]. This means that no matter where the product crosses the EU border, the exporter can expect the same conditions. Thus, the Member States cannot gain a competitive advantage over each other by fixing lower customs duties, but a product from outside the Union, on which customs has been paid in one country, can be freely transported to another Member State.

While at the time the Community was formed, trade in products was predominant, over the last decade or two trade in services has grown to become highly important, to the extent that one quarter of the foreign trade turnover of the EU is now represented by services, and services are the main sector of the economy from the point of view of both GDP and employment. The former Article 113 of the Treaty, however, offered no basis for the Community's authority over foreign trade in services, so the Treaty of Amsterdam amended Article 113 of the Treaty. Under the provisions of this Article (which became Article 133), the Council acting unanimously could extend the application of the Article to trade in services and intellectual property. The Treaty of Nice further developed the contents of this provision, removing the requirement for the Council to take a prior decision, and extended the application of Article 133 unconditionally to services and intellectual property. However, the Treaty of Nice does not place all services under the provisions of Article 133, since the Member States and the Community still share authority in the fields of cultural and audio-visual services, educational services and health services. This means that, in these

---

[5] See Chapter 6.1.1.2. on the Common Customs Tariff, related to the free movement of goods.

areas, the Member States and the Community (i.e. the Commission in the name of the Community) proceed with trade negotiations together; the full agreement of the Member States is necessary for the negotiations, and agreements are concluded jointly.

The main institutions responsible for the implementation of the Common Commercial Policy are the Commission and the Council. The Commission carries out the day-to-day execution of trade policy, while more important decisions are made by the Council, which also monitors the decisions of the Commission.

As from 1970, decisions on the Common Commercial Policy have been adopted with a qualified majority, but the approval of certain broader agreements (e.g. association agreements) is by consensus.

The Parliament participates in trade policy in the case of important international agreements since, under the Treaty, the Parliament too must approve certain agreements (such as association agreements), which have a wider scope[6].

Trade policy is one of the areas where the Commission has greatest independence, and the greatest authority to make and implement decisions.

The role and authority of the Commission is involved in two ways in the implementation of trade policy. On one hand, the Commission, as a delegated decision-making and implementing body, may decide, under the control of the Member States, on the application of anti-dumping and market protection measures. The Commission may initiate a dumping procedure if a product from a country outside the EU is distributed in a Member State at a price lower than the price in the home country or the cost of production, shipping and distribution[7]. In addition, the Commission may order the temporary imposition of custom duties to redress the balance on goods which receive an unreasonable subsidy in the exporting country.

In the case of trade agreements with third countries, the Commission is less independent. For negotiations such as these, the Council delivers the necessary mandate and negotiating guidelines (see below).

---

[6] For a list of the types of agreements to which Parliament must give its assent, see 9.3.

[7] In certain cases, the Commission applies anti-dumping market-protective measures if the product imported into a Member State would seriously disturb the market, regardless of whether the reason for these disturbances actually falls into the dumping category, i.e. whether the product is being distributed at a sales price lower than the cost price.

9.3. The conclusion of trade and other international agreements

Under the EC Treaty, the Community has the right to conclude international agreements in certain areas. The Community can only conclude international agreements in pursuit of the fulfilment of objectives laid down in the EC Treaty, hence it has a functional competence to conclude treaties. Such powers may arise not only from a specific conferral thereof by the Treaty.[8] In areas where the Community has competence (either specifically defined in the EC Treaty or implicitly for the pursuit of the objectives laid down in the EC Treaty), it means that it enjoys both internal powers, for adopting legislation applying to the Member States and their legal subjects, as well as external powers, to act in international organisations or to conclude international agreements. As the Treaty does not clarify the internal and external dimension of implicit powers, the European Court of Justice has played an important role in defining the scope of these powers.
The significance of agreements concluded by the Community lies in the fact that they are binding both on the Community's institutions and the Member States.

Article 300 of the EC Treaty provides for the conclusion of international agreements in general, while Article 310 stipulates complementary provisions in respect of association agreements. Agreements concluded within the independent Common Commercial Policy are regulated separately by Article 133.

Under Article 133 of the EC Treaty on the Common Commercial Policy, the Commission makes a recommendation to the Council, which authorises the Commission to open the negotiations necessary for the conclusion of agreements serving the implementation of the Common Commercial Policy. The Council and the Commission are responsible for ensuring that the agreements negotiated are compatible with internal Community policies and rules. The Commission conducts these negotiations in consultation with a special committee (the so-called 'Article 133 Committee') appointed by the Council to assist the Commission in this task, and within the framework of such directives as the Council may issue to it. The Commission reports regularly to the special committee on the progress of negotiations. The agreement is concluded by the Council. In exercising these powers, the Council acts by a qualified majority.

---

[8] In addition to concluding trade agreements (EC Treaty Article 133), specific powers are conferred upon the Council alone in the areas of monetary policy (EC Treaty Article 111) and research and technological development (EC Treaty Article 170), the environment (EC Treaty Article 174) and development cooperation (EC Treaty Article 181).

According to Article 300, where the Treaty provides for the conclusion of agreements between the Community and one or more States or international organisations, the Commission makes recommendations to the Council, which authorises the Commission to open the necessary negotiations. The Commission conducts these negotiations in consultation with a special committee (responsible for the given subject) appointed by the Council to assist it in this task and within the framework of negotiating directives as the Council may issue to it.

As a general rule, for the conclusion and signature of agreements, the Council acts by a qualified majority on the Commission's proposal. There are two exceptions to this general rule, when the Council acts unanimously: when the agreement covers a field for which unanimity is required for the adoption of internal rules and when an association agreement is concluded. The Council concludes agreements after consulting the European Parliament, which must deliver its opinion within a time limit set by the Council according to the urgency of the matter. In the absence of an opinion within that time limit, the Council may act. By way of derogation from that rule, association agreements, agreements establishing a specific institutional framework by organising cooperation procedures, agreements having important budgetary implications for the Community and international agreements entailing the amendment of an act adopted under the co-decision procedure, can only be concluded after the assent of the European Parliament has been obtained.

If the Council plans to conclude an agreement which makes it necessary to amend the Treaties, such amendments are adopted according to the revision procedure (Article 48 EU Treaty). In practice, this means that amendments can only enter into force after they have been ratified by all Member States according to their constitutional requirements.

9.4. The external relations of the European Community

In spite of the fact that the Treaty of Maastricht founded the European Union, it is still only the Communities that have international legal personality. Among them, the European Community (EC) plays an active role in international relations.

The EC is a unique player in international law. Its legal status is similar to that of international organisations, but since the European Community increasingly speaks out as a Community or Union of its Member States in international relations, its status – in many aspects – is more similar to that enjoyed by states or federations of states. This is shown by the fact that external countries consider the EC as an equal partner, and further proved by the international agreements made with it and diplomatic relations entered into.

The EC Treaty gave the Community legal personality but, in international relations, both the Community and the Member States are protagonists. The question therefore arises as to what competence the EC has in international law. The answer is that, in certain cases, the EC has exclusive competence (e.g. for trade agreements), while in other areas, the Member States have the exclusive right to act (e.g. agreements on human rights or culture). In several cases, the EC and the Member States act together (shared competence) (e.g. as regards association agreements or accession treaties). As a whole, the EC has delegated, and thus only limited international competence.

It should be noted that in first-pillar matters, it is the Commission that normally acts in the name of the Community, while in matters under the second pillar, representation is ensured by the country holding the Council Presidency or by the Council's Secretary General (known as the High Representative for CFSP). In cases when first and second pillar issues are both on the agenda, the Community is represented by the Council's President-in-office or the so-called *Troika* [the President-in-office of the Council (or the President of the European Council), the Secretary General of the Council, and the Commissioner for External Relations from the Commission (or the Commission President, himself)].

While with most international organisations, only states which are members, or wish to become members or which have observer status enter into diplomatic relations with the organisation, more than 160 states have diplomatic representatives accredited to the EC (although it is true that the majority of these are not exclusively accredited to the EC but to Belgium as well).

The Commission of the EC itself also maintains Delegations (similar to diplomatic representations but rather regarded as administrative field offices) in third countries and associated countries, although not to the same extent as the missions which are accredited to it (the Commission operates around 130 delegations in third countries). The European Commission usually opens delegations in countries that are in some kind of contractual and institutionalised relation with the EC.

9.4.1. Characteristics of the EC's multilateral external relations

The Treaty of Rome laid down provisions governing relations between the EC (then EEC) and certain international organisations (the UN, GATT, OECD[9], and the Council of Europe). There is, however, a difference in relations between the various international organisations and the EC, according to whether or not the issues fall under Community competence. If they do, the Commission acts in the name of the Member States (on the basis of a mandate given by the Member States), and, if not, then the Presidency of the Council acts.

---

[9] At the time of the Treaty of Rome, only the OEEC existed (this was the forerunner of the OECD).

While it is normally a representative of the Commission who negotiates with the WTO (formerly GATT), the OECD and the UN Economic Commission for Europe, it is normally the current President of the Council who acts in the name of the EC vis-à-vis other institutions that are part of the UN (e.g. UNIDO).

It is important to emphasise that representatives of the Member States are also present in cases where the Commission or the President of the Council negotiates in the name of the Community with international organisations. The Community endeavours to ensure that the Member States do not enter into debate publicly and that they speak with one voice in relation to international organisations. To this end, the Member States regularly negotiate with representatives of the Commission and the President of the Council.

The World Trade Organization (WTO) has an especially important role in the area of multilateral trade relations. As the world's largest trader, the European Union plays a defining role in the multilateral negotiating rounds of the WTO, which lay down the framework and main rules for world trade. In recent times, the WTO negotiating rounds have been heavily dominated by EU-USA relations and, to a lesser extent, by EU-USA-Japan relations. The conclusion of the Uruguay Round in 1993 was clearly the result of an agreement between the United States and the European Community. Due to their concerted action, developing countries have pushed their interests to the forefront of the WTO agenda, which makes WTO negotiations more complicated and agreement more difficult. This is demonstrated by the multilateral trade round that began in Doha in 2001 (the Doha Development Agenda), which – in addition to the traditional EU-USA dispute – puts great emphasis on improving the trading position of developing countries. The EC (EU) also plays an important role in the Doha round: it wishes to realise its economic policy philosophy, based on sustainable development; it seeks to promote its values (environmental protection, social security, the protection of cultural identity, etc.) and also, in line with its development policy, to act in the interests of the least developed and developing countries, recognising that, while further liberalising trade, the special interests of developing countries must be fully taken into account. With a view to these objectives and policies, the EC (EU) is willing to make major concessions by abolishing a large part of its trade-restricting measures (subsidies to agricultural produce and exports), provided that the other key WTO partners are willing to follow suit and do the same.

9.4.2. The system of agreements defining the bilateral external relations of the EC

The EC develops relations with third countries according to two basic principles. On the one hand, drawing on the instruments of the Common Commercial Policy defined in Article 133 of the Treaty, it may conclude various trade agreements with external states; on the other hand, Article 310 of the Treaty allows the Community to enter into special, closer, preferential forms of cooperation with certain third countries, going beyond trade relations to some extent, and to conclude association agreements.

9.4.2.1. Association agreements and preferential arrangements

On the basis of Article 310, association means that mutual rights and obligations are set up between the EC and a country or group of countries, common actions may be realised, and common procedures applied. Usually, through association, the partner countries gain special conditions from the EC on market access and free trade and, in certain cases, the prospect of future membership. In addition, these agreements are completed by various types of economic and thematic cooperation, special political agreements, as well as the provision of financial aid on the part of the EC. Over the decades, the institution of association has been applied by the EC in five different types of agreement, further complemented by a sixth, unilateral, preferential relationship with the former colonies of the EU Member States.

a.) Association agreements concluded with the countries of Southern Europe
The EC first made special association agreements with two southern European countries: in 1961 with Greece, and in 1963 with Turkey. In theory, these agreements had as their objective complete membership or, more precisely, the implementation of a customs union in line with the level of integration of the sixties. Greece actually became a Member State in 1981. In Turkey, cooperation only went as far as a customs union (and with difficulty, only on 31 December 1995), and because of the lack of development of its economic and political institutions, significant differences in its level of development and for political reasons, it is uncertain when its membership can become reality. Nonetheless, at the Helsinki Summit in December 1999, Turkey was granted candidate status. Moreover, following lengthy debate, at the December 2004 summit, the Member States decided to open accession negotiations with Turkey in October 2005.

On the basis of this type of partnership, similar agreements were concluded in the early seventies with Malta (1971) and Cyprus (1973), which also aimed at a customs union and full membership. As a consequence, the EU began accession negotiations with Cyprus in 1998 and with Malta in 2000, following the successful conclusion of which, both countries joined the European Union on 1 May 2004.

b.) Cooperation with members of EFTA and the European Economic Area
The EC (then EEC) entered into a free trade system with the members of EFTA one by one in the seventies. Due to the strong trade relations and the similar level of development, forming closer cooperation had long been on the agenda, and this finally received more impetus simultaneously with the programme for the single market. In the eighties, the objective of a European Economic Area (EEA) was defined, and this was realised in 1994. The objective of this was to develop internal market relations between the EU Member States and the participating EFTA countries (currently Norway, Iceland and Liechtenstein[10]) without making EC membership a further aim (although Finland, Sweden, and Austria did end up as members on 1 January 1995). In essence, the EEA is about the participating EFTA countries agreeing to adopt a large part of the acquis communautaire concerning the single market.[11]

c.) Europe Agreements concluded with countries of Central and Eastern Europe
Between 1991 and 1996, the EC concluded association agreements with 10 former socialist countries of Central and Eastern Europe (Bulgaria, the Czech Republic, Estonia, Hungary, Latvia, Lithuania, Poland, Romania, Slovakia, Slovenia), which, by virtue of their historical significance, are collectively referred to as the Europe Agreements. The agreements had as their fundamental aim the creation of equal (not unilateral) free trade for industrial products. However, the implementation of this aim was asymmetrical, i.e. the Community removed its protective measures earlier. The agreements did not specify the extent of loans and aid to be provided by the EC, relying on the discretion of the Community, but they did make mention of and confirmed earlier agreements and commitments thereto (e.g. PHARE[12]). Political cooperation, which was to some extent a novelty in association agreements, became a key feature of the Europe Agreements. The introduction of legal approximation and the setting up of common institutions to operate the agreements

---

[10] Following a referendum, the fourth EFTA member state, Switzerland decided not to join the EEA.
[11] For the EEA and its Member States, see 1.9.
[12] See 1.13.1.

were elements through which close relations were formed between the Member States and the CEECs. In the Agreements, the countries of Central and Eastern Europe indicated that their objective was to be full EU members, although the Community made no concrete commitment in this regard in the Agreement provisions. However, this type of agreement included the possibility of accession already at the time when it was signed, especially as it applied to a wide range of cooperation in political, financial, cultural fields as well as to the approximation of legislation. As it turned out later, it provided the best conditions among association agreements for subsequent membership. In 1998, five of the ten countries (the Czech Republic, Estonia, Hungary, Poland, and Slovenia) and, in 2000, the other five, began accession negotiations with the EU. Eight of these ten countries became full members of the EU on 1 May 2004, while Bulgaria and Romania joined on 1 January 2007.[13]

d.) Stabilisation and association process with countries of the Western Balkans
After the end of the wars in the former Yugoslavia, the EU decided to offer a form of cooperation similar to the Europe Agreements to the countries of the Western Balkans (Albania, Bosnia and Herzegovina, Croatia, Macedonia, as well as Serbia and Montenegro, including Kosovo). What the EU had in mind was a form of agreement, which – similarly to the Europe Agreements – could lead these countries all the way to full membership. At the Feira Summit of June 2000, it was formally recognised that all countries of the Western Balkans were potential candidates for EU membership, subject to their fulfilment of the Copenhagen criteria[14] as a precondition for accession. The Thessaloniki European Council of June 2003 offered a real prospect of accession (a 'European perspective') to these countries, although without making a specific promise on membership. The instrument for bringing these countries closer to the EU is the so-called *stabilisation and association process*, which has three elements: the Stabilisation and Association Agreement (SAA), trade measures granting preferential treatment (wider market access), and the CARDS programme. CARDS[15] was an assistance instrument created especially for the Western Balkans (which was designed on the lines of the former PHARE programme) with a EUR 4.65 billion budget for the 2000–2006 period. From 2007, CARDS was replaced by IPA, which united all accession and pre-accession assistance programmes in the form of

---

[13] For the relations of the countries of Central and Eastern Europe with the EU, and the Europe Agreements, see 1.13.

[14] See 1.13.2.

[15] Community Assistance for Reconstruction, Development and Stabilisation.

an Instrument for Pre-Accession providing assistance to candidate and potential candidate countries (i.e. Turkey and the whole Western Balkans). The total budget of IPA for the 2007–2009 period is EUR 4 billion, with 60% earmarked for countries of the Western Balkans and the rest to Turkey. It is worth highlighting the substantial differences between the countries of this region in the pace of their alignment and catching up with the EU. Accession talks with Croatia opened in October 2005, Macedonia officially became a candidate country in December 2005, Albania signed the Stabilisation and Association Agreement (SAA) in 2006, while Bosnia-Herzegovina, Serbia and Montenegro (which became independent in the meantime) are only negotiating such Agreements. Negotiations are especially complicated with Serbia due to the issue of Kosovo (currently under UN administration), although the final status of Kosovo will have to be decided under the auspices of the UN, not of the EU.[16]

e.) Agreements made with Mediterranean countries outside Europe
The bilateral agreements made with the non-European countries of the Mediterranean Basin are unique agreements, and ensure asymmetric free market access to the Mediterranean countries in question. The agreements include concrete loans, credits and aid, and certain provisions are made in relation to labour from the region, but under no circumstances could these countries have a prospect of membership. As part of the Euro-Mediterranean Partnership announced at the Lisbon Summit in June 1992 (which took on concrete form in the Barcelona Declaration of 1995 and became known as the 'Barcelona process'), the EU offered to countries of the region (Algeria, Morocco, Tunisia, Egypt, Jordan, Lebanon, Syria, Israel and the Palestinian Authority)[17] the setting up of a free trade area by 2010.[18] In line with this, the EU has transformed the original cooperation agreements into Euro-Mediterranean Association Agreements which have

---

[16] For more on EU relations with countries of the Western Balkans, on further enlargement and the IPA, see 1.13.8.

[17] The EC has not concluded a bilateral agreement with Libya, and Libya is not part of the Euro-Mediterranean Partnership either. Nonetheless, the recent rapprochement has led to Libya taking part in the Barcelona process as an observer.

[18] There are 37 countries involved in the Barcelona process: the EU-27, the 9 Mediterranean partner countries and Turkey. (Cyprus and Malta used to be involved on the Mediterranean side but, since their accession in 2004, they have been involved on the EU side). Libya has an observer status.

already been signed with all countries of the region, except for Syria. The Euro-Mediterranean Partnership was complemented by the MEDA programme, which had a total budget of EUR 5.35 billion for 2000–2006. From 2007, MEDA was replaced by the new European Neighbourhood and Partnership Instrument (ENPI)[19], which provides assistance to the EU's southern and eastern neighbours without prospects for membership (former MEDA and TACIS countries). The ENPI budget for 2007–2013 is roughly 30% higher than what was spent through MEDA and TACIS in the previous 7-year budgetary period. These countries are also eligible for loans from the European Investment Bank, available in increased sums to Euro-Mediterranean partners from 2007.[20]

f.) The Lomé Conventions and the ACP-EC Partnership Agreement
The institution of association was originally introduced into the Treaty of Rome so that the former colonies of the Member States of the EC, and those states which traditionally had special relations with certain Member States could enjoy favourable treatment on the EC (then EEC) markets. Initially, the colonies were associated areas of the Community but, after becoming independent, the relationship had to be revised. This type of partnership was put into concrete form by the customs union, and – because of its former colonies – the accession of the United Kingdom. As a result of this, in Lomé (Togo) in 1975, the EC signed the Lomé Convention, initially with 46 countries from Africa, the Caribbean and the Pacific (the so-called ACP states), which was gradually extended to more than 70 countries by the turn of the millennium. The 1st Lomé Convention was concluded for five years, and was renewed every five years thereafter (2nd and 3rd Lomé Conventions); the 4th Lomé Convention was concluded for a ten-year period (1990 – 2000). The Lomé Convention was an asymmetric agreement in which the EC provided free market access to the countries in question who, in return, only had to provide the principle of the most-favoured nation clause. In addition, the EC, as part of the agreement, provided guaranteed financial aid to the ACP states, for example Stabex, serving to stabilise the export earnings of ACP countries, and Sysmin, a system to compensate for reducing the yield in mines.

---

[19] See 9.4.2.3.
[20] In 2002, the EIB created a special facility for these countries with the name Facility for Euro-Mediterranean Investment and Partnership (FEMIP), which the EU's southern partners would like to see converted into a Euro-Mediterranean development bank.

Following the 4th Lomé Convention, which expired in 2000, the EC and the ACP countries decided to set a new basis for relations. In this spirit, on 23 June 2000 in Cotonou (Benin), the EC signed the ACP-EC Partnership Agreement with 78 ACP countries[21], which can be considered as a renewed and extended version of the Lomé Convention. The ACP-EC Partnership Agreement is much more than a trade agreement and builds on political and economic cooperation and dialogue, reforming and extending the financial support offered by the EU by giving more direct involvement and responsibility to participating countries. (For example, Sysmin and Stabex were discontinued and the financial engagements, so-called country support strategies (CSS), acting as key elements of the new agreements, were used for this purpose as well.) The Agreement was concluded for 25 years and is reviewed every five years. (The first review was on 23 February 2005.) Every five years, the financial framework of such EC support, primarily the European Development Fund[22], is also reviewed. From 2000 to 2007 EUR 13 billion was available to ACP countries, while between 2008 and 2013, this will go up to 22 billion.

9.4.2.2. Other relations built on the Common Commercial Policy

The Community has institutionalised its trade relations with developing countries which are not participants in the Lomé Convention (i.e. mainly Asian and Latin American states) through the instruments of the Common Commercial Policy. These trade agreements, building on the principle of the most-favoured nation clause, are symmetrical in nature and endeavour to be free of discrimination. However, the Community often offers various forms of aid to these countries too, as well as unilateral preferences through the customs preferences of the Generalised System of Preferences (GSP).[23]

---

[21] Cuba is also considered an ACP country (the 79th), although it has not signed the Cotonou Agreement.

[22] See 9.5.

[23] The GSP may be granted to developing countries on the basis of international agreements. Formerly, for the EU, these were mainly quota preferences but, since the Uruguay Round of GATT, quotas had to be discontinued, and so the EU has redesigned the system. The EU now provides various-sized custom duty preferences to developing countries for different groups of products. However, within the GSP, development policy is steadily being given greater emphasis, and the EU takes other criteria into account besides trade aspects (e.g. respect for fundamental rights, or environmental improvements).

Generally, the EU endeavours to negotiate the same conditions for countries from the same economic region and, if possible, to make group agreements with the member countries of various economic blocs and regional organisations. In this way, the agreement with the countries of the Common Market of Central America in Latin America and of the Southern Common Market (Mercosur) in South America came into being and, similarly, with the members of the Association of Southeast Asian Nations (ASEAN) in Eastern Asia, as well as the Cooperation Council for the Arab States in the Gulf (GCC) in the Middle East.

In the nineties, the EC (EU) endeavoured to develop more intense relations with the independent republics of the former Soviet Union, the countries of the Commonwealth of Independent States (CIS). The EU regards Russia and Ukraine particularly as important partners, but is steadily paying more attention to the other states in the region as well. On the basis of cooperation built on aid and partnership, the EU offered considerable financial support through the TACIS programme (Technical Assistance for the Commonwealth of Independent States) to the countries of Eastern Europe and Central Asia (Armenia, Azerbaijan, Belarus, Georgia, Kazakhstan, Kyrgyzstan, Moldova, Mongolia, Russia, Tajikistan, Turkmenistan, Ukraine and Uzbekistan). TACIS supported institutional, legal and administrative reform, the development of the private sector, the financial sector and the economy, as well as the development of infrastructure networks. For the period 2000–2006, TACIS had a budget of EUR 3.138 billion, which has been increased by about one third for the period 2007–2013 within the framework of the new European Neighbourhood Policy Instrument (ENPI).[24] The EU has also concluded so-called *Partnership and Cooperation Agreements* with most former Soviet Union countries, which provide a framework for bilateral relations.

The EU devotes special attention to Russia, the leading country of the region; EU-Russia summits are held regularly, usually biannually. The Partnership and Cooperation Agreement concluded in 1997 serves as a framework for EU-Russia relations. In addition, the roadmap on the '*Four Common Spaces*' (decided already in May 2003) was adopted in May 2005 following long preparatory talks. This roadmap includes the Common Economic Space, Common Space of Freedom, Security and Justice, Common Space of External Security and the Common Space on Research, Education and Culture. The objective of the common economic space is to create an open and integrated market between the EU and Russia. Work on this space will gradually bring down barriers to trade and investment. The common space of freedom, security and justice includes future agreements on

---

[24] See 9.4.2.3.

visa policy and consultations on combating terrorism, organised crime and corruption. The road map for the common space of external security underlines the shared responsibility of the EU and Russia for crisis management and for combating the proliferation of weapons of mass destruction (WMDs). Work to create the common space of research and education, including cultural aspects, focuses on the convergence of university course formats and qualifications, and visa-free travel for scientific researchers. Energy has come to dominate EU-Russia political and trade relations lately – Russia is the number one energy supplier of the Union and the EU is the biggest buyer of Russian oil and gas. Russia is the only one of the world's leading economies outside the World Trade Organisation, thus Russia's accession to the WTO is an important priority for the EU.

It is characteristic that the Community has not made a special trade agreement with the United States or Japan, its main economic rivals but also its greatest trade partners. With these countries, the Community considers that cooperation based on the most-favoured nation clause, and the regulations of the WTO (GATT) and the OECD is sufficient. These organisations, primarily the WTO, often serve as the site for trade debates between the USA and the EU.

Due to the differences of opinion on trade matters, the relationship of the EU with the United States is to some extent contradictory, since the USA is the main strategic political and economic partner of the EU, and also its main ally, despite the recent disagreement between the USA and some EU Member States over the war in Iraq.[25] Most EU Member States are members of the joint political, military alliance with the United States – NATO – and, in spite of frequent trade disagreements, the EU and the USA cooperate intensively in the area of economic relations, for example at regular (usually annual) EU-US summits. As part of the New Transatlantic Agenda (NTA) of 1995, the European Union and the United States hold institutionalised, continuous and intensive dialogue on economic, political, security and social issues affecting the world and their bilateral relations. This cooperation is complemented by a joint EU-USA action plan. In the spirit of the NTA, the Transatlantic Economic Partnership programme was adopted in London in May 1998, which, as part of an open process, has as its objective further trade liberalisation and, eventually, the creation of free trade.

---

[25] For more on the foreign policy aspects of trans-Atlantic relations, see 23.6. and 23.7.

In addition to the NTA, as a somewhat similar initiative, in 1996 in Bangkok, the EU established the Asia-Europe Meeting (ASEM) with Far Eastern countries with significant economic potential, and this has become a regular forum. In the ASEM, the partners of the Member States of the EU are, on the Asian side, the members of ASEAN (Brunei, Cambodia, Indonesia, Laos, Malaysia, Myanmar, the Philippines, Singapore, Thailand, and Vietnam) and China, Japan and South Korea. The ASEM is a process based on dialogue and cooperation, and its aim is to create a comprehensive partnership, by deepening political dialogue and economic relations and strengthening cultural ties. A biennial summit is organised as part of the ASEM.

The Joint declaration adopted in 1991 and the ten-year EU-Japan Action Plan (bearing the subtitle 'Shaping our common future') adopted in 2001 form the framework for bilateral relations between the EU and Japan. This Action Plan is based on the following four principles: promoting peace and security in the world, developing economic and trade partnership, utilising the dynamism of globalisation to benefit all, and strengthening cultural ties. EU-Japan summits are usually held annually.

China is an increasingly important trade partner of the EU, with its share in EU trade surpassing that of Japan. The basis for trade relations between the EU and China is still the EEC-China Trade and Economic Cooperation Agreement of 1985, although China's WTO membership since 2001 has been the key factor. Negotiations began in 2007 about a comprehensive partnership and cooperation agreement (including political issues). EU-China summits are usually held annually. The recent flood of cheap Chinese products and China's aggressive export policy have caused considerable harm to certain European sectors (especially the clothing industry), which has also ignited a trade row between Brussels and Beijing, influenced by the fact that the EU runs a huge trade deficit with China, importing about twice as much from China as it exports.

*Table 9.2. Share of the most important trading partners of
the EU in its imports, exports and trade in 2005,
by country and by economic region*

Key import partners		Key export partners		Key trading partners	
Country	Share of EU imports	Country	Share of EU exports	Country	Share of EU trade
1. USA	13.9	1. USA	23.7	1. USA	18.5
2. China	13.4	2. Switzerland	7.7	2. China	9.4
3. Russia	9.1	3. Russia	5.3	3. Russia	7.3
4. Japan	6.2	4. China	4.9	4. Switzerland	6.6
5. Norway	5.7	5. Japan	4.1	5. Japan	5.2
6. Switzerland	5.6	6. Turkey	3.9	6. Norway	4.5
7. Turkey	2.8	7. Norway	3.2	7. Turkey	3.4

Import partners		Export partners		Trading partners	
Region	Share of EU imports	Region	Share of EU exports	Region	Share of EU trade
NAFTA	16.1	NAFTA	27.5	NAFTA	21.5
EFTA	11.6	EFTA	11.2	EFTA	11.4
Latin America	5.5	Latin America	5.1	Latin America	5.3
ASEAN	6.0	ASEAN	4.2	ASEAN	5.2
Mediterranean*	4.6	Mediterranean*	5.6	Mediterranean*	5.1
ACP	3.1	ACP	2.9	ACP	3.0

* Turkey not included

9.4.2.3. Neighbourhood policy

The eastward enlargement of the European Union created a new situation in the EU's external relations, posing new challenges and aggravating former ones. Overnight, the EU had borders with new countries to the south and the east, posing security risks related to illegal immigration, organised crime, trafficking in drugs and human beings, or terrorism.

However, these neighbouring countries also offer promising market opportunities and potential for economic growth. It is in the interests of countries on the Union's southern and eastern border, both politically and economically, to forge close ties with the EU, and some of them even nurture the idea of membership, in the long term. The EU also has a vested interest in ensuring that its neighbours are politically stable and safe, and developed in economic terms. Therefore the EU had to make it clear that, although membership was by no means automatic, neighbouring third countries did have a legitimate claim for special relations.

In order to provide a framework for relations with neighbouring countries without the prospect of membership, the EU launched its *European Neighbourhood Policy* (ENP), which was based on the Commission's 'Wider Europe – Neighbourhood' concept of March 2003. The aim of the ENP was to define the relations of the enlarged Union with its eastern and southern neighbours: Russia, the former Soviet republics of Ukraine, Moldova and (upon its democratisation) Belarus, as well as Armenia, Azerbaijan and Georgia in the southern Caucasus, and countries of the Mediterranean (Algeria, Morocco, Tunisia, Egypt, Jordan, Lebanon, Syria, Israel and the Palestinian Authority)[26].
The neighbourhood policy does not cover the candidate countries of Croatia, Turkey and Macedonia, or the countries of the Western Balkans, because the ENP is tailored to the needs of countries which do not have a prospect of becoming potential candidates for membership.

An important feature of the neighbourhood policy is differentiation. Action plans are adopted for each individual country, except for Russia, with which the EU has decided to create the 'Four Common Spaces'.
The action plans set out priorities for political dialogue, institutional reforms, trade measures, justice and home affairs measures, social and cultural issues, and the development of transport and energy infrastructure. The differentiated priorities, tasks and commitments

---

[26] In the Mediterranean region, Libya could also be involved in the EU's neighbourhood policy if it joins the Barcelona process by accepting the values that the EU expects its partners to respect.

are defined with regard to each partner country's geographic location, political and economic situation, reform programmes, needs and capacities. The earlier agreements concluded with these countries (Partnership and Cooperation Agreements with eastern neighbours and Euro-Mediterranean Association Agreements with southern neighbours) remain in force, and are only complemented by the action plans within the context of the ENP.

In order to kit out neighbourhood policy with a specific assistance instrument, for the 2007–2013 period the EU created the European Neighbourhood and Partnership Instrument (ENPI), with a budget of EUR 11.18 billion for the seven years. The ENPI replaced TACIS (for Eastern partners), MEDA (for Southern partners) and some other thematic (e.g. human rights) programmes. The reinforced ENPI budget makes available 32% more funding than its predecessors did in the previous seven years. ENPI assistance is aimed at promoting gradual economic integration between the EU and partner countries, having special regard to the implementation of objectives laid down in the partnership and cooperation agreements (PCAs). In addition, the EU tries to make use of the ENPI to promote good governance, as well as fair social and economic development.

9.5. The development cooperation policy of the EU

The EU pursues a broad development cooperation or development policy to provide subsidies and aid to the developing countries of the world. The Member States of the EU provide around half of world aid, far more than the USA and Japan together. Around 15% of aid financed by EU Member States is made directly by the Union, i.e. from the Community budget. The main task of Community development aid is to complement and balance the aid provided by the development offices of the Member States.

There are historical, strategic and moral reasons for the development of Community development policy. The historical reasons lie in the colonial past of many of the Member States, as a result of which these Member States (particularly the United Kingdom and France, but several others, too) still have strong political and economic ties with countries in the developing world, their former colonies. Strategically, the developing countries are important to the EU, both as the producers of many indispensable raw materials and also as target markets of the EU. From a moral point of view, the EU is obliged, as one of the most developed regions in the world, to assist developing and poor countries, which are marginalised economically and politically.

Development cooperation was not explicitly mentioned in the Treaty of Rome. The Treaty only gave a legal base to the management of relations with the overseas countries and territories (OCT) of the Member States. With the independence of the colonies, however, the significance of this part (EC Treaty, Part Four) diminished.[27] Former Article 238 of the Treaty (currently Article 310) provided the opportunity for the EC to form special relations with former colonies, and to give them special treatment. This is how the Lomé Convention was concluded with ACP countries.

The institutionalisation of development cooperation in the Treaty was implemented by the Treaty of Maastricht. The Treaty of Maastricht embedded the development policy (which had been pursued for decades) as a separate title (currently Title XX, Part Three) in the EC Treaty. Within this, Article 177 of the Treaty defines the objectives of Community development policy. According to this Article, the development activities pursued by the Member States should be complemented in order to strengthen developing countries':

- sustainable economic and social development;
- smooth and gradual integration into the world economy;
- fight against poverty.

Article 177 adds that Community policy should contribute to the consolidation of democracy, the rule of law, and respect for human rights and fundamental freedoms in developing countries.

The Community's development cooperation policy is implemented through five basic principles:

- The principle of *complementarity*: the Community should complement the actions of the Member States (there are cases where, for political or efficiency reasons, joint action brings better results).
- The principle of *coordination*: the Member States and the Community should coordinate their actions, particularly in international organisations.
- The principle of *coherence*: the objectives of development policy should be integrated into other EU policies (e.g. agriculture, transport), and should be taken into account when implementing them.

---

[27] There are, however, still around 20 overseas countries and territories (e.g. Greenland, Bermuda, New Caledonia, etc.) which have special relations with Denmark, the United Kingdom, France or the Netherlands, and in this respect qualify as associated countries and territories of the European Community. The natural and legal personalities of these areas have the same rights as Member States in several respects (e.g. free trade, freedom of establishment).

- The principle of *geographical weighting*: priority should be given to the least developed countries.
- The principle of sound *political conditions*: the provision of aid is linked to the operations of democratic governmental structures in the beneficiary state.

The Community's development cooperation policy comprises two main types of instruments: aid instruments and trade instruments.

Community aid provided to developing countries covers a broad range of areas and, with its subsidies, the EU takes on an active role from developing macroeconomic strategies, reinforcing (political) institutions, developing social (educational, health) care, providing and improving the quality of food and drinking water, making environmental investments, to increasing equality between women and men. For all of these activities, the EU provides aid in two ways. On the one hand, on the basis of an agreement, e.g. to the ACP countries, or to the Mediterranean countries (ACP-EU Partnership, Euro-Mediterranean Partnership) and, on the other hand, on an individual basis, to needy countries anywhere in the world. Financing is made up of three elements: subsidies from the European Development Fund (EDF), preferential loans from the European Investment Bank (EIB) and special items in the common budget. In this context, special mention should be made of the ECHO (Humanitarian Aid Office) of the European Commission, which provides humanitarian aid in times of emergency and catastrophe in the form of food, medicine and other items to those in need, including refugees.[28]

The EDF is not operated from the budget of the EU but from the direct contributions of the Member States and provides aid mainly to the ACP countries. However, the EDF has a Community nature because it is related to the agreements with the ACP countries and the European Commission participates in its operation. In the first years of the Cotonou Agreement (see 9.4.), from 2000 to 2007, the EDF's budget was EUR 13.5 billion, but in the period 2008–2013, 22,68 billion is earmarked for this purpose: with 22 billion going to ACP countries, 286 million to overseas countries and territories, and the rest financing the Commission's EDF-related costs.

---

[28] Recently, ECHO has focused on Africa and Asia, as well as Afghanistan, Armenia, Azerbaijan and in other areas, helping those in emergency situations or refugees; it has also been active in alleviating the consequences of the wars and crises in the former Yugoslavia. About half a billion euros are spent on humanitarian aid from the Community budget annually.

As regards trade instruments, a key role is played by the agreements such as Cotonou Agreement (mentioned in 9.4.), which give preferences and special market access to developing countries, and the unilateral customs preferences of the GSP (Generalised Preference System).

An important step for the future of development cooperation policy came as a result of the 16–17 June 2005 EU summit meeting, where the European Council defined objectives for the Member States for development funding. The Member States agreed to earmark 0.56% of their GNI for official development aid in 2010, and to increase the rate of such assistance to 0.70% of GNI by 2015. For the new Member States, that rate was set at 0.17% in 2010 and 0.33% in 2015, in view of the fact that these countries had only recently ceased being beneficiaries themselves.

CHAPTER 10
COMPETITION POLICY

10.1. The reasons for establishing competition policy at Community level

When establishing the European Communities, the founding Member States highlighted the importance of ensuring competition within the common market. Competition is essential for the effective operation of any healthy economy, including the common market. It is the driving force behind innovation, technical progress, economic growth and the welfare of society. Effective competition is in the fundamental interests of consumers, since it allows them to buy goods and services under the best conditions. Therefore, the Member States did their utmost to design the Founding Treaties in such a way that no new anti-competitive practices – such as market-sharing, restrictive agreements and concerted practices by market participants – should emerge in lieu of the obstacles to trade already removed, which had once impeded competition between the economies of the Member States. Accordingly, the Member States agreed to establish competition policy at Community level. With the liberalisation of markets, companies started engaging in intensive economic activities in several Member States at the same time, certain companies became key players in several national markets all at once and the number of trans-national companies increased. Regulation of competition at national level could no longer guarantee the necessary conditions for competition and effective market monitoring. The design of Community legislation on competition based on a common competition policy became indispensable to ensure healthy market competition.

Competition policy was essentially established as a classic common policy. Article 3 of the EC Treaty stipulated that a system guaranteeing undistorted competition on the internal market should be established. Competition policy is regulated by Articles 81 to 89 of the EC Treaty.
Pursuant to the above provisions, in relation to Community legislation, decisions on Community competition are adopted at Community level, while national authorities of the Member States are responsible for issues that exclusively concern competition within their national markets.[1] Accordingly, competition policy is clearly viewed as a common policy.

---

[1] This is demonstrated by the fact that the subject of state aid has also been relegated to Community level. A subsidy allocated to a national enterprise or sector in a Member State may exert influence on (distort) competition between market participants.

The weight of the Community in the field of competition policy is reinforced by the central role played by the Commission, which acts as the guardian of competition in the Community. It is in this field that the Member States vested in the Commission the greatest degree of independence and the broadest scope of decision-making and executive and monitoring competence.

Although the philosophy behind competition policy highlights the importance of competition, it is not based on the principle of traditional free competition, which emphasises competition under all circumstances and credits all its instruments with beneficial effects. The competition policy of the EC allows for the restriction of competition in certain cases when so required by various social interests (e.g. the improvement of employment levels), long-term economic interests (e.g. the development of SMEs and the incubation of emerging industries) and consumers' interests.

To ensure effective competition, the policy of the EC has two fundamental objectives. On the one hand, it prohibits agreements and concerted practices between market participants that may restrict competition within the common market. On the other hand, it prevents the Member States from discriminating in favour of their own national companies or public enterprises by adopting anti-competitive measures. Along the lines of these two objectives, Community provisions on competition fall into two distinct categories. Provisions in the first category regulate the practices, agreements and mergers of companies, while provisions falling under the second category deal with the Member States, state aids and public enterprises (state-owned enterprises and enterprises in which the state has a controlling stake).

10.2. Community competition rules applying to undertakings

EC competition policy must avoid monopolisation which restricts competition within the internal market. It must prevent companies from sharing the market by means of restrictive agreements and concerted practices. It must also prevent companies in a dominant position from restricting or preventing market competition and prohibit company mergers that may monopolise the market.

10.2.1. Prohibition of agreements and other concerted practices distorting competition

Article 81 of the EC Treaty prohibits "all agreements between undertakings, decisions by associations of undertakings and concerted practices which may affect trade between Member States[2] and which have as their object or effect the prevention, restriction or distortion of competition within the common market". Pursuant to the Treaty, the following activities in particular which fall into this category are those which:
- directly or indirectly fix purchase or selling prices or any other trading conditions;
- limit or control production, technical development, or investment;
- share markets or sources of supply;
- apply dissimilar conditions to equivalent transactions with other trading parties; and
- make the conclusion of contracts subject to acceptance by the other parties of obligations which have no connection with the subject of such contracts.

Community legislation on competition also prohibits any similar non-binding agreements concluded between corporate decision-makers, so-called gentlemen's agreements. The ban applies both to horizontal agreements (between companies at the same stage of production or commercial chain) and to vertical agreements (between firms operating at different stages of the production and commercial chain) which distort competition, as well as to any concerted practices. Agreements between parent and subsidiary companies however are not prohibited. In accordance with Community law, the provisions on competition policy apply to any company that is present in the common market, including companies that are not registered in the Community; it is not the location of the protagonists which is important but the effect of the agreement or practice on competition in the Community which is important.

There are, however, certain exemptions to the provisions on restrictive agreements and concerted practices. Agreements between undertakings, decisions by associations of undertakings and concerted practices that contribute to improving the production or distribution of goods or which promote technical and economic progress (e.g. licensing agreements for technology transfer) and which are beneficial for consumers are authorised, even if they restrict competition. The Commission has the right to grant exemption from the prohibitions in cases where it deems that an agreement or practice has a beneficial effect and only imposes restrictions which are indispensable.

---

[2] Should a certain practice or agreement restrict competition only within a single Member State and not affect trade between Member States, the competition law of the given Member State must be applied.

10.2.2. Prohibition of abuses of dominant positions

Article 82 of the Treaty prohibits any abuse by an undertaking of its dominant position within the common market which may hinder effective competition and trade between the Member States. The Treaty does not prohibit a dominant position of itself, but its abuse, insofar as it affects trade between the Member States. There is an abuse of a dominant position when the conduct of the undertaking in question is such that it influences the structure of the relevant market or its degree of competition. Such conduct is forbidden even if it is favoured by a provision of national law. Such abuse may consist in:
- imposing unfair prices or other trading conditions;
- limiting production or technical development to the detriment of consumers;
- applying dissimilar conditions to equivalent transactions with other trading parties; and
- making the conclusion of contracts subject to the acceptance of obligations which have no connection with the deal in question.

Unlike Article 81, which prohibits restrictive agreements and concerted practices, Article 82 of the Treaty has no exemptions.

10.2.3. The control of concentrations of undertakings

Under Community law, a concentration (or merger) occurs where two previously separate companies merge, or a firm acquires control over another firm, or where one or several firms – which already control at least one other firm – take control of one or more other firms.

The Founding Treaties contained no provisions on the control of concentrations or mergers. Experience, however, showed that competition could be restricted by means of a merger. The Court of Justice ruled to this effect on several occasions. Finally, in 1989, the Council adopted a Regulation[3] on the control of concentrations. The Regulation, subsequently amended by another Regulation[4] in 1997, prohibits 'a concentration with a Community dimension' which may significantly impede competition in the common market through establishing a dominant position. The Regulation applies to companies whose merger has a Community dimension (due to their strengthened position on the internal market) and which may restrict competition within the Community; the Regulation also covers

---

[3] Regulation 4064/89/EEC on the control of concentrations between undertakings.
[4] Regulation 1310/97/EC amending Regulation 4064/89/EEC on the control of concentrations between undertakings.

companies that are not registered in the Community. 'Concentration with a Community dimension' is defined under the Regulation.[5]

The Regulation stipulates that companies proposing a concentration/merger with a Community dimension must notify the Commission before the merger takes place, that is within one week after signing the agreement on the merger. The Commission takes a decision on whether or not to authorise the concentration/merger within an appointed time.[6] The Commission may authorise the merger, ask the participants to amend the preliminary agreement or may prohibit the operation. The proposed concentration/merger cannot go ahead until the Commission's final decision has been taken. It must be emphasised that, unlike when investigating an abuse of a dominant position, in this case the Commission does not examine whether the proposed company concentration will abuse its dominant position on the market but whether a dominant position is created that may alter the structure of the relevant market (and thus potentially distort competition).

10.3. Community competition rules applying to Member States

In addition to the practices of enterprises, certain actions of the Member States may also restrict competition in the common market. Various aids granted by the Member States or resulting from State resources may distort competition on the internal market, since they may discriminate in favour of the subsidised enterprise. As a result of state intervention, public enterprises (state-owned enterprises and enterprises in which the state has a controlling stake) may acquire a competitive advantage that may harm the position or chances of other companies. These issues needed to be addressed by Community competition law.

10.3.1. Community competition rules applying to state aids

Article 87 of the Treaty stipulates that "any aid granted by a Member State or through State resources in any form whatsoever which distorts or threatens to distort competition by favouring certain undertakings or the production of certain goods shall, insofar as it affects trade between Member States, be incompatible with the common market". The

---

[5] In accordance with the 1997 amendment of the Regulation, the Community dimension obtains when the companies concerned have a combined turnover of at least EUR 2.5 billion, or each of the companies concerned generates a turnover of EUR 100 million in each of at least three Member States, or at least two of the companies concerned have a minimum turnover of EUR 25 million in each of at least three Member States, or at least two of the companies concerned have a minimum Community-wide turnover of EUR 100 million respectively.

[6] The Commission has to take a decision within one month; however, the time-limit may be prolonged by a maximum of four months if the Commission decides to carry out a detailed investigation.

Commission and the Court of Justice have placed a very broad interpretation on the concept of 'aid', which includes any aid granted by the government, a local or regional authority, as well as any aid coming from a private source over which the State exercises a dominant influence directly or indirectly. The form and purpose of the aid and the reason for it are irrelevant; all that matters is its effect on competition. Any form of aid is prohibited, including subsidies, soft loans, interest subsidies, tax allowances and the reduction of social security contributions; in other words, any measure that reduces the financial burden on an enterprise, granting it an economic benefit.

On the other hand, Community competition law does not exclude the possibility of state aid in itself, which is a fundamental instrument for reaching certain economic- and socio-political objectives set by the Community. Community competition law permits state aids provided for national enterprises and industries insofar as they serve economic and social interests.

Article 87 of the Treaty provides for a number of exemptions from the prohibition on state aids which are considered to be compatible with the internal market. Accordingly, the following forms of state aid may be granted:

- state aid having a social character granted to consumers, provided that it is granted without discrimination in relation to the origin of the products concerned;
- aid to make good the damage caused by natural disasters or exceptional occurrences;
- aid granted to the economy of certain areas of the Federal Republic of Germany affected by the division of Germany, insofar as such aid is required in order to compensate for the economic disadvantages caused by that division.

Article 87 of the Treaty also lists state aids which – despite the general prohibition – the Commission may declare compatible with the common market. The Commission may permit the following:

- aid to promote the economic development of areas where the standard of living is abnormally low or where there is serious under-employment;
- aid to promote the execution of an important project of common European interest or to remedy a serious disturbance in the economy of a Member State;
- aid to facilitate the development of certain economic activities, where such aid does not adversely affect trading conditions to an extent contrary to the common interest;
- aid to promote culture and heritage conservation;
- such other categories of aid as may be specified by a decision of the Council acting on a Commission proposal by a qualified majority.

In relation to the last situation mentioned, the Council adopted a Regulation[7] in 1998 enabling the Commission to authorise state aids to support small- and medium-sized enterprises, research and development, environmental protection and increased employment, as well as regional aid in certain regions approved by the Commission.

Article 88 (formerly Article 93) of the Treaty stipulates that the Member States must notify the Commission of their intention to provide aid. The Commission examines the form and objective of the given aid and decides whether or not to give its approval. Should a Member State not agree to the Commission's decision and act in non-compliance with it, the Commission will institute legal proceedings against the State before the European Court of Justice.

10.3.2. Community competition rules applying to public enterprises

Under Article 86 of the Treaty, public enterprises (state-owned enterprises and enterprises in which the state has a controlling stake) are subject to the same rules as private undertakings. Member States may not enact or maintain in force any measure and may not engage in any practice that discriminates in favour of a public enterprise. Member States are prohibited from using public enterprises in state ownership or under state control to restrict competition. Enterprises in the common market must be treated on an equal footing irrespective of their ownership.

However Article 86 provides for special treatment for enterprises that are entrusted with the operation of services of general economic interest (for example public utility services) and for monopolies generating public revenue. For such enterprises, the Treaty allows a derogation insofar as their influence on trade is in compliance with Community interests. The purpose of this provision is essentially to reconcile Member State practices of using certain enterprises as an economic or tax policy instrument with general Community interests. However, Article 86 authorises the Commission to issue directives and regulations that are legally binding on the Member States to facilitate the implementation of the objectives of the Article. Thus, in order to prevent public service monopolies within the common market from sharing the market, the Commission may adopt measures for liberalisation. For instance, a Directive[8] issued in 1996 set 1 January 1998 as the date for liberalising the telecommunications market, opening it up to free competition.

---

[7] See Council Regulation 994/98/EC on the Implementation of Articles 92 and 93 of the Treaty establishing the European Community in respect of certain categories of horizontal State aid.

[8] Directive 96/19/EC amending Directive 90/388/EEC with regard to the implementation of full competition in telecommunications markets.

CHAPTER 11
THE COMMON AGRICULTURAL POLICY AND THE COMMON FISHERIES POLICY

11.1. Establishment of the Common Agricultural Policy

Agricultural policy constitutes a key element in every country's economic policy. Agriculture as an economic sector displays distinctive characteristics and is a strategic area in any state's economy, irrespective of its size or share of the national economy. This is attributable to various economic, political and cultural factors, such as, for example, the assurance of food supply and subsistence, the employment of the agrarian labour force, landscape conservation and regional characteristics. This was all the more true a few years after the Second World War, in the cold-war era. The founding Members of the EEC were well aware of this and wanted to introduce agriculture into the future common market under conditions unlike those relating to other sectors of the economy. As a result, Common Agricultural Policy (CAP) established at Community level has become a unique, specific domain within the common market.

The privileged position of agriculture was further reinforced by the fact that France, a major agricultural producer and exporter, wanted to see a common agricultural market system that provided ample support and protection, as well as a substantial market for the agricultural sector and thereby for export-oriented Member States with a traditionally strong agricultural base. The French intention was to provide compensation for the fact that the common market established favourable conditions first and foremost for the strong German industrial economy. Germany, having gained new markets for its manufactured goods, proved willing to endorse French demands in the domain of agriculture.

When setting out the principles of the CAP, the Member States had to bear in mind the historical shortcomings of European agriculture, relying mostly on family holdings compared with overseas economies (especially those of America, Australia and South-America) based on large-scale farming. European agriculture unquestionably needed protection against its more efficient overseas rivals.

Due to the complexity of the area, the Treaty of Rome merely defined the general objectives of the Common Agricultural Policy. The more detailed elaboration of the CAP was a longer process; its mechanisms were set out after the EEC had been established.

Pursuant to Article 39 of the Treaty of Rome establishing the European Economic Community (now Article 33 of the EC Treaty), the five main objectives of the CAP are as follows:

– to increase agricultural productivity;
– to ensure a fair standard of living for the agricultural community;

- to stabilise markets;
- to assure the availability of supplies;
- to ensure that supplies reach consumers at reasonable prices.

The Member States defined separate principles for the Common Agricultural Policy since, as already mentioned, they did not intend to enforce the market conditions pertaining to other products on agricultural products. The principles of the CAP adopted at the 1958 conference held in Stresa in Italy were:

- *The principle of a unified market*: within the area of the Member States, the unified market of agricultural products had to be organised, including the free movement of agricultural products and the unification of competition rules, market mechanisms and price control systems.
- *The principle of Community preference*: the internal market of the Community had to be protected from imported products and the fluctuation of prices on the world market.
- *The principle of financial solidarity*: a common financial fund had to be set up to finance the Common Agricultural Policy.

The Common Agricultural Policy was launched in 1962 along the lines of the principles adopted in Stresa. By 1967, the common agricultural market, based on the elimination of internal customs duties and quotas and the liberalisation of intra-Union trade, had become fully functional. National agricultural preference systems were dissolved and transferred from national to Community level. Agricultural legislation was gradually harmonised and a common organisation of the market was established for agricultural products produced within the Community. The so-called Common Market Organisations (CMOs) laid down the market regime rules protecting the farmers and markets of individual produce or sectors. A common system of protective trade mechanisms was set up to protect the internal market from imported products. To finance the CAP, the European Agricultural Guidance and Guarantee Fund (EAGGF) was set up in 1962. The Guarantee Section of the EAGGF funds expenditure related to the market intervention policy, while the Guidance Section, one of the structural funds, contributes to the structural reform of the agricultural sector.

The Common Agricultural Policy has developed as a true common policy where the Member States have transferred their decision-making powers to Community level, while they themselves remain responsible for the implementation of the decisions adopted.

The Council adopts the main decisions concerning Agricultural Policy. The Commission also plays a vital role as it initiates the decision-making process and, in certain cases, is designated to adopt various executive decisions. Although under the comitology procedure, the Council closely monitors the Commission's executive activities through management committees, the Commission has a more marked and influential role in this sphere compared to other Community policies. The Council adopts its decisions on agricultural policy by a qualified majority. Since the beginning, the Parliament has only been consulted on agriculture.

11.2. Agricultural market organisation in the first thirty years of the CAP

The CAP launched in 1962 was set up as a subsidy policy at Community level. During the first few decades – and, despite subsequent reforms, to an important extent even today – subsidies took the form essentially of price subsidies. In compliance with the objectives set, the foundations of the Common Agricultural Policy were consolidated primarily by giving price advantages to EU agricultural products over imported products. The main basis of the CAP was the maintenance of the stability of internal market prices. Under the CAP, Community agricultural products were assigned unified wholesale prices (so-called limit or threshold prices), which were usually based on the product prices of the Less-Favoured Areas. Since generally these prices significantly exceeded world market prices (by 200 or even 300 per cent), in order to protect Community producers, any Member State that imported produce from the external market was required to pay the difference between the threshold price and the import price into the Community budget (the agricultural levy mechanism). Levies were established by the Commission, which sometimes changed them on a daily basis in function of current world prices.[1]

For many agricultural products, the Community has also assumed a purchase intervention responsibility. In practical terms this means that, when the price of a certain product falls below a given level (the so-called intervention price), the Community automatically purchases the surplus of the producers at the intervention price. Since time and again excessive surplus is created - primarily as a result of intervention - the Community subsidises exports. Nonetheless, as prices on the world market are generally much lower than prices on the internal market, the Community heavily subsidises export activities. The result is a paradox situation, where agricultural produce produced in the EU is sold at much lower prices on external markets than on the internal market itself.

11.3. Results and problems of the CAP in its first three decades

The Common Agricultural Policy succeeded in reaching its initial goals set out in the Treaty of Rome. Nevertheless, along with the success came severe and pervasive problems.

---

[1] In accordance with the decisions adopted at the Uruguay Round of the GATT, the EU had to dismantle the levy system. Instead, the EU now applies the system of variable duties.

Agricultural production and productivity were on the rise, which secured supplies and ultimately made the Community self-sufficient. Furthermore, the EU became the largest exporter of agricultural products in the world. At the same time however it also developed into the world's largest importer, which meant that its agricultural trade balance remained slightly in the red.

Up until the end of the seventies, the rise in farmers' incomes had been similar to that of other segments of the labour force; later, however, it started falling behind, although the different countries and regions showed significant divergences in this respect. Prices of food products were higher than prices on the world market but reasonable in view of consumers' incomes and they remained stable. In the meantime, the weight and role of agriculture within the economy have undergone significant changes. Since the beginning of the sixties, the percentage of the labour force employed in agriculture and the share of agriculture in GDP have plummeted from 20 to 6% and from 7 to under 3% respectively.

In a nutshell, although the CAP seemed to have succeeded in reaching its original goals, the common agricultural market organisation manifested numerous undesirable side-effects, both on internal and external markets, and its maintenance proved to be a hugely expensive mechanism.

The subsidy system of the CAP caused a lot of imbalances. The most severe problem was triggered by the direct subsidy of prices. The guaranteed intervention prices did not encourage productivity but production. As a result, over-production created an excessive surplus costing several billion ECU.

Moreover, the main beneficiaries of the intervention price mechanism were the wholesalers, the large-scale producers and, due to the high prices, the more affluent countries. 80% of the EAGGF subsidies was absorbed by a mere 20% of farmers, who owned 50% of the arable land and were interested in the constant expansion of production; they thus contributed significantly to the creation of product surplus. The preservation of the system became a vital interest for these large-scale farmers, who usually succeeded in asserting their will through agricultural lobbies.

As the CAP in the sixties was set up by the six founding Member States, the range of subsidised products traditionally included the agricultural merchandise of these countries. When the Mediterranean countries joined the Union, further products were added to the list of subsidised produce; nevertheless, intervention prices continued to encourage mostly the producers of traditional temperate products, such as cereals, dairy products and beef. As a result of the above-mentioned anomalies, price subsidies completely dwarfed the objective of structural reforms within the EAGGF. In the eighties, the Guarantee Section consumed 95% of the Fund's resources. The objectives of increasing productivity and establishing a reasonable structure were relegated to the background and the EAGGF was reduced to a mere subsidy system compensating for losses.

Owing to the constant rise in agricultural subsidy demand and the upsurge in the storage and marketing costs of the accumulated surplus, CAP expenditures amounted to two thirds of the Community budget.

From a global point of view, the CAP significantly contributed to the distortion of the agricultural world market. The Community rendered itself independent from international market prices, while at the same time its subsidised export prices often under-cut international prices. As a result, the Community had to face incessant conflicts on the international scene. By the end of the eighties, due to the ever-growing resentment of the USA and the opening of the GATT's Uruguay Round, the situation had become intolerable.

All things considered, at the end of the eighties, for internal and external reasons, the reform of the financing mechanism of the agricultural policy seemed inevitable.

11.4. The 1992 CAP reform

The first attempt at reform came just a few years after the CAP's creation, at the end of the sixties. By that time, it had become obvious that high intervention prices generated over-production. In 1968, the then Commissioner responsible for the CAP, Sicco Mansholt, submitted a proposal on the modernisation of the Community's agricultural structure. To improve productivity, the Mansholt Plan sought to promote the formation of larger units of agricultural production and to reduce the number of people employed in agriculture. The plan of developing larger and more efficient farms however was rejected by both the agricultural organisations and the governments of the Member States.[2] Afterwards, the operating mechanism of the CAP was left essentially untouched until the eighties.

At the beginning of the eighties, the Commission tried to restructure the agricultural market system afresh. A guarantee threshold was introduced for several products, that is, the intervention price was cut back once a certain production threshold had been reached. But these measures proved insufficient and, by the middle of the eighties, huge unsaleable surpluses had been created in the traditionally most problematic product categories, namely dairy products, arable crops and beef. The CAP was on the verge of financial collapse. In 1984, at the Fontainebleau Summit, the Member States agreed that, in future, producers'

---

[2] Farm-structure reform has been permanently struck from the agenda. In fact, in the nineties, the preservation of the European farming model (the family farm) became one of the primary objectives of the CAP.

income could only rise on the basis of improved productivity and purchase prices could not increase as a function of inflation. The most important decision was the introduction of milk quotas. Producers exceeding the set quotas were liable to sanctions in the form of punitive duties. As the action taken had not brought about radical changes, the quota-system was not extended to other products. In 1988, in the framework of the Delors I Package, new provisions were issued to reform the financial mechanism of the CAP. Stricter budgetary discipline was introduced, which limited the annual growth rate of agricultural budgetary expenditures at 74% of the annual GNP growth rate. In the years that followed, the share of farm subsidies in the budget was gradually reduced, although this was more due to increased spending in other areas than a nominal cut in farm support. After 1988, the amount of product surpluses was successfully reduced but the comprehensive reform of the financing mechanism of the CAP was still imperative.

As a result of several years' work and negotiations, the Commission, with the Irishman Ray McSharry as the Agriculture Commissioner, put forward a comprehensive reform package in 1991. The McSharry Plan, aiming at a genuine reform of the CAP, was adopted by the Council in May 1992.
The main elements of the reform were as follows:
- Agricultural support prices were significantly reduced over a period of three years in order to ensure the competitiveness of Community agricultural production on the world market. Thus, for example, the price of cereals fell by 29%, while beef prices dropped by 15% (it was imperative to decrease the purchase prices of these products since the most excessive surpluses had accumulated in these sectors).
- Parallel with the price cutbacks, a direct income support scheme was introduced to compensate farmers for their loss of income. Under the system, farmers are entitled to receive direct payment support irrespective of their volume of production. The main advantage of the income support system over the price support system is that it does not encourage over-production.
- For cereals and other arable crops, payment of compensatory income support was dependent on the withdrawal of land from production, that is, on the obligatory set-aside of a certain percentage of the land.
- Environmental protection featured prominently in the McSharry proposal. Farmers who engaged in environmentally-sound management were supported through various incentives. Over 160 projects were launched, which sought to teach farmers to understand their role not as mere food producers and cultivators of the land but also as environmentalists.

- Early retirement schemes were offered for elderly producers (as an alternative and not as a compulsory measure of the reform package). Member States that offered early retirement schemes for farmers and those employed in agriculture over age 55 were entitled to Community support. This was a measure of particular importance, since 50% of the Union's agrarian labour force was over 55.

The centrepiece of the 1992 McSharry reform was the Community's gradual move away from reliance on price support towards income support based on direct payments, whose effect on market mechanisms was much less distorting. It must be mentioned however that the introduction of direct payments was a gradual process. Initially, the system covered cereals, sheep meat and beef, then vegetables and fruit, while dairy products, sugar and wine were not eligible. A further problem relating to the system of direct payments is that it is a quite complicated and time-consuming administrative process. Nevertheless, since the launch of the 1992 reform, the average annual income of agricultural producers has increased by 4.5%, which shows that the transfer from the price support system to direct income compensation did not have a detrimental effect on producers' income levels but had results more in line with market based conditions.

The most important results of the 1992 reform have been manifest in the arable crops sector. The cereal surplus stored in warehouses fell from 30 million tonnes in 1993 to 3 million in 1996. The set-aside (or fallowing) programme has restored the balance of supply and demand. Community cereal production has become more competitive. The results in the beef sector had also seemed promising before BSE suddenly hit the market, leading to a drastic fall in demand and thus creating new surpluses. As a result of a more environmentally-conscious approach, the quantity of chemicals and fertilisers used has dropped. The percentage of CAP expenditure in the overall budget has been successfully reduced; while in the eighties it had amounted to two thirds of the Community budget, by the late nineties it dropped to 45–50%. This apparent reduction was, however, mainly the consequence of the increase in the aggregate sum of the budget. Agricultural expenditures *per se* continued to escalate; it was only their share of the aggregate sum that showed a decrease. In brief, the reforms failed to prevent the continuous increase of agricultural expenditure. Overall, the introduction of direct payments had a stabilising effect on the Community budget, but it also led to a situation where farmers felt that more radical reforms were against their interests. This problem was particularly accentuated by the challenge of enlargement.

It should be emphasised here that the 1992 reform introduced an entirely novel approach towards the CAP, which in the long term may fundamentally transform European agriculture and rural development. The McSharry proposal identified an important function of agriculture that had not been mentioned in the Treaty of Rome, namely that agriculture has a role beyond the mere production of food; the sector also has responsibility for preserving the rural landscape and cultural values, a task greatly facilitated by the traditional European agricultural model (the family farm). Agriculture offers a whole range of services (in terms of maintaining the landscape in the countryside and preserving traditional cultural values) which constitute a common legacy of society as a whole. This approach provides an excellent basis for the system of direct payments. It embodies the Community objective of maintaining the agricultural population in rural areas.[3] At the same time, by propagating traditional, environmentally sound and extensive production techniques, it discourages intensification and in fact encourages reduced production and improved, wholesome produce.

To sum up, the 1992 reform of the CAP has brought about positive changes within the agricultural support policy of the Community. Nevertheless, since its measures have often proved incomplete and superficial, it has failed to resolve the fundamental conflicts and problems of the sector in the long run. At the turn of the millennium, the Union was forced to face the need for a further reform. In addition, two new factors – the liberalisation of the world market as a result of the GATT/WTO negotiations and the challenges posed by the forthcoming accession of the Central and Eastern European countries – called for the immediate reform of the Common Agricultural Policy.

In accordance with the GATT Agreement adopted in April 1994, the members of the World Trade Organisation (WTO) were required to reduce their agricultural support by 20% for all products, export subsidy spending by 36% and the volume of subsidised exports by 21% over a period of six years. This obligation strongly influenced the agricultural policy of the Union and necessitated a further adjustment of the support system. At the end of the nineties, it became clear that the accession of the Central and Eastern European countries to the European Union would increase the Union's agricultural area by 50% and almost double the agricultural labour force. Consequently, were the CAP to retain its current support system, it would impose a huge burden on the Community budget, which would endanger the financeability of the CAP as a whole. This once again necessitated the radical reform of the support system.

---

[3] This is all the more important as, in the early nineties, urban unemployment increased significantly and, as a consequence, the further migration of an extensive agrarian population to urban areas could have caused social tension.

Bearing in mind the WTO obligations and the challenges of enlargement, the European Commission proposed the deepening of the reform of agricultural policy as a central element of its Agenda 2000 package[4], issued on 16 July 1997.

11.5. A new reform of the CAP – Agricultural provisions of Agenda 2000

In the summer of 1997, within the framework of Agenda 2000, the Commission proposed a further reform of the CAP to deepen, widen and step up the 1992 reform measures by continuing the replacement of price support mechanisms with direct payments. In its proposal, the Commission defined the measures to be implemented in the 2000–2006 budgetary planning term and analysed their probable influence on the Community budget. In accordance with the proclaimed ambitions, the Commission set the primary objectives of the reform as follows: the reinforcement of the competitiveness of Community agriculture through lower product prices, the preservation of the European agricultural model, the fair distribution of support measures, the promotion of a stable income and fair living standards for the farming community, the creation of alternative employment and other sources of income for farmers and their families.

The Commission embarked on various specific measures giving concrete shape to the above objectives. The most radical changes were to be implemented in the beef, dairy and cereals sectors. The Commission warned that – in view of the forthcoming enlargement – adherence to the present price support mechanism would result in an unjustifiable accumulation of the already significant volume of surpluses. The proposed measures included: for beef, a price fall of 30% in the period 2000–2002; for cereals, a reduction in purchase prices of 20% in 2000, and; for dairy products, a reduction of intervention prices of 10% by 2006. Farmers would be compensated for their loss of income by direct payments unrelated to production, which were first introduced in the framework of the 1992 reform. The Commission also proposed the introduction of similar measures for the tobacco, oil and wine regimes.

Further actions were recommended to encourage the use of more extensive farming techniques, agro-environmental measures, further investments in agriculture, the development of farming methods which respect the environment and the improvement of the competitiveness of rural areas. Rural development and tackling the problems of rural areas were central elements of the proposal. The Commission suggested that regions in which development is lagging behind should enjoy priority when receiving support from the Structural Funds, since the promotion of sustainable income sources for farmers and the preservation of rural heritage are fundamental Community objectives.

---

[4] For more on Agenda 2000, see 1.13.3., 1.13.5. and 7.3.4.

All things considered, the specific measures suggested by the Commission did not truly reflect the concepts outlined in the original ambitious objectives. The Commission failed to propose drastic changes fundamentally transforming the prevailing mechanisms. It embarked on schemes that are governed by the principle of progressivity, essentially prolonging the 1992 reforms. Likewise, the changes suggested within the framework of Agenda 2000 were neither comprehensive (various sectors were excluded), nor radical enough (they permitted only moderate reductions). However, the Commission's careful approach was fully justified by the fact that several Member States were expected to (and indeed did) oppose fervently any attempt to institute major changes.

The Member States had to come to an agreement on the proposed reform of the CAP within the framework of Agenda 2000 prior to the commencement of the 2000–2006 budgetary period. Finally, the agreement was concluded at the Berlin European Council on 24–25 March 1999. Beforehand however, negotiations on Agenda 2000, and its most controversial and difficult element, the reform of the CAP, had been going on for one and a half years. Besides complex issues such as the financial aspects of the enlargement of the Union and the reform of Structural Funds, agricultural reform had traditionally posed the most severe problem to be solved.

The original proposal of the Commission issued in July 1997 envisaged an initial growth of agricultural expenditures in the period 2000–2006 as a consequence of the wider application of the income support mechanism. The Commission took the view that the replacement of price support measures with direct payments would prove profitable in the long run. While, initially, it would be more expensive than sustaining the existing price support mechanism, ultimately it would be a cheaper solution since, after reaching a certain level, expenditures would cease to rise and settle at a fixed level.[5] Parallel with the introduction of the direct income support mechanism, the market could be gradually liberalised, which had long been the focal point at the GATT/WTO negotiations with non-Member States. The price support mechanism, by contrast, had encouraged excessive production and an immense upsurge of expenditure. Consequently, the Commission proposed an initial increase of the amount of agricultural support at the beginning of the 2000–2006 period (until 2004 when expenditures would even out at a fixed level), while at the same time converting price support into a direct income support mechanism, thus establishing a more rational and profitable system in the long-term. Most Member States, however, were firmly opposed to this concept.

On the one hand, the Community's proposal, based on the reduction of guaranteed prices was resisted by the main beneficiaries of the CAP, who had been pressured by the strong,

---

[5] The Commission reckoned that the volume of income support might be gradually reduced year by year to motivate farmers to adapt themselves to conditions prevailing on the world market.

organised agricultural lobbies, which mainly represented the interests of large-scale farmers. On the other hand, the proposal was not popular amongst the net contributor Member States either, who interpreted the increase of direct payments essentially as a renewed attempt to entice financing from them to increase expenditure, and not as a restructuring of the support mechanism.

The main contributors to the Community budget, who had in any case perceived the reduction of expenses as the primary objective of Agenda 2000, categorically refused to support the idea of increasing the agricultural budget and demanded a reform to curb costs. As a result, the final agreement was a synthesis of the above conflicting interests. While, under mainly German[6] and British pressure, the increase of expenditure was successfully prevented, the French managed to reduce the extent of price support cutback originally proposed by the Commission.

Finally, in Berlin, the European Council adopted a version of Agenda 2000 that attempted to reflect the opinions of the two interest groups. It aimed to stabilise agricultural expenditure, but reduced price support to a lesser extent than originally proposed by the Commission. In accordance with the agreement of the Heads of State or Government, intervention prices for beef were cut by a mere 20% accompanied by the same rate of increase in income support, while new special support schemes were put in place. For cereals, the Member States agreed on a reduction in intervention prices of 15%, to be implemented in two separate phases of 7.5% during the period 2000–2002, offset by an increase in direct payments. For dairy products, the quota system was extended until 2006, while intervention prices were cut from the marketing year 2005–2006. As a new development, direct payments were introduced in this sector as well.

Reflecting the Community's new approach to agricultural policy, the main objective of the Agenda 2000 reform package, besides the reduction of intervention prices, was the promotion of rural development. The novel approach emphasised not only agriculture's traditional role in producing food but also its environmental function of land conservation and the preservation of the rural and cultural heritage. Its importance was reflected by the fact that rural development had become the second pillar of the CAP. Consequently, its share of overall CAP spending had also grown. To promote rural development and

---

6   Germany proposed the introduction of national co-financing for direct payments. Although this would have meant the end of agricultural policy as a *common* policy, and its re-nationalisation, it could have reduced the ardent agricultural debates raging at Community level. France, along with several other Member States, however, rejected this solution. Instead, the French government suggested the method of digressive payments for direct income aids, entailing an annual reduction of 3% in direct payments with their final termination by the end of a 30-year period, but this proposal failed to receive majority support as well.

the structural reorganisation of farming in the fiscal term commencing 2000, new support schemes were introduced, such as measures for organic farming and non-food producing agricultural activities. Nevertheless, the second pillar of the CAP by itself, amounting to under 10 per cent of the overall agricultural budget, remained of limited significance.

The agricultural reform within the framework of Agenda 2000 essentially preserved the current production and structural mechanisms, fell short in preparing the sector for the challenges to be faced by the Union and failed to remedy several decade-old problems. It did not bridge the gap between EU and lower world market prices and did not resolve the surplus problem. Agenda 2000 only scratched the surface without really remedying the problems of the CAP. In a nutshell, the Common Agricultural Policy, despite the measures introduced by Agenda 2000, continued to be the most controversial issue for the internal market, external trade relations and, most importantly, the enlargement of the Community. As a consequence, the Member States agreed to launch a new CAP reform as early as 2002, even before the duration of Agenda 2000 reached its midpoint. This reform was all the more necessary as the citizens of the Union had been increasingly worried about the series of recent food-safety crises, such as BSE (mad cow disease) and foot-and-mouth disease, which had considerable implications for Community spending as they were managed with the help of resources from the Community budget.[7]

11.6. Eastern enlargement and the Common Agricultural Policy

Overall the reform of Agenda 2000 was less radical but also less expensive than originally intended. However, the potential difficulties were numerous. On the one hand, the reform did not fully comply with the Union's obligations assumed in the framework of the WTO to sharply reduce agricultural support. In addition, the agricultural chapter of Agenda 2000 generated further problems in view of the future enlargement. With regard to the accession of the applicant countries, the reform package anticipated a lengthy transitional period (along the lines of the Commission's proposal); it failed to allocate adequate financial resources for the new Member States and in fact, at the beginning, it did not even include

---

[7] The fact that food safety has become a priority issue is demonstrated by the decision of the Nice European Council in December 2000 to set up a European Food Safety Authority. The institutional establishment of this Authority was actually laid down in a joint Regulation 178/2002/EC of Council and Parliament issued on 28 January 2002, under which the Authority started its work. For more on the activities of the European Food Safety Authority, see 19.2.

plans for extending the direct payments mechanism to farmers of new Member States. That is why among the EU's internal policies, the extension of the Common Agricultural Policy to new Member States proved to be the hardest nut to crack during the course of the accession negotiations. As in the case of all enlargement items, for agricultural expenditures the problem arose that Agenda 2000 foresaw an earliest date of enlargement in 2002 and a maximum number of six new Member States before 2006. However, in the light of the Nice and Laeken Summits in December 2000 and 2001, this hypothesis changed to 2004 as the earliest date of accessions, moreover with up to 10 new members.

In relation to enlargement, the greatest problem was the question of extending direct payments to the new Member States. The debate had been going on since the draft of Agenda 2000 was published as to whether farmers of new Member States should be entitled to direct payments or not. One side argued that the mechanism of direct income support was introduced to compensate for the reduced price support and, since new Member States had never enjoyed the old higher level of guaranteed prices, they were not entitled to such compensation. Candidate countries on the other hand insisted on direct payments on the basis of the principle of equal competition, arguing that, following accession, since they would be producing for the same market, they should be allowed to compete on equal terms and a difference in support would distort the level playing field. In addition, direct income support had come to represent a growing proportion of farm subsidies and had significantly contributed to farmers' improved standard of living, which is exactly why acceding countries insisted on direct payments.

However, the problem was not just about extending the system to new Member States, but rather that net contributors (primarily Germany) expected a new CAP reform to reduce their contributions to the budget. These Member States feared that if farmers in CEECs were granted the same level of direct payments, there would be a conflict of interests: new Member States would not really be interested in reforming the system of agricultural subsidies.[8] This reform was increasingly demanded by net contributors, who did not wish to pay more into the common budget and wanted to complete reforms prior to enlargement.

In the closing stages of the accession negotiations, in order to ensure the financial sustainability of agriculture and to win the support of net contributors for extending the

---

[8] It was evident that the extension of direct payments to CEECs would bring about a significant change in the lives of farmers, whose level of income could rise very considerably.

CAP to new Member States, the Brussels European Council of October 2002 – following a Franco-German deal – forged a political agreement on the long-term financing ceilings of the CAP. The Member States agreed that, until 2006, the ceilings of Agenda 2000 would apply and that, from 2007, CAP spending could gradually increase by not more than 1% a year. Considering enlargement and the extension of the CAP to the new Member States, this implicitly necessitated reforms in farm policy, without which it would be impossible to distribute the same amount of money among farmers of more countries.

The October 2002 summit also proposed a farm subsidy package to the then-candidate countries. According to this package, CAP market regulatory mechanisms (price support, export subsidies, etc.) would apply to farmers from new Member States from day one of membership, but direct payments to them would be phased in gradually. The EU-15 took a firm stance on direct income support, arguing that full direct payments could have been counter-productive, as they would have served as a disincentive to restructure the agricultural sector and would have thereby preserved lower productivity and the old ways of farming; hence they proposed the gradual phasing in of direct payments to farmers in the new Member States over a period of nine years, to reach the full 100% level in 2013. The candidate countries only managed to improve the EU's common position in the final phase of accession talks and practically cut the phase-in period to six years: the final package adopted at the Copenhagen European Council of 12–13 December 2002 granted the option of topping up those payments by 30% from the national budget and partly from EU rural development funding. Based on this agreement, in the first three years after accession, direct payments amounted to 25–30–35% of what farmers from the old Member States were entitled to. From 2007 on, direct payments grow by 10% each year, but national top-ups can come exclusively from the national budget. Under this arrangement, the level of direct income support to farmers of the 10 Member States that joined in 2004 and the 15 'old' Member States can become equal in 2010.

In addition to full market support and reduced direct income support, the new Member States could benefit from rural development funding to a much greater extent than old Member States. Projects in the new Member States are eligible for up to 80% co-financing from the Community budget. For the years 2004 to 2006, the Union earmarked EUR 5.11 billion for rural development aid to the new Member States that acceded to the Union in 2004, which exceeded the 4.7 billion allocated to market support and direct payments.

This was a clear message from the Union that the new Member States should focus on restructuring and establishing efficient production structures.[9]

In the negotiations with Bulgaria and Romania, the European Union used the same solution as it had invented for the ten Member States that joined in 2004. According to the Treaty of Accession signed on 25 April 2005, in the first three years of their membership between 2007 and 2009 these two countries will be eligible for 25–30–35% of direct payments, which will then grow by 10% annually from 40% in 2010 to 100% in 2016. Nonetheless, both countries may add additional top-up payments of up to 30%. With this option, Bulgarian and Romanian farmers may receive payments equivalent to full Community direct support as early as 2013. Similarly to the ten Member States that joined in 2004, Bulgaria and Romania will also be eligible for significant sums of rural development aid: in the period 2007–2009, EUR 3.041 billion will be available to them for restructuring and establishing efficient production structures.

Table 11.1. The level of direct payments to farmers of the 12 new Member States between 2004 and 2016

a) the 10 Member States that joined in 2004

	2004	2005	2006	2007	2008	2009	2010	2011	2012	2013
Without national topping up	25%	30%	35%	40%	50%	60%	70%	80%	90%	100%
With maximum national topping up	55%	60%	65%	70%	80%	90%	100%	100%	100%	100%

b) the 2 Member States that joined in 2007

	2007	2008	2009	2010	2011	2012	2013	2014	2015	2016
Without national topping up	25%	30%	35%	40%	50%	60%	70%	80%	90%	100%
With maximum national topping up	55%	60%	65%	70%	80%	90%	100%	100%	100%	100%

---

[9] For more on the outcome of accession negotiations and the Copenhagen financial package, see Subchapter 1.13.5. and Table 1.4.

11.7. The agricultural reform of 2003

The deal reached in October 2002 on the long-term financial ceilings foreshadowed further reforms of the Common Agricultural Policy. Net contributors to the CAP – particularly Germany – increasingly argued that a gradual re-nationalisation of CAP financing should be considered; financing the CAP exclusively from the Community budget should be reviewed. These proposals were rejected by the main beneficiaries of the CAP, such as France. Nevertheless, these proposals set the agenda and led to reforms focused on decoupling support from production in order to ensure that the CAP could remain financeable in the long run. The negotiations on CAP reforms, which began in the middle of 2002 and went on for almost a year, concentrated on the following priorities:

– decoupling payments and production;
– simplifying the regulatory framework;
– promoting sustainable farming and paying more attention to consumer needs (including, *inter alia*, strengthening the aspects of quality production, food safety, and environmental protection);
– strengthening the role of rural development;
– improving the competitiveness of agriculture;
– meeting WTO obligations;
– ensuring financial discipline with a view to the decisions taken in October 2002.

In line with these priorities, an agreement was finally reached in June 2003 on reforming the CAP by introducing fundamental changes in its financing.[10] The key elements of the 2003 reform package are the following:

– A single farm payment system based on partial decoupling of production and subsidies
This single decoupled farm payment means that various forms of direct aid to farmers are paid in one sum for each farm holding, based on the levels of assistance received under the previous system. The agreed reference period for the calculation of single decoupled farm payments was the 2000–2002 payment entitlements of the farmers concerned. Direct payments are decoupled from production, supporting the producer (farmer) rather than the

---

[10] The reform package of June 2003, which laid down the general framework and the support mechanisms of key commodities, was complemented by a package of measures in April 2004, which included further commodities (e.g. tobacco and olives) in the reforms.

product. However the decoupling is only partial, because the flexible system allows the Member States to decide at their own discretion the extent to which they apply decoupling to various agricultural products (or, in certain cases, even to maintain previous forms of support).

– Reduction in direct payments
Direct payments remained unchanged until 2005, but then the part above EUR 5,000 was reduced by 3% in 2005, 4% in 2006 and 5% from 2007 on. This is also known as the *modulation* mechanism. The Commission proposal for capping annual farm support (at EUR 300,000 / farm / year) to put an end to the excessive subsidies to large farm holdings was rejected.

– Compliance with Community standards
The single farm payment is linked to measures taken to meet environmental, food safety, animal and plant health and animal welfare standards, as well as the requirement to keep all farmland in good agricultural and environmental condition (termed *cross-compliance*).

– Strengthening rural development
A strengthened rural development policy with more EU money is designed to promote the environment, product quality and animal welfare and to help farmers to meet EU production standards; this commenced in 2005.

In line with the decisions taken in June 2003, the implementation of the reforms and of the decoupling of production and direct payments started on 1 January 2005. The Member States were, however, allowed to maintain the old system of payments for a transitional period of two years. Thus, the new system became compulsory from 1 January 2007. The new Member States are an exception; in their case, the reduction of direct payments becomes effective only after the level of those payments has reached the Union level of direct payments. In 2005, ten Member States (Austria, Belgium, Denmark, Germany, Ireland, Italy, Luxembourg, Portugal, Sweden and the United Kingdom) decided to switch over to the single payment scheme (SPS). The remaining five old Member States (Finland, France, Greece, the Netherlands and Spain) changed over in 2006, followed by Malta and Slovenia in 2007. The remaining eight of the ten Member States which acceded in 2004 (Cyprus, the Czech Republic, Estonia, Hungary, Latvia, Lithuania, Poland and Slovakia) will have to change over to SPS from the single area payment scheme (SAPS)[11] adopted upon their accession by December 2010 at the lastest; Bulgaria and Romania have until the end of 2011 to do so.

In terms of its approach, the 2003 reform package can be considered as the most serious reform of the CAP ever, although it was weakened on several points by the compromises necessary for its adoption. Its most controversial element is the option granted to Member States to maintain production-linked aid in certain areas (which happen to be the three, traditionally most problematic sectors: cereals, beef and dairy). It is also rather unfortunate that the proposal for capping subsidy payments to large farmers was torpedoed. These compromises may even jeopardise compliance with the farm spending ceilings adopted in October 2002. The Member States recognised this risk when adopting the reform package, and thus, as part of the reform, a 'financial discipline mechanism' was introduced with a view to ensuring that, from 2007, direct subsidy payment ceilings would not be exceeded. The mechanism allows reductions at source whenever forecasts show that spending on market and direct support is likely to exceed the budget ceiling. It should also be noted that the Member States have much more leeway in applying and combining various forms of funding. On the one hand, this runs counter to the objective of simplification and reduces transparency, while, on the other hand, it is – to a certain degree – a move towards re-nationalising the CAP. Nevertheless, overall, the 2003 CAP reform is a huge step towards ensuring the long-term sustainability of the EU's farm policy. At the same time, gradual decoupling is consistent with the Union's WTO obligations and strengthens the Union's position in the WTO negotiations in the liberalisation of trade in agricultural commodities.

The Commission wanted to further improve the 2003 comprehensive CAP reform by supplementing it with sectoral reform packages. It was in that framework that the new sugar market regime came into effect in July 2006, restructuring a sector untouched

---

[11] The single area payment scheme (SAPS) is a simplified direct payment scheme designed specifically for the new Member States to help them adjust to the complicated procedures of the CAP. Under the SAPS, there is no set-aside obligation, and payments are not linked to production volume or livestock numbers but are instead based on land area only. In essence, the SAPS is a decoupled support scheme which puts farmers under no obligation to produce. Payments are based on national financial envelopes set by the Commission. The level of the per-hectare SAPS payment is calculated by dividing the national envelope by the utilised agricultural area. With the exception of Malta and Slovenia, all new Member States opted for the SAPS at the time of their accession.

Table 11.2. The evolution of CAP expenditure from 1992–2005 (EUR million)

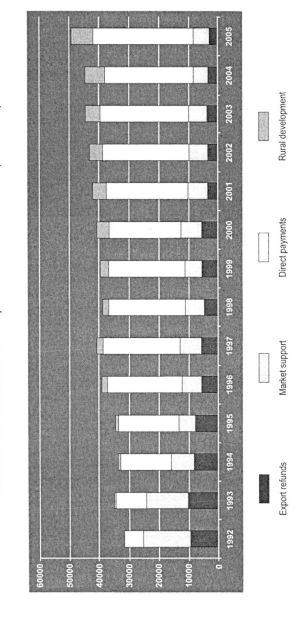

Source: European Commission

for four decades. It lowered the guaranteed price by 36% but offered compensation to farmers in return, and introduced a restructuring fund helping non-competitive market actors to leave the sector. Agreement was reached in June 2007 on the new common market organisation for fruit and vegetables, which brings the sector – formerly managed very separately – closer to the operation of the reformed CAP. The changes will come into effect in 2008 and include integrating the sector into the single payment scheme, scrapping export refunds, encouraging farmers to join producer organisations (which are eligible for substantial funding to cope with crisis periods), strengthening environmental aspects and promoting organic farming. The next Commission proposal in the pipeline affects the wine sector, and is aimed at boosting the competitiveness of European wines by strengthening quality production, introducing simpler and more transparent rules, and finding a better balance between supply and demand. On top of the sectoral reforms, agreement was reached in the Council in June 2007 on replacing the 21 individual sectoral common market organisations with a single common market organisation framework, which is yet another great step in the direction of reforming and simplifying the CAP.

11.8. The Common Agricultural Policy from 2007 to 2013

As the 2003 reform package set the financial framework of the CAP for a decade, there was little room for manoeuvre during the elaboration of the agricultural heading of the 2007–2013 financial perspectives. When the Commission submitted its proposal for the next financial perspective on 10 February 2004, it took these reforms into consideration.[12] Amending this document, the Commission made proposals for the financing instruments of the CAP on 14 July 2004.

The budgetary ceiling adopted in October 2002, which froze the growth of expenditure at a nominal 1%, had an impact on CAP spending as well, which was reflected in the Commission's proposals. Hence, following up the trends of the Delors II package and of Agenda 2000, the ratio of agricultural expenditure was to be further reduced in the budget (from 46.4% to 36.5% between 2006 and 2013). This reduction would be due not only to the significant increase in other budget headings, but also because farm spending would

---

[12] For more on the 2007–2013 financial perspectives, see 7.3.5.

practically remain unchanged in nominal terms. The Commission proposal called for the reinforcement of rural development within the new budgetary heading of natural resources (formerly agricultural policy), which is demonstrated by the increase in its share within CAP spending (as pillar 2) to 27% compared to 14% in 2005.

Although following the 2002 agreement, many considered CAP financing for 2007–2013 a done deal, the UK and some other Nordic countries managed to re-open the debate. The UK was only willing to accept a cut in its rebate[13] – which it secured in 1984 and which has been a thorn in the side of other Member States since – in return for further reforms to the financing of the common farm policy. [14] Linking these two issues was something that France and many other Member States could not accept, referring to the unanimously adopted deal of 2002. Eventually, the final compromise solution does not modify the UK rebate significantly, nor does it unravel the 2002 package deal.

Under the 2007–2013 Financial Perspective adopted by the Member States in December 2005, and approved by the European Parliament in May 2006, the ceiling for the 'preservation and management of natural resources' budgetary heading was set 9% lower than the Commission had proposed (EUR 371.3 billion instead of 404.6 billion). Rural development was trimmed back to a slightly greater extent, but there was a reduction also in CAP market support measures and direct payments from EUR 301 billion to 293 billion. In practical terms this meant that the 2002 agreement was interpreted in a way that Bulgaria and Romania had to be squeezed into the financing framework originally elaborated for 25 members, which entailed a relative drop for the 25 countries concerned. The much higher share of rural development is a novelty. Even though 30% lower than the figure in the original Commission proposal, the total sum is well above what was dedicated to this area before 2007. Over the course of the seven years, EUR 69.25 billion will go to

---

[13] See 7.3.3.

[14] According to the UK position, in the 21st century it is unjustified to spend 40% of the Community budget on a sector which employs 5% of the workforce and produces 3% of GDP. Instead, these funds should be channelled to policies improving the Union's global competitiveness (such as R&D).

rural development (roughly 24% of CAP market support and direct payments), out of which 31 billion is ringfenced for the 12 new Member States that joined in 2004 and 2007, where reinforced rural development funding is badly needed to assist restructuring.

An important element of the compromise on the 2007–2013 Financial Perspective was the so-called review clause, calling for a review of both the revenue and expenditure side of the budget halfway through the financial period. The Commission was entrusted in 2008–2009 with the task of carrying out a comprehensive survey of the two most controversial budgetary issues: the Common Agricultural Policy and the British rebate. The Commission's reports will be taken into consideration in the new financial planning period starting in 2014. It had also been agreed that if, on the basis of the mid-term review, the European Council deemed it necessary, it could also take measures to modify the financial framework before 2013. This leaves the door open for further CAP reforms in the second half of the financial term, but the chances of such reforms are negligible, considering the stubborn positions of the Member States most concerned and the fact that such decisions require unanimity.

The new Financial Perspective also brought a new financing framework for the CAP from 2007. As part of the reinforced role and more independent management of rural development, the European Agricultural Guidance and Guarantee Fund (EAGGF), in existence since the birth of the CAP, is now split in two and the CAP is financed from two funds: the European Agricultural Guarantee Fund (EAGF) – covering the traditional CAP subsidies – and the newly created European Agricultural Fund for Rural Development (EAFRD). The EAGF finances: export refunds; intervention payments; direct payments; information programmes; the marketing of agricultural products; financial contributions to certain veterinary and phytosanitary measures and to food and feed control measures; the conservation, characterisation, collection and utilisation of genetic resources in agriculture; the establishment and maintenance of agricultural accounting information systems, and agricultural testing systems. The EAFRD finances rural development programmes implemented through joint management by the Member States and the Community. In 2007, rural development tasks that used to be implemented within structural operations (e.g. the LEADER Community initiative) were also placed under the EAFRD in a comprehensive rural development framework.

11.9. The Common Fisheries Policy

The Common Fisheries Policy (CFP) was already established under the Treaty of Rome establishing the European Economic Community with the same set of provisions as the ones set out for the Common Agricultural Policy. Nonetheless, the Common Fisheries Policy has developed at a much slower pace than agriculture itself. It was not until 1970 that the first provisions for a Common Fisheries Policy were adopted and although the CFP was already functional in the seventies, it only became a fully-fledged policy as late as 1983.

Decision-making in fisheries is the same as that applied for agricultural policy. The Council acts by qualified majority on the Commission's proposal and after consulting the European Parliament.

The CFP is built on four main elements: the conservation of fish stocks, the common organisation of the markets, structural measures and agreements with third countries.

The depletion of fish stocks is a serious and persistent danger, since fish, unlike agricultural produce, are a limited natural resource. The conservation and management of resources is therefore the cornerstone of the CFP and the EU Member States have assumed joint responsibility in this area. In the framework of the CFP, the maximum quantity of catches is set. The Council sets annual TACs (total allowable catches) by species and determines quotas that allocate the TACs between the Member States. The EU acknowledges the exclusive fishing rights of the Member States in their respective coastal waters. The authorities of the Member States are responsible for monitoring adherence to the set quotas. The Commission monitors the Member States' compliance with relevant legislation.

The common organisation of the fisheries market is based on four instruments: common marketing standards, the operation of producers' organisations (which are exempted from the general rules on competition), a common price mechanism for certain produce and a compensation system similar to that of the CAP, and the introduction of safety measures to manage critical market imbalances.

Structural policy is an important aspect of the CFP since the sector has long been struggling with problems. The fleet capacity of the EU Member States exceeds the available accessible resources. Although the number of fishing vessels has been reduced there is still an imbalance. This problem is all the more urgent as excessive capacities may generate unemployment and, to make matters worse, often in regions which offer no alternative sources of income. The structural policy for fisheries, which aims to modernise the sector, promote structural changes and develop fisheries-dependent areas (and areas where significant fishing activity is pursued), attempts to tackle these problems. Although there had already been structural funding for fisheries in the seventies, support for the sector became prominent with the reinforcement of the Community economic and social cohesion policy in the late eighties and early nineties.[15] With the establishment of the Financial Instrument on Fisheries Guidance (FIFG) in 1993, the amount allocated for the structural support of the sector was doubled. Within the framework of Agenda 2000, the FIFG's budget amounted to EUR 1.1 billion for the period 2000–2006.

Since 1976, fishing agreements on behalf of the Member States have been concluded by the Community. The EU has entered into over two dozen agreements with third countries, whose primary objective is to protect the traditional fishing zones and rights of the Community fleets and to gain access to new fishing waters. Most of these agreements relate to the waters of the North Atlantic, North Africa and the Indian Ocean.

At the turn of the millennium, the time was becoming ripe to reform the fisheries policy inherited from the eighties, which could no longer ensure a sustainable marine environment. Intensive fishing had led to a depletion of fish stocks, which in turn had had a negative effect on the income of fishermen. Reforms were required to ensure biologically, environmentally and economically sustainable fishing. The Commission proposed a series of reform measures, which were adopted by the Council in December 2002 and put the functioning of the Common Fisheries Policy on a new footing. The reform was based on the following components:
 – *long-term approach*: Earlier, actions concerning fishing opportunities and related measures were taken annually. They often resulted in fluctuations which not only prevented fishermen from planning ahead but also failed to conserve fish stocks. Under the new CFP, long-term objectives are adopted for ensuring the sustainability of marine fauna.
 – *new fleet policy*: The chronic overcapacity of the EU fleet led to over-fishing. The new, simpler fleet policy lays responsibility for matching fishing capacity to fishing possibilities on the Member States, and calls for the phasing out of public aid to

---

[15] For more on this topic, see 13.1.

private investors for expanding fishing capacities, while increasing aid for measures to improve vessel security and working conditions on board.

– *better application of the rules*: Measures have to be taken to develop cooperation among the various authorities concerned and to strengthen the uniformity of control and sanctions throughout the EU to ensure more effective enforcement of the rules.

– *stakeholder involvement*: Fishermen need to take a greater part in the CFP management process. Regional advisory councils (RACs) need to be created to bring together the various stakeholders, mainly fishermen but also researchers and scientists, who can help identify the measures that can ensure the sustainability of marine life.

The financing framework of the Common Fisheries Policy is also changed for the 2007–2013 period. Fom 1 January 2007, fisheries policy is financed from a European Fisheries Fund (EFF), which falls in the agricultural policy budgetary heading of the 'preservation and management of natural resources'. The European Fisheries Fund is the successor of the Financial Instrument for Fisheries Guidance (FIFG), with a few new objectives. During the seven years between 2007 and 2013, the EFF will have EUR 3.85 billion at its disposal for the following five priorities:

– matching fleet capacity to available fishery resources
– support to certain industries (aquaculture, processing, marketing)
– support measures of benefit to the entire sector
– sustainable development of areas dependent on fisheries
– technical assistance to Member States.

CHAPTER 12
THE COMMON TRANSPORT POLICY AND TRANS-EUROPEAN NETWORKS

12.1. Developing a Common Transport Policy

The Treaty of Rome establishing the European Economic Community envisaged that transport policy would be based on particularly close cooperation since, with regard to the free movement of goods and persons, this area is of key importance within the Union. Accordingly, the Treaty (Article 3 TEC) identifies transport as one of the common policies. The competence of Community institutions, however, is much more limited in this sphere than in the other so-called 'common' policies of trade, competition, agriculture and fisheries. In contrast to the other common policies, the Community refrains from arbitrating in the day-to-day operation of transport policy. Its role is essentially limited to legislation and policy-making, whereas daily management, pursuant to Article 70 of the Treaty, falls under the competence of the Member States. The Treaty of Rome laid down the specific objectives of the policy, calling for the application of common rules to international and transit transport and, in accordance with the free movement of services, for the adoption of measures that permit non-resident carriers to operate transport services within another Member State.

At the beginning of the sixties, the Commission outlined the framework for the alignment of legal provisions and a comprehensive strategy for implementing legislation. The set objectives primarily aimed at eliminating physical and administrative barriers. Establishing a system of common rules and dismantling the protectionist systems of the Member States proved to be an extremely difficult task. State involvement had traditionally been a feature of the transport sector in all the Member States and, for socio-political or other reasons, most countries insisted on maintaining their role in this sector. Consequently, progress towards even the basic aims of common policy envisaged by the Treaty was extremely slow due to the lack of political will demonstrated by the Council.

The breakthrough came in 1985 when the European Court of Justice ruled in favour of the European Parliament, which had brought a case against the Council for failure to act. The Court found against the Council for breaching the Treaty by having failed to adopt the necessary Community legislation in the transport sector.

The Court ruling and the concept of a single market enshrined in the Single European Act finally provided the long-needed impetus for the harmonisation of regulations in the transport sector. The liberalisation of transport and the free movement and competition of services for all forms of transport became one of the fundamental aims of the Single Market Programme. Although these objectives had not been met by 1 January 1993, the deadline for the implementation of the Single Market Programme, the liberalisation of most modes of transport were finally successfully completed by 1998, the 40th anniversary of the EC (EEC). Today, national carriers are free to set up and operate transport services within any other Member State.[1] Accordingly, any airline of a Member State now has the right to operate flights between any two destinations within another Member State.

For intra-Community transport operations, the Member States cannot impose any rates or conditions involving any element of support or protection favouring one or more particular undertakings, unless authorised by the Commission.

In the framework of the Common Transport Policy, the Community institutions function in compliance with the general institutional and decision-making rules. The Commission as the initiating, advisory body prepares the sectoral provisions and decisions and monitors and manages the resources allocated to transport policy from the Community budget. The Council, as the decision-making body, has a key role in framing transport policy. It generally adopts decisions concerning transport policy by a qualified majority. In the past, the Parliament only had an advisory function; later on, it could influence the Council's decisions under the cooperation procedure. Since the Treaty of Amsterdam, however, in accordance with the co-decision procedure, the Parliament functions as the Council's co-legislator and enjoys equal rank in matters pertaining to transport policy. When the application of Community measures seriously affect the standard of living and level of employment in certain regions, and the operation of transport facilities, such acts are adopted by the Council acting by unanimity in the consultation procedure.

---

[1] It should be noted that restrictions remained in place in certain sectors, for example relating to the use of infrastructure which is particularly of key importance in the railway sector.

12.2. New objectives of the Common Transport Policy

A significant stride forward in the Common Transport Policy was made by the Treaty of Maastricht, which introduced the programme of *trans-European networks* (see the next sub-chapter) as an essential element of the single market in the areas of transport, telecommunications and energy supply. Pursuant to the Maastricht Treaty, fundamental changes have been implemented in the Common Transport Policy. Emphasis has been gradually shifting from legal harmonisation to the development of infrastructure. Environmental protection has also become a major objective, which has made transport policy a more complex field.

In 1992, the Commission published a White Paper, in which it undertook to promote the observation of global aspects, efficiency, safety, social legislation and the protection of the environment in transport policy. Under the new, development-oriented policy, particular emphasis was laid on guaranteeing excellent economic performance, maintaining the rise in the standard of living and paying attention to the social (employment) aspects of transport and environmental protection.

Consequently, by the nineties, the objectives of transport development had undergone major changes. In reference to the new environment- and efficiency-oriented approach, the aim was to shift the focus of long-distance transport and haulage from road to rail and the focus of local transport from private vehicles to public transportation. The above measures endeavoured to reduce air pollution and increase the efficiency and speed of transport networks, above all in large cities.

In connection with the new objectives, the Commission published a transport action programme for the period of 1995–2000, which dealt with three main areas:

– improving quality, based on the introduction of integrated systems using new technologies, which would also contribute to environmental protection and safety;
– improving the operation of the single market by improving the efficiency of transport services, encouraging competition between the various modes of transport and offering more user-friendly services, while safeguarding social standards;
– improving transport links with non-Member States.

Besides infrastructural developments, the action programme (in line with the second objective of improving the operation of the single market) continued to promote the harmonisation of national legislation, which in the liberalised market primarily meant the introduction of new provisions (such as the safeguarding of social standards) into the existing legislative framework. Particular emphasis was laid on the more effective enforcement of competition rules (e.g. monitoring state aids in air transport).

The Commission's 2000–2004 action programme, based on the 1995–2000 action programme, with the strategic objective of 'sustainable mobility', defined the same three areas of action to give substance to a transport policy promoting safe, efficient, competitive, social and environmentally-friendly transportation. The Sustainable Mobility Action Programme aimed to set up integrated transport systems (e.g. a global navigation satellite system and a unified system of air traffic management), to reduce the distortions of competition (e.g. by fair pricing), to give more attention to the social aspects of transport (including working time and working conditions), to improve the safety of transportation (especially by air, sea and road), to reduce air-pollution mainly caused by road traffic (in the spirit of the Kyoto Protocol) and to develop transport links with third countries (principally with Central and Eastern European countries, Switzerland, the United States and the Far East).

In the White Paper „European transport policy for 2010", adopted in 2001, the European Commission proposed about 60 measures for adoption by 2010. The main objective – in line with the sustainable development strategy announced at the Gothenburg Summit of June 2001 – was to establish a more efficient balance of transport in Europe and reduce the proportion of road transport. The burning necessity of such a shift was indicated by the ever-increasing levels of road transport, which in 2000 represented 79% of passenger and 44% of freight traffic. The White Paper proposed to shift the balance between transport modes by revitalising the railways (the proportion of which fell from 20% to 8% in 30 years), promoting maritime and inland waterway transport, linking up the different modes of transport, and keeping a check on the growth of aviation.

For road transport, a key priority was road safety, due to the high number of fatalities. A road safety action programme was adopted for the period 2003–2010.

For rail transport, the task outlined by the Commission was to create the conditions of more efficient, more competitive, more attractive and safer rail transport. The Commission put forward major legislative packages both in 2001 and 2002, which were adopted by the Council and Parliament, and were aimed at creating a more integrated European railway network, particularly for railway freight transport. The third railway package, initiated by the Commission in 2004 and adopted in 2007, places more focus on passenger services. The key elements of the legislative package are the opening-up of the international passenger transport market by 2010, the rules on passengers' rights on international journeys and the quality of services in freight transport.

For maritime and inland waterway transport, the White Paper's priority was to develop infrastructure, simplify the regulatory framework and thereby make the sector more attractive.

For aviation, the priorities for controlling growth included ensuring the efficiency of air traffic control, improving air safety and security, and promoting environmental considerations.

12.3. The trans-European networks programme

By the early nineties, most Member States had established highly advanced transport and other infrastructure networks. This achievement was greatly facilitated by the European integration process.[2] Nonetheless, no adequate link of infrastructures between the individual Member States was set up with regard to the single market. The national networks did not form an integrated system. Therefore, the Maastricht Treaty gave the Community the task of helping to establish and develop trans-European networks (TENs) linking the transport, telecommunications and energy infrastructures of the Member States. Pursuant to the Treaty, the European Union supports the design, establishment and development of TENs, which the Maastricht Treaty defines as a separate title of the EC Treaty (EC Treaty Part III, Title XV, ex-Title XII).

The purpose of these networks lies in the objective of interconnecting existing national and regional networks, building missing links, eliminating bottlenecks and linking peripheral regions with the central regions of the Community. The creation of an inter-operable

---

[2] The development of transport and the European integration process have been closely interlinked from the start. They have mutually reinforced each other: while the integration process facilitates the development of transport infrastructure, the implementation of the latter accelerates European integration. In the less-favoured areas and poorer Member States, infrastructural development has been stimulated by Community funds from very early on.

Community transport network is essential to create new jobs as it allows the free movement of labour, which is a fundamental requirement for boosting employment. The international interests of the Union and the ongoing enlargement process highlight the importance of linking TENs to the networks of Eastern Europe and the Mediterranean countries, thereby creating networks covering the whole continent, and providing a further impetus for the European integration process. On the whole, the trans-European networks are expected to encourage economic competitiveness and growth, increase employment, improve transport safety, reduce air pollution, introduce stricter environmental standards and consolidate inter-regional cooperation and cohesion.

Guidelines and other measures related to trans-European networks are adopted jointly by the Council and Parliament through the co-decision procedure.

With regard to transport generally, the primary objectives of the programme are to link national road systems, to establish a trans-European high-speed railway network and to align national provisions concerning air transport and air traffic management systems. The European Commission has laid down the development strategy outlined in detailed maps and comprehensive network plans. According to the plan, the Community programme will have been implemented by 2010 as the result of an EUR 400 billion investment scheme, which is essentially financed by the Member States and supported by the EU. The Commission's proposal foresees the building, development and reconstruction of a rail network of 70,000 kilometres (including 22,000 kilometres of high-speed links), a 15,000 kilometre-long road system (mainly in peripheral regions) and over 250 airports. The bulk of the TEN budget is allocated to railway development (around 60%). A significant amount (some 25% of the budget) is assigned to the expansion of road networks, while investment in air- and water-borne transport consumes a smaller proportion of the resources.

In December 1994, the Essen European Council adopted a list of 14 priority projects in the field of trans-European transport networks, with a total budget of EUR 110 billion (mainly financed by the Member States), most of which have been implemented. With a view to the forthcoming enlargements, as many as 30 priority projects were named in 2003, the implementation of which had to commence before 2010 and end before 2020. The estimated total cost of these projects is EUR 225 billion. The new priorities were set having regard to the impact of enlargement and sustainable mobility. Two thirds of these priority projects are aimed at developing railway transport (developing railway axes and high-speed railway lines).

The Treaty of Maastricht provides for a Community contribution to the creation of trans-European networks. The Treaty states that the Community may support the public and private investments of the Member States (who foot most of the bill) through feasibility and preparatory studies, and loans for project implementation (primarily with EIB funding). The Maastricht Treaty also set up the Cohesion Fund to support transport infrastructure (especially TENs projects) and environmental investments in the Union's then four least developed countries, Greece, Ireland, Portugal and Spain. In the period of 1993–1999, approximately half of the EUR 15 billion budget of the Cohesion Fund was appropriated to the transport sector. The Cohesion Fund's budget for 2000–2006 for the four countries rose to EUR 18 billion, about half of which was earmarked for financing transport projects. In addition, according to the Copenhagen financial package, the ten Member States that joined on 1 May 2004 were entitled to a further EUR 7.59 billion between 2004 and 2006, with about half the money (approximately EUR 3.8 billion) going to transport infrastructure.[3]

The total cost of priority projects for the 2007–2013 financial period is estimated at EUR 160 billion, with the EU picking up a large chunk of the tab. In these seven years, EUR 8 million will go to developing trans-European networks (mostly for project preparation and less for implementation), up from just over 4 billion in the previous 7-year financial perspective. Cohesion funding has also been reinforced to meet the new demands of an enlarged Union: EUR 35 billion is earmarked in the Cohesion Fund for transport projects, with a strong emphasis on TEN priority projects. In addition, the eligible regions can decide to spend subsidies from the European Regional Development Fund (ERDF)[4] on developing their transport infrastructure (for example between 2000 and 2006, EUR 34 billion went into transport projects, with a substantial proportion of that sum earmarked for trans-European priority projects.) The Member States will also continue to have the option of applying for preferential loans from the European Investment Bank as the EIB's objectives include supporting TEN development (between 2000 and 2006, a total of 38 billion in loans was granted for such purposes).

---

[3] For more on the Cohesion Fund, see the relevant parts of Chapter 13.
[4] For more on the ERDF see Chapter 13.

CHAPTER 13
REGIONAL POLICY –
ECONOMIC AND SOCIAL COHESION IN THE EU

13.1. The evolution and development of the policy of economic and social cohesion

Regional policy and regional support were not included in the Treaty of Rome as a Community objective; the Treaty only stipulated the need to guarantee the harmonious economic development of Member States. This was understandable at the time, since the European Economic Community was rather homogeneous from the point of view of the level of economic development, except for Southern Italian regions. In the sixties, Community support to less developed regions was only provided through the preferential loans of the European Investment Bank and through the Common Agricultural Policy.

In the early seventies, the concept of the monetary union set down in the Werner Plan, the first enlargement, and the consequences of the economic crisis, drew increasing attention to the fact that Community support to backward regions was necessary for the smooth functioning of the common market. As a result, the European Regional Development Fund (ERDF) was set up in 1975, with the aim of reducing economic and social disparities between European regions and promoting restructuring through structural measures. The Fund was established not only to assist the general aim of diminishing differences in the level of development but also to complement the activities of the existing European Social Fund (ESF) and the Guidance Section of the European Agricultural Guarantee and Guidance Fund (EAGGF). These three Funds, and the Financial Instrument for Fisheries Guidance (FIFG), which was created in 1993, were collectively called the Structural Funds.[1]

Enlargement to Mediterranean countries (Greece in 1981 and Portugal and Spain in 1986) entailed major changes in the weight of regional policy and in its place among other Community policies. The accession of the three Southern countries significantly

---

[1] The Structural Funds in this structure were in operation until the end of 2006. The number, structure and functioning of Structural Funds changed from 2007. To learn more about these changes, see 13.4.

increased the economic disparities between the Member States. The accession of these Mediterranean countries increased the Communities' population by 22%, while its GDP only grew by 10%. The European Communities became a rather heterogeneous area, where the GDP of the 10 most developed regions was about three times higher than that of the 10 least developed ones.

When joining the EC, these less developed Southern countries emphasised that they expected Community compensation to assist them to catch up with the rest of Europe. The limited resources of the European Regional Development Fund and its support mechanisms, which were inadequate for comprehensive activities, left little room for manoeuvre in regional development, leading to the launch of a reform of the system of regional aid in 1985. The Single European Act, adopted in 1986, put Community regional development on new foundations. It declared economic and social cohesion as a Community objective, adding this new element to the EEC Treaty (currently Part Three Title XVII of the EC Treaty). In practical terms, this meant that regional support policy was officially recognised as a Community policy.

The provision of regional and structural transfers is also justified by certain impacts of integration. Some Community policies and objectives (such as the single market or the monetary union) themselves can have effects that induce regional disparities. Regions where such disparities occur can justifiably demand compensation. A higher level of integration is more difficult to achieve for less developed countries or backward regions, which are in return entitled to structural aid for their preparation. While the principle of cohesion is manifest in national budgets, which re-channel funds from the richer citizens/ regions to the poorer ones, the same principle of cohesion is implemented in the EU with the help of structural measures (Structural and Cohesion Funds) financed from the common budget.

Structural and cohesion funding mainly focuses on developing infrastructure, because that can create equal conditions in Member States. Levelling differences in infrastructural conditions contributes to the closer cohesion and homogeneity of integration, which is ultimately in the interests of all Member States: the higher the unity, the more they can benefit from integration.

The reform of regional and structural policies in the mid-eighties paved the way for coordinating the activities of the different Funds. The emphasis shifted from financing individual projects to more complex programme-oriented development and, through the overhauling of the Structural Funds, a comprehensive set of objectives was defined for the Funds.

The use of Structural Funds is based on principles laid down for each financial planning period[2], which traditionally include the following[3]:

a) the principle of concentration: This means that the Member States' overall development objectives are set out in national Community Support Frameworks, in which the objectives are matched with appropriate Funds. Under this principle, the Council, with Parliament's assent, adopts a Regulation setting out the objectives that Structural Funds may be used for in a given programming period.

b) the principle of partnership: The Structural Funds contribute to national programmes. Programmes are proposed by the Member States, but they are implemented in cooperation by the national, regional and local authorities. Beneficiaries of regional funding are usually not the Member States' governments but regions or local authorities, which have the ability and the institutional capacity to implement and manage projects.

c) the principle of additionality: Community assistance complements the contributions of the Member States rather than replacing them. National co-financing is a precondition for EU support.

d) the principle of programming and planning: The Member States draw up comprehensive development plans on the basis of priority objectives. These documents are submitted to the Commission, which decides on eligibility for support. Until 2006, the Community Support Frameworks and single programming documents were used to be adopted which laid, laying down the tasks, sources of financing and the modes of implementation used to be adopted for a period usually corresponding to the multi-annual financial plans. From 2007, Member States elaborate their National Strategic Reference Framework for a given financial perspective (multi-annual budgetary framework – currently 2007–2013) on the basis of Community Strategic Guidelines. These Frameworks serve in the Member States as the basis for development strategies – so-called Operational Programmes – which include the detailed priorities. Both National Strategic Reference Frameworks and Operational Programmes require the Commission's approval. The Member State usually runs a few Operational Programmes, each to achieve a certain objective of the Funds.

---

[2] See 7.3.2.

[3] For the 2007–2013 period, the additional principles are proportionality, gender equality, sustainable development and shared management by Member States and the Commission.

Structural Funds are distributed on the basis of the Nomenclature of Statistical Territorial Units called NUTS[4], which is a system introduced and used by Eurostat to classify regions into 5 categories according to their size. In EU regional policy NUTS II denotes the most important level, corresponding to regions that serve as a basis for disbursing the bulk of Structural Funds. NUTS II does not necessarily cover a historical region; it is often only used for planning and statistical purposes and covers a territory typically with a population of 1.5 to 2 million (in the case of smaller states, the whole country forms a NUTS II region). The NUTS I level covers larger geographical units (large regions of big countries or even a whole country of medium-size) while NUTS III, IV and V roughly correspond to counties, micro-regions and towns, respectively.

With the Treaty of Maastricht in 1993, a new source was added to the support policy based on the Structural Funds; this was the Cohesion Fund, which was set up by the Treaty separately from the Structural Funds. The aim of the Cohesion Fund is to help the less developed Member States (Greece, Ireland, Portugal and Spain in 1993) – defined as states with a GNP (calculated at purchasing power parity) below 90% of the Community average – to catch up with the economic and monetary union, in other words to relieve the budget of countries trying to fulfil the convergence criteria[5] of some of the financial burden of investment. Hence, unlike with structural funding, the beneficiaries of the Cohesion Fund are not regions, but countries. The Cohesion Fund provides financial support for investments in infrastructure, with a roughly 50–50% division between large-scale environmental projects and transport projects, particularly the development of trans-European networks (TENs).[6]

The growing importance of the policy of economic and social cohesion is indicated by the sharp increase of its share in Community expenditure since the mid-eighties. While regional policy spending accounted for about 5% of the common budget in the seventies, it rose to 10% in the eighties and 30% in the nineties. This increasing trend was partly attributable to the Delors II package[7], in which Member States agreed that annual Community spending on regional development would be 0.46% of their total GDP.

---

[4] NUTS is a French acronym and stands for Nomenclature des Unités Territoriales Statistiques.
[5] See 8.5.
[6] For details, see 12.3.
[7] For details, see 7.3.3.

By the nineties, economic and social cohesion had undoubtedly become one of the greatest achievements of the Union. It may not have led to a spectacular catching-up of backward and underdeveloped regions, but analysis confirmed that reinforced and extended support prevented the widening of gaps between regions, helped poorer regions in more prosperous countries to make up some of their backlog, and yielded significant progress in less developed Member States. In the three poorest Member States (Greece, Portugal and Spain), per capita GDP grew from 68% of the EU average in 1988 to 79% in 1999. The fourth so-called cohesion country, Ireland, pulled off the biggest success story, by raising its per capita GDP from 68% of the Community average in 1988 to 108% a decade later. After the reinforcement of Structural Funds by the Delors II package, per capita GDP figures of key beneficiary regions started catching up with the EU average. In these regions, per capita GDP growth grew by up to 3% in real terms between 1994 and 2001, while in the rest of the Union the same figure was only 2%.

Table 13.1. Per capita GDP of Member States expressed as a percentage of the Community average in 1988 and 1998
(In purchasing power standard)

Member States	Per capita GDP in % of EU average in 1988	Per capita GDP in % of EU average in 1998
Austria	102.2	111.7
Belgium	103.2	111.3
Denmark	105.3	118.9
Finland	101.6	101.6
France	108.4	98.6
Germany (western Länder)	114.8	116.3
Germany (whole)	–	107.7
Greece	58.1	66.0
Ireland	65.9	108.1
Italy	100.2	101.1
Luxembourg	139.1	175.8
Netherlands	97.7	113.2
Portugal	58.9	75.3
Spain	74.0	81.1
Sweden	109.7	102.4
United Kingdom	98.7	102.2
EU-15	100.0	100.0

Source: European Commission

The programmes implemented by the European Union contributed not only to regional development, but also to the emergence or revival of cross-border regions, enhancing cooperation between neighbouring countries and their border regions and bringing nationals of different countries closer to each other. Nonetheless, the greatest achievement of regional policy is that it has proved that the European Union can function like a federation, redistributing income to regions in need, which reinforces solidarity between Member States and their regions and strengthens the cohesion of European integration.

Regional policy is a classic Community policy, where Community action complements regional support by Member States. However, regional policy stands out from other Community policies, due to its weight in the common budget and its impact on the internal development of Member States.

Setting the budgetary framework for and the operating system of structural and cohesion policy is the task of the Council, although the Parliament also has a say; through the assent procedure, Parliament gives its approval to the Council's decisions on the tasks, priority objectives and the organisation of the Structural and Cohesion Funds, and, through its budgetary powers, it can influence annual spending by the Funds. Through the co-decision procedure, the Council and Parliament together adopt the regulations setting out the implementing measures of the European Regional Development Fund and the European Social Fund.

At present, decisions on the tasks, priority objectives and budgetary framework of the Structural and Cohesion Funds are taken in the Council by unanimity. According to the Treaty of Nice, the Council will be able to take these decisions by qualified majority voting following the budgetary period starting in 2007, i.e. from the period starting in 2013.

The Commission also plays a key role in structural and cohesion policy. In addition to its right of initiative, the Commission is responsible for disbursing aid (according to the framework figures set by the Council), approving specific national programmes (the National Strategic Reference Frameworks and Operational Programmes), and monitoring the implementation of programmes and the use of funds. In addition, every three years the Commission prepares a report on progress in the area of economic and social cohesion.

The results of the policy of economic and social cohesion in the nineties increased the benefits of membership for countries and regions on the periphery of the EU. Community support available to poorer regions and Member States has also been a great attraction for neighbouring countries in Central, Eastern and Southern Europe, who had already had their eyes fixed on the EU. The accession of these countries has meant an enormous challenge for the EU's structural and cohesion policy because taking in countries whose level of development was well below the EU average, demanded a significant increase of resources allocated to the Structural and Cohesion Funds, which has jeopardised the interests of the current main beneficiaries of the Funds. The provisions of Agenda 2000 (the reform package adopted by the Berlin European Council in March 1999) on the Structural and Cohesion Funds are aimed at reconciling enlargement with the sustainability of regional policy by restructuring the system for financing the Funds from 2000 onwards.[8] Agenda 2000, however, only achieved a partial and transitional success in regulating the inclusion of acceding countries in structural and cohesion funding. Hence economic and social cohesion instruments were only fully extended in 2007 to the ten Member States that joined in 2004 through the 2007–2013 financial perspectives. Bulgaria and Romania – which joined in 2007 – benefit from structural and cohesion policy from day one of their membership, but will only enjoy equal treatment from 2010.

13.2. The operation of the Structural and Cohesion Funds before 1999

During the reform of the Structural Funds (called for by the Delors I package) in 1988, the Council set the five Objectives that, along with Objective 6 adopted at the accession of Nordic countries in 1995, formed the set of objectives for the use of Structural Funds, until Agenda 2000 entered into force in 2000:

Objective 1: Helping regions whose development was lagging behind to catch up. Objective 1 areas included NUTS 2 regions whose per capita GDP did not exceed 75% of the Community average. This included, for example, all regions of Greece, Portugal and Ireland, most of Spain, Southern Italian areas (Mezzogiorno), French overseas 'départements' and Corsica, Northern Ireland, some parts of Scotland, Flevoland in the Netherlands and Hainault in Belgium, Burgenland in Austria, and Eastern *Länder* of Germany. Until 1999, this Objective absorbed about 70–73% of the Funds.
Objective 2: Supporting economic and social conversion in regions worst hit by the decline in industrial production. This included traditional (mostly western European) heavy industrial areas where outdated industries needed restructuring. Until 1999, this Objective received about 7–9% of total funding.

---

[8] For more on Agenda 2000, see 1.13.3., 1.13.5. and 7.3.4.

Objective 3: Supporting programmes aimed at helping the young and long-term unemployed. Until 1999, this Objective received about 5–6% of the funding available.

Objective 4: Supporting measures for re-training and promoting the adjustment of the workforce to changes, in order to avoid unemployment (about 5–6% of the Funds).

Objective 5: (a) Supporting the modernisation and structural adjustment of certain agricultural and fisheries sectors (about 4% of the Funds).

(b) Supporting the development of typically agricultural regions with high agricultural employment (about 4–5% of the Funds).

Objective 6: Supporting the adjustment of thinly populated regions. This Objective - which represented about 0.5–1% of Structural Fund spending - served the development of remote, scarcely populated areas (fewer than 8 people per square km) in Northern Finland and Sweden.

As individual Objectives were rather complex and often overlapped, the comprehensive set of Objectives of European structural policy was implemented through the coordinated activities of four Structural Funds.

The *European Regional Development Fund (ERDF)* primarily financed Objectives 1, 2, 5b and 6 until 1999. The *European Social Fund (ESF)* focused on Objectives 3 and 4. The *Guidance Section of the European Agriculture Guidance and Guarantee Fund (EAGGF)*[9] and the *Financial Instrument for Fisheries Guidance (FIFG)* mainly promoted the development and adjustment of agricultural and fisheries structures, primarily serving Objective 5a, but also contributing to developing rural areas under Objectives 1 and 5b.

A certain part (until 1999 about 9–10%) of the funding for the Structural Funds was spent by the Commission within its own competence through the *Community Initiatives,* which seek common solutions to specific problems not covered by the six Objectives. In the 1993–99 period, there were over a dozen programmes running within the framework of Community Initiatives; these financed activities that did not fit into any of the six Objectives, involved more than one region (cross-border, transnational and inter-regional cooperation) or did not feature in the national programmes.

---

[9] The Guidance Section of EAGGF only disposed of a fraction (about 5%) of the Guarantee Section's budget.

Table 13.2. Structural Funds allocation by Objective and by Member State between 1994–1999 (million ECU)

Member States	Objectives								Total	Community Initiatives
	1.	2.	3.	4.	5.a	5.a Fisheries	5.b	6.		
Austria	162	99	329	60	377	2	403	–	1 432	144
Belgium	730	341	396	69	170	25	77	–	1 808	288
Denmark	–	119	263	38	127	140	54	–	741	102
Finland	–	179	254	83	324	23	190	450	1 503	151
France	2 190	3 769	2 562	641	1 746	190	2 236	–	13 334	1 605
Germany	13 640	1 566	1 681	260	1 070	75	1 227	–	19 519	2 211
Greece	13 980	–	–	–	–	–	–	–	13 980	1 154
Ireland	5 620	–	–	–	–	–	–	–	5 620	484
Italy	14 860	1 462	1 316	399	680	134	901	–	19 752	1 897
Luxembourg	–	15	21	1	39	1	6	–	83	19
Netherlands	150	650	923	156	118	47	150	–	2 194	422
Portugal	13 980	–	–	–	–	–	–	–	13 980	1 061
Spain	26 300	2 415	1 474	369	326	120	664	–	31 668	2 781
Sweden	–	157	342	170	88	39	135	247	1 178	126
United Kingdom	2 360	4 580	3 377	–	186	89	817	–	11 409	1 573
EUR 15	93 972	15 352	12 938	2 246	5 251	885	6 860	697	138 201	14 018

Source: European Commission

For the period from 1993 to 1999, the annual budget of the Cohesion Fund gradually increased to an aggregate of ECU 15 billion at 1992 prices (or EUR 16.75 billion at 1999 prices). The annual sums of Cohesion funding that the four eligible countries had at their disposal evolved as follows: ECU 1.5 billion in 1993, 2 billion in 1995, 2.5 billion in 1997 and 2.6 billion in 1999. The four cohesion countries shared these funds as follows: Spain 55.2%, Greece 17.9%, Portugal 17.9% and Ireland 8.9%.

13.3. The Structural and Cohesion Funds between 2000 and 2006

Further enlargement of the EU to the East and the South involved countries whose level of development was well below the Community average. This had several implications for the future of the policy of economic and social cohesion, which the EU had to take into consideration when setting the 2000–2006 financial perspective in Agenda 2000. With the eligibility criteria in place (Structural Funds 'Objective 1': per capita GDP lower than 75% of the Community average; Cohesion Fund: per capita GNP lower than 90% of the Community average), more or less all regions of Central and Eastern European candidate countries would have been eligible for strtuctural assistance following their accession. This had two important implications: on the one hand, all new Member States wanted to enjoy the full benefits of Community funding; on the other hand, as the Community's average level of development fell, former beneficiary regions would no longer be entitled to assistance. This two-fold problem could have been best solved by a drastic increase in the EU's structural and cohesion expenditure, but this was practically unthinkable in the light of the Community's internal financial situation. The issue was further exacerbated by the fact that it came on the agenda at a time when budgetary discipline was a universal requirement due to the introduction of the monetary union, and when net payers were campaigning for the reduction of their contributions to the common budget.

The European Union had to find a solution to this rather complex problem before the 2000–2006 budgetary planning period, when Eastward enlargement would already be imminent. The Commission tried to find an answer to the issue in the draft version of Agenda 2000, published on 16 July 1997, through a number of proposed changes to economic and social cohesion policy, in an attempt to make the amended policy acceptable for both old and new Member States without jeopardising the financial soundness of the common budget. One of the cornerstones of Agenda 2000, adopted by the Heads of State or Government of the EU-15 at the Berlin Summit on 24–25 March 1999, was the decision on the new structural and cohesion policy regulatory and financial framework for the period 2000–2006.

Table 13.3. Annual average of total structural and cohesion assistance by Member State in 1989–1993 and 1994–1999

Member States	EU assistance (annual average)	
	total (million ECU)	in % of GDP
1989–1993		
Belgium	173	0.11
Denmark	86	0.08
France	1 387	0.14
Germany	1 680	0.13
Greece	1 834	2.65
Ireland	980	2.66
Italy	2 374	0.27
Luxembourg	15	0.17
Netherlands	163	0.07
Portugal	1 892	3.07
Spain	3 017	0.75
United Kingdom	1 066	0.13
EU-12	14 666	0.29
1994–1999		
Belgium	349	0.18
Denmark	140	0.11
France	2 491	0.22
Germany	3 622	0.21
Greece	2 956	3.67
Ireland	1 234	2.82
Italy	3 608	0.42
Luxembourg	17	0.15
Netherlands	436	0.15
Portugal	2 940	3.98
Spain	7 066	1.74
United Kingdom	2 164	0.25
EU-12	27 024	0.45
Austria	316	0.19
Finland	331	0.40
Sweden	261	0.37
EU-15	27 932	0.41

Source: European Commission

The Berlin European Council decided to maintain structural and cohesion allocations to the old 15 Member States at the level of previous years but set lower financing terms for the new Member States. According to the Berlin decision, for the period 2000–2006, the EU allocated a total of EUR 260 billion (at 1999 prices) for structural measures; 195 billion for the Structural Funds and 18 billion for the Cohesion Fund in old Member States. An additional 47 billion was set aside for structural measures in the new Member States (40 billion for new Member States between 2002 and 2006[10], and over 7 billion for pre-accession aid to candidate countries.)

It should also be noted that, at the time of the adoption of Agenda 2000, Member States could not calculate exactly the structural and cohesion-related costs of enlargement, since they did not know when and which applicants would become members. Just as for the 'enlargement' item, the assumption was that enlargements could take place from 2002 and that six new countries would become members by 2006. This hypothesis was later over-ridden by the decisions of the Nice, Laeken and Copenhagen European Councils[11]. Therefore, the structural and cohesion expenditure foreseen in the Berlin financial perspectives had to be adjusted according to the accession negotiations. As the most likely date of the first round of enlargement had changed to 2004, and the group of potential first wave countries had grown to 10, the use of the sums outlined in the Berlin framework had to be modified accordingly.

Increasing the efficiency of the use and disbursement of Structural and Cohesion Funds as part of the reform of structural measures was also one of the key objectives of Agenda 2000. Member States agreed on the concentration of financial support, the strengthening of the forms, control, management and assessment of financing, as well as the de-centralisation of decision-making and the streamlining of administrative procedures.

In order to increase the efficiency and concentration of the Structural Funds and to face new challenges (particularly the alarming rate of unemployment), the number of priority Objectives was reduced from 6 to 3, according to the Commission's proposals:

Objective 1: helped development and restructuring in regions whose development was lagging behind. It incorporated former Objectives 1, 6 and, to a certain extent, 5a. Objective

---

[10] As enlargement only took place on 1 May 2004, and since – due to the economic conditions – the Member States were trying to cut spending, the final sum was only EUR 21.7 billion, well below even the EUR 30 billion originally foreseen for the period 2004–2006 in Agenda 2000.

[11] For more on these decisions, see 1.13.5.

1 represented 69.7% of the funding, and covered NUTS 2 regions whose per capita GDP did not exceed 75% of the Community average, as well as the thinly populated regions of Finland and Sweden and the outermost regions (French overseas departments, Canary Islands, Azores and Madeira).

Objective 2: supported economic and social conversion in areas facing structural difficulties, such as: industrial or service sectors subject to restructuring; loss of traditional agricultural activities in rural areas; problems in declining urban or fisheries-dependent areas. Objective 2 practically united and complemented former objectives 2 and 5b, laying special emphasis on sustained unemployment. A maximum of 11.5% of the Funds covering no more than 18% of the EU's population could be used for this objective, with the breakdown of 10% in industrial and service areas, 5% in rural areas, 2% in urban areas and 1% in areas dependent on the fishing industry.

Objective 3: provided funding for all EU measures concerning human resources (former Objective 3 and 4), such as the adjustment and modernisation of systems and structures of education, training and employment. Funding was available for all regions not covered by Objective 1. Depending on their population, all Member States received a certain proportion of financial support available within Objective 3, which ensured that even the most prosperous countries received support from structural funding, while carrying an important message that all European citizens should feel the Funds were their own. Objective 3 received 12.3% of total funding.

Tasks resulting from the three Objectives were carried out by the four Structural Funds, which remained unchanged by Agenda 2000, unlike the Community Initiatives. Agenda 2000 reduced Community Initiatives from 13 to the following four: INTERREG (transnational, cross-border and inter-regional cooperation), URBAN (economic and social regeneration of crisis-hit towns and cities), LEADER (rural development through local initiatives), and EQUAL (transnational cooperation to combat all forms of discrimination and inequality in access to the labour market). While previously, 9–10% of structural funding commitments was allocated to Community Initiatives, these four initiatives received just over 5% of total Structural Funds during the 2000–2006 period.

The EU had to solve another important issue related to the Structural Funds: how to manage the so-called *statistical effect* of enlargement on old Member States. While nearly 70% of the Funds was targeted on Objective 1 regions, the main beneficiaries of the Union's structural policy were areas whose per capita GDP was below 75% of the Community average. It was clear that due to the statistical effect of enlargement caused by a drop in the Community's average GDP (although in some cases, for reasons unconnected to this), certain regions would rise above the 75% threshold and lose entitlement to such funding. To avoid a brutal cut-off of assistance to these regions and the resulting financial and social repercussions, the Commission proposed gradually decreasing payments, with final *phasing out* by the end of 2005 or 2006. Such transitional assistance was introduced in 2000 to regions like Hainault in Belgium, Flevoland in the Netherlands and the Lisbon region in Portugal. In regions that lost eligibility in 1999, the level of transitional support was gradually cut from the year 2000 until 2005 or 2006. This process is referred to as *phasing-out*.

Following lengthy debates, Agenda 2000 finally left the Cohesion Fund unchanged for the period from 2000 to 2006. The Cohesion Fund was originally set up to help the four least prosperous Member States (whose per capita GNP was below 90% of the EU average) prepare for monetary union by co-financing investment projects in the fields of environment and transport infrastructure. Since Ireland, Portugal and Spain, three of the four cohesion states, joined the EMU in 1999, a number of Member States suggested that these countries should no longer be entitled to support from the Cohesion Fund.[12] However, under pressure from the governments of these countries, in the end the European Council decided that the significance of the main priorities of the Fund (improvements in the area of the environment and transport infrastructure) had not been reduced. Eventually, the budget of the Cohesion Fund for the seven years from 2000 to 2006 was even increased – primarily on Spanish demands – to EUR 18 billion (up from 15 billion for 1993–1999), but the allocation of assistance had to take into consideration the development achieved by these countries, as well as their macroeconomic environment. Therefore in 2003, the Commission carried out a mid-term review to check whether all these states were still eligible for support from the Cohesion Fund and as a result, Ireland lost its eligibility from 1 January 2004.[13]

---

[12] Two years later, Greece also joined the eurozone (on 1 January 2001).

[13] It should be noted here that Ireland's GNP had been above 90% of the Community average since the late nineties, but since calculations are always based on previous reference years, Ireland was allowed to keep its entitlement to Cohesion Fund support for a while even after 2000. Another factor was that an overnight cut-off of Community assistance would have had adverse effects both on the national budget and regional development in Ireland.

Table 13.4. Structural and Cohesion Funds preliminary allocation by the 15 'old' Member States for the period 2000–2006 (EUR million, at 1999 prices)

Member States	Objectives								
	Objective 1.	1. (transitional support)	Objective 2.	2. (transitional support)	Objective 3.	FIFG (outside Objective 1)	Community Initiatives	Cohesion Fund	Total
Austria	261	0	578	102	528	4	358	–	1 831
Belgium	0	625	368	65	737	34	209	–	2 038
Denmark	0	0	156	27	365	197	83	–	828
Finland	913	0	459	30	403	31	254	–	2 090
France	3 254	551	5 437	613	4 540	225	1 046	–	15 666
Germany	19 229	729	2 984	526	4 581	107	1 608	–	29 764
Greece	20 961	0	0	0	0	0	862	3 060	24 883
Ireland	1 315	1 773	0	0	0	0	166	720	3 974
Italy	21 935	187	2 145	377	3 744	96	1 172	–	29 656
Luxembourg	0	0	34	6	38	0	13	–	91
Netherlands	0	123	676	119	1 686	31	651	–	3 286
Portugal	16 124	2 905	0	0	0	0	671	3 060	22 760
Spain	37 744	352	2 553	98	2 140	200	1 958	11 160	56 205
Sweden	722	0	354	52	720	60	278	–	2 186
United Kingdom	5 085	1 166	3 989	706	4 568	121	961	–	16 596
EUR 15	127 543	8 411	19 733	2 721	24 050	1 106	10 290	18 000	211 854*

Source: European Commission
* This sum is less than the EUR 213 billion provided for in Agenda 2000, because it does not contain the financing of the network of Community initiatives and innovative actions.

Agenda 2000 also decided on the ceiling figures of Community co-financing of structural and cohesion measures. Accordingly, from 2000, Community assistance could not exceed 75% of total project costs within Objective 1 (80 to 85% for regions of states eligible for Cohesion Fund), and 50% in Objectives 2 and 3. For the Cohesion Fund, the ceiling of Community assistance was kept at 80–85% of public or other comparable co-financing.

In order to limit the amount of Community assistance a Member State could receive, and primarily with a view to the financeability of enlargement, Agenda 2000 introduced the 4% ceiling, which stipulated that each Member State could receive a maximum of 4% of its GDP in support from the Structural and Cohesion Funds.[14]

The financing sources set out in Agenda 2000 had to be finalised for the new Member States in the accession negotiations. During the talks, the acceding countries insisted that they should receive the same support as they would be entitled to under the current rules of the Structural and Cohesion Funds, thereby demanding equal treatment with Objective 1 regions (75% threshold) and cohesion countries (90% limit). The old Member States argued that Agenda 2000 did not provide sufficient financing, also referring to worsening economic conditions and the increase of prospective new Member States from six to ten. Due to the financial reality of Europe, in the end the candidates had to accept a gradual phasing-in of structural and cohesion funding in the period 2004–2006 and being treated equally only from 2007, the first year of the new financial perspectives.

Legally speaking, the 15 old and 10 new Member States became eligible for such Community funding on the same conditions from 2007. According to the Copenhagen financial package[15], the final deal of the accession negotiations adopted on 13 December 2002, in the years 2004 to 2006 the new Member States were only entitled to a much lower level of funding than the old ones. In fact, the funds available for the new Member States in these years remained well below the figures foreseen in Agenda 2000: EUR 21.7 billion instead of 30 billion.

---

[14] This could mean a problem mainly for new (Central and Eastern European) Member States, since their GDP was lower by far than that of the EU-15; therefore, they might more easily reach the level of funding that corresponds to the GDP-ceiling. It is quite paradoxical that, the less prosperous a country was, the more the 4% ceiling limited its opportunities to receive Community funding.

[15] For more on the outcome of the accession negotiations and the Copenhagen financial package, see Subchapter 1.13.5. and Table 1.4.

Table 13.5. Structural and cohesion funding allocated
for 2004–2006 to the ten Member States that joined in 2004
(EUR million, at 1999 prices)

Member States	Objective 1	Objective 2	Objective 3	Fisheries	INTERREG	EQUAL	Cohesion Fund	Total
Cyprus	0	25	20	3	4	2	48	101
Czech Republic	1 286	63	52	0	61	28	836	2328
Estonia	329	0	0	0	9	4	276	618
Hungary	1765	0	0	0	61	27	994	2847
Lithuania	792	0	0	0	20	11	544	1366
Latvia	554	0	0	0	14	7	461	1036
Malta	56	0	0	0	2	1	20	79
Poland	7321	0	0	0	196	119	3733	11369
Slovakia	921	33	40	0	37	20	510	1560
Slovenia	210	0	0	0	21	6	169	405
Total %	61.0	0.6	0.5	0.0	2.0	1.0	35.0	21708

Source: European Commission

During the negotiations with Bulgaria and Romania, the Union sought the same solution as it applied to the ten Member States that joined in 2004. According to the Accession Treaty concluded with these two countries on 25 April 2005, in the first three years of their membership between 2007 and 2009, the two countries are eligible for a fixed amount of support, which is considerably lower than what they would be entitled to under Community rules, and will only receive equal treatment in this field from 2010. Bulgaria will have at its disposal EUR 539, 759 and 1,002 million, while Romania will receive up to 1,399, 1,972 and 2,603 million in the years 2007–2009.

13.4. The Structural and Cohesion Funds between 2007 and 2013

The enlargement of the European Union on 1 May 2004 put the issue of economic and social cohesion in a different light. The disparities in development within the Union grew considerably, which was only further augmented by the accession of Bulgaria and Romania in 2007. On the one hand, this only further justified the existence of the policy of economic and social cohesion, but, on the other hand, it did make this policy rather difficult to finance as the resources needed to be increased significantly.

As a result of enlargement, the gaps between Member States and their regions widened. In 2006, the GDP per capita of the 27 Member States (in PPS) varied from 37% of the Community average in Bulgaria to 280% in Luxembourg. All of the Member States that joined in 2004 and 2007 – with the exception of Cyprus – were below 90% of the average of the Community of 27. Disparities between regions were even bigger: in terms of GDP per capita, in 2004 the poorest region (in North-Eastern Romania) stood at 24% of the EU-27 average while the wealthiest region (Inner London) stood at 303%.
In the EU of 27 members, roughly 10% of the population lives in the most dynamically developing regions accounting for 19% of the EU's GDP, while the 10% living in the poorest regions contributes only 1.5% of the Community GDP.
According to 2004 figures, in the twelve Member States that joined recently, 88% of the population lived in a region with under 75% of GDP per capita of the EU average, (the only exceptions were Prague, Bratislava, Budapest, Cyprus, Slovenia and Mazoviecke Voivodship in Poland), while the same ratio in the old Member States was only 8%. In the Union of 27, almost 25% of citizens (123 million people – 91 million in the twelve recently acceded Member States) lived in regions with below 75% of average per capita Community GDP.

Table 13.6. GDP per capita (in PPS) of EU Member States and candidate countries in 2000 and 2006 as a percentage of the EU average

	2000	2006
EU-27	–	100
EU-25	100	104
Austria	127	129
Belgium	116	123
Bulgaria	27	37
Cyprus	86	94
Czech Republic	65	79
Denmark	126	127
Estonia	43	67
Finland	114	117
France	115	113
Germany	113	113
Greece	72	89
Hungary	53	66
Ireland	126	144
Italy	111	104
Latvia	35	56
Lithuania	38	58
Luxembourg	217	280
Malta	77	77
Netherlands	121	131
Poland	46	53
Portugal	77	75
Romania	25	38
Slovakia	48	63
Slovenia	73	87
Spain	93	102
Sweden	119	121
United Kingdom	114	118
Croatia	41	50
Macedonia	–	27
Turkey	30	29

Source: Eurostat

When adopting the 2007–2013 Financial Perspectives, the Member States had to take into consideration not only the changing allocation levels but also the fact that, according to the Treaties of Accession, the ten Member States that joined in 2004 had to benefit fully from structural and cohesion funding starting from 2007, and Bulgaria and Romania had to enjoy full eligibility from 2010. These facts were also the starting point for the Commission when it drew up its proposal for the new financial perspectives[16] and as a part the heading on structural and cohesion measures, finally submitted (in five draft Regulations) to the Council and Parliament on 14 July 2004.

In this package of Regulations, the Commission proposed a revision of the composition and objectives of the Structural and Cohesion Funds, adjusting them to the new circumstances. In its proposal, the Commission earmarked EUR 344 billion for the seven-year period, with a significant shift towards the new Member States: while in 2006 only 22.5% of the funds were allocated to the new Member States, the Commission initiated increasing this ratio to 44.7% in 2007 and to 53.3% in 2013.

The debate on the seven-year financial perspective revolved partly around the issue of how much cohesion funding would be available and how these funds would be distributed. As a result of the dispute discussed in 7.3.5., under pressure from net contributors, the final deal – laid down in an Inter-Institutional Agreement, which the European Parliament also signed up to – reduced the sums proposed by the Commission by about 10% and set EUR 308 billion (35.6% of the total budget, 0.37% of GNI) as the ceiling for cohesion spending (Heading 1b in the new budgetary classification) over the seven years. The Commission's figures were cut back, but the part of the proposal on restructuring the Funds and revising the objectives were taken on board by the Member States and used for rewriting the eligibility conditions and implementing rules. As a result, in 2007, the four Structural Funds, the Cohesion Fund and the Community initiatives were replaced with a new system consisting of just two of the old Structural Funds – the European Regional Development Fund (ERDF) and the European Social Fund (ESF) – and the Cohesion Fund. The financing instruments related to the Common Agricultural Policy and the Common Fisheries Policy were separated, creating the European Agricultural Fund for Rural Development (EAFRD) to replace the EAGGF Guidance Section and the European

---

[16] For more details see 7.3.5.

Fisheries Fund (EFF) to replace the FIFG.[17] As the latter two Funds both serve economic and social cohesion – only in different budget headings under Heading 2 not 1b – the proportion of cohesion expenditure increased considerably compared to the 2000–2006 period. Including the EAFRD and EFF, between 2007 and 2013, 44% of the Community budget (0.46% of GNI) will serve cohesion, which corresponds to levels of the Delors II package. A major change from the previous period is that 51% of all funding will go to the Member States that joined in 2004 and 2007 (compared with 22.5% in 2006). For the Member States that acceded to the Union in 2004, this means that in the 2007–2013 period, they will have more funding available annually than they received in total during the three years from 2004 to 2006.

The comprehensive reform package defined the priorities of the Structural Funds and of the Cohesion Fund together. From 2007 to 2013, the Structural and Cohesion Funds have to serve three Objectives:

Objective 1: Convergence
Similar to Objective 1 of the 2000–2006 period, this new Convergence Objective supports the least developed Member States and regions through the ERDF, ESF and Cohesion Fund. First and foremost, this objective concerns those NUTS 2 regions with per capita GDP less than 75% of the EU-25 average (measured in purchasing power parities and calculated on the basis of the Community figures for the years 2000–2002). At the same time, temporary *phasing-out* support (gradually decreasing until 2013) is granted to regions where, due to the so-called *statistical effect* of enlargement, per capita GDP has risen over 75% of the Community average in the years 2000–2002. In addition, the Convergence Objective covers support from the Cohesion Fund for those Member States whose GNI is below 90% of the Community average in the three years from 2001 to 2003. The Convergence Objective totals EUR 251 billion, which accounts for 81.54% of all structural and cohesion spending. Within that amount, 70.51% (177.1 billion) goes to regions with GDP below 75% of the EU average, 4.99% (12.5 billion) to phasing-out regions, 23.22% (58.3 billion) to countries benefiting from the Cohesion Fund, and 1.29% (3.25 billion) to Spain, where the Cohesion Fund is phased out (because the statistical effect of enlargement pushed per capita GNI above the 90% threshold).

---

[17] For more on the EAFRD and the EFF, see 11.8. and 11.9., respectively.

Objective 2: Regional competitiveness and employment
This objective is designed to help regions falling outside Objective 1 'Convergence' to increase their competitiveness and employment, in line with the Lisbon strategy. Objective 2 is achieved through the ERDF and the ESF. 15.95% of cohesion policy funds (EUR 49.1 billion) are allocated to this objective, with 78.86% (38.7 billion) going to regions outside the Convergence Objective and with 21.14% (10.4 billion) to regions no longer being eligible for Objective 1 funding due to their natural development. These latter regions are commonly referred to as phasing-in regions, (where per capita GDP exceeded 75% of the EU-15 average) which are compensated through Objective 2.

Objective 3: Territorial cooperation
Based on experiences with the INTERREG Community Initiative, this Objective stimulates cross-border, trans-national and inter-regional cooperation, which it aims to achieve through joint local initiatives. Financial support is provided under the ERDF to NUTS 3 regions on internal and external frontiers, whether on land or sea. Objective 3 receives 2.52% (EUR 7.8 billion) of all cohesion funding.

Reducing national contributions for co-financing EU Funds was an important way of sugar-coating the 2007–2013 financial package for new Member States. The new ceilings for Community co-financing are as follows: for the Structural and Cohesion Funds, the maximum ratio of Community contribution to the public expenditure of a project is 85% for countries where per capita GDP was below 85% of the EU-25 average in 2001–2003 (Greece, Portugal and all new Member States); for Member States eligible for transitional cohesion funding on 1 January 2007 (Spain) the EU contribution can be up to 80%; while for the remaining Member States, the threshold remains at a maximum of 75% for regions under the Convergence Objective and 50% for regions under the Regional Competitiveness Objective.
Another welcome change for Member States that joined in 2004 and 2007 is that, from 2007, ERDF funding can also be used for housing projects, which could be of vital importance for the urban regeneration of prefabricated housing estates in these countries.
It is unfavourable for new Member States, however, that the national support ceiling was reduced in 2007. The original rule introduced in 2000 stipulated that the annual amount of support to a Member State from Community funds must not exceed 4% of its GDP.

Table 13.7. Preliminary allocations of structural and cohesion funding for the 2007–2013 period by Member State (EUR million, at 2004 prices)

	Convergence Objective			Regional Competitiveness and Employment Objective		Territorial Cooperation Objective	Total	Funding per capita over the 7 years	Order in terms of per capita funding
	Cohesion Fund	Convergence	„Statistical phasing out" regions	„Phasing in" regions	Regional Competitiveness and Employment				
Austria			159		914	228	1 301	157	23.
Belgium			579		1 268	173	2 019	192	21.
Bulgaria	2 015	3 873				159	6 047	783	13.
Cyprus	193			363		24	581	758	14.
Czech Republic	7 830	15 149			373	346	23 697	2 312	2.
Denmark					453	92	545	100	27.
Estonia	1 019	1 992				47	3 058	2 273	1.
Finland				491	935	107	1 532	292	17.
France		2 838			9 123	775	12 736	202	19.
Germany		10 553	3 770		8 370	756	23 450	284	18.
Greece	3 289	8 379	5 779	584		186	18 217	1 637	10.
Hungary	7 589	12 654		1 865		343	22 451	2 228	3.
Ireland				420	261	134	815	193	20.
Italy		18 867	388	879	4 761	752	25 647	437	16.
Latvia	1 363	2 647				80	4 090	1 782	9.
Lithuania	2 034	3 965				97	6 097	1 792	8.
Luxembourg					45	13	58	126	25.
Malta	252	495				14	761	1 883	5.
Netherlands					1 477	220	1 696	104	26.
Poland	19 562	39 486				650	59 698	1 565	11.
Portugal	2 722	15 240	254	407	436	88	19 147	1 811	7.
Romania	5 769	11 143				404	17 317	801	12.
Slovakia	3 433	6 230			399	202	10 264	1 905	4.
Slovenia	1 239	2 407				93	3 739	1 867	6.
Spain	3 250	18 727	1 434	4 495	3 133	497	31 536	721	15.
Sweden					1 446	236	1 682	186	21.
United Kingdom		2 436	158	883	5 349	642	9 468	157	24.
Not allocated						392	392	–	–
Total	61 558	177 083	12 521	10 385	38 742	7 750	308 041	625	–

Source: European Commission

The new ceiling is 3.79%, but only for countries with a GDP below 40% of the EU-25 average between 2001 and 2003. The higher the GDP, the lower the funding ceiling: for example for a country with GDP between 70 and 75% of the EU-25 average, it is only 3.24%.

CHAPTER 14
EMPLOYMENT AND SOCIAL POLICY

14.1. The development of social policy up to the nineties

Although the Treaty of Rome dealt extensively with social policy (twelve articles of the Treaty are related explicitly to social policy), no significant progress was made in this field at the Community level for a good decade, because the Member States wished to keep legislation related to social policy within their own jurisdiction. It should, however, be noted that the Member States had independently built up highly developed social welfare systems and it was mainly in this period that the institution of the welfare state was refined in Western Europe.

The Treaty dealt with broad areas of social policy, with its articles on employment, labour law, working conditions, the principle of equal treatment for men and women, vocational training, social security, collective bargaining between employers and employees and the prevention of accidents in the workplace. However, Community legislation proceeded extremely slowly.

In the seventies, Community-level social policy seemed to be gaining ground, when the Member States accepted the first social action programme in 1974. However, the action programme contained general principles that were difficult to translate into Community law, although some directives were issued. On the basis of these directives, measures relating to mass redundancies and certain measures relating to labour law issues arising during company mergers were harmonised. But, in spite of this partial success, social policy brought no further significant results until the eighties; this was because certain Member States, in line with their traditional economic philosophy, saw the Community's role in this field differently. There were constant disagreements between those who wished to liberalise and deregulate, and those who favoured the interventionist role of the state and the Community.

Simultaneously with the conception of the single market, the question arose as to whether the free flow of prcduction factors and liberalisation might have a negative effect on achievements in the social sector. In answer to this question, most Member States judged that the programme laid down in the Single European Act should be counter-balanced with social policy measures. In consequence, in December 1989 in Strasbourg, the Member States, with the exception of the United Kingdom, adopted the Community Charter of Fundamental Social Rights of Workers (the Social Charter), which provided for closer coordination in several areas in order to realise social policy aims. The main aim of the Social Charter was to lay down the basic principles on which the European labour market and the role played by work in society would be built. The Social Charter dealt with the following 12 areas: free movement of workers, employment and remuneration, improvement of living and working conditions, social protection, the freedom of association and collective bargaining, vocational training, equal treatment and pay for men and women, consultation, participation and information of workers on decisions, health and safety at work, as well as the protection of children and adolescents, elderly persons and disabled persons.

To achieve the aims of the Social Charter, the Commission drew up a new social action programme, with 47 concrete measures, 29 of which required the approval of the Council of Ministers. About two thirds of these measures were actually implemented in practice. An interesting point about the Social Charter is that, since the United Kingdom was not a signatory, the Charter did not clearly form part of the Community framework. The signatories however emphasised that they could make use of Community institutions to achieve the objectives of the Social Charter.

After adopting the Social Charter, the eleven signatory Member States wanted to make further progress in this direction and intended to incorporate a social chapter into the Treaty. But the UK maintained its earlier position and, not wishing to further strengthen the competence of the Community institutions in this area, did not support this idea. British opposition meant that the other eleven Member States were limited to merely annexing to the Maastricht Treaty a protocol on social policy, also known as the *Agreement on Social Policy*. The Agreement however authorised the EU Member States to adopt legally binding measures in the sphere of social policy, and in some areas (e.g. improving conditions in the workplace, equal treatment and pay for men and women, involving workers in and informing them about decisions, health and safety at work), even to make a decision with a qualified majority. In 1994, the first Community Directive was drawn up on the basis of the Agreement on Social Policy, and it dealt with European Works Councils.

In the first four decades of European integration, in addition to legislation, the main instrument of social policy was the provision of subsidies by the Community to the Member States. In the Treaty of Rome, the founding Member States had already considered it important to set up a Community fund for social tasks; so the European Social Fund (ESF) was the first of the structural funds to start operating in 1958. However, in the first decade of its operation, since the Fund did not have sufficient resources and its objectives were not expressed clearly, it did not achieve any significant results. The Fund was reformed in 1971 and the criteria for utilising its resources were coordinated. The beneficiaries could now be private companies and this made the operation of the ESF more realistic. In addition, the resources increased six-fold, so its operation became more visible and more successful. In this period, its main task was the management and reduction of unemployment among young people but, from the seventies on, regional issues played an increasing role In 1988, the Council gave a new basis to structural policy by enlarging the resources available and defining integrated objectives for the funds. In the period 1993–1999, the ESF concentrated on structural policy, supporting Objective 3 of the Structural Fund (programmes to curb unemployment among young people and long-term unemployment) and Objective 4 (re-training of employees, adapting to change).[1] In the 2000–2006 period, to a certain extent, the European Social Fund became more significant, because the fight against unemployment played an increasing part in economic and social cohesion. In this period, the task of the ESF was primarily focussed on the Structural Fund policy Objective 3 (adapting and modernising education, training and employment systems and policies) and on financing the Community Initiative EQUAL (equal opportunities in the labour market).[2] The ESF has been further reinforced in the period 2007–2013, playing a major role in both Objective 1 (convergence of backward regions) and Objective 2 (regional competitiveness and employment) mainly by financing projects aimed at improving employment (job creation and modernisation).[3] All in all, although the various budget reforms have continually enlarged the resources of the European Social Fund, the Fund has remained modest compared to the tasks required at Community level. On the other hand, it should be stressed that the Fund is only intended to complement the subsidy systems of the Member States.

14.2. Employment moves to the foreground –
The effect of the Treaty of Amsterdam

By the nineties, unemployment had taken on grave proportions in the countries of the EU and had stabilised at the highest level since World War II, at around an average of 10%. Thus, the issues of increasing employment, reducing unemployment and creating jobs became the main focus of social policy. In recognition of this, a new social action programme

---

[1] For more on the ESF Objectives, see 13.2.
[2] See also 13.3.
[3] See also 13.4.

was launched at the Commission's initiative between 1995–1997, which had as its target the improvement of the employment situation and the reduction of unemployment. But this, too, had little effect. It became clear that the threat of unemployment was the political question that most worried the citizens of the EU and that they expected more action in this area, not just from their national governments, but from the Union too. Recognising this, in the Treaty of Amsterdam (signed on 2 October 1997), the Member States aimed to give special attention to employment policy. As a result, the topic of employment was incorporated into the EC Treaty as a new Title, separate from the other social policy issues.

In the Treaty of Amsterdam, the Member States undertook to coordinate their national strategies in the field of employment, to transform their employment policies in line with broader economic policy objectives and to treat the promotion of employment as a common interest. The Treaty stipulates that it is the task of the European Council to draw conclusions from annual employment reports prepared by the Commission and adopted by the Council. Building on these conclusions and the Commission's proposals (in consultation with the European Parliament, the Economic and Social Committee, the Committee of the Regions and the Employment Committee[4], created by the Treaty of Amsterdam), the Council must adopt employment guidelines with a qualified majority. The Member States must take the guidelines into account in their national employment policies and submit an annual report on their implementation.

As a consequence of the pressing need to complete these tasks, in November 1997, for the first time in the history of the EU, the Heads of State or Government held a special employment summit in Luxembourg, where they confirmed the provisions of the Treaty of Amsterdam and decided to elaborate employment policy guidelines by 1998, in fact before the Treaty entered into force. The policy guidelines were then adopted by the European Council in December 1997.

The first employment policy guidelines in the EU's history, completed in 1998, were built on four pillars:

---

[4] Article 130 of the Treaty provides for the setting up of the Employment Committee. The tasks of this consultative committee are to observe the employment situation and the employment policies of the Community and the Member States, to coordinate the Member States' activities and to consult with employers and employees. The body has two delegates from each Member State and from the European Commission. The Employment Committee forms an opinion on a given issue at the request of the Council, the European Commission or on its own initiative.

- *Improving employability* (for instance this pillar dealt with finding young people a good job quickly and defined strategies related to this);
- *Developing entrepreneurship* (this pillar aimed to simplify the process of starting an enterprise and to make the tax systems enterprise-friendly);
- *Encouraging adaptability of businesses and their employees* (this pillar was directed towards improving the ability to adapt quickly to structural and organisational changes, and defined strategies related to this);
- *Strengthening the policies for equal opportunities* (this pillar aimed primarily at improving the employment prospects of various groups, particularly women, for example by proposing the introduction of flexible working hours).

These four pillars became the basis of the European Employment Strategy, the essence of which was to carry forward the process started in Luxembourg, to achieve the objectives of the guidelines. As a result, these four pillars remained in the employment guidelines in the following years.

As a consequence of the process started by the Treaty of Amsterdam and the 1998 employment guidelines having been judged successful, the Member States not only decided on the 1999 guidelines at the Vienna Summit in December 1998, but also agreed to reinforce joint action against unemployment and to prepare an employment pact, based on the model of the Stability and Growth Pact[5] (i.e. essentially economic policy harmonisation). As a result of this, at the Cologne Summit of June 1999, the European Employment Pact was adopted, which aimed to harmonise the employment policies of the Member States and the Community and to achieve a higher level of employment. It is built on the following three pillars:

1. Coordination of economic policy and improvement of mutually supportive interaction between wage developments and monetary, budget and fiscal policy through macro-economic dialogue aimed at preserving a non-inflationary growth dynamic.
2. Further development and better implementation of the coordinated employment strategy, to improve the efficiency of the labour markets by improving employability, entrepreneurship, adaptability of businesses and their employees, and equal opportunities for men and women in finding gainful employment.
3. Comprehensive structural reform and modernisation, to improve the innovative capacity and efficiency of the labour market and the markets in goods, services and capital.

---

[5] See 8.7.

In addition to reinforcing employment policy, the Treaty of Amsterdam brought significant progress in other areas of social policy. Most importantly, the provisions of the Agreement on Social Policy annexed to the Maastricht Treaty were expanded and enshrined in the Treaty of Amsterdam. Thus, the social policy aims, formerly only partly related to the Community, now became part of the *acquis communautaire*, the body of Community law. The Social Charter, however, was not made part of the Treaty. Nevertheless, the Social Charter became an authoritative document for every Member State when, in the UK, the new Labour government following the 1997 elections decided to adopt the Charter in 1998.

Another key social policy provision of the Treaty of Amsterdam was that it gave special priority to gender equality and made this one of the most important Community objectives in the EC Treaty (Articles 2 and 3 of the Treaty). According to Article 141 of the Treaty, the Council and the Parliament, in the framework of the co-decision procedure, must adopt measures to ensure the application of the principle of equal opportunities and equal treatment of men and women in matters of employment and occupation, including the principle of equal pay for equal work or work of equal value.

As far as decision-making in the field of social policy following Amsterdam is concerned, in the areas listed in Article 137 of the EC Treaty[6], the Community may adopt measures designed to encourage cooperation between Member States through initiatives aimed at improving knowledge, developing exchanges of information and best practices, promoting innovative approaches and evaluating experiences. These measures are adopted jointly by the Council and the Parliament by co-decision, except for the areas of social security

---

[6] In accordance with Article 137 the Community supports and complements the activities of the Member States in the following fields: (a) improvement in particular of the working environment to protect workers' health and safety; (b) working conditions; (c) social security and social protection of workers; (d) protection of workers where their employment contract is terminated; (e) the information and consultation of workers; (f) representation and collective defence of the interests of workers and employers; (g) conditions of employment for third-country nationals legally residing in Community territory; (h) the integration of persons excluded from the labour market; (i) equality between men and women with regard to labour market opportunities and treatment at work; (j) the combating of social exclusion; (k) the modernisation of social protection systems without prejudice to point (c).

and social protection of workers, protection of workers when their employment contract is terminated, representation and collective defence of interests of workers and employers, and conditions of employment for third-country nationals legally residing in Community territory, where the Council acts unanimously in the consultation procedure. Under the Treaty of Nice the Council, however, may – with a unanimous decision – extend the co-decision procedure and qualified majority voting to these areas, with the exception of social security and social protection of workers.

14.3. New directions in Community employment and social policy

Employment and social policy today operate as a typical Community policy, in that the Community actions complement the Member States' own related policies. In parallel with the integration process (e.g. the launching of the monetary union) and the appearance of challenges affecting all Member States (e.g. an ageing population and continuing unemployment), there is a greater need than ever for closer cooperation in this field. The announcement of the employment guidelines had already shown that, as with economic policy, the coordination of national policies was moving into the foreground. Although in one defining aspect of social policy – the operation of social security – the Member States still enjoy total independence, in the last few years they have coordinated their employment and social policy at a Community level, and this process will probably gain in strength. This is primarily due to the fact that, in recent years, the issues of employment and social health of society have become more important from the point of view of global competitiveness. This is indicated by the fact that employment and social policy objectives form the core of the long-term economic strategies adopted at the Lisbon Summit in March 2000 for the next decade until 2010. The original key objective of the Lisbon strategy[7] is to make the EU the most competitive and the most dynamic knowledge-based economy in the world, capable of sustainable development while creating more and better jobs through greater social cohesion. For this to happen, a number of steps must be taken but, more than anything else, the level of employment needs to be raised and workers trained with the necessary skills to meet the challenges. The Member States want to achieve these objectives and

---

[7] See also 1.12.3.1.

increase competitiveness while preserving the values of the European social model (the achievements of the European welfare state) and without damaging them.[8]

At the beginning of the 21st century, the improvement of the employment situation became a strategic objective of the EU, and this, together with the task of preserving the European social model[9], resulted in the adoption by the Member States of the European Social Agenda at the Nice Summit in December 2000. The Agenda defined the framework for employment and social policy for several years. On the basis of this, during the first decade of the new millennium, Community social policy will concentrate on the following six objectives:

1. Creating more and better jobs;
2. Promoting and utilising a work environment built on flexibility and security;
3. Fighting all forms of poverty and discrimination in the interests of stimulating social integration;
4. Modernising social protection;
5. Promoting equality between the sexes;
6. Reinforcing the social dimension of enlargement and EU foreign policy.

In 2005, the Commission published a Communication on launching a new European Social Agenda for 2005–2010 with two key priorities: full employment (by making work a real option for everyone) and a more cohesive society (by strengthening equal opportunities). The Member States, in the framework of the European Social Agenda, seek to achieve results by relying on means such as technical progress, the advantages of monetary union and better exploitation of mobility. One example of exploiting mobility and technical progress is EURES [EURopean Employment Service], a Community database for those offering and seeking work. Essentially, EURES operates as a Community job agency matching jobseekers and employers. But EURES is much more than just a job portal – it has an important role to play in providing information about and helping to solve all sorts of problems related to cross-border working that workers and employers may experience.

---

[8] It should however be noted that, as in the previous forty years of integration, the differing economic and social policy philosophies of the Member States still pose difficulties in terms of defining the role and the tasks of the EU in the area of social and employment policy. Even today, there are often differences of opinion at the Union level between those favouring liberalisation and those favouring the regulatory role of the state (or the Community).

[9] One such task is to maintain the level of the social safety net and to preserve the value of pensions despite the challenges in the labour market (high labour costs) created by globalisation.

The shift of focus in the field of employment and social policy shows that this policy can no longer be examined and pursued as a separate area. In the European Union, in relation to activities to be pursued for a successful future, priority is also given to the principle of sustainable development, expressed in the Lisbon strategy. From 2001, the EU has placed social policy in a new perspective in line with these changes, starting with the preparation of the sustainable development strategy for the Gothenburg Summit in June 2001. The strategy is based on the principle that the economic, social and environmental effects of all policies should be examined in a coordinated way and taken into account in decision-making.

In connection with sustainable development, in the area of social policy, the European Union has identified two challenges: the fight against poverty and social exclusion, and tasks arising from the economic and social consequences of an ageing society. To meet these challenges, the Union defined specific objectives within the framework of the Lisbon strategy. Of these, the following should be highlighted:

- raising the level of employment to 70% by 2010 (60% for women and 50% for the 55–64 age-group), which is a key objective of the Lisbon strategy;
- reducing by 50% the number of 18 to 24 year-olds with only lower-secondary level education who are not in further education and training;
- improving equality between the sexes in access to jobs, vocational training, promotion and working conditions;
- improving the effectiveness of the fight against social exclusion (e.g. through Community programmes);
- improving the adjustment of pension systems to the current situation;
- improving conditions for life-long learning;
- taking into consideration social effects in immigration and refugee policies (demographic challenges).

Since the Lisbon strategy was announced, the Heads of State or Government devote their spring summits exclusively to economic and social issues, thereby regularly revising and updating the strategy. The objective of coordinating sustainable development and employment and social policy with other policies was expressed at the Barcelona Summit on 15–16 March 2002, where the European Council decided that the employment strategy laid down in 1997 in Luxembourg should also be reviewed and revised in line with the Lisbon strategy, with the aim of completion by 2010. As far as activities are concerned, emphasis should be given to increasing employment (to the targeted 70% rate) alongside the high-level protection of the European social model. The Barcelona Summit pointed out the need to coordinate and align broad economic policy guidelines[10] with the priorities and periods of employment policy guidelines.

The Brussels European Council of 20–21 March 2003 reasserted that employment strategy should play a central role in meeting the employment and labour market objectives of the Lisbon strategy, for which coordination between broad economic policy guidelines and employment policy guidelines is indispensable. With a view to the above, the decision was taken to adopt the two packages of guidelines together for the same three-year periods. The employment policy guidelines adopted in 2003 for the following three years laid down the following main objectives:

- *Full employment*: In particular, achieving the employment rates targeted in the Lisbon strategy (70% in 2010, 60% for women, and 50% for workers in the age group 55 to 64);
- *Improving quality of and productivity at work*: This objective encompasses a wide range of areas such as lifelong learning and career development, gender equality, health and safety at work, flexible working time, social dialogue and worker involvement;
- *Strengthening social cohesion and inclusion*: In the framework of this objective, national employment policies should promote access to employment for all women and men, combat discrimination in the labour market, prevent the exclusion of people from the world of work, and reduce regional disparities.

The success of employment policy coordination, as encouraged by the Lisbon strategy, hinges on the Member States' commitment to implementing Community guidelines and national measures. A key tool of cooperation between the Member States is the open method of coordination, whereby they agree on common objectives which they then try to achieve at national level through coordinated efforts. In the first years after Lisbon, the Member States demonstrated little of the required commitment, as the strategy's mid-term review pointed out. The mid-term review of the Lisbon strategy carried out by the Brussels European Council on 22–23 March 2005 therefore brought a new approach to implementing the objectives of the strategy. The new approach brought more direct feedback to facilitate effective Community surveillance of national performances, based on three-year cycles, the first of which commenced in 2005 and will be renewed in 2008. The Council, following the Commission's preparatory strategy paper and the European Council's conclusions, has

---

[10] For more, see 8.7.

to adopt *integrated guidelines* consisting of two parts: the broad economic policy guidelines and the employment guidelines. On the basis of the integrated guidelines, Member States draw up 3-year national reform programmes, while the Commission elaborates its own 'Community Lisbon Programme' covering all the actions at EU level that complement the national programmes. At the end of each three-year cycle, the integrated guidelines, the national reform programmes and the Community Lisbon programme are all updated and revised. The Commission publishes progress reports on the achivements of individual Member States in carrying out their national programmes and in the implementation of the Community programme. The first integrated guidelines for 2005–2008 were adopted at the European Council meeting of 16–17 June 2005. Among others, these guidelines promote policies aimed at achieving full employment, improving quality and productivity at work, ensuring inclusive labour markets, matching labour market needs and adapting education and training systems in response to new competence requirements.

The 2006 spring European Council carried on where the mid-term review left off and set the goal of adding new momentum to employment with the objective of creating 2 million new jobs by 2010 and improving the employability of young people. To this end, an EU average rate of no more than 10% of early school leavers should be achieved and at least 85% of 22 year olds in the European Union should have completed upper secondary education. In addition, every young person who has completed their education should be offered a job, apprenticeship, additional training or other employability measure within six months of becoming unemployed by the end of 2007, and within no more than four months by 2010.

For the future of Community social and employment policies, the 2007–2013 financial perspectives were of paramount importance because of the overhaul of the European Social Fund.[11] As part of the Structural Funds' reforms, the ESF, which has a total budget of EUR 75 billion for these seven years, is supposed to link funding more closely with policies to boost employment and strengthen economic and social cohesion. With less red tape, simpler rules and more decentralisation to the Member States from 2007,

---

[11] For more, see 13.4.

the ESF should be both easier to manage and better equipped to tackle the new challenges arising from enlargement, the ageing population and globalisation.

A new integrated programme, the Community Programme for Employment and Social Solidarity, called PROGRESS, was created for the 2007–2013 period, to focus on five key areas of action: employment (with spcial focus on the implementation of the European Employment Strategy), social protection and inclusion (using the open method of coordination), improving working conditions (concentrating on health and safety at work and reconciling professional and private life), combating discrimination (mainstreaming the princinple of non-discrimination into all EU policies) and promoting diversity and gender equality (mainstreaming the gender issue into all EU policies). For the seven years between 2007 and 2013, PROGRESS has a total budget of EUR 743.25 million.

CHAPTER 15
INDUSTRIAL POLICY

15.1. Industrial policy

During the past decades, Community industrial policy has undergone major transformations and changes in concepts. The Treaty of Rome itself does not make any reference to an independent Community industrial policy. It was presumed that the development of the common market, the removal of internal barriers and the ensuing free competition and Common Commercial Policy of the European Community, as well as the restrictions introduced vis-à-vis external competitors, would sufficiently guarantee the dynamic and sound development of European industry. Accordingly, the European Communities did not assume major responsibilities at Community level over industry, with the exception of certain fields (such as the coal and steel industry in the framework of the European Coal And Steel Community[1]). Industrial policy remained under the competence of the Member States. During this period, Community activities were characterised by attempts to modernise the structure of industry. These efforts however were restricted to a handful of intergovernmental programmes of minor effect, promoting modernisation and company (micro) level integration.

In the sixties and seventies, the conflicting goals and economic philosophies of the Member States posed a major obstacle to the development of a Community industrial policy. While the German, British and Dutch economic policies focused on liberalisation, the French and Italian government strategies highlighted the necessity of state intervention.

The situation was further aggravated by the outbreak of the 1973 oil crisis. The Member States almost uniformly reacted by withdrawing into themselves and intensifying the promotion of their national industries. During this period, industrial policy erroneously focused on protectionism and the reparation of losses through subsidies, which not only failed to alleviate the crisis, mainly manifesting itself in the traditional sectors (e.g. steel and textile industries and ship building), but, through the continuous flow of subsidies, worked rather to conserve outdated structures and stall structural reforms.

---

[1] Although in the framework of the ECSC, the coal and steel industries were put under Community management in the fifties, strategically this development was important as long as the industry struggled with product shortage. During the sixties, when the shortage was remedied, the importance of the ECSC Treaty diminished.

As a result of this policy, by the eighties, European industry had fallen into an unfavourable situation vis-à-vis American and Japanese companies, which handled structural reorganisation in a more effective way. The Japanese and Americans leapt ahead and their advantage over the Europeans was most prominent in the high tech industries. Despite the ongoing European integration process, overseas and Far-Eastern competition managed to exploit the opportunities offered by trans-nationalisation and micro-level integration more efficiently. This phenomenon forced the Member States to re-evaluate their industrial policies and realise that, notwithstanding 25 years of integration, isolation was still a hallmark of European industry. It became evident that competitiveness on the international scene required a more effectively coordinated European industrial policy and that the Communities needed to assume responsibility in this regard. The most important consequence of this realisation was the development of the programme to establish a single market, which aimed at exploiting the advantages offered by integration as opposed to the introverted, protectionist national policies of the seventies. In addition to aspiring to the concept of the single market, at the Community's initiative, the Member States started re-evaluating the objectives set out by their respective national industrial policies, gradually shifting emphasis to structural reorganisation and technological modernisation.

The philosophy of realising development through the liberalisation of markets as an alternative to protectionism progressively gained ground. Competitiveness became the buzzword, which in turn raised the key question for economic strategy and industrial policy, namely what needed to be done to help Community industry and business compete in the global market place?

15.2. Industrial policy in the nineties

The Treaty of Maastricht provided industrial policy with a new basis by introducing it into the EC Treaty (presently Title XVI, Part Three of the EC Treaty). The Treaty called for the creation of the necessary conditions to improve the competitiveness of European industry as the fundamental objective of industrial policy. Article 157 defined four comprehensive objectives:
– speeding up the adjustment of industry to structural changes;
– promoting an environment favourable to the development of undertakings, particularly small- and medium-sized undertakings;
– promoting an environment favourable to cooperation between undertakings;
– fostering better exploitation of the industrial potential of policies of innovation, research and technological development.

According to the provisions of the EC Treaty, the Member States consult with each other involving the Commission, and if necessary, they coordinate their industrial policies. The Commission may take initiatives to promote this coordination. The Council, acting together with Parliament through co-decision, may take measures to implement the objectives laid down in Article 157.

In December 1993, parallel to the entry into force of the Treaty of Maastricht, the Commission submitted its 'White Paper on Growth, Competitiveness and Employment' to the European Council. In accordance with the challenges of the turn of the century, the White Paper did not merely highlight the responsibilities of industrial policy but analysed the fundamental problems of contemporary society, first and foremost rising unemployment, and outlined a comprehensive economic strategy for the EU. The 1993 White Paper proposed practical solutions for achieving dynamic, job-creating growth and referred to the particular importance of expanding information infrastructure networks and markets and increasing the international competitiveness of European companies.

Similarly to the Treaty of Maastricht, the White Paper also called attention to the fact that industrial policy in the nineties could not be defined as an isolated mechanism and could not yield results of itself. Community industrial policy needed to be understood as a policy that aimed at encouraging competitiveness. Consequently, its instruments needed to be defined in a wider context. The new central role of competitiveness entailed the redefinition of tasks and it became clear that realising the objectives of the sector required the coordination of several Community policies (e.g. research and technological development, education and training, competition policy, development of infrastructure and environmental protection).

Thus, from the nineties, industrial policy has undergone a transformation from its traditional role. Along the lines of the above-mentioned new philosophy, the EU has moved away from focusing on industrial development in its strict sense to policies aimed at fostering competitiveness and encouraging a favourable environment at the Community level. The Community's main responsibility now is to define the framework of industrial policy, at the threefold level of undertakings, Member States and the Union, and to ensure the necessary conditions for competition in concert with the Member States. The exploitation of potential and the implementation of practical measures to improve competitiveness fall within the competence of undertakings. To create a favourable environment, the EU has become involved in two kinds of actions: actions relating to the operation of markets and actions relating to factors that affect industry's capacity to adapt to change.

From the mid-nineties, in line with the orientations developed in the 1993 White Paper, the EU's four priorities for creating a favourable environment for industry, have been as follows:

a) Promotion of intangible investment
With the growth of information and knowledge-based competition, areas such as research and technological development and education and training have become vitally important. Sound investment in these fields is a key factor in industrial competitiveness and, therefore, the financing and development of these sectors is crucial to the EU's strategy.

b) Development of industrial cooperation
While decisions to enter into industrial cooperation are the responsibility of businesses, the EU may contribute to fostering relations between participants by employing its legal and organisational means of influence. The Union is involved in the organisation of forums and round tables that encourage cooperation between the representatives of the various industrial sectors.

c) Strengthening of competition
The completion of the internal market, which involves the removal of hidden barriers distorting competition, remains the most important issue in this context. Legislation is still to be implemented in the areas of public procurement, company law and fiscal harmonisation.
This involves the approximation and standardisation of divergent national regulations, standards and certification. In this respect, the EU pays special attention to guaranteeing the free movement of goods and services, which is warranted by the harmonisation approach aimed at standardising essential requirements (for example related to health and consumer protection, etc.) and, by referring to the principle of mutual recognition, at interpreting standards more liberally. The Community promotes the unified application and standardisation of various European systems (for example the GSM system for mobile phones).
The trade policy of the Union vis-à-vis its international competitors should encourage the opening of markets on the basis of reciprocity. The Commission's role is to analyse the effects of removing the various barriers and to take a lead in negotiations aimed at their removal.

d) Modernisation of the role of public administrations
Under the EU's strategy, public authorities must also redefine their role in order to correspond to the needs of the information society, so that they can fulfil their legislative and regulatory responsibilities. Public authorities must make use of the latest developments in information and communication technologies and draw on them in their everyday communication with each other and with business representatives.

15.3. From industrial policy to enterprise policy

The change of concept in industrial policy shifted the EU's focus to the promotion of competitiveness. At the same time, at the turn of the century, activities formerly falling under the competences of industrial policy came to be defined as enterprise policy. This process was further reinforced by the practice of increasing support for small- and medium-sized enterprises (SMEs) and of encouraging a business environment favourable to them, which has now taken root. At the turn of the millennium, there were approximately 18 million such undertakings in the EU-15, which employed 66 per cent of the Community's employees. SMEs have come to the fore primarily because this sector continues to have the most significant potential for increasing employment and has the ability to create the most jobs, which is a crucial factor in the unemployment-stricken Union.

In the framework of Community activities aimed at coordinating various policies, and which became known as enterprise policy, in December 2000, the Council adopted the Multi-annual Programme for Enterprise and Entrepreneurship[2] for the period 2001–2005 with a budget of EUR 450 million, which was then extended until the end of 2006 with an 88.5 million of additional funding.

The 2001–2005 Community programme on enterprise, which put small- and medium-sized enterprises at its core, had the following objectives:
- to enhance the growth and competitiveness of businesses in a knowledge-based international economy;
- to promote entrepreneurship;
- to simplify and improve the administrative and regulatory framework for business, so that research, innovation and business creation in particular can flourish;
- to improve the financial environment for businesses, especially SMEs;
- to give businesses easier access to Community support services, programmes and networks and to improve the coordination of these facilities.

To recognise the increased significance of SMEs and to promote their activities more effectively, in addition to the introduction of the multiannual programme on enterprise, the European Council adopted the European Charter of Small- and Medium-Sized Enterprises in June 2000 at the Feira Summit. The Charter demonstrates the Member States' commitment to improving the business environment of SMEs in the following areas:

---

[2] Decision 2000/819/EC

- education and training for entrepreneurship (particularly for young people);
- cheaper and faster start-up;
- better (more effective and simpler) legislation and regulation;
- availability of skills (training institutions deliver skills adapted to the needs of small enterprises and provide lifetime training and consultancy);
- improving on-line access to public administration;
- enabling SMEs to take more advantage of the opportunities offered by the single market and developing SMEs in accordance with the interests of the single market;
- fostering a favourable fiscal and financial environment;
- strengthening the technological capacity of SMEs;
- making use of e-business and successful e-business models for SMEs;
- developing a stronger, more effective representation of SMEs' interests at national and Union level.

Since the Lisbon strategy[3] was announced in March 2000 – with the primary aim of making the EU the most competitive knowledge-based economy in the world by 2010 – industrial policy has been dominated by the aspiration of improving competitiveness. The concept of sustainable development was incorporated into the Lisbon strategy in 2001, which calls for a balance of social progress, economic development and the environment. Since the Lisbon Summit, the Heads of State or Government have dedicated their annual spring summits exclusively to economic and social issues, where they formulate conclusions complementing the Lisbon strategy and focusing on boosting competitiveness in the EU. The backbone of the Lisbon strategy is the coordination of various Union activities for the achievement of these objectives. In that sense, industrial policy and enterprise policy are viewed as being inseparable from other policies, and are thus no longer really independent but rather increasingly incorporated into other policy areas.

Both the 2003 and 2004 spring summit meetings reasserted that enterprise policy should focus on competitiveness as a factor contributing to growth. At its March 2004 meeting, the European Council singled out four key tasks: completing the internal market, better regulation, stepping up efforts in research and improving the efficiency of the institutions. The significant legislative work of recent years conducted at sectoral level was aimed at creating better and more effective internal market regulation.

---

[3] For details, see 1.12.3.1.

As part of better regulation, several complex pieces of overlapping legislation are being replaced with clearer, less complicated ones. In addition, extra emphasis is being put on the more systematic impact assessment of legislative proposals, exploring the pros and cons of various regulatory alternatives and reducing the administrative burden of undertakings, especially SMEs. Fundamentally, the programme is aimed at the simplification of Union law both in form and content, ensuring transparency without hindering competitiveness.

It should be pointed out, that the Lisbon strategy hinges on coordinating national efforts, which depends mainly on the will of the Member States themselves, something the Union has limited influence over. In most of the areas in question the *open method of coordination* is applied. In the framework of open coordination, the Member States establish their goals jointly, which they then try to achieve by finding and disseminating best practice. The lack of sufficient commitment on the part of Member States was demonstrated in the mid-term review of the Lisbon process at the summit meeting of 22–23 March 2005[4], where the Member States decided to step up national efforts in parallel with the implementation of the Lisbon strategy. From 2005 on, national action should be based on 3-year integrated guidelines (including both economic and employment policy guidelines), which serve as common ground for the national reform programmes for competitiveness, particularly growth and employment.[5]

As part of the efforts to reinvigorate the Lisbon strategy, the European Commission collected various enterprise policy aspirations in a single document, published as a Communication in November 2005, 'A modern SME policy', outlining five key objectives:
- *Promoting entrepreneurship and skills.* Reducing the burden of risk linked to setting up and running a business, eliminating the negative effects linked to business failure, and promoting entrepreneurial skills in particular categories of entrepreneurs (women, young people, old people, and people from ethnic minorities).
- *Improving SMEs' access to markets.* Better access to tenders on the public market and increased awareness of intellectual property rights, to help SMEs to take full

---

[4] The mid-term review admitted that the objective of making the EU the world's most competitive economy by 2010 was unattainable. The backbone of the strategy – improving competitiveness based on sustainable development – was reasserted as the key objective for boosting growth and employment.

[5] See 14.3.

advantage of the opportunities provided by the internal market as well as international markets.

- *Cutting red tape.* It is vital to simplify the regulatory and administrative constraints weighing on SMEs. The principle of giving priority to small enterprises ('Think Small First') are being integrated across all EU policies. The interests of SMEs are systematically taken into consideration when assessing the impact of Community legislation and when preparing forthcoming legislation. In the case of SMEs special attention is given to the flexibility of rules concerning state aid.
- *Improving SMEs' growth potential.* Improving SMEs' access to finance, research, innovation and information and communication technologies (ICT). Better involvement of SMEs in the Competitiveness and Innovation Framework Programme (see below) and in the 7th Research Framework Programme[6] from 2007.
- *Strengthening dialogue and consultation with SME stakeholders.* Better access to information, more direct consultation with the Commission and other measures promoting entrepreneurship, such as the 'European Enterprise Awards' established in late 2005.

With the decisions of the 2006 and 2007 spring summits, the Member States wanted to maintain the momentum of the Lisbon strategy – revitalised in 2005 – and press on with the Commission's policy. The March 2006 Spring Council decided that the Member States should establish, by 2007, a one-stop-shop, or arrangements with equivalent effect, for setting up a company and take steps to cut down the administrative time needed for setting up a business to one week by the end of 2007.

The March 2007 summit also focused on improving the regulatory environment. As part of the 'better regulation' objective, the European Council decided to reduce the administrative burden[7] put on companies by European legislation by 25% by 2012 and encouraged Member States to set similarly ambitious objectives for simplifying national law and cutting red tape by 2008. The Commission estimates that this could lead to an increase of 1.5% in EU GDP. The European Council also instructed the Commission to launch together with the Member States an Action Programme aimed at reducing administrative burdens on businesses.

---

[6] See 17.2.

[7] Administrative burden means information obligations (permit/licence applications, data provision, etc.) stemming from but not essential to achieving the goals of relevant law.

The growing importance of enterprise policy is demonstrated by the budget of the Entrepreneurship and Innovation Programme – EIP (the successor of the Multi-annual Programme for Enterprise and Entrepreneurship), which was significantly increased to EUR 2.14 billion for the period 2007–2013. The increased budget – however – has to cover a wider range of tasks as some (innovation- and environment-related) objectives formerly attributed to other budget lines were integrated into the EIP. Accordingly, 20% of the Programme's budget is earmarked for so-called eco-innovation projects. Alongside supporting innovation in 'green' technology, the main focus of the Entrepreneurship and Innovation Programme is to facilitate access to finance for the start-up and growth of SMEs and to provide information to enterprises on the operation of and opportunities in the internal market and on Community rules and future legislative developments, so that SMEs understand their regulatory environment and can prepare for changes. The EIP was set up as part of the Competitiveness and Innovation Framework Programme, running from 1 January 2007.[8]

---

[8] The Entrepreneurship and Innovation Programme (EIP) is part of the Competitiveness and Innovation Framework Programme (CIP), which also contains the ICT Policy Support Programme (ICT PSP) and the Intelligent Energy – Europe Programme (IEE). The former promotes the application of information and communication technology, the latter promotes sustainable energy management. For the period 2007–2013, CIP has a total budget of EUR 3.621 billion, divided among its constitutive programmes as follows: 60% (EUR 2.17 billion) to the Entrepreneurship and Innovation Programme, 20% (EUR 730 million) to ICT Policy Support Programme and 20% (EUR 730 million) to Intelligent Energy – Europe Programme.

CHAPTER 16
ENERGY POLICY

16.1. Development of energy policy

Even though two of the founding treaties of the European Community concerned energy policy, namely the 1951 Treaty of Paris establishing the European Coal and Steel Community and the Treaty establishing the European Atomic Energy Community (Euratom), signed in 1957 in Rome just like the EEC Treaty, in the past fifty years the Member States have been reluctant to 'communitise' this area, and energy policy has essentially remained under the competence of the Member States. One explanation for this reluctance may be that the most important Treaty, the EC Treaty, did not have a part devoted specifically to energy; it only mentioned energy in Article 2 as one of the areas of Community action.[1] Hence, rules pertaining to energy policy only occur when incorporated into other areas.

In the fifties and sixties, the pattern of energy use underwent major changes, which greatly affected the energy policies of the Member States of the European Communities. Coal consumption decreased, and with it the significance of the ECSC, while crude oil became the number one energy resource. As a result, the energy supply of the Member States became dependent primarily on imports.

With the outbreak of the 1973 oil crisis, the energy supply situation of the Member States met with a major setback. The national economies depending on imported crude oil were weakened by the drastic rise in oil prices. In the wake of the crisis, national governments resorted to state intervention, which reinforced national sovereignty and hindered the realisation of energy policy at Community level. While the Member States tried to join forces in solving the crisis, the measures taken were overwhelmingly national ones. During this period, the Community's role was mainly limited to the adoption of common guidelines and joint target figures.

In 1974, the European Commission presented a common energy strategy, which was approved by the Council. The strategy proposed the rational utilisation of energy, the reduction of oil imports, the promotion of the growth of national energy production and, more importantly, the stabilisation of coal production and the promotion of investment in the nuclear sector. In the seventies, internal energy consumption was successfully

---

[1] Although Declaration I annexed to the Maastricht Treaty called on the IGC preceding the Amsterdam Treaty to examine whether energy policy should be included in the Treaty under a separate Title, no agreement was actually reached on this issue.

reduced and energy saving programmes proved effective; nevertheless the development of nuclear power production faced both political opposition (by various green movements) and economic difficulties. Since then, the significance of Euratom, similarly to the ECSC, has decreased significantly.

With the onset of the second oil crisis, the need for strengthening Community energy policy re-emerged. At the 1980 Venice Summit, the Heads of State or Government stated that the rate of growth of internal energy consumption must not exceed 60% of Community economic growth. During the eighties, the Member States were successful in observing this target figure. Energy consumption – primarily crude oil consumption – plummeted, while the Community became less dependent on outside resources as a result of the exploration and exploitation of North Sea oil reserves.

In 1986, the Commission submitted its White Paper, which set out comprehensive energy policy objectives. It focused on further rationalisation, the reduction of energy consumption and the structural reorganisation of the energy sector. Nonetheless, the development of nuclear power production was not included among the objectives, as the focus of energy policy had shifted.

From the mid-eighties, the nature of the energy market fundamentally changed, which had a profound effect on energy policy. Energy supply was abundant, the price of oil plummeted and electric energy surpluses were created. Consequently, energy policy aimed at the reduction of prices and, in line with the objective of production rationalisation, the notion of privatising the energy sector came to the fore.

During this period, the concept of developing an internal market emerged and transformed the energy objectives of the Community. Energy policy was understood as an essential part of a unified internal market, since an internal energy market was clearly likely to improve the competitiveness of European industry. Accordingly, the Commission gradually shifted the focus of energy policy to objectives dictated by the development of the internal market, such as the harmonisation of rules in the field of energy subsidies, state monopolies and price transparency.

Proposals for the monitoring of state subsidies in the field of energy met with opposition from the Member States. Like the harmonisation of national energy policies, this issue was also relegated to the background. The most significant result with a view to establishing an internal energy market was achieved through the standardisation of norms.

When the programme introduced in the middle of the eighties expired in 1995, the Commission set out new energy policy guidelines. A new White Paper in 1995 defined

an overall energy framework with three strategic objectives, which remain the basis of all energy policy programmes and actions even today:
- competitiveness;
- security of energy supply;
- environmental protection.

Although environmental protection had featured prominently among the 1986 objectives, it was the 1995 programme that gave it ranking of equal importance.

The Energy Charter

The experience of the past decades has shown that it is expedient to coordinate energy policy at an international level. Extensive global cooperation promotes the rationalisation and sustainable provision of energy supply. Accordingly, 56 countries have signed the Energy Charter, originally adopted in 1991 in The Hague, which plays an important complementary role to Community energy policy. The Energy Charter was originally designed to promote cooperation with the former Communist countries – in particular with the Republics of the former Soviet Union – and develop energy infrastructure in the participating countries. The Charter aims at providing the necessary conditions for Western investments in Central and Eastern Europe and in Central Asia and facilitates market developments in the energy sector and the establishment of a modern and secure energy sector in the former Communist countries. Furthermore, the Energy Charter strives to help the signatory countries to improve energy efficiency and step-up environmental measures. In 1995, the signatories of the Charter adopted a legally binding agreement, which provides legal safeguards in the areas of trade, competition and investment. The EU also provides assistance to the participating countries outside the framework of the Energy Charter. One of the aims of the TACIS programme, for instance, was modernising and improving the safety features of Soviet-type nuclear power stations in the CIS republics. Following the accession of Central and Eastern European countries to the Union, the added value of the Charter lies in energy policy relations with former Soviet republics. However, it greatly detracts from its value that Russia, the region's main energy supplier, has failed to ratify the Charter despite repeated requests by the EU. Nevertheless the bright future of the Charter is demonstrated by the growing number of signatories and the recent expansion of its geographical scope to include Pakistan.

16.2. Energy policy at the turn of the millennium

In accordance with the completion of the single market, since the second half of the nineties, the primary objectives of EU energy policy have included the closer coordination of national energy policies, the liberalisation of the energy sector and more emphasis on environmental aspects. These policy strands have been completed by the energy network development projects and investments introduced in the framework of the trans-European networks, which promote the development of cross-border gas and electricity networks and aim at the establishment of a single energy market.

The liberalisation of the energy market is a fundamental element of the completion of the internal market, which the EU failed to realise by the turn of the century. To remedy this problem, following the economic policy strategy for the period 2000–2010, which was adopted in March 2000, the Lisbon strategy continued to call for the liberalisation of the gas and electricity markets. In this respect, the first successful step was taken at the Barcelona Summit on 15–16 March 2002, where the Member States agreed that, from the year 2004, non-household consumers would have the right to choose their gas and electricity suppliers freely. In 2003, the Council and Parliament adopted Directives 2003/54/EC and 2003/55/EC, which laid down the exact schedule for liberalisation in the electricity and gas sectors. These two Directives extended liberalisation to include household consumers too. Accordingly, non-household consumers have had the right to choose their electricity and gas suppliers freely since 1 July 2004, while household consumers have had the same right of option from 1 July 2007. Liberalisation is expected to create more competition in the single market, and thereby contribute to a better and cheaper service for consumers.

The work on completing the single energy market has also been facilitated by the development of trans-European energy networks.[2] In 1996, the Member States adopted guidelines for this area and agreed to put 74 projects in place. The guidelines were reviewed and modified in 2003, setting 12 new priority projects (7 in the electricity and 5 in the gas sector). The guidelines were reviewed and modified again in 2006, and 15 priority projects were set (9 in the electricity and 6 in the gas sector), which should be implemented by 2010 and will require a total investment of roughly EUR 28 billion. Within the priority projects for large networks, 42 specific development objectives – so-called projects of European interest – were identified as being necessary for the operation of true trans-European energy networks.

---

[2] For more on trans-European networks, see 12.3.

The new common priorities defined by the guidelines (which also served as the basis for identifying the priority projects and in their framework the projects of European interest) stipulated that trans-European energy networks should be developed in a way that they can contribute to:
- reducing energy prices for household users, diversifying energy sources and encouraging greater use of renewable energy;
- reducing the isolation of less-favoured, island or remote regions;
- improving security of energy supply, primarily through deepening relations with third countries within the framework of the Energy Charter and cooperation agreements concluded by the Community;
- promoting sustainable development and protecting the environment, inter alia by the increased use of renewable energy sources.

The guidelines also defined the special priorities of: adapting and developing both electricity and gas networks to ensure interoperability and interconnectivity with candidate countries, other European countries, Mediterranean countries and countries of the Black Sea region, and for gas networks with countries of the Caspian basin, the Middle-East and the Persian Gulf.

In recent times, the financing of energy policy has been guaranteed by multi-annual framework action programmes. In December 1998, the Council adopted a multi-annual (1998–2002) framework programme for the development of the energy sector in line with the objectives set out in the 1995 White Paper (overall competitiveness, security of energy supply and environmental protection). The framework programme aimed at improving efficiency, transparency and coordination within the energy sector and strengthening coherence between Community and national measures.

For the 2003–2006 period, the EU adopted a new multi-annual action programme, with the name of Intelligent Energy – Europe Programme (IEE) and a budget of EUR 200 million, focusing on the following objectives:
- promoting energy efficiency and the use of renewable energy sources, in particular with a view to energy saving and reducing carbon-dioxide emissions;
- developing instruments for assessing and monitoring measures taken by Member States;
- promoting efficient and intelligent methods of energy production and consumption.

The Intelligent Energy – Europe Programme 2003–2006 was divided into the following four specific sub-programmes:
- SAVE – promotion of energy efficiency (with a budget of EUR 69.8 million);
- ALTENER – promotion of renewable energy sources (with a budget of EUR 80 million)
- STEER – energy aspects of transport and fuel diversification (with a budget of EUR 32.6 million);
- COPENER – promotion of renewable energy sources and energy saving in developing countries (with a budget of EUR 17.6 million).

The Intelligent Energy – Europe Programme continues in the 2007–2013 period as part of the Competitiveness and Innovation Framework Programme (CIP). The Intelligent Energy – Europe Programme 2007–2013 (IEE II) has a total budget of EUR 730 million for the seven years. The objectives of IEE II are similar to those of IEE I and include improving energy efficiency, promoting renewable energy sources and supporting energy diversification. IEE II covers five priority areas: energy efficiency (SAVE), renewable energy (ALTENER), transport (STEER), developing countries and horizontal issues.

Energy Community

The EU's aspiration to create a pan-European energy market is key to the future of its energy policy. The most important step in this direction was the Treaty, signed on 25 October 2005, to create an Energy Community extending the European Community's energy market to South-East Europe. The Treaty, with a historic mission reminiscent of the ECSC, entered into force on 1 July 2006 with 34 parties to it: the EU's current 27 Member States plus Albania, Bosnia-Herzegovina, Croatia, Macedonia, Montenegro, Serbia and the United Nations Interim Administration Mission in Kosovo. Apart from market opportunities, the Energy Community guarantees the Union a direct link with countries lying next to reserves in the Caspian Sea and the Middle East and extends the application of internal market rules on energy and the environment to neighbouring countries. For the countries of South-East Europe, in political terms, the Energy Community serves as a forerunner of integration and, in economic terms, makes a significant contribution to boosting investment in energy infrastructure and to ensuring non-interrupted energy supply. The Energy Community has its own Secretariat, seated in Vienna, to coordinate its operation.

16.3. The beginning of a new European energy policy

In the first years of the new millennium, several important steps were taken in the field of energy policy but, compared to the size of the challenges, they were of minor impact, as it became apparent by the middle of the decade. The urgent need for a complete overhaul of energy policy was made painfully clear by the environmental impacts of climate change – which were no longer ignorable – and the burning issue of energy security underscored by uncertainties of supplies from Russia.[3]

The magnitude of the challenge is demonstrated by the EU's persistently growing dependency on imported energy. Unless the Union can make internally available energy competitive, in the next 20 to 30 years it will have to import 70% of its energy (compared to today's 50%), and a major share of these imports come from insecure sources from unstable regions. For its reserves Europe relies on a handful of countries. At present, half of all European gas imports are supplied by three countries (Russia, Norway and Algeria), while current trends indicate that gas consumption will increase by up to 80% in the coming 25 years. A serious challenge stems from the fact that 80% of energy consumption in the EU comes from fossil fuels (oil, natural gas and coal). If current trends continue, in 2030 the EU will depend on imports for 93% of its oil and 84% of its gas requirements, which not only makes the Union vulnerable but represents an unsustainable energy mix against the backdrop of climate change. If the EU wants to act against global warming, it must radically reduce the share of fossil fuels in its energy mix.

These challenges were summarised clearly in the Commission Green Paper "A European strategy for sustainable, competitive and secure energy", published on 8 March 2006,

---

[3] In the consecutive winters of 2005–2006 and 2006–2007, Russia and its neighbours (first Ukraine then Belarus) fell out over gas prices and transit fees. As efforts to resolve the energy dispute failed, Russia cut off supplies, which had serious implications for Europe (especially Central and Eastern Europe). It became clear that Russia was using gas and oil as a political lever. When the gas pipeline ran dry in Lithuania in early January 2007, due to bilateral political and economic rows, it became clear that this can happen to the Union. In addition, Russia began major network and pipeline developments on its eastern frontiers, which raised concerns that some of the gas sold to Europe could be diverted to China. These developments drew attention to the fact that the EU needs to show more solidarity between its Member States in energy policy negotiations with external partners and in any partnership agreements it concludes.

which proposed a framework for developing an energy policy for the European Union. The Green Paper identified six priority areas where urgent action was needed:

- *Completing the internal energy market*, which – according to the Commission – requires the following steps: developing the gas and energy grids, establishing a common European energy regulator, better coordination of trans-European network development, full application of rules already in force, supporting new initiatives, creating a level playing field.
- *Security of supply and solidarity between the Member States*, which – according to the Commission – can be achieved by ensuring technical and physical security of networks, creating a European Energy Supply Observatory, re-examining existing legislation with a view to managing supply disruptions (particularly with regard to the EU's oil and gas stocks), investing in storage infrastructure and creating emergency stocks.
- *Towards a more sustainable, efficient and diverse energy mix.* Currently, each Member State is free to choose its own energy mix from the sources available, which will remain unchanged. However these choices by individual countries can have an impact on the energy security of their neighbours and of the whole Union, and therefore should be coordinated at European level by means of a Strategic EU Energy Review based on comprehensive analysis and detailed impact assessment.
- *Tackling climate change.* The Commission proposed an Action Plan on Energy Efficiency to achieve a 20% energy saving by 2020. The Commission also proposed that the EU should elaborate a Renewable Energy Road Map by 2020.
- *Setting up a strategic energy technology plan.* The Commission believes that such a Plan can enable European companies to become market leaders in the dynamically growing sector of the latest generation of energy efficient and low-carbon technologies.
- *Coherent action in external energy policy.* Growing demand, rising prices, increasing import dependency and climate change mean that Europe must speak with one voice on the international scene. According to the Commission, the key tasks are supporting investment in infrastructure required for security of supply, reinforcing the EU-Russia dialogue, ratifying the Energy Charter and elaborating response mechanisms for crisis situations outside the Union.

On the basis of the Green Paper, the EU began to give some thought to the issue – it transpired that Community institutions, market leaders and even Member States wanted to go down the route of change. The European Council of 8–9 March 2007 brought a new turn in energy policy. Realising that climate change and energy policy were closely interrelated, the Heads of State or Government decided to launch a new, integrated climate change and energy policy. Within that framework, the summit adopted a new Energy Policy Action Plan for the period 2007–2009, which can be considered as the beginning of a true Community energy policy. The Action Plan outlined five priority areas:

a) *The internal market for gas and electricity*
Following the market liberalisation of 2007, the key task is the effective separation of supply and production activities from network operations ('unbundling'). This means full ownership unbundling, which can force large energy firms to sell off some of their stakes to comply with requirements. This is necessary to protect consumers' interests and indirectly to slash prices. In addition, further harmonisation of the powers and strengthening of the independence of national energy regulators is needed. To enhance competition and security of supply, the EU must facilitate the integration of new power plants into the electricity grid in all Member States. Better consumer protection also requires the development of an Energy Consumers' Charter for the customers of suppliers.

b) *Security of supply*
The Action Plan, which maintains most of the former priorities, underlines the need for improving effective diversification of energy sources and transport routes, developing more effective crisis response mechanisms, improving oil data transparency, reviewing EU oil supply infrastructures and oil stocks mechanisms and conducting a thorough analysis of the availability and costs of gas storage facilities in the EU.

c) *External energy policy*
More intensive and unified common action is required, which the EU can achieve by the means of: negotiating a new partnership and cooperation agreement with Russia; intensifying the relationship with Central Asia, the Caspian and Black Sea regions, with a view to diversifying energy sources and routes; strengthening cooperation with the USA, China, India and other emerging economies, focusing on the reduction of carbon emissions, energy efficiency and renewable energy sources; possibly extending the Energy Community to Norway, Turkey, Ukraine and Moldova.

d) *Energy efficiency*
The most important element of the entire programme is the target of a 20% share of renewable energies in overall EU consumption by 2020 and a 10% minimum target for the share of biofuels in overall transport petrol and diesel consumption by 2020. On top of these targets, the Action Plan urges Member States to achieve an energy saving potential of 20% compared to projections for 2020.

e) *Energy technologies*
The Union set itself the objectives of elaborating a European Strategic Energy Technology Plan; establishing a mechanism to stimulate the construction and operation by 2015 of up to 12 demonstration plants of sustainable fossil fuel technologies in commercial power generation; launching wide-ranging dialogue on the opportunities offered and the risks posed by nuclear energy.

The most important result and challenge of the integrated climate change and energy policy will undoubtedly be to achieve the 20% share of renewable energies (mainly wind, water, photovoltaic and biomass) by 2020, especially in the light of the environmental commitment in the framework of the integrated policy to reduce CO_2 emissions by 20% by 2020 in an effort to tackle climate change.[4]
The integrated climate change and energy policy is one of the most outsanding decisions of recent years. It should, however, be noted that the 20% target for renewables will not be easy to achieve because the March 2007 summit did not set any national quotas or other specific details. This is important, as the EU average of renewable energy sources was 6.4% in 2005 but with considerable disparities between the Member States: four European countries (Austria, Finland, Latvia and Sweden) had achieved or even surpassed the 20% target by 2005. Consequently, differentiated obligations will have to be determined otherwise some Member States will surely be unable to meet the target. The last word, of course, belongs to the Member States themselves, thus any obligation or national target will require their agreement. This is a good indication of why the integrated policy is only the first step on the road leading to a true Community energy policy, and will have to be followed by many other measures in the years to come.

---

[4] For more, see 18.2.5.

CHAPTER 17
RESEARCH AND TECHNOLOGICAL DEVELOPMENT POLICY

17.1. The beginnings of Community research and technological development

Two of the Founding Treaties, the Treaties establishing the ECSC and Euratom, contained provisions on research and technological development. In other words, Community research and technological development (RTD) essentially existed from the beginning. Research in the coal and steel sector was supported by an assistance programme as early as 1955, while a Joint Research Centre was set up within the framework of the Euratom. In the area of nuclear energy, however, Community programmes did not prove especially successful, since the Member States tended to focus on their own national projects. On the whole, coordinated Community research activities conducted within the framework of the two energy programmes were of limited significance.

Although from the seventies on, the Member States endeavoured to include further RTD areas (such as biotechnology, environmental protection and information technology), Community programmes all in all carried little weight.

By the eighties, the European Communities had fallen behind the United States and Japan in the field of technology. While, in the Communities, the number of patented inventions in high tech industries, such as electronics, pharmaceuticals and biotechnology, was decreasing year by year, Japan was registering a dynamic growth. Characteristically, in the USA and Japan, high tech products constituted half of the goods exported, while they represented a mere third of the EU's exports. The EU also spent less on RTD: 2% of its GDP was allocated for research purposes, while at the same time the United States and Japan both assigned 3% of their GDP to research and technological development.

By the eighties, it had become clear that the isolated RTD activities of the relatively small European states, characterised by outdated structures and obsolete organisational and marketing principles, could not be a match for the concentrated research potential of the American and Japanese competitors. This policy area also required more intense coordination and cooperation, while the Communities needed to assume more extensive responsibilities. The Treaty of Rome establishing the European Economic Community, however, had not provided a solid legal basis for a Community RTD policy. Therefore, recognising the need for concerted actions in the area, the Single European Act amended the Treaty by introducing research and technological development as a separate Title (presently Part III Title XVIII of the EC Treaty).

17.2. The system of research framework programmes

Pursuant to the Single European Act, Community RTD policy is implemented through multiannual framework programmes. The framework programmes outline the scientific and technological objectives for a period of several years and allocate the necessary financial resources. The framework programmes are put forward by the Commission and adopted by a qualified majority by the Council together with the Parliament (within the scope of the co-decision procedure). Within the framework programmes, several sub-programmes aimed at various fields or priorities are launched, which are presented by the Commission and adopted by the Council by a qualified majority vote following consultation with the Parliament. The Commission is responsible for the implementation of the programmes.

Three instruments assist the implementation of the framework programmes:
– The bulk of the budget of the framework programmes is allocated to so-called co-financed research activities. Here, research projects are partly financed by the Commission, up to a maximum level of 50%, and partly by companies, institutions and universities from the Member States.
– In certain cases, the Commission does not contribute financially to the research activities themselves but coordinates the concerted projects and bears the full cost of coordination.
– The EU also carries out its own research projects, which are implemented by the already-mentioned Joint Research Centre and 2,000 researchers working in its seven institutes located in five European cities.

The First Framework Programme was conducted prior to the Single European Act, between 1983 and 1987. The Second Framework Programme covered the period 1987–1991, the Third Framework Programme the period 1991–1994, and the Fourth Framework Programme 1994–1998. The Fourth Framework Programme brought major changes concerning the size and influence of the programmes. Its four-year budget amounted to ECU 13.1 billion compared to the previous budget of ECU 5.7 billion available for the period 1991–1994. The Fifth Framework Programme (1999–2002), introduced in 1999, was provided with a budget of EUR 15 billion. As the figures demonstrate, RTD has become one of the central EU policies, not least in view of its share of the overall EU budget. Following agricultural policy and structural and cohesion measures, RTD has been the third biggest expenditure of the Union.

Subject to the same conditions as the Member States, the Union's research framework programmes were also opened to non-member states that contribute financially[1]. Sixteen[2] non-member countries joined the EU's Fifth Research Framework Programme.

The first five framework programmes focused on information and communication technologies, industrial technologies, and research on the environment, biotechnology, energy and transportation. Attention was also paid to the management of intellectual resources, such as the training and mobility of researchers and cooperation between them. Growing emphasis has been laid on SMEs, which lack the necessary resources to conduct research and development activities. The Union provides financial assistance for SMEs to submit research proposals and to carry them out in specialised research institutions.

In the early 21st century, research policy – just like most European policy areas – is heavily influenced by the all-pervasive objective of the Lisbon strategy to turn the European Union into the most competitive knowledge-based economy in the world by 2010.[3] Naturally, research and technological development have a fundamental role to play in building this European knowledge-based society. On that basis, the European Commission, the European Parliament and the Member States committed themselves to creating a European Research Area (ERA). The Sixth Research Framework Programme, adopted in 2002 for the period 2002–2006, was primarily aimed at creating a real European Research Area.

The Sixth Framework Programme focused on three key objectives, within which there were various themes for specific programmes:

1. *Integrating and concentrating Community research:* This heading, which made up the bulk of the framework programme, covered activities aimed at integrating research at the European level. It focused on seven priority areas: 1) life sciences, genomics and biotechnology; 2) information society technologies; 3) nanotechnologies, knowledge-based multifunctional materials and new production processes; 4) aeronautics and space; 5) food safety and risks to health; 6) sustainable development, global change and ecosystems; 7) citizens and governance in a knowledge-based society.

---

[1] The associated countries' financial contributions to the framework programmes are supported also by Community resources.

[2] The then 12 candidate countries carrying on accession negotiations with the European Union, as well as Iceland, Liechtenstein, Norway and Israel.

[3] For more on the Lisbon strategy, see 1.12.3.1.

2. *Structuring the European Research Area:* This heading covered activities aimed at eliminating existing structural weaknesses and shortcomings in order to create a true European Research Area, such as: 1) research and innovation; 2) human resources and mobility; 3) research infrastructures; 4) science and society.

3. *Strengthening the foundations of the European Research Area:* The activities carried out under this heading were intended to step up coordination and to support the coherent development of research and innovation-stimulating policies and activities in Europe.

The Sixth Framework Programme had a total budget of EUR 17.5 billion, 13.345 billion of which was for Heading 1, 2.605 billion for Heading 2 and 320 million for Heading 3. An additional EUR 1.23 billion was earmarked within the framework of Euratom for research on nuclear energy.

In order to complement the objectives of the Lisbon strategy and to improve European competitiveness (in particular by catching up with Europe's main competitor: the USA), in March 2002, the European Council set the objective of increasing investment in research and technological development to 3% of GDP by 2010, one third financed by public funds and two thirds by the private sector. The EU has a large gap to close, since it has fallen behind the USA and Japan who, in 2001, invested 2.8% and 3.1% of their GDP (respectively) in research and development, while in the same year R&D spending in the EU was a measly 1.9%.

The 3% target was reconfirmed at the mid-term review of the Lisbon strategy and has become an emblematic Lisbon objective. Nonetheless, it is a fair bet to say that neither the EU as a whole nor many of the Member States will be able to meet that target. In 2004 the accession of ten new Member States – which are less developed and devote less of their limited resources to research – even pulled down the EU R&D spending average to 1.86%.[4] If anything, the gap between the two sides of the Atlantic has only widened: in 1994, European R&D expenditure (as a share of GDP) was 77% of that of the USA, which fell to 72% by 2004. The most disappointing trend is that the private sector has really fallen behind in recent years: in 2004, R&D investment by European companies (as a share of GDP) was 66% that of the American corporate sector. (For the public sphere this ratio was 86%.) Consequently, research and development has to be promoted both in the public but especially the private sector.

If the Union wants to narrow the gap between itself and its main rivals and boost its competitiveness – as the Lisbon strategy aspires to – then research and technological

---

[4] Realistic calculations based on current trends project an EU average of 2.2% for 2010.

development activities must intensify at the Community, national as well as the micro-economic level. It is against this backdrop that the Seventh Research Framework Programme was adopted in late 2006 for a period of seven years, corresponding to the 2007–2013 Financial Perspective.

When drawing up the budget of the new Framework Programme, it was clear that the funds available in the EU budget would not bring about drastic improvement in research at Union level (after all, the EU budget amounts to no more than 1% of the Member States' GDP, and only 4% of that EU budget is allocated to research, which means that Community funding for research is 0.04% of the Union's GDP). Despite their limited resources, the role of Community research programmes should not be underestimated – they coordinate national efforts and stimulate the Member States, thereby creating a multiplier effect and influencing national and corporate decisions. In its proposals for the 2007–2013 Financial Perspective published in February 2004, the Commission significantly increased spending on research, technological development and innovation compared to previous years, as these areas have a key role in strengthening the Union's competitiveness. The Commission put forward a total draft budget of EUR 72.7 billion for the seven-year Framework Programme, more than 10 billion annually (up from 4 billion in the previous period).

The Financial Perspective finally adopted by the Member States in December 2005[5] was considerably less ambitious than the Commission's original proposal. Spending was trimmed back heavily, and most of the cuts affected the Heading 'Competitiveness', which includes research funding. On this basis the Council and Parliament adopted the Seventh Research Framework Programme in December 2006 with a total budget of EUR 50.5 billion – over 7 billion per year, almost double than in the previous period – which is supplemented in the framework of Euratom with another EUR 2.7 billion for nuclear research for the years 2007–2011. As a general rule, the Framework Programme co-finances 50% of project costs, which can go up to 75% in the case of SMEs.

The Seventh Research Framework Programme is implemented through four specific programmes:

Cooperation
The Cooperation programme supports cross-border research projects contributing to sustainable development and improving competitiveness. It fosters collaboration between

_____
[5] For more details see 7.3.5.

industry and academia for Europe to gain leadership in key technology areas, such as: health; food, agriculture and fisheries, biotechnology; information and communications technologies; nanosciences, nanotechnologies, materials and new production technologies; energy; environment (including climate change); transport (including aeronautics); socio-economic sciences and the humanities; space; security. *Cooperation* has a total budget of EUR 32.4 billion.

Ideas
The Ideas programme is aimed at boosting the dynamism and promoting the excellence of European basic research through creating centres of excellence. By supporting basic research, it fosters healthy competition between Europe's best researchers. It is implemented by the new European Research Council (ERC), which in practice functions like a European research agency, and finances investigative research at the forefront of science and technology with great potential but no guarantee of success. The strategy and policy of the European Research Council is defined by a so-called Scientific Council, consisting of 22 independent scientists. The 7.5 billion *Ideas* budget is managed by the ERC.

People
The People programme is aimed at human resources development in research through activities focussing on training, career development, attracting scientists to Europe and retaining Europe's researchers. EUR 4.75 billion is earmarked for *People*.

Capacities
The Capacities programme is designed to help strengthen and optimise the knowledge capacities that Europe needs if it is to become a competitive knowledge-based economy. The programme is aimed at developing and optimising the use of research infrastructures, strengthening the innovation capacity of SMEs, creating regions of knowledge and bringing science closer to society. Its budget is EUR 4.1 billion.

In addition to the four specific programmes, the EU Joint Research Centre (JRC) has at its disposal EUR 1.7 billion for non-nuclear research. The JRC also oversees nuclear research funding from the Euratom Framework Programme (2.7 billion to be spent over the period 2007–2011), which focuses on fusion energy and developing the International

Thermonuclear Experimental Reactor. ITER could revolutionise nuclear power plants and the use of nuclear energy, and as such is the European Union's flagship research venture.

In addition to FP7, research and technological development in Europe could greatly benefit from the future European Institute of Technology. The idea of the EIT was proposed by the Commission in 2005 at the mid-term review of the Lisbon strategy. The Council reached an agreement on the Institute in June 2007, committing EUR 308.7 million for the years 2008–2013. The EIT should be able to begin operations in 2008 with its headquarters to be established from the above budget. Another six knowledge and innovation communities would operate in various locations, with the task of finding the answers to strategic long-term economic and social challenges. The Union expects the public and private sectors of Member States to contribute to the financing of the Institute and the network around it.

CHAPTER 18
ENVIRONMENTAL POLICY

18.1. Development of Community environmental policy

When the founding Member States drafted the Treaty of Rome in the fifties, they did not think it necessary to develop an environmental policy at Community level. Nonetheless, intensive economic growth, the fast pace of industrialisation and increasing energy consumption resulted in rising levels of environmental pollution. As damage to the environment was growing steadily worse all over Europe, at the beginning of the seventies the Member States came to recognise environmental protection as one of the areas that called for concerted Community efforts.

In October 1972, at the Paris Summit, the Heads of State or Government decided that a Community environmental policy was essential and initiated the process of designing the necessary legislative framework and common action programmes in the field of environmental protection. However, the effect and scope of the first two action programmes – introduced in 1973 and in 1977 – were limited. The objectives and basic principles of the Community environmental policy started to gain their true shape under the Third Action Programme set up in 1983. The Third Action Programme shifted the emphasis from treatment to prevention, which has been the guiding principle of the sector ever since.

The breakthrough came with the Single European Act, which amended the Treaty of Rome with new articles on environmental protection. The new provisions institutionalised Community environmental policy and its objectives under the Treaty (Part Three Title XIX of the EC Treaty). In accordance with the objective of establishing a single market, the emphasis of the policy has shifted to the introduction of common provisions (for example Community standards and quantifiable limits on air and water pollution).

The Treaty of Maastricht expanded the scope of environmental policy and supplemented it with new objectives. The increasing importance of environmental policy is shown by the fact that the Treaty of Maastricht incorporated into the EU Treaty the objective of environmental protection, linking the *principle of sustainable development* to the need to respect the environment. In compliance with the Treaty of Maastricht and the Treaty of Amsterdam, one of the fundamental principles now is to take account of environmental protection in all sectoral policies, namely to integrate environmental considerations into all other Community policies (Article 6 of the EC Treaty).

The main objectives of the Community environmental policy, as set out in the EC Treaty (Article 174), are:
- preserving, protecting and improving the quality of the environment;
- protecting human health;
- encouraging prudent and rational utilisation of natural resources; and
- promoting measures at international level to deal with regional or worldwide environmental problems.

As an established EU practice, in addition to the pursuit of the above objectives, Community environmental policy also observes the following basic principles:
- *the principle of prevention* (which has priority over remediation);
- *the principle of rectifying environmental hazards at source*;
- *the 'polluter pays' principle*;
- *the integration principle* (the need to integrate environmental considerations into all Community sectoral policies);
- *the principle of avoidance* (whereby, in relation to activities that may be environmentally hazardous, intervention measures must be taken prior to the manifestation of damage).

Thus, environmental policy has become a Community policy institutionalised by the Treaties. In the area of environmental protection, the Community's main responsibility is to provide a legislative framework for the activities of the Member States, to ensure the conditions that facilitate the cooperation of the Member States and the improvement of the quality of the environment at European and international levels. To this end, the EU adopts Community legislation and action programmes and provides the necessary financial instruments for the implementation of Community objectives.

The Commission plays a key role in environmental policy-making. On the one hand, it makes proposals for Community legislation on the environment and for Community action programmes while, on the other hand, it monitors their implementation by the Member States. The decisions on the protection of the environment are jointly adopted by the Council and the Parliament under the co-decision procedure, apart from a few exceptions[1]

---

[1] These exceptions are the following: issues primarily of a fiscal nature (environmental levies); measures related to spatial planning and water supply management; land use matters (except for waste management); the choice of a Member State between various energy sources and the general structure of its energy supply.

when the Council has the exclusive right of decision and the Parliament is only consulted. It must be noted that the environment is an area of Community law where the Treaty allows the Member States to adopt and apply rules stricter than those of the Community. Nonetheless, these measures must always be compatible with the Treaty.

18.2. Instruments of Community environmental policy

18.2.1. Environmental legislation

Environmental legislation in the EU is based on secondary legal sources, primarily directives. Since 1972, the Community has adopted several hundred pieces of legislation (mainly directives), chiefly concerned with limiting pollution by introducing minimum levels of protection and product specifications. Environmental legislation primarily covers air pollution control, water pollution control, waste management, noise reduction, nuclear safety, protection of flora and fauna and provisions on chemicals. Traditionally, the three key areas are waste management, water pollution and air pollution.

Community policy on waste management involves three strategies: eliminating and reducing waste at source, encouraging the recycling and re-use of waste and reducing pollution caused by waste incineration. The Community's approach has been to assign more responsibility to the producer. For instance, in accordance with a Directive adopted in 1997, end-of-life vehicles are to be collected and recycled at the manufacturer's expense. In the field of water pollution, Community legislation focuses on two objectives: the introduction of quality requirements and minimum quality levels of drinking water and the monitoring and reduction of emission limits. Wastewater management is regulated by strict Community rules.

Community policy on air pollution primarily involves the introduction of minimum levels of protection and the reduction of hazardous emissions. Recently, Community legislation has been particularly concerned with transport, where three objectives have been set up: the reduction of polluting emissions (e.g. through the use and development of catalytic converters), the reduction of fuel consumption (in collaboration with car manufacturers) and the promotion of "clean" vehicles through tax incentives. The Community underlines that combating air pollution is a world priority, as global warming and the growing depletion of ozone in the atmosphere are issues that require global cooperation. To this end, the EU is making serious efforts to be party to the drafting and implementation of international conventions and legislation. In this respect, the Union plays a leading role amongst the world's most powerful economic regions – for instance in the enforcement and implementation of the Kyoto Protocol – and is firmly committed to keeping the issue of environmental protection on the agenda of international talks. For instance, the EU tried on a number of occasions to persuade the United States to implement the Kyoto Protocol after the US announced, at the start of 2001, that it did not wish to ratify the Protocol. The issue has been a cause of severe friction in EU-USA relations. The Kyoto Protocol entered into force in February 2005, thanks to the Union's continuous efforts; the EU managed to convince Russia to ratify the Protocol, thereby achieving the required limit for the Kyoto Protocol to enter into force.[2] In the Kyoto Protocol, the EU undertook to reduce greenhouse gas emissions from the 1990 level by 8% during 2008–2012.

In recent years, the application of Community legislation has featured prominently among Community objectives in the field of environmental protection. While Community legislation on environmental issues has become extensive, its transposition into national law and its enforcement at national level have been lagging behind and in some cases have never come about, which has impeded the realisation of sectoral objectives. The Sixth Action Programme for the Environment for the period 2002–2010 therefore establishes as priority issues the improvement of the application of environmental legislation and the more effective monitoring of the Member States and various polluting sources.

Within the framework of harmonising environmental legislation, modernising the regulatory framework for chemicals has increasingly been on the agenda. The most important development on this front was when, in October 2003, the European Commission adopted a proposal for a new EU regulatory framework for chemicals. The so-called REACH (Registration, Evaluation and Authorisation of CHemicals) Directive was adopted by the Council and the European Parliament in December 2006, following lengthy debates and negotiations.

---

[2] The Kyoto Protocol annexed to the UN Framework Convention on Climate Change was opened for ratification in 1998. The required limit for its entry into force was that 55 of the parties ratified it, which should include those countries that were responsible for at least 55% of pre-1990 carbon-dioxide emissions. For a long time, it seemed that the Protocol would not enter into force; even though 120 countries ratified the Protocol, in the absence of the USA (the world's biggest CO_2 emitter), the second criterion was not fulfilled until Russia decided to sign up to it. By 2007, close to 170 countries (responsible for 60% of all carbon emissions) had signed up to Kyoto – the USA and Australia remain the only two developed industrial countries that have failed to ratify the Protocol.

REACH has two aims. Firstly, it hopes to make European chemical legislation more uniform and effective, by centralising the registration and evaluation of chemical substances. Secondly, it is aimed at protecting human health and the environment by introducing a more structured system for the registration and handling of chemicals and by introducing better risk analysis. The Directive will enter into force gradually from 2007; it will be phased in over a period of 11 years at the end of which, in 2018, all chemicals will have to be registered with the European Chemicals Agency (ECHA) in Helsinki.

In the field of nature protection, the Natura 2000 European ecological network is an important part of the Community efforts for harmonisation. Natura 2000 ensures the preservation and recovery of biodiversity through the protection of natural habitat and wildlife fauna and flora. The task of the Member States is to designate protected areas and cooperate according to predefined rules.

18.2.2. Environmental action programmes

Community action programmes define the framework of the Community environmental policy. They set out the challenges and priorities for a given period and constitute a framework for Community measures on the environment, from legislation to the implementation of common projects. The Fifth Action Programme of the nineties and the Sixth Action Programme, which was introduced in the new millennium, presented a new, more complex and comprehensive Community strategy on the environment and developed the protection of the environment as one of the Community's priority objectives.

18.2.2.1. The Fifth Environmental Action Programme

The Fifth Environmental Action Programme of the EU, for the period 1992–2000, adopted a new approach to the problems of the sector. Pursuant to the provisions of the Maastricht Treaty, the programme focused on guaranteeing the necessary conditions for sustainable development. The programme concentrated on the following priorities:
- improving the sustainable management of natural resources (soil, water, forests, etc.);
- promoting an integrated approach to combating pollution;
- stepping up recycling activities;
- reducing the consumption of energy from non-renewable sources;
- promoting prudent, environment-conscious mobility management;

- improving the quality of urban environment;
- improving health, reducing industrial hazards and improving nuclear safety.

The priority objectives of the programme were to integrate environmental concerns into other policy areas and establish the concept of shared responsibility with national governments, the business sector and the public. The programme particularly underlined the importance of Community intervention to preserve and improve the environment in the following identified target sectors: industry, energy, transport, agriculture and tourism. These policy areas have a particularly large impact on the environment and may be more effectively regulated by concerted Community actions.

To facilitate the achievement of the set objectives, the programme provided for the development of new instruments, such as the promotion of the introduction of environment taxes and incentives for producers who respect the environment and who produce environmentally friendly products.

18.2.2.2. The Sixth Environmental Action Programme

The Fifth Environmental Action Programme brought about a reduction in trans-boundary air pollution, better water quality and a reduction in substances that deplete the ozone layer. On the other hand, less progress was made than had been foreseen, the integration of environmental concerns into other Community policies was slow and the Union was still far from achieving the objective of sustainable development. Therefore, in the Sixth Environmental Action Programme for the period 2002–2010, the Community seeks to give further impetus to environmental policy by pursuing its action in the areas already covered by the Fifth Action Programme, addressing the same priority objectives (the principles of sustainable development and integration of environmental aspects into other policy areas), while also defining new targets.

The Sixth Action Programme focuses on four priority areas:
- climate change,
- nature and biodiversity,
- environment and health,
- natural resources and waste.

In the above four areas, the Sixth Action Programme proposes five priority strategic actions:
- improving the implementation of existing legislation;
- effectively integrating environmental concerns into all relevant policy areas;
- encouraging closer cooperation with the business sector and consumers;
- improving the quality and accessibility of information provided to people as private citizens;
- promoting environmentally-conscious behaviour towards land-use.

The Sixth Action Programme was drawn up in the light of the Community's strategy of sustainable development, elaborated in 2001, which further increases the importance of environmental policy among Community priorities. The Union's sustainable development strategy is based on the principle that the economic, social and environmental effects of all policies should be examined in a coordinated way and taken into account in decision-making.[3]

18.2.3. The European Environment Agency

One of the primary objectives of environmental policy during the last decade has been to ensure that the public is properly informed on the state of the environment and effectively educated about environmental matters and that public awareness of environmental problems is improved. In this respect, the unobstructed flow of information and data is of fundamental importance. To this end, in 1990, the Council adopted a Regulation[4] establishing the European Environment Agency. The Agency started its operations in 1994 with its headquarters located in Copenhagen. Its main objectives are: to provide the Community, the Member States and third countries with information on the state of the environment; to gather, evaluate and disseminate data for the countries concerned; to direct the countries' attention to the need for effective implementation of environmental policies, and; to develop forecasting techniques to enable preventive measures to be taken. A key objective of the Agency is to assist the EU in promoting sustainable development.

18.2.4. Financial instruments

The EU allocates financial resources to sustain the objectives and action programmes implemented within the framework of the Community environmental policy.

Regional support is available from the Structural Funds for projects that aim to improve the state of the environment in a particular region. The Cohesion Fund, supporting the less prosperous Member States, allocates half of its total budget to environmental investments (between 2000 and 2006, Greece, Ireland, Portugal and Spain were eligible for support totalling EUR 9 billion, while the 10 new Member States received up to EUR 3.8 billion between 2004 and 2006). Due to enlargement, the Cohesion Fund has a reinforced budget for the period 2007–2013: in these seven years, EUR 26.5 billion will be available for environmental projects in the 15 eligible countries. In addition, regions under the Convergence Objective can decide to use the financial support of the European Regional Development Fund for environmental investment.[5]

---

[3] See 1.12.3.1.
[4] Regulation 1210/90/EEC, amended by Regulation 933/99/EC.
[5] For details, see 13.4.

Research projects on environmental protection also receive substantial financial support within the framework of Community research and development programmes.

The European Investment Bank issues loans for environmental development and investment projects. Some 20% of the projects financed by the Bank are connected with environmental protection.

In addition, in 1992, the EU set up a fund for the environment, the LIFE[6] programme, which co-finances environmental activities in the Community and in certain non-Community countries (Eastern European and Mediterranean countries). For these countries, participation in the programme is subject to the condition that they participate financially. LIFE has completed three phases: the first phase, from 1992 to 1995, was granted EUR 400 million, the second phase, between 1996 and 1999, was granted EUR 450 million, the third phase, for the period 2000–2004, had a total budget of EUR 640 million. The third phase was extended until the end of 2006, to coincide with the Union's financial perspectives, with additional funding of EUR 317.2 million. In these years, LIFE essentially consisted of three thematic components: LIFE-Nature (47% of the total budget), which financed mostly nature conservation projects; LIFE-Environment (47% of the total budget), which granted support to demonstration projects that integrated considerations relating to the environment, and; LIFE-third countries (6% of the total budget), which financed projects implemented in regions bordering the EU.

The European Commission submitted its proposals for the 2007–2013 financial perspectives in 2004. In its proposals, the Commission put forward the idea of launching a new, more comprehensive environmental facility with the name LIFE+. Council and Parliament finally adopted the Regulation on launching LIFE+ in May 2007, committing EUR 2.14 billion to the programme for seven years, more than double LIFE's budget in the previous period. LIFE+ seeks to strengthen EU action in fields such as: combating climate change, addressing threats to human health, preserving biodiversity, and managing natural resources and waste in a sustainable manner. LIFE+ consists of three elements: 'LIFE+ Nature and Biodiversity', 'LIFE+ Environmental Policy and Governance', 'LIFE+ Information and Communication'. Participation in LIFE+ is open to neighbouring countries.

18.2.5. Integrated action against climate change

The Integrated Climate Change and Energy Policy[7], launched at the European Council of 8–9 March 2007, can be considered a new pillar of Community environmental policy and a key EU achievement of recent years. The integrated policy is aimed at tackling climate

---

[6] The English acronym 'LIFE' comes from the abbreviation of the French "l'instrument financier pour l'environnement" (meaning: financial instrument for the environment).

[7] For more, see 16.3.

change and global warming and reflects the conviction that successful environmental protection should be aimed at integrating environmental aspects into all other policies, in particular the transport and energy sectors, as the main polluters. This is what makes the Integrated Climate Change and Energy Policy a milestone.

We have been hearing for a long time that the world's countries must join hands in the fight against global warming and climate change. The European Union has been playing a leading role in the application of the Kyoto Protocol, arguing in multilateral talks for its extension beyond its expiry in 2012. However, some important countries (especially the two biggest polluters: the USA and China) are reluctant to engage in increased global action.

The EU has recognised that the best way of putting pressure on its partners is to lead by example and make a voluntary commitment to tackle climate change. The Union's target is to limit the global average temperature increase to 2°C compared with pre-industrial levels. To this end, the Member States made a unilateral strategic pledge at the March 2007 summit to increase the share of renewable energy in their consumption to 20% by 2020 and to cut carbon-dioxide emissions from the 1990 level by 20% by 2020 (the Kyoto target was only 8% by 2012).

The European Council also set the objective of reducing the emission of greenhouse gases from the 1990 level by 60–80% by 2050. Alongside these objectives and voluntary limitations, the EU made global target commitments a key agenda item of the June 2007 G8 summit (uniting the world's leading powers). Due to the pressure applied by the EU, the G8 finally agreed to set specific targets, if less ambitious than Europe's, and that greenhouse gas emissions must be halved by 2050 and pledged to act jointly for the adoption of this objective in a UN framework.[8]

---

[8] Putting the agreement into a UN framework is important because emerging, developing countries have become big emitters (China has caught up with the USA in emission levels), but are not required to cut emissions under the Kyoto Protocol (that is why easily agreed to ratifiy it). Kyoto will require a major overhaul after 2012, when it is due to expire.

CHAPTER 19
CONSUMER POLICY

19.1. The evolution of Community consumer policy

The primary objective of the Treaty of Rome was to establish the common market, removing economic barriers, broadening the range of products and services, improving their quality, and thus promoting the needs of consumers. Nonetheless, the Treaty of Rome did not enshrine consumer protection as a community policy in its own right when setting the objectives of the common market. Without a Community consumer policy, each Member State adopted its own set of rules on consumer protection. However, the diversity of national product specifications and safety requirements to a certain extent contributed to inhibiting the development of a true common market.

It was not until the Paris Summit in 1972 that the Heads of State or Government first called for the development of a Community-level policy of consumer protection. The Member States sought to bring the integration process closer to the citizens by highlighting the areas directly affecting their daily lives. As a result, in 1975, the Commission adopted the first action programme on consumer policy in compliance with the Council's decision. The programme set out the five fundamental principles, which became the basis for Community legislation in this area:
- *The right to the protection of health and safety* (when properly used, no product or service may pose any danger to consumers or else it must be withdrawn from the market).
- *The right to the protection of economic interests* (consumers are entitled to protection against certain sales practices with regards to loans, credits, contracts and follow-up services).
- *The right to damages* (consumers are entitled to compensation for damage caused by faulty services or products).
- *The right to information and education* (consumers must be informed about product and service features and their safe use).
- *The right to representation* (consumers' interests must be represented in the development of Community policies).

In addition, the action programme highlighted the horizontal quality of consumer protection and the need to integrate consumers' interests into Community policies.

In addition to launching the first Action Programme, the Member States at the Paris Summit also decided to establish a committee to assist Community decision-making in relation to consumer affairs. The Committee, which was set up in 1973 and since 2003 has been called the European Consumer Consultative Committee, comprises one representative from each national consumer protection authority and European consumers' organisations. The European Commission consults the Committee regularly (four times a year) on decisions concerning consumer interests.

As a result of the first action programme, Community legislation on consumer protection was put in place. Initially, the Community legislated in the field of cosmetic safety, food labelling and misleading advertising. It was not until the Single European Act that Community legislation on consumer protection really got under way. With the development of the common market, there was a greater need than before to enact common measures on consumer protection. The Single European Act incorporated the notion of the high-level protection of consumers' interests into Article 100a of the Treaty on the harmonisation of legislation on the internal market (now Article 95 of the EC Treaty). Hence, consumer policy became a fundamental instrument for completing the single market. Within the framework of the general policy of establishing the single market, legislation on consumer protection - in compliance with the overall Community harmonisation process - shifted from the former product and sector-oriented approach to horizontal regulation. Legislation gathered new momentum in the areas of general product safety, cross-border payments, unfair contract terms, and distance selling. In parallel with the completion of the single market, the corpus of Community consumer protection law was instituted.

Notwithstanding the results achieved by the Single European Act, the real breakthrough in institutionalising consumer protection policy came with the Treaty of Maastricht. The Treaty of Maastricht introduced a separate title on consumer protection (Part Three Title XIV of the EC Treaty) and thus enshrined consumer protection as a fully-fledged Community policy, establishing the concrete legal basis for Community action. The need to strengthen consumer protection was also included among the fundamental principles of the Treaty (Article 3 of the EC Treaty). The Maastricht Treaty gave new momentum to Community consumer policy in various fields, such as financial services, foodstuffs and guarantees. The focal importance of consumer policy is demonstrated by the fact that, in 1995, the Commission set up an autonomous Directorate-General for Consumer Protection.

In the mid-nineties, following the Treaty of Maastricht, consumer policy faced new challenges arising from globalisation, the emerging information society and the development of new industries (e.g. biotechnology). Accordingly, the action programme for the period 1996–1998 focused on three priorities:

- financial services, essential public utility services and food products as sectors of primary importance;
- consumer education (aimed mainly at encouraging sustainable consumption behaviour and facilitating access to the information society);
- assistance for the countries of Central and Eastern Europe and developing countries in order to help them to develop their own consumer-oriented policy.

However, in the middle of the nineties, the BSE crisis (mad cow disease) had significant effects on consumer policy. It put the above priorities on the back burner and placed food safety on the political agenda as the number one priority. In order to boost consumer confidence shaken by the BSE crisis, at the Luxemburg Summit in December 1997, the Member States stated that the production and supply of safe food must be one of the EU's policy priorities.

Accordingly, the Treaty of Amsterdam gave fresh impetus to Community consumer policy. It amended the relevant provision of the Treaty (Article 153 of the EC Treaty), providing a more precise definition of consumer policy activities, and stated that the Community must contribute to the protection of the health, safety and economic interests of consumers and promote their right to information and education. The Treaty of Amsterdam also introduced the notion that consumer protection requirements must be taken into account in other Community policies and activities under the EC Treaty.

In the area of consumer protection, the Council adopts necessary measures jointly with Parliament through the co-decision procedure. However, these measures cannot prevent the Member States from maintaining or adopting stricter provisions, which must – nevertheless – be compatible with the EC Treaty.

In certain cases, in the interests of consumer protection, the Member States have the right to restrict the free movement of goods in the single market. Article 30 of the Treaty states that, on the grounds of protecting the health of humans, animals or plants, the Member States may adopt protective provisions against the trade of certain products. For instance, following the outbreak of the BSE (mad cow disease) crisis in the UK, the Member States imposed a total export ban on British beef. Citing consumer protection as a reason, the Member States may also challenge the application of the principle of mutual recognition, and in so doing may restrict the free movement of goods in line with the 1979 'Cassis de Dijon' ruling of the European Court of Justice (which referred to the so-called mandatory requirements of the Community).[1]

---

[1] See 6.1.2.

19.2. Current trends in Community consumer policy

The 1999–2001 action programme on consumer protection was adopted against the background of the new challenges and the provisions of the Amsterdam Treaty, with the following major fields of activity:

- *consumer representation and education* (entailing more systematic and effective dialogue between consumer associations and between consumers and business, the expansion of information and advice centres and the launch of appropriate information campaigns);
- *consumer health and safety* (based on the best possible scientific advice on consistent analysis of risks);
- *the economic interests of consumers* (with steps being taken to ensure that the existing legislation is properly applied and keeps pace with developments in products and services, with particular reference to financial services, telecommunications, transport and the reform of the Common Agricultural Policy).

In January 1999, the joint decision of the Council and the Parliament established the *General Framework* for Community Activities in Favour of Consumers until 31 December 2003. The programme, with a budget of EUR 112 million, identified the following four areas where Community actions were to be taken:

- protecting the health and safety of consumers as regards trade of products and services;
- protecting the economic and legal interests of consumers, including access to dispute resolution;
- educating and informing consumers about their protection and rights;
- promoting the representation of consumers' interests.

Under the framework programme, the European Union provided support to non-governmental non-profit-making organizations representing the interests of consumers at European level, which contribute to the realization of the set objectives at Community level.

Following this general framework, the consumer policy strategy for 2000–2006 set three key objectives:

- *Ensuring a high common level of consumer protection*: This objective means harmonising not just the safety of goods and services, but also those economic and legal aspects that give consumers the confidence necessary to conduct transactions anywhere in the internal market.
- *Effective enforcement of consumer protection rules*: This objective focuses on administrative cooperation between the Member-State authorities.
- *Involvement of consumer organisations in EU policies*: The main actions for achieving this objective are the revision of mechanisms for the participation of consumer organisations in EU policy-making and the establishment of education and capacity-building projects with such organisations (for example through training).

The Parliament and the Council adopted a new general framework for implementing the strategy. This general framework serves as a financing instrument for the implementation of the strategy, making available EUR 72 million for the years between 2004 and 2007, with EUR 54 million until the end of 2006. Within this Framework, four areas of action were set, which were essentially the same as those defined in the previous general framework.

Recently, the most important result achieved in the area of consumer protection has undoubtedly been the reform of food safety legislation adopted by the Parliament and the Council in January 2002, which aims at improving food safety in Europe and providing it with a new framework. The primary objective of the reform, which focuses on the greatest recent challenge of consumer protection, namely the restoration of consumer trust in food safety[2], is to ensure that, in the food industry, only safe foodstuffs and raw materials are marketed and enter the food chain. The Regulation[3] for setting up the European Food Safety Authority (EFSA), which was initiated by the Nice Summit of December 2000, constitutes the key element of the package of laws adopted. Pursuant to the Regulation, the Authority was set up in 2002 and is located in Parma. The responsibility of the European Food Safety Authority is to provide information for consumers as an independent organization, to provide scientific advice for Community legislation and to alert relevant Community and national bodies promptly in the case of a food safety emergency. Overall, the Authority serves as a point of reference in the area of consumer protection. Legislative work in this field did not stop with the setting up of the EFSA; the *acquis* now covers the entire process of food production ('from farm to fork', 'from stable to table'), harmonising food hygiene rules.

In April 2005, the European Commission submitted its proposal for a Community action programme for health and consumer policy in the next financial perspectives. The proposal, bearing the title 'Healthier, safer and more confident citizens – health and consumer protection programme 2007–2013', indicated the new approach of combining health and consumer policy. However taking into account Parliament's opinion, the Council and Parliament finally decided to continue the practice of managing the two areas separately

---

[2] Consumer trust has been shaken by events such as the BSE crisis or the dioxin crisis in Belgium, which became Europe-wide scandals and shattered the image of the European food industry.

[3] Regulation 178/2002/EC of the European Parliament and of the Council of 28 January 2002 laying down the general principles and requirements of food law, establishing the European Food Safety Authority and laying down procedures in matters of food safety.

under two distinct action programmes. As a result, an independent Community action programme on consumer protection was adopted in December 2006, with a budget of EUR 156.8 million for the period 2007–2013. The programme is based on the following two objectives:

- ensuring a high level of consumer protection, notably through improved information on consumer-related data, better consultation and better representation of consumers' interests;
- ensuring the effective application of consumer protection rules, notably through cooperation between authorities and organisations responsible for the implementation of consumer legislation, information and education.

The programme is open for participation for EEA countries, candidate countries, countries of the Western Balkans, as well as the Union's eastern and southern neighbours included in the European Neighbourhood Policy.

Following the adoption of the Action Programme, in March 2007 the Commission published a Community Consumer Policy Strategy for 2007–2013, which was endorsed by the Council. The strategy outlined three main objectives:

- To empower EU consumers, by offering them real choices, accurate information, market transparency and the confidence that comes from effective protection and solid rights.
- To enhance EU consumers' welfare in terms of price, choice, quality, diversity, affordability and safety.
- To protect consumers effectively from the serious risks and threats that they cannot tackle as individuals.

According to the strategy, when putting forward legislative proposals, the Commission will try to take into consideration new market trends, changed retail and marketing practices and shopping habits (such as cross-border online shopping or new types of financial services) and update existing legislation accordingly.

CHAPTER 20
PUBLIC HEALTH POLICY

20.1. The evolution of Community public health policy

For a long time, health policy was not developed at Community level and each Member State pursued its own course of actions in the area. The breakthrough came with the Treaty of Maastricht, which sought to deepen the European integration process, which had been focussing mainly on economic aspects, by introducing various policies that were not explicitly economic, including health policy. The Maastricht Treaty introduced public health policy as a separate title (now Part Three Title XIII of the EC Treaty).

Public health policy aims to improve the health of all citizens, and includes comprehensive and complex activities aimed at improving public health and preventing human illness and diseases. This is reflected in the EC Treaty, pursuant to the provisions of which the Community must contribute to ensuring a high level of human health protection by complementing the actions of Member States.

Hence the legal base of Community public health policy was created in Maastricht. Nevertheless, the importance of this step was diminished by the fact that the need to harmonise legislation was not incorporated into the relevant provisions of the EC Treaty. As a result, public health policy at the Community level has been limited essentially to encouraging cooperation between the Member States in various fields. While the Community contributes to improving the state of public health in the Community by implementing incentive measures, the management of health services and the provision of health care have remained the exclusive responsibility of the Member States.

Community public health policy – unlike consumer and environment policies, which are regulated by a common legislative framework – is only concerned with lending support to the efforts of the Member States in developing strategies, implementing common objectives and encouraging the flow of information within the Community; accordingly, it is primarily based on adopting and pursuing Community action programmes.

The Treaty of Amsterdam did not introduce very important changes in Community public health policy either; nonetheless, as a matter of principle, it is of significance that the Treaty of Amsterdam amended the EC Treaty by incorporating into it the provision that a high level of human health protection must be ensured in the definition and implementation of all Community policies and activities. Yet, the harmonisation of national legislation as an instrument was still not included and thus health policy remained a Community activity of lesser weight. Health policy at EU level has continued to focus on managing Community programmes that promote cooperation between the Member States in certain areas, with the aim of meeting some common objectives.

In the areas of public health policy that fall within the competence of the Union[1], the Council acts jointly with the Parliament through the co-decision procedure. The Council may also adopt recommendations acting by a qualified majority on a Commission proposal.

20.2. The main trends of Community action in the field of public health

In the nineties, within the framework established by the Maastricht Treaty, EU action focused on formulating Community public health programmes. In the decade following the adoption of the Treaty, Union action was primarily taken in the form of the following eight health programmes:

 - *Health promotion*: the programme focused on improving the general state of health in the EU by raising public awareness of risk factors and encouraging healthy lifestyles, through information and education campaigns (particularly in the areas of nutrition, smoking, alcohol consumption, drug abuse, mental health, physical training, etc.).
 - *Health monitoring*: the programme aimed at establishing a Community monitoring system, to enable the measurement of health indicators and trends, promote the development, monitoring and evaluation of Community programmes and provide information to the Member States, in order to help them to develop their own health policies.
 - *AIDS and other communicable diseases*: the programme focused on preventing the spread of AIDS and other communicable diseases (and on reducing mortality rates); emphasis was placed on the promotion of cooperation between the Member States, the coordination of their preventive policies and measures and support for NGOs.
 - *Cancer*: the programme promoted various activities to help combat cancer (such as information campaigns, professional training, research, early detection, etc.).
 - *Rare diseases*: the programme focused on improving the flow of information and raising awareness of rare diseases.

---

[1] These are the following: measures setting high standards of quality and safety of organs and tissues of human origin, blood and blood derivatives; measures in the veterinary and phytosanitary field which have as their direct objective the protection of public health; incentives for protecting and improving human health.

- *Injury prevention*: the programme supported public activities aimed at the prevention of injuries, in particular domestic and leisure-related accidents.
- *Pollution-related diseases*: the programme promoted measures aimed at reducing exposure to pollution (e.g. the Community proposal on reducing electro-magnetic radiation).
- *Prevention of drug-dependence*: the Treaty of Maastricht defined combating drug addiction as a priority area within public health policy; accordingly, the programme focused on a better understanding of the problem of drug-dependence (its reasons, consequences and prevention) and on stepping up information, education and training campaigns, particularly among young people.

Community-level legislation in the area of public health was relatively limited in the beginning. Nonetheless, during the past decade, health-related Community provisions and measures pursuing the objectives of public health policy have been regularly adopted, since in the framework of completing the single market, several other Community policies which also have a significant health impact (agriculture, consumer protection, environment, transport, etc.) have been the subject of extensive legislation. Legislative activities have been particularly intensive in the area of phytosanitation, veterinary hygiene and the control of medicinal substances.

Various Community or coordinated activities pursued in the framework of other Community policies also facilitate the implementation of health objectives. For instance, health and biotechnology are priority areas within the Research Framework Programmes while, in the context of the third pillar, the police, customs and judiciary of the Member States cooperate closely to combat drug trafficking and drug consumption. The above-mentioned Community activities adhere to the provisions of the Treaty of Amsterdam calling for the integration of health concerns into other EU policy areas.

At the turn of the millennium, the European Commission proposed the development of a new public health strategy for the European Community. The strategy has two major instruments: an action programme with comprehensive objectives based on the Community public health programmes and an integrated health strategy which, in accordance with the provisions of the Treaty of Amsterdam, calls for the integration of the principle of health protection into all sectoral policies (particularly the single market, environmental protection, consumer protection and employment and social policy).

The action programme for 2003–2008, which was adopted in 2002 based on the strategy and whose total budget amounts to some EUR 312 million, contained three main policy aspects:

- improving health information and awareness at all levels of society;
- creating a mechanism for responding rapidly to major health threats;
- addressing health determinants, notably harmful factors linked to lifestyle.

The action programme is open also to EEA and candidate countries.

Recently, especially since food safety issues have been at the forefront of public attention, the objectives of public health and consumer policy have become increasingly inter-related. This was demonstrated by the European Commission's proposal for a Community action programme for 2007–2013 in the area of health and consumer policies, which was submitted in April 2005 and has the title 'Healthier, safer, more confident citizens: a health and consumer protection strategy'. However taking into account Parliament's opinion, the Council and Parliament finally decided to continue the practice of managing the two areas separately under two distinct action programmes. The action programme for health is based on the following three objectives:

- improving citizens' health security;
- promoting health to improve prosperity and solidarity;
- generating and disseminating health knowledge.

The action programme has a budget of EUR 365.6 million, its implementation will start in 2008 when the previous action programme runs out.

CHAPTER 21
EDUCATION, VOCATIONAL TRAINING AND YOUTH POLICIES

21.1. The creation of education, vocational training and youth policies at Community level

Education, vocational training and youth policies first appeared at the Community level in the Treaty of Maastricht. The Member States sought to deepen the European integration process that had been focusing mainly on economic aspects by introducing various policies directly concerning the citizens of the Union. This aspiration was expressed by the Maastricht Treaty, which highlighted the importance of areas such as education, culture and health.

The EC Treaty, as amended by the Treaty of Maastricht and the Treaty of Amsterdam (Articles 149 and 150), stipulates that in the field of education, vocational training and youth policies, the Community should contribute to the development of a high standard of education and the implementation of vocational training policy, by encouraging cooperation between the Member States and by supporting and complementing their action. The Treaty underlines that each State retains exclusive responsibility for the content of teaching and the organisation of its education system, whereas the Community has to respect the cultural and linguistic diversity of the Member States.

Pursuant to the Treaty, in the field of education and vocational training, the Community (the Council and the Parliament jointly under the co-decision procedure) may adopt incentive measures; however, it is not entitled to approximate the laws of the Member States in this field. Given the exclusion on harmonisation, the scope of Community education policy is essentially limited to launching Community programmes and initiatives and establishing objectives that facilitate cooperation between the Member States. The education policy of the EU supplements and supports the national policies of the Member States, who retain their exclusive right to decision-making.

It must be noted that, besides supplementing national activities, Community education policy also aims at promoting the implementation of other Community activities. On the one hand, it supports study abroad - the mobility of students and teachers - which strengthens the feeling of unity among the citizens of the Union and reinforces the process of European integration. On the other hand, it contributes to the successful implementation of other Community policies (e.g. social policy and employment, research and technological development, environment, etc.). The latter is becoming increasingly important, since the expansion of globalisation, modern technologies and information society bring about the inter-penetration of various sectoral policies. No results can be achieved without synchronising the objectives and instruments of the Union's policies, in which process education and training, which affect nearly all Community activities, take a prominent part.

Although harmonisation of the legal provisions of the Member States is excluded from the scope of Community education policy, the extensive approximation of legislation concerning the free movement of persons is closely interlinked with this field. The free movement of workers can only be guaranteed if the Member States recognise each other's certificates and degrees; without any type of recognition, study abroad would also be less attractive. Therefore, the Community sought to enforce the concept of mutual recognition from the beginning; however, progress was slow. Ultimately, a Directive concerning the general system for the recognition of higher education degrees, diplomas and certificates was adopted in 1989, while another Directive adopted in 1992 covered diplomas and certificates at a lower level.[1] This framework legislation virtually grants "semi-automatic" accreditation, which means that the Member States recognise each other's diplomas if there is no significant discrepancy between their educational systems regarding duration and content; if the divergence is considerable, the applicant may be required to undertake further professional experience, an adaptation period or an aptitude test.[2]

21.2. The functioning of Community education, vocational training and youth policy

Devoid of legislative harmonisation, education, vocational training and youth policies have been pursued through Community programmes since the Treaty of Maastricht. The programmes created in the nineties functioned as follows, until the turn of the millennium:
- *Socrates* was the Community programme in the field of education. It encouraged study abroad, student mobility, exchange programmes for students and teachers, language learning and the exchange of information and good practice at all levels of education. In the period 1995–1999, the Socrates budget amounted to EUR 850 million. Support was allocated to finance the studies and employment of 275,000 students and teachers

---

[1] See 6.2.1.2.
[2] Special directives concerning the recognition of diplomas such as lawyers and doctors have also been adopted.

in host Member States, and to assist 1,500 universities, 850 schools and 500 cross-border projects.
- The *Leonardo* programme sought to promote cooperation in the field of vocational training, mostly in relation to activities designed to increase the EU's competitiveness and facilitate the development of the information society. Between 1995 and 1999, it supported over 3,000 projects with a total investment of EUR 730 million and encouraged the mobility of 130,000, mainly young people.
- In the period 1995–1999, the *Youth for Europe* programme supported the education of young people outside the formal educational system. Its total budget of EUR 126 million supported projects involving over 400,000 young people. In 1998, an additional new programme, the *European Voluntary Service for Young People* (EVS) was established, which allocated EUR 47.5 million between 1998 and 1999 to support young people engaging in unpaid, voluntary activity in a host Member State.

By the end of the nineties, in the context of improving EU competitiveness, the two areas of maintaining a high level of employment and developing the information society – which are inseparable from education policy – had become increasingly prominent. In these areas, the EU sought to reinforce Community actions, which called for the adjustment of education policy objectives. To improve the competitiveness of the present and future work force, two new initiatives were highlighted: lifelong learning and *e*-Learning, which are essential instruments for the extension of a knowledge-based society in the 21st century.

The Lisbon strategy adopted at the EU summit in March 2000 outlined the new priorities for education policy, emphasising the objective of the EU to become the most competitive and dynamic knowledge-based economy in the world.[3] In compliance with this fundamental concept, the Lisbon strategy established various objectives relating to education policy to be achieved by 2010, the most important of which were the following:
- halving the number of persons aged 18–24 who have completed only the first stage of secondary education and who are not continuing their studies;
- ensuring that at least 85% of 22-year-olds complete upper-secondary education;
- bringing about an increase of at least 15% in the number of graduates in maths, science and technology;

---

[3] See 1.12.3.1.

- promoting lifelong learning and achieving an average level of participation in lifelong learning of 12.5% of the adult working age population (age 25–64);
- developing a European certificate of competence in information technology;
- promoting the mobility of students, teachers, trainers and researchers;
- improving the synergy of employment and education markets, ensuring that every young person is offered a job, apprenticeship or additional training or other employability measure within four months of completing their studies.

In accordance with the new challenges and tasks outlined by the Lisbon strategy, the Council and the Parliament adopted a reform of the Community's education, vocational training and youth programmes for the period 2000–2006. As a result of the reform, since 2000, Community programmes have been implemented on the basis of more focussed objectives, simplified procedures, decentralised management, more flexible and closer relationships between programmes, the application of new technologies and the accentuation of lifelong learning. Support for the 2000–2006 period was focused on the following activities:

- Within the framework of the *Socrates* programme, promoting lifelong learning was highlighted alongside encouraging mobility, enhancing the quality of education and furthering the process of educational innovation. The programme, which consisted of five sub-programmes and three pilot programmes, was allocated a budget of EUR 1.85 million for the period 2000–2006. Erasmus – which was the dominant sub-programme of Socrates[4], receiving half of the total budget – sought to enhance higher education[5], Comenius focused on school education, Grundtvig on adult education, Lingua on language learning, while Minerva sponsored Information and Communication Technologies (ICT) in education. The pilot programmes aimed to enhance innovation in educational systems, coordinate joint actions with other Community programmes and support other accompanying measures.
- The *Leonardo* programme concentrated on the improvement of technical knowledge (mainly of young people), continuous education, the promotion of an entrepreneurial spirit, innovation and language learning. For the period 2000–2006, the programme had a budget of EUR 1.15 billion.
- In 2000, the two former programmes 'Youth for Europe' and EVS were merged into a single programme under the name of *Youth*. The new programme sought to develop

---

[4] Since its creation in 1987, over 1.5 million students have participated in Erasmus.

[5] Within higher education, we should also mention the Jean Monnet Project, which promotes the introduction of European integration studies (courses, modules, centres) at universities. Full-time teaching posts devoted to the teaching of European integration may be awarded the title 'Jean Monnet Chair'. Professors and researchers of European integration studies are brought together by ECSA (European Community Studies Association), which is independent of, but supported, by the EU.

stronger coherence in the youth policy of the EU. *Youth* was set up with a total budget of EUR 520 million for 2000–2006.

EEA and candidate countries had the right to participate with full powers in all three programmes, on condition that they contributed financially.

In order to facilitate the implementation of the Lisbon objectives, in December 2003, the Council and Parliament – acting on a Commission initiative – decided to set up the *e-Learning* programme, which aims to integrate information and communication technology into vocational training and education. For the 2004–2006 period, the programme had a total budget of EUR 44 million.

In addition, the *Erasmus Mundus* programme was created in December 2003. Erasmus Mundus seeks to contribute to the Bologna process[6] by improving the quality of Europe's tertiary education and intercultural understanding through promoting cooperation with third countries. This programme facilitates the inclusion of students and teachers from all over the world into European postgraduate education, as well as supporting student and teacher mobility from Europe to third countries. For the period 2004–2008, the programme has a budget of EUR 230 million.

In the early nineties, the EU launched the *Tempus* programme to provide support to the restructuring of educational systems in the former communist countries. At the beginning, the key objectives of the programme were to encourage the mobility and exchange of students and university staff from Central and Eastern European countries to the EU Member States and to promote the development of educational institutions in the countries concerned. Once these countries were successfully integrated into the Community's own programmes, the focus of Tempus shifted to the republics of the former Soviet Union, the CIS-countries. Tempus III, launched in 2000, is specifically aimed at providing support to non-candidate countries (countries of the Western Balkans, CIS-countries and Mongolia and, from 2002, Mediterranean countries of North Africa and of the Middle-East). In its first 16 years until 2006, Tempus financed 6,500 projects involving over 2,000 institutions of higher education.

---

[6] The Bologna process was launched by 29 European countries in 1999, and now 45 countries are involved in it (the 27 Member States and another 18 countries). Its main goal is to facilitate the compatibility and comparability – and thus recognition – of tertiary qualifications, by creating a two-tier ('bachelor-master') structure in higher education, consisting of a minimum three-year basic (so-called Bachelor) level, and a subsequent (so-called Master) level. The key elements of the process also include the transferability of credits earned, student and teacher mobility as well as cooperation in quality assurance.

In addition to the Tempus programme and the involvement of candidate states and EEA countries in Community education programmes, the EU set up the European Training Foundation (ETF) as an independent agency to establish cooperation in the field of education with third countries. The ETF, which has its headquarters in Turin, opened on 1 January 1995. Its key objectives are to contribute to the reform of education and vocational training systems in the partner countries[7], to impart Community experience to the countries concerned, to support the Tempus programme by practical activities and to enhance cooperation between the EU and the partner countries in the field of education and vocational training.

The Europass system, which was launched in 2004, is designed to encourage occupational and educational mobility. The Europass is a single framework for the transparency of diplomas, certificates and competences; it is a portfolio of skills and qualifications acquired in various EU countries and presented in a common format. A Europass consists of five documents: Europass CV, Europass Language Portfolio, Europass Mobility (recording experiences of transnational mobility for learning purposes), Europass Diploma Supplement (recording the holder's higher educational record), and Europass Certificate Supplement (a supplement to a vocational education and training certificate, clarifying the holder's professional qualifications).

21.3. Education, vocational training and youth programmes 2007–2013

In the context of the 2007–2013 financial perspectives, the Commission proposed reforms in the field of education. The Commission proposal aimed to incorporate European education and training programmes in an integrated action programme, hinging on the concept of life-long learning and supporting the fulfilment of the key Lisbon objective of making Europe the world's most competitive knowledge-based society by 2010.
On the basis of the Commission proposal, Council and Parliament adopted the 2007–2013 Lifelong Learning Action Programme in November 2006, with a budget of EUR 7 billion (an almost twofold increase from the previous period). The programme consists of four sub-programmes: Comenius (for schools), Erasmus (for higher education), Leonardo da Vinci (for vocational training) and Grundtvig (for adult education).

---

[7] Applicant countries, countries of the Western Balkans, the CIS republics and Mongolia and the Mediterranean countries.

- Comenius continues to promote cooperation between schools and teachers. It aims to involve at least three million pupils in joint educational activities, over the seven-year period. A minimum 13% of the Action Programme budget is earmarked for Comenius.
- Erasmus remains the flagship educational programme, with at least 40% of the total budget (EUR 3 billion). It promotes student mobility and cooperation between institutions of higher education, financing the foreign studies of 150,000 students annually. Erasmus Mundus is also maintained, helping 2,000 students from all parts of the world to participate in Masters level programmes offered by a consortium of universities from at least three different European countries.
- Leonardo da Vinci remains the Community's vocational training programme, promoting professional experience of young workers and apprentices by funding transnational work placements, exchanges and cooperation between institutions or enterprises of different Member States providing vocational learning opportunities. Leonardo has at its disposal at least 25% of the total budget of the Action Programme.
- Grundtvig promotes adult education with an emphasis on mobility through transnational cooperation and networking. It aims to support the mobility of 7,000 individuals involved in adult education per year, by 2013. At least 4% of the Action Programme's total budget is ring-fenced for Grundtvig.

The sectoral programmes are complemented by so-called transversal programmes, which aim to: support policy development and cooperation at European level in lifelong learning, notably in the context of the Lisbon strategy, as well as the Bologna and Copenhagen processes[8]; ensure an adequate supply of comparable data, statistics and analyses to underpin lifelong learning policy development, as well as to monitor progress towards objectives and targets in lifelong learning, and to identify areas for particular attention; promote language learning and support linguistic diversity in Member States; support the development of innovative ICT-based content; and ensure that the results of the Lifelong Learning Programme are appropriately demonstrated. Transversal projects must cover at least two (or more) sectoral sub-programmes. The Lifelong Learning Action Programme is open for participation to candidate countries, EEA members, Switzerland and countries of the Western Balkans.

---

[8] The Copenhagen process, similar to the Bologna process, is a form of European cooperation in the area of vocational training with the participation of 32 countries. It is aimed at facilitating the mutual recognition of vocational qualifications and improved transparency/compatibility of educational systems.

According to the decision of the Council and Parliament – based on the Commission's proposal – in the period 2007–2013 an integrated action programme serves youth policy. The general objectives of the new programme are, inter alia, to promote young people's (aged between 13 and 30 years) active citizenship in general and their European citizenship in particular (strengthening young people's feeling of belonging to European Union, promoting their participation in Europe's democratic life, facilitating youth mobility within Europe), to develop young people's solidarity and tolerance, to foster European cooperation in youth policy, to promote mutual understanding between young people of different Member States, and to contribute to developing the quality of support systems for youth activities and the capabilities of civil society organisations in the youth field. *Youth in Action* supports exchange projects aimed at improving youth mobility and projects facilitating the exchange of information within the EU and between Member States and partner countries. The *European Voluntary Service* continues to be a part of the Programme. *Youth in Action* has a budget of EUR 885 million, which is a considerable increase compared to the previous seven-year period. The Programme is also open for participation to candidate countries, EEA members, Switzerland and countries of the Western Balkans.

Tempus continues from 2007 with the participation of neighbouring countries. Tempus IV, which now involves the 27 Member States and 26 beneficiary countries, has a budget of EUR 50 million at its disposal until 2013. Its main objective is to improve cooperation between institutions of higher education in the EU and its partner countries.

CHAPTER 22
CULTURAL AND AUDIOVISUAL POLICY

22.1. EU cultural policy

Cultural policy, similarly to education, first appeared at the Community level in the Treaty of Maastricht. The Member States sought to provide a broader base for European integration, which was historically concerned mainly with economic and commercial benefits, by introducing various policies involving citizens to a greater degree and strengthening the feeling of belonging to the European Union; this approach would also help to reinforce the message of the legitimacy of European integration. In this respect, cultural policy plays a prominent role. This development is reflected in the Treaty of Maastricht, which amended Article 3 of the EC Treaty on the objectives of the Community with the stipulation that the Community should make a contribution to the promotion of the cultures of the Member States. The Treaty also defines cultural policy as a separate title of the Treaty (now Part Three Title XII of the EC Treaty).

Article 151 of the EC Treaty sets out the specific objectives of cultural policy. Pursuant to this article, the Community should contribute to the "flowering" of the cultures of the Member States, while respecting their national and cultural diversity and bringing their common cultural heritage to the fore. This is the objective that later gave birth to the motto of the European Union, 'United in diversity', which emphasises the existence of a multicultural but unified EU.

Under Article 151, the Community should enhance cooperation between the Member States and, when necessary, supplement and support their actions in the following areas: disseminating and promoting a wider knowledge of European culture and history, conserving and safeguarding cultural heritage, promoting non-commercial cultural exchanges and supporting artistic and literary creation (including the audiovisual sector). Article 151 requires the Community to take cultural aspects into account when defining other Community activities, in order to promote and respect cultural diversity.

To realise the objectives set out in the Treaty, incentive measures may be adopted jointly by the Council and the Parliament under the co-decision procedure; however, the Community is not allowed to approximate the laws of the Member States in this field. Given the exclusion on harmonisation, the scope of Community cultural policy, just like education policy, is essentially limited to launching Community programmes and initiatives. The Member States retain their sovereignty, while the Community aims at promoting and supporting cooperation between the Member States.

In the field of culture, the Member States are particularly determined to maintain their sovereignty, which is shown by the fact that, while the adoption of proposals comes under the co-decision procedure, as a rare exception, unanimity in the Council is required in the procedure.

The EU seeks to meet the objectives of its cultural policy through Community programmes. These aim at developing *ad hoc* cultural cooperation activities, encouraging broad multi-annual cultural cooperation agreements (cultural networks, partnerships), promoting projects and supporting symbolic cultural initiatives.

Following the entry into force of the Maastricht Treaty, the Community launched the first Community programmes on culture in the middle of the nineties, lasting until 2000:

- The *Kaleidoscope* programme was set up in 1996 and aimed to encourage artistic creation, to widen the market for cultural products and to promote the development of a cultural market on a European scale, in order to improve the knowledge and dissemination of the works of the European peoples. The budget of the programme between 1996 and 1999 amounted to EUR 36.7 million, which was allocated to 518 projects.

- The *Ariane* programme was adopted in 1997 and was intended to promote the dissemination and translation of literary works of the European peoples into the Union's other languages, in order to promote a wider knowledge and dissemination of literary works. The total budget of the programme for the period 1997-1999 was EUR 11.1 million, funding 767 projects.

- The *Raphäel* programme was launched in 1997 and aimed at the conservation and restoration of the European cultural heritage. Between 1997 and 2000[1], it supported over 360 projects, with a total investment of EUR 30 million.

In 2000, pursuant to the joint decision of the Council and the Parliament, the three Community programmes on culture were merged into a single programme under the name of *Culture 2000*, which brought together their respective objectives. Culture 2000 was first launched for the period 2000-2004 and was later extended until 2006. Its total budget for the years between 2000 and 2006 was EUR 236.5 million.

The objectives of the *Culture 2000* programme set for the period 2000-2006 were to promote artistic creativity and disseminate cultural knowledge in the fields of music, literature, fine arts, cultural heritage and new forms of cultural expression. The programme aimed at meeting these objectives by promoting cooperation between cultural organisations,

---

[1] The Raphäel programme expired in 1999 and, similarly to the other two action programmes, was merged into the Culture 2000 programme in the year 2000.

institutions and representatives of the Member States and by implementing support measures of a European dimension to foster the dissemination of European culture both within and outside the Union. Culture 2000 provided support for three types of actions:
- innovative and experimental actions with participants from at least three different Member States;
- integrated actions covered by structured, multi-annual cultural cooperation agreements with participants from several Member States;
- special cultural events with a European or international dimension.

Culture 2000 also recognised culture as an economic factor and an instrument of social integration, and therefore sought to strengthen its relationship with other Community areas and measures having an effect on culture. The programme was open to participation by the countries of the European Economic Area and the candidate countries, which, similarly to the education and youth action programmes, had the right to participate with full powers.

In the context of the 2007-2013 financial perspectives, the Commission proposed the Culture 2007 programme as a follow-up to Culture 2000. Council and Parliament decided in December 2006 to launch the new seven-year programme with an increased budget of EUR 400 million. The specific objectives of the programme are:
- to promote the transnational mobility of people working in the cultural sector;
- to encourage the transnational circulation of works and cultural and artistic products;
- to encourage intercultural dialogue.

The objectives of the programme are pursued through measures in the following fields of action:
- support for cultural actions;
- support for cultural organisations active at European level;
- in the area of European cultural cooperation and cultural policy support for analyses and the collection and dissemination of information and for activities maximising the impact of cultural projects.

Culture 2007 is also open to the participation of EEA countries, candidate countries, countries of the Western Balkans, as well as third countries whose association or cooperation agreements concluded with the EU include a clause on cultural cooperation.

Another important cultural initiative of the EU is the European Capital of Culture Programme, launched in 1985. The European Capital of Culture is a city – recently two cities – designated by the European Union for a period of one year during which it is supported by the Culture programme. However, most of the investment in infrastructure needed for implementing the associated cultural projects is financed by the respective Member State and the Structural Funds. The European Capital of Culture is given an opportunity to showcase the cultural heritage of the city and its region, as well as to provide a venue for artists from all corners of the continent to present their talents. This is a great opportunity to transform a city in terms of culture, tourism and infrastructure. From 2009 on, two cities will share the title: one from the EU-15 and one from the 12 Member States that joined in 2004 and 2007.

22.2. EU audiovisual policy

The audiovisual sector constitutes a unique section within culture. It is an area where culture and business meet; its economic significance matches its cultural importance. In addition, it has great socio-cultural implications since, for a large part of the population, it is the main pastime, the most important instrument of entertainment and the primary source of information. It plays a decisive role in the future development of society and the conservation of national culture. It is also crucial in determining what kind of programmes are offered to viewers/listeners and who is responsible for creating these programmes, which may also produce substantial financial profits.

It is therefore logical that audiovisual policy, whose course of development in the EU has been different from other areas of cultural policy, should be treated as a separate field. In addition to measures on culture, audiovisual policy is also affected by legal provisions implemented in other Community policies, first and foremost by the regulatory framework of the single market (in particular in the context of the freedom to provide services[2]).

In recent years, the market for the audiovisual industry (film, television and radio) has broadened enormously all over the world and turned the sector into one of the leading industries. The European audiovisual industry, however, has not profited greatly from the

---

[2] The scope of the freedom of establishment and the freedom to provide services was interpreted by the European Court of Justice as extending to audiovisual services (to broadcasting and programme service provisions alike).

profound changes of the last couple of decades. On the contrary, it has suffered a major crisis, particularly in the nineties.[3] Community action can be essential to lead the industry out of the slump, as the problems of the sector stem primarily from the fragmentation of the European market. The industry is in desperate need of structural reform, incentive measures and financial support. Despite the fact that the European audiovisual sector started falling behind the United States as early as the start of the eighties, the Community could take no real initiatives in response, since audiovisual policy was not defined as a policy in its own right either in the Treaty of Rome, or in the Treaty's subsequent amendments. However, the situation changed when audiovisual policy was incorporated into the EC Treaty as part and parcel of culture by the Treaty of Maastricht.

In the absence of a Community legal basis, the aspects of audiovisual policy that came to the fore were those that were inextricably interlinked with the general operation and development of the Union, i.e. with the operation of the single market. The spread of modern technologies (satellites, cables, etc.) turned broadcasting into a transnational activity. As a result, its status within the single market had to be regulated with regard to the freedom of establishment and the freedom to provide services. In 1989, responding to this need and in accordance with the programme of the single market, the Council adopted the Community framework legislation on audiovisual policy, the 'Television without Frontiers' Directive[4]. In addition to laying down provisions at European level, the Directive also introduced support measures to protect the troubled European audiovisual industry from international competition. The Directive's measures were based on two fundamental principles. The first objective aimed at ensuring the free movement and the provision of equal opportunities for television broadcasts from the Member States. The second objective sought to introduce essentially protectionist measures in defence of the European audiovisual industry. In addition, the Directive defined a framework for the regulation of TV commercials within the Community and the moral, mental and physical protection of minors and of human dignity.

---

[3] In the audiovisual sector, the common (single) European market played into the hands of the USA. American films tend to recover their production costs on the buoyant domestic market and, as a result, their export means sure profit. By contrast, European films tend to be distributed exclusively within their countries of production. Due to the relatively small size of national markets, profit is hardly ever generated. This explains why distribution on the internal market should be conducted through a trans-European distribution network. The establishment of such a network however requires Community action. Trans-European cooperation would also contribute to the promotion of the manufacture of audiovisual products and the spread of advanced technologies.

[4] Directive 89/552/EEC.

As the most important harmonisation measure, the Directive – based on the 'country of origin' principle – provided that the Member States could not restrict the reception or broadcast of programmes from other Member States. This essentially corresponded to the enforcement of the principle of mutual recognition in the audiovisual sector. The only exceptions to the rule related to programmes that might seriously impair the physical, mental or moral development of minors.

In the context of protecting the industry, the Directive stipulated that broadcasters within the EU must reserve for European works a majority proportion of their transmission time, excluding the time appointed to news, sports events, games, advertising and teletext services (a 50% quota).

As this is one of the most dynamically evolving sectors of the 21st century, a review of the Directive – only updated once in the mid-nineties since its adoption in 1989 – had long been on the agenda. The Directive needed to be amended to take into account the new requirements of the digital age, the immense technological and market changes of the audiovisual industry, and the sector's increasing convergence with telecommunication services. Council and Parliament finally arrived at an agreement on how to amend the Directive in May 2007. Accordingly, the updated provisions (such as the country of origin principle) of the new Directive will apply from 2009 not only to traditional television broadcasting but will cover all audiovisual media services (such as on-demand video, news, sport broadcasts and the provision of content downloadable to mobile phones). The amendments also seek to simplify advertising rules and make them more flexible for producers of audiovisual programmes. The Directive maintains the twelve-minutes-per-hour limit on commercials, the provisions on the protection of minors from harmful content, measures promoting European and independent programmes, as well as the ban on content inciting religious or racial hatred.

The Treaty of Maastricht extended the range of instruments available for audiovisual policy beyond single market regulation. Maastricht brought about a change in the status of audiovisual policy by including a specific reference to the sector in Article 151 of the EC Treaty, which deals with culture. It established the legal basis for introducing incentive actions and support measures. The *MEDIA* programme, established on this base, which is the second pillar of audiovisual policy alongside the 'Television without Frontiers' Directive, is the Community support programme for the sector, similar to the Community's programmes on culture.

By launching the MEDIA programme, the EU wanted to increase the competitiveness of the European audiovisual industry. In accordance with this objective, the programme sought:

- to encourage, by providing financial and technical assistance, an environment favourable to the development of audiovisual companies;
- to promote the development of production projects;
- to strengthen the European distribution sector by encouraging European distributors to invest in production;
- to promote wider transnational distribution of European films;
- to actively support the linguistic diversity of audiovisual works;
- to promote the training (particularly in relation to economic and commercial knowledge and the utilisation of new technologies) of audiovisual professionals.

The MEDIA programme mainly supports projects with participants from several Member States. The first phase of the programme, launched prior to the Treaty of Maastricht, was allocated ECU 200 million for the period 1991-1995, whereas the total budget of the MEDIA II programme between 1996 and 2000 amounted to EUR 310 million. The funding of the MEDIA+ programme for the period 2001-2005 was earmarked at EUR 350 million, but when the programme was extended to 2006, the budget was raised to 453.6 million.

The MEDIA programme, in the same way as the Community programmes on culture, was open to both EEA and candidate countries.

In addition to the MEDIA programme, MEDIA Training was launched in 2001 to provide training for professionals in the audiovisual sector to increase the competitiveness of the European audiovisual industry. These training programmes focused on new technologies, economic, financial and commercial management and script-writing techniques. Originally, EUR 50 million was earmarked for MEDIA Training 2001-2005, but when the programme was extended until the end of 2006, its budget was also increased to 59.4 million.

Although the Community succeeded in reversing the under-performance of the European audiovisual industry to a certain extent, by means of the support measures of the MEDIA programme and the protectionist provisions of the 'Television without Frontiers' Directive, a boom has never occurred. The annual Community funding of EUR 70-80 million served as a mere "cosmetic treatment" and the 50% European quota by itself could not provide the necessary impetus for the dissemination of European works, since the transmission time allocated to the quota was usually reserved for national productions. Nonetheless, amongst the Community's objectives, the audiovisual sector continues to be a major development area, which has substantial job-creating potential and strategic importance in preserving and disseminating cultural values.

On this basis, and in the context of the 2007-2013 financial perspectives, the Commission proposed a budget of EUR 1.055 billion for the next seven years of MEDIA 2007, merging the former MEDIA+ and MEDIA Training programmes. Council and Parliament made their final decision on the budget and objectives of MEDIA 2007 in November 2006. The final budget – EUR 755 million for the seven years – was lower than the Commission's original proposal, but still an increase compared to the previous programming period. The key objectives of MEDIA 2007 are the following:

- promoting European cultural and linguistic diversity, preserving the heritage of the European film and audiovisual industry and making it available to the public, encouraging inter-cultural dialogue;
- increasing the circulation and audience of European audiovisual works inside and outside the EU;
- improving the competitiveness of the European audiovisual industry within the framework of an open European market, which – inter alia, through promoting exchanges of expertise between audiovisual experts – improves employment opportunities.

MEDIA 2007 continues to be open to the participation of EEA and candidate countries, countries of the Western Balkans, as well as third countries whose association or cooperation agreements concluded with the EU include cultural cooperation clauses.

CHAPTER 23
THE COMMON FOREIGN AND SECURITY POLICY AND THE EUROPEAN SECURITY AND DEFENCE POLICY

23.1. The evolution of cooperation in the field of foreign and security policy

At the foundation of the European Communities, a foreign policy aim was out of the question and there was no reference of any kind to foreign policy cooperation in the Treaties.[1] The Communities only agreed upon their external economic relations in respect of matters concerning the customs union and common market.[2] However, seeing the success of economic cooperation, it quickly became obvious that the European Communities – that had become a "giant" of the world economy – could not remain a political "dwarf" and that it should have a political role to match its economic potential.

This realisation was only slowly turned into practice for two major reasons: first of all, Member States, even today, see an independent foreign policy as the most important element and measure of sovereignty and, because of this, they will not easily give up direct control; secondly, for a long time, several Member States did not regard the Communities as competent in foreign and security policy matters, but rather emphasised the roles of other organisations – primarily NATO – in these fields.

The first specific step towards the construction of a common foreign policy emerged at the December 1969 Hague Summit, where the Member States agreed to hold consultations at different political levels in order to lay the foundations for foreign policy cooperation. After the summit, the so-called Davignon Report was adopted in 1970, which launched the project of the European Political Cooperation (EPC), which was the conciliation mechanism for the European Communities for two decades. The Single European Act of 1986 eventually institutionalised the existing *de facto* cooperation. European Political Cooperation was directed towards the coordination of national foreign policies in order that Member States could develop a common standpoint on a given matter, based on intergovernmental consultation, and in this way act together.

---

[1] As separate Communities in the early fifties (before the EEC and Euratom), there were attempts to establish a European Defence Community and a European Political Community but they failed (see 1.3.). Finally, the three established Communities were integrated purely on economic grounds.

[2] See Chapter 9.

EPC operated at several levels: its highest forum was the meeting of Heads of State or Government (the European Council); but the meetings of Foreign Ministers played an important role as well. The continuous operation of EPC and day-to-day relations in Foreign Ministries were ensured by the Political Committee, which was the body of the political directors appointed for foreign policy consultation. EPC was based on consensus between Member States; no voting took place.

23.2. Second pillar of the Maastricht Treaty: establishing the Common Foreign and Security Policy

Although EPC had several practical advantages, it could not ensure that Member States always had common positions and could take joint actions. The larger Member States especially tended to act autonomously.

In the eighties, it was felt that there was an increased need for the European Communities to have a common foreign policy and a single voice and that they should try to build upon the foreign policy potential of joint actions. Trends in the world economy were also proving that acting as a block of countries could be much more effective than acting alone.

The turning point in the debate surrounding the establishment of a common foreign policy came with the collapse of the Soviet system, the political turnaround in Central and Eastern Europe and – as a part of this – the question of a unified Germany. On the one hand, it became clear for the leaders of the Member States that, with its increased size, Germany should be anchored more firmly to European integration[3] while, on the other hand, paradoxically, the feeling of stability decreased within the European Community, due to the end of the Cold War and the uncertain political future of the Central and Eastern European countries. These two inter-twining factors played a crucial role in the decision to create a common foreign and security policy and the construction of a political union.

The Treaty on European Union adopted in Maastricht placed Member States' foreign policies on a new basis, because the States moved from political cooperation towards a "common foreign policy" (which had a federal ring to it) and made the so-called Common Foreign and Security Policy (CFSP) the second pillar of the newly established European Union.

---

[3] It should be mentioned that Germany also saw the need to progress towards political union; moreover, it was the main driving force behind it. It was willing to introduce Monetary Union and give up the Deutsch Mark. In exchange, it asked the French, the main supporters of the single currency, for the creation of a political union.

However, we should emphasise here that although its name is Common Foreign and Security Policy, it should not be understood as a "common" policy in the strict sense of the word. Like the EPC, the Common Foreign and Security Policy was still not Community-based and was certainly not exclusively Community-based, as was the case with the 'real' common policies (e.g. commercial policy); rather, it remained a mechanism operating at intergovernmental level. This is true, despite the fact that common elements were strengthened, several instruments were assigned to the Common Foreign and Security Policy and the members accepted that cooperation covered all fields of foreign and security policy, including the need for a common defence policy to be established at a later date. However, the initial Common Foreign and Security Policy was established on a purely intergovernmental level and was therefore different from the Community pillar.

According to the Treaty on European Union established in Maastricht, the main aims of Common Foreign and Security Policy (Article 11, EU Treaty, former Article J.1) were – in harmony with the fundamental principles of the UN Charter – to safeguard the Union's common values, fundamental interests, independence and integrity, to strengthen its security, to preserve peace and strengthen international security, to promote international cooperation, and to consolidate democracy and the rule of law, including respect for human rights and fundamental freedoms.

The Treaty on European Union bound Member States to harmonise their actions in relation to international organisations. The Treaty laid down that Member States should avoid all actions that would be contrary to the interests of the Union or which might impair its effectiveness as a cohesive force in international relations. At the same time, the Treaty underlined that the policy of the Union should not prejudice the specific character of the defence policy of individual Member States (including their obligations as NATO members).

According to the Maastricht Treaty, the second pillar was created solely at an intergovernmental level. This meant that the governments of the Member States, the European Council and the institutions of the Council played the leading role in the control of CFSP. Except for procedural matters, the Maastricht Treaty made unanimity-based decision-making the norm within the second pillar.

The Maastricht Treaty was also a step forward in the field of defence policy, as it defined the Western European Union (WEU) as an integral part of the development of the European Union, underlining the necessity for cooperation between the two organisations. According to the Treaty, Common Foreign and Security Policy covered all security questions of the Union including the possible development of a common defence policy, which might lead to common defence in the future. In practice, this meant that, while the European Communities formally held the view that the WEU was solely responsible for military cooperation (while political and economic matters were within the competence of the Communities), at the same time, the Maastricht Treaty called the WEU an integral part of the development of the Union and asked the WEU to occasionally implement EU decisions related to defence tasks.

The Western European Union until the end of the nineties

Following the failure to establish the European Defence Community[4], the Western European Union was created in 1954 through the so-called modified Brussels Treaty[5], signed by the six countries of the European Coal and Steel Community and the United Kingdom. The WEU was formed with much less institutional potential than the EDC's plan – dropping the idea of a common armed force – with its main aim similar to the EDC's – namely to ensure European defence. However, the WEU could not become a key player in the Western European defence system, since this was built on NATO. Although it played an important role in some historic issues after its formation (e.g: integration of the Federal Republic of Germany, settling the problem of Saarland, mediating between the EC and the United Kingdom), by the seventies, its activity and importance had dropped to a minimal level.

The WEU was revived from its decade-long hibernation through the 1984 Rome Declaration, which set new aims for the organisation: the definition of the identity of European security policy and the gradual harmonisation of Member States' defence policies. The WEU was strengthened by the fact that, in 1990, as a result of the EC's southern enlargement, Spain and Portugal joined.

Following the WEU's revival, the definition of its roles and tasks, as distinct from those of NATO and the European Union, remained the most important question. At the Maastricht Summit, in December 1991, WEU members issued a declaration on the WEU's relationship with the EU and NATO, emphasising that the WEU should become the defence component of the EU and the European pillar of NATO.

Another declaration was also issued at Maastricht about the relationship of the WEU to European countries. EU Member States were offered the possibility of joining or the status of observer, while non-EU European members of NATO were offered the status of associated

---

[4] See Chapter 1.3.

[5] The Brussels Treaty was signed on 17 March 1948 by Belgium, the United Kingdom, France, the Netherlands and Luxemburg. In this Treaty, the parties – who at that time were especially aiming to prevent Germany's re-armament - expressed their commitment towards common defence. This treaty was modified on 23 October 1954 in Paris (modified Brussels Treaty), when Germany and Italy joined (basically extending common defence to these two countries as well) and thus the Western European Union was created.

members, with somewhat wider rights than those of an observer. Among the EU's non-WEU members, Greece chose to join the WEU, while EU and NATO member Denmark and the only neutral EU-member at that time – Ireland – chose observer status. At the same time, non-EU European NATO members Iceland, Norway and Turkey became associated members. On 1 January 1995, the number of observers grew to five as the three neutral countries joining the EU, namely Austria, Finland and Sweden, received this status as well.

Since the publication of the Maastricht Declaration it has been an unwritten rule that membership of the WEU is only open to EU Member States that are also members of NATO.

In 1994, the WEU offered another kind of status, the so-called associated partnership (with less rights than an observer), for Central and Eastern European countries which had already signed Association Agreements with the EU: Bulgaria, the Czech Republic, Estonia, Hungary, Latvia, Lithuania, Poland, Romania, Slovakia, and Slovenia. These countries could automatically enter into higher positions when they became NATO and/or EU members. This was the situation with the Czech Republic, Hungary and Poland when, following their NATO entry on 12 March 1999, they became associate members of the WEU on 23 March 1999.

By the late nineties, the WEU – with its four different levels – included 28 European states (10 Member States, 6 associated members, 5 observers and 7 associated partners).

The direction of the WEU's operation in the nineties was mainly determined by the so-called Petersberg Declaration, which was issued by the Council of the WEU on 19 June 1992 in order to define more specifically the role of the organisation. The Declaration laid down all cases where the WEU's role was necessary.

The aims included in the 'Petersberg–type missions' or 'Petersberg tasks' are the following: 1. humanitarian and rescue tasks; 2. peacekeeping tasks; 3. tasks of combat forces in crisis management, including peacemaking. The Petersberg missions, which mainly mean crisis management tasks, are sometimes called the new acquis of the WEU, as opposed to the old acquis of the WEU originating from the modified Brussels Treaty concerning collective defence. In the nineties – besides managing relations with non-EU members – the operation of the WEU was justified by this new acquis: the question of crisis management (since collective defence was provided by NATO).

The main achievement of the Common Foreign and Security Policy established by Maastricht was that it made significant progress compared to the EPC because it provided a previously non-existent legal framework. It placed legal obligations on Member States in the field of foreign and security policy and defined the instruments for CFSP. All in all, it defined the legal conditions for the EU to be able to take concerted action in international politics and, in some cases, this brought specific results (e.g: various humanitarian actions, assistance in the democratisation process of South Africa, joint action against landmines).

However, it cannot be said that a true Common Foreign Policy was realised in the first few years of CFSP's operation. Joint action failed in several cases. First of all, the failure to determine a unified standpoint concerning the future of the former Yugoslavia cast a shadow over progress during the first half of the nineties. Due to the particular interests of the largest Member States (the United Kingdom, France and Germany), coordination between the Member States often failed. Each of these three states ignored, at least once, the rules of reconciliation; memorable cases were Germany's individual action in recognising Croatia (even if this occurred before the entry into force of the Maastricht Treaty), France's resumption of nuclear testing and the UK's policy towards Iraq (with the unconditional support of the USA). However, it should be pointed out that, occasionally, certain smaller Member States were also reluctant to surrender their individual interests to the common will.

Above all, the CFSP's smooth operation was obstructed by its institutional shortcomings. The continuous struggle to achieve a consensus made the adoption of common positions difficult or even impossible. The CFSP received further criticism as evidence of Europe's inability to speak with one voice, as there was no institution or person who could competently represent the European position.

23.3. The novelties of the Amsterdam Treaty

Through assessing the above-mentioned failures and problems, one of the main aims of the 1996–1997 Intergovernmental Conference was to strengthen the CFSP's Community nature and to make progress towards a real Common Foreign Policy, by enhancing the system of decision-making and joint action and by achieving a more meaningful foreign policy image.

As a result of the Intergovernmental Conference, the Amsterdam Treaty was signed on 2 October 1997 and it included several elements that might have improved CFSP's efficiency in practice. However, these could not be considered as very radical steps towards the creation of a Common Foreign Policy. Nevertheless, the Amsterdam Treaty included several new elements and organisational changes, which enriched the operation of CFSP and, given sufficient political will, carried the potential of the EU having a more unified and distinct voice.

In order to create a more efficient Common Foreign and Security Policy image, the Amsterdam Treaty modified legal sources and decision-making mechanisms in the area of CFSP and redefined the role of particular institutions. Since Amsterdam, the task of the European Council has been primarily to adopt the *common* strategies, introduced as a new type of legal act. With considerable restrictions, it nevertheless allowed for qualified majority voting for decisions of an implementing nature. The Treaty of Amsterdam also introduced the institution of constructive abstention, according to which if, for some reason, a Member State does not want to take part in a joint action but does not want to hinder it either, the other states can take action without the abstaining state having to participate.

In order to give a more unified and characteristic appearance and a single voice to the Common Foreign and Security Policy, the Amsterdam Treaty introduced the position of High Representative for CFSP. This person is the foreign policy representative of the Member States who represents and communicates the EU's position to the rest of the world. However, contrary to the original French initiative, this office is not a wholly new position. Rather, the tasks had already been imposed upon the Council's Secretary General, who previously had mainly bureaucratic functions and who led the Council's apparatus. This position was reformed and divided. Since the Amsterdam Treaty entered into force, the Secretary General's new task has been mainly to help the Presidency of the Council on foreign and security policy issues and to communicate on a political basis with outside partners, while the former tasks of the Secretary General have been carried out by a Deputy Secretary General.[6] However, the scope of the Secretary General's tasks is problematical, since the EU Treaty does not define exactly the range of authority. In fact, it only mentions assisting the Council's President as the representative of CFSP. As a result, in some cases, there might be a clash of competences between the Council's Secretary General and the Commissioner responsible for External Relations of the European Commission, as has already happened.

According to the Amsterdam Treaty, the renewed *Troika* also became more important to the realisation of the Common Foreign and Security Policy. Previously, this body consisted of the Member States holding the previous, current and subsequent Presidency of the Council, but, since Amsterdam, the body consists of the President of the Council, its Secretary General and the Commissioner for External Relations. This body is very important in the event of crises, but its tasks of representing the EU and its common position at international level and in the world at large are important as well.

In order to ensure the more efficient prevention and management of crises, a Declaration annexed to the Amsterdam Treaty called for the establishment of a Policy Planning and Early Warning Unit (PPEWU) within the General Secretariat of the Council. Its tasks are to monitor, and assess international trends and events relevant to the CFSP, analyse the Union's foreign and security interests, identifying the future key areas of CFSP, and to

---

[6] The first High Representative for CFSP – Javier Solana, former Secretary General of NATO – started work on 19 October 1999. His mandate was renewed in 2004.

issue early warnings of potential crises and events with a significant impact on the Union's foreign and security policy. In addition, the Unit also develops recommendations on political measures and strategies. The Unit cooperates with the European Commission in order to adequately coordinate foreign policy with trade and development policies.

Strengthening Common Foreign and Security Policy and improving joint actions was the aim of the Treaty's clause on operating expenses for CFSP purposes (except for military and defence expenses), which stipulates that these should come from the budget of the European Communities (Maastricht had only provided for administrative expenses). Occasional military and defence expenses are still financed by contributions from the budgets of the Member States, generally determined on the basis of their GDP.

Due to the implementation of the long-term goals of the Maastricht Treaty, integrating the WEU into the EU became a much-debated issue at the 1996–1997 Intergovernmental Conference. However, as the United Kingdom, Denmark and the neutral countries (Ireland, Sweden, Finland and Austria) were against the WEU's assimilation, the Amsterdam Treaty only declared the need for the further strengthening of relations between the two organisations. It also stipulated, however, that the EU should build closer institutional relations with the WEU, having regard to its possible integration into the EU. This question was simplified by the Amsterdam Treaty, which provided that such integration only required the decision of the European Council. Thus, while the integration of the WEU did not actually take place, it required only a simple political decision without amending the EU Treaty.

23.4. The instruments and decision-making order of the Common Foreign and Security Policy

According to the provisions of the EU Treaty, in the spirit of loyalty and mutual solidarity, the Member States support the Common Foreign and Security Policy created in Maastricht and supplemented in Amsterdam. The Member States must refrain from any action that is contrary to Union interests. Within the Council, the Member States mutually inform each other about and discuss all foreign and security policy issues of general interest, to ensure that the Union can exert its influence effectively through concerted action.

The Member States coordinate their action in international organisations and at international conferences. In international organisations where not every Member State is a member, the participating Member States represent the common positions. The Member States that are members of the United Nations Security Council consult each other and keep the other Member States fully informed. Member States that are permanent members of the UN Security Council[7] are responsible for ensuring that the Union's position and interests are defended.

In the second pillar, the Union has the following legal acts as instruments at its disposal: *principles and general guidelines, common strategies, joint actions* and *common positions* as well as *decisions*.[8]
The European Council defines the principles and general guidelines for the Common Foreign and Security Policy, including for matters with defence implications. The European Council also decides on common strategies to be implemented by the Union, which set the political guidelines for a given country, region, foreign policy area or theme.
The Council of Ministers adopts joint actions for a specific situation requiring operational action by the Union. The Council also adopts common positions defining the Union's position on issues of a geographic (applying to a country, region or area) or thematic nature. The Council may also adopt implementing decisions.

In summary, while the European Council conducts the Common Foreign and Security Policy at a strategic level, the Council ensures that Union action is united, coherent and effective. Hence, the decisions needed for the operation of the CFSP are taken by the Council.
The involvement of the Commission and the Parliament are much more limited than in first-pillar policies. The Commission's right of initiative is not exclusive; it is shared with the Member States.
The Council Presidency consults the European Parliament on the main aspects of CFSP, and ensures that the Parliament's views are duly taken into consideration. However, this consultative obligation is much looser than in the case of first-pillar policies; it is of a general character and does not apply to individual decisions; nor is there any time limit imposed. In addition, the Presidency and the Commission inform Parliament regularly about developments in the Union's Common Foreign and Security Policy.

The Council takes decisions in the second pillar acting by unanimity. Abstentions do not block decisions; abstaining Member States do not have to apply the decision but accept that the decision is binding on the Union (this is known as constructive abstention).

---

[7] France and the United Kingdom
[8] For more on legal acts of the second pillar, see 5.2.2.2.

Qualified majority voting is also used, but only to a limited extent. The Council acts by a qualified majority when adopting joint actions, common positions or any other decision based on a common strategy, or when adopting decisions for the implementation of joint actions or common positions. The Council also acts by a qualified majority when appointing a special representative for a geographic or thematic issue, and when approving the conclusion of an international agreement related to the second or third pillar requiring a qualified majority for its internal implementation.[9] The Council may apply unanimity in these cases as well (allowing for a special, limited right of veto): if a member of the Council declares that, for vital and stated reasons of national policy, it intends to oppose a European decision to be adopted by a qualified majority, the vote is not taken; the Council, acting by a qualified majority, may request that the matter be referred to the European Council for a decision by unanimity.

The mechanism for the conclusion of international agreements is also different from that applied in the first pillar.[10] When the Union wants to conclude an agreement with one or more states or international organisations for implementing the Common Foreign and Security Policy, the Council may authorise the Presidency (but not the Commission) to begin negotiations to that end. The Presidency may, however, request the help of the Commission. The agreements are concluded by the Council acting on the basis of the Presidency's recommendation.

Upon the entry into force of the Maastricht Treaty, the General Affairs Council, consisting of Ministers for Foreign Affairs, became the competent Council formation in the second pillar. The Seville Council of June 2002 introduced reforms to the Council's structure, renaming the General Affairs Council the General Affairs and External Relations Council (GAERC), and stating that it must hold separate meetings for general affairs and external relations. The GAERC is responsible for all aspects of the Union's external relations, such as second pillar Common Foreign and Security Policy and European security and defence policy (see 23.6.), as well as first pillar policies such as foreign trade, development cooperation and humanitarian aid (see Chapter 9).

---

[9] The latter two cases (i.e. the appointment of special representatives and the conclusion of specific types of international agreements) were transferred to QMV by the Treaty of Nice.

[10] For more on international agreements in the first pillar, see Chapter 9.3.

The Council structure established following Maastricht relied heavily on the structures of the EPC. The Political Committee, consisting of political directors (senior officials of foreign ministries), was retained, with the task of monitoring the international political situation, conducting political dialogue and preparing political decisions. The Helsinki Summit of December 1999 decided to set up the *Political and Security Committee* (PSC) in spring 2000, which was later institutionalised by the Treaty of Nice (see 23.6.). The Political and Security Committee replaced the Political Committee, taking over its tasks and becoming a body that meets on a weekly basis. As a consequence, officials of ambassadorial rank at the permanent representations in Brussels replaced the political directors as members of the Political and Security Committee.

Nevertheless, the position of political directors was maintained; the members of the PSC work under their direction and oversight (and theoretically the PSC can be convened at the level of political directors as well). Below the level of political directors is the network of *European correspondents*, who are in daily contact with each other, forming a kind of hotline between the foreign ministries.

The Political and Security Committee is assisted in the area of ESDP by two military bodies composed of defence personnel: the European Union Military Committee (EUMC) and the European Union Military Staff (EUMS), whose role is discussed in detail in 23.6.

COREPER is also involved in decision-making in the second pillar, as it is responsible for preparing the Council's meetings. COREPER has the final say before Council meetings concerning the draft agenda and proposals for a decision, but it usually does not reopen discussion on issues already negotiated in the Political and Security Committee; unless, of course, there is no agreement in the PSC on a question, when COREPER plays an important role, acting as a mediator.

Since the Amsterdam Treaty, the High Representative for CFSP has also played an important role in the work of the Council in the area of the Common Foreign and Security Policy by assisting the formulation, preparation and implementation of political decisions and negotiating with third parties at the Council's request.

The Council may also appoint a special representative with a specific mandate for a given issue.[11]

---

[11] It appointed such special representatives for example after the Bosnia and Kosovo crises, to lead EU action and act as the head of the international interim administration.

23.5. Key issues of the Common Foreign and Security Policy after Amsterdam

The need for further strengthening of the Common Foreign and Security Policy remained on the agenda after the Amsterdam Treaty, as well. As a result of its still unclear nature, a common defence policy, which was laid down as early as the Maastricht Treaty, continued to be a major concern and an unresolved question for several Member States. The importance of this lies in the fact that only a foreign and security policy backed up by serious defence capability can be really effective; only with real military capability could the policy become as important a factor in world politics as the EU wished and its economic potential justified. Although the unified European military and defence potential (primarily initiated by the French) was on the agenda for a long time, the EU's common defence policy (the first logical step of which would have been the WEU's integration into the EU) was not defined by the Amsterdam Treaty either. The reason for this was that some countries – led by the UK – did not want the EU to develop in this direction, as they saw common defence as best guaranteed within NATO (with the United States taking a leading role). These countries also wanted to avoid an overlap or duplication of NATO and EU activities. In Amsterdam the countries that emphasised the importance of trans-Atlantic cooperation and NATO[12], together with the neutral countries (which, because of their special situation, represented the position that it would be incompatible with the EU's character as an organisation to take an active role in defence), prevented the decision on common defence from being taken. The first step of such a defence policy could have been the WEU's integration into the EU. The new Treaty left some room for manoeuvre, in particular the placing of the question of the WEU's integration within the Council's scope of competence.

Throughout the nineties, the WEU continuously played a kind of balancing role between the EU and NATO, and its members were unable to make up their minds on a key issue - with which of the two organisations the WEU should build closer relations: whether it should become the defence wing of the EU, or the European pillar of NATO, or whether these two aims could be incorporated in some way. The problem of the WEU was further aggravated by the fact that it did not have its own military and armament potential – although some

---

[12] Generally, the United Kingdom is considered the country most unconditionally committed to close trans-Atlantic relations, but the Netherlands, Portugal, Denmark and Italy also tend to share similar sentiments. The 8 CEECs that became EU members in 2004 and 2007 are all NATO members and pursue a rather pro-Atlantic foreign policy.

troops might have been deployed to serve WEU's aims[13]. Furthermore, the EU Member States were generally reluctant to invest in the development of the necessary resources. As a result, the WEU became dependent on NATO, which is primarily based on US assets. This was a major impediment to the initiative – mainly supported by France – according to which Europe (i.e. the EU) should build its own common defence potential and should reduce its dependence on America, to give it greater weight in world politics. According to this concept, the incorporation of the WEU should have been the EU's first step towards creating the necessary defence and military background.

Immediately after the Amsterdam Treaty, as a result of the EU's decision on the WEU's integration, it seemed that the WEU preferred building closer institutional relations with NATO. This direction was changed at the end of 1998, as the British Labour government changed Britain's former position and started to support WEU's integration within the EU. The background to this change of position was that the UK realised that the WEU's integration within the EU – resulting from its institutional weakness – would not be a real challenge for NATO's domination in the field of common defence, but it would nevertheless strengthen Europe's (and the EU's) weight in world politics. The British position was built on the notion that, if the organisation ceased to exist, relations between the EU and NATO would be clearer and the division of authority and competences would become easier. Although the British position – opposing the former Conservative position – was clearly in favour of strengthening Europe's unity and creating a "unified European voice" in the field of security policy, at the same time – according to the traditional British concept – collective defence was still seen as more achievable within NATO, within which Europe would be able to represent a common position and take joint actions in a more pronounced way. This would contribute to the enhancement of the notion of the European Security and Defence Identity (ESDI)[14] that had been on the agenda of NATO, the EU and WEU for a long time.

---

[13] These were the so-called Forces Answerable to WEU (FAWEU), the forces available for the WEU's aims, which were usually multinational troops. These included German-French Eurocorps and Spanish-Italian-French Eurofor. Their significance, however, was weakened by the fact that WEU never had its own command and control system.

[14] ESDI is a notion used within NATO, the WEU and EU, meaning the organisation and development of a European countries' Common Security and Defence Policy that is separable from NATO but which may use its assets. ESDI's exact content, however, is not well defined and particular countries interpret it differently.

The basis for the new British approach was that the CFSP could no longer be effective without a military force of adequate weight. Thus, according to the British, an independent defence policy could be the EU's fourth pillar. The UK also encouraged the restructuring of the defence industry. However, the initiative clearly declared that decisions concerning defence policy should be made by the national governments, that the establishment of a joint European defence force was out of the question and that the duplication of NATO's structure and activities should be avoided. British ideas were supposed to begin a debate, which they did, as the French government showed interest in them. Although it was clear that the British position was not supportive of the individual European direction suggested by the French, it was seen as a progressive step and as a basis for achieving the French position or at least for developing an acceptable compromise. The French wanted to avoid the integration of the WEU into the EU because they were afraid that under British leadership it would only mean the end of the WEU, without the creation of a real European defence policy, which was traditionally the key element of the French position.

The British and French positions were finally reconciled at Saint Malo on 3–4 December 1998. The differences were clarified during discussions and, as a result, a common declaration was issued. The declaration issued by the two major military powers of the Community emphasised that the EU should have an international influence commensurate with its economic weight, the Common Foreign and Security Policy provisions of the Amsterdam Treaty should be realised as soon as possible and the EU's individual operational capacities should be established based on a credible military force. The Declaration of Saint Malo also suggested that structures necessary for executing the military tasks should be built within the EU on top of the WEU's existing assets. The EU would act in all areas where America was reluctant to interfere and European actions would be carried out without duplicating NATO's capacities.

The process begun at Saint Malo gathered momentum and started to move more dynamically. The question of European defence was a key issue in the first half of 1999 during the German Presidency, which was fundamentally supportive of the concept put forward at Saint Malo, and turned the process into a direction which would lead to the gradual integration of the WEU. Despite British hopes, however, the Member States thought that the WEU should be integrated as part of the second pillar and not as a separate pillar. The idea of an extended second pillar was reinforced by the fact that the question of European defence seemed to be moving away from the WEU and starting to become an individual policy. This was the situation before the June 1999 Cologne European Council.

23.6. The birth of a European Security and Defence Policy

Following the British initiative, and parallel to the debate on European defence, the 1998–1999 Kosovo crisis and war was an important influence on the Cologne Summit. The events strengthened the view that the Union should have a stronger international presence and a more determined and defined common position on European defence policy. The conflict revealed that the capabilities of the EU and NATO were very different and that the EU, without the USA, had its limits and impediments when trying to play a determining role. Furthermore, there was a shift towards the view that, at the turn of the millennium, crisis management was the key issue and the problem which required resolution, rather than collective defence. It became clearer and clearer that the basis for respect in world politics was the ability to manage crises successfully. In the light of the events of the nineties in the Balkans, the Union in particular and Europe in general had clearly failed in this area.

As the British were willing to develop the CFSP further and thereby integrate the WEU into the Union, the most important issue was to convince the neutral states about the necessity for this decision and to find an acceptable alternative for them. Against that backdrop, on 3–4 July 1999, the European Council decided to adopt a declaration that enabled the EU to perform its duties declared in the Common Foreign and Security Policy.

At the Cologne Summit, the Member States decided that the WEU as an organisation "had fulfilled its historic mission" and would cease to exist; by the end of 2000, the necessary decisions would be taken about integrating the tasks of the WEU into the EU, in order to enable the Union to perform the so-called Petersberg tasks. These crisis management tasks were already included in the Treaty on European Union (Article 17): humanitarian and rescue missions, peacekeeping and deployment of combat forces in crisis management, including peacemaking. This meant that the European Council supported the WEU's integration in a way that did not include the WEU's principle of Common Defence, primarily due to the opposition of neutral states and, secondarily, because of arguments against the duplication of NATO's tasks in the EU. Thus, under pressure from neutral states and with the tacit approval of the more transatlantic-minded countries, the Member States in Cologne in practice decided that, of the two types of WEU functions, the newer ones (Petersberg missions) would be integrated into the EU, while the older ones concerning Common Defence would not. Thus, in the field of security policy, the Cologne Declaration first of all entrusted the EU with conflict-prevention and crisis management tasks, but did not create a common defence policy. However, it did note that in order to be able to perform these tasks, the EU should have an effective military force that was not dependent on NATO. In Cologne, the European Council urged the establishment of the necessary institutional framework, including not only the development of the necessary military forces, but also the setting up of new institutions. The European Council moved to include Defence Ministers in the Council of Ministers, establish a Political and Security Committee based in Brussels, create a Military Committee (whose leaders would make recommendations to the Political and Security Committee), recruit EU military staff and establish other institutions, including a satellite centre and an institute for security studies.

The Cologne decisions also underlined the need for Member States to establish crisis management units with their own headquarters. There would be two options in the event of an EU operation: either an EU operation with the use of NATO capacities and assets (based on an agreement with NATO), or an EU operation without the use of NATO capacities and assets.

The Declaration of the European Council called for crisis management to be developed in a way whereby all Member States would receive the same, full and unbiased treatment, whether they were NATO members or not. In addition, the Declaration of Cologne emphasised that non-EU NATO European allies and other EU applicant countries should be granted the opportunity to benefit from the closest possible cooperation, taking into consideration the consultation practice applied earlier in the WEU, and having regard to the EU's decision-making autonomy. The European Council underlined that this would require effective consultation, cooperation and transparency between NATO and the EU. However, the Cologne Summit did not provide guidelines for the practical implementation of cooperation with NATO and the involvement of non-EU members.

In the Cologne Declaration, the Heads of State or Government of the Member States supported a more coordinated development of the industrial and technological background of European defence, although they did not place the military industry within the Community's scope of authority.

To summarise, we can say that Cologne's greatest achievement was that it laid down the framework determining the cooperation mechanism called the European Security and Defence Policy (ESDP). However, specific details of cooperation were not elaborated at Cologne and basic questions were left open, namely the establishment of military capabilities, NATO-EU relations and the involvement of non-EU countries.

The European Council in Helsinki on 10–11 December 1999 tried to convert the Cologne objectives into specific tasks.

The most important decision of the Helsinki Summit concerned the creation, by 2003, of a rapid reaction force of 50–60,000 troops that could be deployed within 60 days and sustained for at least one year. The establishment of an independent European military capability with the necessary command, control, logistics and intelligence capacities would aim at the goal of being able to manage all of the Petersberg tasks – the so-called *'Headline Goal'*[15] of the ESDP. Member States confirmed that the rapid reaction force would not be a European Army, rather an operational and deployable multinational military force for crisis management (with the necessary command, control and logistics capability, etc.).

The European Council in Helsinki underlined that, in addition to the Headline Goal, non-military crisis management mechanisms should be established, which would enable a more effective use of civil assets and resources.

Furthermore, Helsinki ordered that, for the fulfilment of new tasks, new political and military structures should be built within the Council. In this new institutional set-up, regarding defence questions, the Defence Ministers of Member States are involved in the sessions of the Foreign Ministers' Council. The new permanent bodies responsible for the implementation of ESDP have been created within the Council. Specifying the decisions of the Cologne Summit, the Helsinki Summit decided upon the establishment of the following bodies within the Council:

- *Political and Security Committee (PSC)*: a body at ambassadorial level falling under the authority of the Council, to carry out political and strategic control in the whole field of ESDP and CFSP. PSC primarily monitors international trends and events, coordinates ESDP and CFSP issues, provides continuous dialogue between Member States and prepares recommendations for the Council. PSC also takes over the tasks of the former Political Committee as well and controls the work of the Military Committee.

- *European Union Military Committee (EUMC)*: a body consisting of military representatives of the Chiefs of Staff of the Member States' forces, which makes proposals to the Political and Security Committee and works beside it as a military consulting body. If needed, the body can meet at the level of Chiefs of Staff as well. It controls the EU Military Staff. Its president may participate at the Council's sessions if defence questions are on the agenda.

---

[15] The concept of 'Headline Goal' refers specifically to the creation of a rapid reaction force.

- *European Union Military Staff (EUMS):* a body consisting of military experts and responsible for the military planning, situation analysis and implementation of crisis management actions. This body designs the actions necessary for the Petersberg tasks and earmarks the capacities needed to perform them. The body performs its duties under the control of the EUMC.

The Helsinki European Council decided that temporary pre-institutions of these bodies should be set up from March 2000 (and this took place on 1 March 2000).

At the Helsinki Summit, the EU also tried to respond to US worries that the Cologne decisions foreshadowed a future neglect of NATO. The American position after Cologne stated that the EU could not 'own' all the Petersberg-type tasks and should only take independent steps in these fields if NATO did not wish to act. Eventually, in Helsinki, the Council accepted a formula that acknowledged NATO's primary competence in the field of crisis management and declared that the EU would carry out independent actions only if NATO (i.e. the USA) did not wish to act. However, there was no specific decision taken in Helsinki concerning the form of EU-NATO cooperation or about the specific conditions for the involvement of the non-EU European NATO allies in the ESDP.

Following Helsinki, in the first half of 2000, the EU continued with the development of ESDP. Tangible signs of this were the creation of ESDP's temporary institutions on 1 March, the establishment of the EU Civilian Crisis Management Committee and the fact that the first informal Council meeting of Defence Ministers took place on 28 February 2000. The end of this phase was marked by the Feira Summit on 19–20 June 2000, which also took some decisions supplementing Helsinki. The most important of these was that, in order to support the Headline Goal, the Member States would establish a police force of 5,000 troops, contributed from their respective forces, to be deployed as part of international missions for the prevention of crises and crisis management operations; Member States would be expected to deploy 1,000 policemen within 30 days.

In the second half of 2000, the development of the ESDP's operational framework and the EU's military capabilities continued. On 20 November 2000 in Brussels, Member States held a so-called 'capabilities commitment conference' concerning the realisation of the

Headline Goal, where 100,000 troops, 400 aircraft and 100 ships were pledged to the future rapid reaction force by different Member States, which would make it possible for the Headline Goal to be operational by 2003, if the other necessary structures (command, control, logistics, etc.) were in place. The latter, which many consider more difficult than declaratory offers, is essential to create a really effective military force. From this perspective, the availability of NATO assets was of crucial importance.

Apart from the Member States' pledged assets, non-EU European NATO members and candidate countries for EU membership also defined military capabilities that they could contribute to the European rapid reaction force.

As part of the process launched in Cologne, an important event was the Marseilles session of the WEU's Council of Ministers on 13 November 2000. At the Cologne Summit, the Member States had decided to wind up the WEU by integrating it into the EU, for which the related decisions were to be taken by the end of 2000. However, the EU did not want the ESDP to look like a direct successor of a relatively impotent WEU and thus wished to emphasise the fact that it had been established on a new basis. Therefore, at the Marseilles meeting of November 2000, the Member States decided that the WEU would not be directly subsumed into the EU, but its activities would be wound up first while the former WEU tasks would be incorporated into the EU at a higher level. In fact, this was indicated earlier by the fact that, following the Cologne Summit, the EU had started to build the capabilities and institutions that had formerly existed within the WEU. In this way, the process was directed towards the winding up of the WEU, rather than its integration within the EU. However, several Member States rejected the complete winding up of the WEU, as that would have also meant the denunciation of the modified Brussels Treaty creating the WEU, which at the same time had provided for the collective defence of ten WEU members. Although collective defence was provided for all WEU members within NATO, such a step would have been contrary to the principle of European integration, as it would have led to the winding up of an existing symbolic European achievement. In this way, the WEU members wanted to emphasise that they would like to keep collective defence within the European framework as well and maintain the modified Brussels Treaty, even if it was impossible within the EU framework – primarily because of the neutral countries. As a result, a formula concerning the WEU was adopted, calling for the winding up of the operation of the WEU, while retaining the modified Brussels Treaty. This was outlined eventually in the WEU's Marseilles Declaration. In Marseilles, the Member States decided that the practical operation of the WEU would cease on 1 July 2001, but that the organisation itself would not be wound up because the modified Brussels Treaty (primarily because of its Article V on collective defence) would stay in force, with some residual functions and limited institutional structure. This meant that some WEU institutions were kept[16], while others were incorporated into the EU (Institute for Security Studies, Satellite Centre). WEU bodies that had been duplicated in the EU ceased operation (essentially the governmental dimension disappeared, and with it the WEU Council). The process that had kicked off in Amsterdam came to an end and the organisation that had functioned for almost five decades was in practice wound up in 2001.

It was considered important to institutionalise certain elements of the process that had begun in Cologne and Helsinki and incorporate them into the EU Treaty through the Treaty of Nice. Accordingly, The Treaty of Nice, adopted at the Nice Summit on 7–10 December 2000, included several changes concerning ESDP and CFSP. According to the Treaty of Nice, due to the end of the WEU's operation, provisions concerning the WEU's integral role were to be taken out of the EU Treaty. As an institutional change, the Treaty of Nice introduced the Political and Security Committee instead of the Political Committee in the Treaty on European Union. Apart from the former tasks of the Political Committee – under the supervision of the Council – the Treaty placed political control and strategic direction within the Political and Security Committee's scope of authority. As an innovation, the Treaty of Nice introduced the possibility of enhanced cooperation[17] in the second pillar, although under much stricter conditions than in the first pillar: only for decisions adopted by unanimity on joint action and common positions, excluding defence and military issues.

The Nice Summit did not solve the question of how the establishment of EU operational capacity would avoid a duplication of existing NATO capabilities and create a cost-effective structure beneficial to all. Another question was how to involve non-EU European NATO allies and other states such as non-NATO candidate countries in EU operations.
For the EU, access to NATO assets, especially to planning capabilities, was of primary concern. For the practical operation of the ESDP, the conclusion of an agreement between the EU and NATO on the specific operational details seemed essential, but proved to be a tall order.

---

[16] The only WEU body still functioning on a regular basis is the Parliamentary Assembly, whose work mostly focuses on activities relevant to the EU.

[17] See 4.1.1.2. for details.

Europe had to reassure the United States that rivalry with NATO could be ruled out. But it was not only the USA that had reservations concerning such an agreement; Turkey – a European NATO ally but not an EU member – was not keen on allowing the Union to use NATO capabilities without it having a say in the decision-making process. It took the EU longer than expected to sort out Turkish reservations, which delayed the conclusion of the NATO-EU agreement. Finally, a political agreement was reached in December 2002, and the so-called Berlin Plus NATO-EU security agreement was signed on 17 March 2003. Under the terms of this agreement, the EU can make use of NATO assets and have access to NATO planning capabilities for EU-led crisis management operations. The agreement also established the appropriate NATO-EU consultation mechanisms[18], which provide guarantees for non-EU NATO members too. The agreement paved the way for independent EU crisis management operations, which began in early 2003, thereby fulfilling the Helsinki Headline Goal by the 2003 target date.

Overall, the process launched in Cologne – put into a final shape in Helsinki and confirmed in the Treaty of Nice – laid the foundations of a new European security and defence policy, aimed more at crisis management operations than common defence. It should be noted, however, that even the establishment of such a system was already a huge leap forward for Europe; its smooth operation could earn the EU authority and political capital on the international scene, and it could also boost the CFSP's image, which was relatively feeble (with mainly economic instruments) and controversial (with Member States frequently divided).

23.7. Recent developments in the Common Foreign and Security Policy; the European Security and Defence Policy in practice

The first EU operation launched under the aegis of the ESDP was the EU Police Mission (EUPM) in Bosnia-Herzegovina, which took over the task of UN peacekeepers, i.e. the blue helmets. The first phase of EUPM lasted until the end of 2005, when it was renewed and extended till the end of 2007.

---

[18] The levels of consultation: EU Political and Security Committee, NATO North-Atlantic Council, the EU and NATO Military Committees, NATO Secretary General and EU Secretary General (CFSP High Representative).

The EU launched its second ESDP operation and first military operation – *Concordia* – in Macedonia on 31 March 2003, which replaced the NATO-led mission, and was transformed into a police mission – *Proxima* – on 15 December 2003. Proxima was followed up by a police advisory mission – *EUPAT* – for a duration of six months. The EU terminated its crisis management activities in Macedonia in June 2006.

Concurrently, the EU carried out the *Artemis* humanitarian rescue mission in the Democratic Republic of Congo (DRC) between 30 May and 1 September 2003, followed up by the *Eupol-Kinshasa* police mission in 2004, which was succeeded by the *EUPOL RD Congo* mission. Following an official request by the DRC government, the EU decided to establish an EU advisory and assistance mission for security reform: *EUSEC - DR Congo*. In July 2004, the first so-called 'rule of law' mission was successfully launched in Georgia under the name *EUJUST/THEMIS*, which lasted one year. A decision was made in March 2005 on a similar mission in Iraq with the name *EUJUST/LEX*, whose mandate expires at the end of 2007. The European Union deployed a monitoring mission (*AMM*) in Aceh (Indonesia), designed to monitor the implementation of the peace agreement between the Indonesian Government and the Free Aceh Movement on 15 August 2005. The AMM became operational in September 2005, and was successfully concluded in December 2006. In response to the request of the African Union (AU), the European Union established in July 2005 an EU civilian-military supporting action to AMIS II, the AU peacekeeping mission in Darfur. The EU launched its Border Assistance Mission to Moldova and Ukraine (*EUBAM*) on 1 December 2005 with a two-year mandate to assist the two countries' border management authorities in fighting smuggling, trafficking in drugs and human beings, and customs fraud. The EU Border Assistance Mission at Rafah crossing point (Gaza) – code-named *EU BAM Rafah* – was launched in November 2005 for a duration of 12 months, which has been extended once until May 2008. In November 2005, the Council established an EU Police Mission in the Palestinian Territories (*EUPOL COPPS*) for an initial duration of 3 years to provide enhanced support to the Palestinian Authority in establishing sustainable and effective policing arrangements. The EU Police mission in Afghanistan (*EUPOL Afghanistan*) was launched in June 2007 for a period of at least 3 years with a similar aim.

The first few EU crisis management operations involved a few hundred troops. The most ambitious and biggest task so far is the *Althea* military operation, which began on 2 December 2004, under which the EU-led forces (EUFOR) took over the baton from the NATO-led SFOR troops in the peacekeeping mission in Bosnia-Herzegovina, safeguarding the implementation of the Dayton/Paris peace accords. Althea is carried out within the framework of the EU-NATO agreement with NATO assets and capabilities. Within the framework of Althea, 7,000 troops from 22 EU Member States and 11 other countries have been deployed. Due to the success of the mission and the stabilisation of the political and security situation, in February 2007 the EU decided to gradually scale back EUFOR's presence to some 2,500 troops.

The EU is preparing for an enhanced crisis management role in Kosovo. In this context, an EU planning team (*EUPT Kosovo*) – was set up in May 2007 regarding a possible future EU crisis management operation and a smooth transition from the United Nations Interim Administration Mission in Kosovo (UNMIK). As part of a possible EU crisis management operation in the field of rule of law and other areas, the EU is ready to deploy 2,000 policemen, judges, prosecutors and customs experts in Kosovo.

At its meeting in December 2003, the European Council decided that it was necessary to set up an intergovernmental defence agency for creating more flexible and effective military assets. Accordingly, on 12 July 2004, the Council established the *European Defence Agency*, with its seat in Brussels. The task of the Agency is to develop defence capabilities in crisis management, to promote European cooperation in military technology, to strengthen the industrial and technological bases of European defence, and to encourage technological research in the European defence industry.

In May 2004, the General Affairs and External Relations Council decided to adopt the 2010 Headline Goals, which added new objectives to the 1999 Helsinki Headline Goals (e.g. reinforcing strategic air, surface and sea transport). The 2010 Headline Goals focus on establishing so-called rapid deployment combat units. To fulfil this objective, in November 2004, the Ministers for Defence of the EU Member States announced their capabilities commitments for setting up combat units of 1,500 troops deployable within 5 to 10 days. Based on the capabilities pledged at the commitments conference, 13 combat units were set up, which can perform peacekeeping operations even in remote areas outside Europe.[19] By 2007, the EU had achieved one of the key 2010 Headline Goals of becoming capable of deploying two combat units at the same time.

In parallel with making the ESDP operational, the Member States decided to elaborate a European security strategy. The European Security Strategy adopted by the European Council of 12–13 December 2003 takes stock of the key security challenges the EU has to face (terrorism, the proliferation of weapons of mass destruction, regional conflicts,

---

[19] The full operational capacity of combat units had to be ensured by 2007, when they had to be deployable anywhere within 6,000 kilometres of Brussels. The United Kingdom, France, Italy and Spain pledged to also establish their own combat units, while the remaining combat units consist of the common commitments of various make-up of Member States.

weak governments and organised crime) and the strategic answers to those challenges. The EU must give a resolute response to these threats, promote security in neighbouring regions (particularly in the Balkans, the Mediterranean and the Middle East) and contribute to strengthening the international order based on multilateral cooperation ('effective multilateralism'), with cooperation with the UN as a priority. According to the strategy, the EU must be capable of deploying all means available, including economic, diplomatic, military and civilian means, to attain its objectives. If necessary, the EU must also be able to act quickly and effectively to prevent threats in time. The strategy allows pre-emptive strikes if necessary to avoid humanitarian disasters.

The strategy stipulates that the NATO-EU agreement provides the framework of crisis management operations. The strategy also devotes special attention to strengthening trans-Atlantic links within multilateral relations. The US has welcomed the adoption of the strategy and its objectives, particularly because it clarifies Europe's security policy ambitions and does not foresee the building-up of an independent, all-European operational capacity competing with the US.[20]

The European Security Strategy has enabled the EU to strengthen its relations with the United States in foreign, security and defence policy, which was needed and welcome on both sides of the Atlantic in the wake of the Iraqi crisis and following the disagreements of early 2003 on how to respond to and handle the situation in Iraq. NATO allies were divided on how to assess and manage the situation in Iraq, which caused the biggest rift in EU-US relations since World War II and caused internal conflicts within the Union. Some of the Member States strongly opposed the invasion of Iraq (mainly France, Germany, Belgium and Luxembourg), while others (the UK, Spain, Italy, Denmark, and acceding CEECs) supported the US openly, some even participating in military operations on the ground. This division over Iraq dealt a huge blow to the CFSP, because the Member States took opposing stances on the most important topical question of world politics, which questioned the very existence of the CFSP. Fortunately, the success of the first ESDP operations

---

[20] The Union began the implementation of the strategy in 2004. In that framework, the European Council adopted a Declaration on terrorism, reinforced and reasserted its action plan on combating terrorism, and adopted an EU strategy on the proliferation of weapons of mass destruction (WMDs).

counterbalanced the conflict to some extent. By the turn of 2003 and 2004, the functioning of the CFSP was returning to normal; once again, it was 'business as usual'.

The internal tensions of the CFSP created by the disagreement over intervention in Iraq eased as was demonstrated in 2004 when the Member States managed to come to an agreement on the CFSP reforms in the Constitutional Treaty. Reforming the Common Foreign and Security Policy has been on the European agenda since the Treaty of Amsterdam. The Member States tried to bring this process to a conclusion in the Constitutional Treaty, which had CFSP and ESDP reforms as one of its key elements.

However the ratification of the Constitutional Treaty signed on 29 October 2004 was not successful in all Member States and therefore, at their summit on 21–22 June 2007, the Heads of State or Government decided to abandon the constitutional path and place the Union's operation on new foundations by adopting a Reform Treaty amending the EU and EC Treaties in force. Nonetheless the Reform Treaty is largely based on the Constitutional Treaty and borrows a good part of its provisions, but in the area of CFSP and ESDP it waters down the reforms enshrined in the Constitutional Treaty and to some extent is therefore a step backwards. However, its provisions (on abolishing the pillar structure, merging the positions of the CFSP High Representative and the External Relations Commissioner under the new title of *High Representative of the Union for Foreign Affairs and Security Policy*, setting up a European External Action Service, establishing a separate Foreign Affairs Council and the incorporation of the principle of collective defence) will bring some progress insofar as decision-making could become more efficient in the area of CFSP compared to the current practice. Since the changes introduced by the Reform Treaty will probably only become effective in 2009, they are discussed in detail separately, in Point 23 of the Annex.

It should be noted that the Common Foreign and Security Policy will not change fundamentally upon the entry into force of the Reform Treaty (in fact, the element hindering results the most – decision-making by unanimity – will be maintained), but a special passarelle clause leaves open the option of switching to qualified majority voting – without amending the Treaties – by a unanimous decision of the Member States. This is worth pointing out because, as was indicated by the creation of the ESDP, due to the intergovernmental nature of cooperation, all decisions in this area depend on the political will of the Member States. By creating the ESDP, the EU already took a huge step forward in resolving the 'economic giant – political dwarf' paradox. Nevertheless, due to the decision-making framework (the need for unanimity), the EU may easily find itself in a situation where it is unable to speak with a single voice, take a united stance, respond effectively to political developments in the world and demonstrate that it is a political force to be reckoned with on the global stage.

CHAPTER 24
JUSTICE AND HOME AFFAIRS IN THE EUROPEAN UNION

24.1. The beginnings of cooperation in justice and home affairs: the third pillar of the Maastricht Treaty

The Treaty establishing the European Economic Community included no provisions to establish the necessary legal basis for cooperation in justice and home affairs (JHA). Nonetheless, the need for such cooperation would be inevitable, given the logical outcome of the main goal of the Community: the single market characterised by the principle of the unrestricted free movement of workers. With the evolution of European integration, this principle was interpreted increasingly broadly, extending free movement to all persons and, in this context, the aim was to dismantle physical and technical internal borders. The rationale behind this objective is that the removal of these barriers and the free movement of persons enables citizens to fully enjoy the benefits of integration. However, the free movement of persons carries a number of security risks, which necessitates cooperation and coordination between JHA bodies and the approximation of JHA legislation. The need to create a single market without border controls, which was growing stronger in the late eighties, led logically to the idea that the Member States should institutionalise their cooperation in the field of justice and home affairs. This idea was reinforced by the recognition that, in the age of globalisation, EU Member States can only combat illegal immigration, organised crime and terrorism endangering their security through concerted action.[1] On this basis, and led by the objective of creating a political union, the Member States decided to introduce justice and home affairs cooperation as a new element of the Treaty on European Union. However, as this field impinges on national sovereignty, similarly to the Common Foreign and Security Policy, they did not want to transfer it from national competence to Community institutions, but only to intergovernmental cooperation.

---

[1] As part of the fight against terrorism, the so-called TREVI cooperation was created in the mid-seventies, which led to continuously expanding police cooperation through various working groups (on organised crime, internal security, etc.); the TREVI cooperation was a forerunner of what later became the third pillar.

This led to the establishment of Cooperation in the field of Justice and Home Affairs as the third pillar of the European Union, separate from the Community first pillar and also from the intergovernmental second pillar of Common Foreign and Security Policy.

The Maastricht Treaty, signed on 7 February 1992, institutionalised JHA cooperation at the level of European integration. JHA cooperation was provided for in Article K of the Treaty on European Union, and Article K.1 listed those areas that belonged to the scope of third pillar intergovernmental cooperation:

1. asylum policy;
2. the control of external borders of Member States (namely borders with non-EU states);
3. immigration policy and questions relating to nationals of third (non-member) countries (entry into, exit from and movement within the Member States, residence, immigration, establishment, family reunion and employment of such people);
4. the fight against drugs;
5. the fight against international fraud;
6. judicial cooperation in civil matters;
7. judicial cooperation in criminal matters;
8. customs cooperation;
9. police cooperation on preventing and combating terrorism, illicit drug trafficking and other serious forms of international crime.

Due to the intergovernmental nature of cooperation in justice and home affairs, according to the Maastricht Treaty, the Council became the key body in relation to third pillar issues. In the Council, following consultations, the Member States' Ministers for Justice and Home Affairs could adopt the following legal acts: common positions, joint actions and conventions. As justice and home affairs cooperation was a sensitive area in terms of Member States' national sovereignty, the Maastricht Treaty stipulated that decisions were to be taken unanimously, except in relation to procedural questions and the implementation of joint actions. According to the provisions of the Treaty, the Council had to act by unanimity for the adoption of conventions, but measures concerning the implementation of conventions only required a two-thirds majority.

The COREPER assisted the work of the Council of Ministers in this field too, primarily by preparing the Council's meetings. However, just as in the second pillar, the main consultative technical forum was not COREPER, but the Coordination Committee, which was also known as the K.4 Committee, after the relevant Article of the Maastricht Treaty. Within the Coordination Committee, separate working groups were set up to deal with specific technical issues and to serve as consultative forums between Member-State officials.

By putting the Council in charge of the third pillar, the Maastricht Treaty gave all other Community institutions a limited role. The Treaty stipulated that the Member States could involve the Commission in JHA cooperation. The Commission could make proposals in the first six points listed in Article K.1, but its power of initiative was not exclusive as under the first pillar, being shared instead with the Member States, while only the Member States could make proposals on the last three points of Article K.1. Under the Maastricht Treaty, the Council was obliged to inform the European Parliament about decisions taken under the third pillar. The Parliament also had the right to pose questions, and in certain cases, it even had a consultative role, but it had to deliver its opinions within a limited period and the Council had no obligation to take them into consideration. The Court of Justice had no jurisdiction over activities in the third pillar, but the Council could authorise it to give a preliminary ruling in relation to certain conventions.

The source of law and decision-making mechanisms established by the Maastricht Treaty functioned in unchanged form until the entry into force of the Amsterdam Treaty, which brought fundamental changes to the sources of law and amended the decision-making rules as well. (See 24.3.3.)

Within the framework of JHA cooperation but related to Community law (EC Treaty), it should be noted that the Treaty of Maastricht introduced a new Article (Article 100c), which created the basis for a common visa policy. According to the provisions of this Article, the Council, acting on the Commission's proposal, sets the list of third countries whose citizens need a visa for entering EU Member States. All Member States are obliged to check the visas of citizens from countries on this list.

24.2. The Schengen Agreement and the Schengen acquis

Concerning the free movement of persons, some of the Member States had decided to establish a type of cooperation in justice and home affairs before the Maastricht Treaty, though outside the framework of the Community. The Schengen Agreement, signed on 14 June 1985 by France, Germany, Belgium, Luxembourg and the Netherlands, can be considered a type of 'enhanced cooperation'[2] initiated by a group of Member States. The Schengen Agreement on the abolition of checks at internal borders was supplemented by

---

[2] For more on enhanced cooperation, see 4.1.1.2.

the Convention Implementing the Schengen Agreement on 19 June 1990. On this basis, the Agreement and the Implementing Convention finally entered into force in 1995.
The Schengen Implementing Convention provided for the setting up of an Executive Committee, with one delegate from each Member State, for the purposes of overseeing the implementation of the Agreement and further decision-making necessary for its implementation.
The five original signatories to the Agreement and the Implementing Convention were later joined by Italy (1991), Portugal and Spain (1991), Greece (1992), Austria (1995), Denmark, Finland and Sweden (1996), who abolished checks at internal borders with a few years' delay. Out of the EU-15, only two Member States, namely the United Kingdom and Ireland, opted to stay out, while non-members Iceland and Norway joined as associated countries at the same time as the three Scandinavian Member States.[3] The ten Member States that joined the EU in 2004[4] are expected to become fully-fledged members of the Schengen area from 31 December 2007, which means that in practice checks of persons at internal borders[5] will be abolished on 1 January 2008. Non-EU member Switzerland is also expected to become part of the Schengen area in 2008.[6] Bulgaria and Romania, who became EU members on 1 January 2007, will probably be able to join the Schengen area in a few years.

With the entry into force of the Schengen Implementing Convention, checks at the common borders of participating countries were abolished and transferred to the external EU borders, which meant the adoption of common visa, asylum and border control provisions. In order to compensate for the increased risks to security, the free movement of persons entailed certain 'compensation measures', which necessitated closer

---

[3] Since Iceland and Norway, in cooperation with Denmark, Finland and Sweden, had established the so-called Nordic Passport Union earlier, thereby abolishing border checks among the five of them, it was a logical step to allow Iceland and Norway to join the Schengen zone with the three Scandinavian Member States. These two countries take part in the work of the Schengen Executive Committee and in developing the legal acts related to the Schengen Agreement (the so-called Schengen *acquis*), but have no voting rights.

[4] Cyprus is the only one of the ten Member States that acceded to the Union in 2004 which is not planning to join Schengen on the above date.

[5] For air traffic – checks at airports – the introduction of the Schengen system is programmed for 29 March 2008 when the new airline timetables take effect.

[6] The accession of Switzerland to the Schengen area inevitably means the same for Liechtenstein, as there are no border controls between the two countries.

coordination between judicial, police and customs authorities. The so-called Schengen Information System (SIS) was also set up to facilitate the exchange of information for the identification of persons, stolen or lost goods. The functioning of the SIS is assisted by a network called SIRENE, which comprises representatives of national and local judicial, police and customs authorities and operates a non-stop ('24/7') mutual information exchange service. Since SIS was designed for the needs of a pre-enlargement Union, the EU decided to develop SIS II to meet the new requirements.[7]

As a result of the Schengen Implementing Convention, and particularly the work of the Executive Committee, the Member States adopted a number of supplementary implementing measures, which - together with the Convention itself - created a comprehensive body of legislation, called the Schengen *acquis*. However, as it was created outside the European Union and European Community framework, it did not become part of the *acquis communautaire*. In addition to the dismantling of internal border controls, the Schengen *acquis* included provisions on the following areas:
– the rules applicable to external border controls;
– the separation of passengers from within and outside the Schengen area at airports and sea ports;
– the harmonisation of legislation on entry and short-term visas;
– coordination between border guards;
– the role of haulage operators and carriers in the fight against illegal immigration;
– the reinforcement of legal cooperation for faster extradition and information provision;
– asylum issues.

The asylum legislation adopted within the framework of the Schengen Agreement was replaced by the provisions of the Dublin Convention, which was signed by the EU Member States on 15 June 1990. The Convention entered into force on 1 September 1997. The key provision of the Dublin Convention is that an application for asylum submitted in the

---

[7] SIS II should have been operational by March 2007, but it became clear in 2006 that the original deadline was not feasible, thus the Ministers of Justice and Home Affairs decided at their meeting in December 2006 that the ten new Member States would not have to wait for SIS II and could become part of the Schengen area with the current improved version of SIS I (SIS One4All). SIS II is expected to be introduced in 2008 in the enlarged Schengen area.

area of the EU only has to be examined by one Member State, and if rejected, does not have to be processed again by other Member States.[8]

24.3. The Treaty of Amsterdam: an overhaul of the third pillar, 'Communitising' part of the cooperation in justice and home affairs

Article K.9 of the Maastricht Treaty stipulated that, if the Council deems it necessary, it may unanimously decide to take the issues listed in points 1–6 of Article K.1 into the first pillar (and apply Article 100c of the Treaty establishing the European Community to them), and at the same time define the voting rules applicable to these issues. It was the 1996–1997 intergovernmental conference and the Amsterdam Treaty it prepared that finally brought a breakthrough in this area by introducing fundamental changes in JHA cooperation, based on the principle laid down in Article K.9. Arguably the greatest achievement of the Amsterdam Treaty was to lay the new foundations for cooperation in justice and home affairs.

The Treaty of Amsterdam inserted into Article 2 of the Treaty on European Union the objective of developing the Union as an 'area of freedom, security and justice' based on the free movement of persons and on concerted action in the first, third (and to some extent the second) pillar.

To this end, the Treaty overhauled the system of cooperation in justice and home affairs. The changes introduced by the Amsterdam Treaty focused on three elements:

- Transferring some JHA questions (asylum and immigration policy, internal and external border controls, judicial cooperation in civil matters) into the first pillar.
- Incorporating the Schengen Agreement, the Schengen Implementing Convention and the Schengen acquis into the legal and institutional framework of the European Union.

---

[8] The Dublin Convention was replaced in 2003 by Regulation 343/2003/EC ('Dublin II"), which clarifies and specifies the responsibilities of Member States for processing applications for asylum.

- Reinforcing and restructuring the legal sources of the remaining third pillar (police and judicial cooperation in criminal matters).

As justice and home affairs became fragmented between two pillars after Amsterdam, activities in this area are now usually referred to as the area of freedom, security and justice.

24.3.1. Justice and home affairs questions transferred into the first pillar

The Treaty of Amsterdam 'Communitised' many of the former third pillar areas (asylum and immigration policy, external and internal border controls, judicial cooperation in civil matters), transferring them to the competence of the Community institutions. The Amsterdam Treaty incorporated the area of "Visas, asylum, immigration and other policies related to free movement of persons" as a separate title (EC Treaty Part Three Title IV Articles 61–69). To mitigate the impact of changes and to ensure continuity, the Amsterdam Treaty provided for a five-year transitional period for drafting Community legislation in this field. Accordingly, within five years after the entry into force of the Treaty (by 1 May 2004), the EU had to establish a uniform border control procedure and a common visa policy, adopt the necessary Community legislation (minimum requirements) on asylum and immigration policy, as well as draw up uniform conditions for the entry and residence of third-country nationals. The necessary legal measures were to be adopted through the legal sources of the first pillar (regulations, directives, and decisions).

In 'Communitised' areas, the Commission gradually acquired the main and exclusive right of initiative.[9] The Treaty also gradually introduced the jurisdiction of the Court of Justice. At first, the European Parliament had a consultative right only but, since the end of the five-year transitional period, the Council, acting unanimously, may introduce co-decision in certain areas. In the Council, decision-making by unanimity remained the general rule in the area of justice and home affairs (except for certain elements, such as visa policy, where qualified majority voting was introduced); since the end of the five-year period, the Council may also change this requirement, following a unanimous decision, and introduce qualified-majority voting.[10] The Treaty of Nice brought further progress in this respect. (See 24.5.)

---

[9] Following the extension of the Commission's scope of competence, a separate Directorate-General for Justice and Home Affairs (DG JHA) was set up within the Commission in late 1999.

[10] According to the Amsterdam Treaty, such decisions by the Council had to be ratified by the Member States in accordance with their own constitutional requirements. This was amended by the Treaty of Nice. (See 24.5.)

Overall, since the end of the five-year period, the visa, asylum, immigration and other policies related to the free movement of persons have been functioning entirely according to the institutional and decision-making rules of the first pillar. With these achievements, the Amsterdam Treaty took a great step towards creating a political union, and also created precedence in European integration by bringing intergovernmental areas under the scope of Community competence. The 'Communitisation' of justice and home affairs demonstrated that intergovernmental cooperation is not an alternative to but rather a forerunner of the Community system, and that the pillar structure is not a rigid system, but rather a process leading from intergovernmental to Community cooperation.

24.3.2. Incorporating the Schengen acquis into the framework of the European Union

The Schengen Agreement, which was signed by 13 states, dismantled internal borders and was thus one of the most tangible results of integration. Placing this Agreement into the Community's or Union's legal and institutional competence would be a logical consequence of transferring the area of free movement of persons into the first pillar. A major step forward was taken when, in order to 'Communitise' border controls by abolishing internal border checks and unifying external border controls, one of the Protocols to the Treaty of Amsterdam incorporated the Schengen Agreement and related *acquis* into the EU framework. The Member States implemented this provision after the entry into force of the Amsterdam Treaty on 1 May 1999 while, with its decision of 20 May 1999, the Council incorporated the Schengen *acquis* into the first and third pillars (depending on the nature of the relevant legislative provisions). This meant that, since that time, countries wishing to join the EU have also had to accept the Schengen Agreement as part of Community legislation.

Due to their special insular status, the UK and Ireland, which had opted to stay out of the Schengen area, did not have to adopt the Agreement or the Schengen *acquis*. Under the Amsterdam Treaty, Denmark, although a full member of the Agreement, could reserve the right to decide on a case-by-case basis whether it wanted to implement a new piece of legislation adopted by the EC or EU in this field.

24.3.3. Police and Judicial Cooperation in Criminal Matters – The third pillar after the Amsterdam Treaty

Due to the changes introduced by the Treaty of Amsterdam, the third pillar, i.e. Title IV of the EU Treaty, and the amended Article K.1 (after Amsterdam, Article 29 of the EU Treaty) now only included Police and Judicial Cooperation in Criminal Matters (PJCC).
However, even the narrowed-down third pillar was not left untouched: the Amsterdam Treaty brought some progress towards closer and more successful cooperation.

In order to create an 'area of freedom, security and justice', cooperation on combating crime became more intensive following Amsterdam. Priority areas now include the fight against organised crime, terrorism, trafficking of children and human beings generally, illicit trafficking in drugs and arms, fraud and corruption. The Amsterdam Treaty specified the measures that Member States should take for such purposes: the Treaty called for closer cooperation between police forces, customs, judicial and other authorities, the approximation of criminal laws of Member States where necessary and the strengthening of the role of Europol.

Europol

The Council decided on the establishment of a European Police Office (Europol) on 26 July 1995. Europol, which started operating on 1 July 1999 with headquarters in The Hague, replaced the Europol Drugs Unit (EDU) created in 1995 for an interim period with limited competence. Europol is an intergovernmental agency based on the cooperation of Member State police authorities and aimed at improving the efficiency of cooperation. Europol, unlike Interpol, has no investigative and law enforcement competence of its own, although the issue of giving Europol such powers has been raised recently. The task of Europol is to facilitate the exchange, collection, analysis, maintenance and dissemination of information, to inform competent authorities and to support the investigation activities of Member States. Each of the Member States has set up a national liaison unit to liaise between Europol and national authorities.

> The competence of Europol extends to combating terrorism, drug trafficking, trade in human beings, illegal immigration, illicit trafficking in radioactive and nuclear substances, trafficking of stolen vehicles, money laundering and counterfeiting of the euro.

As a fundamental change, the Amsterdam Treaty introduced a new system of legal sources in the restricted third pillar. Out of the three legal acts indicated in the Maastricht Treaty, it abolished joint actions, retained conventions and common positions, and introduced the so-called framework decisions and other decisions. The four legal acts of the third pillar are discussed in detail in Chapter 5.2.2.3.

The Amsterdam Treaty did not change the system of decision-making in the third pillar laid down in the Treaty of Maastricht, maintaining the leading role of the Council as the exclusive decision-making body. As far as decision-making is concerned, the Council acts by unanimity when adopting any of the four types of legal acts in the third pillar, with the exception of measures necessary for the implementation of decisions, which are adopted by a qualified majority.

It should also be mentioned that, due to the new numbering of Articles in the Amsterdam Treaty, the K.4 Committee was renamed the Article 36 Committee.

The Treaty also clarified the Parliament's consultative role: the Council now has to consult the EP before taking a binding decision on any third-pillar question. Nevertheless, the Parliament still has to issue its opinion by the deadline set by the Council, which cannot be shorter than three months.[11]

The Commission's role has also grown, as it was granted the right of initiative in respect of all issues in the third pillar, although it still shares this with the Member States.

The Amsterdam Treaty did not give the Court of Justice full jurisdiction in the third pillar, but gave the Court the power of delivering preliminary rulings on new pieces of legislation.

---

[11] It is worth noting that, due to its consultative right, the Parliament's competence is somewhat wider than in the second pillar, where it is only informed about decisions in addition to its right to pose questions.

24.4. Building an area of freedom, security and justice after Amsterdam

In the area of justice and home affairs, the overall objective of the Amsterdam Treaty was to create an area of 'freedom, security and justice', which gave a common frame to future tasks in both 'Communitised' and third pillar areas.

The building of the area of freedom, security and justice had begun well before the Amsterdam Treaty entered into force. In July 1998, the European Commission had issued a Communication which laid down the foundations, conditions and instruments of implementing this objective. On the basis of this Communication, the Council adopted an Action Plan, on 3 December 1998, on the area of freedom, security and justice, which was confirmed by the Vienna European Council a few days later. The Action Plan gave substance to the objectives of the Amsterdam Treaty, set deadlines for a period of five years and specified a list of priorities with measures necessary for establishing an area of freedom, security and justice. The Action Plan pointed out that the underlying aim of this objective was to guarantee the free movement of persons as well as to safeguard their security by combating crime. The Action Plan defined what the Union meant by an area of freedom, security and justice. An area of freedom meant the free movement of persons based on the Schengen model, the protection of fundamental rights and the combating of all forms of discrimination. An area of security meant the fight against all forms of crime, for which a separate Action Plan was adopted at the Amsterdam Summit in June 1997; Europol had a key role to play in establishing an area of security. An area of justice reflected the EU's aim to guarantee equal access to justice for all citizens, and to promote cooperation between judicial authorities; in practical terms, the latter meant simplifying the legal environment for citizens in civil matters, improving coordination between prosecuting authorities in criminal matters, and elaborating uniform principles and rules, particularly in relation to procedures and sentences.

The Action Plan was based on a coordinated set of measures of first and third pillar JHA areas. Within that framework it was decided that:

– in the area of asylum, a uniform procedure based on common standards would be developed (clarifying the procedures for examining applications for asylum), and the Eurodac Convention (which compares the fingerprints of refugees) would be put into practice;

- in the area of immigration, common rules would be adopted on entry, residence, and refusal of entry, action against illegal immigration would be improved, and the rules on free movement of non-Member State nationals within the EU would be elaborated;
- in the area of visa policy, a standard visa would be introduced;
- in the area of judicial cooperation in civil matters, problems arising from the conflict of national laws would have to be sorted out, particularly in the fields of various contractual relationships, marriage, divorce and inheritance;
- in the area of police cooperation, the emphasis would be on extending cooperation between authorities, reinforcing the operational capabilities of Europol, developing cooperation between Europol and judicial authorities, and elaborating the conditions for action and intervention by Member State authorities in another Member State;
- in the area of judicial cooperation in criminal matters, the focus would be on mutual assistance by national authorities, simplifying extradition procedures, mutual acceptance and enforcement of decisions and sentences and approximating criminal law.

The priority of justice and home affairs and the weight of the objective of establishing an area of freedom, security and justice were demonstrated by the fact that the extraordinary European Council meeting of Tampere on 15–16 October 1999 was fully dedicated to these issues. The Tampere Summit pointed out that establishing the area of freedom, security and justice was as important a task as the creation of the single market had been previously. Thus, the Heads of State or Government requested the Commission to develop a so-called 'scoreboard' on the basis of the Action Plan, which would serve as an instrument to monitor the progress made on the priority tasks over the next five years. The Commission completed the scoreboard by March 2000, which served as an instrument to monitor the implementation of the package of measures – which became known as the Tampere programme following the Tampere Summit – in the Commission's bi-annual reports.

At the Tampere Summit, the Heads of State or Government decided to set up Eurojust, a unit modelled on Europol, giving it the task of facilitating cooperation and the exchange of information between national authorities responsible for prosecution. Eurojust's purpose is to promote coordination between national judicial, prosecuting and police authorities in the fight against organised crime, relying on Europol analyses and closely cooperating with the European Judicial Network, which was set up in 1998 to facilitate judicial cooperation in criminal matters.

24.5. The provisions of the Treaty of Nice affecting justice and home affairs

The Treaty of Nice, which was signed three and a half years after Amsterdam on 26 February 2001 and which entered into force on 1 February 2003, amended some Treaty provisions pertaining to policies in the area of justice and home affairs both in the first and third pillar.

In the first pillar, the changes introduced by the Treaty of Nice concerned decision-making. The Treaty of Nice extended the scope of qualified majority voting and the co-decision procedure and made further extensions easier. The Treaty of Nice extended co-decision and QMV to judicial cooperation in civil matters (with the exception of family law) upon its entry into force, and to certain other areas from 1 May 2004; in other areas, it allowed further extensions to be made by a unanimous decision of the Council.[12]

In the third pillar the Treaty of Nice brought two important changes.
Firstly, it institutionalised Eurojust, as had been decided in Tampere, by incorporating its establishment both into Article 29 defining third-pillar activities and into Article 31 providing for cooperation in criminal matters. The amended EU Treaty defined the scope of competence of Eurojust as decided in Tampere, i.e. strengthening cooperation between national prosecuting authorities, promoting investigations against organised crime based on analyses by Europol, and enhancing cooperation with the European Judicial Network. Secondly, the Treaty of Nice revised the conditions for enhanced cooperation in the third pillar.[13] The Treaty allowed for initiatives for enhanced cooperation in any area of the third pillar. Similarly to the first pillar, the right of veto was abolished in the third pillar too, which means that enhanced cooperation between at least 8 Member States in the area of

---

[12] Regulating the conditions of the free movement of third country nationals in possession of a visa (from 1 May 2004), illegal immigration (from 1 May 2004), procedures for checks of persons at external borders (with unanimous Council decision), asylum (following the adoption of a Community framework agreement), refugees/'temporarily protected persons' (following the adoption of a Community framework agreement). In the above areas, the introduction of co-decision and QMV does not require ratification by the Member States.

[13] For more on enhanced cooperation, see 4.1.1.2.

police or judicial cooperation in criminal matters requires the qualified majority approval of the Member States. The request for enhanced cooperation has to be submitted to the Commission, which formulates an opinion and submits its recommendation to the Council. During this endorsement procedure, the European Parliament has to be consulted and its opinion is sought.

24.6. Further steps in the creation of an area of freedom, security and justice

The terrorist attacks against the United States on 11 September 2001 brought about a decisive turning point in the creation of an area of freedom, security and justice, necessitating a brand new approach to the issue. Following the events of 11 September, the fight against terrorism gained new momentum, which opened new dimensions not only in international cooperation but also in cooperation inside the European Union, particularly in areas where a lack of sufficient political will had prevented real progress in previous years. The attacks of 11 September indicated that, for their domestic security, individual states depend on each other more than ever; this gave a push to the deepening of integration in a number of areas.

At the extraordinary summit meeting in Brussels on 21 September 2001, the EU Heads of State or Government took a common stand on taking all measures possible to increase security. As a first step, they asserted the need to implement the conventions that had been concluded earlier to curb terrorism, such as the conventions of 1995 and 1996 on extradition, the decisions on setting up Europol and Eurojust, and the one signed in May 2000 on mutual assistance in criminal matters. In addition, the events of 11 September 2001 triggered a number of other initiatives and measures, which also led to the setting up of Eurojust (on 6 March 2002), the creation of a Police Chiefs Task Force, the strengthening of cooperation between intelligence services, the judiciary and the police, the adoption of a European arrest warrant, and efforts to cut the financing of channels of terrorism, in particular the amendment of the Anti-Money-laundering Directive.

From 2002, the implementation of the Tampere programme accelerated; according to plans, the objectives had to be fulfilled by the end of the five-year transitional period in May 2004. The Commission published its assessment report on the Tampere programme on 2 June 2004. The report delivered a positive overall assessment, dealing with issues such as laying the foundations for a common asylum and immigration policy, preparing the harmonisation of external border control, developing police cooperation, establishing judicial cooperation and approximating legislation on cross-border crime and terrorism. Although the report acknowledged the fact that not all objectives had been achieved, it emphasised the progress made by comprehensive and coordinated action in those five years. The report pointed out that, in the wake of the terrorist attacks in the USA on 11 September 2001 and closer to home in Madrid on 11 March 2004, citizens expect the European Union to develop a more effective, common approach for managing and preventing cross-border problems (terrorism, organised crime, immigration, trafficking in human beings), while continuing to guarantee fundamental rights and liberties. In that respect, the report also underlined the rigidity of decision-making mechanisms, which made cooperation and prompt action difficult, and thus proposed the extension of co-decision and qualified majority voting to this area by applying the relevant clause of the Treaty of Nice. The Commission also proposed the adoption of another multi-annual programme as a follow-up to Tampere.

The Heads of State or Government of the EU met in The Hague on 4–5 November 2004 for a summit devoted to justice and home affairs (similarly to the Tampere Summit), where they adopted the so-called Hague programme (also known as the Tampere II programme). The Hague programme is a multi-annual justice and home affairs programme dealing with all aspects of the area of freedom, security and justice, which is complemented by an Action Plan, adopted by the Council.

The key objective of the Hague programme is to develop the common capabilities of the Union and its Member States to guarantee fundamental rights, minimum procedural guarantees and access to justice, provide protection to asylum seekers under the Geneva Convention and other international conventions, regulate flows of immigration, safeguard the Union's external borders, combat cross-border organised crime, prevent terrorist threats, make greater use of Europol and Eurojust, ensure the mutual recognition of court rulings in civil and criminal cases, and remove legal and judicial obstacles from civil and family law proceedings with cross-border implications. Among the objectives to be achieved in five years, the Hague programme sets ambitious goals, including to:

– establish a Common European Asylum System, with a common procedure and a uniform status for those who are granted asylum; as part of this objective, the European Refugee Fund was set up in 2005;

- elaborate an effective policy to expel and return illegal immigrants to their country of origin;
- abolish checks at internal borders and make the new Schengen Information System (SIS II) operational in 2007[14];
- gradually establish the integrated management of external border controls, set up a European Agency for the Management of Operational Cooperation at the External Borders (FRONTEX) by 2005[15] and establish a Community border control fund;
- integrate biometric data into travel documents, visas, residence permits, passports of Union citizens and information systems, as well as elaborate minimum rules for national identity cards;
- establish, in the long-term, common visa application centres;
- step up efforts in the fight against terrorism, draw up a long-term strategy by 2005 and address the factors that contribute to fundamentalism and to the involvement of individuals in terrorist activities;[16]
- establish a European Area for Justice to ensure cross-border litigation and enforcement of judgements in civil matters among European states.

The European Drugs Strategy for 2005–2012 was annexed to the Hague programme in December 2004.

At its Hague Summit, the European Council requested the Commission to draw up annual reports on the basis of information provided by the Member States, which assess the implementation of the Hague programme in the same scoreboard format as in the case of the Tampere programme.

---

[14] As explained in 24.2., SIS II is expected to become operational only in 2008.

[15] FRONTEX was established in 2005 with its headquarters in Warsaw.

[16] The EU's Counter-Terrorism Strategy was adopted at the European Council meeting of December 2005. The Strategy covers four strands of work: *Prevention* (to prevent people turning to terrorism by tackling the factors or root causes that can lead to radicalisation and recruitment), *Protection* (to protect citizens and infrastructure and reduce vulnerability to attack), *Pursuit* (to pursue and investigate terrorists, bring them to justice, to impede their planning, travel and communications, to disrupt their support networks and to cut off their funding) and *Response* (to prepare to manage and minimise the consequences of a terrorist attack in the spirit of solidarity, should the other three strands fail).

Migration has become a key issue of justice and home affairs in recent years, partly because of its security implications and partly because of its links with the fight against organised crime (trafficking in drugs and human beings) and terrorism. While the EU, with its aging and shrinking population, needs migrants to reinvigorate its labour market, but uncontrolled waves of migration could jeopardise the jobs of many Europeans and thereby create social tensions. To make things more complicated, migration carries with it a number of potential clashing points due to differences in cultural traditions and identity. In that context – and having regard to the principle of the free movement of persons – the EU's key task is to establish a comprehensive European immigration policy.

As illegal immigration has been a growing problem for several Member States in recent years[17], the European Council meeting of 14–15 December 2006 – which devoted special attention to immigration issues – identified this issue as one of the EU's key priorities for the 21st century. The European Council pointed out that the EU must step up international cooperation with countries of origin and between the Member States themselves to combat illegal immigration. International cooperation should focus on: linking immigration to aid and development, and elaborating country-specific forms of cooperation; improving bilateral cooperation in readmission and return issues, with an emphasis on reintegrating returned emigrants; ensuring that action along the main immigration routes is more effective to prevent people smuggling and human trafficking. Intra-Community cooperation between Member States should encourage more effective action against illegal employment, improved policing of external borders by reinforcing FRONTEX capacity, and better control of marine borders to the south. In line with the European Council's decisions, the European Commission took a number of specific initiatives in 2007 to reinforce Union action, including a draft Directive on sanctioning employers of illegal workers and a proposal for offering countries of origin so-called mobility partnerships (which would provide a legal framework for managing legal migration to the EU, offer immigrants legal employment in sectors facing labour shortages and the opportunity to return to their home country with the experience they gained in Europe).

---

[17] There are currently between five and eight million illegal immigrants residing in the EU, and that figure grows by about 400,0000 to 500,000 each year.

The EU has also set up a Community framework programme for the period 2007–2013 under the name on 'Solidarity and management of migration flows', to help improve the management of migratory flows at the level of the European Union and to strengthen solidarity between Member States, with the aim of the better management of immigration, asylum and border control. The framework programme, which has a total budget of EUR 4 billion, operates financial solidarity mechanisms through the following four funds: the European Refugee Fund (budget: EUR 700 million), the External Borders Fund (EUR 1.82 billion), the European Fund for the Integration of Third-country Nationals (EUR 825 million) and the Return Fund (EUR 676 million)

An important recent development in the area of justice and home affairs is the Treaty of Prüm, signed by seven Member States (Austria, Belgium, France, Germany, Luxembourg, the Netherlands and Spain) on 27 May 2005 in the German city of Prüm. Similarly to the Schengen Agreement, this Treaty was born outside the EU framework, and is aimed at stepping up the fight against terrorism, cross-border crime and illegal immigration by means of improved exchange of information relating to DNA, fingerprints, vehicle registration, personal and non-personal data. A number of other Member States had indicated their wish to sign the Prüm Treaty, while the June 2007 JHA Council adopted a third-pillar Decision to incorporate the majority of the Prüm provisions into the EU's legal framework. The Prüm Decision aims to improve and accelerate the exchange of information between national law-enforcement authorities.[18] This correspond to the Hague programme, which set 1 January 2008 as a deadline for implementing the availability principle (which means that information held by any EU law enforcement authority must be made available to all the others).

Owing to the implementation of the Tampere and Hague programmes – aimed at creating an area of freedom, security and justice – justice and home affairs has been the most dynamically developing area of EU legislation.[19] However, the biggest obstacle hampering even more dynamic legislative progress in justice and home affairs remains the cumbersome (unanimity-based) system of decision-making. In order to facilitate the

---

[18] The provision of the Prüm Treaty which allows armed uniformed police officers to cross from one country to another and take appropriate measures was not incorporated into the EU framework.

[19] In recent years, one out of five EU legislative proposals has related to justice and home affairs.

implementation of the Hague programme and decision-making related thereto, the Hague European Council requested the Council to adopt a decision within the framework provided by the Treaty of Nice on extending the co-decision procedure and qualified majority voting. On the basis of this request, the Council introduced co-decision and qualified majority voting with effect from 1 January 2005 in the following areas: abolition of checks at internal borders, the management of external borders, free movement of third-country nationals within the EU and the division of labour in asylum and illegal immigration matters. This significant development will undoubtedly contribute to more efficient legislative work in these areas and hence to deepening integration. Nonetheless, due to the requirement of unanimity, decision-making is still rather cumbersome when it comes to justice and home affairs in the third pillar.

The Constitutional Treaty signed on 29 October 2004 was of particular importance for justice and home affairs, as it would have brought significant changes on its entry into force, amending the current EC and EU Treaty provisions in many respects. However, the Constitutional Treaty was not successfully ratified in all of the Member States and, therefore, at their summit on 21–22 June 2007, the Heads of State or Government decided to place the Union's operation on new foundations by the means of a Reform Treaty amending the EU and EC Treaties in force. It must be noted that the Reform Treaty is largely based on the Constitutional Treaty and borrows the majority of its provisions. In the area of justice and home affairs, the Reform Treaty – on its entry into force – will bring changes comparable to those of the Treaty of Amsterdam. These changes will include the abolition of the pillar structure and a number of other novelties. As the Reform Treaty is expected to enter into force only in 2009, its JHA provisions are discussed separately in Point 24 of the Annex.

The momentum of the reform of decision-making and operation of cooperation in justice and home affairs is likely to continue in coming years. As the proposed amendments to the Treaties will have a major effect on the area of freedom, security and justice, it will probably remain the most dynamically evolving area of integration.

ANNEX

REFORM TREATY
BASED ON THE CONSTITUTIONAL TREATY

What changes will the Reform Treaty bring on its entry into force compared to the treaty framework currently in effect?

1. The new Treaty framework:
a Reform Treaty instead of a Constitutional Treaty

At the European Council meeting of 21–22 June 2007, a decision was made on the new treaty framework of the Union, which put an end to the "treaty crisis", the uncertainty brought about by the French and Dutch referenda rejecting the Constitutional Treaty. It was decided that the Constitutional Treaty would not enter into force but the Member States would draft a so-called Reform Treaty.[1]

Unlike the Constitutional Treaty, the Reform Treaty does not replace the Treaty on the European Union (EU Treaty) and the Treaty establishing the European Community (EC Treaty); it only amends them and renames the latter the Treaty on the functioning of the European Union. The Reform Treaty is an amending Treaty in the classical sense, just as the Treaty of Amsterdam or the Treaty of Nice: it amends but does not replace the Treaties in force.

Unlike the Constitutional Treaty, the new Treaty does not use the term 'constitution', considered as the symbol of a European "superstate", nor does it take on a constitutional form, and the text does not include any reference to some sort of statehood. The Reform Treaty does not include the state-like symbols of the anthem and the flag and does not use terms such as 'European law' or 'Union Minister for Foreign Affairs'.

Nonetheless, the Reform Treaty does maintain the overwhelming majority of the Constitutional Treaty's achievements and thereby brings more fundamental reforms than previous amending Treaties – with possibly one exception: the Treaty of Maastricht. The main purpose of the Reform Treaty is to ensure that the provisions laid down in the Constitutional Treaty, which were born out of a compromise between the Member States after three years of negotiations, are not lost, but incorporated into the current Treaties. Drafting the Reform Treaty is the job of the Intergovernmental Conference convened by the June 2007 European Council, which began work on 23 July 2007.

According to the mandate agreed by the European Council on 22 June 2007, in practice the IGC has legal and technical tasks aimed at transposing the majority of the Constitutional Treaty's provisions and the changes containing the 'final' political compromises into the EU Treaty and the EC Treaty (which will emerge as the Treaty on the functioning of the European

---

[1] For more on the decision on the Reform Treaty and the unsuccessful ratification of the Constitutional Treaty, see 1.12.2.

Union). The IGC has been given a strictly worded remit, which does not allow it to stretch beyond its mandate. The IGC must conclude its work, before the end of 2007, to leave the Member States ample time to ratify the Reform Treaty, so it can enter into force before the elections to the European Parliament in June 2009.

The manuscript of this Handbook was completed when the IGC began its work. As a result, the provisions of the Reform Treaty are not presented with precise references to the Treaty Articles. However, the mandate adopted by the Heads of State or Government at the June 2007 European Council did specify which provisions of the Constitutional Treaty are to be incorporated into the Reform Treaty and in what ways, and which provisions are to be deleted.

Consequently, this Annex presents the changes which can be expected in various areas by comparing the Constitutional Treaty and the mandate for the IGC agreed by the Heads of State or Government on 22 June 2007. This Annex follows the chapter structure of the Handbook for easy reference, hopefully making it simple to check what changes the Reform Treaty will bring upon its entry into force in the Treaty framework and how the Union's functioning will be different in a specific area.

2. The institutional framework

2.1. Changes affecting the Commission

2.1.1. The role and competence of the Commission

The Reform Treaty, similarly to the provisions of the Constitutional Treaty, will not bring about fundamental changes in the role and competences of the European Commission, but will reinforce the Parliament's oversight of the Commission. The Reform Treaty stipulates that the European Council has to propose to the European Parliament a candidate for the Presidency of the Commission "taking into account the elections to the European Parliament".[2] Although the composition of the European Commission will not depend on the outcome of the EP elections, as other members of the Commission will still be nominated by the Member States – obviously on the basis of domestic political balance (probably proposing a leading figure from the political forces in power), which will lead to a politically mixed Commission – a closer

---

[2] This principle was already applied during the nomination of the President of the Commission who took office in November 2004, when the Heads of State or Government proposed José Manuel Durão Barroso, a politician belonging to the European People's Party, which won the most seats in the European Parliament in the June 2004 elections.

political link and responsibility between Parliament and Commission will be established. According to the Reform Treaty, the European Parliament will no longer just "approve" but will "elect" the Commission President-designate (on the European Council's qualified majority proposal), which is more a question of principle than a substantial change.

2.1.2. The composition of the Commission

The key issue concerning the Commission during the drafting of the Constitutional Treaty was the number of its members, i.e. how long the 'one country – one Commissioner' principle should be maintained, and on what conditions the transition to the rotational system should happen. According to the Treaty of Nice, the Commission taking office in 2009 was supposed to have fewer members than Member States, but the Constitutional Treaty would have postponed that date by another term by stipulating that the first Commission to take office following the entry into force of the Constitutional Treaty should consist of one member from each Member State, and only the second Commission (which – with the Constitutional Treaty's entry into force forecast for 2006 – was to take office in 2014) should be appointed according to the system of rotation. The Reform Treaty also calls for the introduction of the system of rotation to be introduced from 2014. From this time on, the number of Commissioners will equal two thirds of the number of Member States, unless the European Council alters that by a unanimous decision. The rotation mechanism must respect the equality of Member States. This system of rotation will be defined by the European Council based on two principles. First of all, each successive Commission must be so composed as to reflect satisfactorily the demographic and geographical range of all the Member States. Secondly, the difference between the total number of terms of office held by Commissioners nominated by any given pair of Member States may never be more than one.

A key provision of the Reform Treaty relating to the Commission involves the creation of the office of the High Representative of the Union for Foreign Affairs and Security Policy, which is the former High Representative for Common Foreign and Security Policy with a new status in a new set-up. The High Representative will also be one of the Vice-Presidents of the Commission, a fact which will have to be considered during his appointment. The High Representative will be appointed by the European Council, acting by a qualified majority, with the agreement of the President of the Commission. The revamped High Representative will take over the job of the Commissioner for External Relations and of the Council's Secretary General, i.e. the High Representative for Common Foreign and Security Policy.[3]

---

[3] For more on the office of the High Representative, see Point 2.4. of this Annex.

2.2. Changes affecting the European Council

One of the most significant changes introduced by the Constitutional Treaty was to elevate the European Council to the level of an independent institution, and detach it from the Council of Ministers. The Constitutional Treaty completely separated the tasks of the European Council and the Council, making it clear that the European Council would have no legislative power of its own. Its main task would be to provide the Union with the necessary impetus for its development and to define the general political directions and priorities thereof. The Reform Treaty borrows this provision and incorporates the European Council as an independent institution into Title III of the EU Treaty on the institutional framework.

Unlike the present system of rotating Presidencies, the European Council will have a standing President, but no administrative staff of its own (its work will be assisted by the Secretariat General of the Council). The European Council will elect its President, by a qualified majority, for a term of two and a half years, renewable once. The President will not be able to hold a national office; thus the current practice of a Head of State or Government in office presiding over the European Council will disappear.[4] The task of the President of the European Council will be to chair it and drive forward its work, guarantee the preparation and continuity of its work and ensure – at his level (that is without prejudice to the powers of the EU High Representative for Foreign Affairs and Security Policy) – the external representation of the Union.

Decisions of the European Council will continue to be taken by consensus, except where the Treaties provide otherwise (for example in the case of electing its President, when it acts by a qualified majority). During voting, a Member State will be able to cast votes on behalf of another Member State.[5] Abstention by a member will not prevent the European Council from making a decision. Decisions will also be adopted in the absence of some members, with the consensus of the members present or through representation by a member present.

2.3. Changes affecting the Council

2.3.1. The status of the Council

The Reform Treaty – like the Constitutional Treaty – defines the Council of Ministers (in short, the Council) as the institution – jointly with the European Parliament – exercising legislative

---

[4] The Treaty will, however, allow the European Council President to hold some other EU office, leaving open the option of merging the posts of Commission President and European Council President some time in the distant future. There were fears that maintaining these two separate Presidents could give rise to rivalry and power struggles.

[5] Similarly, Member States may act on behalf of each other in the Council as well.

and budgetary functions, which also carries out policy-making and coordinating functions as laid down in the Treaties.

In order to ensure greater transparency of Union decision-making, the Reform Treaty aims to make Council meetings public when it deliberates and votes on a draft legislative act.

2.3.2. Council Presidency

When drafting the Constitutional Treaty, the Member States agreed that the Council Presidency would work on the basis of equal rotation. This new system was partially introduced on 1 January 2007[6] and is maintained by the Reform Treaty. The Presidency of Council formations will be held by groups of three Member States for a period of 18 months in a predetermined order. These groups of three will be drawn up taking into consideration the differences between Member States and with a view to a geographical balance. Within each group, the three Member States will hold the Presidency of Council formations in rotation for periods of six months. The other two members of the group will help the Presidency in performing its task. The Foreign Affairs Council, which was proposed by the Constitutional Treaty, is an exception: it will not be chaired by a Member State minister, but instead by the High Representative for Foreign Affairs and Security Policy. Concerning Council configurations, it should be noted that, at the IGC in 2004, the Member States agreed to have ten configurations: the current nine will be maintained but the General Affairs and External Relations Council will be divided into a General Affairs Council and a Foreign Affairs Council. This agreement is respected by the Reform Treaty.

2.3.3. Voting in Council

A key provision of principle in the Constitutional Treaty – which is borrowed by the Reform Treaty according to the mandate of the 2007 IGC – was the general rule that the Council would act by a qualified majority. Thus, the new Treaty considers the Council acting by unanimity as an exception to the rule, significantly reducing the scope of such decision-making, but keeping unanimity as the dominant form of decision-making in a few areas.[7]

When the Constitutional Treaty was being drafted, the most controversial question was the definition of qualified majority voting, particularly in the light of the fact that the Constitutional

---

[6] See 2.3.4.
[7] For more, see Point 4.1. of this Annex. For a complete list of areas falling under the scope of unanimity according to the Reform Treaty, see Appendix II.

Treaty wanted to extend QMV to so many areas. It was due to the difficulties in agreeing on the weighting of the votes in qualified majority voting that the draft Constitutional Treaty was not adopted by the end of 2003, and negotiations dragged on into the first half of 2004. The European Convention and the subsequent IGC had to live up to the complex expectations of ensuring more transparency, more efficient and less cumbersome decision-making procedures (with fewer opportunities for vetoing or blocking decisions), which would also be simpler and easier to understand for the citizens, with voting procedures not based on artificial weightings but on the number of Member States and proportional to population, and – the most difficult of them all – acceptable for small- and medium-sized as well as large Member States.

Finally, as a result of lengthy negotiations, a formula acceptable to all parties at the time was found and agreed upon. According to this formula, the Constitutional Treaty sought to introduce a new voting system on 1 November 2009, which would be based on the principle of 'double majority' (the majority of Member States + the majority of population). A double majority was defined as at least 55% of the members of the Council, comprising at least fifteen of them and representing Member States comprising at least 65% of the population of the Union, when the Council was deciding on a proposal from the Commission or from the Union Minister for Foreign Affairs (replaced by the High Representative for Foreign Affairs and Security Policy in the Reform Treaty).[8] When the Council was not acting on a proposal from the Commission or from the Union Minister for Foreign Affairs (High Representative), the qualified majority was defined as at least 72% of the members of the Council, representing Member States comprising at least 65% of the population of the Union.
The definition of qualified majority was complemented by the specific provision that a blocking minority must include at least four Council Member States, failing which the qualified majority was deemed attained and the decision adopted, even if the three blocking states represented over 35% of the Union's population.
The Constitutional Treaty included a transitional rule on the blocking majority, according to which until 2014, Member States forming 75% of the necessary blocking minority (either population-wise or number-wise) could demand the decision to be postponed and the negotiations to be resumed after a reasonable period, in order to build wider consensus in the Council.

The introduction of the double majority rule was deemed the single most important element of the Constitutional Treaty, which – due to the hard-forged compromise of 2004 – also looked

---

[8] The original formula proposed by the 2003 Convention included a 50% figure for Member States and a 60% threshold for population, but under pressure from Poland and Spain, the two countries most adversely affected, the population limit was raised to 65%. At the same time, to ensure that smaller countries are not disadvantaged, compared to the Convention proposal, the member-state limit was also raised by 5% to 55%.

to be the most robust provision of the Treaty. When it became apparent that the Constitutional Treaty might have to be reworked, few thought that this provision could come under scrutiny again. Poland, however, placed the voting system at the heart of the negotiations and, just as in 2004, it insisted on maintaining the system enshrined in the Treaty of Nice. The Nice formula is especially advantageous to Poland, giving it an almost equal say with Germany despite having half its population. (Under the Nice arrangement, Poland has 27 votes and Germany has 29.) But as Poland found itself alone in its endeavours to renegotiate the voting system, as a compromise the Heads of State or Government agreed at the 21–22 June 2007 summit to preserve the double majority system put forward by the Constitutional Treaty (55% of Member States, 65% of population) in the Reform Treaty too, but to introduce it only on 1 November 2014, and keep the Nice system till then. Another concession was made to Poland by creating the possibility for any Member State to request Nice-type qualified majority voting on an issue until 31 March 2017. In addition, the transitional rule on the blocking majority – originally foreseen until 2014 – was also extended until 31 March 2017, enabling Member States forming 75% of the necessary blocking minority (either population-wise or number-wise) to demand a decision and negotiations thereon to be postponed.[9]

This double majority formula will also be applied in the European Council when it acts by a qualified majority, with the obvious proviso that the President of the European Council and the President of the Commission do not take part in the vote.

Compared to the system of qualified majority set forth in the Treaty of Nice and currently effective, the key novelty of the double majority formula is the elimination of the weighting of the votes, while the limits of supporting Member States and population are slightly raised (from 50% + 1 to 55%, and from 62% to 65%). With the disappearance of weighted votes, small- and medium-sized countries will lose some of their weight, while the increased importance of population limits will add to the influence of bigger countries. However, considering that currently there are 6 larger and 21 medium-sized or smaller countries in the Union, while at least 15 Member States are needed to adopt a decision, the balance of interests between smaller and bigger countries seems guaranteed. The more muscle that larger Member States have due to their population will play a more important role in the blocking of decisions: while three big ones united with just one small country or four big countries will easily be able to

---

[9] This is really a modernised version of the 'Ioannina compromise' (see 2.3.5.), extended until 2017. In a Union of 27, such a postponement will require 10 Member States or enough countries to represent 26.26% of the Union's population.

block a decision, smaller Member States will have to forge much wider alliances and coalitions if they want to establish a sufficient percentage population-wise. Another consequence of the increased importance of population as a factor is that, for the first time, Germany's advantage in population size will be recognised (especially vis-à-vis France). Ever since the beginnings of European integration, it had always been taken for granted that Germany and France should have the same weight; the new system of double majority will put an end to that parity.

2.4. The High Representative of the Union for Foreign Affairs and Security Policy

The Constitutional Treaty sought to create the office of the Union Minister for Foreign Affairs, merging the current CFSP High Representative and the External Relations Commissioner. This is important, because with the abolition of the pillar structure[10], the economic and political aspects of foreign policy – currently divided – would be united in one person, who would be the single representative of the Union on the international political scene.

At the end of the period of reflection, the Czech Republic demanded that the federal-sounding name of Union Minister – also disliked by the United Kingdom – be scrapped in the Reform Treaty. At the summit of June 2007, the decision was made to replace the title of 'Union Minister for Foreign Affairs' with 'High Representative of the Union for Foreign Affairs and Security Policy'. The provisions on the High Representative are incorporated into the EU Treaty under Title III – institutional provisions.

The High Representative for Foreign Affairs and Security Policy will be a so-called 'double-hatting' post, acting both as Commission Vice-President and the President of the Foreign Affairs Council. He or she will also take part in the work of the European Council.

This double hatting (between Council and Commission) is due to the fact that, even with the abolition of the three-pillar structure, the area of Common Foreign and Security Policy will remain a Council monopoly, with the Commission playing a limited role. The double-hatted nature of the job is demonstrated by the fact that the High Representative will only be bound by the rules governing the Commission in his work when acting as a member of the Commission, and that if the Commission resigns or is dismissed, he will only lose his mandate as a Commissioner but keep his job in the Council.

The High Representative will be assisted in his work by the European External Action Service, to be created by the Reform Treaty. The Service, which will operate in cooperation with the diplomatic services of the Member States, will consist of officials from the Council Secretariat General, or the Commission or seconded from the Member States' services. The organisational and operational arrangements of the European External Action Service will be decided by the Council on the proposal of the High Representative, after consulting the European Parliament and obtaining the Commission's agreement.

---

[10] See Point 3 of this Annex.

2.5. Changes affecting the European Parliament

2.5.1. The status and competences of the European Parliament

As far as the European Parliament is concerned, the most significant provision of the Reform Treaty – borrowed from the Constitutional Treaty – stipulates that "the European Parliament shall, jointly with the Council, exercise legislative and budgetary functions", which clearly underlines Parliament's role as a co-decision-maker. In addition, "it shall exercise functions of political control and consultation" as laid down in the Constitutional Treaty, and "it shall elect the President of the Commission". Unlike the present EC Treaty – which does not define Parliament's role, only stating that it exercises the competences conferred upon it by the Treaty – the Reform Treaty stipulates that the European Parliament is to have real parliamentary powers in the areas of legislation, adoption of the budget, and appointments and control functions, even though it will exercise decision-making competences jointly with the Council.

As an expression of Parliament's role as a co-legislator, and as one of the most significant practical implications, the Reform Treaty – just like the Constitutional Treaty – will make co-decision the general legislative procedure, significantly extending its scope and specifying the exceptional areas where other procedures (special legislative procedures) remain applicable. According to the mandate of the IGC, the Reform Treaty will incorporate into the EU Treaty all the areas that the Constitutional Treaty would have brought under the scope of co-decision. This means that the Parliament and the Council will adopt legislation in most cases, hence the European Parliament will become part and parcel of Community decision-making in almost all areas, and Community decision-making will be placed in a much more transparent framework: as a general rule, Parliament and the Council will legislate through co-decision (with other procedures applied only in exceptional cases), while decision-making in the Council will be generally by qualified majority voting, with unanimity as an exception to the rule.[11]

2.5.2. The composition of the European Parliament

The Constitutional Treaty was to bring a slight change in the composition of Parliament by stipulating that the number of its members could not exceed 750 and, entitling Member States to a minimum of 6 and a maximum of 96 seats in the EP. Within this set framework, it would

---

[11] See also Point 4.1. of this Annex.

have been up to the European Council to decide on the precise allocation of seats, acting on the European Parliament's proposal and in unanimity. The Reform Treaty adopts the same solution. Accordingly, the European Council of 21–22 June 2007 asked the European Parliament to make a proposal for its composition by October 2007 with a view to the European elections of 2009, which would enable the European Council to make its decision in time.

2.6. Changes affecting the Court of Justice

The Reform Treaty – taking up the proposals of the Constitutional Treaty – renames the Court of Justice of the European Communities as the Court of Justice of the European Union[12], consisting of the Court, the General Court (the new name of the Court of First Instance) and the Specialised Courts (currently called judicial panels).

The competence of the Court of Justice will be broadened in the area of police and judicial cooperation in criminal matters, and to a lesser extent in foreign and security policy, although mainly in current second- and partly in third-pillar areas, its jurisdiction will remain limited.[13] An important novelty will be the Court's new competence to revise all decisions by the European Council (which will become an institution proper), other than those in the field of foreign and security policy. Another new element will allow for a certain degree of individual access to the Court, giving any natural or legal person the opportunity to institute proceedings against regulatory acts that are of direct concern to the person in question and that do not entail implementing measures.

3. The definition of competences – the abolition of the system of three pillars

One of the main motivations behind the Constitutional Treaty was to define the Union's powers more clearly, to reduce the number of potential clashes between national and Union competences and to solve the problems created by the three-pillar division. The Reform Treaty sets itself the same objectives, amending the provisions of the Constitutional Treaty only to prevent the Union from over-reaching its competences.

When the Constitutional Treaty was being drafted, in order to clarify the Union's competences the Member States were given the tasks of:

---

[12] This is possible because, with the entry into force of the Reform Treaty, the European Union will have a legal personality of its own and the three-pillar system will disappear.

[13] See Points 23 and 24 of this Annex.

1. Laying down principles for the limits and use of Union competences, as well as the terms and conditions required to ensure that these principles are observed, in particular the role of national parliaments.
2. Replacing the system of three pillars, providing more precise definitions of and distinctions between Member-State and Union competences (by means of a kind of catalogue of competences).
3. Ensuring flexibility in the course of exercising these competences for the sake of achieving the goals of the Union.

These are the areas where the Reform Treaty will bring changes.

3.1. The principles governing the limits and exercise of competences

The Constitutional Treaty stipulated that the limits of Union competences were to be governed by the principle of *conferral*. Under the principle of conferral, the Union was to act within the limits of the competences conferred upon it by the Member States in the Treaty to attain the objectives set out therein. The Reform Treaty adopts the principle of conferral but with a small clarification, adding that the Union will act exclusively within the limits of the competences conferred upon it by the Member States in the Treaty. This also means that competences not conferred upon the Union in the Treaties will remain with the Member States.

The Constitutional Treaty also stipulated that the use of Union competences should be governed by the principles of *subsidiarity* and *proportionality*.
Under the principle of subsidiarity, in areas that do not fall within its exclusive competence, the Union acts only if and insofar as the objectives of the intended action cannot be sufficiently achieved by the Member States, either at central level or at regional and local level, but can rather, by reason of the scale or effects of the proposed action, be better achieved at Union level.
Under the principle of proportionality, the content and form of Union action cannot exceed what is necessary to achieve the objectives of the Treaties.

The two Protocols annexed to the Constitutional Treaty ('Protocol on the role of national parliaments in the European Union' and 'Protocol on the application of the principles of subsidiarity and proportionality') provided for the monitoring of compliance with these two principles.
While, at the moment, it is the Commission's responsibility to ensure the application of these two principles when making legislative proposals, the second Protocol stipulates that each institution have to ensure constant respect for the principles of subsidiarity and proportionality. Nonetheless the Protocol aims to give national parliaments a lead role in monitoring compliance with the principle of subsidiarity. According to the provisions of the Protocol, the Commission has to send all its legislative proposals and amended proposals to the national parliaments of the Member States at the same time as to the Union legislators (the Council and the Parliament). In all such cases, national parliaments have six weeks to assess whether the given proposal

complies with the principle of subsidiarity.[14] If at least one third of the national parliaments find that the Commission proposal does not comply with the principles of subsidiarity, the Commission has to review its proposal.[15] This threshold is one quarter in the case of a Commission proposal in the area of police and judicial cooperation in criminal matters (current third-pillar area). After such review, the Commission may decide to maintain, amend or withdraw its proposal, but giving reasons for its decision.

The subsidiarity Protocol guarantees legal control over the application of the principle of subsidiarity by stipulating that the Court of Justice has jurisdiction to hear actions on grounds of infringement of the principle of subsidiarity by a legislative act of the Union. Such action can be brought to the Court of Justice by Member States, or – in accordance with their domestic legal order – by Member States on behalf of their national parliament or a chamber of it. The Committee of the Regions may also bring such actions in respect of legislative acts whose adoption it must be consulted on.

The Reform Treaty amends the subsidiarity Protocol annexed to the Constitutional Treaty on two points, further strengthening the role of the national parliaments. Firstly, national parliaments will have eight instead of six weeks to respond to Commission proposals. Secondly, if the national parliaments oppose a legislative proposal with a simple majority of the votes but the Commission decides not to withdraw it, then the Council and Parliament give their opinion on the proposal. If the proposal is deemed incompatible with the principle of subsidiarity by a 55% majority in Council or a majority in Parliament, the proposal must be withdrawn.

---

[14] The Protocol on the role of the national parliaments in the European Union aims to reinforce the role of national parliaments by guaranteeing their right to information on the Union's decision-making process and by enabling them to monitor and influence actions by their national government in the Council. The Protocol requires the Commission to forward to Member States' national parliaments all Commission consultation documents (green and white papers and communications), the annual legislative programme, all draft legislative acts as well as any other instrument of legislative planning or policy strategy submitted to the European Parliament and to the Council of Ministers, at the same time as the Commission submitted them to those institutions. In order to give the national parliaments enough time to provide an input in the decision-making process, the Protocol stipulates that a six-week period has to elapse between a draft European legislative act being made available to national parliaments in the official languages of the Union and the date when it is placed on a provisional agenda for the Council for its adoption. These six weeks are to give national parliaments time to formulate their position and communicate it to their governments.

[15] National parliaments with a unicameral system have two votes, while each chamber of a bicameral parliamentary system has one vote.

Emphasising the role of national parliaments, the Reform Treaty introduces a new provision into the EU Treaty, which – in essence – enumerates the areas where the national parliaments have a role to play in Union decision-making.

3.2. Categories of competence

During the course of the drafting of the Constitutional Treaty in 2002 and 2003, there was profound debate in the Convention on Union competences, which showed a sweeping demand for the introduction of a much more transparent system of competences. The starting point proposed by many was the abolition of the three-pillar system, thereby eliminating the distinction between Community and Union competences. Abolishing the system of pillars and defining competences more rationally was possible due to the single legal personality declared by the Constitutional Treaty; this has been taken up by the Reform Treaty.[16] However, a Declaration is annexed to the Reform Treaty stipulating that the Union's legal personality does not authorise it to legislate or to act beyond the competences conferred upon it by the Member States in the Treaties.

The analytical work of the Convention drafting the first version of the Constitutional Treaty identified three basic categories into which Union competences can be grouped: areas where the Union has exclusive competence, areas where the Union and Member States have shared competence and areas within national competence. Nonetheless, the Union does carry out actions with the aim of supporting, supplementing and – occasionally – coordinating Member-State actions. The debate in the Convention, and later at the IGC, revealed that there are also areas that Member States do not wish to place into any of these precise categories. One such area was Common Foreign and Security Policy (currently the second pillar) and the related field of common defence policy. The Member States did not want to declare that conducting foreign affairs should be an exclusive Union competence and wanted to avoid even hinting that foreign policy should be a shared competence, or that the EU would only have complementary tasks, as that could politically devalue the CFSP. As a result, it was decided to create a separate category of competence for Common Foreign and Security Policy. This decision was also justified by the fact that, despite the dismantling of the pillar system, Member States wished to continue operating foreign policy according to special methods. The coordination of economic and employment policies was also defined

---

[16] For more on the Union's legal personality, see Point 5.1. of this Annex.

as a special area of competence. Here tasks arise at the Union level, but implementation takes place at Member-State level, and – due to its nature – this policy area does not fit into the category of actions coordinating sectoral policies, because it is more than mere supplementing action; comprehensive national economic policies are coordinated.

The Constitutional Treaty provided for – and the Reform Treaty maintains this decision – the abolition of the three-pillar division (although slightly different rules will apply to certain areas now belonging to the second and the third pillar[17]) and Union competences will be divided into the following five categories:
– exclusive competences;
– shared competences;
– coordinating economic and employment policies;
– common foreign and security policy;
– supporting, coordinating and supplementing actions.

When the Reform Treaty confers on the Union *exclusive competence* in a specific area, only the Union may legislate and adopt legally binding acts, the Member States being able to do so themselves only if empowered by the Union or for the implementation of acts adopted by the Union. According to the Reform Treaty, the Union will have exclusive competence in the following areas:
– customs union;
– the establishment of competition rules necessary for the functioning of the internal market;
– monetary policy for the Member States whose currency is the euro;
– the conservation of marine biological resources under the common fisheries policy;
– Common Commercial Policy.
The Reform Treaty also grants the Union exclusive competence for the conclusion of an international agreement, when its conclusion is provided for in a legislative act of the Union or is necessary to enable the Union to exercise its internal competence, or insofar as its conclusion may affect common rules or alter their scope.

When the Reform Treaty confers on the Union a *competence shared* with the Member States in a specific area, both the Union and the Member States will be able to legislate and adopt legally binding acts in that area. The Member States will be able to exercise their

---

[17] See Points 4.1., 23. and 24 of this Annex. It must be noted here that the third pillar will disappear to the degree that the contents of Title VI of the EU Treaty containing the current third-pillar provisions (police and judicial cooperation in criminal matters) will be fully transferred to the Treaty on the functioning of the European Union (current EC Treaty) in the Title on the area of freedom, security and justice, while the Common Foreign and Security Policy under the second pillar will remain in the EU Treaty (and thereby remain the only policy not regulated in the Treaty on the functioning of the European Union).

competence to the extent that the Union has not exercised, or has decided to cease exercising, its competence. Shared competence thus means that both the Union and the Member States can adopt legal acts, but the Member States can only do so if the Union has not done so or has decided not to. In areas already regulated by the Union, that is in areas where the Member States have already decided once on the need for Community action, the Member States lose their competence and only recover it if the Union has explicitly relinquished its right to exercise its competence. This also means that in areas of shared competence, as a result of the legislative process, the competences exercised by the Union can continuously expand. For this reason, the Reform Treaty adds a new provision to the text of the Constitutional Treaty, contained in a separate Protocol, which states that "when the Union has taken action in a certain area, the scope of this exercise of competence only covers those elements governed by the Union act in question and therefore does not cover the whole area.".

According to the Reform Treaty, shared competence between the Union and the Member States will apply in the following areas:
- internal market;
- social policy, for the aspects defined in Part III of the Constitutional Treaty;
- economic, social and territorial cohesion;
- agriculture and fisheries, excluding the conservation of marine biological resources;
- environment;
- consumer protection;
- transport;
- trans-European networks;
- energy;
- area of freedom, security and justice;
- common safety concerns in public health matters.

Shared competences will also include the following areas, but with special rules:
- research, technological development and space;
- development cooperation and humanitarian aid.

In the latter two areas, the Union will have competence to carry out activities, in particular to define and implement programmes in the first area and to take action and conduct a common policy in the second; however, the exercise of that competence cannot result in Member States being prevented from exercising their own competence. In summary, these two areas are an exception to the rule that if the Union begins to regulate an area, it automatically becomes an area falling within Union competence. In these two areas, the Member States will maintain their competence to adopt legally binding acts.

Under the Reform Treaty, the Member States will coordinate their *economic and employment policies* within the rules set out in the Treaties. The Council will adopt measures for coordinating economic policies, in particular broad economic policy guidelines. In order to ensure the functioning of the monetary union, the Reform Treaty stipulates that specific provisions can apply to those Member States whose currency is the euro. The Reform Treaty will empower the Union to take measures to ensure the coordination of the employment policies of its Member States, in particular by defining guidelines for these policies, and also to take initiatives to ensure the coordination of Member States' social policies. Thus, while in the area of economic and employment policies, the Union will adopt guidelines, in social policy areas, it will be able to take initiatives.

Under the Reform Treaty, the European Union will conduct a *Common Foreign and Security Policy*, based on the development of mutual political solidarity among Member States, the identification of questions of general interest and the achievement of an ever-increasing degree of convergence of Member States' actions. The Union's competence in matters of Common Foreign and Security Policy will cover all areas of foreign policy and all questions relating to the Union's security, including the progressive framing of a common defence policy that might lead to a common defence structure. The same Article also calls upon the Member States to actively and unreservedly support the Union's Common Foreign and Security Policy in a spirit of loyalty and mutual solidarity and to comply with the Union's action in this area, as well as to refrain from action which is contrary to the Union's interests or likely to impair its effectiveness.

In specific areas determined by the Reform Treaty, the Union will have competence to carry out *supporting, coordinating or complementary action* without thereby superseding the competence of the Member States in these areas. A major difference compared to shared competences is that legally binding acts adopted by the Union in these areas will not result in approximation of legislation. The areas where the Union will have competence to carry out actions to support, coordinate or supplement the actions of the Member States at European level are:
- protection and improvement of human health;
- industry;
- culture;
- tourism;
- education, youth, sport and vocational training;
- civil protection;
- administrative cooperation.

3.3. Flexibility in exercising competences

Article 308 of the current EC Treaty allows the Community to take appropriate measures even when the Treaty does not provide the necessary powers, if action by the Community should prove necessary to attain, in the course of the operation of the common market, one of the objectives of the Community. In such cases, the Council adopts measures acting unanimously, on a proposal from the Commission and after consulting the European Parliament.

During the analytical work of the Convention when drafting the Constitutional Treaty, it became apparent that the Member States wanted to maintain this option in the new Treaty, enabling the Union to act even in cases when there was no specific legal base in the Treaty but where action was necessary to attain its objectives. This is of particular importance because the Member States were aware of the fact that the new Treaty was unlikely to be amended for a long while once it entered into force, and therefore such flexibility was required to guarantee the stability of the Treaty. On that basis, the Constitutional Treaty preserved and further developed the underlying concept of Article 308 of the EC Treaty in the form of a 'flexibility clause'. This flexibility clause empowers the Council to take decisions in policy areas when it wants to attain one of the objectives set out in the Treaty (no longer only the operation of the common market) for which the Treaty provides no powers. In such cases, the Council, acting on a proposal from the Commission and after obtaining the consent of the European Parliament (this is also a new feature), can take the necessary measures by unanimity. The Reform Treaty adds some minor changes: firstly, the flexibility clause will not be permitted to serve as the basis for implementing CFSP-related objectives; secondly, it will not be able to lead to an extension of Union competences beyond the general framework laid down by the Treaty provisions (particularly the provisions on the Union's tasks and activities) – in other words, the clause cannot be used for adopting decisions amounting to an amendment of the Treaties.

4. Decision-making and legislation

4.1. The decision-making order

The obvious aim of adopting the Constitutional Treaty was to introduce decision-making reforms to lay the foundations for a simpler, more transparent and more efficient functioning of the Union. To that end, the Constitutional Treaty attempted to set up a uniform and general decision-making system and define any deviation from that system as an exception to the rule. The first step towards more transparent decision-making was the abolition of the pillar structure, although, due to the special nature of certain areas – primarily the Common Foreign and Security Policy – some special decision-making solutions were to remain in place under the Constitutional Treaty. The main thrust of these reforms was aimed at re-fashioning the voting arrangements of the Council and laying down Parliament's role as a co-decision-maker in clear terms. In that spirit, the institutional provisions of the Constitutional Treaty stipulated that the Council and the Parliament perform legislative tasks jointly, in practice defining the two institutions as co-decision-makers on an equal footing. Accordingly, the Constitutional Treaty went on to stipulate that the *ordinary legislative procedure* of the European Union was the co-decision procedure. The Constitutional Treaty also stipulated that, as a general rule, the Council should make its decisions by qualified majority. Thus other decision-making procedures were only to be applied when the Treaty so stipulated for individual cases.

Despite the number of special exceptional cases, the decision-making system introduced by the Constitutional Treaty making co-decision and qualified majority a general rule would have a huge symbolic value to the evolution of European integration. Moreover, this reform would make Union decision-making more transparent and understandable for the citizens. With that aim in mind, the Member States have agreed to preserve in the Reform Treaty the decision-making reforms set forth in the Constitutional Treaty.

On the basis of the mandate adopted by the European Council on 22 June 2007, the Reform Treaty transposes into the current Treaties the decision-making reforms proposed in the Constitutional Treaty, with some conceptual changes and a handful of minor changes in content. As part of the conceptual changes, the Reform Treaty avoids using terms and concepts of a constitutional nature, such as law or law-making. Instead it sticks to the terminology, using 'legislative act' and referring to co-decision as an 'ordinary legislative procedure'. Substantive changes in content are few and far between; they concern just a handful of policy areas. These changes are outlined in this Annex under the Points dealing with specific policies.

One element of the decision-making reforms to be introduced by the Reform Treaty is the transformation and extension of the system of qualified majority voting. Defining decision-making mechanisms proved to be the most difficult issue during the drafting of the Constitutional Treaty. The so-called double majority voting (55% of the Member States + 65% of the population) – discussed in detail in Point 2.3.2. of this Annex – emerged as a result of lengthy and heated debates. The Constitutional Treaty wanted to introduce this new system of voting on 1 November 2009, but the Reform Treaty will postpone it until 1 November 2014. This reform is by no means only about the introduction of a new qualified majority; the extension of the scope of such voting is an equally important new feature. The significance of this reform is accentuated by the fact that, following the entry into force of the Reform Treaty (foreseen for 2009), qualified majority voting will be applied in 80% of policy areas, and the extension of its scope will take effect immediately and not in 2014 like the double majority rule. Unanimity will only be upheld for about 50 issues that for various reasons were considered sensitive by the Member States. These include issues such as determining own resources for the EU budget, social security, family law or taxation. For a complete list of areas placed under unanimity by the Constitutional Treaty – and transposed into the current Treaties by the Reform Treaty – see Appendix II.

In addition to the reform of qualified majority voting, another novelty of the decision-making reform is its definition of co-decision as the ordinary legislative procedure. This will not only simplify Union decision-making but will also considerably change the institutional balance by significantly strengthening Parliament's role. While emphasising the Union's federative nature, this will also broaden the democratic legitimacy of decisions. The system based on the joint decision-making of Council and Parliament reflects the Union's dual nature by expressing the common will of the Member States (represented by the Council) and of the citizens (represented by the Parliament).

Defining co-decision as the ordinary legislative procedure (i.e. the general rule) naturally entails a considerable extension of its scope. The number of areas under co-decision will nearly double. Following the entry into force of the Reform Treaty[18], decisions will have to be taken by the co-decision procedure in about three quarters of all policy areas, putting the Parliament on an equal footing with Council as an unavoidable co-legislator in areas such as agriculture or the former third-pillar area of judicial cooperation in the field of criminal matters. Following the entry into force of the Reform Treaty, there will be about twenty areas left where the Council will retain its lead legislative role with Parliament playing a merely consultative role in the current consultation procedure. The cooperation procedure, which is hardly ever used anyway, will disappear. The assent procedure, in which the Council will continue to have to obtain Parliament's assent before it can take its final decision, will survive with changes to its scope: it will be used in some new areas while certain areas will be transferred to co-decision. The Reform Treaty stipulates some rare issues pertaining to the European Parliament's operation (such as the statute and duties of MEPs), where the Parliament will have the right of initiative and final decision and will need to obtain the Council's consent (assent). For a complete list of areas under various legislative procedures as laid down in the Constitutional Treaty and to be transposed into the Treaties by the Reform Treaty, see Appendix IV.

Important changes affecting decision-making procedures will result from the fact that the Reform Treaty will abolish the three-pillar-based decision-making system, but maintain some exceptional rules, due to the special status of the former intergovernmental pillars, particularly the Common Foreign and Security Policy. This is demonstrated by the fact that while current third-pillar provisions (police and judicial cooperation in criminal matters) will be fully transferred to the Treaty on the functioning of the European Union (the current EC Treaty) under the Title on the area of freedom, security and justice, current second-pillar CFSP is the only policy area which will remain in the EU Treaty.

---

[18] The extension of the scope of co-decision will be immediate, as soon as the Treaty enters into force.

From the viewpoint of decision-making, third pillar areas will be incorporated into the general structure; so much so, that in the area of judicial cooperation in criminal matters, the ordinary legislative procedure will be introduced. Moreover, for police cooperation too, the ordinary legislative procedure will be the general rule, with the exceptional application of the consultation procedure. However, for judicial cooperation in criminal matters, the Reform Treaty will introduce a so-called *emergency brake clause* (discussed in detail in the next Point), which will enable any Member State – if it considers that a given legislative act would affect fundamental aspects of its criminal justice system – to request the Council to suspend the decision-making procedure and refer the issue to the European Council. The provisions of the Constitutional Treaty appear in the Reform Treaty with a slightly amended wording (for more, see Points 4.2. and 4.3. of this Annex).

In the area of police and judicial cooperation in criminal matters, we can see another exception to the general rule of initiative; in this area, acts can be adopted on a proposal from the Commission or on the initiative of a quarter of the Member States (maintaining, to a certain extent the parallel right of initiative of the Commission and the Member States, but setting a minimum threshold on the number of Member States).[19]

Significantly, bigger differences will remain in place in the current second pillar, the area of Common Foreign and Security Policy, which is primarily attributable to the special nature of this field; there is no legislative work in the area of Common Foreign and Security Policy. Unless the Treaties provide otherwise, the European Council and the Council will set the Common Foreign and Security Policy by unanimity. The CFSP will be implemented by the Union High Representative for Foreign and Security Policy and the Member States. The European Parliament will continue to have merely a consultative role. As a peculiar feature, the Commission will lose its right of initiative in this area, which will be transferred to the High Representative. When adopting the mandate for the IGC elaborating the Reform Treaty, the Member States agreed that provisions on the CFSP should not bestow upon the Commission new competences for initiating Decisions and extending the role of the European Parliament. As before, the Court of Justice will have no competence in this field, except to review the legality of acts in certain cases. The Reform Treaty, like the Constitutional Treaty includes a so-called *special passarelle clause* or *special bridging clause*, which will enable the European Council to introduce QMV in a field normally under unanimity (except for military and defence issues) simply by a unanimous decision and without convening an IGC.[20]

---

[19] For more on decision-making in the area of police and judicial cooperation in criminal matters, see Point 24 of this Annex.

[20] For more, see the next Point as well as Point 23 of this Annex.

4.2. The revision of the decision-making order

During the drafting of the Constitutional Treaty, it was clear that, on the one hand, there were areas where the Member States lacked the political will to apply the ordinary legislative procedure and qualified majority voting, while, on the other hand, in certain areas the political will was insufficient even for ensuring Union action. Nonetheless, the Member States also recognised that for 27 or more countries – partly because of the lengthy process of ratification – it would be very difficult to amend the Constitutional Treaty. Thus they wanted to leave open the possibility of reforming the decision-making system without amending the Constitutional Treaty and convening an IGC, and of changing the conditions of Union action in various policy areas. To that end, the Constitutional Treaty was to introduce a number of review instruments; these are maintained in the Reform Treaty and will be incorporated into the current Treaties.

Like the Constitutional Treaty, the Reform Treaty will introduce two simplified revision procedures into Article 48 of the EU Treaty, in addition to the ordinary revision procedure.
In order to facilitate the future extension of decision-making reforms to new areas, the *simplified revision procedure* will be introduced. This procedure, instead of the lengthy and cumbersome revision of the Treaties, will enable the European Council, by a unanimous decision, to authorise the Council to act by a qualified majority and to apply the co-decision procedure in areas for which the Treaties still provide for unanimity or a special legislative procedure. Such decisions will be subject to the consent of the European Parliament (given by a majority of its component members) and will only be deemed adopted in the absence of any objection by national parliaments within six months. This is also called the *general passarelle clause* or *general bridging clause*.
Maintaining the relevant provisions of the Constitutional Treaty, the Reform Treaty will also enact a simplified revision procedure concerning internal Union policies and action[21]. In internal policy areas, the European Council will be able to adopt a decision amending all or part of the relevant provisions of the Treaty on the functioning of the European Union acting by unanimity, with the proviso that such a decision may not increase the competences conferred on the Union. Prior to taking its decision, the European Council will consult the European Parliament and the Commission, and the European Central Bank in the case of institutional changes in the monetary area. Such a decision will not enter into force until it

---

[21] All areas where the Union has some kind of competence, with the exception of policies related to the Union's external action, are considered *internal policies*.

has been approved by the Member States in accordance with their respective constitutional requirements. As we can see, unlike the situation for the revision of decision-making rules, in this case national ratification will be required. The significance of this procedure is that it will allow for the amendment of internal policies without the need to convene an IGC.

In addition to the general bridging clause, the Reform Treaty – following the proposals of the Constitutional Treaty – will introduce several special passarelle clauses into the Treaty on the functioning of the European Union, allowing – in some specific areas – for a swift changeover to the ordinary legislative procedure with a unanimous decision of the Council. The Council will consult the European Parliament prior to such decisions. Compared to the mechanism of the general bridging clause, an important difference is that, in this case, the national parliaments will not be involved; they will be unable to veto the application of the special bridging clause by officially objecting to the Council's decision. The Constitutional Treaty allowed for a changeover from the special to the ordinary legislative procedure following a unanimous Council decision in one Article in each of the following three areas: social policy, environment and family law. However, according to the mandate on the Reform Treaty, national parliaments must be given a role in the special passarelle clause for family law.
Similarly to the Constitutional Treaty, the Reform Treaty will introduce into the Treaty on the functioning of the European Union a special passarelle clause that will enable the European Council, acting by a unanimous decision, to authorise the Council to adopt multi-annual financial frameworks with a qualified majority in the future.
In the area of the Common Foreign and Security Policy too, the Reform Treaty like the Constitutional Treaty will introduce a special passarelle clause in the EU Treaty, enabling the European Council to unanimously adopt a decision authorising the Council to act by a qualified majority. The European Parliament and national parliaments will not be involved in this procedure either.[22]

As a tally to the special bridging clause, the Constitutional Treaty created the novel instrument of the *emergency brake clause*, which is applied for three Articles (two cases of

---

[22] Due to the deep division among Member States at the 2004 IGC (or, to be more precise, the strong resistance of some countries, e.g. the United Kingdom), it was impossible to introduce qualified majority voting in CFSP, but each Member State acknowledged the future necessity of doing so. Thus, with the special bridging clause, they wanted to make it possible to change their minds and give up their right of veto in this area with a simple decision of the European Council, avoiding the lengthy revision procedure.

judicial cooperation in criminal matters and the free movement of migrant workers), where the Member States only agreed to use qualified majority voting if guaranteed the right of veto under certain conditions. Under the Constitutional Treaty's emergency brake clause, any Member State could request the Council to suspend the decision-making procedure and submit the issue in question to the European Council, which had four months to either send the proposal back to the Council where the suspension would be lifted, or ask the Commission or the Member States activating the emergency brake clause to submit a new proposal.

The Reform Treaty modifies the procedure slightly applied to the two Articles on judicial cooperation in criminal matters: firstly, it does not mention the option of submitting a new proposal and secondly, it stipulates that "if there is a consensus" within four months the European Council will send the proposal back to the Council, where the suspension of the ordinary legislative procedure will be lifted. If there is no consensus by the end of the four months, then at least one third of the Member States will be able to request enhanced cooperation, and in this case the authorisation to proceed with enhanced cooperation will be deemed granted.[23]

In the Article on the free movement of migrant workers, the Reform Treaty adds a new option to the emergency brake procedure, which will enable the European Council to decide not to act.

4.3. The instruments of flexible integration: enhanced cooperation and permanent structured cooperation

Due to the recent significant increase in the number of Member States and the likely continuation of enlargement, during the drafting of the Constitutional Treaty great emphasis was put on flexible integration. It was considered important to allow a group of Member States wishing to forge closer integration in an area without all the Union's Member States necessarily wishing to do so, to be able to cooperate within the institutional and legal framework of the Union, so that they did not establish new institutional frameworks of

---

[23] Enhanced cooperation will be initiated in a similar, simplified manner in areas of police and judicial cooperation in criminal matters where unanimity is upheld. In these areas, if there is no unanimous consensus in Council, one third of the Member States will be able to request that the legislative proposal be submitted to the European Council and the procedure in Council be suspended. The European Council will have four months to discuss the issue, arrive at a consensus and send the proposal back to the Council for adoption. If there is no consensus within four months, at least one third of the Member States will be able to request to proceed with enhanced cooperation, the authorisation for which will be deemed granted.

integration, which might jeopardise the unity of the Union. In order to ensure the possibility of such closer cooperation, the Constitutional Treaty modified the existing instrument of *enhanced cooperation*, and introduced for the Common Foreign and Security Policy the instrument of permanent *structured cooperation*. The Reform Treaty transposes into the EU Treaty the provisions of the Constitutional Treaty on enhanced cooperation and structured cooperation, slightly modifying the conditions for proceeding with enhanced cooperation.

The current principles of enhanced cooperation were upheld by the Constitutional Treaty and are maintained in the Reform Treaty. Thus enhanced cooperation will be open to all Member States from the beginning and must remain open later as well. Enhanced cooperation may not have a detrimental effect on the functioning of the internal market or the economic and social cohesion of the Union. Authorising enhanced cooperation can only be a last resort, once it has become clear that the objectives of such cooperation cannot be attained within a reasonable period by the Union as a whole. Within the framework of enhanced cooperation, only participating Member States can take part in the actual decision-making or votes. Acts adopted in the framework of enhanced cooperation bind only participating states.

While currently, a minimum of eight Member States is needed to initiate enhanced cooperation, the Constitutional Treaty stipulated that at least one third of the Member States would be required to participate in enhanced cooperation. The Reform Treaty sets the threshold for the number of Member States required for enhanced cooperation at nine.

The Treaty simplifies the use of different procedures for different pillars. Generally, a qualified majority vote will be required for an authorisation to proceed with enhanced cooperation, except for the area of Common Foreign and Security Policy, where the Council will continue to act unanimously. In the area of police and judicial cooperation in criminal matters, initiating enhanced cooperation will be even simpler; if the Member States fail to find a compromise either in Council or in the European Council, then a minimum of one third of the Member States will be able to request enhanced cooperation, and the authorisation to proceed with such cooperation will be deemed granted.

The Council will only be able to grant such authorisation after consulting and obtaining the consent of the European Parliament, except for CFSP, where the Parliament will only be informed of such a decision. Contrary to present rules, defence issues will not be excluded from the scope of enhanced cooperation.

Member States participating in enhanced cooperation will be able to apply the bridging clause, i.e. decide with unanimity to switch to qualified majority voting and the ordinary legislative procedure in their decision-making. The bridging clause will not apply to decisions having military or defence implications. In order to ensure the unity of the Union, the Reform Treaty clearly puts emphasis on making it easier for Member States to join enhanced cooperation subsequently, calling on the Commission and the participating Member States to promote participation in enhanced cooperation in progress by as many Member States as possible.[24]

In the area of Common Security and Defence Policy, the Reform Treaty – like the Constitutional Treaty – introduces and incorporates into the EU Treaty the instrument of flexible integration called permanent structured cooperation. Under this procedure the Council will be able to entrust the implementation of a task to a group of Member States within the Union framework. Countries meeting the criteria of higher military capabilities will be able to establish structured cooperation for the implementation of more complex tasks or more demanding missions. Unlike in the case of enhanced cooperation, the Reform Treaty does not require at least nine Member States to participate; as few as two countries will be able to initiate permanent structured cooperation. The Council will adopt its decision on authorising permanent structured cooperation by qualified majority and after consulting the Union High Representative for Foreign Affairs and Security Policy. Permanent structured cooperation will be open only to those Member States that make a political commitment to develop their military capabilities and that have the capacity to supply rapid-response combat units.[25]

5. The legal order of the EU

5.1. The introduction of the single legal personality and the interrelationship of the Treaties

One of the key provisions of the Constitutional Treaty was to confer a single legal personality upon the European Union. This provision is maintained by the Reform Treaty, which will incorporate into the EU Treaty a new Article stipulating that "the Union shall have legal personality". In that spirit, the Reform Treaty will rename the EC Treaty, giving it the new name of Treaty on the functioning of the European Union. Article 1 of the EU Treaty will be amended and the following supplementary sentence added: "The Union shall be founded on the present Treaty and on the Treaty on the functioning of the European Union. It shall replace and

---

[24] Countries wishing to participate in enhanced cooperation in progress will have to notify the Council and the Commission. If the Commission considers that the conditions for participation have been fulfilled, within four months of receipt of the notification, it will confirm the participation of the Member State concerned. However, if the Commission considers that the conditions of participation have not been fulfilled, it will indicate the arrangements to be adopted to fulfil those conditions and set a deadline for re-examining the request. If, upon re-examining the request, the Commission considers that the conditions have still not been met, the Member State concerned will be able to refer the matter to the Council, which will decide on the request, adopting transitional measures. When taking such a decision, only Member States participating in the enhanced cooperation in question will take part in the vote.

[25] For more, see Point 23.2. of this Annex.

succeed the European Community." Throughout the Treaty on the functioning of the European Union, the term Community is replaced by Union; Article 1 of this Treaty lays down the objective of the Treaty and its relationship with the EU Treaty and stipulate that the two Treaties have the same legal value.

The European Union's legal personality in essence will replace the legal personality of the European Community. The particular importance of this change is that, currently, only the European Community has legal personality, while the European Union does not.[26] In practice this means that, until the European Union has legal personality, it is only the European Community that can conclude international agreements and act as a self-contained entity vis-à-vis third countries in areas where it has competence. By conferring legal personality upon the Union, the Reform Treaty aims to put an end to the current division between first-pillar foreign trade activities[27] and second-pillar foreign and security policy activities[28], and reinforce the Union's clout on the international scene. With the conferral of legal personality, the Union – as a subject of international law – would be able to avail itself of all means of international action (such as the conclusion of international agreements, membership in international organisations, accession to international conventions, etc.).

The amendments to the current EU and EC Treaties do not concern the substance of the Euratom Treaty, but the Reform Treaty will make some necessary technical amendments, as agreed in the 2004 IGC. The new Protocols agreed in the 2004 IGC will be annexed to the existing Treaties (e.g. Protocol on the role of national parliaments, Protocol on the application of the principles of subsidiarity and proportionality, Protocol on the EuroGroup, Protocol on permanent structured cooperation in the field of defence and Protocol on the accession of the Union to the European Convention for the Protection of Human Rights and Fundamental Freedoms). The Reform Treaty will amend some existing Protocols and delete others. Similarly, some Declarations will be amended or deleted, and several new Declarations will be annexed to the Reform Treaty.[29]

---

[26] In addition to the European Community, Euratom also has a legal personality of its own.

[27] See Chapter 9.

[28] See Chapter 23.

[29] Provisions of Protocols have the same binding force as provisions in the main text of the Treaties. The same cannot be said about Declarations, which are not binding or enforceable; they are only declarations of political positions. Declarations usually interpret certain Treaty provisions. Their political weight is determined by the number of signatories. There are Joint Declarations signed by all Member States and Declarations with one or more signatories.

5.2. The primacy of Union law

The Constitutional Treaty clearly stipulated the primacy of Union law over national law. This unambiguous reference sought to incorporate the principle established by the judicial practice of the Court of Justice into a primary source of Union law.

At the European Council meeting of 21–22 June 2007, the Heads of State or Government decided not to include in the Reform Treaty an explicit mention of the primacy of Union law. Instead, a Declaration recalls the existing case law of the Court of Justice, which lays down the primacy of the Treaties and the law adopted by the Union over the law of the Member States.

5.3. Accession to and withdrawal from the Union

Like the Constitutional Treaty, the Reform Treaty amends the conditions of accession to the Union. Article 49 of the currently effective EU Treaty stipulates that any European state may apply for membership if it respects the fundamental principles of the Union (the principles of freedom, democracy, human rights, fundamental freedoms and the rule of law). Under the Reform Treaty, this reference to the Union's principles will be replaced by a reference to the Union's values, which is an extension of the current conditions of eligibility for accession: the current principles do not include a number of the values defined by the Constitutional Treaty which are inserted by the Reform Treaty into the new Article 2 of the EU Treaty. In the future, potential applicant countries will have to respect values such as respect for human dignity, protecting the rights of persons belonging to minorities, pluralism, non-discrimination and gender equality.

The Reform Treaty introduces into Article 49 of the EU Treaty the corresponding text of the Constitutional Treaty, inserting a new last sentence: "The conditions of eligibility agreed upon by the European Council shall be taken into account." This will integrate into the Treaties and thereby institutionalise the practice of referring to the currently applied Copenhagen criteria[30], and will allow the European Council to add new – even country-specific – conditions for accession. This reflects the new approach, which emphasises the Union's absorption capacity for future enlargements.

---

[30] See 1.13.2.

A novel feature of the Constitutional Treaty, unprecedented in the history of European integration, was that it defined the conditions and procedures for voluntary withdrawal by a Member State from the Union. The current Treaties do not contain any provisions on the possibility of withdrawal from the Union.[31]

The Reform Treaty incorporates into the EU Treaty the procedure on voluntary withdrawal from the Union, as had been proposed in the Constitutional Treaty. The following procedure is laid down for a withdrawal. Any Member State will be able to decide to withdraw from the European Union in accordance with its own constitutional requirements. When a Member State notifies the European Council of its wish to withdraw from the Union, negotiations will begin on an agreement setting out the arrangements of its withdrawal and the framework for its future relationship with the Union. Such negotiations will be conducted on behalf of the Union not by the Commission, but by a chief negotiator appointed by the Council. That agreement will be concluded on behalf of the Union by the Council, acting by a qualified majority, after obtaining the consent of the European Parliament. In this case, a qualified majority will require the vote of at least 72% of the Member States representing a minimum of 65% of the Union's population. The membership of the relevant Member State will cease upon the entry into force of that agreement. If no withdrawal agreement is concluded within two years of the notification, the Treaties will cease to apply to the Member State in question, unless the European Council, in agreement with the Member State concerned, decides to extend this period. If a state which has withdrawn from the Union decides to rejoin, its application for membership will be subject to the same accession criteria as any other applicant country.

5.4. Secondary legal acts

According to the Laeken mandate[32], one of the key objectives during the process of drafting the Constitutional Treaty was to simplify the system of legal instruments in the Union. Simplification was justified by: i) the need to reduce the excessive number of legal instruments to ensure transparency, as currently there are 15 different legal instruments available in the three pillars (see 5.2.2.), not counting the non-typical legal norms (such as declarations, conclusions, guidelines) of *soft law* unspecified in the Treaties but adopted by the institutions; ii) the need for a clearer distinction between, and more transparent hierarchy among, the original legislative, delegated and executive-type acts, which are currently slightly muddled and obscure, as legal acts can be used for almost any purpose. A good example of how complicated and foggy the current system is, are the four different types of decisions; while the first-pillar decision alone is used in a myriad of cases from laying down the rules of European Parliament elections to common anti-dumping measures.

---

[31] Up until now, no Member State has decided to withdraw from the Union, but an autonomous region of a Member State has withdrawn: it was agreed in 1985 that Community law would not apply to the island of Greenland, a part of Denmark.

[32] See 1.12.2.

The abolition of the three-pillar system allowed the Constitutional Treaty to significantly cut the number of legal acts the Union could adopt and to create a single uniform system of the sources of Union law. In the spirit of simplification, the Constitutional Treaty provided for four binding and two non-binding legal acts: European law (to replace the current regulation), European framework law (to replace the current first-pillar directive and the third-pillar framework decision), European regulation (an implementing version of the current regulation), European decision (to replace the current four types of decisions, second-pillar joint actions and second- and third-pillar common positions) and recommendation and opinion (equivalent to the current recommendation and opinion).

For the first time in the history of European integration, the Constitutional Treaty – in addition to the new denominations – aimed to establish a hierarchy of legal acts. The aim of this hierarchy was to define and separate legislative and executive tasks and legislative acts thereof. This was particularly important because, currently, the same nomenclature and legal value (binding force and rules of application) is used for legal acts adopted by the Council or jointly by the Council and the Parliament for regulating a legislative issue of some gravity and for those legal acts of a lower level that are adopted by the Commission for implementing or amending the very framework acts described above. Consequently, a Council and Parliament directive can be implemented by a Commission regulation. In order to eliminate this problem, the Constitutional Treaty differentiated between legislative acts and non-legislative acts, as two separate categories. The Constitutional Treaty defined European laws and framework laws as *legislative acts* while other legislative acts, i.e. European regulations, European decisions, recommendations and opinions, were defined as *non-legislative acts*. The Constitutional Treaty also defined so-called *delegated European regulations*, thereby aiming to give the Commission the legal instrument to supplement or – in certain cases – amend a law or framework law. Equally, the Constitutional Treaty defined *implementing acts* as European implementing regulations and European implementing decisions. When responsibility for implementing legally binding Union acts did not lie with the Member States but uniform conditions for implementing legally binding Union acts were needed, those acts could confer implementing powers on the Commission, or – in duly justified specific cases and in the area of CFSP – on the Council. The Constitutional Treaty stipulated that for the purposes of implementing acts, European laws should lay down in advance the rules and general principles concerning mechanisms for the control by the Member States of the Commission's exercise of implementing powers.

In the mandate for the IGC on the Reform Treaty agreed on 22 June 2007, the Member States decided not to retain the new denominations proposed by the Constitutional Treaty in an attempt to remove from the text of the new Treaty all the terms and references reminiscent of a constitution or state. As a result, it was decided that the denominations used by the current EC Treaty for EU legal acts would remain in use. Consequently, the legal acts of the Union will remain: regulation, directive and decision. However, the definition of decision will be amended to reflect the definition used by the Constitutional Treaty for what it would have called European decision.

Although the Reform Treaty does not maintain the denominations of legal acts proposed by the Constitutional Treaty, it does retain the distinction between legislative and non-legislative acts as well as their hierarchy. Accordingly, after Article 249 of the current EC Treaty three new Articles will be inserted covering, respectively, acts which are adopted in accordance with a legislative procedure, delegated acts and implementing acts. The Article on legislative acts will state that acts (regulations, directives or decisions) adopted under a legislative procedure (ordinary or special) are legislative acts. The wording of the Articles on delegated and implementing acts will be based on the wording proposed by the Constitutional Treaty.

5.5. Provisions concerning the Charter of Fundamental Rights

The Convention and the subsequent IGC incorporated the full text of the Charter of Fundamental Rights into the proposed Constitutional Treaty as Part II. The question whether to include the explanatory parts interpreting the provisions of the Charter in the Constitutional Treaty and, if so, what their legal status would be was a major sticking point at the 2004 IGC. The Convention that drafted the Charter, in an attempt to make the Charter easier to understand, annotated the Articles. These explanatory annotations were based on the interpretative rulings of the European Court of Human Rights in Strasbourg. The importance of these annotations is that they tie the hands of courts in interpreting the Charter when referring to it. In the end, primarily due to the demands of the United Kingdom, a rather restrictive compromise was adopted: "the explanations drawn up as a way of providing guidance in the interpretation of the Charter of Fundamental Rights shall be given *due regard* by the Courts of the Union and of the Member States".

When it became clear that the Constitutional Treaty would not enter into force, the UK reopened the issue of the Charter, its binding force and the justiciable rights therein, which they had opposed but finally accepted in 2004 – with the proviso already mentioned. The British position was that the Charter should be removed from the text of the new Treaty and should only become legally binding under certain conditions.

The final compromise forged by the European Council of 21–22 June 2007 was that the Charter would not be formally incorporated into the text of the Treaties, but that Article 6 of the

EU Treaty on fundamental rights would include the following reference: the Union recognises the rights, freedoms and principles set out in the Charter of Fundamental Rights, which shall have the same legal value as the Treaties. Consequently, the Charter will have legal effect with the entry into force of the new Treaty. Nevertheless, according to the amended Article 6, "the provisions of the Charter shall not extend in any way the competences of the Union as defined in the Treaties".

The interpretation of the Charter was a contentious issue at the June 2007 summit too. When the Charter becomes legally binding, it will become justiciable (applicable in Court), but the Reform Treaty maintains that "the rights, freedoms and principles in the Charter shall be interpreted with due regard to the explanations referred to in the Charter". The UK managed to obtain another opt-out in this field, according to which the Charter will only be justiciable to a limited extent (in practice, non-applicable to the UK). The details of this opt-out are laid down in a Protocol annexed to the Treaty.[33]

Another issue linked to the Charter is the new provision of Article 6 of the EU Treaty, stipulating that the Union will accede to the European Convention for the Protection of Human Rights and Fundamental Freedoms of the Council of Europe on the entry into force of the Reform Treaty. This is of symbolic importance, as all Member States are already signatories to the Convention, and the rights set out in the Convention form the basis of the Charter of Fundamental Rights. The new Article 6 does stipulate that "such accession shall not affect the Union's competences as defined in the Treaties" but recognises that the fundamental rights, as guaranteed by the European Convention for the Protection of Human Rights and Fundamental Freedoms and as they result from the constitutional traditions common to the Member States, constitute general principles of the Union's law.

---

[33] This implies that neither the European Court of Justice, nor any British court will be able to rule that laws or practices in the UK are in violation of the Charter. Concerning the social rights set out in the Charter (Title IV) "nothing ... creates justiciable rights applicable to the United Kingdom except in so far as the United Kingdom has provided for such rights in its national law". If a provision of the Charter includes a reference to national law or practice, it will be applicable to the UK only in so far as the rights and principles in it are recognised in UK law and practice. The UK was not alone in seeking to secure special treatment. According to the agreement reached on 21–22 June 2007 Poland annexes a unilateral Declaration to the Reform Treaty in which it states its position that "the Charter does not affect in any way the right of Member States to legislate in the sphere of public morality, family law as well as the protection of human dignity and respect for human physical and moral integrity". The Polish government was keen on this additional Declaration, because it wanted to secure a loophole against subsequent attempts to introduce same-sex marriages in Poland.

6. The functioning of the single market

Apart from certain amendments necessitated by legal technicalities, the Constitutional Treaty did not seek to amend the substantive nature of the provisions on the four fundamental freedoms. The Reform Treaty maintains the provisions of the Constitutional Treaty in this field, incorporating them into the current Treaty framework.

The following changes should be highlighted:
For the free movement of goods there will be no substantive amendments.
For the free movement of persons, the scope of application of harmonising measures in the field of social security will be extended to include employed as well as self-employed persons. In the field of social security of migrant workers, the current unanimity will be replaced with qualified majority voting, and a special emergency brake clause (already discussed in detail in Point 4.2. of this Annex), allowing Member States to use their right of veto under certain conditions and to a limited extent.
For the freedom to provide services, the Reform Treaty takes on board the provisions of the current EC Treaty, and will extend the ordinary legislative procedure to two new areas: i) extending the freedom to provide services to service provision by third-country nationals established within the Union; and ii) adopting measures to achieve the liberalisation of a specific service.
For the free movement of capital, the Reform Treaty will introduce the ordinary legislative procedure for capital movements to and from third countries. In order to improve the efficiency of the fight against terrorism, the Treaty creates a legal base for the Union to freeze the funds and financial assets of natural or legal persons.

For taxation, the Reform Treaty takes on board all the provisions of the EC Treaty with one amendment, which will enable the Union to establish measures for the harmonisation of legislation concerning taxation, provided that such harmonisation is necessary to ensure the establishment and functioning of the internal market and to avoid a distortion of competition. During decision-making however, without exception, the Council will act unanimously after consulting the European Parliament and the Economic and Social Committee.

7. The Union budget

7.1. The institutionalisation of multi-annual financial frameworks

Like the Constitutional Treaty, the Reform Treaty will institutionalise the now standard practice of multi-annual financial planning, which currently has no legal base in the Treaties, and incorporate it into the primary sources of EU law under the name of multi-annual financial *framework*. Accordingly, the Union's annual budget will have to be drawn up on the basis of the multi-annual financial framework. Following the practice of financial perspectives, the multi-annual financial framework will determine the annual ceilings on commitment appropriations by headings.

The Council and the Parliament will adopt multi-annual financial frameworks jointly. It took a long and heated debate at the IGC finalising the Constitutional Treaty to decide whether the Council should switch to QMV and, if so, from what date. A few Member States refused to give up their right of veto in this area before the system of own resources was reformed. Consequently, unanimity remains the applicable procedure in budgetary issues. Nonetheless, like the Constitutional Treaty, the Reform Treaty includes a special bridging clause, which will allow the European Council acting by unanimity to authorise the Council to switch to qualified majority voting when adopting a multi-annual financial framework.

7.2. The new budgetary procedure

Like the Constitutional Treaty, the Reform Treaty will also amend the budgetary procedure used for adopting the Union's annual budget. The new budgetary procedure will be introduced as a special modified version of the ordinary legislative procedure. The new procedure, which has strict deadlines, will consist of a single reading and a conciliation phase (so far only used for co-decision). Another step toward simplification is that the annual budget will no longer differentiate between compulsory and non-compulsory expenditure. This will have two consequences: i) it will reinforce Parliament's role, which will enable it to deal with all expenditure items in the same way; ii) Parliament will no longer have the final say in non-compulsory expenditure. The Reform Treaty allows for only one case when Parliament will have the final say: if the Council rejects the budget after an agreement has been reached in the conciliation committee (which is most unlikely to happen in practice).

Having regard to these changes, following the entry into force of the Reform Treaty, the Union's annual budget will be established through the following procedure:

1. Each institution, before 1 July, will draw up estimates of its expenditure for the following financial year. The Commission will consolidate these estimates in a draft budget containing an estimate of revenue and an estimate of expenditure.
2. The Commission will submit a proposal containing the draft budget to the European Parliament and to the Council not later than 1 September of the year preceding that in which the budget is to be implemented. The Commission will be able to amend the draft budget during the procedure until such time as the Conciliation Committee is convened.
3. The Council will adopt its position on the draft budget and forward it to the European Parliament not later than 1 October of the year preceding that in which the budget is to be implemented.

4. If, within forty-two days of such communication, the European Parliament: (a) approves the position of the Council, the budget will be adopted; (b) has not taken a decision, the budget will be deemed to have been adopted (c) adopts amendments by a majority of its component members, the amended draft will be forwarded to the Council and to the Commission. The President of the European Parliament, in agreement with the President of the Council, will immediately convene a meeting of the Conciliation Committee. However, if within ten days of the draft being forwarded, the Council informs the European Parliament that it has approved all its amendments, the Conciliation Committee will not meet.

5. The Conciliation Committee, composed of the members of the Council or their representatives and an equal number of members representing the European Parliament, will have the task of reaching agreement on a joint text within twenty-one days of its being convened. The Commission will take part in the Conciliation Committee's proceedings and take all the necessary initiatives in order to reconcile the positions of the European Parliament and the Council. If, within the twenty-one days, the Conciliation Committee does not agree on a joint text, a new draft budget will have to be submitted by the Commission.

6. If, within the twenty-one days the Conciliation Committee agrees on a joint text, the European Parliament and the Council will each have a period of fourteen days from the date of that agreement in which to approve the joint text.

7. If, within the period of fourteen days: (a) the European Parliament and the Council both approve the joint text or fail to take a decision, or if one of these institutions approves the joint text while the other one fails to take a decision, the budget will be deemed to be definitively adopted in accordance with the joint text, or (b) the Parliament, and the Council both reject the joint text, or if one of these institutions rejects the joint text while the other one fails to take a decision, a new draft budget will have to be submitted by the Commission, or (c) the Parliament, acting by a majority of its component members, rejects the joint text while the Council approves it, a new draft budget will be submitted by the Commission, or (d) the Parliament approves the joint text whilst the Council rejects it, the Parliament will be able, within fourteen days from the date of the rejection by the Council and acting by a majority of its component members and three fifths of the votes cast, to decide to confirm all or some of the amendments referred to in paragraph 4(c). Where a European Parliament amendment is not confirmed, the position agreed in the Conciliation committee on the budget heading which is the subject of the amendment will be retained. The budget will be deemed to be definitively adopted on this basis.

8. When the procedure provided is completed, the President of the European Parliament will declare that the budget is definitively adopted.

8. Economic and monetary union

8.1. Provisions affecting monetary policy

Like the Constitutional Treaty, the Reform Treaty stipulates that the Union has exclusive competence over monetary policy for the Member States whose currency is the euro. Upon its entry into force, in addition to the necessary modifications amounting to legal technicalities, the Reform Treaty will amend the provisions of the EC Treaty in several respects. It will make qualified majority voting the general rule for monetary policy issues, stipulating unanimity in only three areas.[34]

The Reform Treaty institutionalises the cooperation of eurozone countries by creating the *EuroGroup*, and enabling them to adopt acts in certain areas that are legally binding in the whole area of the eurozone. Eurozone members will be able to elect a president for a period of two and a half years. The President will chair the monthly EuroGroup meetings, represent the eurozone on the international scene and liaise with the European Central Bank. A President will be permitted to be re-elected once.

Eurozone members will be able to adopt specific measures – without the other members of the Council participating in the vote – to strengthen the coordination and surveillance of their budgetary discipline, and to set out economic policy guidelines for them, while ensuring that they are compatible with those adopted for the whole of the Union and are kept under surveillance. Eurozone members will also be able to decide among themselves what position the EuroGroup should represent within international financial institutions and conferences. Decisions on the accession of new members to the eurozone will continue to be taken by the full Council, but the EuroGroup will have a larger say, as in such cases the Council will act on the recommendation of the EuroGroup adopted by a qualified majority of its members.

As proposed by the Constitutional Treaty, the Reform Treaty will reinforce the role of the Commission in the excessive deficit procedure. When deciding whether an excessive deficit exists, the Council will act on a proposal by the Commission. Under the current EC Treaty, the Commission can only make recommendations to the Council concerning excessive deficits. The significance of this difference between the two treaties lies in the fact that the Council can modify Commission recommendations acting by a qualified majority, while a Commission proposal can only be modified with unanimity.

8.2. Provisions affecting the coordination of economic policies

The Reform Treaty, like the Constitutional Treaty, defines the coordination of economic policies (and of employment policies) as an area where tasks occur at the Union level but which, due to its character, does not fit into the category of activities aimed at coordinating sectoral policies,

---

[34] These are the following: amending the Protocol on the excessive deficit procedure; conferring on the European Central Bank the task of prudential supervision of credit institutions and other financial organisations; setting the exchange rate of the currency of a country joining the eurozone.

because it entails the establishment of harmonious comprehensive national economic policies and is not a simple supporting action.

Coordinating economic policies will continue to contribute to the achievement of the Union's objectives, particularly those aimed at the harmonious, balanced and sustainable development of economic activity, a high degree of competitiveness, a high level of employment and social protection, sustainable and non-inflationary growth respecting the environment, and a high degree of competitiveness and convergence of economic performance.

Broad economic policy guidelines will remain the main tool of economic policy coordination. The Treaty introduces two new elements in that context. Firstly, the Commission will be able to address a warning directly to a Member State whose economic policies are not consistent with the broad guidelines. Secondly, similarly to the excessive deficit procedure, the Member State concerned will not be able to take part in the vote when a decision is taken on whether its economic policy is consistent with the BEPGs.

9. The Union's external relations – the Common Commercial Policy and the conclusion of international agreements

The abolition of the system of three pillars will pave the way for much more concerted external action (the Common Foreign and Security Policy, the Common Commercial Policy, cooperation with third countries, development cooperation and humanitarian aid, international agreements and the Union's relations with international organisations and third countries). To this end, Title V of the EU Treaty will include both general provisions on external action and provisions on the Common Foreign and Security Policy. The detailed rules of those aspects of external relations that are currently under the first pillar will remain in the amended EC Treaty, which becomes the Treaty on the functioning of the Union, but in a separate new part of the text. The key novelty of this new part of the Treaty will be that for the first time humanitarian aid will be institutionalised in the EC Treaty.

In accordance with the Constitutional Treaty, the current General Affairs and External Relations Council will be split up and the Foreign Affairs Council will be set up. The Foreign Affairs Council will be responsible for elaborating the Union's external action, on the basis of strategic guidelines laid down by the European Council, and for ensuring that the Union's action is consistent. It will also be the task of the Union Minister for Foreign Affairs to ensure the consistency of the Union's external action.

9.1. Provisions affecting the Common Commercial Policy

The Reform Treaty defines the Common Commercial Policy as an area of exclusive Union competence. Upon its entry into force, the Reform Treaty will bring the following changes in Common Commercial Policy:
- the Common Commercial Policy will include negotiating and concluding agreements on foreign direct investment; for decisions on the conclusion of such agreements, the Council will act unanimously;
- the special procedure for concluding agreements will be maintained in the areas of trade in cultural and audiovisual services and trade in social, education and health services, according to which the Member States and the Union will conduct negotiations jointly and by the full common accord of the Member States. The Reform Treaty will bring a slight change, by stipulating that this special procedure will apply to cultural and audiovisual services where these agreements risk prejudicing the Union's cultural and linguistic diversity; and for social, education and health services, where these agreements risk seriously disturbing the national organisation of such services and prejudicing the capability of Member States to deliver them.
- a key institutional change is that all international agreements will require the consent of the European Parliament, which will have to be regularly informed about the progress of negotiations.

9.2. Provisions affecting other international agreements

Like the Constitutional Treaty, the Reform Treaty will institutionalise the case law of the Court of Justice on the Union's implicit external powers. Accordingly, the Union will be able to conclude an agreement with one or more third countries or international organisations in one of the following four cases:
- when the Treaties so provide;
- when an agreement is necessary in order to achieve one of the objectives referred to in the Treaties;
- when an agreement is provided for in a legally binding Union act; or
- when an agreement is likely to affect common rules or alter their scope.

Besides the Commission, the High Representative of the Union for Foreign Affairs and Security Policy will also play a role in the conclusion of international agreements. The High Representative must submit recommendations to the Council if the planned agreement is exclusively or mainly related to Common Foreign and Security Policy and, in other cases, the recommendations must be submitted by the Commission. The Reform Treaty will not provide for a chief negotiator, but will confer competence for taking that decision on the Council. The Council may appoint a special committee, which the chief negotiator will have to consult during the course of the negotiations.

The Treaty will maintain the two types of voting procedures in Council. As a general rule, the Council will act by a qualified majority, except for areas where unanimity is required for the adoption of internal rules. For association agreements and agreements with candidate countries on economic, financial or technical issues, the Council will act by unanimity.

10. Competition policy

The Reform Treaty stipulates that the Union has exclusive competence in the area of establishing the competition rules necessary for the functioning of the internal market. Provisions of the EC Treaty on competition policy will be retained with some minor amendments.

Like the Constitutional Treaty, the Reform Treaty will reinforce the Commission's role of implementation in competition policy by enabling it to adopt supplementary implementing regulations on agreements restricting competition for which the Council has already adopted a regulation. Similarly, the Commission will be able to adopt supplementary implementing regulations for state aids which Council has exempted from the authorisation rule in a specific regulation.

The Reform Treaty will amend the list of state aids which are compatible with the internal market in relation to cases when a Member State may grant aid automatically, and when the Commission may authorise such aid. The first group includes three cases: a) aid having a social character, granted to individual consumers, provided that such aid is granted without discrimination related to the origin of the products concerned; b) aid to make good the damage caused by natural disasters or exceptional occurrences; and c) aid granted to the economy of certain areas of the Federal Republic of Germany affected by the division of Germany, insofar as such aid is required in order to compensate for the economic disadvantages caused by that division. However, five years after the entry into force of the Reform Treaty, the Council, acting on a proposal from the Commission, may adopt a decision repealing this latter category, (obviously, depending on the development of the East German Länder). In the category of non-automatic aid, for which the Member State requires permission from the Commission, the Reform Treaty will add aid to promote the economic development of the overseas territories of Guadeloupe, French Guiana, Martinique, Réunion, the Azores, Madeira and the Canary Islands.

A symbolic change affecting competition policy included due to the insistence of France, is the deletion from the Article on the Union's objectives (TEU Article 3 under the Reform Treaty) the objective of ensuring free and undistorted competition in the internal market, which is included both in the current Treaties and in the Constitutional Treaty. Instead, a

Protocol on competition in the internal market will be attached to the Reform Treaty, which will declare that the internal market provided for in Article 3 of the EU Treaty includes a system ensuring that competition is not distorted. In this Protocol the Member States also agree that to attain this objective the Union may take measures as provided for by the Treaties. Since Protocols attached to Treaties have the same legal value as the Treaties themselves, what the provisions of this Protocol mean in practical terms is that the Union will have the necessary legal base for adopting such measures. This change is more about satisfying France's desire to not include free competition among the key, outstanding objectives of the Union but hide it somewhere less obvious. France insisted on this because a key criticism voiced during the referendum rejecting the Constitutional Treaty was that the Union is too liberal and pro-competition and not social enough. Nonetheless, it was also clear that a key pillar underpinning the operation of the internal market could not be removed altogether, which has led to this peculiar arrangement, which is not the most fortunate solution either politically or legally speaking.[35]

11. The Common Agricultural Policy and the Common Fisheries Policy

Like the Constitutional Treaty, the Reform Treaty defines the Common Agricultural Policy and the Common Fisheries Policy as areas of shared competence. It should be noted, however, that both policies will belong to an area of shared competence, where – according to the principal of conferral – most decision-making competences will be exercised at the Union level.

In decision-making, the Reform Treaty will bring about major changes compared to the EC Treaty. Provisions necessary for the pursuit of the objectives of the Common Agricultural Policy and the Common Fisheries Policy will be adopted through the ordinary legislative procedure. The significance of this is that, for the first time in the history of European integration, the European Parliament will play a real role in the shaping of agricultural policy. However, the Council – on a proposal from the Commission – will adopt the decisions on fixing prices, levies, aid and quantitative limitations and on the fixing and allocation of fishing opportunities, without having to consult the European Parliament.

It is also interesting to point out that while, like the Constitutional Treaty, the Reform Treaty – emphasising the Union's responsibility – makes specific reference to the conservation of marine biological resources under the Common Fisheries Policy as an area of exclusive competence, it does not stipulate directly what measures can be taken and in what form.

---

[35] Following the unsuccesful French referendum the greatest headache for the EU – and even more so for French political leaders – was how to amend the Constitutional Treaty, because the various 'NO' camps used contradictory critical remarks. The end result is this unique solution.

12. Transport policy and trans-European networks

Like the Constitutional Treaty, the Reform Treaty defines the Common Transport Policy and the development of trans-European networks as a shared competence. Apart from repealing outdated provisions, the Reform Treaty will maintain the relevant provisions of the current EC Treaty with no substantive changes for TENs and with minor amendments for Common Transport Policy.

13. The policy of economic, social and territorial cohesion

According to the Reform Treaty – as proposed by the Constitutional Treaty – economic and social cohesion will be complemented by the objective of territorial cohesion. The Reform Treaty defines economic, social and territorial cohesion as an area of shared competence.
In addition to the main objective of reducing disparities between the levels of development of the various regions and the backwardness of the least favoured regions, the Constitutional Treaty will extend the scope of economic, social and territorial cohesion to include rural areas, areas affected by industrial transition, and regions which suffer from severe and permanent natural or demographic handicaps, such as northernmost regions with very low population density and island, cross-border and mountain regions.
According to the Treaty of Nice, in the budgetary planning period following the financial perspective beginning in 2007 (i.e. after 2013), a qualified majority in the Council is required for decisions concerning the objectives, tasks and financial framework of Structural and Cohesion Funds. The Reform Treaty maintains the introduction of qualified majority at a later date. It is also stipulated that, at the same time, the ordinary legislative procedure will replace the current assent procedure in this area.

14. Social policy and the coordination of employment policies

14.1. Provisions affecting social policy

Like the Constitutional Treaty, the Reform Treaty defines social policy as an area of shared competence and will reinforce the Union's role in this area.
The general principles applicable to the Union's policies and functioning will include the guarantee of adequate social protection and the fight against social exclusion. The significance of this is underscored by the fact that the European Court of Justice can annul any legal act or draft legislation contrary to these provisions with reference to this clause.

Gender equality will become a fundamental value of the Union, and thus indirectly it will also become an accession criterion and its violation could even be a legal base for suspending membership rights.

A new element in social policy is that, in the interest of achieving social policy objectives, the Commission will be able to encourage cooperation between the Member States and facilitate the coordination of their action, particularly in matters relating to employment; labour law and working conditions; basic and advanced vocational training; social security; prevention of occupational accidents and diseases; occupational hygiene; the right of association and collective bargaining between employers and workers.

Upon its entry into force, the Reform Treaty will reinforce the provisions of the EC Treaty, with more emphasis on social aspects at the level of principles. It should be noted here that the Reform Treaty will include a reference to the Union's Charter of Fundamental Rights as a document with equivalent legal value to the Treaties. Since many of the provisions of the Charter of Fundamental Rights are based on the Social Charter, a wide range of social rights will be incorporated into Union primary law.[36]

14.2. Provisions affecting the coordination of employment policies

Like the Constitutional Treaty, the Reform Treaty defines the task of coordinating employment policies (and economic policies) as an area of competence at the Union level. However, it does not fit into the category of coordinating sectoral policies, as this is more than a supporting activity; it involves the alignment of comprehensive national employment policies. The Union will be explicitly given the specific competence of coordinating the employment policies of the Member States, in particular by defining guidelines for these policies.

The Reform Treaty otherwise maintains the provisions of the EC Treaty on employment policy without any substantive changes.

15. Industrial policy

Like the Constitutional Treaty, the Reform Treaty defines industrial policy as a means of supporting, coordinating or complementary action by the Union. Upon its entry into force, the Reform Treaty will maintain all the provisions of the EC Treaty with one amendment, which takes into consideration the practical instruments of cooperation already applied in the Lisbon process and based on the method of open coordination. In the area of industry, the Commission will be able to take any useful initiatives to promote the coordination of Member-State action, in particular initiatives aimed at establishing guidelines and indicators or promoting the exchange of best practices.

---

[36] It should be noted that a separate Protocol will stipulate that concerning the social rights enshrined in the Charter "nothing ... creates justiciable rights applicable to the United Kingdom except in so far as the United Kingdom has provided for such rights in its national law".

16. Energy policy

Like the Constitutional Treaty, the Reform Treaty defines energy policy as an area of shared competence. Unlike the current EC Treaty, the Reform Treaty will devote a separate Article in the Treaty on the Functioning of the Union to the energy policy of the Union, providing a legal base. This mostly takes on board the objectives laid down in the 1995 White Paper on Energy Policy: ensuring the functioning of the energy market, ensuring security of energy supply, promoting rational and efficient energy use, promoting environmentally sound energy use and production, and developing new and renewable energy sources. These objectives will be achieved by measures adopted by the Council and Parliament through the ordinary legislative procedure. By way of derogation, for the adoption of energy rules primarily of a fiscal nature, the Council will act unanimously after consulting the European Parliament. Measures adopted in the field of energy can not affect a Member State's right to determine the conditions for exploiting its energy resources, its choice between different energy sources and the general structure of its energy supply.

Reflecting the latest developments in energy policy, at the time of the adoption of the mandate for the IGC drafting the Reform Treaty, it was decided that in addition to the taking on board the above provisions of the Constitutional Treaty, a reference to solidarity and promoting interconnectivity would also be included in the new Article on energy policy. In the area of coordinating economic policies, the current Article 100 will also stipulate that, according to the principle of solidarity, it may become necessary for the Council to adopt measures in the field of energy supply.

17. Research and technological development policy and space policy

Like the Constitutional Treaty, the Reform Treaty defines research and technological development as an area of shared competence. In addition to the provisions of the EC Treaty, the Reform Treaty – upon its entry into force – will create the legal base for the Union to draw up a European space policy.

Within the framework of open coordination, the Commission – in essence – will be able to propose the establishment of guidelines and indicators, and the organisation of exchange of best practices in order to facilitate the coordination of member-state RTD policies.

The Reform Treaty specifically mentions the concept of the European Research Area, for the creation of which measures will be adopted by the ordinary legislative procedure.

The multi-annual framework programmes will be adopted by the ordinary legislative procedure. When adopting other programmes, the Council will only have to consult Parliament.

Upon its entry into force, the Reform Treaty will provide the Union with a legal base for elaborating its own space policy, within the framework of which it will coordinate the efforts needed for the exploration and exploitation of space. The aim of space policy will be to support scientific and technical progress, industrial competitiveness and the implementation of Union policies. To contribute to attaining these objectives, legal acts will be adopted within the framework of the ordinary legislative procedure to establish the necessary measures, which can take the form of a European space programme.

18. Environmental policy

Like the Constitutional Treaty, the Reform Treaty defines the environment as an area of shared competence. According to the mandate of 22 June 2007, there will be only one substantive amendment to the relevant provisions of the current EC Treaty: a reference to the necessity of international measures to combat climate change will be included.

19. Consumer policy

Like the Constitutional Treaty, the Reform Treaty defines consumer protection as an area of shared competence, and will take on board the relevant provisions of the EC Treaty without any substantive amendments.

20. Public health policy

Like the Constitutional Treaty, the Reform Treaty will retain the health clause introduced in the EC Treaty by the Treaty of Amsterdam, which stipulates that a high level of human health protection must be ensured in the definition and implementation of all the Union's policies and activities. As a new element, and in an attempt to distinguish between Union and Member State competences, the Treaty will stipulate that the Member States have responsibilities for the organisation and delivery of health services and medical care, including the allocation of resources assigned to them. The Union, on the other hand, will have dual responsibility in the field of public health. Firstly, it will have shared competence in the area of common safety concerns, and secondly, it will have supporting, complementary and coordinating competence in the area of protection and improvement of human health.

21. Education, vocational training, youth and sport policy

Like the Constitutional Treaty, the Reform Treaty will maintain the relevant provisions of the EC Treaty. In addition, it will create a new legal base for Community action in the field of sport, by stipulating that Community action should be aimed at developing the European dimension in sport by promoting fairness and openness in sporting competitions and cooperation between bodies responsible for sports.

A new objective of education and youth policy will be "encouraging the participation of young people in democratic life in Europe".

The Reform Treaty defines education, youth, sport and vocational training as a policy area where the Union may take coordinating, complementary or supporting action.

22. Cultural and audiovisual policy

Like the Constitutional Treaty, the Reform Treaty defines culture as an area where the Union has coordinating, complementary or supporting competence. The new Treaty will maintain all relevant provisions of the EC Treaty without any substantive amendments. The only exception will concern decision-making: while co-decision (the ordinary legislative procedure) will be maintained in cultural and audiovisual policy, the Council will act by a qualified majority instead of the former rule of unanimity.

23. The Common Foreign and Security Policy

23.1. Provisions affecting foreign and security policy

The Reform Treaty – building considerably on the Constitutional Treaty – will bring a number of fundamental changes in the field of foreign and security policy, but not a complete overhaul of the current decision-making system. It will put an end to the pillar structure and the fragmentation it entails (enabling a much more effective coordination of current first and second pillar foreign affairs), but foreign policy will remain fundamentally intergovernmental with separate decision-making and operating rules.

Extending qualified majority voting is an essential element of building a common foreign policy and ensuring united action. The Reform Treaty will not bring a real breakthrough on this front, but leaves open the opportunity for future changes. The Reform Treaty will also maintain the institution of constructive abstention and the option of requesting a postponement of a decision due to vital national interests and referring that decision to the European Council. In addition to the cases provided for in the EU Treaty, qualified majority voting will be extended to one more case: when adopting a decision defining a Union action or position, on a proposal which the High Representative of the Union for Foreign Affairs and Security Policy presents following a specific request to him or her from the European Council. Nonetheless the Reform Treaty contains a special passerelle clause – potentially opening the way for deep reforms – which will enable the European Council to take a unanimous decision on acting by qualified majority voting, without having to convene an IGC. This passerelle clause will not apply to decisions having military or defence implications.

In the area of CFSP, the key novelties of the Reform Treaty concern the institutional set-up. It will create the office of the Union High Representative for Foreign Affairs and Security Policy (renamed from the Union Minister for Foreign Affairs as it was called in the Constitutional Treaty), who will be assisted by a European External Action Service. According to the Reform Treaty, the Foreign Affairs Council will meet in a separate formation and will be chaired by the High Representative, who will also serve as the Vice-President of the Commission and as such will represent the Union on the international scene single-handedly.[37]

Compared to the current EU Treaty, the Reform Treaty – in accordance with the Constitutional Treaty – will reduce the range of legal acts that can be adopted in the field of CFSP. The European Council and the Council will be able to adopt decisions, and the Union will be able to conclude international agreements. Upon the entry into force of the Reform Treaty, the Council will be able to adopt a decision on the Union's common position and joint action, as well as the implementation thereof.

The European Commission – as a body – will no longer have a right of initiative; the European Council and the Council will be able to act on an initiative from a Member State or on a proposal from the High Representative or from the High Representative with the Commission's support.

While the current EU Treaty limits enhanced cooperation only to the implementation of some joint action or common position and excludes areas with military or defence implications, the Reform Treaty will allow enhanced cooperation in the whole field of CFSP, though still requiring a unanimous decision by the Council.

23.2. Provisions affecting security and defence policy

In the new EU Treaty, the Reform Treaty will deal with the Common Security and Defence Policy[38] in a separate section of the chapter on Common Foreign and Security Policy. In the area of Common Security and Defence Policy, the Council will be able to adopt decisions and recommendations, acting by unanimity as a general rule.

In relation to missions, the Reform Treaty makes reference to the new task of the fight against terrorism, and also reasserts the Petersberg tasks.

One of the most important symbolic provisions of the Reform Treaty is the incorporation of the much-debated collective defence clause, which stipulates that if a Member State is the victim of armed aggression on its territory, the other Member States will have an obligation to provide aid and assistance by all the means in their power. But since the Member States did not want to compete with NATO in the area of collective defence, the Reform Treaty – maintaining the

---

[37] For more on the High Representative of the Union for Foreign Affairs and Security Policy, see Point 2.4. of this Annex.

[38] As in the Constitutional Treaty, the Reform Treaty introduced the concept of a *Common* Security and Defence Policy instead of the currently widely used term of *European* Security and Defence Policy.

wording of the current EU Treaty – also stipulates that the Union must "respect the obligations of certain Member States, which see their common defence realised in the North Atlantic Treaty Organisation, under the North Atlantic Treaty". In order to allay fears by neutral states, the Reform Treaty adds that the collective defence clause cannot "prejudice the specific character of the security and defence policy of certain Member States".

The Reform Treaty also introduces the solidarity clause, which stipulates that if a Member State is the object of a terrorist attack or the victim of a natural or man-made disaster, the other Member States will be obliged to act jointly in the spirit of solidarity to assist that Member State. Under the provisions of this clause, the Union will have to mobilise all the instruments at its disposal, including the military resources made available by the Member States, to prevent the terrorist threat in the territory of the Member States, to protect democratic institutions and the civilian population from any terrorist attack, and to assist the Member State concerned at the request of its political authorities.

The Council will be able to entrust the execution of a task, within the Union framework, to a group of Member States in order to protect the Union's values and serve its interests. Those Member States whose military capabilities fulfil higher criteria will be able to establish appropriate forms of cooperation for the execution of more demanding missions. To this end, the Reform Treaty introduces *permanent structured cooperation*, open to participation by those Member States that make political commitments to improve their military capabilities. Within the framework of permanent structured cooperation, the Member States will cooperate to fulfil the objectives on defence spending and align their defence equipment. Specific measures will be taken to improve the availability, interoperability, flexibility and deployability of their armed forces.

The Reform Treaty incorporates the European Defence Agency into the EU Treaty, with responsibilities in field of defence capabilities development, research, acquisition and armaments.

24. Provisions affecting the area of freedom, security and justice

In accordance with the Constitutional Treaty, the Reform Treaty defines the policy area of freedom, security and justice as an area of shared competence. Upon its entry into force, the Reform Treaty will bring fundamental changes in this field, amending current EC Treaty and EU Treaty provisions and introducing new ones.

The key change will be the abolition of the three pillar system, and the introduction of the ordinary legislative procedure as a general rule in the whole spectrum of the area of freedom, security and justice.[39] The only exception will be operational police cooperation and cooperation on family law[40], where the Council will continue to take decisions acting by unanimity.

As a reflection of the current different status of third-pillar judicial and police cooperation, in these areas not only the Commission, but also at least one fourth of the Member States will be able to make a legislative proposal.

The Reform Treaty will extend the competence of the European Court of Justice to current third-pillar justice and home affairs, but the Court of Justice will only have competence in police cooperation in criminal cases where the application of the *acquis* is concerned.

With the end of the pillar system, the secondary sources of law will also change: there will be regulations, directives and decisions adopted in this area as well.

As far as individual fields affecting the area of freedom, security and justice are concerned, this may be where the Reform Treaty will bring the most substantive changes compared to the current Treaties. For example, it will:

- allow the gradual introduction of an integrated management system for external borders;
- call for a Common European Asylum System comprising a uniform status of asylum, and common procedures for the grant and withdrawal of subsidiary protection and temporary protection;
- focus a common immigration policy on the following four areas: the efficient management of migration flows, fair treatment of third-country nationals residing legally in Member States, the prevention of and enhanced measures to combat illegal immigration and trafficking in human beings. The Union may conclude agreements with third countries for the re-admission to their countries of origin or provenance of third-country nationals who do not or who no longer fulfil the conditions for entry, presence or residence in the

---

[39] Nevertheless, in the area of judicial cooperation in criminal matters, a so-called *emergency brake clause* will apply, which will allow any Member State – if it feels that a proposed legislative act would affect the fundamental principles of its internal criminal justice system – to request the suspension of the decision-making process and refer the draft to the European Council. (For a detailed description of the emergency brake clause, see Point 4.2. of this Annex)

[40] In the area of family law, a special 'passerelle clause' will allow the Member States to change over to the ordinary legislative procedure with a unanimous decision.

territory of one of the Member States. However, the Member States will continue to have the right to determine volumes in relation to the admission of third-country nationals coming from third countries to their territory in order to seek work, whether employed or self-employed;

– extend judicial cooperation in civil matters to the following areas: effective access to justice, the elimination of obstacles to the proper functioning of civil proceedings, the development of alternative methods of dispute settlement, and support for the training of the judiciary (judges and prosecutors) and judicial staff;

– strengthen judicial cooperation in criminal matters by establishing minimum rules concerning the definition of criminal offences and sanctions in certain areas, such as serious crimes with a cross-border dimension resulting from the nature or impact of such an offence;

– create the possibility for establishing a European Public Prosecutor's Office, a highly controversial proposal during the elaboration of the Constitutional Treaty, which the Member States could not agree on definitively. Therefore this Office can be established by a decision with the Council acting unanimously after obtaining the consent of the European Parliament. When established, the European Public Prosecutor's Office will take over the tasks of Eurojust and will have competence to investigate and prosecute the perpetrators of offences against the Union's financial interests.

The Reform Treaty will incorporate, with some minor amendments, the two Protocols regulating the special participation of Denmark and the United Kingdom and Ireland in justice and home affairs cooperation.

Overall, in the area of freedom, security and justice, the provisions of the Reform Treaty abolishing the third pillar and reforming decision-making will follow up and conclude the steps taken in that direction by the Amsterdam Treaty, which – upon the entry into force of the Reform Treaty – will contribute to strengthening the political union.

ABBREVIATIONS AND GLOSSARY OF TERMS

ABBREVIATIONS

ACP	African, Carribean, Pacific Countries
AP	Accession Partnership
ASEAN	Association of South-East Asian Nations
ASEM	Asia-Europe Meeting
BEPGs	Broad Economic Policy Guidelines
CAP	Common Agricultural Policy
CARDS	Community assistance for reconstruction, development and stabilisation
CFP	Common Fisheries Policy
CFSP	Common Foreign and Security Policy
CIP	Competitiveness and Innovation Framework Programme
CMOs	Common Market Organizations
COREPER	COmité des REprésentants PERmanents [Committee of Permanent Representatives]
DG	Directorate-General
EAFRD	European Agricultural Fund for Rural Development
EAGF	European Agricultural Guarantee Fund
EAGGF	European Agricultural Guidance and Guarantee Fund
EC	European Community
ECB	European Central Bank
ECOFIN	Economic and Financial Affairs Council
ECSC	European Coal and Steel Community
ECU	European Currency Unit
EDC	European Defence Community
EDF	European Development Fund
EEA	European Economic Area
EEC	European Economic Community
EFF	European Fisheries Fund
EFSA	European Food Safety Authority
EFTA	European Free Trade Association
EIB	European Investment Bank
EIF	European Investment Fund
EIP	Entrepreneurship and Innovation Programme
EMI	European Monetary Institute
EMCF	European Monetary Cooperation Fund
EMS	European Monetary System
EMU	Economic and Monetary Union
ENPI	European Neighbourhood and Partnership Instrument

EP	European Parliament
EPC	European Political Cooperation
ERDF	European Regional Development Fund
ERM	Exchange Rate Mechanism
ESC	Economic and Social Committee
ESCB	European System of Central Banks
ESDI	European Security and Defence Identity
ESDP	European Security and Defence Policy
ESF	European Social Fund
ETF	European Training Foundation
EU	European Union
EUMC	European Union Military Committee
EUMS	European Union Military Staff
Euratom	European Atomic Energy Community
EURES	European Employment Service
EVS	European Voluntary Service
FIFG	Financial Instrument for Fisheries Guidance
G-7	Group of Seven
GATT	General Agreement on Tariffs and Trade
GDP	Gross Domestic Product
GNI	Gross National Income
GNP	Gross National Product
GSP	Generalized System of Preferences
ICT PSP	Information and Communication Technologies Policy Support Programme
IGC	Intergovernmental Conference
IIE	Intelligent Energy – Europe Programme
IIA	Interinstitutional Agreement
IPA	Instrument for Pre-Accession Assistance
ISPA	Instrument for Structural Policies for Pre-Accession
JHA	Justice and Home Affairs
LLL	Lifelong Learning
NTA	New Transatlantic Agenda
NATO	North Atlantic Treaty Organization
NPAA	National Programme for the Adoption of the Acquis
NUTS	Nomenclature des Unités Territoriales Statistiques [Nomenclature of Statistical Territorial Units]
OCT	Overseas countries and territories
OECD	Organisation for Economic Cooperation and Development

OEEC	Organization for European Economic Cooperation
OP	Operational Programme
PHARE	Poland and Hungary Assistance for the Restructuring of the Economy
PJCC	Police and Judicial Cooperation in Criminal Matters
PSC	Political and Security Committee
SAA	Stabilisation and Association Agreement
SAPARD	Special Accession Programme for Agriculture and Rural Development
SAPS	Single Area Payment Scheme
SEA	Single European Act
SIS	Schengen Information System
SPS	Single Payment Scheme
TACIS	Technical Assistance for the Commonwealth of Independent States
TEN	Trans-European Networks
UNIDO	United Nations Industrial Development Organization
VAT	Value-Added Tax
WEU	Western European Union
WTO	World Trade Organization

GLOSSARY OF TERMS
(The most important EU terms used in the book)

'A' points: Decision-making or legislative proposals that the *Council* of Ministers adopts without discussion because they have already been fully agreed at COREPER or a lower level.

Accession Partnership (AP): As part of the enlargement process, the *EU* and the candidate countries draw up a bilateral programme for the timetable and financial support of the pre-accession preparations for each country according to its own merits. The EU side of this programme, the Accession Partnership, coordinates the aid provided by the European Union and has to be in agreement with the candidate country's own programme and timetable for the adoption and implementation of the *acquis communautaire*, the so-called *National Programme for the Adoption of the Acquis*. Under the AP, the *EU* provides technical and financial assistance for the candidate country, the latter mainly in the form of *pre-accession funds*. The implementation of the APs and NPAAs – which are essentially mirror images – is monitored by the association institutions established under the *Europe Agreements*.

ACP countries: The group of African, Caribbean and Pacific countries which are former colonies of and thus have had traditionally strong ties to certain *EU* Member States. They belonged formerly to the *Lomé Conventions*, which granted free market access to the *EC* on a non-reciprocal basis, and are now parties to the *ACP-EC Partnership Agreement* currently in effect. The Member States also offer the ACP countries direct financial assistance from the *European Development Fund* and under the *Stabex* and the *Sysmin* systems.

ACP-EC Partnership Agreement: The Partnership Agreement concluded in Cotonou (Benin) on 23 June 2000 by the *EU* Member States and the *ACP countries*, which expands and renews the scope of the original *Lomé Conventions*. The ACP-EC Partnership Agreement is based on new, more extensive, political and economic cooperation and dialogue, extending significantly beyond trade agreements, as well as reforming and extending the financial assistance offered by the EU. The Agreement runs for 25 years and is reviewed every five years. The budget of the reviewed Agreement is also earmarked every five years. All 79 ACP countries, except for Cuba, have joined the Partnership Agreement.

Acquis communautaire: The term is of French origin and means Community patrimony, i.e. the entire body of Community law which binds all the Member States. It is based not only on the common objectives laid down in the *Founding Treaties* of the *European Communities* (the *EC, Euratom* and *ECSC* Treaties) and their amendments, but also on all legal acts adopted by the Community institutions under so-called secondary legislation. It comprises every legal act, principle, agreement, declaration, resolution, opinion, objective and practice (including the case law of the *Court of Justice*), relating to the *European Communities*, irrespective of whether it is legally binding or not. The *acquis communautaire* is the set of legal obligations that applicant countries have to accept, adopt and implement before they can accede to the European Union. Recently, the use of the short version of the term 'acquis' has become common, which is used to refer to not just the first Community pillar, but the Union as a whole, i.e. all three pillars.

Acquis screening: The screening of Community law, which takes place in the first, preliminary phase of the accession negotiations. It entails an examination of the extent to which the laws, regulations and institutions of the candidate country comply with the individual chapters of the *acquis communautaire*. The screening process, which precedes the substantive accession negotiations, is undertaken by the *Commission* and the governments of the candidate countries in bilateral meetings.

Advocate General: The work of the *European Court of Justice* is assisted by 8 advocates general, whose status and appointment are similar to that of judges. They are appointed for a term of 6 years, with half of the advocates general appointed every three years. The task of an advocate general is to give a summary of a particular case and submit an opinion in writing to the Court, although the opinion is not binding on the Court.

Agenda 2000: Agenda 2000 is a programme package adopted by the *European Commission* on 16 July 1997 as an official response to the request by the *European Council* to present a general document on the Union's future financial framework for the period 2000–2006, on enlargement, the reform of *Community policies* and the reconciliation of these problems. The primary importance of Agenda 2000, which bears the subtitle 'For a Stronger and Wider Union', is that it tackles the reform of the EU, its future strategy and the challenges of enlargement at the same time. Attached to it are the Commission's opinions on the 10 Central and Eastern European countries that had then applied for Union membership (see also *Avis*). Pursuant to Agenda 2000, on 25 March 1999, the Berlin *European Council* adopted the Union's financial perspectives for the period 2000–2006.

ALTENER: A component of the *Intelligent Energy – Europe (IEE)* Community programme aimed at promoting the use of new and renewable sources of energy.

Althea: The EU's peacekeeping military mission in Bosnia-Herzegovina, which was launched on 2 December 2004. The EU-led forces (EUFOR) deployed 7,000 troops from 22 Member States and 11 third-countries, which are gradually reduced to 2,500 troops from 2007.

Amsterdam leftovers: Questions of institutional reform which were left unsettled by the *Treaty of Amsterdam* and which were finally resolved by the *Intergovernmental Conference* in 2000 and its closing document, the *Treaty of Nice*.

Antici Group: The Antici Group, which was named after its first chairman and set up in the seventies, decides on the organisation of *COREPER II* proceedings and also conducts important preparatory work for *European Council* meetings. It is made up of officials working at the permanent representations, who are also known as Antici diplomats.

Area of freedom, security and justice: Following the entry into force of the Treaty of Amsterdam, justice and home affairs issues are divided between the first and third pillar. The EU uses the collective term of 'area of freedom, security and justice', which is based on the free movement of persons and is implemented through coordinated action in the first and third (and to some extent the second) pillars.

Artemis: The EU'S humanitarian mission in the Democratic Republic of Congo, carried out between 30 May 2003 and 1 September 2003.

Article 36 Committee: See *Coordinating Committee.*

Article 133 Committee: A special committee, which the *European Commission* regularly consults when negotiating agreements aimed at implementing the Common Commercial Policy. (Although negotiated by the Commission, these agreements are ultimately concluded by the Council.) Its members are Member-State officials appointed by the *Council.* Its name comes from Article 133 of the *EC Treaty,* which regulates trade policy.

Asia-Europe Meeting (ASEM): A forum established by the Member States of the *EU* and a number of Far Eastern countries (the ASEAN States, Japan, China and South Korea) in Bangkok in 1996. ASEM is a process based on dialogue and cooperation. Its objective is to develop comprehensive partnership through intensifying political dialogue and strengthening economic relations and cultural links. Summits are held bi-annually.

Assembly: The original name of the joint parliamentary assembly of the three *Communities* (*ECSC, EEC* and *Euratom*) used by some languages. In 1962, it was renamed the *European Parliament* in all official languages.

Assent procedure: One of the *EU*'s decision-making procedures introduced by the *Single European Act.* Under the procedure, the Parliament may accept or reject a proposal but cannot amend it. The object of the procedure is that the *Council* must obtain Parliament's assent before it takes its final decision, in practice giving Parliament a right of veto in areas falling within the scope of the assent procedures.

Association Agreements: International agreements between the *European Community* and third countries, under which the *EC* establishes special relations (e.g. mutual or non-reciprocal trade preferences, financial assistance, customs union, etc.) with the parties concerned. Several types of Association Agreements exist. Generally, the EC enters into a similar type of agreement with states from the same region.

Barcelona process: See *Euro-Mediterranean Partnership.*

Benelux Union: The *customs union* established by Belgium, the Netherlands and Luxembourg in 1948. In 1944, the governments-in-exile of the three countries entered into an agreement to establish closer economic cooperation under which, four years later, internal customs duties were abolished and common external tariffs were introduced.

Better regulation: The programme of better regulation, announced in the framework of the *Lisbon strategy,* aims to simplify and improve the regulatory environment. Complicated, often overlapping legislative acts are replaced by simple, transparent ones, both at the national and Community level. The programme is aimed primarily at simplifying EU law both in content and form, making it more transparent, to reduce the administrative burden and improve competitiveness.

Blocking minority: In *qualified majority voting*, the minimum number of votes needed to prevent the adoption of a decision, i.e. to block it.

Bologna process: A European initiative in the area of higher education, which was launched in 1999 by 29 European countries and which now involves about 45 European states (the 27 Member States and another 18 countries). Its key goal is to promote the compatibility and comparability of tertiary degrees, by creating a two-tier higher education system, consisting of a first (undergraduate or Bachelor) level of at least three years and a subsequent second (graduate or Master) level. Other key elements of the process include credit transferability, student, teacher and researcher mobility and cooperation in quality assurance.

Broad Economic Policy Guidelines (BEPGs): Within the framework of economic policy coordination, *the Council* formulates broad economic policy guidelines for the Member States to follow. Currently, BEPGs are adopted for three-year periods (they were adopted annually before 2003).

Budgetary procedure: The procedure for adopting the *European Union*'s budget, which is different from any other Community decision-making procedure. The preliminary draft budget submitted by the *Commission* is adopted jointly by the *Council* and the *Parliament*.

Budgetary Treaties: The *Treaties* stipulating the Community budgetary system, adopted in 1970 and 1975, which amended the *Founding Treaties* (establishing the *EEC, ECSC* and *Euratom*).

CARDS (Community Assistance for Reconstruction, Development and Stabilisation): CARDS is an assistance instrument created especially for the Western Balkans (Albania, Bosnia-Herzegovina, Croatia, Macedonia, Montenegro and Serbia, including Kosovo), which was designed on the lines of the former PHARE programme to support reconstruction, development and stabilisation in the region in the framework of the *Stabilisation and Association Agreements* (SAAs). CARDS was replaced by *IPA* on 1 January 2007.

Charter of Fundamental Rights: This charter aims at consolidating the fundamental rights of *EU* citizens. It was drawn up by the Member States in 2000 and was proclaimed at the Nice Summit in December 2000. It was deemed necessary because, while close economic integration and comprehensive related legislation had been established in the EU, the definition of human rights and fundamental liberties of the citizens at Union level had hitherto lagged behind. Nonetheless, the Charter did not become binding or legally enforceable upon its proclamation; hence it remained a political declaration. The Reform Treaty, which is expected to enter into force in 2009, includes a reference to the Charter; therefore the Charter will become binding on the entry into force of the Treaty.

Citizenship of the Union: Everyone who is a citizen of a Member State is also a citizen of the Union. Union citizenship does not replace national citizenship; rather, it is complementary and grants extra rights. Union citizenship grants four specific rights: a citizen of the Union can 1. move freely, travel and stay in any country of the EU; 2. participate in municipal and European Parliamentary elections in the Member State in which he resides, and participate as a candidate and be elected; 3. request protection while in a country outside the Union from diplomatic bodies or consulates of any other EU Member State, if his own country has no representation there; 4. submit a petition to the European Parliament and contact the European Ombudsman for legal assistance.

Co-decision procedure: One of the most often used Community decision-making procedures (alongside *consultation)* in the *EU*, which can consist of up to three readings. In the areas falling under the scope of the co-decision procedure, which was introduced by the *Treaty of Maastricht*, the *Parliament* participates in the decision-making process as the *Council*'s co-legislator on an equal footing. If the two institutions cannot agree on a compromise in the first two readings, the final conciliation between the two institutions is effected in the Conciliation Committee. The *Treaty of Amsterdam* significantly extended the scope of co-decision, which was further extended by the *Treaty of Nice*. The *Reform Treaty* defines co-decision as the *ordinary legislative procedure*, and would make co-decision a general rule for decision-making on its entry into force.

Cohesion Fund: Under the *Treaty of Maastricht*, the Cohesion Fund was set up in 1993 independently of the *Structural Funds*. It provides financial help for less prosperous Member States whose per capita GNP rate calculated at purchasing power parity amounts to less than 90 percent of the Union average. It grants major financial assistance for projects in the fields of the environment and transport infrastructure.

Comenius: An education sub-programme of the *Life-long Learning Programme* focusing on pre-school, primary and secondary education.

Comitology: The *Council* may delegate certain implementing and executive decision-making powers to the *Commission*, but may also exercise control, or even the right of veto, over any such activities of the Commission through various Committees, which consist of the representatives of the Member States. In Community jargon, this procedure is known as Comitology.

Commission: See the *European Commission*.

Commissioners: The members of the *European Commission*, whose portfolios are similar to those of national ministers and who perform their duties in a given area (e.g. agriculture, environmental protection, competition, etc.). The Commissioners pledge to perform their duties independently of their national governments and the *Council* and to act in the interests of the *Community*. At present, the Commission has one member per Member State, altogether 27 members, including the President and the five Vice-Presidents.

Committee of Permanent Representatives (COREPER – Comité des REprésentants PERmanents): A body that assists and prepares the work of the *Council*. It consists of the Heads of the Permanent Representations (ambassadors) of the Member States in Brussels or their Deputies. Its principal responsibility is to try to reconcile and harmonise the positions of the Member States on the questions discussed at this expert, diplomatic level and to prepare draft proposals for political decision by the Ministers. Furthermore, COREPER is responsible for maintaining communication between the governments of the Member States and the institutions of the Union and for mediation and coordination between Community and national administrations. COREPER meets weekly. It has two levels: **COREPER II** is the forum of the Permanent Representatives, while **COREPER I** consists of their Deputies. The two fora also divide the thematic issues between themselves.

Committee of the Regions: One of the two advisory committees of the *EU* (the other being the *Economic and Social Committee*), which was set up by the *Treaty of Maastricht*. In the Union of 27, the Committee of the Regions consists of 344 representatives of local and regional authorities, mainly mayors, municipal and provincial leaders. This consultative body functions as a forum where local and regional authorities can have a direct say in the *Communities*' work.

Common Agricultural Policy (CAP): The Common Agricultural Policy established in 1962, under which agriculture as a whole was elevated from national to Community level. Agricultural Policy became a distinct and separate area of the *common market*, functioning mainly as a preference policy. Its primary objectives are to enhance productivity, ensure fair living standards for farmers and their families, stabilise agricultural markets, ensure quality supply at reasonable prices and support rural development.

Common European Asylum System: One of the key objectives of The *Hague Programme*, the 2005–2010 justice and home affairs action programme, is the creation of a Common European Asylum System, which would establish a common asylum procedure and a uniform status for those who are granted asylum.

Common Foreign and Security Policy (CFSP): Common Foreign and Security Policy was established by the *Treaty of Maastricht* as the second pillar of the *EU* within the framework of intergovernmental cooperation. It replaced *European Political Cooperation* (*EPC*) and elevated it to 'common foreign policy'. CFSP, however, cannot be understood literally as a common foreign policy, since it does not mean that the Member States have a single, joint, foreign policy. Neither can it be seen as a Community policy, since it works entirely on an intergovernmental basis. The principles of CFSP call for an ongoing exchange of information on foreign policy and security issues between the Member States and for aligning national positions. These objectives are to be attained and put into action through the legal instruments of *general guidelines*, *common strategies*, *common positions* and *joint actions*.

Common market: A broader form of economic integration than a *customs union*, in which, besides guaranteeing the free movement of goods and services, the movement of productive factors (capital and labour) is also liberalised, and thus the four fundamental freedoms (free movement of goods, services, capital and persons) are realised.

Common policies: The common policies of the *EC* include areas where, pursuant to the *Treaty*, the legislative competence of the *Community* is dominant; decisions are mostly made at the level of the Community and not at the level of the Member States. In the EC, such areas include e.g. trade policy, monetary policy and competition. The concept of common policies must be distinguished from the concept of *Community policies*, where decisions are taken both at the Community and the Member-State level.

Common position: Firstly, in the *second pillar*, the *CFSP*, the common position means a legal act which outlines the common position of the Member States on a specific foreign policy issue, which then serves as the main guideline for further action. Secondly, in the third pillar, a common position means a legal act which defines the EU's approach and opinion on a given issue. Common positions are adopted by the *Council* in both pillars.

Common strategy: A legal act under the *second pillar*, the *CFSP*. Common strategies outline the policy guidelines on a state, region or specific issue to be followed by the Member States. Common strategies are adopted by the *European Council*.

Communities: See *European Communities*.

Community: On the one hand, the term may denote one of the three Communities of the *European Communities* (*ECSC, EEC and Euratom*) but, more often than not, only the *European (Economic) Community* (when not otherwise indicated). On the other hand, it may refer to the Member States as a whole.

Community Lisbon programme: On the basis of the *integrated guidelines* on the implementation of the *Lisbon strategy*, adopted by the *Council* every three years, Member States draw up 3-year national reform programmes, while the Commission elaborates its own Community Lisbon Programme, covering all Community-level activities aimed at boosting growth and employment. The Heads of State or Government of EU Member States decided on this 3-year-cycle approach at their summit meeting on 22–23 March 2005, when the mid-term review of the Lisbon strategy was carried out.

Community policies: The Community policies of the *EC* include Community actions under the *Treaty*, which – unlike the *common policies* – run in parallel with the actions of the Member States or complement national policies in a specific area. Community policies include e.g. research and technological development, environmental or social and employment policy.

Competitiveness and Innovation Framework Programme (CIP): A framework programme established for the period 2007–2013 with a view to implementing the Lisbon objectives. It is implemented through three specific programmes: the *Entrepreneurship and Innovation Programme*, the *ICT Policy Support Programme* and the *Intelligent Energy – Europe Programme*.

Concordia: The EU Mission in the Former Yugoslav Republic of Macedonia (FYROM), which was launched on 31 March 2003 as the first ever EU military mission, and which was converted into a policing mission (*Proxima*) on 15 December 2003.

Consolidated Treaties: The terms *Treaty* and *Treaties* always refer to the amended versions of the Founding Treaties, namely the provisions that are in force at that time. These Treaties are published in a consolidated form (Consolidated Treaties), and references are also made to the consolidated text. However, legally speaking, the consolidated texts of the Treaties have never been adopted.

Constitutional Treaty: Its exact title was 'Treaty establishing a Constitution for Europe'. The Constitutional Treaty, designed to replace the current *EC Treaty and EU Treaty*, was adopted at the Brussels Summit on 17–18 June 2004 following 18 months of drafting in the *Convention* on the Future of Europe and 8 months of negotiations in the subsequent *Intergovernmental Conference*. It was signed on 29 October 2004 in Rome, and was originally supposed to be ratified by 1 November 2006. 18 Member States successfully ratified the Constitutional Treaty, while the French and Dutch electorate rejected it in national referenda in May and June 2005. This created considerable uncertainty, as all Member States would have had to ratify the Treaty for it to enter into force. Following the two failed referenda, seven Member States suspended ratification. After a two-year period of reflection, at the summit of 21–22 June 2007, the Member States decided to abandon the Constitutional Treaty and place the enlarged *European Union* on new foundations by means of a *Reform Treaty*. This Reform Treaty will maintain the majority of the Constitutional Treaty's provisions and incorporate these reforms – primarily affecting the institutional and decision-making machinery of the EU – into the current Treaties.

Consultation procedure: One of the most common decision-making procedures of the *EU* (alongside *co-decision*). Under this procedure, established by the *Treaty of Rome*, the *Council* must consult the *European Parliament* and take its views into account. However, it is not bound by Parliament's position but only by the obligation to consult it. Parliament has the least power to influence decisions under this legislative procedure.

Convention (full name: Convention on the future of Europe): The body that drafted the *Constitutional Treaty* and prepared the work of the 2003–2004 *Intergovernmental Conference* between its opening session on 28 February 2002 and its closing session on 10 July 2003. It was set up in December 2001 by the Laeken European Council with a view to the involvement of a wider European public. The Convention, in addition to its President (Valéry Giscard d'Estaing) and two Vice-Presidents (Giuliano Amato and Jean-Luc Dehaene), comprised the delegates of the 15 then Member States and 13 candidate countries: 1 representative from each government, 2 representatives from each of the 28 national parliaments, 16 members of the *European Parliament* and 2 members of the *European Commission*. The Convention formulated the draft of the Constitutional Treaty, which was amended slightly by the subsequent IGC before the final text was adopted by the Heads of State or Government at their Brussels Summit of 17–18 June 2004.

Cooperation in the fields of Justice and Home Affairs (JHA): Cooperation on Justice and Home Affairs at the EU level was institutionalised by the *Treaty of Maastricht*, due to the desire to establish the *single market* without internal borders and border controls, and the need to take joint action against illegal immigration, organised crime and terrorism, which were an increasing threat to the Member States. Establishing cooperation on JHA has been an important step on the road to developing political union. Until the *Treaty of Amsterdam* entered into force, JHA had been known as the *third pillar* of the EU and worked exclusively on an intergovernmental basis. After Amsterdam, however, the cooperation was split into two: many fields (asylum and immigration policy, external and internal border control and judicial cooperation in civil matters) were brought under the *first pillar* within the Community framework, while *police cooperation and cooperation in criminal matters* remained under the third pillar.

Cooperation procedure: A decision-making mechanism of the *EU* introduced by the *Single European Act*, which is now applied only in a few areas concerning the *EMU*. In the cooperation procedure, which is a more developed version of the *consultation procedure* and has two readings, if the *Parliament* rejects the Council's common position, in the second reading the *Council* may only adopt it by unanimity. With the entry into force of the Reform Treaty, the application of the cooperation procedure will be discontinued.

Coordinating Committee: A conciliatory forum of senior officials which prepares the meetings and decisions of the *Council of Ministers* within the *third pillar* of the *European Union*. It executes duties in addition to and similar to those of *COREPER* in the *first pillar*. Following from the relevant article of the *Treaty of Maastricht*, the Coordinating Committee was termed the *K.4 Committee* while, under the *Treaty of Amsterdam*, it was renamed the Article 36 Committee.

COPENER: A Community programme for promoting the use of renewable energy and improvements in energy efficiency in developing countries, which operated as part of the first *Intelligent Energy – Europe* programme until 2006.

Copenhagen Criteria: The accession criteria laid down by the June 1993 Copenhagen European Council with a view to the accession of the Central and Eastern European countries. In accordance with the Copenhagen Criteria, candidate countries must meet the following criteria:
– the stability of democracy and institutions (the rule of law, respect for human rights, the protection of minorities);
– a functioning market economy, which is able to cope with the competitive pressures of the single market;
– the ability to assume the obligations arising from Community membership: to adopt and implement the *acquis communautaire*, including adherence to the aims of *political union* and *economic and monetary union*.

Copenhagen Process: The Copenhagen process, similar to the *Bologna process*, is a form of European cooperation in the area of vocational training with the participation of 32 countries. It is aimed at the mutual recognition of vocational qualifications and improved transparency/compatibility of educational systems.

COREPER: See *Committee of Permanent Representations*.

Council: See *Council of the European Union*.

Council of Ministers: See *Council of the European Union*.

Council of the European Union: The *Union's* principal, but not exclusive intergovernmental decision-making and legislative body, with the *European Parliament* acting as a co-legislator in certain cases. The Council is composed of one representative at ministerial level from each Member State, usually the minister responsible for the subject discussed; therefore it is often referred to as the Council of Ministers.

As the Council meets in the configuration of the agenda and the policy area under discussion at a given meeting, the name of the Council of Ministers varies depending on which ministers are to meet. The bodies of the competent ministers are the so-called sectoral Councils (e.g. Economic and Financial Affairs Council, Justice and Home Affairs Council, etc.). The *General Affairs and External Relations Council* falls into a separate category: it deals with politically more significant, general and sensitive issues and often also functions as an appeal forum for the sectoral Councils. The smooth running of the Council is assisted by the so-called *Council working groups, COREPER* and the Council's own administration, theGeneral Secretariat headed by the Secretary General (See also *High Representative for CFSP*).

Council Presidency: The Presidency of the *Council of the European Union*, which rotates between the Member States every six months. *The President in office* convenes the *Council* and the relevant Member State's representatives preside not only over the *Council of Ministers* but also over other bodies related to the Council (*European Council, COREPER, working groups*); the Presidency also presides over the voting and signs the adopted acts. Since, during its Presidency, the presiding Member State plays a decisive role in the arrangement of the agenda and in the preparation of voting, it has significant influence over the issues discussed. The State holding the Presidency of the Council also plays a key role in the international representation of the Union and its position on CFSP issues. From 2007 onwards, the Member States assume the responsibilities of the Presidency in groups of three for periods of 18 months. Within every such group of three, each Member State still holds the Presidency for six months, while the other two members in the group help the country in question run the Presidency according to the common programme.

Council working groups: The work of the *Council* and *COREPER* is assisted by permanent and *ad hoc* working groups arranged according to specific subjects. The members of these working groups are 2–3 officials from the Member States' governments and relevant *Commission* representatives. The number of Council working groups varies according to the topics under discussion at any given moment; currently there are about 250 of them.

Court of First Instance: As the *European Court of Justice* became increasingly overloaded with cases, the Court of First Instance was established in 1989 to relieve the Court by assuming some of its tasks. The Court of First Instance is composed of one judge per Member State. Appeals against the rulings of the Court of First Instance may be submitted to the Court of Justice. With the entry into force of the *Reform Treaty*, it will be renamed the General Court.

Court of Justice of the European Communities (European Court of Justice – ECJ): The supreme judicial forum of the *European Communities*, comprising one judge from each Member State, which sits in Luxembourg. As an independent body, the Court ensures that Community law is uniformly interpreted and implemented in each Member State, supervises the observance of Community law and monitors and ensures that the Community institutions act in line with their competences stipulated by the Treaties. Upon its entry into force, the *Reform Treaty* will rename the Court of Justice of the European Communities the *Court of Justice of the European Union*.

Court of Justice of the European Union: The new name of the *Court of Justice of the European Communities* under the *Reform Treaty*, which will be used when the Treaty enters into force. The Court of Justice of the European Union will consist of the Court of Justice, the *General Court* (the current *Court of First Instance*) and *specialised courts* (the current *judicial panels*).

Culture Programme: The Community cultural framework programme, launched in 2000, which merged the three former cultural programmes of the EU, *Kaleidoscope, Ariane and Raphäel.* For the period 2000–2004, its objectives were to encourage artistic activities, strengthen cultural awareness of music, literature, arts and new forms of culture and conserve cultural heritage. For the 2007–2013 financial perspective, the **Culture 2007** programme focuses on facilitating the mobility of artists and works of art and on encouraging inter-cultural dialogue.

Customs Union: An area where trade between member states is liberalised, customs duties and quotas are abolished, and goods and services move freely between member countries. In a customs union, members pursue a common commercial policy and common customs tariffs are set for products from third countries.

Decision: A fully binding Community legal act pertaining to specific issues, and addressed to specific addressees.

Delors Plan: A package of proposals put forward by the *European Commission* in 1989, then headed by Jacques Delors. It developed the concept of monetary union and thus laid down the foundations of the programme of *economic and monetary union* (EMU), later institutionalised by the *Treaty of Maastricht.*

Democratic deficit: The term is principally understood to be shorthand for the argument that the representation of ordinary citizens is rather indirect in the *EU*'s main decision-making body, the *Council*, as well as in the *Commission*, which also has major influence on the decision-making process through its preparatory and delegated executive powers. Furthermore, too much power is concentrated in the hands of officials who are appointed and not elected, while a more direct participation of the Union's citizens in decision-making is not adequately guaranteed. Firstly, the *European Parliament*, which is directly accountable to the citizens, does not have sufficiently broad decision-making powers, and secondly, the direct involvement of the national parliaments in Community decision-making is not guaranteed.

Derogation: A mitigation of the strict application of or an exemption from certain requirements arising from Union membership; a derogation is, in principle, of a temporary nature.

Direct applicability: Certain elements of *EC* law must be applied directly in the national law of Member States, which means that these Community legal acts are integrated into domestic law without the need for further national legislative acts, just like in the case of *directives*. Among secondary legal acts, *regulations* fall within the principle of direct applicability.

Direct effect: The principle of direct effect became widely known as a result of the interpretations of the *European Court of Justice*. It permits natural and legal persons to invoke Community law before their national courts and ask the national court to base its ruling on Community law. Under the principle of vertical direct effect, a natural or legal person may invoke Community law before his national court vis-à-vis a domestic legal act. Under the principle of horizontal direct effect, natural or legal persons may invoke Community law before their national court in legal relationships between each other.

Direct payment: The income policy instrument of the *Common Agricultural Policy*. Its objective is to grant income support in the form of direct payments to farmers cultivating specific products, irrespective of their volume of production. The main objective and advantage of this system, compared to price support, is that since it is decoupled from production, it does not encourage over-production or distort the market.

Directive: A Community legal act which is binding upon the Member States, but usually in the form of a general instruction as to the goal to be achieved. The way in which the goal is to be attained, the selection of national procedures to be used and the method of incorporation into national jurisdiction are left to the discretion of each Member State, albeit with a specific deadline for transposition.

Directorate-General (DG): The administrative structure of the *European Commission* is composed of the Directorates-General (DGs) and similar services under the *Commissioners'* control. The allocation of the Directorates-General and other services to the Commissioners, similarly to the national Ministries, takes place in the framework of the division of portfolios, such as agriculture, trade, environmental protection, etc. The Directorates-General and the Commissioners' portfolios nevertheless do not necessarily correspond to each other; there are usually fewer Commissioners than DGs, and thus some Commissioners are responsible for more than one DG. The DGs are further divided into Directorates, which in turn are divided into Units.

Double majority: the principle of double majority, which means the majority of Member States + population, will be introduced by the *Reform Treaty* upon its entry into force from 1 November 2014 for *qualified majority voting* in the *Council*. In the Reform Treaty, a double majority is defined as at least 55% of the members of the Council, comprising at least 65% of the population of the Union, when the Council decides on a proposal from the *Commission* or from the *High Representative of the Union for Foreign Affairs and Security Policy*; when the Council does not act on a proposal from the Commission or from the High Representative, the qualified majority is defined as at least 72% of the members of the Council, representing Member States comprising at least 65% of the population of the Union.

Dublin Convention: A Convention, which was signed by the EU Member States on 15 June 1990 and entered into force on 1 September 1997. The key provision of the Dublin Convention is that an application for asylum submitted in the area of the EU only has to be examined by one Member State, and if rejected, does not need to be processed again by other Member States. The Dublin Convention was replaced in 2003 by Regulation 343/2003/EC ('Dublin II'), which clarifies and specifies the responsibilities of Member States for processing asylum applications.

ECHO (Humanitarian Aid Office): The Office of the *European Commission* responsible for managing humanitarian aid to third countries, providing help – in the form of food, medicine, etc. – to victims of natural disasters or humanitarian crises.

Economic and monetary union (EMU): The programme outlined by the *Treaty of Maastricht*, whose third and final phase was launched when 11 Member States (Austria, Belgium, Finland, France, Germany, Ireland, Italy, Luxembourg, the Netherlands, Portugal and Spain) introduced the single European currency, the *euro* on 1 January 1999. (Greece joined on 1 January 2001, followed by Slovenia on 1 January 2007 and by Cyprus and Malta on 1 January 2008). The *EMU*, as shown by its name, does not only imply monetary union and the introduction of the single currency, but also the harmonisation and coordination of the economic policies of the Member States, i.e. the realisation of *economic union.*

Economic and Social Committee: One of the *EU's* two advisory committees, (the other being the *Committee of the Regions)* which represents the interests of various economic and social groups. It was set up by the *Treaty of Rome* and presently consists of 344 members falling into three categories: employers, workers and the representatives of other interest groups (representing particular types of activities outside the scope of the first two categories). The decision-making bodies of the EU consult the Economic and Social Committee on a wide range of issues to familiarise themselves with the opinions of the various economic and social interest groups of the Union.

Economic Union: Close economic integration, not only involving the realisation of the *common market* or *single market*, but the integration of the economic policies of the Member States as well. It entails the harmonisation and coordination of national economic policies, and as a final goal, their unification at a Community level. The *single currency* constitutes an important element of *economic union*, which thus becomes essentially inseparable from the monetary union.

EC Treaty: Its full name is 'Treaty establishing the European Community', namely the Treaty in force for the European Community, which was originally established in 1957 by the *Treaty of Rome* as the *European Economic Community*, and renamed the *European Community* by the *Treaty of Maastricht*. Upon its entry into force, the *Reform Treaty* will rename it as the *'Treaty on the functioning of the European Union'*.

Emergency Aid Reserve: The Emergency Aid Reserve, a novel feature of the 2007–2013 Financial Perspective, enables the Union to respond rapidly to crisis situations in third countries and provide assistance for humanitarian aid, civil crisis management and civil protection.

Emergency brake clause: Upon its entry into force, the *Reform Treaty* will introduce the emergency brake clause, allowing Member States to use their right of veto under certain conditions and, to a limited extent, in areas falling within the scope of qualified majority voting (such as two specific fields of judicial cooperation in criminal matters as well as the free movement of migrant workers within the Union).

Employment guidelines: Since the *Treaty of Amsterdam*, the *Council* has adopted employment guidelines (formerly annually, but for three-year periods since 2003). According to the conclusions of the Brussels Summit on 22–23 March 2005, which carried out the mid-term review of the *Lisbon strategy*, from 2005 on, the Council must adopt *integrated guidelines*, incorporating *broad economic policy guidelines* and employment guidelines.

Energy Charter: The Energy Charter, dating from 1991, was designed to promote cooperation between the participating countries of Western Europe and the ex-Communist bloc on developing their energy infrastructures. The Charter, which now has over 50 signatories, aims at providing the necessary conditions for western investment in Eastern Europe and Central Asia (former Soviet Republics) and at facilitating market development in the energy sector. Furthermore, the Energy Charter strives to help the participating countries to improve energy efficiency and step-up environmental measures.

Energy Community: The Energy Community extends the Community energy market to South-East Europe. Reminiscent of the ECSC in having an historic mission, the Energy Charter entered into force on 1 July 2006 with 34 signatories: the 27 EU Member States, Albania, Bosnia-Herzegovina, Croatia, Macedonia, Montenegro, Serbia and the UN Interim Administration in Kosovo.

Engrenage: This term, of French origin, denotes the interweaving of the national and Community administrative systems, which has occurred increasingly with the development of the integration process, as the decision-making elite at the two levels has become increasingly inter-twined.

Enhanced cooperation: An instrument of flexible integration, enhanced cooperation is applied when, in a specific area, certain Member States wish to establish closer integration and make faster progress, while other Member States are reluctant or unable to follow. The objective of enhanced cooperation is that, within the institutional framework of the *EU*, some Member States strengthen their cooperation, while others prefer to opt-out but may freely join the "forerunners" at a later date.

ENPI (European Neighbourhood and Partnership Instrument): ENPI is a support instrument established in the framework of the *European Neighbourhood Policy* for the 2007–2013 period, replacing the former *TACIS* (for eastern partners), *MEDA* (for Mediterranean partners) and other thematic (e.g. human rights) programmes.

Entrepreneurship and Innovation Programme (EIP): A Community programme running from 1 January 2007 and set up as part of the Competitiveness and Innovation Framework Programme. Its main focus is to facilitate access to finance for the start-up and growth of SMEs, to promote eco-innovation and to provide information to SMEs on the operation of and opportunities in the internal market and on Community rules and future legislative developments.

EQUAL: A *Community initiative* financed from the *European Social Fund*, which aims at strengthening cooperation between the Member States in order to fight any form of discrimination on the labour market.

Erasmus: The biggest sub-programme of the *Life-long Learning Programme*, focusing on tertiary education, promoting student mobility and cooperation between institutions of higher education. Erasmus finances 150,000 foreign study trips a year.

Erasmus Mundus: A programme linked to *Erasmus*, which is aimed at promoting mobility and cooperation with third countries in the area of higher education.

ERM (Exchange Rate Mechanism): The exchange rate mechanism of the *European Monetary System*. It was based on the central parity-grid established by the national central banks for the participating currencies. A grid of bilateral rates was calculated for all the currencies. The basis of the mechanism was that the national central banks were obliged to intervene before the limits set out in the parity grid were breached.

ERM II (Exchange Rate Mechanism II): The Exchange Rate Mechanism of the *European Monetary System* was replaced by ERM II with the introduction of the *euro*. ERM II provides a link between the currencies of Member States that opted out of the *eurozone*, but which wish to participate in the exchange rate mechanism. ERM II membership is a pre-condition for eurozone membership.

EU Treaty: Its full name is the 'Treaty on European Union'. It is the Treaty version in force created by the *Treaty of Maastricht* and supplemented by subsequent amendments.

EUBAM: The EU Border Assistance Mission to Moldova and Ukraine, launched on 1 December 2005, with a two-year mandate to assist the two countries' border management authorities in fighting smuggling, trafficking in drugs and human beings, and customs fraud.

EU BAM Rafah: The EU Border Assistance Mission at the Rafah crossing point between Gaza and Israel, launched in November 2005 for a duration of 12 months, which has been extended once until May 2008.

EUJUST/THEMIS: The EU's 'rule of law' mission in Georgia, launched in 2004 with a one-year mandate.

EUJUST/LEX: The EU's 'rule of law' mission in Iraq, which was decided upon in March 2005 and whose mandate expires at the end of 2007.

EUPM: An EU police force deployed in Bosnia-Herzegovina. The operation, which was launched in January 2003, was also the first mission of the *European Security and Defence Policy*. Its first phase ended at the end of 2005, and its mandate was renewed and extended until the end of 2007.

EUPOL Afghanistan: The EU Police mission in Afghanistan, which was launched in June 2007 for a period of at least three years with the aim of assisting the Afghan authorities in establishing effective police forces.

EUPOL COPPS: The EU Police Mission in the Palestinian Territories established for a duration of at least three years from 1 January 2006 to provide enhanced support to the Palestinian Authority in establishing sustainable and effective policing arrangements.

EUPOL RD Congo: The EU launched a police mission in the Democratic Republic of Congo under the name of Eupol-Kinshasa, which was later renamed EUPOL RD Congo. It has been complemented by the operation EUSEC RD Congo, an EU advisory and assistance mission for security reform.

EUPT Kosovo: The EU planning team in Kosovo, which was set up in May 2007 regarding a possible future EU crisis management operation that would take over some of the tasks from the United Nations Interim Administration Mission in Kosovo (UNMIK).

EURES (European Employment Service): A Community database for workers and employers. EURES functions as a Community job centre, since it provides information and counselling to potentially mobile employees about job opportunities within the *EU* and assists employers in recruiting workers from other countries.

Euro: The European single currency, the key element of the *economic and monetary union*. Under the timetable of the *EMU* outlined in the *Treaty of Maastricht*, the Euro (€) was introduced in 11 Member States (Austria, Belgium, Finland, France, Germany, Ireland, Italy, Luxembourg, the Netherlands, Portugal and Spain) on 1 January 1999. Greece joined the monetary union on 1 January 2001, Slovenia on 1 January 2007, to be followed by Cyprus and Malta on 1 January 2008. Before 2002, the euro existed only as an accounting unit; banknotes and coins denominated in euros were put into circulation on 1 January 2002. As of 1 January 1999, the euro replaced the *ECU* in the accounting mechanisms of the Community.

EuroGroup: The informal economic policy forum of the Financial Ministers of the Member States of the single currency zone. The EuroGroup's primary objective is to provide an exclusive forum for the participating Member States to coordinate their economic and monetary strategies. The *Reform Treaty*, upon its entry into force, will institutionalise the cooperation of *eurozone* countries, enabling them to adopt acts in certain areas that are legally binding in the whole area of the eurozone. Eurozone members will be able to elect a president for a period of two and a half years. The President will chair the monthly EuroGroup meetings, represent the eurozone on the international scene and liaise with the European Central Bank. A President will only be able to be re-elected once.

Eurojust (European Judicial Cooperation Unit): An intergovernmental unit established on 6 March 2002 following the model of *Europol*. Its objective is to facilitate cooperation and the exchange of information between national prosecuting and judicial authorities and police officers of the Member States. Its set-up was adopted at the Tampere Summit in October 1999; it was institutionalised in the *EU Treaty* by the *Treaty of Nice*. Eurojust contributes to improving coordination between national prosecutors, criminal investigation bodies and police in combating organised crime on the basis of Europol analyses, as well as to developing cooperation with the *European Judicial Network*.

Euro-Mediterranean Partnership: A programme for the non-European countries of the Mediterranean basin (Algeria, Morocco, Tunisia, Egypt, Jordan, Lebanon, Syria, Israel and the Palestinian Authority) announced at the Lisbon Summit in June 1992, which took on concrete form in the Barcelona Declaration of 1995 and became known as the 'Barcelona process'. Within the framework of this Partnership, the EU offered to countries of the region the setting up of a free trade area by 2010. In line with this, the EU has transformed the original cooperation agreements into Euro-Mediterranean Association Agreements with all countries of the Mediterranean, except for Syria. The Euro-Mediterranean Partnership was complemented by the *MEDA* programme, through which the EU offered financial and technical assistance to the countries of the region. *MEDA* was replaced by the *European Neighbourhood and Partnership Instrument* (*ENPI*) on 1 January 2007, which provides a single instrument for countries covered by the *European Neighbourhood Policy*. Countries of the Mediterranean are also eligible for loans from *the European Investment Bank*.

Europass: Designed to encourage occupational and educational mobility, Europass is a single framework for the transparency of diplomas, certificates and competences; it is a portfolio of skills and qualifications acquired in various EU countries and presented in a common format for easy comparability. Its key element is the Europass CV.

European Agency for the Management of Operational Cooperation at the External Borders (FRONTEX): A Community agency with its seat in Warsaw set up in 2005 pursuant to the justice and home affairs package known as the Hague programme, which was adopted by the *European Council* meeting of 4–5 November 2004. Its key task is to reinforce cooperation between Member States in border management.

Europe Agreements: The Europe Agreements – whose title was chosen to distinguish them from other association agreements and to emphasise their historic significance – provided the framework for bilateral relations between the *EC*, its *Member States* and Central and Eastern European countries. The Europe Agreements signed with the 10 Central and Eastern European countries (Bulgaria, the Czech Republic, Estonia, Hungary, Latvia, Lithuania, Poland, Romania, Slovakia and Slovenia) aimed progressively to establish a free trade area between the EU and the associated countries over a given period, on the basis of reciprocity but applied in an asymmetric manner (i.e. more rapid liberalisation on the EU side than on the side of the associated countries). The Europe Agreements covered trade-related issues, political dialogue and legal approximation. While, in the Agreements, the associated countries expressed their intent to become members of the EU, the EC did not enter into an obligation in this respect in the Agreements. The Agreements signed with Hungary and Poland were the first ones to enter into force on 1 February 1994.

European Agricultural Fund for Rural Development (EAFRD): The fund financing rural development objectives within the *Common Agricultural Policy (CAP)* became operational from 1 January 2007. This comprehensive rural development framework also took over the rural development activities of structural measures (e.g. *LEADER* Community initiative) and relevant budgetary items.

European Agricultural Guidance and Guarantee Fund (EAGGF): The fund financing the EU's *Common Agricultural Policy (CAP)* was established in 1962 and terminated at the end of 2006. It was divided into two sections: the Guarantee Section financed interventions, market support and direct payments, while the Guidance Section – as one of the *Structural Funds* – disbursed subsidies for structural improvements in farming. The Guidance Section budget amounted to only a fraction of the Guarantee Section budget. From 1 January 2007, the EAGGF was split into two: the *European Agricultural Guarantee Fund* and the *European Agricultural Fund for Rural Development*.

European Agricultural Guarantee Fund (EAGF): In essence the successor of the EAGGF, the fund financing the traditional payments of the EU's *Common Agricultural Policy (CAP)* from 1 January 2007. It finances export subsidies, interventions, direct payments, as well as contributions to veterinary and phytosanitary control measures.

European Area for Justice: A key objective of the justice and home affairs package known as the Hague programme, which was adopted by the *European Council* meeting of 4–5 November 2004. Its aim is to eliminate the remaining obstacles to cross-border judicial procedures, in particular as regards litigation in civil cases, the launch of court proceedings and the enforcement of court decisions in civil cases.

European Atomic Energy Community (Euratom): One of the three organisations of integration in the *European Communities*. It was established by the members of the *ECSC* (Belgium, France, Germany, Italy, Luxembourg and the Netherlands) on 25 March 1957 – at the same time as the *EEC* – through the signature of one of the *Treaties of Rome*, which entered into force on 1 January 1958. The main objectives of the Treaty of Rome establishing Euratom were to develop the nuclear energy industry, to conduct Community research, to ensure the effective use of atomic energy and to maintain nuclear safety.

European Central Bank (ECB): The central bank of the *EU*, which is responsible for managing the *economic and monetary union (EMU)* and the single currency. Its main tasks are to manage the *euro* and to maintain its stability. As part of the *EMU*, the ECB was established on 1 June 1998. The European Central Bank is a completely independent institution; it may not seek or take instructions from the governments of the Member States. Although the National Central Banks cannot be seen as mere subordinates of the ECB, they perform their duties in compliance with the ECB's guidelines and instructions; they are authorised to issue banknotes and coins exclusively with the ECB's consent. The decision-making process of the *European System of Central Banks* (ESCB) is centralised through the European Central Bank. The ECB, assisted by the National Central Banks, guarantees that the duties assigned to the ESCB are carried out.

European Coal and Steel Community (ECSC): The *ECSC*, the first Treaty organisation of the three *European Communities*, was established by the signatories (Belgium, France, Germany, Italy, Luxembourg and the Netherlands) of the *Treaty of Paris* on 18 April 1951. The Treaty entered into force on 23 July 1952 and expired on 23 July 2002. The expiry of the *ECSC Treaty* itself however has not presented a serious problem, as most of the Treaty's provisions have been sustained within the framework of the *EC*, due to the general effect of the *EC Treaty* over the *common market*. The financial consequences of the expiry of the Treaty were settled by a protocol attached to the *Treaty of Nice*. The idea of creating a European Coal and Steel Community was proposed by the French Minister for Foreign Affairs, Robert Schuman, on 9 May 1950. Under the so-called *Schuman Plan*, French-German coal and steel production was pooled under a joint High Authority in the framework of an organisation that other European countries were free to join.

European Commission: The European Commission is the *EU*'s body that has responsibility for preparing decisions and making proposals and, in certain cases, for performing monitoring and executive duties. The 'Commission' may denote either the institution's leading political body, the so-called college of Commissioners, with 27 officials called *Commissioners*, who function similarly to national Ministers, or may denote both the Commissioners and the institution itself with an administrative staff of nearly 30,000. The Commission's responsibility is to guard Community interests and to observe and execute Community policies. It performs its duties independently of the national governments and the *Council*.

European Communities (EC): The term has been used since 1967, since the entry into force of the *Merger Treaty*, which established a joint *Council* and *Commission* for the three *Communities* (the *European Coal and Steel Community*, the *European Economic Community* and the *European Atomic Energy Agency)*, in addition to the already-joint Assembly (the *European Parliament*) and the *Court of Justice*. As the Treaty entailed the merger of the institutions of the three Communities, the term *European Communities,* (the *EC)* became widely used from that time on, although the three Communities continued to retain their own independent international legal status. Since the *Treaty of Maastricht*, the European Communities are generally referred to as the *first pillar of the European Union.* The Treaty of Maastricht renamed the European Economic Community as the *European Community;* therefore, today, the European Communities consists of the European Community and the European Atomic Energy Community (the ECSC disappeared in 2002, following the expiry of the ECSC Treaty). The *Reform Treaty* will rename the Treaty establishing the European Community as the *Treaty on the functioning of the European Union*, thereby abolishing the name European Community. With the entry into force of the Reform Treaty, the *European Union* will become the legal successor of both the European Community and the European Communities. The European Atomic Energy Community will remain in existence as an independent Community.

European Community (EC): The *Treaty of Maastricht* renamed the *European Economic Community* as the European Community, thus signifying that the *Community* is not a mere framework for economic cooperation and indicating its general competence on the territory of the *common market* vis-à-vis the more limited and functional competences of the two other Communities (*ECSC, Euratom*). The *Reform Treaty* will rename the Treaty establishing the European Community as the *Treaty on the functioning of the European Union*, thereby abolishing the name European Community. With the entry into force of the Reform Treaty, the *European Union* will become the legal successor of the European Community.

European company: known formally by its Latin name of 'Societas Europeae' (SE), a European company can be established on the basis of the European Company Statute adopted at the Nice Summit in December 2000. The advantage of forming European companies is that they are able to operate throughout the EU on the basis of a single set of rules and a unified management and reporting system.

European Consumer Consultative Group: A consultative body dealing with consumer protection, consisting of one delegate from each national consumer body and one delegate from each European consumer organisation. The European Commission regularly consults it before taking decisions with an impact on consumer interests.

European Convention (Convention on the Future of Europe): See *Convention*.

European Council: The European Council is the body consisting of the Heads of State or Government of the *EU* Member States and the President of the *European Commission*, which functions as the top forum of the Union. The European Council did not feature in the *European Communities'* first *Treaties*. Nevertheless, it evolved from the practice of organising meetings of the Heads of State or Government of the Member States, which became regular meetings following the Paris Summit of December 1974. This arrangement of the European Council was formalised by the *Treaty of Maastricht*. The Member States' Ministers of Foreign Affairs and a Member of the Commission assist the European Council's work. The European Council settles vital, strategic issues and defines the general policy guidelines for the EU's development. Most important compromises between the Member States are made at this level. The European Council meets at least four times a year. Upon its entry into force, the *Reform Treaty* will elevate the body to the rank of a proper institution with a permanent President.

European Court of Auditors: The European Court of Auditors was established in 1977 as the independent body entrusted with the revision of Community finances. The Court sits in Luxembourg and consists of one member from each Member State. Its task is to examine the sound financial management of the revenues and expenditure of the *Communities* and their institutions.

European Court of Justice: See *Court of Justice of the European Communities*.

European Currency Unit (ECU): The currency basket created in 1979, in which each national currency was weighted according to its country's economic strength. The ECU, which was an important instrument of the *European Monetary System*, never existed as tangible cash. It played a vital role in laying down the foundations of the European single currency, the *Euro*, as its forerunner. On 1 January 1999, with the introduction of the Euro, the ECU ceased to exist. Its exchange rate to the Euro (€) was set at 1:1.

European Defence Agency: An intergovernmental agency with its seat in Brussels, which was set up by the *Council* by its decision of 12 July 2004. The task of the Agency is to develop defence capabilities in crisis management, promote European cooperation in military technology, strengthen the industrial and technological bases of European defence, and encourage technological research by the European defence industry. Upon its entry into force, the *Reform Treaty* will institutionalise the Agency in the text of the *Treaty on the functioning of the European Union*.

European Defence Community (EDC): In 1950, the *Pléven plan* aimed at creating an integrated European defence force under joint command. The Treaty establishing the European Defence Community was signed by the Member States of the *European Coal and Steel Community* in 1952. However, the EDC never came to fruition, since it was rejected by the French National Assembly on 30 August 1954. Essentially, the *Western European Union* was established in place of the EDC, but with a far more modest capacity and institutional structure than outlined in the original plan.

European Development Fund (EDF): A fund providing financial assistance to the *ACP countries*. It is not funded from the *EU* budget but from direct contributions from the Member States. It qualifies as a Community instrument, since it functions under the agreements signed by the EU with the ACP countries and the *European Commission* participates in its work.

European Economic Area (EEA): The Treaty establishing the European Economic Area was signed by the then twelve members of the *EC* and six members of the EFTA (Austria, Finland, Iceland, Norway, Switzerland and Sweden) on 2 May 1992 and entered into force on 1 January 1994. The importance of the EEA is that many provisions and rules of the EU's *single market* were also extended to these EFTA members, i.e. to a wider European area. Since Switzerland rejected joining the EEA at a referendum, the EEA was finally established with 17 participating States. Liechtenstein entered the EEA in 1995; therefore, the number of members rose to 18. The enlargements of 2004 and 2007 increased membership to 30. The EEA lost much of its importance when three former EFTA-members (Austria, Finland and Sweden) joined the European Union in 1995 and EFTA came to be represented by only three states in the EEA, two of them very small.

European Economic Community (EEC): The original term for one (the most important) of the three organisations of the *European Communities*. The EEC was established by the *Treaty of Rome,* which was signed by the six members of the *ECSC* (Belgium, France, the Netherlands, Luxembourg, Germany and Italy) on 25 March 1957 and entered into force on 1 January 1958. The Treaty of Rome establishing the EEC stipulated the development of the *common market* as the general objective of the *Community*. The term 'European Economic Community' was changed to *European Community* by the *Treaty of Maastricht,* thus indicating the general competence of this Community on the territory of the common market, as opposed to the former term emphasising only its economic nature, and the more limited and functional competences of ECSC and Euratom.

European Employment Pact: The Pact adopted at the Cologne Summit in June 1999 aims at closer coordination of the employment policies of the Member States and the *Community* in order to strengthen Europe's ability to boost employment.

European Environment Agency: An *EU* agency established in 1994, with its headquarters located in Copenhagen. Its main objectives are to provide the Community, the Member States and third countries with information on the state of the environment and to direct their attention to the need for the effective implementation of environmental policies.

European External Action Service: A foreign service, which will be created upon the entry into force of the *Reform Treaty* to support the work of the *High Representative of the Union for Foreign Affairs and Security Policy*; it will comprise officials of the *Council*, the *Commission* and the Member States.

European Fisheries Fund (EFF): This new structural fund, which became operational on 1 January 2007, replacing the *Financial Instrument for Fisheries Guidance*, supports restructuring in the fisheries sector.

European Food Safety Authority (EFSA): The European Food Safety Authority was set up in 2002 to restore consumer trust in the safety of foodstuffs (which had been shaken, for example by the BSE crisis). The responsibility of the Authority, which has its seat in Parma, is to provide information for consumers as an independent organisation, to provide scientific advice for elaborating Community legislation and to alert relevant national and Community authorities promptly in cases where there is a food safety emergency.

European Globalisation Adjustment Fund: A Community fund established in 2007 to provide complementary assistance for the restructuring efforts aimed at counterbalancing the negative impacts of globalisation and of world trade flows endangering European jobs.

European Institute of Technology: To be established in 2008 in accordance with the Lisbon strategy, the EIT and its six knowledge and innovation communities in various locations will have the task of finding the answers to strategic long-term economic and social challenges. The Union expects the public and private sectors of Member States to contribute to the financing of the Institute and the network around it.

European Investment Bank (EIB): The European Investment Bank was created under the *Treaty of Rome*. The Luxembourg-based EIB's objective is to contribute to the balanced economic development of the *Communities* through financing capital investments. The Member States subscribe jointly to the EIB's capital. The EIB's task is to grant loans to finance projects that are in accordance with the economic policy aims of the Community, both within and outside its borders.

European Judicial Network: A network of judicial contact points designated by the Member States and the European Commission, which was set up in 1998 with the aim of facilitating cross-border investigations and criminal proceedings in order to improve the fight against international crime. After the creation of the criminal judicial network, the EU Member States decided to set up another judicial network in 2001 for cooperation between competent national authorities on civil and commercial matters.

European Monetary Cooperation Fund (EMCF): The fund of reserves established in the framework of the *European Monetary System*, whose task was to issue short-term *ECU* credit facilities in order to assist the financial interventions of the national central banks.

European Monetary Institute (EMI): Under the programme of the *economic and monetary union*, the EMI was the precursor of the *European Central Bank* from 1 January 1994 to 1 June 1998. The tasks of the Frankfurt-based EMI were, on the one hand, to make preparations for the conducting of the single monetary policy through strengthening monetary cooperation and convergence between the Member States and, on the other hand, to establish the necessary institutional foundations for launching the *European System of Central Banks* and for establishing the European Central Bank.

European Monetary System (EMS): The EMS was set up in 1979 to guarantee the sustainable monetary cooperation of the Member States of the *European Economic Community*. The main objective of the European Monetary System (EMS) was to create exchange rate stability within the Community.

It was based on three elements: the *Exchange Rate Mechanism (ERM)*, the *European Currency Unit (ECU)* and the *European Monetary Cooperation Fund* (EMCF).

European Neighbourhood Policy (ENP): The EU launched its European Neighbourhood Policy, which was based on the Commission's 'Wider Europe – Neighbourhood' concept of March 2003, in order to provide a framework for relations with countries neighbouring the EU which, although not prospective members, are strategic partners of the Union. The aim of the ENP was to define the relations of the enlarged Union with its eastern and southern neighbours: Russia, the former Soviet republics of Ukraine, Moldova and Belarus, as well as Armenia, Azerbaijan and Georgia in the southern Caucasus, and countries of the Mediterranean (Algeria, Morocco, Tunisia, Egypt, Jordan, Lebanon, Syria, Israel and the Palestinian Authority).

European Ombudsman: The Ombudsman of the *European Union* is appointed by the *European Parliament*. He is empowered to receive complaints from any citizen of the Union or any natural or legal person residing in a Member State about alleged misconduct or maladministration by Community institutions or bodies.

European Parliament (EP): The European Parliament (EP) is a representative body elected directly by the citizens of the *Union*. The current (January 2007–June 2009) 785 Members of the European Parliament (MEPs) perform their duties working in transnational political groups. The EP is not the main legislative body of the EU, since its legislative and decision-making role is limited. Originally, the Parliament only performed consultative and limited monitoring functions. Over the years, its powers have been gradually extended. Its transformation into a true legislative body did not begin until the *Single European Act*, the *Treaty of Maastricht*, the *Treaty of Amsterdam* and the *Treaty of Nice* progressively expanded its role as the co-legislative and co-decision-making institution of the Union, alongside the *Council*. Today, in a significant part of the Community's legislative process, the Parliament is an equal partner of the *Council* as a co-legislator, and in several areas its role is decisive.

European Political Cooperation (EPC): The EPC, as the *European Communities'* mechanism for coordinating the foreign policies of the Member States, was superseded by the introduction of the *Common Foreign and Security Policy (CFSP)* under the *Treaty of Maastricht*. It was introduced informally in 1970 and formalised by the *Single European Act* with effect from 1986. Its objects were to facilitate intergovernmental consultations between the Member States in foreign policy matters and to assist them in reaching common positions and, wherever possible, in presenting a united front on foreign policy issues.

European Public Prosecutor's Office: The Reform Treaty provides for the option of the establishment of this new body. The Office could be established through a decision by the *Council* acting unanimously, after obtaining the consent of the *European Parliament*. If established, the European Public Prosecutor's Office would take over the tasks of Eurojust and would have competence to investigate and prosecute the perpetrators of offences against the Union's financial interests.

European Refugee Fund: A fund established in 2005 and linked to the creation of the *Common European Asylum System.* See *Solidarity and management of migratory flows.*

European Regional Development Fund (ERDF): The biggest of the *EU*'s *Structural Funds,* which was established in 1975 and designed to reduce regional, economic and social disparities and strengthen economic and social cohesion within the *Community.*

European Research Area (ERA): A key objective of the EU's research activities is the establishment of a European Research Area based on linking together European researchers to facilitate cooperation between them, in line with the principles of the *Lisbon strategy,* which underscores the special role of research and technological development in creating a knowledge-based society.

European Research Council (ERC): A body established within the framework of the 'Ideas' programme of the Seventh Research Framework Programme, which in practice functions like a European research agency, and finances investigative research at the forefront of science and technology with great potential but no guarantee of success. The strategy and policy of the ERC is defined by a 22-member Scientific Council.

European Security and Defence Identity (ESDI): A concept used within NATO, the *WEU* and the *EU* alike, which denotes the joint development and organisation of security and defence actions of the European states (distinct from NATO but having access to its military capacity). The concept of ESDI has been rarely used since the creation of the *European Security and Defence Policy.*

European Security and Defence Policy (ESDP): The process officially started at the Cologne Summit in June 1999, which aimed at putting increasing emphasis on defence issues within the scope of the *Common Foreign and Security Policy* of the EU. Under ESDP, the *EU* decided to establish its own military capacity in order to handle crisis management and assume the tasks of the *Western European Union* (*Petersberg tasks*). ESDP, however, does not signify common defence in its traditional sense, since it focuses mainly on crisis management. The collective defence of the NATO members of the EU remains the responsibility of the North Atlantic Treaty Organisation, while the neutral Member States act autonomously in this regard. The key element of ESDP was the so-called Headline Goal, which stated that, by 2003, the EU should be able to deploy a rapid reaction force of up to 50,000–60,000 troops committed by the Member States. In the framework of ESDP, new institutions were set up (the *Political and Security Committee, Military Committee* and *Military Staff*) or transferred from the WEU (the Satellite Centre and the Institute for Security Studies).

European Security Strategy: The European Union's Security Strategy adopted by the *European Council* of 12–13 December 2003. It takes stock of the key security challenges the EU has to face (terrorism, the proliferation of weapons of mass destruction, regional conflicts, weak governments and organised crime) and the strategic answers to those challenges. ESS concludes that the EU must give a resolute response to these threats, promote security in neighbouring regions (particularly in the Balkans, the Mediterranean and the Middle East) and contribute to strengthening the international order based on multilateral cooperation ('effective multilateralism'), with cooperation with the UN as a priority.

European Social Fund (ESF): The ESF is one of the *European Union*'s four *Structural Funds*, which was set up in 1958 as a Community fund undertaking social responsibilities. Its main objective is to reduce unemployment and stimulate job creation through support for adapting and modernising education, training and employment policies. The ESF is intended to function as a supplement to the national support systems of the Member States.

European System of Central Banks (ESCB): The ESCB, established on 1 June 1998, is composed of the *European Central Bank* and the national central banks (NCBs) of the Member States. With the adoption of the *single currency*, the European System of Central Banks became the leading institution of the Union's monetary policy. The primary objective of the ESCB is to maintain price stability. The basic tasks carried out by the ESCB are to: define and implement the monetary policy of the *Community*, conduct foreign exchange operations, hold and manage the official foreign reserves of the Member States and promote the smooth operation of payment systems.

European Training Foundation (ETF): An *EU* agency, which aims at establishing cooperation with third countries in the field of education. The ETF, which has its headquarters in Turin, opened on 1 January 1995. Its key objectives are to contribute to the reform of education and vocational training systems in the partner countries (candidate countries, countries of the Western Balkans, CIS countries and Mongolia, countries of the Mediterranean), impart Community experience to the countries concerned, support the *Tempus* programme by practical activities and improve cooperation between the EU and the partner countries in the field of education and vocational training.

European Union (EU): The integration framework currently involving 27 European countries was established by the *Treaty of Maastricht* with effect from 1 November 1993. The Treaty of Maastricht created a unique three-pillar structure. The *first pillar* of the EU became the *European Communities* (incorporating the three *Communities* of the *EC, ECSC and Euratom*) alongside a few new Community policies and the programme of the *economic and monetary union*. The *second pillar*, the *Common Foreign and Security Policy*, and the *third pillar*, *Justice and Home Affairs* (today limited to *Police and Judicial Cooperation in Criminal Matters*), function on the basis of intergovernmental cooperation. The Union itself does not have legal personality in international law, since the three separate Communities retained their legal personalities after Maastricht; nevertheless, the Union acts through the institutions of the European Communities. When it enters into force, the *Reform Treaty* will abolish the pillar structure and bestow legal personality on the Union, which will thereby become the legal successor of the European Community.

European Union Military Committee: See *Military Committee*.

European Union Military Staff: See *Military Staff*.

European Voluntary Service (EVS): A programme promoting the voluntary work of young people abroad. From 2000 to 2006, it was part of the Youth programme; from 1 January 2007, it operates within the framework of the Youth in Action integrated action programme.

Europol (European Police Office): Europol is the European Union's intergovernmental police organisation, which sits in The Hague. Its aim is to improve effectiveness and cooperation between the competent authorities of the Member States in preventing and combating serious forms of international crime. Europol functions as an office of cooperation, facilitating the exchange of information between the Member States; it has no independent investigative or prosecuting mandate.

Eurozone: The group of countries that adopted the single currency, the euro. In 2007, the eurozone consists of 13 countries (Austria, Belgium, Finland, France, Germany, Greece, Ireland, Italy, Luxembourg, the Netherlands, Portugal, Slovenia and Spain), who will be joined by Cyprus and Malta on 1 January 2008.

Financial Instrument for Fisheries Guidance (FIFG): One of the *EU's* former four *Structural Funds. FIFG* was launched in 1993 to develop and assist the adaptation of the fisheries structures. It was replaced by the *European Fisheries Fund* on 1 January 2007.

Financial perspectives: Multi-annual budgetary packages or financial frameworks, which are not institutionalised in the Treaties and thus have no primary legal base. Financial perspectives are adopted at summit level meetings of Heads of State or Government by a unanimous vote. Their aim is to ensure the stable operation and financing of EU policies for longer periods by using multi-annual budgetary planning. Financial perspectives are adopted – recently for 7-year periods – on the basis of estimated *own resources*. These financial perspectives include ceilings for the overall budget and its key headings, which then serve as a framework for the annual budgets of subsequent years. Upon its entry into force, the *Reform Treaty* will institutionalise the now standard practice of multi-annual financial planning and incorporate it into the Treaties under the name of *multi-annual financial framework*.

First Pillar: Since the *Treaty of Maastricht*, the first pillar is the common term referring to areas falling under the competences of the three *Communities (EC, Euratom, ECSC)*, in other words the *European Communities*, as distinct from the *second and third pillars* established by the Treaty of Maastricht, which operate on an intergovernmental basis, outside the Community dimension. While the first pillar is operated by the Community institutions, only the *Council and the European Council*, which work on an intergovernmental basis, play a decisive role in the second and third pillars. The pillar structure will disappear with the entry into force of the *Reform Treaty*. The current mechanisms of the first pillar will be extended to the third pillar, while the second pillar of foreign and security policy will remain intergovernmental.

Flexibility instrument: An instrument established with the aim of supplementing depleted headings of expenditure of the EU budget without a need for transfers.

Founding Treaties: The treaties establishing the three Communities (ECSC, EC and Euratom) and the Treaty on European Union adopted in Maastricht.

Four freedoms: The free movement of goods, services, capital and persons. The four freedoms are one of the primary objectives of the *Communities*, since they constitute the essence of the *single market*. Legislation to facilitate the exercise of the four freedoms is a vital part of the *acquis communautaire*.

Framework decision: One of the legal acts of the *third pillar*. Framework decisions are adopted by the *Council* by unanimity for the purpose of approximating the laws, regulations and administrative provisions of the Member States. Framework decisions – similarly to first-pillar *directives* – are binding upon the Member States as to the result to be achieved but leave to the national authorities the choice of form and method of implementation, albeit with a specific deadline for transposition.

Free Trade Area: An area where all customs duties and other measures restricting trade between members have been removed and thereby trade between members is liberalised. Countries in a Free Trade Area retain their own national customs duties and trade policy vis-à-vis third countries. It is not understood as a genuine form of integration.

FRONTEX: See *European Agency for the Management of Operational Cooperation at the External Borders.*

General Affairs and External Relations Council (GAERC): The *Council* formation dealing with general affairs (horizontal dossiers which affect several of the Union's policies and key strategic issues) and external relations. The General Affairs and the External Relations sections meet separately. Each government is usually represented by its Minister for Foreign Affairs, but some Member States choose to delegate their Minister or State Secretary for European Affairs to the general affairs section. It deals with the preparation and follow-up of European Council meetings, institutional and administrative questions, horizontal dossiers which affect several of the Union's policies as part of general affairs and with the whole of the Union's external action, namely *Common Foreign and Security Policy* (CFSP), *European Security and Defence Policy* (ESDP), foreign trade, development cooperation and humanitarian aid as part of external relations. Upon the entry into force of the *Reform Treaty*, this Council formation will be divided into a General Affairs Council and a Foreign Affairs Council. See also the *Council of the European Union.*

General Court: The name by which the current *Court of First Instance* will be known, following the entry into force of the *Reform Treaty.*

General guidelines: A type of legal act, applied in the *second pillar* and adopted by the *European Council* for the implementation of the principles of the *Common Foreign and Security Policy.*

Generalised System of Preferences (GSP): General customs preferences beyond the most-favoured nation clause, which the *EU* grants unilaterally to certain (usually developing) countries and regions.

Green Paper: *Commission* Green Papers are documents intended to stimulate debate. Their objectives are to highlight the most pressing problems of a sector and to launch a process of consultation at European level (between Community institutions, national government offices, NGOs, lobbies, and the private sector) on what kind of Community actions are needed in a given area. These consultations may result in the conversion by the Commission of the conclusions of the debate into practical proposals for Community action.

Grundtvig: The adult education sub-programme of the *Life-long Learning Programme.*

Hague programme: The justice and home affairs programme for the period 2005–2010, a follow-up to the *Tampere programme*. The Hague programme, which was decided at the *European Council* meeting of 4–5 November 2004, deals with all aspects of the *area of freedom, security and justice*.

High Representative for the Common Foreign and Security Policy: The position of High Representative for the *Common Foreign and Security Policy* was created by the *Treaty of Amsterdam*, in order to entrust a single person with the uniform representation of the common position of the Union on foreign policy matters. This position is held by the Secretary General of the *Council* (while responsibility for running the Council's General Secretariat since Amsterdam rests with the Deputy Secretary General). The High Representative's task is to assist the Presidency of the Council in matters relating to Common Foreign and Security Policy and to conduct political dialogue with third parties on behalf of the Union. With the entry into force of the *Reform Treaty*, this job will be assumed by the *High Representative of the Union for Foreign Affairs and Security Policy*.

High Representative of the Union for Foreign Affairs and Security Policy: An office to be created by the *Reform Treaty* upon its entry into force. The High Representative will also be one of the Vice Presidents of the *European Commission*, and the President of the Foreign Affairs Council. The High Representative will be appointed by the *European Council*, acting by a qualified majority after obtaining the consent of the Commission President. The procedure for withdrawing his/her mandate will be the same. The High Representative of the Union for Foreign Affairs and Security Policy will take over the job of both the External Relations *Commissioner* and the *High Representative for CFSP* acting as the Council's Secretary General.

ICT Policy Support Programme (ICT PSP): Part of the *Competitiveness and Innovation Framework Programme* serving the implementation of the *Lisbon strategy*, the ICT PSP promotes the wider application of information and communication technology by business, public administration and citizens.

Indirect effect: A legal principle laid down by the *European Court of Justice*, under which national courts must interpret national law in such a way as to ensure that the objectives of *directives* are achieved. Every national court must, in a case within its jurisdiction, apply Community law in its entirety and protect rights which the latter confers on individuals; therefore, it must set aside any provision of national law which may conflict with Community law, for example due to the failure of a Member State to properly incorporate a given directive into national law.

Information procedure: A decision-making procedure, which is applied in the case of certain financial and economic measures taken by the *Council* (or the *Commission*), such as the adoption of *broad economic policy guidelines* or certain trade agreements. The objective of the procedure is that the Council (or the Commission) must notify the *European Parliament* of the decision or measure taken.

Integrated guidelines: At the mid-term review of the *Lisbon strategy*, at the 22–23 March 2005 summit, the formal decision was taken that the *Council* should adopt three-year *integrated policy guidelines*, consisting of *broad economic policy guidelines* and *employment policy guidelines*. On the basis of the integrated guidelines, the Member States elaborate *national reform programmes* and the Commission draws up a *Community Lisbon programme* covering all Community-level activities boosting growth and employment. At their annual spring summit, the Heads of State or Government take stock of the progress made and decide on the modification of the integrated guidelines if necessary. At the end of each three-year programme, the integrated guidelines have to be renewed, along with the national reform programmes and the Community Lisbon programme.

Intelligent Energy – Europe (IEE) Programme: An energy action programme launched in 2003 and operating as part of the *Competitiveness and Innovation Framework Programme* in the 2007–2013 period. The IEE 2 programme for 2007–2013 has similar aims as the IEE 1 for the 2003–2006 period: energy efficiency, renewable energy resources and energy diversification. IEE 2 covers five priority areas: energy efficiency (SAVE), renewable energy sources (ALTENER), transport (STEER), developing countries and horizontal issues.

Intergovernmental Conference (IGC): Negotiations between the Member States' governments with a view to amending the *Treaties*. Examples of IGCs include negotiations on strengthening European integration and the establishment of new forms of closer cooperation between the Member States (such as the introduction of the *EMU* or *CFSP,* prior to the *Treaty of Maastricht*). Accession negotiations are also undertaken in the framework of IGCs; the outcome of these conferences has included the accession treaties, which entail amendments of the EU/EC Treaties. IGCs are not conducted within the institutional framework of the Union or the *Communities*, but are viewed rather as traditional diplomatic negotiations, where each state acts as a sovereign power and decisions are adopted by unanimity. The outcome of the Conferences, namely the ensuing agreements, must be ratified by each signatory Member State in line with its national constitutional provisions.

Inter-institutional Agreement (IIA): A long-term agreement between any two or all of the three main Community institutions, the *Council*, the *Parliament* and the *Commission*, under which the institutions agree on certain procedures and cooperation between themselves.

Internal market: See *Single market.*

INTERREG: One of the *Community initiatives,* financed by the *European Regional Development Fund*, which supported cross-border cooperation between nations and regions until 2006. From 2007, cross-border territorial cooperation became an independent Objective (3.) of structural and cohesion policy, which is still financed by the ERDF.

IPA (Instrument for Pre-Accession Assistance): The Instrument for Pre-accession Assistance became operational from 1 January 2007, and covers candidate countries (Croatia, Macedonia and Turkey) as well as potential candidates (Albania, Bosnia-Herzegovina, Montenegro and Serbia, including Kosovo). With its creation, all existing pre-accession-type funds (PHARE, ISPA, SAPARD, Turkey's pre-accession support and CARDS for the Western Balkans) were merged into a single instrument. The IPA has five constituent strands, each supporting one priority area: transition assistance and institution building, regional development, cross-border cooperation, human resources development and rural development. The latter three are only available to candidate countries and are aimed at preparing them for the management of Structural Funds.

ISPA (Instrument for Structural Policies for Pre-Accession): One of the Union's three *pre-accession funds* granted to the Central and Eastern European candidate countries for the period 2000–2006. As the precursor of the *Cohesion Fund*, it provided financial assistance for transport and environmental infrastructure development. ISPA was replaced by the IPA on 1January 2007.

Joint Action: One of the legal sources of the *second pillar,* the *Common Foreign and Security Policy.* It means coordinated action by the Member States to attain specific objectives. The *Council* defines the scope and objectives of joint action.

Joint Research Centre: The EU's own network of research institutes with 2,000 researchers working in its 7 institutes located in five European cities.

Judicial panel: In order to reduce the case overload of the *Court of Justice* and the *Court of First Instance,* the *Treaty of Nice* introduced the possibility of setting up judicial panels with special competences, to act as specialised courts and deliver rulings in the first instance. Such judicial panels can be set up by the *Council* acting unanimously on a proposal from the *Commission* or on a request from the Court of Justice, after consulting the *European Parliament.*

K.4 Committee: See *Coordinating Committee.*

LEADER: One of the *Community initiatives* of the Structural Funds designed to encourage rural development. In 2007, it was incorporated into the European Agricultural Fund for Rural Development.

Legal harmonisation: The approximation of national legislation and the alignment of national legal systems in order to realise the objectives of the integration process, such as the *single market* and the *economic and monetary union.* The need for approximating the national laws of the Member States first emerged upon the establishment of the *EEC.* The *Treaty of Rome* institutionalised legal harmonisation as the principal form of the approximation of laws. Since then, the primary goal of the *EC* has been to harmonise rather than develop common legislation, although *regulations* result in national laws with uniform texts. The main instruments of legal harmonisation under the Treaty of Rome are *directives,* as they facilitate the approximation of national legislation with a minimum amount of conflict.

Leonardo: The vocational training sub-programme of the *Life-long Learning Programme.*

LIFE: A Community programme for the environment, established in 1992 and renamed LIFE+ in 2007, which co-finances environmental activities in the *EU* and in neighbouring countries. For these third countries, participation in the programme is subject to the condition that they participate financially. LIFE+ essentially consists of three thematic components: Life+ Nature and Biodiversity, Life+ Environmental Policy and Governance, and Life+ Information and Communication.

Lifelong Learning: The *EU*'s integrated action programme on education for the period 2007–2013. Its four sub-programmes are *Erasmus,* focusing on higher education, *Comenius,* focusing on pre-school, primary and secondary education, *Grundtvig,* on adult education, and *Leonardo da Vinci* on vocational training.

Lisbon strategy: The process launched at the 23–24 March 2000 Lisbon European Council, aimed at coordinating the economic policies of the Member States. Its primary goal is to make the *EU* the world's most competitive and dynamic knowledge-based economy by 2010, and an economy which is capable of sustainable development and which creates more and better employment opportunities through stronger social cohesion. To attain these goals, the Member States coordinate their economic policies and formulate specific objectives with specific deadlines. The Lisbon strategy focuses on improving competitiveness and growth. At the Lisbon European Council, the Heads of State or Government agreed to monitor and supplement the decade-long strategy at their regular spring summits. At the Gothenburg Summit of June 2001, the Lisbon strategy was amended to include the new aim of sustainable development, combining the aspects of economic growth, the environment and social progress.

Lomé Convention: The non-reciprocal agreements between the *EC* and the *ACP* countries, under which the EC granted free market access to the ACP countries under the *GSP*, in return for only the most-favoured nation clause. The first Lomé Convention was signed in 1975, while the fourth Lomé Convention expired in 2000; its scope was renewed and extended by the *ACP-EC Partnership Agreement* concluded in 2000.

Maastricht convergence criteria: Under the *Treaty of Maastricht*, in order to join the *single currency* of the *eurozone*, the economies of the Member States must fulfil certain conditions vital to the monetary union, these being the stability of the economy, mature conditions for currency union and excellent monetary results. Criteria were established to ensure that these objectives were met. The relatively strict standards to be met by the Member States for the adoption of the single currency, the so-called Maastricht convergence criteria, have been set as follows:
- Price stability. This is considered to be achieved when a country's inflation rate exceeds the average inflation in the three best-performing Member States by no more than 1.5%.
- The convergence of interest rates. This condition is measured by nominal long-term interest rate levels, which may not be more than two percentage points higher than the average of, at most, the three countries with the lowest rates of inflation.
- Exchange rate stability. Currencies are required to remain within the exchange rate mechanism (formerly *ERM I*, now *ERM II*) for at least two years without devaluing against the currency of any other Member State.
- The sustainability of the government's financial position. This condition is fulfilled when the annual government budget deficit is no more than 3% of GDP and total public debt does not exceed 60% of GDP.

MEDA: Community aid programme, under which the *EU* granted financial and technical assistance to non-European countries of the Mediterranean. In 2007, it was replaced by the *ENPI* created in the framework of the *European Neighbourhood Policy*.

MEDIA: The *EU*'s audiovisual policy programme, whose primary objectives are to establish competitive structures in the European audiovisual industry (film making, distribution and dissemination), to protect Europe's audiovisual heritage and to promote inter-cultural dialogue. The MEDIA 2007 programme for the 2007–2013 period unites the MEDIA programme running since 1991 and the MEDIA Training programme launched in 2001.

Merger Treaty: The Treaty provides for the merger of the institutions of the *ECSC*, *EEC* and *Euratom*, which formerly functioned in parallel. It was adopted in 1965 and entered into force in July 1967. It established a joint *Council* and *Commission* for the three *Communities*, in addition to the already-joint Assembly (the *European Parliament*) and the *Court of Justice*. As the Treaty entailed the merger of the institutions of the three Communities, the term *European Communities, (the EC)* became widely used from that time on. Although their institutions were merged, the three Communities continued to retain their own independent international legal status.

Mertens Group: The Mertens Group, which was named after its first chairman and set up in the early nineties, prepares *COREPER I* meetings. It is made up of officials working at the permanent representations, who are also known as Mertens diplomats.

Military Committee (EUMC): The European Union Military Committee, established in the framework of *ESDP*, is composed of the military representatives of the Chiefs of Defence Staff of the Member States. It gives military advice and makes recommendations to the *Political and Security Committee*. In the case of an emergency, the Committee may also hold meetings at the level of the Chiefs of Staff. The Committee also provides military direction to the EU *Military Staff*. The chairman of the EUMC attends the meetings of the *Council*, when decisions with defence implications are to be taken.

Military Staff (EUMS): The European Union Military Staff is a body of military experts set up in the framework of *ESDP*. It performs early warning tasks, situation assessments and strategic planning of military activities in crisis management. The EUMS designs actions in relation to the *Petersberg tasks* and designates the force capacity to implement them. It implements policies and decisions as directed by the *Military Committee*.

Modified Brussels Treaty: The Brussels Treaty was signed by Belgium, the UK, France, the Netherlands and Luxembourg on 17 March 1948, under which the signatory states agreed to establish a collective defence system. On 23 October 1954, the Paris Agreements amended the Brussels Treaty (modified Brussels Treaty). The German Federal Republic and Italy joined the Treaty (and the area of collective defence) and the *Western European Union* was then established.

Modulation: A mechanism for reducing *direct payments*, introduced by the 2003 agricultural reforms. According to this mechanism, direct payments to farms remained unchanged until 2005, but then the part above EUR 5,000 was reduced by 3% in 2005, 4% in 2006 and 5% from 2007 on.

Multi-annual financial framework: Upon its entry into force, the *Reform Treaty* will institutionalise the now standard practice of multi-annual financial planning for the EU budget and incorporate *financial perspectives* into the Treaties under the name of 'multi-annual financial framework', but with a five-year cycle instead of the current seven-year practice.

Mutual recognition: Under this principle, the *European Court of Justice* ruled in the Cassis de Dijon case in 1978, that the free movement of goods within the Union may only be subject to restrictions as a consequence of the divergence of national rules if these restrictions are necessary to satisfy mandatory requirements relating to: the effectiveness of fiscal supervision, the protection of public health, the fairness of commercial transactions and the defence of the consumer. The ruling was a cornerstone in widening the process of legal harmonisation, since mutual recognition in *EC* law became a flexible instrument for harmonisation and was extended to other areas too (such as diplomas).

National Programme for the Adoption of the Acquis (NPAA): The action programme adopted by the governments of the candidate countries for the adoption and implementation of the *acquis communautaire*, outlining the timetable for fulfilling the requirements of EU membership. Its corresponding programmes on behalf of the Union are the *Accession Partnerships*.

National reform programmes: On the basis of the *integrated guidelines* on the implementation of the *Lisbon strategy*, adopted by the *Council* every three years, Member States draw up 3-year national reform programmes. The Heads of State or Government of EU Member States decided on this three-year-cycle approach at their summit meeting on 22–23 March 2005, when the mid-term review of the Lisbon strategy was carried out.

National Strategic Reference Framework: Strategic programmes of individual Member States for the use of *Structural and Cohesion Funds* for a given financial perspective requiring the approval of the European Commission.

Natura 2000: A European ecological network, which ensures the preservation and recovery of biodiversity through the protection of natural habitats and fauna and flora.

New Transatlantic Agenda (NTA): In the framework of this process, launched in 1995, the *European Union* and the United States of America hold a continuous, institutionalised, intensive dialogue on global and bilateral economic, political and social issues. The cooperation is complemented by a joint EU-USA Action Plan. Under the NTA in London in May 1998, the parties adopted the programme called the Transatlantic Economic Partnership, an open cooperation process, which aims at the further liberalisation of trade relations and, as a final goal, the development of free trade.

NUTS (Nomenclature des Unités Territoriales Statistiques): The French acronym, which denotes the Nomenclature of Statistical Territorial Units, is a system introduced by Eurostat, the *European Commission's* Statistical Office, to classify regions into a hierarchy of five levels on the basis of their size. NUTS I is the top level, which covers big regions of large countries or in the case of small- and medium-sized countries, the whole country. NUTS II is the level of regions used for the purposes of Objective I of the *Structural Funds*, in terms of planning and statistics; NUTS II regions generally have a population of 1.5 to 2 million. NUTS III regions more or less correspond to counties, NUTS IV regions are also known as micro-regions, while the NUTS V level denotes towns.

Open method of coordination: In certain policy areas, the Member States may formulate common goals, which they then try to achieve through national measures. In the open method, the Member States coordinate their action to achieve better results.

Operational Programme (OP): The objectives of the *Structural and Cohesion Funds* are achieved through development strategies (called operational programmes) enumerating the priorities for a given budgetary planning period elaborated in accordance with the *National Strategic Reference Framework*. Each Member State runs a fewl of operational programmes for implementing major objectives of the Funds. Operational programmes require the Commission's approval.

Opinion: A non-binding Community legal act, giving an assessment of a given situation, often at someone's request.

Opt-out: Opting out is an exemption granted by the *Treaties* to a country that does not wish to join the other Member States in a particular area of Community cooperation. Under the *Treaty of Maastricht*, the United Kingdom and Denmark, for instance, were granted an opt-out for the third stage of *EMU*, (and in justice and home affairs in the case of Denmark). These two states may freely decide whether to join the monetary union and replace their national currencies with the single European currency. The other Member States fulfilling the necessary financial criteria are legally bound to do so.

Ordinary legislative procedure: Upon its entry into force, the Reform Treaty will make *co-decision procedure* the EU's ordinary legislative procedure, i.e. the general rule for legislative work, with other procedures applied only in special cases.

Own resources: Own resources were introduced in 1970 to finance Community expenditure. Presently, own resources available for the EU budget are: traditional own resources (customs duties, agricultural variable duties and sugar levies), the VAT resource (calculated from value-added tax revenues of the Member States) and the GNI resource, based on the gross national income of the Member States.

Package deal: The term generally refers to compromise decisions made at the meetings of the *European Council*. During the meetings, the Member States put (sometimes only remotely) related issues into so-called baskets, in order to create discussion packages and to reach a compromise on the package as a whole. To reach a compromise, the Member States relinquish their positions on some issues so as to maintain their interests on others.

Parliament: See *European Parliament.*

Passerelle clause (bridging clause): *See Simplified revision procedure*

Permanent structured cooperation: An instrument of flexible cooperation in the area of *European Security and Defence Policy*, which will be created upon the entry into force of the *Reform Treaty*. Permanent structured cooperation will allow the *Council* to entrust the execution of a task to a group of Member States and Member States whose military capabilities fulfil higher criteria, to establish such cooperation for the execution of demanding missions. Unlike in the case of enhanced cooperation, which was introduced with a similar aim and where at least nine Member States must be involved, there will be no minimum requirement for the number of participating states: as few as two Member States will be able to initiate permanent structured cooperation. When deciding on permanent structured cooperation, the

Council will act by a qualified majority after consulting the *High Representative of the Union for Foreign Affairs and Security Policy.*

Petersberg Tasks: The Petersberg Declaration, adopted by the Council of the *WEU* on 19 June 1992, defined the guidelines for the future development of the WEU. The Declaration outlined the responsibilities of the WEU under the so-called Petersberg tasks (or Petersberg-type missions). The different types of military tasks were defined as follows: 1) humanitarian and rescue tasks; 2) peace-keeping tasks; 3) tasks of combat forces in crisis management, including peacemaking. In the framework of developing *ESDP*, the EU has been creating its own military capacity for crisis management and has gradually taken charge of the Petersberg tasks.

PHARE: The *EU*'s financial assistance programme for Central and Eastern European countries. The PHARE programme was launched at the G7 summit on 14 July 1989 under the coordination and guidance of the *European Commission.* The acronym stands for 'Poland and Hungary Assistance for Restructuring of the Economy". Originally, it affected only Poland and Hungary but, from 1990 on, it was gradually extended to cover all Central and Eastern European countries. After 1998, PHARE became the main financial instrument for the pre-accession strategy for the ten Central and Eastern European countries which applied for membership of the *European Union* (Bulgaria, the Czech Republic, Estonia, Hungary, Latvia, Lithuania, Poland, Romania, Slovakia and Slovenia), providing assistance for institution building in public administration and the judiciary and for the adoption and implementation of the *acquis communautaire.* As of 2000, new forms of pre-accession aid, the *ISPA* and *SAPARD* programmes, were added to those already provided by PHARE. In 2007, PHARE was replaced by the *IPA.*

Pléven Plan: The programme named after René Pléven, the then French Prime Minister, launched in October 1950, which aimed at creating an integrated European defence force under joint command. It introduced the concept of the *European Defence Community*, which never came to fruition, since it was rejected by the French National Assembly.

Police and Judicial Cooperation in Criminal Matters (PJCC): The area of the *third pillar* under the *Treaty of Amsterdam.* Since Amsterdam, the third pillar has been limited to police cooperation and judicial cooperation in criminal matters; Amsterdam left these matters to be covered in an intergovernmental framework and did not elevate them to Community level, into the *first pillar*, where the other issues covered by Justice and Home Affairs now belong.

Political and Security Committee (PSC): An ambassadorial-level body supervised by the *Council*, with a policy-making role in political and strategic areas within the framework of the *second pillar*, the *CFSP* and the *ESDP.* It also monitors the international situation in fields covered by the *CFSP*, coordinates issues under CFSP and ESDP, conducts political dialogue between the Member States and makes proposals to the *General Affairs and External Relations Council.* The Political and Security Committee assumed the responsibilities of the former Political Committee and controls the work of the *Military Committee.*

Political union: The highest level of integration. The majority of executive and legislative powers, including foreign policy and justice and home affairs, are largely transferred to Community level.

Pre-accession funds: Financial assistance provided by the *EU* for the candidate countries, aimed to facilitate pre-accession preparation. In the 2000–2006 budgetary planning period, there were three such funds: *PHARE* and the *SAPARD* and *ISPA* programmes, the latter two having been established in 2000. All the three programmes were replaced on 1 January 2007 by IPA, which has a wider scope and covers all forms of pre-accession aid to candidate countries and potential candidates.

Pre-accession strategy: The strategy outlined by the *EU* to support the accession of the Central and Eastern European countries, which was adopted at the Essen Summit in December 1994.

Pre-emption: A principle linked to the supremacy of Community law, according to which, in certain areas which are fully regulated by Community law or which fall under the exclusive competence of the *Community*, no further laws may be enacted at the national level.

President in office: See *Council Presidency.*

President of the European Council: Upon the entry into force of the *Reform Treaty,* the *European Council* will have a permanent President, elected by the European Council acting by a qualified majority. The President will be elected for a term of two and a half years, renewable once. His/her task will be to chair and prepare the European Council meetings, ensure continuity, seek and facilitate compromises, and represent the Union at his/her level (i.e. without prejudice to the powers of the *High Representative of the Union for Foreign Affairs and Security Policy*). The European Council President will not be permitted to hold a national office (which will mean that – contrary to current practice – the Member States will not be able to appoint a head of state or government in office).

Principle of conferral: A principle laid down in the *Reform Treaty,* which will be applied on its entry into force, governing the limits of Union competences. Under the principle of conferral, the Union acts exclusively within the limits of the competences conferred upon it by the Member States in the Treaties, to attain the objectives defined therein. Competences not conferred upon the Union by the Treaties remain with the Member States.

Principle of equivalence: The principle was first established by the *European Court of Justice* in the Cassis de Dijon case in 1978, when the Court's ruling stated that when a product is lawfully produced and marketed in a Member State, it is freely marketable on the entire territory of the *Communities*. This ruling finally prevented the Member States from protecting their national products by applying diverse national rules and standards.

Progress (PROGRamme for Employment and Social Solidarity): An integrated employment and social solidarity programme of the *Community* for the 2007–2013 period. Its five key areas of action are: employment, social protection and inclusion, improving working conditions, combatting discrimination and promoting gender equality.

Proportionality principle: One of the fundamental principles in the functioning and decision-making of the Union, next to *subsidiarity*. The principle of proportionality stipulates that *EU/Community* actions should only extend as far as is necessary to achieve the objectives set out in the *Treaty*.

Proxima: The EU police operation in Macedonia, launched on 15 December 2003, which superseded the EU military mission (*Concordia*) started on 31 March 2003. Proxima ended after two years in 2005.

Qualified majority voting (QMV): A voting procedure in the Council, which requires a set qualified majority number of votes for a decision to be adopted. The threshold for a qualified majority is currently set at 255 of the total 345 votes of the 27 Member States. Member States' votes are weighted on the basis of their population, but are not directly proportional to their size, as political considerations also play a role. With the entry into force of the Reform Treaty the current weightings of qualified majority voting will be replaced by *double majority* voting on 1 November 2014.

Rapporteur: A Member of the *European Parliament* (MEP) entrusted with a specific dossier or issue. In the European Parliament, decisions are always prepared by one MEP. The rapporteur prepares a draft text, which is discussed in the competent EP Committee and then submitted to the vote in plenary session. Rapporteurs are appointed through a system based on the weight of the political groups and as a result of a political deal between them.

REACH (Registration, Evaluation and Authorisation of Chemicals): A Directive on the registration, evaluation and authorisation of chemicals. The Directive will enter into force gradually from 2007; it will be phased in over a period of 11 years by the end of which, in 2018, all chemicals will have to be registered with the European Chemicals Agency (ECHA) in Helsinki.

Recommendation: A non-binding Community legal act, which nonetheless has to be observed by the national courts of the Member States when deliberating on cases relating to Community law. Recommendations, as a rule, set out the action or behaviour which is expected of the addressees.

Reform Treaty: As the *Constitutional Treaty* could not be ratified successfully in all Member States, it became clear that it would not enter into force. Therefore, at the *European Council* meeting of 21–22 June 2007, the Member States decided to place the Union on a new basis by means of a Reform Treaty, which – unlike the Constitutional Treaty – will not replace the *EU and EC Treaties*, but only amend them and rename the latter as the *Treaty on the functioning of the European Union*. The Reform Treaty is an amending treaty in the classical sense, which discards the concept of 'Constitution' (considered a symbol of a European "superstate" by many) and all elements of a constitutional nature or reminiscent of statehood, but which still manages to maintain the majority of the Constitutional Treaty's achievements. The main task of the Reform Treaty is to salvage the majority of the Constitutional Treaty's provisions by incorporating them into the current *Treaties*. Upon its entry into force, it will abolish the complex pillar structure, bestow legal personality on the Union, simplify decision-making by making *co-decision* the *ordinary legislative procedure* (i.e. the general rule for legislative work) and by extending *qualified majority voting* to new areas rather than unanimity. It will significantly widen the competences of the *European Parliament* and create two new positions: the permanent President of the European Council and the *High Representative of the Union for Foreign Affairs and Security Policy*. The plan is for ratification by the Member States to be completed in time for the Reform Treaty to enter into force before the elections to the EP in 2009.

Regulation: A Community legal act of general application, which is binding in its entirety and directly applicable in all Member States.

SAPARD (Special Accession Programme for Agriculture and Rural Development): A pre-accession fund for Central and Eastern European candidate countries set up in 2000 to provide financial support for structural changes in agriculture and rural development. It was replaced in 2007 by the *IPA*.

SAVE: A Community programme, operating within the framework of the *IEE* programme, promoting energy efficiency and rational energy use.

Schengen acquis: The *Schengen Agreement* and other related legal acts make up what is known as the Schengen *acquis*. In May 1999, with the entry into force of the *Treaty of Amsterdam*, the *Council* incorporated this *acquis* into the *EU* framework.

Schengen Agreement: Under the Agreement signed at Schengen in Luxembourg on 14 June 1985, the Benelux countries, France and the Federal Republic of Germany agreed that they would gradually remove their internal border controls and introduce freedom of movement for all individuals. The Agreement was supplemented by the Convention implementing the Schengen Agreement (Schengen Implementing Convention), which laid down the rules for implementing the Agreement. According to the provisions of the Convention, the Agreement and the Implementing Convention entered into force on 26 March 1995, with Spain and Portugal having joined the original five signatories. Further Member States joined the Schengen zone soon after. While removing internal border controls, the members of the Agreement reinforced external *EU* border controls. The *Treaty of Amsterdam* incorporated the Schengen Agreement and the *Schengen acquis* into the EU framework and extended it to all the *EU* Member States. However, under the Treaty, the United Kingdom and Ireland may continue to preserve their border control systems, while Denmark has reserved the right to decide on a case-by-case basis whether it wishes to adopt a new piece of legislation in the *Schengen acquis*. New Member States must adopt the Schengen Agreement and the *Schengen acquis*. Most of the ten countries that acceded to the EU in 2004 will become part of the Schengen area on 1 January 2008, while Bulgaria and Romania – who joined in 2007 – are expected to follow with a few years' delay.

Schengen Information System (SIS): A joint information database for police, customs and judicial authorities, established by the signatories to the *Schengen Agreement*. Its object is to make border controls at the external *EU* borders more effective. The system is being modernised and SIS II is expected to be operational by 2008.

Schuman Plan: On 9 May 1950, the French Foreign Minister, Robert Schuman, unveiled a plan, which laid down the foundation stone of European integration (the future *European Union*). The plan set in motion the process leading to the creation of the *European Coal and Steel Community*, by bringing the French and German coal and steel industries under joint control under an organisation which other European countries were free to join. To commemorate the Schuman Plan, the first step of European integration, 9th May has been designated Europe Day and is the official holiday of the EU.

Second pillar: The second pillar of the *EU*, the *Common Foreign and Security Policy* was created by the *Treaty of Maastricht* in an attempt to keep it out of the *competence of* Community institutions and preserve it on an intergovernmental basis with mechanisms differing from those of the *first* and *third pillars*. Upon its entry into force, the *Reform Treaty* will abolish the pillar structure, but in the area of *CFSP*, different rules will continue to apply.

Simplified revision procedure: A procedure to be introduced upon the entry into force of the *Reform Treaty*. Instead of the lengthy and cumbersome revision of the Treaties, this procedure will enable the *European Council*, acting by a unanimous decision, to authorise the Council to act by a *qualified majority* and/or the *ordinary legislative procedure* in areas for which the Treaties provide for unanimity and/or a *special legislative procedure*. Such decisions will be subject to the consent of the *European Parliament* (given by a majority of its component members) and will only be deemed adopted in the absence of any objection by national parliaments within six months. This is also called the *passerelle clause* or general bridging clause.

Single currency: See *euro*.

Single European Act (SEA): A Treaty amending the *Founding Treaties* of the *European Communities*. It was signed by the members of the European Communities on 18 February 1986 and entered into force on 1 January 1987. Its most important provision concerned the setting of the deadline of 31 December 1992 for the completion of the *single market*, which marked the onset of an intensive legislative and legal approximation programme within the *Communities*. Its various amendments to the *Treaty of Rome* brought about fundamental institutional changes: it strengthened the influence of the *European Parliament*, extended the competence of the *European Commission* and increased the importance of *qualified majority voting* in the voting system of the *Council*.

Single farm payment: See *Single payment scheme*.

Single market (internal market): The developed concept of the *common market* where, besides customs duties and quantitative restrictions, so-called 'non-customs' barriers are also abolished, be they physical (border formalities, border checks), financial (budgetary or fiscal rules) or technical (resulting from the differences in Member State laws, standards and other regulations), insofar as they obstruct the free movement of goods, services, capital and workers.

Single payment scheme (SPS): A scheme introduced by the 2003 reform of the *CAP*, which merges direct payments of various entitlements into a single lump-sum payment calculated on the basis of payments received in previous years.

Single area payment scheme (SAPS): A scheme introduced by the 2003 *CAP* reform for the new Member States, which was designed to facilitate their soft landing in the complicated system of the CAP. Single area payments are not based on production or livestock numbers but exclusively on the size of the cultivated area. Member States that acceded to the EU in 2004 have to switch to the *single payment scheme* by the end of 2010, while the Member States that joined in 2007 have until the end of 2011 to do so.

Social Charter: All the *EC* Member States, except the United Kingdom (which joined later), adopted the Charter of the Fundamental Social Rights of Workers, commonly known as the Social Charter, in 1989. The Charter aims at the closer coordination of twelve social policy areas.

Socrates: The *EU*'s Community programme on education until 2006, which was replaced by the *Lifelong Learning* action programme in 2007.

Solidarity and management of migration flows: a Community framework programme fcr the period 2007–2013 on immigration, asylum and border control. It operates financial solidarity mechanisms through the following four funds: the European Refugee Fund, the External Borders Fund, the European Fund for the Integration of Third-country Nationals and the Return Fund.

Solidarity clause: A clause to be applied upon the entry into force of the Reform Treaty, which stipulates that if a Member State is the object of a terrorist attack or the victim of a natural or man-made disaster, the other Member States will be obliged to act jointly in the spirit of solidarity to assist that Member State.

Specialised court: The current *judicial panels* will be renamed specialised courts by the *Reform Treaty*, upon its entry into force.

Special legislative procedure: Special legislative procedures will be applied in specific cases defined in the *Reform Treaty*, following its entry into force. Under the Reform Treaty, there will be about 20 areas where, instead of the *ordinary legislative procedure* (i.e. *co-decision*), the current *consultation procedure* or the *assent procedure* will apply.

Special passerelle clause (special bridging clause): In addition to the general *passerelle clause*, the *Reform Treaty* stipulates a special passerelle clause for certain cases. When the Treaty enters into force, this clause will enable the *European Council* to act by a *qualified majority* or the *ordinary legislative procedure* in areas for which the Treaties provides for unanimity or a special legislative procedure. Such decisions to switch over to QMV will be taken by unanimity after consulting the *European Parliament*. Compared with the general *passerelle clause*, the key difference is that, in this case, the national parliaments will not be involved and thus will be unable to object to and veto the application of the special passerelle clause.

Special representative: Within the framework of the *Common Foreign and Security Policy*, the *Council* may appoint special representatives with a mandate in specific areas. Such special representatives were appointed for leading EU action and managing the international administration following the crises in Bosnia and Kosovo.

Stabilisation and Association Process: An instrument designed to bring the Western Balkans (Albania, Bosnia-Herzegovina, Croatia, Macedonia, Montenegro and Serbia, including Kosovo) closer to the EU. It consists of three elements: the Stabilisation and Association Agreements (SAA) concluded with individual countries, the trade measures granting preferential treatment (broad market access) and the *IPA (formerly the CARDS* assistance programme).

Stability and Growth Pact: The Pact, adopted at the June 1997 Amsterdam *European Council*, whose objective is to safeguard the monetary stability of the eurozone. Its aim is to ensure that the Member States continue to fulfil the *Maastricht convergence criteria* once the *single currency* has been introduced. For instance, the Stability and Growth Pact opens the way for penalising any participating Member State, up to a certain percent of its GDP, where that State fails to take appropriate measures to end an excessive budget deficit.

STEER: A Community programme in the area of transport and energy aspects of fuel diversification, operating within the framework of the *IEE* programme.

Structural Funds: The Structural Funds are intended to reduce the gap in terms of development between different regions and between Member States of the European Union and thereby promote economic and social cohesion. The primary objective of the Structural Funds is the development and structural adjustment of regions whose development is lagging behind, and whose per capita GDP is less than 75% of the European Union average (Objective 1). Other objectives include competitiveness and employment (Objective 2) and cross-border territorial cooperation (Objective 3). For the 2007–2013 period, there are two Structural Funds: the *European Regional Development Fund* and the *European Social Fund*. Until 2006, there were another two Structural Funds, the Guidance Section of the *European Agricultural Guidance and Guarantee Fund*, and the *Financial Instrument for Fisheries Guidance*. Currently, the Community budget allocated to the Structural Funds and the *Cohesion Fund* (similar in its objectives and nature) is more than one third of the EU's total budget.

Subsidiarity principle: The subsidiarity principle is intended to ensure that decisions are taken as closely as possible to the citizen and are not dealt with at the higher level, unless that approach is more effective than action taken at lower levels. The *Treaty of Maastricht* has incorporated this principle into Community decision-making. Under the Treaty, a decision is taken at Community level when an objective cannot be better achieved at national level or when the means employed by the Community are better suited in proportion to the size, effect and transboundary nature of the issue in question.

Sui generis decision: A type of legal act that evolved because Article 249 of the *EC Treaty* gave a narrow scope of definition to Community legal acts, including *decisions*, without providing for separate legal acts for decisions of a certain type (for example, decisions relating to the Community institutions' internal procedures or staff-related matters).

Sustainable Development Strategy: On 15–16 June 2001, at the Gothenburg European Council, the Member States agreed on outlining a Community strategy for sustainable development. Following suit, the Member States must develop their own national strategies for sustainable development. The concept of sustainable development revolves around the need for all future EU strategies to build on the combination and unity of the three priority areas of environmental protection, economic growth and social development. The strategy is to be revised every five years.

TACIS (Technical Assistance for the Commonwealth of Independent States): The *EU* financial assistance programme for the ex-Soviet, newly independent states (NIS) now in the Commonwealth of Independent States (CIS) and Mongolia, which was based on aid, partnership and cooperation. In

2007, TACIS was replaced by the *ENPI* launched within the framework of the *European Neighbourhood Policy*.

Tampere programme: The justice and home affairs programme for the period 2000–2005, with the goal of facilitating the creation of an *area of freedom, security and justice*. It was adopted at the Tampere *European Council* of 15–16 October 1999.

Tempus: In response to the opening up of Central and Eastern Europe in the early nineties, the *EU* established the *Tempus* programme to provide assistance for education in the former communist countries. Initially, the programme supported the mobility and exchange of students and teachers of the region and the development of educational institutions. Once these countries became integrated into the EU's own programmes on education and youth, Tempus's focus shifted to the former republics of the Soviet Union, the CIS countries. The Tempus III programme, launched in 2000, covers the non-candidate countries (southern and eastern neighbours of the Union).

Third pillar: The third pillar of the *EU* was established by the *Treaty of Maastricht* and, until the entry into force of the *Treaty of Amsterdam,* denoted *Cooperation in the fields of Justice and Home Affairs*. After Amsterdam however, the third pillar was narrowed down to *Police and Judicial Cooperation in Criminal Matters,* since the Treaty communitised a part of justice and home affairs (namely asylum and immigration policy, external and internal border control and judicial cooperation in civil matters), bringing it under the *first pillar* within the *Community* framework. Upon its entry into force, the *Reform Treaty* will abolish the pillar structure and introduce current first-pillar mechanisms in what is currently the third pillar.

Trans-European networks (TEN): The *Treaty of Maastricht* established the programme of trans-European networks (TENs), the trans-frontier development of transport, telecommunications and energy infrastructures. The purpose of these networks is to inter-connect existing national and regional networks, build missing links, overcome bottlenecks and link peripheral regions with the central regions of the Community. Another important objective of the programme is to link TENs to the networks of Eastern Europe, South-east Europe and Mediterranean countries.

Treaties: The *Treaties* of the *European Union* and the *European Communities* and their amendments. The *Founding Treaties* include the *Treaty of Paris* and the two *Treaties of Rome* establishing the three *Communities* (*ECSC, EEC* and *Euratom*), as well as the *Treaty of Maastricht* establishing the European Union (the Treaty of Maastricht is an amending treaty, as well as a founding treaty, since it renamed the former EEC Treaty as the EC Treaty). The amending Treaties include the Treaties amending any or all four of the Founding Treaties, namely the *Merger Treaty,* the *Single European Act,* the Treaty of Maastricht, the Treaty of *Amsterdam,* the *Treaty of Nice,* the *Budgetary Treaties* and the Accession Treaties on the entry of new Member States. The amending Treaties overwrite the original Treaties; nevertheless, at any given moment, there is only one version in effect, namely the latest amended version of the previous text. Therefore, at any time the following Treaties are in force: the *EU* Treaty, the *EC* Treaty (formerly *EEC* Treaty) and the *Euratom* Treaty (the ECSC Treaty expired in 2002); they are collectively known as the Treaties.

Treaty: A reference to one of the *Founding Treaties* of the *European Union* and the *European Communities* in force. The Treaty in question is clearly identified by the context. If the context is unclear, the term generally denotes the version of the *EC Treaty* currently in force. The *EU*, the *ECSC* (now expired) and the *Euratom* Treaties are generally mentioned by name.

Treaty of Amsterdam: A Treaty amending the *EU Founding Treaties*. It was signed on 2 October 1997 and entered into force on 1 May 1999. Among others, it brought about progressive changes in the *Common Foreign and Security Policy*, strengthened *Cooperation in the fields of Justice and Home Affairs*, elevated employment policy coordination to the Union level and extended the *European Parliament's* decision-making powers.

Treaty of Maastricht: The Treaty of Maastricht was signed on 7 February 1992 and entered into force on 1 November 1993; it established the *European Union*, amended the *Founding Treaties* and renamed the *European Economic Community* as 'the *European Community*'. The Treaty was an important milestone in establishing closer European integration and in developing the *economic union* and *political union*. It set up the three-pillar structure of the European Union: the *European Communities, Common Foreign and Security Policy* and *Cooperation in the field of Justice and Home Affairs*. Under the *first pillar*, it outlined the programme of the *economic and monetary union (EMU)* and the *single currency*. Furthermore, it introduced *Union citizenship*, launched several new *Community policies*, significantly extended the competences of the *European Parliament*, widened the scope of *qualified majority* voting in the *Council* and incorporated the principle of *subsidiarity* in the Community decision-making process.

Treaty of Nice: A Treaty amending the *EU Founding Treaties*, and the closing document of the 2000 *Intergovernmental Conference*. It was signed on 26 February 2001 and entered into force on 1 February 2003. The Treaty of Nice outlines the institutional and decision-making reforms of the EU needed in particular in view of eastern enlargement. Its most important provisions concern the re-weighting of votes in the *Council*, the extension of the scope of decision-making by *qualified majority*, the modification of the *Commission*'s composition and the restructuring of the other Community institutions with a view to enlargement.

Treaty of Paris: The Treaty establishing the *European Coal and Steel Community*. It was signed on 18 April 1951 for a period of 50 years and entered into force on 23 July 1952. The Treaty of Paris expired on 23 July 2002.

Treaty of Prüm: originally signed by seven Member States (Austria, Belgium, France, Germany, Luxembourg, the Netherlands and Spain) in 2005 in the German city of Prüm. The Treaty of Prüm – similarly to the *Schengen Agreement* – was born outside the EU framework. It is aimed at stepping up the fight against terrorism, cross-border crime and illegal immigration by means of improved exchanges of information relating to DNA, fingerprints, vehicle registration, personal and non-personal data. A number of other countries had indicated their wish to sign the Prüm Treaty until the June 2007 JHA Council adopted a *third-pillar* Decision to incorporate the majority of the Prüm provisions into the EU's legal framework. The Prüm Decision aims to improve and accelerate the exchange of information between national law-enforcement authorities.

Treaty (Treaties) of Rome: The Treaties of Rome are the treaties establishing the European Economic Community (*EEC*) and the European Atomic Energy Community (*Euratom*). They were signed on 25 March 1957 in Rome and entered into force on 1 January 1958. When no specific reference is made to the EEC or the Euratom Treaty, the term is invariably understood as the Treaty on the EEC (*the current EC Treaty*).

Treaty on the functioning of the European Union: The new name of the current Treaty establishing the *European Community* (*EC Treaty*) to be introduced by the *Reform Treaty*. Upon its entry into force, the Reform Treaty – in accordance with abolishing the pillar structure and giving the *European Union* a legal personality – will abolish the name 'European Community' and replace it with 'European Union'. At the same time, the European Union will become the legal successor of the European Community.

Troika: The Troika is a group representing the *EU* at meetings with third countries, which – at summit level meetings of the Heads of State or Government – consists of the President of the *European Council*, the Secretary General of the *Council (the High Representative for CFSP)* and the President of the *Commission*. At lower (e.g. ministerial) level meetings, the Troika consists of the President-in-office of the *Council* (usually the President of the *General Affairs and External Relations Council*), the *Commissioner* for External Relations and the Secretary General of the Council.

URBAN: One of the Community initiatives financed by the *European Regional Development Fund*, which aims at the economic and social regeneration of cities in crisis.

Werner Plan: The plan was drafted in 1970 by the Werner group, headed by Pierre Werner, the then Prime Minister of Luxembourg. The plan, which envisaged the establishment of monetary union within the *European Communities*, can be seen as the precursor of the *economic and monetary union* (EMU). However, the first oil crisis and the ensuing financial crisis brought an abrupt halt to the realisation of the Werner Plan in its initial stage.

Western European Union (WEU): The organisation which was set up in 1954 by the *modified Brussels Treaty*, after the collapse of the nascent *European Defence Community*, for the purposes of cooperation on defence and security by the six members of the *ECSC* and the United Kingdom. Its original objective was to foster the military integration of West Germany and to establish the foundations of common European defence. Portugal, Spain and Greece joined the WEU later on. For non-member countries, there were different types of status in the WEU: the non-EU member European countries of NATO became associate members, those countries which were members of the *EU* but not of NATO had observer status, while the EU-associated (albeit not NATO member) Central and Eastern European countries had associated partner status. To strengthen its security policy potential (*ESDP*), at the June 1999 Cologne *European Council*, the Member States agreed on the gradual incorporation of the WEU into the EU. At the meeting of the WEU Council of Ministers on 13 November 2000 in Marseilles, the members agreed to terminate the day-to-day operation of WEU as of 1 July 2001. Nonetheless, technically, the organisation itself was not liquidated, since the *modified Brussels Treaty* and its Article V on collective defence remained in effect.

White Paper: In Community jargon, *Commission* White Papers are documents containing proposals for strategic Community action in a specific area. Examples include the 1985 White Papers compiled by Lord Cockfield, on the completion of the *single market* of the *EC* by 1993, and the 1995 Cannes White Paper, on the approximation of the laws of the associated states of Central and Eastern Europe in areas of relevance to the *internal market*, which included nearly 1,100 actions to be completed.

Youth: The *EU*'s action programme on youth, which in 2000 merged the former **Youth for Europe** programme, which supported activities targeting young people who had dropped out of the school system, and the **European Voluntary Service** programme, which promoted the voluntary work of young people abroad. It was replaced by the *Youth in action* integrated action programme in 2007.

Youth in action: The *EU*'s integrated action programme on youth for the 2007–2013 period, which is the successor of the *Youth* Programme, and as such includes the *European Voluntary Service*.

APPENDIX

I. Areas requiring a unanimous decision by the Council under the Treaties currently in force

I/a. EU Treaty

- TEU Article 23(1): decisions under the Title 'Common Foreign and Security Policy' (in issues falling under this title, the only exceptions – when the Council acts by qualified majority – are the following cases: when adopting joint actions, common positions or taking any other decision on the basis of a common strategy; when adopting any decision implementing a joint action or a common position; when appointing a special representative).
- TEU Article 24(2): agreements concluded with one or more states or international organisations for the implementation of the Title CFSP, when the agreement covers an issue for which unanimity is required for the adoption of internal decisions.
- TEU Article 28(3): the Council acting unanimously may decide that operating expenditure incurred by the implementation of the provisions of CFSP should not be charged to the budget of the European Communities.
- TEU Article 28(3): in cases where expenditure is not charged to the budget of the European Communities, it shall be charged to the Member States in accordance with the gross national product scale, unless the Council acting unanimously decides otherwise.
- TEU Article 30: common action in the area of police cooperation.
- TEU Article 31: common action in the area of judicial cooperation in criminal matters.
- TEU Article 32: laying down the conditions and limitations under which the competent authorities referred to in Articles 30 and 31 may operate in the territory of another Member State in liaison and in agreement with the authorities of that State.
- TEU Article 34(2): in the area of police and judicial cooperation in criminal matters the Council always acts by unanimity (only measures necessary for the implementation of decisions are adopted by a qualified majority).
- TEU Article 41(3): by way of derogation from the provisions of Title VI Article 41(2), the Council acting unanimously may decide that operating expenditure to which the implementation of provisions on police and judicial cooperation in criminal matters gives rise should not be charged to the budget of the European Communities. The Council acting unanimously may also decide to derogate from the provision that in cases where such expenditure is not charged to the budget of the European Communities, it shall be charged to the Member States in accordance with the gross national product scale.
- TEU Article 42: the Council, acting unanimously on the initiative of the Commission or a Member State, and after consulting the European Parliament, may decide that action in the area of police and judicial cooperation in criminal matters shall fall under Title IV of the Treaty establishing the European Community, and at the same time determine the relevant voting conditions relating to it. That decision must be ratified by the Member States in accordance with their respective constitutional requirements.

- TEU Article 44a: expenditure resulting from implementation of enhanced cooperation, other than administrative costs entailed for the institutions, shall be borne by the participating Member States, unless all members of the Council, acting unanimously after consulting the European Parliament, decide otherwise.
- TEU Article 49: deciding on the application for membership of a state.

I/b. EC Treaty
(according to decision-making procedure)

Consultation procedure:

- TEC Article 13: without prejudice to the other provisions of this Treaty and within the limits of the powers conferred by it upon the Community, the Council, acting unanimously on a proposal from the Commission and after consulting the European Parliament, may take appropriate action to combat discrimination based on sex, racial or ethnic origin, religion or belief, disability, age or sexual orientation.
- TEC Article 19(1): the right of every citizen residing in a Member State of which he is not a national to vote and to stand as a candidate at municipal elections.
- TEC Article 19(2): the right of every citizen residing in a Member State of which he is not a national to vote and to stand as a candidate in elections to the European Parliament.
- TEC Article 22: provisions to strengthen or to add to rights related to Citizenship of the Union (EC Treaty Part Two).
- TEC Article 63(3) a): conditions of entry and residence, and standards on procedures for the issue by Member States of long-term visas and residence permits, including those for the purpose of family reunion.
- TEC Article 63(4): measures defining the rights and conditions under which nationals of third countries who are legally resident in a Member State may reside in other Member States.
- TEC Article 65: measures in the area of judicial cooperation in family law.
- TEC Article 71(2): provisions concerning the principles of the regulatory system for transport that would be liable to have a serious effect on the standard of living and on employment in certain areas and on the operation of transport facilities.
- TEC Article 93: provisions for the harmonisation of legislation concerning turnover taxes, excise duties and other forms of indirect taxation necessary to ensure the establishment and the functioning of the internal market to the extent stipulated in Article 14.
- TEC Article 94: directives for the approximation of such laws, regulations or administrative provisions of the Member States as directly affect the establishment or functioning of the common market.
- TEC Article 104(14): provisions replacing the Protocol on the excessive budgetary deficit procedure.
- TEC Article 107(5): amending certain Articles and provisions of the Statute of the ESCB with the recommendation of the ECB.
- TEC Article 111(1) sentence 1: concluding formal agreements on an exchange-rate system for the ECU (euro) in relation to non-Community currencies.

- TEC Article 133(5): the Council acts unanimously when negotiating and concluding an agreement in one of the fields of trade in services and the commercial aspects of intellectual property, where that agreement includes provisions for which unanimity is required for the adoption of internal rules or where it relates to a field in which the Community has not yet exercised the powers conferred upon it by this Treaty by adopting internal rules.
- TEC Article 133(7): without prejudice to Article 133(6) subparagraph 1), the Council – acting by unanimity – may extend the application of paragraphs (1)–(4) to international negotiations and agreements on intellectual property, if they do not fall within the scope of paragraph (5).
- TEC Article 137(1) c), d), f), g): social security and social protection of workers; protection of workers where their employment contract is terminated; representation and collective defence of the interests of workers and employers, including co-determination; conditions of employment for third-country nationals legally residing in Community territory.
- TEC Article 175(2): adopting provisions in the following areas of the environment: provisions of a fiscal nature, measures concerning town and country planning, management of water resources (including measures affecting directly or indirectly the availability of such resources), and land use (with the exception of waste management), measures significantly affecting a Member State's choice between different energy sources and the general structure of its energy supply.
- TEC Article 181a(2): the Council acts unanimously for the association agreements referred to in Article 310 and for the agreements to be concluded with the States which are candidates for accession to the Union.
- TEC Article 225a: establishing judicial panels.
- TEC Article 229a: adopting provisions to confer jurisdiction – to the extent that the Council determines – on the Court of Justice in disputes relating to the application of acts which create Community industrial property rights.
- TEC Article 245: amending the Statute of the Court of Justice (with the exception of Title I.).
- TEC Article 266: amending certain provisions of the European Investment Bank.
- TEC Article 269: provisions relating to the system of own resources of the Community.
- TEC Article 279: procedures for establishing and implementing the budget and for presenting and auditing accounts, determining the methods and procedure whereby the budget revenue provided under the arrangements relating to the Community's own resources shall be made available to the Commission, laying down rules concerning the responsibility of financial controllers (QMV from 1 January 2007).
- TEC Article 308: taking the appropriate measures necessary to attain, in the course of the operation of the common market, one of the objectives of the Community, when the EC Treaty does not provide a specific legal base.

Assent procedure:

- TEC Article 105(6): conferring upon the European Central Bank specific tasks concerning policies relating to the prudential supervision of credit institutions and other financial institutions with the exception of insurance undertakings.

- TEC Article 161: defining the tasks, priority objectives and the organisation of the Structural Funds and Cohesion Fund; (QMV from 1 January 2007 if the multi-annual financial perspective applicable from 1 January 2007 and the related Inter-Institutional Agreement have been adopted by that time).
- TEC Article 190(4): adopting a uniform procedure for the elections to the European Parliament.

Co-decision procedure:

- TEC Article 42: social security arrangements, as are necessary to provide freedom of movement for migrant workers in the Community.
- TEC Article 47(2) sentence 2: directives the implementation of which involves the amendment of the existing principles laid down by law governing the professions with respect to training and conditions of access for natural persons pursuing activities as self-employed persons.
- TEC Article 151(5): cultural policy (incentive measures).

Other:

- TEC Article 57(2) sentence 2: measures which constitute a step back in Community law as regards the liberalisation of the movement of capital to or from third countries.
- TEC Article 72: without the unanimous approval of the Council, no Member State may make the various provisions applicable to transport service operators on the date of their accession less favourable in their direct or indirect effect on carriers of other Member States as compared with carriers who are nationals of that State.
- TEC Article 88(2): on application by a Member State, the Council may, acting unanimously, decide that aid which that State is granting or intends to grant shall be considered to be compatible with the common market, in derogation from the provisions of Article 87 or from the regulations provided for in Article 89, if such a decision is justified by exceptional circumstances.
- TEC Article 117(7): conferring upon the EMI tasks for the preparation of the third stage of the EMU.
- TEC Article 123(4): at the starting date of the third stage of the EMU, adopting the conversion rates at which the currencies of participating states are irrevocably fixed and at which irrevocably fixed rate the single currency will be substituted for these currencies and become a currency in its own right.
- TEC Article 123(5): adopting rates at which the single currency will be substituted for the currencies of the Member States joining the monetary union.
- TEC Article 139(2): implementing agreements on social policy concluded at Community level, in matters requiring unanimity covered by Article 137.
- TEC Article 186: agreements governing freedom of movement within Member States for workers from overseas countries and territories, and within overseas countries and territories for workers from Member States.
- TEC Article 187: provisions as regards the detailed rules and the procedure for the association of the overseas countries and territories with the Community.
- TEC Article 190(5): all rules or conditions relating to the taxation of Members or former Members of the European Parliament.

- TEC Article 202: laying down principles and rules for the procedure of conferring implementing powers on the Commission.
- TEC Article 203: deciding the order of the rotating Presidency of the Council.
- TEC Article 213(1): altering the number of Members of the Commission.
- TEC Article 215: the Council may, acting unanimously, decide that a vacancy in the Commission need not be filled.
- TEC Article 222: increasing the number of Advocates-General upon the request of the Court of Justice.
- TEC Article 223: appointing the Judges and Advocates-General.
- TEC Article 224: appointing members of the Court of First Instance.
- TEC Article 225a: appointing the members of judicial panels.
- TEC Article 289: determining the seat of the Community institutions.
- TEC Article 290: rules governing the languages of the institutions of the Community.
- TEC Article 296(2): making changes to the list of the products important for the protection of the essential security interests of the Member States.
- TEC Article 300(2) sentence 2: concluding international agreements that cover a field for which unanimity is required for the adoption of internal rules.

II. Areas requiring a unanimous decision by the Council upon the entry into force of the Reform Treaty (according to the articles of the former Constitutional Treaty)[*]

Legislative areas:

- Article I-18: flexibility clause (If action by the Union should prove necessary to attain one of the objectives set out in the Treaty, and the Treaty has not provided the necessary powers).
- Article I-54(3): provisions relating to the system of own resources of the Union.
- Article I-55(2): laying down the multiannual financial framework (according to Article I-55(4) the European Council may, unanimously, adopt a decision authorising the Council to act by a qualified majority).
- Article I-58: the accession of a new Member State to the Union.
- Article III-124(1): measures needed to combat discrimination based on sex, racial or ethnic origin, religion or belief, disability, age or sexual orientation.
- Article III-125(1) and (2): measures concerning passports, identity cards, residence permits or any other such document and measures concerning social security or social protection (if action by the Union should prove necessary to facilitate the exercise of the right, referred to in Article I-10(2)(a), of every citizen of the Union to move and reside freely and the Treaty has not provided the necessary powers).
- Article III-126: the detailed arrangements for exercising the right, referred to in Article I-10(2)(b), for every citizen of the Union to vote and to stand as a candidate in municipal elections and elections to the European Parliament in his or her Member State of residence without being a national of that State.
- Article III-129: adding to the rights laid down in Article I-10 (rights enjoyed by the citizens of the Union).
- Article III-157(3): measures which constitute a step backwards in Union law as regards the liberalisation of the movement of capital to or from third countries.
- Article III-171: measures for the harmonisation of legislation concerning turnover taxes, excise duties and other forms of indirect taxation provided that such harmonisation is necessary to ensure the establishment and the functioning of the internal market and to avoid distortion of competition.

---

[*] As this book went to press, the text of the Reform Treaty had not been adopted; therefore, this list uses the numbering of the Articles of the former Constitutional Treaty. On the basis of the mandate of the Intergovernmental Conference, as agreed on 22 June 2007, the Reform Treaty will adopt the provisions of the Constitutional Treaty on extending qualified majority voting and incorporate them into the EU and EC Treaties currently in force. The articles listed will be renumbered in the EU and EC Treaties by the Reform Treaty (which will also differ from the numbering used currently due to the many new or reformulated Articles.)

- Article III-173: measures for the approximation of such laws, regulations or administrative provisions of the Member States as directly affect the establishment or functioning of the internal market.
- Article III-176: measures for the creation of European intellectual property rights to provide uniform intellectual property rights protection throughout the Union and for the setting up of centralised Union-wide authorisation, coordination and supervision arrangements.
- Article III-184(13): laying down the appropriate measures to replace the said Protocol on the excessive deficit procedure.
- Article III-185(6): conferring specific tasks upon the European Central Bank concerning policies relating to the prudential supervision of credit institutions and other financial institutions with the exception of insurance undertakings.
- Article III-198: adopting rates at which the single currency will be substituted for the currencies of the Member States that are part of the eurozone.
- Article III-210(1) c), d) f) g): social security and social protection of workers; protection of workers where their employment contract is terminated; representation and collective defence of the interests of workers and employers, including codetermination; conditions of employment for third-country nationals legally residing in Union territory.
- Article III-234(2): provisions in the following areas of the environment: provisions primarily of a fiscal nature; measures affecting town and country planning; measures affecting quantitative management of water resources or affecting, directly or indirectly, the availability of those resources; measures affecting land use (with the exception of waste management); measures significantly affecting a Member State's choice between different energy sources and the general structure of its energy supply.
- Article III-256(3): measures in the area of energy policy (ensuring the functioning of the energy market; ensuring security of energy supply in the Union; and promoting energy efficiency and energy saving and the development of new and renewable forms of energy) when they are primarily of a fiscal nature.
- Article III-269(3): measures concerning family law with cross-border implications.
- Article III-274(1): establishing a European Public Prosecutor's Office in order to combat crimes affecting the financial interests of the Union.
- Article III-275(3): measures concerning operational cooperation between the Member States' competent authorities, including police, customs and other specialised law enforcement services in relation to the prevention, detection and investigation of criminal offences.
- Article III-277: laying down the conditions and limitations under which the competent authorities of the Member States referred to in Articles III-270 (judicial cooperation in criminal matters) and III-275 (police cooperation) may operate in the territory of another Member State in liaison and in agreement with the authorities of that state.
- Article III-291: the detailed rules and the procedure for the association of overseas countries and territories with the Union.
- Article III-330(1): the necessary measures for the election of the Members of the European Parliament by direct universal suffrage in accordance with a uniform procedure in all Member States or in accordance with principles common to all Member States.
- Article III-330(2): all rules or conditions relating to the taxation of Members or former Members of the European Parliament.
- Article III-393: amending the Statute of the European Investment Bank.

Other areas:

- Article I-40(6): decisions relating to the Common Foreign and Security Policy (except in the cases referred to in Part III).
- Article I-41(4): decisions relating to the common security and defence policy (including those initiating a mission as referred to in this Article)
- Article III-158(4): in the absence of a regulation or directive provided for in Article III-157(3), the Commission or – in the absence of a decision of the Commission within three months from the request of the Member State concerned – the Council may adopt a decision stating that restrictive tax measures adopted by a Member State concerning one or more third countries are to be considered compatible with the Treaties insofar as they are justified by one of the objectives of the Union and compatible with the proper functioning of the internal market.
- Article III-168(2): decisions declaring that aid which a State is granting or intends to grant shall be considered to be compatible with the internal market, if such a decision is justified by exceptional circumstances.
- Article III-212: agreements concluded with the social partners at Union level if they contain one or more provisions relating to one of the areas for which unanimity is required pursuant to Article III-210(3).
- Article III-237: unless the Council has unanimously adopted a decision granting a derogation, no Member State may make the various provisions governing transport on the date of their accession less favourable in their direct or indirect effect on carriers of other Member States as compared with carriers who are nationals of that State.
- Article III-270(2) d): establishing minimum rules concerning other specific aspects of criminal procedure, which the Council has identified in advance by a decision.
- Article III-271(1): on the basis of developments in crime, the Council may adopt a decision identifying other areas of crime that meet the criteria specified in this paragraph.
- Article III-312: the decisions and recommendations of the Council within the framework of permanent structured cooperation, other than those provided for in paragraphs 2 to 5, are to be adopted by unanimity. (For the purposes of this paragraph, unanimity shall be constituted by the votes of the representatives of the participating Member States only.)
- Article III-315(4): the negotiation and conclusion of agreements in the fields of trade in services and the commercial aspects of intellectual property, as well as foreign direct investment, where such agreements include provisions for which unanimity is required for the adoption of internal rules; the negotiation and conclusion of agreements in the field of trade in cultural and audiovisual services, where these agreements risk prejudicing the Union's cultural and linguistic diversity; and the negotiation and conclusion of agreements in the field of trade in social, education and health services, where these agreements risk seriously disturbing the national organisation of such services and prejudicing the responsibility of Member States to deliver them.
- Article III-325(8): the conclusion of agreements between the Union and third countries or international organisations, when the agreement covers a field for which unanimity is required for the adoption of a Union act, as well as for association agreements and the agreements referred to in Article III-319 with the States which are candidates for accession.

- Article III-326(1): by way of derogation from Article III-325, the Council, either on a recommendation from the European Central Bank or on a recommendation from the Commission and after consulting the European Central Bank, in an endeavour to reach a consensus consistent with the objective of price stability, may conclude formal agreements on an exchange-rate system for the euro in relation to the currencies of third States.
- Article III-348(2): in the event of a vacancy in the European Commission, the Council may, acting unanimously on a proposal from the President of the Commission, decide that such a vacancy need not be filled, in particular when the remainder of the member's term of office is short.
- Article III-354: if the Court of Justice so requests, the Council may, acting unanimously, adopt a decision to increase the number of Advocates-General.
- Article III-359(4): the appointment of members of the specialised courts.
- Article III-381: amending the provisions of the Statute of the Court of Justice of the European Union, with the exception of Title I and Article 64.
- Article III-386: determining the composition of the Committee of the Regions.
- Article III-412: until 31 December 2006, the Council acts unanimously when adopting the financial rules which determine in particular the procedure to be adopted for: establishing and implementing the budget and for presenting and auditing accounts; establishing rules providing for checks on the responsibility of financial actors, in particular authorising officers and accounting officers; and laying down the methods and procedure whereby the budget revenue provided under the arrangements relating to the Union's own resources shall be made available to the Commission, and the measures to be applied, if need be, to meet cash requirements. (Thereafter the Council will act by a qualified majority.)
- Article III-419(2): the granting of authorisation to proceed with enhanced cooperation within the framework of the Common Foreign and Security Policy.
- Article III-420: within the framework of the Common Foreign and Security Policy, if the Council considers that the conditions of participation in enhanced cooperation have not been fulfilled, it indicates the arrangements to be adopted to fulfil those conditions and shall set a deadline for re-examining the request for participation.
- Article III-421: expenditure resulting from implementation of enhanced cooperation, other than administrative costs entailed for the institutions, shall be borne by the participating Member States, unless all members of the Council, acting unanimously after consulting the European Parliament, decide otherwise.
- Article III-422: where a provision of the Treaties which may be applied in the context of enhanced cooperation stipulates that the Council shall act unanimously (or that the special legislative procedure be applied), the Council, acting unanimously in accordance with the arrangements laid down in Article I-44(3), may adopt a decision stipulating that it will act by a qualified majority (or that the ordinary legislative procedure be applied).
- Article III-433: laying down the rules governing the languages of the Union's institutions, without prejudice to the Statute of the Court of Justice of the European Union.
- Article III-436: making changes to the list of 15 April 1958 of the products to which the provisions of paragraph 1 (b) apply.
- Article IV-440(7): amending the status, with regard to the Union, of a Danish, French or Netherlands country or territory referred to in paragraphs 2 and 3, on the initiative of the Member State concerned.

III. The scope of application of legislative procedures under the Treaties currently in force

III/a. EU Treaty

The European Parliament is consulted:

- TEU Article 21: The Presidency consults the European Parliament on the main aspects and the basic choices of the Common Foreign and Security Policy.
- TEU Article 30: Prior to adopting framework decisions, adopting decisions and establishing conventions in the area of police and judicial cooperation in criminal matters.
- TEU Article 40a: Prior to establishing enhanced cooperation in the area of police and judicial cooperation in criminal matters.
- TEU Article 42: Prior to the application of Title IV of the EC Treaty (i.e. deciding that a given area is transferred to the first pillar) in the area of police and judicial cooperation in criminal matters.
- TEU Article 44a: Prior to deciding that expenditure resulting from implementation of enhanced cooperation, other than administrative costs entailed for the institutions, shall be borne by the participating Member States.
- TEU Article 48: Prior to convening an intergovernmental conference for the amendment of the Treaties.

The assent of the European Parliament must be attained:

- TEU Article 7(1): in determining that there is a clear risk of a serious breach by a Member State of principles mentioned in Article 6(1).
- TEU Article 7(2): in determining the existence of a serious and persistent breach by a Member State of principles mentioned in Article 6(1).
- TEU Article 49: in deciding on the application for membership of a state (prior to the signing of a treaty of accession).

III/b. EC Treaty

The scope of application of the consultation procedure:

- TEC Article 11(2): authorisation to establish enhanced cooperation (except for areas covered by the co-decision procedure, when the assent of the European Parliament is required.)
- TEC Article 13: action to combat discrimination based on sex, racial or ethnic origin, religion or belief, disability, age or sexual orientation.
- TEC Article 19(1) and (2): adopting detailed arrangements concerning the active and passive electoral rights (at municipal elections and elections to the European Parliament) of Union citizens residing in a Member State of which they are not a national.
- TEC Article 22: adopting provisions to strengthen or add to the rights laid down in Part II of the EC Treaty on Union citizenship.
- TEC Article 37(2) and (3): submitting proposals for working out and implementing the Common Agricultural Policy, making regulations, issuing directives, or taking decisions.

- TEC Article 52(1): issuing directives in order to achieve the liberalisation of a specific service.
- TEC Article 62(2) b) i): establishing the list of third countries whose nationals must be in possession of visas when crossing the external borders and those whose nationals are exempt from that requirement.
- TEC Article 62(2) b) iii): establishing a uniform format for visas.
- TEC Article 63(3) a): conditions of entry and residence, and standards on procedures for the issue by Member States of long-term visas and residence permits, including those for the purpose of family reunion.
- TEC Article 63(4): measures defining the rights and conditions under which nationals of third countries who are legally resident in a Member State may reside in other Member States.
- TEC Article 65: adopting measures in the field of judicial cooperation in family law.
- TEC Article 66: measures to ensure cooperation between the relevant departments of the administrations of the Member States in the areas covered by the title 'Visas, asylum, immigration and other policies related to free movement of persons', as well as between those departments and the Commission.
- TEC Article 71(2): adopting measures where the application of provisions concerning the principles of the regulatory system for transport would be liable to have a serious effect on the standard of living and on employment in certain areas and on the operation of transport facilities.
- TEC Article 83: laying down the appropriate regulations or directives to give effect to the principles of competition rules applying to undertakings set out in Articles 81 and 82
- TEC Article 89: making regulations for the application of rules on state aid, and determining the categories of aid exempted from these rules.
- TEC Article 93: adopting provisions for the harmonisation of legislation concerning turnover taxes, excise duties and other forms of indirect taxation to the extent that such harmonisation is necessary to ensure the establishment and the functioning of the internal market.
- TEC Article 94: issuing directives for the approximation of such laws, regulations or administrative provisions of the Member States as directly affect the establishment or functioning of the common market.
- TEC Article 104(14): laying down detailed rules and definitions for the application of the provisions of the Protocol on the excessive budget deficit procedure.
- TEC Article 107(6): adopting certain provisions of the Statute of the ECB.
- TEC Article 110(3): limits and conditions within and under which the ECB is entitled to impose fines or periodic penalty payments on undertakings for failure to comply with obligations under its regulations and decisions.
- TEC Article 111(1): concluding formal agreements on an exchange-rate system for the ECU (euro) in relation to non-Community currencies.
- TEC Article 111(4): deciding on issues related to the external representation of the economic and monetary union.
- TEC Article 121(3) and (4): deciding whether it is appropriate for the Community to enter the third stage of the economic and monetary union.
- TEC Article 122(2): deciding which Member States with a derogation fulfil the necessary conditions for the introduction of the single currency and abrogating the derogations of the Member States concerned (authorising their accession to the eurozone).

- TEC Article 128(2): drawing up guidelines in the field of employment policy on the basis of the conclusions of the European Council.
- TEC Article 133(7): Without prejudice to the first subparagraph of paragraph 6, the Council may extend the application of paragraphs 1 to 4 to international negotiations and agreements on intellectual property in so far as they are not covered by paragraph 5.
- TEC Article 137(1) c), d), f), g): social security and social protection of workers; protection of workers where their employment contract is terminated; representation and collective defence of the interests of workers and employers, including co-determination; conditions of employment for third-country nationals legally residing in Community territory.
- TEC Article 144: establishing a Social Protection Committee with advisory status to promote cooperation on social protection policies between Member States and with the Commission.
- TEC Article 166(3) and (4): adopting specific research programmes.
- TEC Article 172(1): adopting provisions on joint undertakings or any other structure necessary for the efficient execution of Community research, technological development and demonstration programmes.
- TEC Article 175(2): adopting provisions in the following areas of the environment: provisions primarily of a fiscal nature; measures affecting town and country planning, quantitative management of water resources or affecting (directly or indirectly) the availability of those resources and land use (with the exception of waste management); measures significantly affecting a Member State's choice between different energy sources and the general structure of its energy supply.
- TEC Article 181a: economic, financial and technical cooperation measures with third countries.
- TEC Article 225a: creating judicial panels.
- TEC Article 229a: provisions to confer jurisdiction, to the extent determined by the Council, on the Court of Justice in disputes relating to the application of acts which create Community industrial property rights.
- TEC Article 245: amending the Statute of the Court of Justice (with the exception of Title I).
- TEC Article 247(3): appointing the members of the Court of Auditors.
- TEC Article 266: amending certain provisions of the Statute of the European Investment Bank.
- TEC Article 269: laying down provisions relating to the system of own resources of the Community
- TEC Article 279: determining the procedures for establishing and implementing the budget and for presenting and auditing accounts; determining the methods and procedure for making the Community's own resources available to the Commission; laying down the rules concerning the financial controllers.
- TEC Article 283: laying down the Staff Regulations of officials of the European Communities and the Conditions of employment of other servants of those Communities.
- TEC Article 299(2): adopting measures serving the interests of ultraperipheral, overseas regions of the EU.
- TEC Article 300(2): the signing, provisional application, conclusion and suspension of international agreements.
- TEC Article 308: taking the appropriate measures to attain, in the course of the operation of the common market, one of the objectives of the Community, when the EC Treaty dos not provide the necessary powers.

The scope of application of the cooperation procedure:

- TEC Article 99(5): adopting rules for the multilateral surveillance procedure.
- TEC Article 102(2): specification of definitions for the application of prohibitions of privileged access to the services of financial institutions.
- TEC Article 103(2): specification of definitions for the application of prohibitions under Articles 101 and 103 of the EC Treaty (prohibition of assumed commitments or overdraft facilities).
- TEC Article 106(2): harmonisation of the denomination and technical specifications of coins of the single currency.

The scope of application of the assent procedure:

- TEC Article 11(2): granting authorisation to establish enhanced cooperation, when it relates to an area covered by the co-decision procedure.
- TEC Article 105(6): conferring upon the ECB specific tasks concerning policies relating to the prudential supervision pf credit institutions and other financial institutions, with the exception of insurance undertakings.
- TEC Article 107(5): amending certain provisions of the Statute of the ESCB.
- TEC Article 161: defining the tasks, priority objectives and the organisation of the Structural Funds and the Cohesion Fund.
- TEC Article 190(4): adopting a uniform procedure for elections to the European Parliament.
- TEC Article 214: nominating and appointing the President and members of the European Commission.
- TEC Article 300(3): the conclusion of association agreements, other international agreements establishing a specific institutional framework, agreements having important budgetary implications for the Community and agreements entailing amendment of an act adopted under the co-decision procedure.

The scope of application of the co-decision procedure:

- TEC Article 12: anti-discrimination rules.
- TEC Article 13(2): the adoption of Community incentive measures, excluding any harmonisation of the laws and regulations of the Member States, to support action taken by the Member States in order to contribute to combating discrimination based on sex, racial or ethnic origin, religion or belief, disability, age or sexual orientation.
- TEC Article 18(2): if action by the Community should prove necessary to attain the objective of ensuring the right of every Union citizen to move and reside freely within the territory of the Member States and the EC Treaty has not provided the necessary powers, the Council may adopt provisions with a view to facilitating the exercise of the rights.
- TEC Article 40: the adoption of measures to bring about freedom of movement for workers.
- TEC Article 42: the adoption of measures in the field of social security as are necessary to provide freedom of movement for workers.
- TEC Article 44: issuing directives to bring about freedom of establishment for a specific branch of activity.
- TEC Article 46(2): issuing directives for the coordination of provisions providing for special treatment for foreign nationals on grounds of public policy, public security or public health.

- TEC Article 47(2) sentence 2: deciding on directives the implementation of which involves, in at least one Member State, the amendment of the existing principles laid down by law governing the professions with respect to training and conditions of access for natural persons.
- TEC Article 55: the liberalisation of services.
- TEC Article 62(1): adopting measures with a view to ensuring the absence of any controls on persons, be they citizens of the Union or nationals of third countries, when crossing internal borders.
- TEC Article 62(2) a): standards and procedures to be followed by Member States in carrying out checks on persons on the crossing of external borders.
- TEC Article 62(2) b) ii): the procedures and conditions for issuing visas by Member States
- TEC Article 62(2) b) iv): rules on a uniform visa.
- TEC Article 62(3): measures setting out the conditions under which nationals of third countries shall have the freedom to travel within the territory of the Member States during a period of no more than three months.
- TEC Article 63(1): criteria and mechanisms for determining which Member State is responsible for considering an application for asylum submitted by a national of a third country in one of the Member States, minimum standards on the reception of asylum seekers in Member States, minimum standards with respect to the qualification of nationals of third countries as refugees, and minimum standards on procedures in Member States for granting or withdrawing refugee status.
- TEC Article 63(2) a): minimum standards for giving temporary protection to displaced persons from third countries who cannot return to their country of origin and for persons who otherwise need international protection.
- TEC Article 63(2) b): promoting a balance of effort between Member States in receiving and bearing the consequences of receiving refugees and displaced persons.
- TEC Article 63(3) b): illegal immigration and illegal residence, including repatriation of illegal residents.
- TEC Article 65: measures in the field of judicial cooperation in civil matters having cross-border implications (with the exception of family law cases).
- TEC Article 71(1): laying down common rules applicable to international transport to or from the territory of a Member State or passing across the territory of one or more Member States, the conditions under which non-resident carriers may operate transport services within a Member State, measures to improve transport safety and any other appropriate provisions.
- TEC Article 80(2): deciding whether, to what extent and by what procedure appropriate provisions may be laid down for sea and air transport.
- TEC Article 95: adopting the measures for the approximation of the provisions laid down by law, regulation or administrative action in Member States which have as their object the establishment and functioning of the internal market.
- TEC Article 129: adopting incentive measures designed to encourage cooperation between Member States and to support their action in the field of employment, through initiatives aimed at developing exchanges of information and best practices, providing comparative analysis and advice, as well as promoting innovative approaches and evaluating experiences, in particular by recourse to pilot projects.

- TEC Article 135: measures to strengthen customs cooperation between Member States and between the latter and the Commission.
- TEC Article 137: supporting and complementing the activities of the Member States in the following fields: improvement in particular of the working environment to protect workers' health and safety; working conditions; the information and consultation of workers; the integration of persons excluded from the labour market; equality between men and women with regard to labour market opportunities and treatment at work; the combating of social exclusion; the modernisation of social protection systems.
- TEC Article 141: adopting measures to ensure the application of the principle of equal opportunities and equal treatment of men and women in matters of employment and occupation, including the principle of equal pay for equal work or work of equal value.
- TEC Article 148: implementing decisions concerning the European Social Fund.
- TEC Article 149(4): incentive measures in the area of education.
- TEC Article 150(4): supporting and complementing Member-State activities in the area of vocational training.
- TEC Article 151(5): incentive measures in the area of culture (excluding any approximation of such laws, regulations or administrative provisions of the Member States).
- TEC Article 152(4): adopting measures contributing to the achievement of the public health objectives set out in Article 152.
- TEC Article 153: provisions concerning consumer protection.
- TEC Article 156: guidelines and other measures concerning trans-European networks.
- TEC Article 157(3): specific support measures in the area of industry.
- TEC Article 159(3): specific actions outside the Structural Funds aimed at economic and social cohesion.
- TEC Article 162: implementing Decisions concerning the European Regional Development Fund.
- TEC Article 166: adopting multi-annual research framework programmes.
- TEC Article 172: adopting the programmes and provisions necessary for the efficient execution of the multiannual research framework programme.
- TEC Article 175(1): action to be taken by the Community in order to achieve the environmental objectives referred to in Article 174.
- TEC Article 175(1) and (3): general action programmes in the area of the environment.
- TEC Article 179: in the area of development cooperation, adopting the measures necessary to further the objectives referred to in Article 177
- TEC Article 191: laying down the regulations governing political parties at European level and in particular the rules regarding their funding.
- TEC Article 255: general principles and limits on grounds of public or private interest governing the right of access to European Parliament, Council and Commission documents.
- TEC Article 280: measures to prevent and counter fraud affecting the financial interests of the Community.
- TEC Article 285: measures for the production of statistics where necessary for the performance of the activities of the Community.
- TEC Article 286: data protection (setting up an independent supervisory body).

IV. The scope of application of legislative procedures upon the entry into force of the Reform Treaty (according to the articles of the Constitutional Treaty)[**]

IV/a. Ordinary legislative procedure[***]

- Article I-37(3): laying down the rules and general principles concerning mechanisms for control by Member States of the Commission's exercise of implementing powers.
- Article I-47(4): the provisions for the procedures and conditions governing the exercise of the citizens' initiative, enabling Union citizens to invite the Commission, within the framework of its powers, to submit any appropriate proposal on matters where they consider that a legal act of the Union is required for the purpose of implementing the Treaties.
- Article I-50(3): laying down the general principles and limits which, on grounds of public or private interest, govern the right of access to documents of the Union institutions, bodies, offices and agencies.
- Article I-51(2): the rules relating to the protection of individuals with regard to the processing of personal data by Union institutions, bodies, offices and agencies, and by the Member States when carrying out activities which fall within the scope of Union law, and the rules relating to the free movement of such data.
- Article III-122: the principles and conditions of the operation of services of general economic interest.
- Article III-123: rules prohibiting discrimination on grounds of nationality.
- Article III-124(2): Union incentive measures supporting action by Member States to combat discrimination based on sex, racial or ethnic origin, religion or belief, disability, age or sexual orientation and basic principles for such measures.
- Article III-125(1): action to facilitate the exercise of Union citizens to move and reside freely.
- Article III-134: measures needed to bring about freedom of movement for workers.
- Article III-136: measures in the field of social security necessary to bring about freedom of movement for workers (with an emergency brake clause).
- Article III-138(1): measures to attain freedom of establishment as regards a particular activity.
- Article III-139: excluding certain activities from the application of the freedom of establishment.

[**] As this book went to press, the text of the Reform Treaty had not been adopted; therefore, this list uses the numbering of the Articles of the former Constitutional Treaty. On the basis of the mandate of the Intergovernmental Conference, as agreed on 22 June 2007, the Reform Treaty will adopt the provisions of the Constitutional Treaty on extending the application of the ordinary legislative procedure (the current co-decision procedure) and on defining the scope of application of the special legislative procedures and incorporate them into the EU and EC Treaties currently in force. The articles listed will be renumbered in the EU and EC Treaties by the Reform Treaty (which will also differ from the numbering used currently due to the many new or reformulated Articles.)

[***] The current co-decision procedure.

- Article III-140(2): coordinating national provisions providing for special treatment for foreign nationals on grounds of public policy, public security or public health.
- Article III-141: making it easier for persons to take up and pursue activities as self-employed persons (the mutual recognition of diplomas, certificates and other evidence of formal qualifications; the coordination of relevant Member-State provisions).
- Article III-144: extending the application of the freedom to provide services.
- Article III-147(1): measures to achieve the liberalisation of a specific service.
- Article III-152: measures to strengthen customs cooperation between Member States and between them and the Commission.
- Article III-157(2): measures on the movement of capital to or from third countries involving direct investment – including investment in real estate, establishment, the provision of financial services or the admission of securities to capital markets.
- Article III-160: defining a framework for administrative measures with regard to capital movements and payments, in order to achieve the objectives set out in Article III-257, as regards preventing and combating terrorism and related activities.
- Article III-172(1): measures for the approximation of the provisions laid down by law, regulation or administrative action in Member States which have as their object the establishment and functioning of the internal market.
- Article III-174: measures necessary to eliminate the distortion of the conditions of competition in the internal market resulting from differences between the provisions laid down by law, regulation or administrative action in Member States.
- Article III-176: measures for the creation of European intellectual property rights to provide uniform intellectual property rights protection throughout the Union and for the setting up of centralised Union-wide authorisation, coordination and supervision arrangements (with the exception of language arrangements for the European intellectual property rights).
- Article III-179(6): rules for the multilateral surveillance procedure in the area of the economic developments in the Union and the consistency of economic policies with the broad guidelines.
- Article III-187(3): amending certain provisions of the Statute of the European System of Central Banks and of the European Central Bank.
- Article III-191: measures necessary for use of the euro as the single currency (without prejudice to the powers of the European Central Bank).
- Article III-207: incentive measures designed to encourage cooperation between Member States and to support their action in the field of employment through initiatives aimed at developing exchanges of information and best practices, providing comparative analysis and advice as well as promoting innovative approaches and evaluating experiences.
- Article III-210(1) a), b), e), i), j), k): improvement of the working environment to protect workers' health and safety; working conditions; the information and consultation of workers; the integration of persons excluded from the labour market; equality between men and women with regard to labour market opportunities and treatment at work; the combating of social exclusion; the modernisation of social protection systems.

- Article III-214(3): measures to ensure the application of the principle of equal opportunities and equal treatment of men and women in matters of employment and occupation, including the principle of equal pay for equal work or work of equal value.
- Article III-219(3): implementing decisions concerning the European Social Fund.
- Article III-221: establishing any specific measure outside the Funds, without prejudice to measures adopted within the framework of the Union's other policies.
- Article III-223: defining the tasks, the priority objectives and the organisation of the structural funds.
- Article III-223: setting up a Cohesion Fund.
- Article III-224: establishing implementing measures relating to the European Regional Development Fund.
- Article III-231(2): establishing the common organisation of the market provided for in Article III-228(1) and the other provisions necessary for the pursuit of the objectives of the Common Agricultural Policy and the common fisheries policy.
- Article III-234(1): establishing what action is to be taken in order to achieve the environmental objectives referred to in Article III-233 (preserving, protecting and improving the quality of the environment; protecting human health; prudent and rational utilisation of natural resources; promoting measures at international level to deal with regional or worldwide environmental problems).
- Article III-234(3): establishing general action programmes which set out priority environmental objectives to be attained.
- Article III-235(3): measures which support, supplement and monitor the policy pursued by the Member States in the area of consumer protection.
- Article III-236: rules of the common transport policy (railway, road and inland waterways).
- Article III-245(2): measures for sea and air transport.
- Article III-247(2): guidelines and other measures in the sphere of trans-European networks.
- Article III-251(1): establishing a multiannual framework programme for research and technological development, setting out all the activities financed by the Union.
- Article III-251(4): establishing the measures necessary for the implementation of the European research area, as a complement to the activities planned in the multiannual framework programme.
- Article III-252(1): for the implementation of the multiannual framework programme, establishing the rules for the participation of undertakings, research centres and universities and the rules governing the dissemination of research results.
- Article III-252(2): in implementing the multiannual framework programme, establishing supplementary programmes involving the participation of certain Member States only, which will finance them subject to possible participation by the Union.
- Article III-252(3): in implementing the multiannual framework programme, making provision for participation in research and development programmes undertaken by several Member States.
- Article III-254(2): in drawing up a European space policy, establishing the necessary measures.
- Article III-256(2): measures in order to ensure the functioning of the energy market, ensure security of energy supply in the Union, and promote energy efficiency and energy saving and the development of new and renewable forms of energy.

- Article III-265(2): establishing measures concerning: the common policy on visas and other short-stay residence permits; the checks to which persons crossing external borders are subject; the conditions under which nationals of third countries shall have the freedom to travel within the Union for a short period; any measure necessary for the gradual establishment of an integrated management system for external borders; the absence of any controls on persons, whatever their nationality, when crossing internal borders.
- Article III-266(2): laying down measures for a common European asylum system.
- Article III-267(2): establishing measures in the following areas: the conditions of entry and residence, and standards on the issue by Member States of long-term visas and residence permits, including those for the purpose of family reunion; the definition of the rights of third-country nationals residing legally in a Member State, including the conditions governing freedom of movement and of residence in other Member States; illegal immigration and unauthorised residence, including removal and repatriation of persons residing without authorisation; combating trafficking in persons, in particular women and children.
- Article III-267(4): establishing measures to provide incentives and support for the action of Member States with a view to promoting the integration of third-country nationals residing legally in their territories.
- Article III-269(2): establishing measures aimed at ensuring the mutual recognition and enforcement between Member States of judgments and decisions in extrajudicial cases; the cross-border service of judicial and extrajudicial documents; the compatibility of the rules applicable in the Member States concerning conflict of laws and of jurisdiction; cooperation in the taking of evidence; effective access to justice; the elimination of obstacles to the proper functioning of civil proceedings, if necessary by promoting the compatibility of the rules on civil procedure applicable in the Member States; the development of alternative methods of dispute settlement; support for the training of the judiciary and judicial staff.
- Article III-270(1): establishing measures to: lay down rules and procedures for ensuring recognition throughout the Union of all forms of judgments and judicial decisions; prevent and settle conflicts of jurisdiction between Member States; support the training of the judiciary and judicial staff; facilitate cooperation between judicial or equivalent authorities of the Member States in relation to proceedings in criminal matters and the enforcement of decisions.
- Article III-270(2): establishing minimum rules to the extent necessary to facilitate mutual recognition of judgments and judicial decisions and police and judicial cooperation in criminal matters having a cross-border dimension, concerning: the mutual admissibility of evidence between Member States; the rights of individuals in criminal procedure; the rights of victims of crime; any other specific aspects of criminal procedure which the Council has identified in advance by a decision (an emergency brake clause exists!).
- Article III-271(1): establishing minimum rules concerning the definition of criminal offences and sanctions in the areas of particularly serious crime with a cross-border dimension resulting from the nature or impact of such offences or from a special need to combat them on a common basis (an emergency brake clause exists!).

- Article III-271(2): if the approximation of criminal laws and regulations of the Member States proves essential to ensure the effective implementation of a Union policy in an area which has been subject to harmonisation measures, establishing minimum rules with regard to the definition of criminal offences and sanctions in the area concerned (an emergency brake clause exists!).
- Article III-272: establishing measures to promote and support the action of Member States in the field of crime prevention, excluding any harmonisation of the laws and regulations of the Member States.
- Article III-273: determining Eurojust's structure, operation, field of action and tasks.
- Article III-273: determining arrangements for involving the European Parliament and national parliaments in the evaluation of Eurojust's activities.
- Article III-275(2): establishing measures concerning the collection, storage, processing, analysis and exchange of relevant information; support for the training of staff, and cooperation on the exchange of staff, on equipment and on research into crime-detection; common investigative techniques in relation to the detection of serious forms of organised crime.
- Article III-276(2): determining Europol's structure, operation, field of action and tasks.
- Article III-276(2): laying down the procedures for scrutiny of Europol's activities by the European Parliament, together with national parliaments.
- Article III-278(4): establishing measures setting high standards of quality and safety of organs and substances of human origin, blood and blood derivatives; measures in the veterinary and phytosanitary fields which have as their direct objective the protection of public health; measures setting high standards of quality and safety for medicinal products and devices for medical use; measures concerning monitoring, early warning of and combating serious cross-border threats to health.
- Article III-278(5): establishing incentive measures designed to protect and improve human health and in particular to combat the major cross-border health scourges, as well as measures which have as their direct objective the protection of public health regarding tobacco and the abuse of alcohol.
- Article III-279(3): establishing specific measures in support of action taken in the Member States to achieve the objectives of the Union's competitiveness (set out in III-279(1))
- Article III-280(5): establishing incentive measures contributing to the flowering of the cultures of the Member States and facilitating cooperation between them.
- Article III-281(2): establishing specific measures to complement actions within the Member States to achieve the objectives of encouraging the creation of a favourable environment for the development of undertakings in this sector; promoting cooperation between the Member States, particularly by the exchange of good practice.
- Article III-282(3): establishing incentive measures in the area of education, youth and sport.
- Article III-283(3): establishing incentive measures in the area of vocational training.
- Article III-284(2): establishing incentive measures in the area of civil protection.

- Article III-285(2): establishing the necessary measures to support the efforts of Member States to improve their administrative capacity to implement Union law.
- Article III-315(2): measures defining the framework for implementing the Common Commercial Policy.
- Article III-317(1): measures necessary for the implementation of development cooperation policy.
- Article III-319(2): economic, financial and technical cooperation measures, including assistance, in particular financial assistance, with third countries other than developing countries.
- Article III-321(3): measures defining the framework within which the Union's humanitarian aid operations shall be implemented.
- Article III-321(5): the rules and procedures for the operation of the European Voluntary Humanitarian Aid Corps.
- Article III-331: regulations governing the political parties at European level, and in particular the rules regarding their funding.
- Article III-359(1)-(2): establishing specialised courts attached to the General Court to hear and determine at first instance certain classes of action or proceeding brought in specific areas.
- Article III-364: conferring on the Court of Justice of the European Union jurisdiction in disputes relating to the application of acts adopted on the basis of the Treaties which create European intellectual property rights.
- Article III-381: amending the provisions of the Statute of the Court of Justice of the European Union, with the exception of Title I and Article 64.
- Article III-398(2): establishing provisions to ensure an open, efficient and independent European administration of the institutions, bodies, offices and agencies of the Union in carrying out their missions.
- Article III-412: establishing the financial rules which determine in particular the procedure to be adopted for establishing and implementing the budget and for presenting and auditing accounts; rules providing for checks on the responsibility of financial actors, in particular authorising officers and accounting officers.
- Article III-415(4): laying down the necessary measures in the fields of the prevention of and fight against fraud affecting the Union's financial interests, with a view to affording effective and equivalent protection in the Member States and in all the Union's institutions, bodies, offices and agencies.
- Article III-427: laying down the Staff Regulations of officials and the Conditions of employment of other servants of the Union.
- Article III-429: measures for the production of statistics.

IV/b. Special legislative procedures

Consultation with the European Parliament [****]

- Article I-54(3): laying down the provisions relating to the system of own resources of the Union.
- Article III-125(2): measures concerning passports, identity cards, residence permits or any other such document and measures concerning social security or social protection.

[****] The current consultation procedure

- Article III-126: determining the detailed arrangements for exercising the right, referred to in Article I-10(2)(b), for every citizen of the Union to vote and to stand as a candidate in municipal elections and elections to the European Parliament in his or her Member State of residence without being a national of that State.
- Article III-127: adopting the necessary provisions to secure diplomatic and consular protection of citizens of the Union in third countries.
- Article III-157(3): measures which constitute a step backwards in Union law as regards the liberalisation of the movement of capital to or from third countries involving direct investment – including investment in real estate, establishment, the provision of financial services or the admission of securities to capital markets.
- Article III-171: measures for the harmonisation of legislation concerning turnover taxes, excise duties and other forms of indirect taxation, provided that such harmonisation is necessary to ensure the establishment and the functioning of the internal market and to avoid distortion of competition.
- Article III-173: measures for the approximation of such laws, regulations or administrative provisions of the Member States as directly affect the establishment or functioning of the internal market.
- Article III-176: establishing language arrangements for the European intellectual property rights.
- Article III-184(13): laying down the appropriate measures to replace the Protocol on the excessive deficit procedure.
- Article III-185(6): conferring specific tasks upon the European Central Bank concerning policies relating to the prudential supervision of credit institutions and other financial institutions, with the exception of insurance undertakings.
- Article III-210(1) c), d) f) g): social security and social protection of workers; protection of workers where their employment contract is terminated; representation and collective defence of the interests of workers and employers, including codetermination; conditions of employment for third-country nationals legally residing in Union territory.
- Article III-234(2): adopting provisions in the following areas of the environment: provisions primarily of a fiscal nature; measures affecting town and country planning; measures affecting quantitative management of water resources or affecting, directly or indirectly, the availability of those resources; measures affecting land use (with the exception of waste management); measures significantly affecting a Member State's choice between different energy sources and the general structure of its energy supply.
- Article III-256(3): measures in the area of energy policy (ensuring the functioning of the energy market; ensuring security of energy supply in the Union; and promoting energy efficiency and energy saving and the development of new and renewable forms of energy) when they are primarily of a fiscal nature.
- Article III-269(3): measures concerning family law with cross-border implications.
- Article III-275(3): measures concerning operational cooperation between the Member States' competent authorities, including police, customs and other specialised law enforcement services in relation to the prevention, detection and investigation of criminal offences.
- Article III-277: laying down the conditions and limitations under which the competent authorities of the Member States referred to in Articles III-270 (judicial cooperation in criminal matters) and III-275 (police cooperation) may operate in the territory of another Member State in liaison and in agreement with the authorities of that state.

– Article III-291: the detailed rules and the procedure for the association of overseas countries and territories with the Union.
– Article III-393: amending the Statute of the European Investment Bank.
– Article III-419: the granting of authorisation to proceed with enhanced cooperation.
– Article III-424: adopting directives, regulations and decisions aimed, in particular, at laying down the conditions of application of the Treaty, including common policies in Guadeloupe, French Guiana, Martinique, Réunion, the Azores, Madeira and the Canary Islands.
– Article IV-443(2): convening a Convention prior to convening an Intergovernmental Conference on amending the Treaties.

Consent of the European Parliament *****

– Article I-18: flexibility clause (if action by the Union should prove necessary, within the framework of the policies defined in Part III, to attain one of the objectives set out in the Treaty, and the Treaty has not provided the necessary powers).
– Article I-54(4): laying down implementing provisions relating to the system of own resources of the Union.
– Article I-55(2): laying down the multiannual financial framework.
– Article I-58: the accession of a new Member State to the Union.
– Article III-124(1): measures needed to combat discrimination based on sex, racial or ethnic origin, religion or belief, disability, age or sexual orientation.
– Article III-129: adding to the rights laid down in Article I-10 (rights enjoyed by the citizens of the Union).
– Article III-274(1): establishing a European Public Prosecutor's Office in order to combat crimes affecting the financial interests of the Union.
– Article III-325(6): conclusion of international agreements in the following cases: association agreements; Union accession to the European Convention for the Protection of Human Rights and Fundamental Freedoms; agreements establishing a specific institutional framework by organising cooperation procedures; agreements with important budgetary implications for the Union; agreements covering fields to which either the ordinary legislative procedure applies, or the special legislative procedure where consent by the European Parliament is required.
– Article IV-443(2): deciding not to convene a Convention prior to convening an Intergovernmental Conference to amend the Treaties.
– Article IV-444: simplified revision procedure.

Own initiative and consent of the European Parliament

– Article III-330(1): establishing the necessary measures for the election of the Members of the European Parliament by direct universal suffrage in accordance with a uniform procedure in all Member States or in accordance with principles common to all Member States. The Council acts unanimously on initiative from, and after obtaining the consent of, the European Parliament, which acts by a majority of its component members.

***** The current assent procedure.

Own initiative of the European Parliament and consent of the Council

– Article III-330(2): laying down the regulations and general conditions governing the performance of the duties of its Members.
– Article III-333: laying down the detailed provisions governing the exercise of the right of inquiry of a temporary Committee of Inquiry set up by the European Parliament to investigate alleged contraventions or maladministration in the implementation of Union law.
– Article III-335(4): laying down the regulations and general conditions governing the performance of the Ombudsman's duties.

BIBLIOGRAPHY

- Balázs, Katalin – Szalóki, Katalin: Balkáni viszonyok – Az EU és a nyugat-balkáni országok kapcsolata (The Balkan connection - Relations of the EU with the countries of the Western Balkans). _Európai Tükör_, 2006/7–8
- Balázs, Péter: Az Európai Unió jogi személyiségének és egységes külpolitikájának problémája az Európai Konvent munkájában. (The issues of the Union's legal personality and uniform foreign policy in the work of the Convention). _Európai Jog_, 2003/2
- Corbett, R. – Jacobs, F. – Shackleton, M.: _The European Parliament (7th ed)_. John Harper, London 2007
- Cram, Laura: _Policy-making in the European Union: Conceptual lenses and the integration process_. Routledge, London 1997
- Christiansen, Thomas – Kirchner, Emil (eds.): Committee _Governance in the European Union_. Manchester University Press, Manchester 2000
- Commissariat Général Du Plan: _L'élargissement de l'Union européenne a l'est de l'Europe_. La Documentation française, Paris 1999
- Czuriga, Eszter: Az Európai Unió kohéziós politikája 2007 után. (The European Union's cohesion policy after 2007). _Európai Tükör_, 2005/2
- Dehousse, Renaud (ed.): _Europe After Maastricht_. LBE, München 1994
- Dehousse, Renaud.: European Institutional Architecture after Amsterdam: Parliamentary System or Regulatory Structure. _Common Market Law Review_ 35., 1998
- Durousset, Maurice: _Les politiques communautaires_. Ellipses-Marketing, Paris 1998
- Dinan, Desmond: _Europe Recast: A history of European Union_. Palgrave Macmillan, London 2004
- Edwards, Geoffrey - Spence, David (ed.): _The European Commission (3rd ed)_. John Harper, London 2006
- Ficsor, Mihály: Megjegyzések az európai közösségi jog és a nemzeti alkotmány viszonyáról I-II. (Notes on the relation between Community law and national constitutions I-II). _Magyar jog_ 1997/8–9
- Gordos, Árpád – Ódor, Bálint: Az Európai Alkotmányos Szerződés születése. (The birth of the European Constitutional Treaty) HVG-Orac, Budapest 2004
- Halmai Péter: A reform ökonómiája: EU közös agrárpolitika: fordulópont vagy kiigazítás? (The economy of reform: The EU's Common Agricultural Policy: a turning point or adjustment?). KJK-Kerszöv, Budapest 2004
- Hayes-Renshaw, F. – Wallace, H.: _The Council of Ministers (2nd ed)_. Palgrave Macmillan, London 2006
- Hix, Simon: _The Political System of the European Union (2nd ed)_. Palgrave Macmillan, London 2005
- Horváth, Jenő: _Az európai integráció története napról napra, 1945–2002: kronológia. (The history of European integration 1945–2002: chronology.)_ Osiris, Budapest 2003
- Horváth, Zoltán: _Az Európai Parlament együttdöntési szerepe. (The co-decision role of the European Parliament)_. Magyar Országgyűlés, Budapest 2003
- Horváth, Zoltán - Ódor, Bálint: _Az Európai Unió alkotmánya – Mi és hogyan változik az Alkotmányszerződés hatására? (A Constitution for the European Union – What will the Constitutional Treaty change and how?)_. HVG-Orac, Budapest 2005
- Horváth, Zoltán – Sinka, László: Az Európai Unió és a tagállamok közötti hatáskörmegosztás problematikája a Konventben folyó vitában. (The issue of division of competences between the European Union and its Member States during the debate in the Convention). _Európai Tükör_ 2002/3

- Horváth, Zoltán – Sinka, László: Az EU jövőjéről szóló vita Laeken után. (The debate on the future of the EU following Laeken). *Európai Tükör* 2002/1–2
- Horváth, Zoltán – Sinka, László: Az Alapvető Jogok Kartája megszületésének fő kérdései. (The key issues surrounding the conception of the Charter of Fundamental Rights). *Európai Tükör* 2001/1
- Horváth, Zoltán – Sinka, László: A Nizzai Szerződés fontosabb rendelkezései. (The key provisions of the Treaty of Nice). *Európai Tükör* 2001/2–3
- Horváth, Zoltán – Tar, Gábor: Az Európai Parlament az európai demokráciában. (The European Parliament in European democracy). Magyar Országgyűlés, Budapest 2006
- Horváth, Zoltán – Tar, Gábor: *Nemzetközi szervezetek kislexikona. (Manual for International Organizations).* HVG-ORAC, Budapest 2006
- Judge, D. – Earnshaw, D.: From cooperation to co-decision: The European Parliament's path to legislative power, in: Richardson, J. (ed.): *European Union: power and policy-making.* Routledge, London 1996
- Kecskés, László: *EU jog és jogharmonizáció. (második, bővített kiadás) (EU law and approximation of legislation 2nd enlarged ed.).* Budapest: HVG-Orac, 2005
- Kende, Tamás – Szűcs, Tamás (szerk.): *Európai közjog és politika. (European public law and policy).* Osiris-Századvég, Budapest 2002
- Kiss J., László (szerk.): *A huszonötök Európái. (The Europe of 25).* Osiris, Budapest 2005
- Lenaerts, K. – van Nuffel, P.: *Constitutional Law of the European Union (2nd ed).* Sweet & Maxwell, London 2004
- Lőrincné Istvánffy, Hajna: *Pénzügyi integráció Európában. (Financial integration in Europe).* KJK-Kerszöv, Budapest 2001
- Masika, Edit – Harmati, Gergely (szerk.): Egységes belbiztonsági és jogi térség Európában. (Single area of internal security and justice in Europe). Miniszterelnöki Hivatal ISM, Budapest 1999
- Mathijsen, P. S. R. F.: *A Guide to European Union Law* (8th ed). Sweet & Maxwell, London 2004
- McDonagh, Bobby: *Original sin in a brave new world – An Account of the negotiations of the Treaty of Amsterdam.* Institute of European Affairs, Dublin 1998
- Nagy, Tibor: *Pénzügyi jog.* (Finance law). Osiris, Budapest 2005
- Navracsics, Tibor: Európai belpolitika: Az Európai Unió politikatudományi elemzése. (European domestic politics: analysing the European Union from the perspective of political science). Korona, Budapest 1998
- Nugent, Neil: The Government and Politics of the European Union 6th ed). Palgrave Macmillan, London 2006
- Oppenheimer, Andrew (ed.): The relationship between European Community law and national law. The cases *(2nd ed).* Cambridge University Press, Cambridge 2003
- Palánkai, Tibor: *Az Európai integráció gazdaságtana. (The economics of European integration).* Aula, Budapest 2004
- Palánkai, Tibor: *Economics of enlarging European Union.* Akadémiai Kiadó, Budapest 2004
- Peers, Steve: *EU Justice and Home Affairs Law. (2nd ed).* Oxford University Press, Oxford 2006
- Práger, László: A világ(gazdaság) és Magyarország a XXI. század elején. (The world [economy] and Hungary at the beginning of the 21st century). Unió Kiadó. Budapest. 2003
- Práger, László: A magyar felzárkózás: versenyképesség, érdek- és értékrendek a XXI. század elején a globális világ és az Európai Unió terében. (Hungary's catch-up: competitiveness, trends in interests and values in the early 21st century in the global world and the European Union). *Politikatudományi Szemle.* 2004/1–2
- Prechal, Sacha: *Directives in EC Law.* , Oxford University Press, Oxford 2005
- Sidjanski, Dusan: *L'avenir fédéraliste de l'Europe – La Communauté européenne, des origines au Traité de Maastricht.* Presses Universitaires de France, Paris 1992
- Szalayné Sándor, Erzsébet: *Az Európai Unió közjogi alapjai (I. kötet). (The fundamentals of European Union public law – Vol. I.).* Dialóg Campus, Pécs 2003
- Tar, Gábor: *Útmutató az Európai Unió hivatalos dokumentumaihoz. (A guide to official EU documents).* Országgyűlési Könyvtár, Budapest 2004

- Torma, András: *Európai közigazgatás, régiók, önkormányzatok. (European public administration, regions, local governments).* Virtuóz kiadó, 2001
- Tóth Árpádné Masika, Edit: *A szabadság, biztonság, jog európai térségének reformja az európai alkotmányozás tükrében. (The reform of the area of freedom, security and justice in light of the European constitutional process).* Európai Műhelytanulmányok 97., MEH, Budapest 2004
- Wallace. H. – Wallace W.: *Policy-making in the European Union (5th ed.).* Oxford University Press, Oxford 2005
- Weatherill, Stephen: *Cases and materials on EC law (7th ed.).* Blackstone Press, London 2005
- Weatherill, Stephen – Beaumont, Paul: *EU law.* Penguin Books, London 1999
- Welsh, Michael: Europe United? The European Union and the Retreat from Federalism. Macmillan, London 1996
- Westlake, M. - Galloway, D.: *The Council of the European Union (3rd ed.).* John Harper, London 2004
- The sources of primary and secondary legal acts and other EU documents referred to in the book are the Official Journal of the EC/EU, the EUR-Lex database (http://www.europa.eu /eur-lex), and the Europa website (http://www.europa.eu)